Self-Assessment and Career Development

SECOND EDITION

James G. Clawson

John P. Kotter

Victor A. Faux

Charles C. McArthur

SELF-
ASSESSMENT
AND
CAREER
DEVELOPMENT

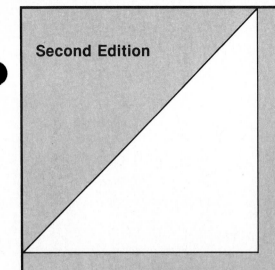

Second Edition

SELF-ASSESSMENT AND CAREER DEVELOPMENT

James G. Clawson

*Colgate Darden Graduate School of Business
University of Virginia*

John P. Kotter

Harvard University

Victor A. Faux

University of Hartford

Charles C. McArthur

Management Consultant

PRENTICE-HALL, INC., Englewood Cliffs, New Jersey 07632

Library of Congress Cataloging in Publication Data
Main entry under title:

Self-assessment and career development.

    Rev. ed. of: Self-assessment and career
development/John P. Kotter, Victor A. Faux,
Charles McArthur. c1978.
    Bibliography: p.
    1. Vocational guidance. 2. Self-evaluation.
3. Job hunting. I. Clawson, James G. II. Kotter,
John P., (date). Self-assessment and career
development
HF5381.S473 1985   331.7'02   84-26641
ISBN 0-13-803107-X

Editorial/production supervision and
    interior design: *Esther S. Koehn*
Cover design: *Lundgren Graphics, Ltd.*
Manufacturing buyer: *Ed O'Dougherty*

The authors are pleased to acknowledge the support for this work provided by the
Sponsors of the Colgate Darden Graduate School of Business Administration, the
University of Virginia, through the School's Case Research Program. The text and
cases from this source are copyrighted by the Sponsors and are used here by permission.

Printed in the United States of America

10 9 8 7 6 5 4 3 2 1

ISBN 0-13-803107-X 01

Prentice-Hall International, Inc., *London*
Prentice-Hall of Australia Pty. Limited, *Sydney*
Editora Prentice-Hall do Brasil, Ltda., *Rio de Janeiro*
Prentice-Hall Canada Inc., *Toronto*
Prentice-Hall Hispanoamericana, S.A., *Mexico*
Prentice-Hall of India Private Limited, *New Delhi*
Prentice-Hall of Japan, Inc., *Tokyo*
Prentice-Hall of Southeast Asia Pte. Ltd., *Singapore*
Whitehall Books Limited, *Wellington, New Zealand*

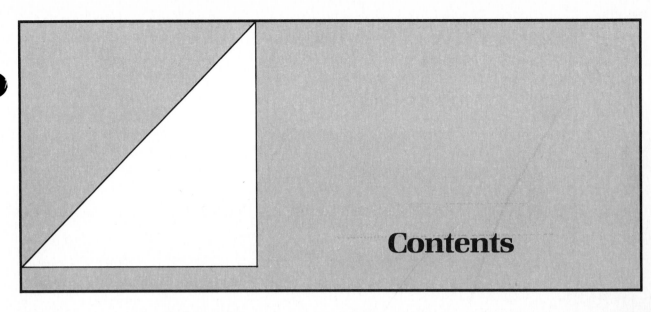

Contents

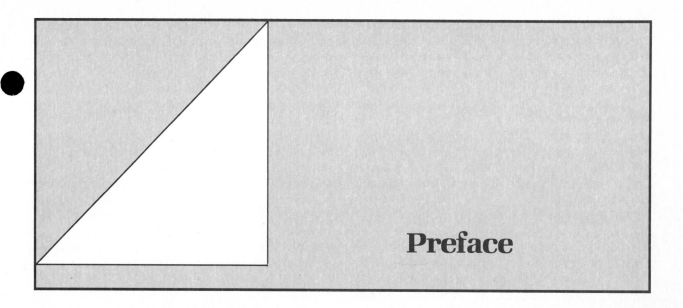

Preface

In 1975, a new second-year MBA elective being taught at the Harvard Business School was awarded the EXXON award for the most creative course in business management. In 1978, Prentice-Hall published the first edition of *Self-Assessment and Career Development,* which summarized major features of that course. The first edition was a result of six years of work and involved the creative and administrative input of a number of people, including Rod Hodgens, Warren Wilhelm, Eileen Morley, Frank Leonard, Allen Froman, and the creative force that launched the book, Tony Athos.

Since the first edition, the course as it was taught at the Harvard Business School has undergone a great deal of development—first by Victor Faux, then by Jim Clawson, and most recently by Jeffrey Sonnenfeld, as each of these have had responsibility for the development and direction of the course.

In addition, every year dozens of students, friends of students, family of students, people who have read about the course, and a variety of public media have contacted the teaching faculty to inquire how they might participate in an exercise similar to the one outlined by the course. The first edition was constructed more for use in the course and did not lend itself well to these individual inquiries.

As a result of this ongoing course development activity and pressure from people who had not taken the course, as well as from faculty members and teachers from other institutions who wanted to teach the course, Jim Clawson undertook to write a second edition.

This edition of *Self-Assessment and Career Development* seeks to make the major parts of the course available to individuals who are willing to spend the time and energy working through the comprehensive self-assessment and career development process. This is not a weekend activity, but requires one or two months of concerted effort.

Other people who have used the book strongly recommended that the focus be shifted to include non-Harvard Business School students and undergraduates as well. This edition broadens the examples used in the cases to include students from other institutions, but the focus still remains clearly with graduating MBAs. This focus on graduate business students does not reduce the applicability of the approach to undergraduates or job hunters in other occupational areas. The process, we believe, is broadly applicable. The examples are specific to the graduate business student.

We have also attempted to broaden the perspective of the book to include more women in management and to give a more detailed consideration of the difficulties of couples making career decisions, both those with more traditional relationships and those with a dual career relationship.

Some controversy has grown up at several institutions across the country around the academic respectability of a course like this. Our belief is that the course stands squarely in the center of courses which teach essential managerial skills.

First, the course is primarily a course in inductive logic—that is the skill required when one must sift through large volumes of disparate data and induce or infer from them patterns or trends from which one can draw one's conclusions. This is a reverse of the common American educational system approach of deductive reasoning, in which the textbook or the teacher will present a theory or a model and ask the student to apply it to particular problem sets or situations. The theories or models developed by working through this book or the course which is associated with it are the individuals' own theories and models about themselves, about career development, and about managing careers in organizations. For this reason, we believe that the course teaches key critical managerial skills, perhaps better than many of the more traditional courses.

Second, the course and the book, although entitled *Self-Assessment and Career Development,* really take two perspectives on the topic of managing careers. The first, obviously, is the focus on one's own career, and in that sense participants in the course generate a great deal of enthusiasm and energy around the assignments and activities outlined in the book. But an equally important and carefully addressed perspective is that of the manager in an organization who must work with, counsel, evaluate, and by raises, promotions, changing assignments reward people working in the organization. This managerial perspective requires an ability to put an individual's talents, characteristics, and personality into the perspective of the organization.

The book also asks individuals to do as careful an analysis of the organizational context as they do of their own careers. Without both analyses, first the individual and second the organizational, it is impossible to develop a complete and carefully thought out choice that will match the strengths and weaknesses of both the individual and the organization.

We believe this matching process is essential in making well-informed and accurate career decisions both on the part of the individual and on the part of the recruiter or manager, who must weigh the appro-priateness not only of the person's managerial style, but also of his or her overall personal style and the demands and requirements of the job in the organization.

The book will outline in basically chronological order the steps in a self-assessment and career development process one is likely to encounter in life. We believe the process to be a cyclical and an ongoing one, in the sense that although one will not continuously be generating self-assessment data so intensively as one will be while working through this book, there will come times in life when a reassessment of one's basic life themes and motivations will be appropriate. The proceduures and the approach outlined in this book will serve the individual well throughout a lifetime of self-assessment and career development.

Acknowledgments

The work of many people has gone into the second edition of the book. The authors wish to acknowledge the helpful suggestions of Ray Hill of the University of Michigan, Tim Hall of Boston University, Paul Thompson of Brigham Young University, and Judy Gordon of Boston College. The editors and staff of Prentice-Hall have also been helpful in shaping the direction of this second edition. Finally, the authors wish to acknowledge Donna Sager's efforts in preparing, retyping and reediting the manuscript.

Reader Feedback

We want to continue to revise and update *Self-Assessment and Career Development* so that it will continue to meet reader needs. If you have *specific* suggestions for how the book might be improved in its next edition, please write them below, tear out this page, and send it to

Mr. James G. Clawson
Colgate Darden Graduate School of Business
University of Virginia
Box 6550
Charlottesville, Virginia 22906

1. What, specifically, did you like about the book and feel should not be changed?

2. What, specifically, did you not like about the book and feel should be changed?

3. What, specifically, do you think should be added to the book?

Your name and address (optional):

SELF-

ASSESSMENT

AND

CAREER

DEVELOPMENT

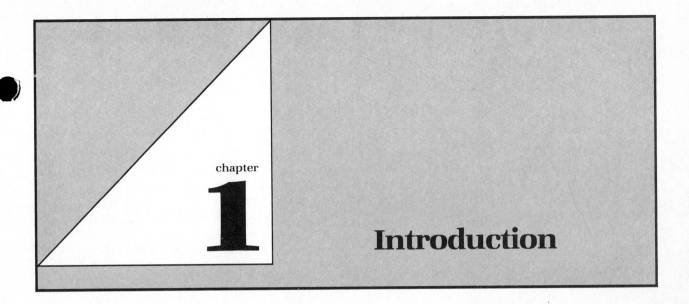

chapter

1

Introduction

"Cheshire Puss," she began, rather timidly, as she did not know whether it would like the name; however, it only grinned a little wider. "Come, it's pleased so far," thought Alice, and she went on. "Would you please tell me, please, which way I ought to walk from here?"

"That depends a good deal on where you want to get to," said the Cat.

"I don't much care where," said Alice.

"Then it doesn't matter which way you walk," said the Cat.

"—so long as I get somewhere," Alice added as an explanation.

"Oh, you're sure to do that," said the Cat, "if only you walk long enough!"

—Alice in Wonderland

A sign beside a freeway in the middle of a large desert in southeastern Idaho reads

ARE YOU LOST?
Keep on going. You're making good time!

These two notes reflect, unfortunately, the kind of thinking that goes into career planning for many of us. Given the press of time and economic circumstance, we often plunge ahead into a job or a "career" without giving much thought to whether or not it is right for us or where it will lead us. We fail to anticipate where our career decisions, both small and great, will take us. And worried by the uncertainty of knowing ourselves and the future, we forge on—hoping that, if we just keep going we will get somewhere, and the sooner the better.

Later, many of us find ourselves in jobs, places, and careers that we did not imagine. In some cases, that is good—we are happy with the result. In other cases, the realization is accompanied by remorse and the wish for a chance to do it over again. What we needed—what we still need—is a systematic way to think about the career decisions we make so that in both the short and the long runs, the result will be what we more or less anticipated and worked toward. Furthermore, this systematic way should not preclude flexibility in the face of changing circumstances. If the opportunities of the future change, our method of thinking about our career decisions should help us compare who we were, who we are, and who we are becoming in the midst of those environmental changes and make decisions that will be appropriate for us and the times.

This book has been written for people who, for whatever reason, wish consciously and explicitly to manage their careers. Our experience has been that people who have already decided on a career (or a job), as well as people who are uncertain about what to do next, have benefited greatly from the process outlined here. The self-assessment process will leave you with a very specific and detailed profile of the things that matter most to you in life and in work. The career development process will help you generate skill at using that profile not only to make reasonable job- and career-related decisions, but also to know what facets of the decision present potential danger areas and what facets will fit you naturally. The process will also help you develop skill in assessing job and career opportunities in dimensions that are specifically relevant to you. Your career planning and activities will be based on information that will help you to develop a greater sense of direction and purpose and of what to look for along the way.

The purpose of the book is to help you develop concrete skills for managing your career—skills at assessing yourself, assessing opportunities, making career- and job-related choices, and managing this process in both the short and long run. The examples and the situations we rely on to present and discuss our approach come primarily from the business world, but the approach is as useful for someone considering a nonbusiness career as it is for someone in business. The book is intended for use in formal courses, but if you are serious about wanting to make a career or job decision that is appropriate for you, and if you have the self-discipline to work on your decision carefully, then this book can help you a great deal.

When we speak of job- and career-related decision making, we are talking about a wide range of important choices that people make during the course of a lifetime. Such decisions include:

1. The selection of type of career
2. The selection of what job to seek next
3. The selection of a strategy for getting a particular type of job
4. The selection of a job offer from among alternatives
5. The selection of assignments, locations, and so on within a job when options are offered
6. The selection of an approach to a job
7. The selection of career goals or a sequence of desired promotions
8. The choice of a life style that surrounds and influences a career
9. The relationship between one's partner and all these choices

It is our observation that people often make these decisions with considerably less care and expertise than they use in the selection of a television or a vacation. Even people who have professional training in analysis and decision making often spend a great deal of time making decisions that, in the context of their lives, may be of little significance, while slipping semiconsciously into major life decisions whose implications are not at all clear to them. Compared to less important decisions, their data-collection methods tend to be less thorough, their analyses more superficial, and their choice processes more random.

There are undoubtedly many reasons why people behave in this way. For most people, assessing something "outside" themselves is a great deal easier, psychologically, than assessing themselves. The latter creates discomfort, which people often deal with by avoiding it. At the same time, our educational institutions have historically provided courses for helping us learn how to make "good" management decisions, legal decisions, engineering decisions, financial decisions, medical decisions—but not career and job decisions.

Some people, of course, manage to go through life quite happily without ever seriously assessing themselves or their opportunities, or making explicit job and career choices. Whether because of luck or very good intuitive decision-making capabilities, they do very well. Many other people behave that way but find the results highly unsatisfying. They often slip into boring or frustrating careers. They sometimes find themselves faced with conflicting job and family demands that are unreasonable. Many discover, to their horror, that they will never achieve the position or professional reputation they had been seeking for years. Some go through the trauma of being fired. Others find themselves securely locked into a job and life style that is no longer satisfying, but from which escape seems impossible. In the words of one 49-year-old individual: "I woke up one day and just sat in bed thinking, how in the hell did I ever get myself into this mess?"

Although this book offers no easy answers, it does try to bring to bear the best technology and insight that exists today on the subject. Like any management task in which the manager does not have absolute control of all the relevant variables, success is not guaranteed. Nevertheless, our experience over the past eight years with the materials and approach presented in this book has convinced us that they are effective, and that they can be of significant help to most people in a variety of ways. The comments of some who have worked through the process may help you anticipate what you can expect to get out of the effort:

This has been the most valuable course I've taken. I maintain that the lack of skills/abilities taught by this course is more often the cause for lack of success than any other subject or skill.

I do know that I will take with me (from this course) a set of tools and a level of self-awareness and sensitivity that will undoubtedly have a profound impact upon my life.

Understanding now that everyone has strengths and weaknesses due to cognitive style, value systems, etc., I've become less judgmental of myself and others in areas of intelligence, and put more emphasis on what a person would be good at doing because of the person's (or own) cognitive style, values, etc.

I gained a fantastic understanding of the *criteria* upon which I will make my job decision. I learned a great deal about what I *really* want out of a job. I learned a great deal about the potential pitfalls of the job hunt and later career development.

I have been forced to formalize a previously semiconscious awareness of myself. This has forced me to acknowledge certain characteristics as important enough to choose a career around. Before taking this course I was boxed into a narrow idea of what were acceptable courses, and viewed incompatible characteristics as sources of tension and discontent that I would just have to live with. Now I've reassessed my priorities, and am taking a much more imaginative approach to finding a job.

I feel like I've gained a whole lot from the course. I was very confused and worried about the job-hunting process at the beginning of this year. Now, I feel I have a good focus and a lot more *self-confidence* in dealing with the whole career selection process.

This course was a lot of work but it was worth three times the work it demanded.

Who Can Use the Book

This book was written primarily for graduate students of business administration, so many of the examples and cases are set in circumstances relevant to that group. The process of self-assessment and career development outlined and developed here, however, is applicable to a much broader audience. In fact, you will probably find these exercises and readings useful regardless of the career area you have decided to pursue or of the point in your career—early, middle, or late.

UNDERGRADUATES. Undergraduates will be able to use the self-assessment exercises in virtually the same way that MBA students do. The details of the job search process may be somewhat different, but the ways in which undergraduates can use self-assessment materials to guide their job search and decision-making activities are not different from those described here. If you have not worked full time before, you may not be able to draw on your work experiences as much as older people, but if you take into account the career stage theories and the tasks associated with them as outlined in Chapter 34, you will be able to get a perspective on how your own goals, values, and career inclinations will evolve over the next few years. An introduction to this material now will better prepare you to make sense of your first experiences.

Again, the process will be helpful even if you are not interested in a career in business. Students considering any career area who work through the book carefully will gain greater insight into the kinds of work, work settings, colleagues, and organizations that would suit them best.

PEOPLE MAKING CAREER CHANGES. If you have been working for some time and are considering a major career change, the process outlined here can be of enormous help. We have found that many people leave one job because they are somehow dissatisfied with the work, the people, or the organization, but *lacking a sufficiently clear and detailed self-assessment,* often put themselves in new situations no better suited to

their interests, skills, and desires. In a sense this is like trying to find what one wants by knowing what one doesn't want. That takes a lot of trial and error. It is much more efficient to begin with a vision of the kind of work you *should* be seeking, given who you are, and to avoid getting sidetracked by "interesting" opportunities that do not really fit you. This book will help you to do that. We will not spend any time discussing the significant emotional issues of leaving a job in which you may have invested a great deal of time and energy. If you are in this category, you may be interested in the work of Meryl Louis. See, for instance, "Career Transitions: The Missing Link in Career Development," published in the Spring 1982 issue of *Organizational Dynamics.*

DUAL CAREER COUPLES. If you are trying to make career decisions in tandem, this book can be a great help. We have found that many of our students ask for copies of the materials and work through them with their spouses or close friends. The process can be even more exciting when you work through it with someone and can talk at leisure about the things you will be learning and doing. The book is organized primarily as a self-assessment exercise for individuals, but there are a few explicitly couple-oriented exercises. In addition to these, we encourage couples to compare their findings on each of the instruments and the implications of those findings for work and to discuss the meanings for their joint relationship, job search, and career development activities.

One of the basic premises of this book is that people are multidimensional and that the various dimensions are closely connected. If working through the exercises with another person will help you to keep in mind the other, noncareer aspects of your life and to make decisions that will balance those aspects in a way that is most appealing to you, then working together can be very beneficial.

One word of caution: Sometimes in discussing very personal data with other people, even those we have known for a long time and with whom we feel very comfortable, we may try to be to those people what we have come to know that they expect. In other words, we may distort our own data or our interpretations of those data for the sake of the relationship and the roles we play within it. This is a manageable danger if you are aware of it and are willing to look at yourself and your relationship openly and honestly. If you plan to work through the book with another person, we advise you to analyze each instrument and exercise alone first, perhaps making notes that you can keep in reserve and do not feel compelled to share with the other person. Then you can compare your private notes with the feedback you get from the other person and note any differences. If there are differences, you may want to think about how, if at all, and in what ways you would like to address those differences in your relationship.

Organization of the Book

The first part of this book deals with the process of self-assessment. It is designed to help you learn how to assess yourself effectively for career and job decision-making purposes, and to help you produce a usable self-assessment. The second part focuses on career development. It is designed to help you assess job and career opportunities, get a job, and deal with the challenges and problems encountered in different stages of a career.

The book was intended primarily for use in a classroom setting, but has been organized to help individuals who want to attack the self-assessment process on their own. This process will require a great deal of discipline and time, so whether you are approaching it in a class or alone, you should plan to spend ample time and energy. Self-assessment should not be rushed. The quick answers are often not the most valid nor the most useful.

The self-assessment portion of the book will help you to generate a great deal of data. We encourage you to purchase a 2-inch three-ring binder and a set of colored index tabs with which to organize your data. The pages of this book are perforated so that you can tear them out and put them in your notebook.

Since our approach is one of self-assessment, we've asked *you* to manage the data-generation process. We will guide you through that process, but at this point we advise you to *not skip ahead* in the book. Proceed sequentially. The next chapter will outline more carefully the self-assessment process we will use and help you prepare to begin.

Your Expectations

Before you begin, however, we ask you to pause for a moment and write down your expectations for this self-assessment and career development project/course. This brief exercise will help you to clarify your goals and also provide an interesting means of reviewing your progress later on. Please be as explicit and specific as you can as you consider the following questions:

Why did you select this course/book?

What do you want to get out of the course/book?

What do you think we will be doing in this course/book?

What do you expect from the faculty/authors?

How does this course fit into your present and future plans?

Any other expectations, feelings?

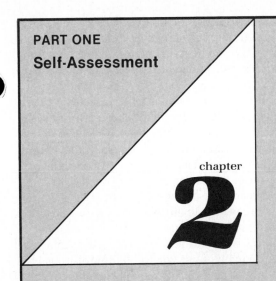

PART ONE
Self-Assessment

chapter

2

The Self-Assessment Process

The self-assessment method presented here is a systematic process designed to generate the type of accurate self-awareness needed to make rational job and career decisions. This approach is similar to that used by many professional career management consultants, with one important exception. The process described here is not just a human assessment process, it is a self-assessment process. You will not only acquire skills in assessing other people for career decision-making purposes, you will learn how to assess yourself.

Our underlying philosophy here is that with some guidance and understanding of the process, any careful and thoughtful person can generate personal information, assess its usefulness, and draw conclusions from it that will be helpful, even extremely helpful, in making career-related decisions. Professional counselors could no doubt interpret any single instrument with a greater degree of skill than we will develop here, and if you have access to them, we encourage you to seek their assistance. *You,* however, will be making the decisions and living with them. We believe that since the consequences of your decisions will affect you, you should maintain the primary responsibility for generating, evaluating, and using the data that affect those decisions. Hence, our focus on *self*-assessment.

We realize that your lack of professional training in career counseling and your own biases and preconceptions about who you are may leave you uneasy as you contemplate a self-assessment process. We have taken these things into account and have provided ways of compensating. First, we will explain in nontechnical terms the strengths and weaknesses of the process and the instruments we will use so that you can make an informed and conservative use of the data. Second, we will provide a way of allowing for the impact of your preconceptions. Third, we will use a variety of instru-

ments so that we will not have to rely on any single data-generating device, but rather will be able to take a multifaceted view and therefore one that is less susceptible to distortion.

We also expect that you may become impatient with this process. In our graduate program, we spend a full semester working through this book. Our experience has been that at first the data-generation process seems disjointed and unconnected. Do not let that disturb you. Before long it will begin to come together, and you will understand more clearly what is happening. It *is* a rigorous process, though, so you should be committed to following through. You can learn something by doing bits and pieces of the self-assessment, but the real strength of the process lies in the integration of the various exercises we will ask you to do. We promise you, as did some of *our* students in the introduction, that it will be worth your time and effort.

The Basic Approach

We will utilize a five-step approach to each of the exercises in the self-assessment process. As you go through the first part of this book, you will be repeating the following cycle a number of times:

1. First, you will use some data-generating device.
2. Then you will be asked to record your reactions to the exercise in a Feelings Record or journal.
3. You next will read the chapter that explains how to score and interpret the scores from that device.
4. You will then practice interpreting the data supplied by that instrument, using data from one or more cases.
5. Finally, you will do an initial interpretation of your own data.

The fourth step in the cycle is particularly important. Developing your skills at assessment requires practice. The case material in the first part of the book is carefully chosen with that requirement in mind.

Generating Useful Data

Rational assessment, of necessity, begins by generating or gathering information. This book contains and describes a number of different mechanisms that can elicit potentially useful information about a person. These include devices we have created for use here, as well as some standard psychological instruments. None of these methods alone can come close to capturing all there is to know about a person. But as a group, they will provide a rich and diverse pool of data tailored for our purposes.

Throughout the first stages of the self-assessment process, you will be asked to use the devices in the book to generate useful data about yourself. Most of these exercises will require only 30 to 60 minutes of your time. (One exception is the written interview, which will require considerably more time and effort and which we will explain later.) You will probably find some of the exercises fun, or at least interesting. And you will probably find some of the exercises boring, or anxiety-producing. These feelings can be useful data too, and we will ask you to record them as well.

One of the reasons people often feel anxious while using these devices is because they assume these mechanisms are evaluating them. They consciously, or more often unconsciously, believe that the devices will tell them if they are "dumb" or "smart," whether they have any chance at all of becoming a CPA, or whether or not they are "sane." As a result, they approach these devices with ambivalence, and they find using them to be somewhat anxiety-producing.

It is very important for you to recognize at the outset that these data-generating mechanisms *do not analyze you*. They do not tell you what you can or cannot do with your life or how good a person you are. All they do is supply potentially relevant information that *you* can use to create a self-assessment, which then can help you make better job- and career-related decisions. *You* have to make sense out of the information. *You* have to do the analysis. *You* are in charge. That's what self-assessment is all about.

Recording Your Feelings

Despite what we have just said, you will no doubt have a variety of emotional reactions to the various instruments in the self-assessment process. These reactions will be in large part due to the nature of the instrument, but other things will affect your feelings as well. The way the instrument is introduced to you, your physical and emotional state when you receive the instrument, what you were doing before you received it, interruptions while you are taking the test, and many other factors will influence your response to each instrument.

A careful recording of your reactions to each device can help in several ways. First, since each of the instruments is different in some way, a Feelings Record will help you to analyze your responses to different kinds of situations. This will help you to anticipate your responses to similar situations on the job. Second, since there are so many different factors that influence your reaction to any particular data-generating device, a record of the most salient will help you to sort out any distortions you feel have occurred in your test results. Finally, since you will be doing the analysis and will draw conclusions based only on data in which *you* have confidence, a detailed Feelings Record can help you to calibrate the validity a particular set of test data has for you. Your notes will remind you of your concerns about an instrument and to put its results in a reasonable perspective.

Understanding the Data-Generating Devices

In order to utilize the information supplied by any data-generating device, it is crucial that you understand the strengths and weaknesses of the device. Your data are only as good as the instrument used to generate them. The *kind* of information, the *accuracy* of the information, and the *use* of the information will all be affected by the nature of the instrument.

We have provided chapters that will give you some insight into the instruments we will be using. These chapters are not designed to make you an expert in measuring techniques; instead, they are designed to provide you with enough information so that you can reasonably and intelligently interpret the output of those devices. Remember, *do not read these chapters before you have completed the test or exercise associated with them*. If you do, your responses may be distorted by your knowledge of the scoring system and your beliefs about what constitutes a "desirable," "right," or "socially acceptable" response.

Practicing Interpretation

Once you have taken a test or exercise and read the note accompanying it, you will be asked to practice interpreting someone else's data—in most instances a case included in the book. This will give you a chance to develop some skill in using each set of data before you begin working on your own.

Our approach is fundamentally a process of inductive logic. That is, it starts by focusing on specifics (data generated by the various devices) and from that slowly develops generalizations (themes). This is in contrast to a deductive process, in which we would begin with a set of generalizations (a model) about the behavior of all human beings, and then use them to generate more specific generalizations about a specific person. (For example, if a model says that "all people with red hair are temperamental" and Joe has red hair, we would *deduce* that Joe is temperamental.[1])

This inductive process of thematic analysis is, in a sense, systematic detective work. It involves sifting through large amounts of information looking for clues (to potential themes), drawing tentative conclusions (about what the themes might be), and then testing those conclusions against still more data. And like detective work, it can be fun.

When you make observations from another person's data (the cases), strive to be conservative and to keep your inferences closely connected to the data. It is easy to let our own values, beliefs, habits, and views of the world color what we might say about another person—and what we might conclude about ourselves. One of the major objectives of the "practicing interpretation" step is to develop skill in drawing simple, conservative inferences from the data. We will have more to say about this later on, but be sure to keep it in mind as you begin.

You might ask: "How do I go about generating conservative inferences?" Generally, you will be asked to do two things. First, you will be asked to *observe* and *cite* a specific bit of evidence (a score on a test, for example) and then to draw an *inference* about what that datum might mean. These inferences are very simple, tentative statements, closely connected to the datum, that attempt to clarify the meaning of the datum. The note that accompanies each instrument will help you make these observations and inferences.

We also encourage you to think carefully about the strengths and weaknesses of each data-generating device. Ask yourself what kind of data it is producing. How accurate is it? To what kinds of distortions is it susceptible? What does it add to what I already know (or suspect about myself?) How might I use the data in conjunction with the other data I have generated?

---

[1]It would be nice if we could use a deductive approach to self-assessment, particularly because most of us have been educated more in deduction than induction. Unfortunately, however, we cannot. There exists today no single model of human behavior that is of the quality necessary for our purposes. The very best psychological or behavioral models are very limited in their scope and applicability. The behavioral sciences might some day create a truly general-purpose model of human behavior, but it most certainly does not exist now. An alternative method that would still allow deduction would be to study *all* the current models of human behavior and how and when each can be useful. But that is a task far beyond our scope here.

The answers to these questions will help you put the data you generate from each instrument into perspective.

If you are working through the self-assessment process alone, we encourage you to work through the cases too. Somehow it is much easier to be "objective" about someone else's data than it is about your own. We would also encourage you in your discussions with friends or spouses or counselors to seek feedback that will add to and complement your conclusions rather than that which will only confirm your views of yourself.

Interpreting Your Own Data

Now, once you have generated some data, read the note, and practiced interpreting a case, you will be asked to begin drawing inferences from your own data. Again, the principles of conservatism, tentativeness, and careful, logical connection should hold. Do not be concerned about drawing sweeping generalizations early in the process. The broader conclusions will come later. This we call "identifying themes."

Identifying Themes

Gradually, as you generate and sift through more and more data, you will begin to see inferences that recur or bits of data that seem to be connected in some way. These connections may be reflections of central themes that are characteristic of your life.

Keep in mind that our purpose is to use a self-assessment as an aid in making career and job decisions. That is, we seek to create a product that can help to discriminate among a set of potential or real career- and job-related options. We need something that can be used to help "predict" what might happen if a person chooses one career or job option over another: Will the individual be happier with job 1 or job 2? Will she be promoted faster at company A or company B? Will he be more likely to succeed with option 1 or option 2? Will she feel more family/job conflicts with offers 1, 2, or 3?

A self-assessment that can help answer these questions must focus on a person's central and stable characteristics. An assessment which says that an individual likes X, or tends to behave like Y, is not very useful if both X and Y can change within a month. Although human beings do change rather drastically in some ways in a short period of time, all people tend to change slowly or not at all in other ways. It is this latter set of characteristics that one searches for in the data.

To get at these more stable, central, and important aspects of a person that in daily conversation we often call "interests," "values," "skills," or "motives," we will be helping you develop skills at thematic analysis. In this type of analysis, we sort through data and inferences from the various devices looking for recurring ideas (themes). The underlying logic is straightforward and compelling: If evidence pointing to a particular theme ("likes to be in charge," for instance) is found a significant number of times in data generated from numerous devices, then it is probably justifiable to conclude that the evidence is saying something important about the person. With the systematic use of this type of analysis, you can find most of the important themes in your life and be well on your way toward a sound self-assessment.

Identifying Implications

The final step in the process is to identify the basic job, career, and life style implications of the themes you have located. This step involves translating that which you have found in the data into a form and format that is not only accurate, but easy to use in job or career decision making. We will help you as you make that translation.

Some Caveats

The process we will repeat with each instrument is outlined in Exhibit 2–1. The self-assessment checklist included at the end of this chapter is provided as a guideline to help you follow the procedure and track your progress.

Human beings are incredibly complex. You could spend your entire life learning about yourself. With varying degrees of awareness, you probably will. To undertake a self-assessment like the one presented here is an opportunity to learn a great deal about yourself in a relatively short time, and in a structured and carefully guided way. It requires a significant commitment of time and energy. Perhaps at no other time in your life will you take or make the opportunity to do what you are about to do. But there are some things you should think about before beginning.

Learning self-assessment is as intellectually demanding as learning marketing, or finance, or art history. But unlike most other subjects, self-assessment can also be *emotionally demanding*. It is useful to recognize this aspect of the process from the beginning. It is relatively easy to be objective and calm when we are asked to evaluate someone else's strengths and weaknesses. Assessing ourselves is quite a different matter. Virtually everyone finds engaging in self-assessment difficult. It is only natural to worry about how the assessment will turn out. It is normal to find yourself occasionally angry about one of the data-generating devices or cases. It is also common for people

Exhibit 2–1
The Self-Assessment Process

1. Complete the test or instrument without understanding its intent or objectives so as not to bias or distort your responses.
2. Record your reactions in your Feelings Record. How did you *feel* about taking the test? Where and when did you take it? How did that influence your results?
3. Read the accompanying note. Find out as much as you can about the instrument. How was it constructed? What is it trying to measure? How are the responses scored? What are the instrument's strengths and weaknesses?
4. Practice interpreting a sample case. Note a piece of data (a score, for example) and then draw a *simple, conservative, tentative, and logically connected* inference from it. "This is a person who..." may help you get started.
5. Interpret your own data using the principles and skills developed in item 4.

LATER

6. Use all the data (including your Feelings Record and your inferences) to *inductively* identify themes that run through the data.
7. Develop a set of *implications* for job- and career-related decisions.

sometimes to see nothing but "good" or nothing but "bad" things in their data, and to feel either very high or very low. That is just the way we are. Again, we encourage you to resist the evaluative posture and to adopt a descriptive one. Do not allow yourself to be always judging. Rather, *describe* and then use that description to make decisions.

Second, self-assessment can be very time-consuming. Sometimes, anxiety pushes people to spend inordinate amounts of time in the pursuit of the "final answer" or of every nuance in the "full story" of their lives. No known process can do that for you. You will not be able to "know all" as a result of this experience. Consequently, we urge you to think carefully about your schedule, your other responsibilities, and your self-discipline as you approach this process. Plan to spend enough time to allow you to work through the exercises, but also discipline yourself to say "Enough is enough." At every step, we will suggest assignments and activities to guide you through the process. These will generate enough data and enough skill in using the data to develop a personal profile that will identify most of the relevant themes in your life. You may feel compelled to go further. We caution: Be reasonable.

You should also know that there are no magic answers to the career-related questions that face you. We offer no crystal balls or predictions about "the perfect job" for you. We do offer a time-tested approach to generating and using extremely useful career data. But you must do the analysis. Do not expect miracles; expect instead an intense and very rewarding exercise in learning or articulating or confirming some important things about you.

This course is also not therapy. You should not consider the book or the process outlined in it to be a substitute for professional counseling. If it is feasible, we encourage you to take the course under the guidance of a trained faculty or in conjunction with other forms of career counseling. If you feel a need for in-depth, personal counseling, seek it. This book will not replace the benefits of that kind of assistance.

Consider these caveats carefully. Remember too, that as of December 1983, more than 1,500 of our students and hundreds of students in other settings have successfully carried out this self-assessment process and have utilized it productively. Seldom has anyone found the process too demanding emotionally. Most have felt that the process, though intense and demanding, yielded extremely useful information about themselves, about jobs in business management, about making career-related decisions, and about the impact of those decisions on their lives and on the organizations for which they work.

First Assignment

With this background, we hope you are eager to proceed. If so, we would like to introduce you to the data-generation part of the self-assessment process by asking you to read the case material that follows. The Dan and Mandy case which follows will help you to think about the *kinds* of information you will want to generate in your self-assessment process. As you read, ask yourself the following questions, and then note your answers on a piece of paper:

1. What decisions do Dan and Mandy need to make?
2. What *kinds* of information do Dan and Mandy need in order to make their decisions? (Consider not only data relating to them as individuals and as a couple, but also to the specific options they face.)
3. Assuming that Dan and Mandy have been able to collect the information you identified in question 2, *how* should they make their decision(s)? What *process* should they use to decide?

DAN AND MANDY

Dan and Mandy were second-year students at the Harvard Business School. On April 15 they were sitting in Mandy's living room discussing the decisions that were facing them. They had met in the first year of the MBA program and in the fall of the second year had become engaged to be married. They faced several different career and life style options and were wrestling with the choices they had to make.

Dan's Background

Dan was raised in an upper middle-class suburb of Philadelphia. His father had an M.D. and was a teaching doctor at a prestigious university. His mother had earned a Ph.D. in Social Research. Dan was the middle child of three boys. He had attended an exclusive boys prep school from the third grade through his high school graduation and gone on to Harvard College, taking a year off to "find himself" while working off and on as a short order cook. Dan worked for several years as a teacher of Transcendental Meditation, most recently to professional sports teams. After an attempt to write a book, Dan had decided to attend the Harvard Business School to gain more professional business education and to broaden his skills. He was 31 when he was graduated.

Dan's Options

In April, Dan had several job options.

NON-PROFIT DATA SERVICES. NPDS, a relatively new Boston firm engaged in fundraising for non-profit organizations and direct mail marketing for private sector companies, had offered Dan the

This case was prepared by Assistant Professor James G. Clawson as a basis for class discussion rather than to illustrate effective or ineffective handling of a career-related situation. Copyright © 1980 by the President and Fellows of Harvard College. Harvard Business School case 9-481-016.

position of Marketing Manager for Sports. Dan's responsibilities would be to work with professional sports organizations to develop computer-assisted means of generating income from alternatives to paid gate attendance at sporting events.

ATLANTIC ASSOCIATES. The AA offer was in Washington, D.C., where Dan would be working with public sector clients as a salesman and trainer/consultant. Dan expected that he would be traveling to visit clients at least two or three days out of every week.

NEW ENGLAND CONSULTING. NEC offered Dan a position in Boston in their Organizational Development and Executive Education group. Dan was to be a consultant traveling about 50% of the time.

EXECUTIVE EDUCATION. Dan had also received an offer from another business school to be an assistant program manager for a series of executive education courses conducted by the University. Implicit in the offer was the understanding that after six months to a year of experience Dan would be made the Program Manager. It was also understood that the job would probably not extend beyond five years. The school was located within an hour's drive of Boston.

A MAJOR BROADCASTING COMPANY. One of the major TV-Radio networks had offered Dan his choice of two positions, one in sales and one in advertising and promotion, both located in New York. The jobs held the promise of a possible move into sports in the future.

SOLAR ENERGY CORPORATION. Dan's last offer came from SEC. The firm was young, comprised of engineers working on problems associated with the large-scale generation of solar produced electrical energy. The small firm wanted Dan to be its Business Manager. The firm was located in a rural setting west of Boston.

Mandy's Background

Mandy was born and raised an only child in a blue collar neighborhood "15 miles geographically but 850 million light years culturally" removed from New York City. Mandy's parents both worked in public education—her father as an administrator and her mother as a teacher. After she graduated from high school, Mandy went to Barnard College and in her second year married her high school boyfriend. After giving birth to two children, Mandy was divorced from her hus-

band and left school to work on Wall Street for a well-known stockbroker. She rose very quickly in the organization and received large salary increases beyond her expectations. Working at night, she finally completed her undergraduate degree when she was 28. Then, with the financial support of the company, she applied to the Harvard Business School and was admitted.

Mandy's Options

Having met Dan and become engaged, Mandy faced several career options as well.

WALL STREET. Mandy's first option was to return to the Wall Street firm where she had been employed before coming to the MBA program at a greatly increased salary but to work for the same supervisor she had had when she left.

HOUSEWIFE AND MOTHER. Alternately, Mandy could stay at home while Dan worked and attend to raising her two daughters and to managing the household affairs. This alternative would provide her children with a "traditional home life" that they had not yet experienced.

UNIVERSITY ADMINISTRATION. Mandy also had received an offer to work as an Assistant Director of Admissions at a Boston university, a position that would include the supervision of the processing of thousands of applications on an annual basis.

Additional Issues and Concerns

In the midst of their career decision making, Dan and Mandy also faced some other major questions.

MARRIAGE. Dan and Mandy had set May 30 as the date for their wedding. Aside from the significant time and energy required to plan the event, they were thinking about adjusting to their new life style—indeed, about *shaping* it. Questions about family finances, education for the two children, friendship networks, commuting and travel time, recreation, and others bubbled up frequently in their conversations.

HOUSING. Since at the outset their marriage would involve four people, they had thought seriously about purchasing a home. Interest rates at the time were rising, and it seemed economically wise to invest in a house as soon as possible. Mandy, given her background, had had a childhood dream of living in a well-groomed, suburban neighborhood. An opportunity had arisen in a community 30 minutes west of Boston to purchase a home which seemed to meet both of their life style interests, and in fact, they had signed a purchase and sale agreement with a probable closing date of May 30. The house had over an acre of land and was set in a thickly wooded area.

The home was 10 minutes from SEC's offices and about 45 minutes each from Atlantic Associates and Dan's Executive Education offer. It took an hour to reach Boston's Logan Airport.

Making Their Decisions

As Mandy and Dan talked, the options that faced them raised a complex set of decisions that had to be made. They wrestled with their decision to purchase the house, with which of the job opportunities would make the most sense as a family, and with the kind of life style that they would like to forge out of their new marriage, their new family, and their new career opportunities.

3 The Written Interview Assignment

The intent of the Dan and Mandy assignment was to get you thinking about the *kinds* of information that will be useful for you to generate in your self-assessment experience. This will be helpful to you as you begin the next assignment, the written interview.

When an individual begins career counseling, the usual first step is a lengthy, in-depth discussion about the person's background. This interview provides a context and typically generates rich data about topics important to consider in making career decisions.

Since we are unable to have this interview with you personally, we have designed a means to simulate the interview and to generate that data. We have constructed some questions that will lead you through a typical background career counseling interview. Writing your answers to the questions will take a good deal of time—how much will depend on you. If you write too much, you may feel overwhelmed in the analytic stage. How much is too little or too much? That's up to you. Our experience has been that somewhere between 25 and 75 handwritten pages is a useful amount. That may seem like a lot, but it will become apparent how easy it is to talk (in this case, write) about yourself.

If you would rather dictate your answers, feel free to do so, but we strongly encourage you to make arrangements to have a written or typed transcript made. This written copy will be invaluable later on. You will need to be able to go back and read your answers.

If you decide to type your answers, don't worry about typographical errors or neatness. Going back to correct or to tidy up will tend to break the flow of your thoughts—and the natural flow is important.

There are 11 questions, one each on the 11 pages that follow. The point of using separate pages is that our dialogue is going to proceed in stages, as a good dialogue should. The natural development of your in-terview and the purity of your answers will be enhanced if you do *not* look ahead. Read the contents of each page only after you have responded completely to the previous question we, your interviewers, have posed. The point is not to spring any great surprises, but to facilitate an interview-like sequence in your ideas. To do that, we have to provide a series of cues, one at a time, so that the effect is one of question, then reply, then question, then reply.

Your replies will be much longer than the questions, of course. As is the case with any good data-generating interview, this one is going to consist of much more of *your* talk than of our talk. When you have finished what you have to say in response to each of our questions and are ready to go on, turn to the next page. We will get a few remarks of our own into the conversation, and then ask another question.

Do not feel that you have to complete the written interview in one sitting. In fact, after question 4 we encourage you to leave it for a day or so. Feel free to leave your writing at *any* point and then to come back and resume.

Occasionally the questions may seem a bit redundant. That really depends on what you've said in response to the previous questions. If you come to a question you have already answered completely, then go on.

When you have set aside some time for your first sitting and are ready to start this "interview," please turn the page to question 1. Relax, and write as you "talk" in reply to the question.

> NOTE:
> DO NOT SKIP AHEAD IN THE INTERVIEW.
> READ THE FOLLOWING PAGE FIRST, AND THEN ANSWER EACH
> QUESTION SEQUENTIALLY.

The goal you and we now share is to generate good data from which you can make valid inferences about your own career. In the end it is you who will make the inferences, so in one sense, all through this exercise or even all through this course, you will be talking to yourself. We are, however, going to listen in. Our presence may enable you to talk to yourself in a more useful way. We will try to steer your soliloquy away from running around in circles. Which direction its tangent should take is not, however, something we intend to dictate or direct. Our job is to show you how to generate good information about yourself, for yourself.

What you are going to need is an account of your life more structured than free association, more personal than a résumé or vita. The level of discourse will be that of personal history—an overview of all those years' diaries that you didn't keep (or at least the parts suitable for public consumption).

Just let it flow. If you belatedly realize you've left something out, put it in when you think about it. This is a *rough* manuscript! Order and method come later.

How long should your story be? As long as it takes to tell. Although an autobiography is usually book length, you may be able to tell your story in the equivalent of a chapter or two.

Tell away!

---

[1]This material was revised by Assistant Professor James G. Clawson. Copyright © 1980 by the President and Fellows of Harvard College. Harvard Business School case 9-481-012.

How late did you start your story? Most people get themselves born and then jump to age 20 when they began their official "career." In a résumé you would lump all the distant past into a few lines under "miscellany." But if you want to collect the facts you'll need later to analyze your own career path, you should fill in some of the things that happened before you were an adult.

Not that we care if you fell in love with your rocking horse at the age of 4. But if your story begins with "I graduated at Michigan," it probably leaves out some facts that are both public and pertinent. What do you remember about primary school or before? How about secondary school? What were your hobbies and avocations? What were the things you had to do but didn't like? What about . . . well, you tell us. This is your life.

What else went on long ago?

Set aside your rambling account of your life from question 1, and go ahead and write some more about the beginning of your life story.

Unless you've already said all that need be said. If so, go on to the next question.

Now, what about the unaccounted-for times? Perhaps there are none in your answers so far, but that would be unusual. Most people leave out little bits and pieces here and there. What went on during your summers? Was there a two-month gap between graduation and a first job? Did those four years at school include one spent abroad? Were there jobs that filled your evenings or weekends?

These odds and ends of living often teach lessons that matter. They often contain data you can use now even though you saw no relevance in the experience back then.

Set aside question 2 and write some bits and pieces about the little odds and ends of living that got tucked in between the major activities you already have described.

Of course, if you have already covered everything, you won't have much work to do for this step in our conversation.

Question 4

What about the jobs you have had so far, both the full-time and the part-time ones? You may have mentioned most of them already. Think back and tell us what it was that you liked and disliked about those jobs. Was it the people? The location? The daily tasks? The pay? Or something else?

If you've already done that carefully, go on. Otherwise, take some time with this one. It can help later.

When you've completed your answer to this question, take a break. Don't go on to the next one just yet. Let it all sit for a day, and then come back to Question 5.

Question 5

Hi again! Last time we asked you about your life and the jobs you've had to this point. Today we'd like to get a little more personal. Talk a little, if you already haven't, about the people in your life. At least the public facts. Who were you closest to, and why? Who used to bug you? What did each of your parents do? Tell us about other members of your family. Were there any major changes in your family structure? What about marriage? And your friends, who are they? What is it that draws you together? In other words, who are the people in your life, and how have you arranged your life around them?

We'll make good use of all these data later on. We ask no judgments of these people, only description. They were there in your life. They're a part of the picture. Tell us about them.

Now, what about the future? Of course, that's the question we're working on in this course, so you may not have any clear answers. But sit back and try to imagine what your ideal future would be like and write it down. What's the happy ending?

Maybe there is more than just one dream. If so, tell us about them. Or if the future is too unclear, tell us about the uncertainties you see, the tradeoffs, the dilemmas.

Question 7

If we read back over the exchanges in your written interview, we can surely find a series of points when your situation changed. You left secondary school to go to college, college to go to graduate school. You may have entered one or another of the armed services from which you subsequently departed, presumably making a decision not to stay when your hitch was over. Perhaps during your college years you transferred, took a year elsewhere, or dropped out. Or simply changed major field. At the very least, you picked a summer job or school or vacation spot.

Before we go on with our written interview, please go back over your story and pick out these points of change. Make a list of them. Add some others that we haven't discussed if others now occur to you. This list will be the backbone of our discussion as we continue our written interview.

You may have already said something about the turning points you've just listed, but there is much to be learned by talking at greater length and in a more systematic way about them. Please go back and tell us a couple of things about each turning point.

First, what were the other options? Even in situations in which you thought you had no choice at all, in all likelihood you did. Maybe you applied only to one college; even so, what others did you consider? Did you have more than one acceptance? One's major field is not usually the one and only possibility ever thought about. Tell us about these other paths you did not take.

Second, tell us about the pros and cons of each of these options. It would be useful to know what the criteria were, the formal ones, the ones other influential people in your life were citing, and the real ones that determined which way you went.

Third, tell us how you arrived at your decisions. Were they easy choices? Perhaps some were made in large part for you? How long did they take? Did you talk to lots of other people? Maybe none? As you look back now, how did you wind your way through each of those turning points to where you are now?

Your life changed in some ways after each of these turning points. After the turning point, what new things had importance? How was living different than it had been before? What new things stood out for you?

External circumstances presumably differed in obvious ways. A dormitory is not the same as your own home. But the point is, what changed *for you*? Was there in some ways a new you? More subtly, was there a new texture of living? How did you react to it?

As a part of your response, you might also want to reflect on which parts of your previous life are still with you, which have withered away, and which are locked up in a "wait until later" mode. Maybe electronics was a high school diversion, or skiing, or drama. Is it still? What effect did these turning points have on those interests?

Again thinking about the turning points, what disillusionments did you suffer? Can you recall your expectations about college, or the army, or a job, and how these expectations contrasted with the event? Perhaps you were utterly realistic in advance—if so, that is a datum about you well worth recording.

Try to recall what you thought each situation was going to be like before you confronted it and then how it in fact turned out. Perhaps your expectations were dead wrong, perhaps they were right on target. Probably there were aspects of the new situation that would never have occurred to you even in your wildest imaginings!

At any rate, please try a little retrospection on the before-and-after view of each listed event. Perhaps even a table is indicated—As Seen Before and After—but a little narrative will serve too.

The emphasis here is on cognitive awareness, not on values. Did you know the facts?

By now you must be aware of some repetition in what you've been saying. There probably are themes. What patterns do *you* see? In the past you have been basing your actions on certain kinds of considerations. Do they still hold true? Were the same criteria used in several decisions? Were your choices derived from similar processes? Can you see trends over time?

If you want to be systematic, you can make some tables showing the plus and minus factors, and perhaps also their weight, in each decision. What factors recur? Can you conceptualize a common factor that underlies apparently distinct events? If you arrange the decisions chronologically, do the choices evolve with time?

This last point is of special interest, since being able to observe yourself acting as if you held consistent values and beliefs is one thing and deciding to base your next decision on these same considerations is quite another. There are two sides to a career: where it has been and where it is going.

Can the array of ins and outs of your actions in the past reveal to you something of the direction of time's arrow?

When you have completed this reply, you are done with the interview. Put your replies together here in your notebook. It's been an exhausting experience, but we hope a very interesting one so far. We've enjoyed helping you generate this rather detailed and lengthy account of your life.

We'll both be referring to this written interview over and over again as the course progresses, so before you put it in your notebook, please go back and number each paragraph sequentially. You may have as much as 60 or 70 pages with 4 or 5 paragraphs per page. That's over 300 paragraphs. It will take a few minutes to do this, but it will really help later on. When you've numbered your paragraphs, you've completed your written interview.

We appreciate the time and effort it has taken to write it and trust that it will serve you well.

The Written Interview Assignment   **35**

Upon Finishing the Written Interview

Now that you have completed your written interview, you probably are a little tired of it—even though it has no doubt generated a lot of fond (and maybe not so fond) memories and feelings. In order to get some distance from the written interview and to let your emotions settle a little, we ask you to set it aside for a while. We will go on with other parts of the self-assessment process and then come back to the written interview data.

Before we leave it, however, we would like to have you begin your Feelings Record. This will be a journal of your experiencing of the self-assessment process that will help you think more clearly—now and later—about what you are doing. It will also provide some valuable data later on.

Feelings Record—Written Interview

Take a few minutes and write down on the following page your reactions to the written interview. Did you enjoy it? Why or why not? How did you feel while you were writing it? How do you feel now?

Along the way, we will remind you to make note of your reactions to each instrument, but we encourage you to make notes of your feelings at any point in the process. Feel free to expand upon our reminders as much as you like.

We also encourage you to collect your entries in one place in order to make them easier to use later on. If you are using a three-ring binder, we suggest you make a separate index tab for the Feelings Record.

When you're done making your Feelings Record entry and have set aside an hour or so, turn the page and begin working on our next data-generating device, Sorting Life and Career Values.

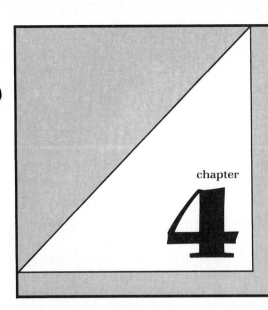

chapter

4

Sorting Career and Life Values

You will need from one to two hours to complete this exercise. *Please make sure that you will not be interrupted,* for although the exercise is relatively simple, it will require careful concentration. Select a space that is quiet—no music please—and that has a minimum of visual stimuli. The intent here is to reduce all external stimuli as much as possible so that you are left with your thoughts and feelings as your primary focus.

You will also need a large flat table or countertop the size of a large desk. A card table is about as small a surface as will function well. You will also need a pencil, an eraser, several sheets of 8 ½ " × 11" typing paper, and maybe some 3 × 5 cards, scissors, and cellophane tape.

The thicker pages at the end of the book contain two kinds of cards—blue "aspect" cards and white "values" cards. Remove these pages from the book and separate the cards by tearing them carefully along the perforated lines. Note that there are several blank blue aspect cards and several blank white values cards.

Sorting the Blue Aspect Cards

Your first task is to arrange the blue aspect cards at the top of your table from left to right in descending order of their importance to you now. As you sort the blue cards, you may feel that two or more are equally important. Think carefully about such groups of cards

and try to rank them. If you cannot, cluster the two or more equally important cards together by leaving a space between them and the next card or cards. An alternative method is to cluster cards within three groups—Most Important, Moderately Important, and Least Important. But do not feel any pressure to use this division.

If you have sorted the cards into clusters, go back to each cluster and force yourself to set priorities *within* each cluster. This may be difficult. Nevertheless, *do it.* Ask yourself the question: "If I could have everything I wanted in just *one* of these categories, which one would I choose?" Then, having chosen one aspect card and placed it on the left-hand side of that cluster, ask yourself the same question for the cards remaining in that cluster.

If you think of aspects of your life that are not included in the blue aspect cards, feel free to label a blank card and include it in the exercise.

As you sort the cards from left to right, use the width of the table to provide a rough guide of importance. If one value or cluster of values is much more important than the next value or cluster, separate them by a wider space than the space between two equally important values.

Once you have carefully sorted the blue aspect cards, note their order and relative spacing at the top of the long side of a piece of typing paper. Your diagram may look something like this:

If the paper is not long enough, tape another sheet to the right-hand edge and continue.

Sorting the White Values Cards

Now that you have the blue aspect cards arranged in order of importance, sort the white values cards beneath them, toward you from top to bottom, in descending order of importance. This exercise is intended to help you identify both *what* is important within each aspect of your life and *how important* those things are. We have provided a number of white values cards to help you get started, but we encourage you to write in your own answer to the question:

WHAT IS IT ABOUT THIS ASPECT OF MY LIFE THAT IS IMPORTANT TO ME?

At first, do not worry about sorting the values cards in order of importance. Rather, just stack them (using either our printed cards or your own written ones) beneath each blue aspect card. Some values may seem to relate primarily to one aspect or another. Other cards may seem to apply to several aspects. Feel free to duplicate cards in more than one stack if you choose.

Once you have what is a relatively complete stack of things that are important to you in *each* aspect of your life, you are ready to sort each stack in order of its importance to you. Do so for each aspect, placing the most important value at the top just beneath the blue aspect card and the least important value closest to you at the bottom of the column. Again, use spaces to reflect the relative strength of the values you have selected. Try to be strictly honest with yourself. Do not order the cards according to what you think you *should* value, but what you *do* value. Think about choices you have made, the way you spend your time, your language, your emotions, your private thoughts—and what they tell you about the values you now hold.

When you have finished, your table will look something like this:

The cards will be sorted according to this value structure:

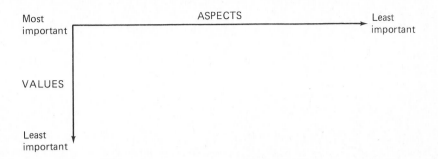

Now, *write down* the arrangement you have on the sheet where you recorded your aspect values. The values in the upper left-hand or northwest quadrant will be your most important values, while those in the lower right-hand or southeast quadrant will be your least important values. You are now ready to begin interpreting your values structure.

Interpreting Career and Life Values Structures

> NOTE:
> DO NOT READ THIS UNTIL YOU HAVE COMPLETED
> THE CAREER AND LIFE VALUES CARD SORT.

Identifying and ranking personal values is one of the most difficult tasks in making career decisions. The task is difficult because values shift in peripheral ways from day to day, and in moderately deep ways from "chapter" to "chapter" in one's life. But at the core, many of our values are remarkably stable over the years. A few core values may change, some with dramatic effect on our lives, but most will continue to guide our choices and activities throughout our lives. Our intent in this exercise is to help you gain a clearer picture of your own value structure in terms of the aspects of your life you value most highly and of the values you hold in each of them. We have included as a practice exercise Tom Wilson's value structure (see case, p. 42). If you are in a regular course, answer the questions below for Wilson's data first, and use your analysis for class discussion. Having practiced it once and learned from the comments of your classmates, analyze your own value structure.

Before you do, though, take a few minutes to record your reactions to this test in your Feelings Record (see page 42).

Step One

First, notice the array of aspects across the top of the page. Is there a pattern? Are the "personal" aspects clustered? If so, are they higher or lower than the "professional" aspects or the "family" aspects? Or are the various aspects mixed in a seeming attempt to find a relatively even balance among them all? How are the aspects spaced? Where are the gaps? What inferences could you draw from these data about this person? Write them down on the Career Values Sort Inferences sheet.

Step Two

Next, look at the white values cards *horizontally* across aspects. Which ones appear most often? Which ones least often? What does this tell you? Write down your inferences.

Step Three

Finally, look at the vertical columns of values. Where are the gaps? Where are the most values listed? Which ones are at the top of each column? What do these things tell you about this person?

TOM WILSON: LIFE AND CAREER VALUE CARD SORT

Primary Value Cluster

A1. Marital

Being independent
Being close
Organizing
Providing
Focus
Set schedules

A2. Parental

Being responsible
Being close
Watching people grow
Teaching

A3. Social

Part of group
Being close
Meeting others
Fun

A4. Professional

Seen as expert
Using energy resources
  wisely
Being praised
Being rewarded

A5. Financial

Planning
Deciding what to do
Getting ahead
Working on details

Secondary Value Cluster

B1. Familial

Being praised
Being encouraged

B3. Intellectual

Learning

B5. Physical

Creating
Building

B7. Political

Recognition
Expanding

B2. Recreational

Enjoying
Relaxing

B4. Identity

Being free
Feeling as an expert

B6. Emotional

Building
Confidence
Influence

Tertiary Value Cluster

C1. Ecclesiastical

Helping others

C3. Societal

Helping others
Working on the broad is-
  sues

C2. Spiritual

Admiring the beauty of it
  all

C4. Material

Having as much as pos-
  sible

This case was prepared by Kevin E. Sachs, research assistant, under the direction of Associate Professor James G. Clawson, as a basis for class discussion. © 1982 by the Sponsors of The Colgate Darden Graduate School of Business, the University of Virginia, Charlottesville, Virginia.

Inferences from the Career and Life Values Sort

This is a person who   *Data*

Sorting Career and Life Values   **43**

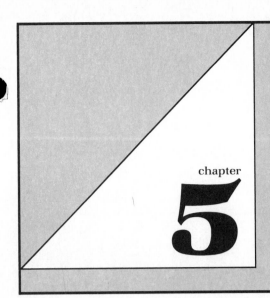

Interpersonal Style Inventory

The following test will help you to learn more about your interpersonal style, an important dimension in a social world.

Administration

First, complete the Current Self report form by circling the number that most describes you as you see yourself now on each dimension. Then complete the Desired Self report form by circling the number that most describes you as you would *like* to be.

When you have completed both forms, select five people from among your acquaintances. It is preferable that these people be colleagues at work, or if you are a student, people who know you reasonably well from class. Do not choose total strangers or more than two or three of your closest friends. The objective is to select a group of people who have interacted with

you or observed you frequently, but who are also willing to be very honest with you.

Next, select a person who is willing to collect the data from the five people in your interpersonal sample. This is important to insure a degree of anonymity for your chosen respondents. This person might be one of the five. Give the "data collector" a list of the names of the people you have selected.

Fourth, give each person in your sample a copy of the Acquaintance's Report and ask him or her to circle the number by each dimension that best describes you as you are now. Explain that it will only take five minutes to complete. *Be sure that you have written your name and the name of the data collector at the top of the page.* Ask the person to give (send) the completed form to your data collector. Explain that the data collector will assemble the data and pass it on anonymously to you in a set of five. Or, you may ask your respondents to mail the completed forms to you.

Interpersonal Style Inventory
CURRENT SELF

Circle the number beside each dimension that you feel best describes you as you are now.

	Never		Average		Always
Takes the lead	1	2	3	4	5
Needs support	1	2	3	4	5
Seeks recognition	1	2	3	4	5
Works alone	1	2	3	4	5
Helps others	1	2	3	4	5
Follows the rules	1	2	3	4	5
Listens well	1	2	3	4	5
Is willing to learn	1	2	3	4	5
Trusts others	1	2	3	4	5
Gets defensive if criticized	1	2	3	4	5
Discusses emotions	1	2	3	4	5
Discusses personal things	1	2	3	4	5
Is easy to talk to	1	2	3	4	5
Is docile, self-effacing	1	2	3	4	5
Gives praise	1	2	3	4	5
Is consistent	1	2	3	4	5
Is conceited	1	2	3	4	5
Can adapt to different social settings	1	2	3	4	5
Is competitive	1	2	3	4	5
Makes *own* decisions	1	2	3	4	5
Is calm	1	2	3	4	5
Is mechanical	1	2	3	4	5
Is tolerant of others	1	2	3	4	5
Is patient	1	2	3	4	5
Keeps promises	1	2	3	4	5
Is cheerful	1	2	3	4	5

Interpersonal Style Inventory
DESIRED SELF

Circle the number beside each dimension that you feel best describes you as you would like to be. (Note this is not necessarily different from the Current Self answers.)

	Never		Average		Always
Takes the lead	1	2	3	4	5
Needs support	1	2	3	4	5
Seeks recognition	1	2	3	4	5
Works alone	1	2	3	4	5
Helps others	1	2	3	4	5
Follows the rules	1	2	3	4	5
Listens well	1	2	3	4	5
Is willing to learn	1	2	3	4	5
Trusts others	1	2	3	4	5
Gets defensive if criticized	1	2	3	4	5
Discusses emotions	1	2	3	4	5
Discusses personal things	1	2	3	4	5
Is easy to talk to	1	2	3	4	5
Is docile, self-effacing	1	2	3	4	5
Gives praise	1	2	3	4	5
Is consistent	1	2	3	4	5
Is conceited	1	2	3	4	5
Can adapt to different social settings	1	2	3	4	5
Is competitive	1	2	3	4	5
Makes *own* decisions	1	2	3	4	5
Is calm	1	2	3	4	5
Is mechanical	1	2	3	4	5
Is tolerant of others	1	2	3	4	5
Is patient	1	2	3	4	5
Keeps promises	1	2	3	4	5
Is cheerful	1	2	3	4	5

Interpersonal Style Inventory
AQUAINTANCE REPORT 1

This brief exercise is intended to collect some descriptive information on
_____, *an acquaintance of yours. Please CIRCLE the number by*
each item that you feel best describes this person and then hand (or send) the completed
form to _____, *who has agreed to collect several forms and return*
them anonymously to your acquaintance. Thank you for your assistance.

	Never		Average		Always
Takes the lead	1	2	3	4	5
Needs support	1	2	3	4	5
Seeks recognition	1	2	3	4	5
Works alone	1	2	3	4	5
Helps others	1	2	3	4	5
Follows the rules	1	2	3	4	5
Listens well	1	2	3	4	5
Is willing to learn	1	2	3	4	5
Trusts others	1	2	3	4	5
Gets defensive if criticized	1	2	3	4	5
Discusses emotions	1	2	3	4	5
Discusses personal things	1	2	3	4	5
Is easy to talk to	1	2	3	4	5
Is docile, self-effacing	1	2	3	4	5
Gives praise	1	2	3	4	5
Is consistent	1	2	3	4	5
Is conceited	1	2	3	4	5
Can adapt to different social settings	1	2	3	4	5
Is competitive	1	2	3	4	5
Makes *own* decisions	1	2	3	4	5
Is calm	1	2	3	4	5
Is mechanical	1	2	3	4	5
Is tolerant of others	1	2	3	4	5
Is patient	1	2	3	4	5
Keeps promises	1	2	3	4	5
Is cheerful	1	2	3	4	5

Interpersonal Style Inventory
ACQUAINTANCE REPORT 2

This brief exercise is intended to collect some descriptive information on
_____, *an acquaintance of yours. Please CIRCLE the number by*
each item that you feel best describes this person and then hand (or send) the completed
form to _____, *who has agreed to collect several forms and return*
them anonymously to your acquaintance. Thank you for your assistance.

	Never		Average		Always
Takes the lead	1	2	3	4	5
Needs support	1	2	3	4	5
Seeks recognition	1	2	3	4	5
Works alone	1	2	3	4	5
Helps others	1	2	3	4	5
Follows the rules	1	2	3	4	5
Listens well	1	2	3	4	5
Is willing to learn	1	2	3	4	5
Trusts others	1	2	3	4	5
Gets defensive if criticized	1	2	3	4	5
Discusses emotions	1	2	3	4	5
Discusses personal things	1	2	3	4	5
Is easy to talk to	1	2	3	4	5
Is docile, self-effacing	1	2	3	4	5
Gives praise	1	2	3	4	5
Is consistent	1	2	3	4	5
Is conceited	1	2	3	4	5
Can adapt to different social settings	1	2	3	4	5
Is competitive	1	2	3	4	5
Makes *own* decisions	1	2	3	4	5
Is calm	1	2	3	4	5
Is mechanical	1	2	3	4	5
Is tolerant of others	1	2	3	4	5
Is patient	1	2	3	4	5
Keeps promises	1	2	3	4	5
Is cheerful	1	2	3	4	5

Interpersonal Style Inventory
ACQUAINTANCE REPORT 3

This brief exercise is intended to collect some descriptive information on
_____, *an acquaintance of yours. Please CIRCLE the number by*
each item that you feel best describes this person and then hand (or send) the completed
form to _____, *who has agreed to collect several forms and return*
them anonymously to your acquaintance. Thank you for your assistance.

	Never		Average		Always
Takes the lead	1	2	3	4	5
Needs support	1	2	3	4	5
Seeks recognition	1	2	3	4	5
Works alone	1	2	3	4	5
Helps others	1	2	3	4	5
Follows the rules	1	2	3	4	5
Listens well	1	2	3	4	5
Is willing to learn	1	2	3	4	5
Trusts others	1	2	3	4	5
Gets defensive if criticized	1	2	3	4	5
Discusses emotions	1	2	3	4	5
Discusses personal things	1	2	3	4	5
Is easy to talk to	1	2	3	4	5
Is docile, self-effacing	1	2	3	4	5
Gives praise	1	2	3	4	5
Is consistent	1	2	3	4	5
Is conceited	1	2	3	4	5
Can adapt to different social settings	1	2	3	4	5
Is competitive	1	2	3	4	5
Makes *own* decisions	1	2	3	4	5
Is calm	1	2	3	4	5
Is mechanical	1	2	3	4	5
Is tolerant of others	1	2	3	4	5
Is patient	1	2	3	4	5
Keeps promises	1	2	3	4	5
Is cheerful	1	2	3	4	5

Interpersonal Style Inventory
ACQUAINTANCE REPORT 4

This brief exercise is intended to collect some descriptive information on
_____, *an acquaintance of yours. Please CIRCLE the number by*
each item that you feel best describes this person and then hand (or send) the completed
form to _____, *who has agreed to collect several forms and return*
them anonymously to your acquaintance. Thank you for your assistance.

	Never		Average		Always
Takes the lead	1	2	3	4	5
Needs support	1	2	3	4	5
Seeks recognition	1	2	3	4	5
Works alone	1	2	3	4	5
Helps others	1	2	3	4	5
Follows the rules	1	2	3	4	5
Listens well	1	2	3	4	5
Is willing to learn	1	2	3	4	5
Trusts others	1	2	3	4	5
Gets defensive if criticized	1	2	3	4	5
Discusses emotions	1	2	3	4	5
Discusses personal things	1	2	3	4	5
Is easy to talk to	1	2	3	4	5
Is docile, self-effacing	1	2	3	4	5
Gives praise	1	2	3	4	5
Is consistent	1	2	3	4	5
Is conceited	1	2	3	4	5
Can adapt to different social settings	1	2	3	4	5
Is competitive	1	2	3	4	5
Makes *own* decisions	1	2	3	4	5
Is calm	1	2	3	4	5
Is mechanical	1	2	3	4	5
Is tolerant of others	1	2	3	4	5
Is patient	1	2	3	4	5
Keeps promises	1	2	3	4	5
Is cheerful	1	2	3	4	5

Interpersonal Style Inventory
ACQUAINTANCE REPORT 5

This brief exercise is intended to collect some descriptive information on _____, an acquaintance of yours. Please CIRCLE the number by each item that you feel best describes this person and then hand (or send) the completed form to _____, who has agreed to collect several forms and return them anonymously to your acquaintance. Thank you for your assistance.

	Never		Average		Always
Takes the lead	1	2	3	4	5
Needs support	1	2	3	4	5
Seeks recognition	1	2	3	4	5
Works alone	1	2	3	4	5
Helps others	1	2	3	4	5
Follows the rules	1	2	3	4	5
Listens well	1	2	3	4	5
Is willing to learn	1	2	3	4	5
Trusts others	1	2	3	4	5
Gets defensive if criticized	1	2	3	4	5
Discusses emotions	1	2	3	4	5
Discusses personal things	1	2	3	4	5
Is easy to talk to	1	2	3	4	5
Is docile, self-effacing	1	2	3	4	5
Gives praise	1	2	3	4	5
Is consistent	1	2	3	4	5
Is conceited	1	2	3	4	5
Can adapt to different social settings	1	2	3	4	5
Is competitive	1	2	3	4	5
Makes *own* decisions	1	2	3	4	5
Is calm	1	2	3	4	5
Is mechanical	1	2	3	4	5
Is tolerant of others	1	2	3	4	5
Is patient	1	2	3	4	5
Keeps promises	1	2	3	4	5
Is cheerful	1	2	3	4	5

Scoring and Interpreting the
Interpersonal Style Inventory

Scoring

When the data collector has accumulated all five reports and given them to you, take a few minutes to write your reactions to this exercise in your Feelings Record. How did you feel about asking acquaintances for feedback? What about asking a friend to collect the data? How do you feel, having collected the data but not yet analyzed it? Any other thoughts or feelings?

Now, transfer the data to the Interpersonal Style Inventory Scoring Form. Sum the scores for each di-mension and find the simple average (mean) and standard deviation for each dimension.

Then, plot your Current Self, Desired Self, and Acquaintances' Report scores on the Interpersonal Style Inventory Profile. Draw lines to connect each score sequentially, using a red line for your Current Self, a blue line for your Desired Self and a black line for the Acquaintances' Report.

Interpretation

The interpretation of the interpersonal style inventory consists of a series of comparisons among the three profiles you have plotted. Look first at the differentials or gaps between your Current Self profile and the Acquaintances' Report. Where are the largest gaps? Which is most accurate? Where are the smallest ones? On which dimensions did you describe yourself as being higher than your acquaintances did? On which ones lower? What do these results tell you about your interpersonal style? Write down your answers.

Then, compare your Desired Self profile with the

INTERPERSONAL STYLE INVENTORY SCORING FORM

ITEM	ACQUAINTANCE					SUM	MEAN	S.D.
	1	2	3	4	5			
Takes lead								
Needs support								
Seeks recognition								
Works alone								
Helps others								
Follows rules								
Listens well								
Willing to learn								
Trusts others								
Defensive								
Emotional								
Discusses personal								
Easy to talk to								
Docile								
Praises								
Is consistent								
Is conceited								
Adapts								
Competitive								
Own decisions								
Calm								
Mechanical								
Tolerant								
Patient								
Keeps promises								
Cheerful								

—X—X— = Current Self, ———— = Desired Self, — — — — = Acquaintances' Report

ITEM	ACQ. S.D.	Never 1	2	Average 3	4	Always 5
Takes lead		•	•	•	•	•
Seeks recognition		•	•	•	•	•
Is conceited		•	•	•	•	•
Is competitive		•	•	•	•	•
Defensive		•	•	•	•	•
Works alone		•	•	•	•	•
Own decisions		•	•	•	•	•
Mechanical		•	•	•	•	•
Consistent		•	•	•	•	•
Keeps promises		•	•	•	•	•
Praises		•	•	•	•	•
Cheerful		•	•	•	•	•
Calm		•	•	•	•	•
Patient		•	•	•	•	•
Listens well		•	•	•	•	•
Easy to talk to		•	•	•	•	•
Tolerant		•	•	•	•	•
Helps others		•	•	•	•	•
Trusts others		•	•	•	•	•
Follows rules		•	•	•	•	•
Willing to learn		•	•	•	•	•
Docile		•	•	•	•	•
Needs support		•	•	•	•	•
Discusses emotions		•	•	•	•	•
Discusses personal		•	•	•	•	•
Adapts		•	•	•	•	•

other two profiles. Again, note the largest and smallest gaps and whether the Desired Self was higher or lower than the other profiles. What do these results tell you about growth? Write your answers.

Now look at the standard deviations of the Acquaintances' Report. Note which ones are high and which ones are low. What does this tell you about the consistency of your interpersonal style? (Remember that others do not see us perfectly accurately.)

Next, look down the list of dimensions on the profile sheet. Do the dimensions seem to be clustered in any way? Are your scores consistent for each cluster? What does this tell you about yourself?

Finally, list the ten or so clearest findings from this exercise. These should be written down in the form of descriptive statements about yourself. You might begin each inference with "I am a person who _____."

Practicing Drawing Inferences

Look at Tom Wilson's ISI profile (case, p. 64). What inferences can you draw about him? What inferences can you draw about the kind of work he should seek?

For Couples

The ISI is an instrument that can obviously be of help to people who are working through the self-assessment exercises together. You might, for instance, discuss the differences in your profiles, in the gaps you observe, and in how other people see each of you. Then note how these observations might affect your relationship and the relationship between your relationship and the world of work.

Feelings Record: Interpersonal Style Inventory

Inferences from the Interpersonal Style Inventory

This is a person who   *Data*

Tom Wilson: Interpersonal Style Inventory Scoring Form

ITEM	ACQUAINTANCE					SUM	MEAN	S.D.
	1	2	3	4	5			
Takes lead	5	3	3	3	4	18	3.6	.8
Needs support	3	2	2	2	3	12	2.4	.5
Seeks recognition	4	1	2	3	2	12	2.4	1.0
Works alone	4		3	4	3	14	3.5	.5
Helps others	4	5	4	4	5	22	4.4	.5
Follows rules	5	4	4	3	4	20	4	.6
Listens well	3	4	3	5	5	20	4	.9
Willing to learn	4	4	3	5	4	20	4	.6
Trusts others	3	4	3	4	4	18	3.6	.5
Defensive	3	2	2	2	3	12	2.4	.5
Emotional	1	3	2	3	3	12	2.4	.8
Discusses personal	2	3	1	2	4	12	2.4	1.0
Easy to talk to	3	5	4	4	5	21	4.2	.75
Docile			3	3	3	9	3	0
Praises	2	4	3	4	3	16	3.2	.75
Is consistent	4	5	3	4	4	20	4	.6
Is conceited	1	1	1	2	1	6	1.2	.4
Adapts	2	4	3	3	4	16	3.2	.75
Competitive	5	4	3	3	4	19	3.8	.75
Own decisions	4	4	4	4	4	20	4	0
Calm	5	4	4	5	5	23	4.6	.5
Mechanical	1	3	4	3	3	14	2.8	1.0
Tolerant	3	5	4	4	4	20	4	.6
Patient	3	4	4	4	4	19	3.8	.4
Keeps promises	5	4	4	5		18	4.5	.5
Cheerful	3	4	4	4	4	19	3.8	.4

This case material was prepared by Kevin E. Sachs, research assistant, under the direction of Associate Professor James G. Clawson, as a basis for class discussion. © 1982 by the Sponsors of The Colgate Darden Graduate School of Business, the University of Virginia, Charlottesville, Virginia. UVA case OB-203.

Tom Wilson: Interpersonal Style Inventory Profiles

Note that the sequence of items has changed. Transcribe the plots carefully!

—X——X— = Current Self, ——————— = Desired Self, — — — — = Acquaintances' Report

ITEM	ACQ. S.D.		Never 1	2	Average 3	4	Always 5
Takes lead	.8	3.6					
Seeks recognition	1.0	2.4					
Is conceited	.4	1.2					
Is competitive	.75	3.8					
Defensive	.5	2.4					
Works alone	.5	3.5					
Own decisions	0	4					
Mechanical	1.0	2.8					
Consistent	.6	4					
Keeps promises	.5	4.5					
Praises	.75	3.2					
Cheerful	.4	3.8					
Calm	.5	4.6					
Patient	.4	3.8					
Listens well	.9	4					
Easy to talk to	.75	4.2					
Tolerant	.6	4					
Helps others	.5	4.4					
Trusts others	.5	3.6					
Follows rules	.6	4					
Willing to learn	.6	4					
Docile	0	3					
Needs support	.5	2.4					
Discusses emotions	.8	2.4					
Discusses personal	1.0	2.4					
Adapts	.75	3.2					

This case material was prepared by Kevin E. Sachs, research assistant, under the direction of Associate Professor James G. Clawson, as a basis for class discussion. © 1982 by the Sponsors of The Colgate Darden Graduate School of Business, the University of Virginia, Charlottesville, Virginia. UVA case OB-203.

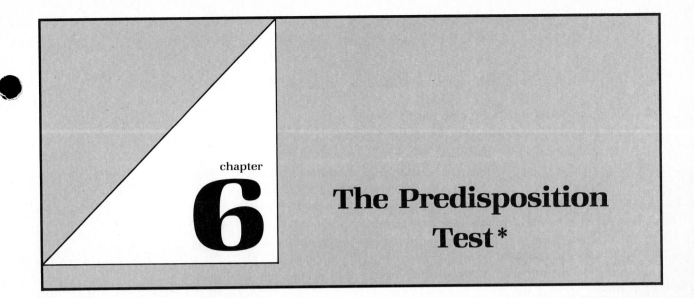

Next we will explore psychological predispositions. We feel this is important, because our psychological tendencies shape our behavior, especially in the workplace. Again, remember that there is no right or wrong answer. The best answer is the one that most accurately describes the way you are, not the way you want to be, or the way you think you should be.

Follow the instructions carefully. When you have completed the test, as before, we will outline the dimensions measured in this exercise and explain how to record and interpret your scores.

For each of the statements below, please draw an "X" through:

DA if you *definitely agree* with the statement,

IA if you are *inclined to agree* with the statement,

ID if you are *inclined to disagree* with the statement,

DD if you *definitely disagree* with the statement.

---

*J. W. Lorsch and J. J. Morse, *Organizations and Their Members: A Contingency Approach* (New York: Harper & Row, 1974). Material reprinted by permission.

1. If a person is satisfied with the kind of job he has done, he shouldn't get upset if colleagues criticize it.   DA   IA   ID   DD

2. The most interesting life is to live under rapidly changing conditions.   DA   IA   ID   DD

3. One often has to be told what to do in order to do a good job.   DA   IA   ID   DD

4. It's satisfying to know pretty much what is going to happen on the job from day to day.   DA   IA   ID   DD

5. Off with the old, on with the new, even though a person rarely knows what the "new" will be.   DA   IA   ID   DD

6. One should never go with a group if the crowd means little to one.   DA   IA   ID   DD

7. Doing the same things in the same places for long periods of time makes for a happy life.   DA   IA   ID   DD

8. A person gets more satisfaction out of reading an enjoyable book than from talking to friends about their vacations.   DA   IA   ID   DD

9. Adventurous and exploratory people go farther in this world than do systematic and orderly people.   DA   IA   ID   DD

10. When planning a vacation, a person should have a schedule to follow if he's really going to enjoy himself.   DA   IA   ID   DD

11. The best work is done with some close supervision.   DA   IA   ID   DD

12. Others' thoughts of one's actions are of great importance.   DA   IA   ID   DD

13. It's better to walk along a beach alone than to sit on a beach blanket with friends.   DA   IA   ID   DD

14. Even if a man loves a girl, he ought not to marry her if his friends don't approve of her.   DA   IA   ID   DD

15. One should welcome suggestions, but resent even reasonable orders.   DA   IA   ID   DD

16. Even children know they must decide their actions; their fathers and mothers do not know best.   DA   IA   ID   DD

17. The least possible governmental and social controls are best for all.   DA   IA   ID   DD

18. A really satisfying life is a life of problems. When one is solved, one moves on to the next problem.   DA   IA   ID   DD

19. Schools which force conformity stifle creativity.   DA   IA   ID   DD

20. Teachers who force students to use prescribed methods of study make it difficult for them to learn.   DA   IA   ID   DD

21. A person usually can get a job done faster and better by working alone than with a group.   DA   IA   ID   DD

Scoring and Interpreting the Predisposition Test*

Introduction

Jobs have a variety of dimensions, many of which will have an effect on how much at home you feel in your work and perhaps on how well you perform. Three such dimensions are the amount of uncertainty or change, the degree of supervision, and the amount of required interaction with others. These were the un-

derlying beliefs of a study conducted in the early 1970s by Professors Jay Lorsch and John Morse of the Harvard Business School. They wanted to understand the impact of the fit between individual characteristics and job characteristics on the effectiveness of companies.

This study represented an extension of contingency theory from its former focus on the organization-environment interface (see *Organization and Environment* by Paul Lawrence and Jay Lorsch, Irwin, Homewood, Illinois, 1969) to include the organization-individual interface. Contingency theory, of course, is the set of ideas surrounding the notion that there is no one best way to organize, rather that the most effective organizational form depends on a variety of factors and constraints. The Lorsch-Morse study suggested that there is no one best individual employee profile, but that individual effectiveness in a job depends on the fit between an individual's characteristics and the demands made of him or her by the job.

---

*Much of this material is based on J. W. Lorsch and J. J. Morse, *Organizations and Their Members: A Contingency Approach* (New York: Harper & Row, 1974). It was prepared by Mark P. Kriger, research assistant, and revised by Ellen Porter Honnet, research assistant, under the direction of Assistant Professor James G. Clawson, as the basis for class discussion. Copyright © 1979 by the President and Fellows of Harvard College. Harvard Business School case 1-480-017.

The Development and Scoring
of the Predisposition Test

As part of this study, the researchers designed a questionnaire that measures personality predispositions along three dimensions:

1. Tolerance for ambiguity
2. Preference for autonomy
3. Predisposition toward solitude in a work situation

All three dimensions are what psychologists call *personality predispositions*—that is, they are tendencies for you to think and act in certain ways which arise from your own particular personality development. For example, if your parents encouraged you as a child to make your own decisions rather than to look to them for the final say in all matters, then you may be predisposed to solving problems on your own and might prefer to work in jobs with less, rather than more, supervision. Likewise, if you were raised an only child or in such a way that you spent a good deal of your time alone, you may be predisposed to working alone more than with others. Or the opposite effect could occur, and you may prefer to be surrounded by people constantly.

There are a variety of personality predispositions which Lorsch and Morse could have explored. These three (along with one or two others), however, seemed to offer the best way to demonstrate their thesis that organization (job)-individual fit did affect effectiveness. The next problem, the most common one in social science research, was how to measure these dimensions in individuals and in jobs.

Lorsch and Morse collected a number of statements they believed described values or behaviors relating to these personality predispositions from a variety of generally accepted personality inventories. To these they added a number of statements of their own invention. They then distilled the number of statements down to 21 by means of factor analysis. Each of these 21 statements represented one of the three dispositions (a "positive" statement) or its opposite (a "negative" statement). Respondents would mark the degree of their agreement or disagreement with each statement, and then the researchers, knowing which statements were the "positive" ones and which were the "negative" ones, could add up the respondents' scores on each dimension. The positive statements were scored as follows:

DA Definitely Agree	IA Inclined to Agree	ID Inclined to Disagree	DD Definitely Disagree
4	3	2	1

They reflect one's agreement with the statement. Negative statements were scored this way:

DA	IA	ID	DD
1	2	3	4

These reflect one's disagreement with the statement. For example, one item in the questionnaire is, "The most interesting life is to live under rapidly changing conditions." This is a positively scored statement for tolerance for ambiguity. If you indicated that you definitely agreed with that statement by putting an X through DA, your tolerance for ambiguity score would increase by 4. There are seven statements for each dimension. After each statement has been scored, you can add the seven scores and calculate an average for each dimension. We have developed a scoring sheet that matches the dimensions and scores with the questions and your answers. Once you have identified your numerical score, you can then transcribe it onto the tally sheet under the appropriate dimension.

Interpretation of Scores

The first personality predisposition, tolerance for ambiguity, measures your preference for a more changing set of conditions as opposed to well-defined, stable, and relatively unchanging conditions. The higher your score on this dimension, the greater your tolerance for ambiguity. As you might expect, if you work in an uncertain environment, you will need a greater tolerance for ambiguity on the whole than if you work in a more certain environment. Less defined work and greater uncertainty of information will produce a higher level of ambiguity with which you must cope. Your tolerance for ambiguity will also be related to the speed and quantity of feedback you receive. When feedback is frequent, you will not require as high a tolerance for ambiguity as when feedback takes longer.

The second personality predisposition, preference for autonomy, measures your preferred ways of relating to authority. The higher your score on this dimension, the greater your disposition toward working *without* supervision. Individuals with higher scores probably will prefer to have more direct influence over defining their work roles and providing their own direction and would feel more at home in jobs that do not require subordinate relationships with strong authority figures.

The third personality predisposition, predisposition toward solitude, measures your attitude towards being alone in a work situation. A higher score on this dimension indicates that you prefer to work more individualistically and to be more alone than with others.

If you have a preference for being and working alone, you will probably enjoy and be more competent in a job where little interaction with others is required. Alternatively, if you prefer spending time with others, you will prefer a work environment which requires more coordination and communication with others.

The usual way of making relative sense of scores like these is to compare them with the scores of various reference groups. For the present, scores for a wide variety of reference groups do not exist for the predisposition test. Nevertheless, after scoring your responses, you will have personal scores along three interesting and provocative personality dimensions which you can utilize in two ways.

First, you can compare your results to the two reference groups used in the Lorsch and Morse study for which we do have data: (a) scientists and engineers working in research organizations, and (b) managers and supervisors working in manufacturing organizations. In these two organizations, chosen because they represented extremes of environmental ambiguity, Lorsch and Morse found that the employees in the jobs in the uncertain environment (R&D organizations) tended to score higher on all three dimensions than the employees working in the more certain environment (manufacturing). See Exhibit 6–1. If your scores for the three dimensions are closer to the scores in a more uncertain environment, such as an R&D laboratory, a consulting firm, or marketing company, you might conclude that you would feel constrained in a more structured industry like durable goods manufacturing. If your scores are mixed—that is, one or two of them are high and the remaining score or scores are low— you should consider each dimension first individually and then in combination with the other two scores.

Exhibit 6–1
A Note on the Predisposition Test
PERSONALITY DIMENSIONS
OF MEMBERS IN RESEARCH
AND MANUFACTURING ENVIRONMENTS:
OVERALL MEANS FOR COMBINED HIGH-
AND LOW-PERFORMING SITES

	Research Organization	Manufacturing Organization
Tolerance for ambiguity	2.91	2.57
Preference for autonomy	2.83	2.17
Predisposition toward solitude	2.96	2.40

J. W. Lorsch and J. J. Morse, *Organizations and Their Members: A Contingency Approach* (New York: Harper & Row, 1974), pp. 53, 55.

The implications one could draw from these scores are fairly straightforward. If, for example, you scored high in tolerance for ambiguity, you *might* prefer working in an uncertain environment, but not necessarily so. Your score indicates that you are tolerant of ambiguity, not that it is essential to you. If, however, you scored high on both the tolerance for ambiguity and the preference for autonomy scales, the implication might be that you *would* prefer working in an environment which is both uncertain and unsupervised. Finally, if your solitude score were low, you would probably conclude that you would feel most at home in a job in which you could work together with others in a collegial, rather than a hierarchical, way on unusual and varied tasks with uncertain results.

Your score on the autonomy scale has implications not only for the kind of organization and the job you may want to work in, but also for the kind of person who will be your supervisor. While it is not wise to judge a whole potential career on the merits of one's first supervisor, that relationship has been shown to significantly affect young managers' success. (See *Formative Years in Business: A Long-Term AT&T Study of Managerial Lives,* by Douglas Bray et al., Wiley, New York, 1974.) Your preference for autonomy or attitude toward authority may suggest some implications about the kind of supervisory relationship that would be most effective for you and your career development in the early years.

These comments on the implications of your scores are intentionally vague. Taken alone, these scores are not accurate enough or descriptive enough to provide the basis for a job decision. When they add to and confirm trends or patterns that run through other bits of data, these scores can help to crystallize important personal characteristics.

The second way you can use your results is to compare them to the mean scores of other Harvard Business School students. By analyzing your scores in relation to those of other students, you can gain a further indication of the direction and strength of your own personality predispositions for these three dimensions (see Exhibit 6–2).

Summary

An individual's predispositions can have a great effect on that person's sense of competence and satisfaction derived from work. While there are many predispositions in one's personality, three key ones are tolerance for ambiguity, preference for autonomy, and preference for solitude. Although the measurement of these predispositions is imprecise, the results from the predisposition test can add to your pool of personal data and can suggest both singly and in combination with each other some implications for the kind of or-

Exhibit 6–2
A Note on the Predisposition Test
PERSONALITY DIMENSION OF HBS STUDENTS*

Dimension	Your Score	Overall	Men	Women	Married	Single	USA	Foreign	Age 20–25	Age 26–30	Age 31–40
Tolerance for ambiguity		2.84	2.82	2.86	2.77	2.87	2.82	2.91	2.86	2.80	2.84
Preference for autonomy		2.61	2.58	2.66	2.61	2.61	2.59	2.70	2.58	2.62	2.64
Predisposition toward solitude		2.62	2.60	2.64	2.65	2.61	2.59	2.78	2.60	2.58	2.71
(Number of students in group)	(1)	(120)	(75)	(43)	(40)	(79)	(102)	(17)	(51)	(42)	(26)

*This information has been taken from the average test scores of the 1978 Self-Assessment and Career Development class at the Harvard Business School.

ganization and job in which you would like to work and would feel most at home.

Predisposition Test Scoring Instructions

1. Tear out scoring sheet on page 73.
2. Cut or fold margins on page 73.
3. Place scoring sheet over the test on page 68.
4. Write the scores corresponding to the letters you circled on the tally sheet, page 72, under the column matching the dimension of each question.
5. Sum the scores for each dimension.
6. Divide your total scores by seven to get your average score.

Assignment

Once you have scored your Predisposition Test, turn to page 72 and read Tom Wilson's scores. What inferences do you draw about Tom from these data?

Predisposition Test Tally Sheet

Tolerance for Ambiguity (Questions 2, 4, 5, 7, 9, 10, 18)	Preference for Autonomy (Questions 3, 11, 15, 16, 17, 19, 20)	Predisposition toward Solitude (Questions 1, 6, 8, 12, 13, 14, 21)
_____	_____	_____
_____	_____	_____
_____	_____	_____
_____	_____	_____
_____	_____	_____
_____	_____	_____
_____	_____	_____

Total

÷ 7   ÷ 7   ÷ 7

Average

TOM WILSON: PREDISPOSITION TEST

	Tolerance for Ambiguity	Preference for Autonomy	Predisposition toward Solitude
Tom Wilson	2.86	2.57	2.57
Research organization	2.91	2.83	2.96
Manufacturing organization	2.57	2.17	2.40

This case was prepared by Kevin E. Sachs, research assistant, under the direction of Associate Professor James G. Clawson, as a basis for class discussion. © 1982 by the Sponsors of The Colgate Darden Graduate School of Business Administration, the University of Virginia, Charlottesville, Virginia. UVA case OB-206.

From J. W. Lorsch and J. J. Morse, *Organizations and Their Members: A Contingency Approach* (New York: Harper & Row, 1974). Research and manufacturing data from a working paper, Personality Dimensions of Members in Research and Manufacturing Environments: Overall Means for Combined High- and Low-Performing Sites, pp. 53, 55.

Predisposition Test Scoring Sheet

Ques. Number	Dimension	Score			
		DA	IA	ID	DD
1.	Predisposition toward solitude	4	3	2	1
2.	Tolerance for ambiguity	4	3	2	1
3.	Preference for autonomy	1	2	3	4
4.	Tolerance for ambiguity	1	2	3	4
5.	Tolerance for ambiguity	4	3	2	1
6.	Predisposition toward solitude	4	3	2	1
7.	Tolerance for ambiguity	1	2	3	4
8.	Predisposition toward solitude	4	3	2	1
9.	Tolerance for ambiguity	4	3	2	1
10.	Tolerance for ambiguity	1	2	3	4
11.	Preference for autonomy	1	2	3	4
12.	Predisposition toward solitude	1	2	3	4
13.	Predisposition toward solitude	4	3	2	1
14.	Predisposition toward solitude	1	2	3	4
15.	Preference for autonomy	4	3	2	1
16.	Preference for autonomy	4	3	2	1
17.	Preference for autonomy	4	3	2	1
18.	Tolerance for ambiguity	4	3	2	1
19.	Preference for autonomy	4	3	2	1
20.	Preference for autonomy	4	3	2	1
21.	Predisposition toward solitude	4	3	2	1

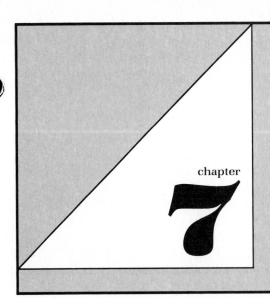

chapter

7

The 24-Hour Diary

Your task in this exercise is to make an accurate record of your activities—what you do. You are to keep a 24-hour diary, a log of your comings and goings and doings, on at least two different days: a weekday and a weekend day. If you would like to monitor more than two days, feel free to do so, but be sure you get at least two days' worth as a minimum.

Do not wait until the end of the 24-hour period to make your diary; make your entries as the day progresses. This will alter your activities a little, but that's okay. You decide how often you will make an entry, but do not wait more than three hours before going back to make your notes.

Make your entries as complete as you can, and fill in the details and events that were significant to you.

When you have completed the diaries, insert them in your notebook and go on to the note on interpretation.

Interpreting The 24-Hour Diary

NOTE:
DO NOT READ THIS UNTIL YOU HAVE COMPLETED THE 24-HOUR DIARY ASSIGNMENT.

As social scientists have discovered over the years, one useful way to learn about a person or a group of people is to obtain information regarding what they actually do on a daily basis. What type of activities do they engage in? How do they allocate their time among job, family, entertainment, sleep, and other activities? With whom do they interact, in what ways, and how often?

Even in situations that are highly structured by others (such as the army), or on the most "atypical" days, the way in which an individual adapts and behaves says something about him or her. Regardless of the setting, we are always faced with choices regarding what to do, how to do it, and when. Patterns in those choices can tell us something about ourselves.

There are a number of different ways one can collect information about an individual's daily activities, but most are not useful for our purposes. An anthropological methodology, for example, in which a second "observer" follows the individual throughout the day, is impractical. Simply asking a person what he or she does on a daily basis is practical, but research has shown it to be not very reliable. People's impressions of what they normally do are often quite inaccurate.

A method we have found to be both feasible and reasonably reliable is to ask an individual to keep a log or diary of his or her activities throughout the day. It is not very difficult or time-consuming to pause every hour or so and to make a few notes regarding what you have been doing. (The entries do not have to be particularly lengthy.) Most people can remember in some detail what they have been doing for the past hour or two. While this method loses the "objectivity" of a second-person observer, it gains an additional type of useful information. One cannot record everything. Consequently, what a person chooses to record and how it is recorded becomes potentially useful information in itself.

Interpreting a 24-Hour Diary

Taking into account how and why it was created, you can examine a 24-hour diary for patterns and draw inferences from those patterns. For example, some diaries have all their entries recorded at regular intervals (perhaps every 30 minutes); others do not. Sometimes entries are given very specific times (5:47, 8:54, 10:01), sometimes not (10:00, 10:15, 11:40). Some diaries will be full of human interaction. Others will not. A few might describe each person mentioned in the diary in great detail. Some will not mention any names. Some diaries are recorded in short, cryptic phrases; others read like a novel. Some describe an incredibly fast-moving, active person. Others do not. Some describe people who sleep exactly eight hours a night (invariably 11:30 P.M. to 7:30 A.M.). Some describe people who jump from one activity to another; others describe people who concentrate on one thing until the task is completed. And so on.

To help you develop some skill in using 24-hour diaries, we have included the diaries of three different individuals (starting below). Study each of them carefully. What might those people be like? What kind of work might they like?

By identifying patterns in a diary and drawing careful inferences from those patterns, you can corroborate or contradict themes that have emerged in other sources, as well as identify new themes. All that is needed is some time, patience, and a modicum of skill.

THREE 24-HOUR DIARIES

Jon Williams

3:55 P.M.	Typed up handwritten comments on my life style and turned in copy.
4:30 P.M.	Ran two and a half miles, stretched, and took a shower.
5:30 P.M.	Studied Service Operations case while cooling down and letting hair dry.
6:00 P.M.	Dinner with Timothy Plain and Jim Falcone, discussed how students are motivated to study and how they decide the amount of time to commit.
6:45 P.M.	Watched news on Mideast and Watergate affair, ate an apple.
7:00 P.M.	Read and completed analysis of Service Operations Case, Victoria Station, Inc.
8:30 P.M.	Read first section of case for Marketing Mgt.
9:00 P.M.	Break for cookies and ice cream.
9:15 P.M.	Completed study first of two cases for Marketing.
10:10 P.M.	Studied second of two cases for Marketing.
10:40 P.M.	Rapped with roommate about Thanksgiving break plans and upcoming papers due.
11:00 P.M.	Continued study of second marketing case.
11:30 P.M.	Slept.

7:30 A.M.	Woke up, showered, dressed and to Serv. Ops.
8:30 A.M.	Management of Service Operations class.
9:50 A.M.	Light brunch.
10:10 A.M.	Completed reviewing appendix surveys for marketing.
10:30 A.M.	Perused today's *Wall Street Journal.*
11:00 A.M.	Chatted with roommate about something happening in his class and wrote out some thoughts on General Foods case.
11:30 A.M.	Marketing Management class.
12:50 P.M.	Listened to professor chat with students after class.
1:05 P.M.	Lunch, alone.
1:40 P.M.	Begin reading Business Policy case for Thursday.
2:05 P.M.	Typed out this diary.
2:30 P.M.	Self-Assessment and Career Development class.

Stephie Rosenbloom

4:00 P.M.	Left Self-Assessment. Bopped down to Course Material Supply Room. Ran into Irv and got my creature contact (lots of nice pats while walking through the library). Dumped my overdue consumer behavior paper in Scott's office. Went to bookstore, ran

---

This case was prepared by Kevin E. Sachs, research assistant, under the direction of Associate Professor James G. Clawson, as a basis for class discussion. © 1982 by the Sponsors of the Colgate Darden Graduate School of Business Administration, the University of Virginia, Charlottesville, Virginia. UVA case OB-206.

into Jimmy Losick who told me Dick Nelson wanted to talk about the communication course I'm trying to develop. Ran into Jim Lane and Mac, talked about Danny Kirsch. Volunteered to go see him and Evelyn. Back to room. Beer. Reflected on the course I'm trying to get started, have to face fact the faculty members all seem to want to take my course development away from me. Called Dick, set up appointment. Should try to get Miles first. Won't be able to. Plan tonight's studying. Not much today. Read USA news. Crud, won't be able to keep appointment with B. C. Allday & Co. here tomorrow, will have to cancel.

4:30 P.M. Cleaned desk. Filed today's cases, looking for tomorrow's. Can't find [expletive deleted] Self-Assessment assignment. Read *Marketing Management* for tomorrow. Can't find my felt tip marker either.

5:00 P.M. Betsy called. Wants to play bridge tonight. OK. Not much work. More *Marketing Management.* Out to eat so I don't miss Betsy's return call. Borrowed dollar, went over to Galley. Eating hamburger on way back. Ran into Tony. Told him it didn't matter how "screwed up" he was as long as he was attractive that way. *Marketing Management* again.

5:30 P.M. *Marketing Management.* Maureen going shopping, had to make list.

6:00 P.M. Spent 15 minutes on phone trying to find fourth for bridge. Bridge off. Good. After you've spent so much time talking about it you don't want it. *Marketing Management.*

6:30 P.M. *Marketing Management.* Helped Mo in with the groceries.

7:00 P.M. *Marketing Management.* Betsy called back, found fourth. On her way to get me.

7:30 P.M. Spent 10 minutes waiting for Betsy, 15 minutes to her place. Waiting for fourth to show up. Reading *Marketing Management.*

8:00 P.M. Made 5 no trump. Still reading *Marketing Management.*

8:30 P.M. Lost rubber. Still playing. Still reading *Marketing Management.* Betsy's a stewardess, so's Kathy. John's the fourth. We picked him up somewhere. Who cares where. New on. I think Nixon's psychotic.

9:00 P.M. Still playing bridge. Both vulnerable.

9:30 P.M. Just made 1,000 hand. Still playing. Betsy and I are having trouble at the two level. We're getting used to making slam.

10:00 P.M. Still playing bridge. Have finished Policy.

10:30 P.M. Still playing bridge.

11:00 P.M. Still playing bridge.

11:30 P.M. Finish the last rubber, we win by piles of points. John's taking me home.

12:00 Home. Talked to John about product management possibilities at Gilberts.

12:30 A.M. Continue talking to John. He left. Talked to Maureen about ESP possibilities. Would be great for bridge.

1:00 A.M. Still talking to Maureen. Munching on cheese and crackers.

1:30 A.M. Still talking with Mo. To bed at two.

2:00 A.M. Bed.

5:00 A.M. Wake up. Not sleepy. Bored. Nothing to do.

5:30 A.M. Go back to sleep.

8:30 A.M. Mo wakes me up. Get dressed.

9:00 A.M. Still get dressed. Walk over bridge to Administration Center to negotiate loan terms. Always horrible ladies there.

9:30 A.M. Still at Center. Head down to bank.

10:00 A.M. Bank. Walk back across to dorm.

10:30 A.M. Spend about 5 minutes talking with maid. Drink some milk (breakfast and lunch).

11:00 A.M. Gather cases together. Head for class. Review *Marketing Management* with Ann. Call Dick Nelson's office. Cancel appointment. Can't get another one till Monday. And he wants to see me. What would happen if I wanted to see him? Can call Miles first then. Fool around with regular premarketing management group doing Al Pesky imitations. Hope Sonny brings his St. Bernard to class. Get coffee.

11:30 A.M. Ahah. There is no Self-Assessment assignment. Won't have to do it in class now. Spent first half hour of MM writing self-assessment diary. Writing note to Sonny, too.

12:00 *Marketing Management* class.

12:30 P.M. *Marketing Management* class. I think I'm hung over, but it could be the class. Had case smashed. Good feeling.

1:00 P.M. Business Policy, bored. This is a dumb course. Anyone who doesn't know about strategy, shouldn't be here.

1:30 P.M. Policy. Bored to death. Although cases better than usual.

2:00 P.M. Policy. Bored to death again. Enjoy watching Dennis Anderson laugh.

2:30 P.M. Self-Assessment.

3:00 P.M. Self-Assessment. (There will be no editorial comments made in this class.)

Tom Wilson

Thursday

6:00 A.M. Woke to WINA, turned off alarm so not to wake Susan or Tommy. Sneaked out of room and downstairs to review Policy assignment. Turned on kettle for a cup of tea. Settled down by 6:15.

7:00 A.M. Finished review. Woke up Susan & Tommy, Jr. Took shower, got dressed, changed and dressed Tommy, went to U-Hall to catch bus.

8–9:30 A.M. Policy class. Nothing too exciting. Took notes; joked with Thompson, chipped in a few comments, too tired to say anything substantial. Talked to Sally about one of our peers.

Saw Jim outside—decided to go to breakfast at Cafe North. Went downstairs to get a cup of coffee and remembered that I was supposed to meet with Mr. Hawkins at coffee to discuss assignment sheets I'm supposed to write for him and discuss problem with one of the programs in the Operations Planning course. Found Hawkins and talked to him until 10:00.

10:00 A.M. Wandered by mailboxes and saw Marketing Research information publications copied. Distributed material to group members boxes.

10:10 A.M. Went to library to sort out work for Hawkins and see what other work I have to do for Friday. I bought some folders to organize my material for classes yesterday and thought I'd do that. I discovered that I had bought legal size instead of letter. I got out the work to do for Friday—Policy/Marketing Research and the notes for the Hawkins assignment.

10:30 A.M. Decided to return folders to bookstore. Caught bus and went downtown. Returned folders and stopped in clothing store. Saw a black sweater I liked—too much. Drove back to U-Hall. Caught bus to school.

11:30 A.M. Back in library. Looked over case for 2:00 P.M. Marketing Research. Read Policy case for Friday. Still couldn't get going on Hawkins's work.

2:00 P.M. Marketing Research Class. Good class. Sat in front of Bruce & Cindy. Expressed views on concept test—not substantial. Pat had good airtime—I even agreed with him.

3:30 P.M. Back to library after checking box. Talking to Bruce about backing out of golf match. Reread Policy Case—Motorcycles.

5:00 P.M. Finally sat down to write Hawkins assignment. I've put it off long enough. Decided to write a case plus instructions. Had a good time writing it. Finished around 7:00 P.M.

7:15 P.M. Home. Tommy is glad to see me. Susan's making pizza, asks how much I want—haven't eaten all day. I say more. Call Mr. Hawkins to tell him I'm through. He says to meet him at coffee the next day. Put Tommy to bed. Sit down to eat pizza. Read Susan my case about Hawkins.

8:30 P.M. Flip on the TV to catch Thursday night football. Bills vs. Eagles. Start copying over Hawkins's work so Donna can type it on Friday.

10:00 P.M. Finished copying paper—surprised Bills haven't done anything yet. Good defensive game. Grab a beer to watch end of half and highlights (interview with Sugar Ray).

11:00 P.M. Into the second half—pick up Policy case to jot down some notes. Remembered that I need to call A&P in morning to order keg for Volleyball Tournament—they usually have an extra one anyway.

11:45 P.M. Turn off game, turn off Tommy's light, set alarm, go to bed.

Saturday

8:00 A.M. Tommy woke up around 7:00 A.M. Susan said she'd get up. I told her that Mom (my parents came in for weekend visit on Friday) would probably be up and she could feed him. I go back to sleep and wake up around now—Tommy sounds like he's going nuts downstairs. I go downstairs and discover all the toys Mom and Dad brought are now open. Play with him for a little while then go to couch and read paper. Suggest Susan fix pancakes when Dad gets up. I'm feeling lazy today—Susan usually cooks when my parents are here.

9:00 A.M. Dad's awake—go upstairs to take a shower.

9:30 A.M. Get out accounting readings due on Monday—try to read one while Dad reads paper out loud and Tommy Jr.'s running around.

10:00 A.M. Breakfast ready—waffles instead. We keep Tommy somewhat quiet by feeding him some. My mom spoils him more than us. Dad has been quiet so far—I'm waiting though.

10:15 A.M. Dad explains account he's been working on who makes stereo and TV stands. He explains his Creative Living Center concept and shows me some brochures. We discuss furniture marketing for a few minutes. I'm interested in what he has to say but am not enthusiastic about the consultation. I add a few "B School" buzz words. I ask Mom to fix some pants of mine. I go up and get them to try on.

10:30 A.M. Steve calls about 1:00 P.M. softball game. I say I'll be there. I'm supposed to play soccer at 4:00 P.M. and decide that I better not do both. I tell Dad that I have to go into school for a couple of hours. He wants to go out to book store.

11–12:20 P.M. He follows me to bookstore. I go to school. Start sorting out what cases are due Monday and decide it's good time to organize all the material that's been stacked up on my desk. Run into John in library who's working away at the adjacent table. Briefly discuss Colts. I threw all my papers (cases, notes, handouts) on the table and start sorting everything out. Guinee comes by and asks me what I'm doing, Carel follows. I pay Daron for volleyball league and say I'll be there tomorrow at 4:00 P.M. for practice. I finish sorting, put information in folders, and label. Carel is now organized.

12:30 P.M. Back home—change clothes for softball.

1–2:00 P.M. Softball game. Go 3 for 4 and score 3 runs. Those guys were terrible. Don Cox goes 3 for 4 scores 3 runs, starts talking who'll win player of the game. I tell him that I'll have to make a spectacular catch. Last inning I'll dive in front of him for a ball—miss—he catches it anyway. We won 10-2.

2–4:00 P.M. Back home—watch Notre Dame-Michigan game. Susan takes nap. I

tell Mom about Eljo's sale. I want to go downtown to get a couple more folders. Dad bought a calculator from the same place earlier that day (bookstore) and wants to go back to get a catalogue.

4:45–5:30 P.M. We drop Mom off at Eljo's and we go to bookstore. It's closed. We go to Eljo's. I try on a couple pair of pants. Dad wants to buy me a wool suit on sale that I don't really like. No sale. Mom buys some shirts.

5:35–7:00 P.M. We decide to go to 6:00 P.M. Mass. Susan decided to go too. Tommy has a good time in church, not too disruptive.

7–8:00 P.M. Dad's trying to figure out how his calculator works. I'm trying once again to read the same accounting article. Mom and Susan are feeding Tommy and fixing dinner. Mom and Dad bought some scallops on way from Chesapeake Bay.

8:30 P.M. Tommy's in bed. We sit down to eat. Two girls come down and ask to use the phone. Scallops are good. I like them broiled in butter better.

9:30 P.M. We've cleared dishes and retired to living room. I pick up same article to read and fix a bourbon. Dad goes on about his stomach problem and how its heredity and I have it (I've heard this millions of times) and about heart condition (ditto on # of times). While he's on the subject he says Claude Bradley only has a few weeks. I'm wondering now how I thought I could work for him if I wanted to in 2–3 years.

10:30 P.M. I'm tired, go to bed.

chapter

8

Creating Life Style Representations

One hears a lot of talk about life style these days. People talk of liking or disliking their current life style, of the merits of various alternative life styles, of how Mary and Tim Jones have changed their life style.

The *American Heritage Dictionary* defines *life style* as "an internally consistent way of life or style of living that reflects the attitudes and values of an individual or a culture." That is, life style is someone's way of life. It is the pattern of how one relates to key parts of external reality; how one uses time; whom one relates with and how; how one uses or relates to objects and possessions; how one reacts to geography and space generally; what one does. Second, one's life style, insofar as there is choice in its establishment, reflects some of the things inside the person. It is, in a sense, a mapping out of who one is into what one does, how one does it, and with whom or what.

Life style relates to our present purposes in two ways. First, career- and job-related decisions are a subset of the total life style decisions that people make, whether consciously or not. It would certainly make things easier if we could treat job and career decisions independently from other life style decisions, but we really can't—they are interdependent. If one chooses to live in a cabin in Maine, that choice makes the possibility of working as a loan officer in a bank in Los Angeles impractical. If one chooses to work for a consulting firm in a job that takes 60 hours a week, one-third of it out of town, one probably cannot spend 7 hours a day, every day, with one's spouse and children. If one chooses to be surrounded by expensive art and yet has no independent source of funds, it is probably impractical to seek a job as the executive director of the local community chest.

Second, one's past and current life styles, in that they reflect attitudes and values, can provide us with data. No matter how constrained one is by economics or institutional requirements, one always has some choice about how to adapt to those constraints. And the form or pattern of adaptation says something about the person.

Assignment

The assignment is to produce on paper a representation, nonnarrative in nature, that will reflect as accurately as you can your life style and provide you with data useful for analysis. Your life style representation should include a consideration of your past life style, your current life style, and your desired future life style.

There are a number of alternative ways you might approach this assignment.

Open-Ended Option

This first option is opened-ended. You may let your creative side run free in selecting your approach to the assignment. You may choose without restraint the shape or the form of your representation. If you choose this option, feel free to use any media, any material, and any approach that you feel captures more, rather than less, of the complexity of the detail and shape of your life style. The only constraint should be that your work can be viewed while sitting at a desk. Exhibit 8–1 is one example of a free-style life style diagram.

Exhibit 8–1
An Open-Ended Life Style Diagram
(BETSY DRAKE)

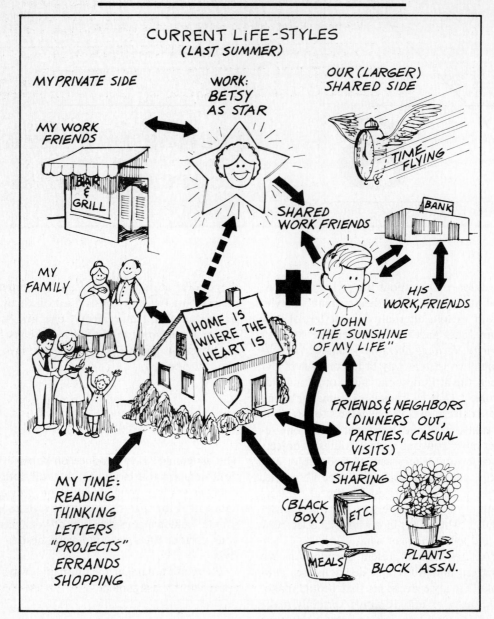

CURRENT LIFE-STYLES
(LAST SUMMER)

MY PRIVATE SIDE

WORK: BETSY AS STAR

OUR (LARGER) SHARED SIDE

MY WORK FRIENDS

BAR & GRILL

TIME FLYING

SHARED WORK FRIENDS

BANK

MY FAMILY

HIS WORK FRIENDS

HOME IS WHERE THE HEART IS

JOHN "THE SUNSHINE OF MY LIFE"

FRIENDS & NEIGHBORS (DINNERS OUT, PARTIES, CASUAL VISITS)

MY TIME: READING THINKING LETTERS "PROJECTS" ERRANDS SHOPPING

OTHER SHARING

(BLACK BOX)

ETC.

MEALS

PLANTS BLOCK ASSN.

Current.

I used last summer just because it is a little more compact, a little less geographically and emotionally fragmented than my life here at school. The fundamentals are the same, and have been for as long as I've been making my own life: a place of my own, suited to my taste; John and our shared time/place/experiences/feelings/intellects; time of my own; lots of reading; work which is satisfying and visible.

In the Next Few Years.

Lots of the same elements. The only significant difference is right now a big question mark: kid or kids? If so, will I feel that I can still work?

Time-Oriented Representations

Time-oriented life style representations begin with a consideration of the finite amount of time an individual has and attempt to reflect the personal allocations of that time. Exhibit 8–2 is an example done by a student who chose a bar graph structure. Pie charts or other graphic means are also appropriate. Exhibit 8–3 shows a life style diagram that reflects major interests and activities chronologically.

Relationships-Orientation Option

Another way to approach representing your life style is to begin with your relationships. Photograph collages; network diagrams with degrees of strength, intimacy, frequency of interaction, and other related variables indicated; or cluster diagrams are appropriate ways of using this option. You may be able to think of others.

Activities

Another way to approach this assignment is to think of the things you do and to represent those activities in ways that reflect who you are.

Aspects

Another approach is to begin with the list of aspects of our lives shown in Exhibit 8–4. This list is similar to the one we used in the Values Sort. For each aspect, write down your interests, goals, characteristics, and needs. Then use that list to devise a graphic representation of the life style (yours) that incorporates all the items on the list.

Things to Remember

Whichever option you choose, there are some things you should keep in mind. Your representation should reflect the past, the present, and the future. It should have some means of indicating the strength or the importance of a particular object or activity or person in your life style. It should reflect as accurately as possible the level of congestion or complexity you experience in your life. Last, it should feel comfortable to you when you have finished it. In other words, when you look at your life style representation, your diagram or representation should communicate a sense of who you are in such a way that you feel comfortable with it, that it seems to be "you," and that it reflects the major issues and aspects of your life.

Exhibit 8–2
A Time Allocation Life Style Representation

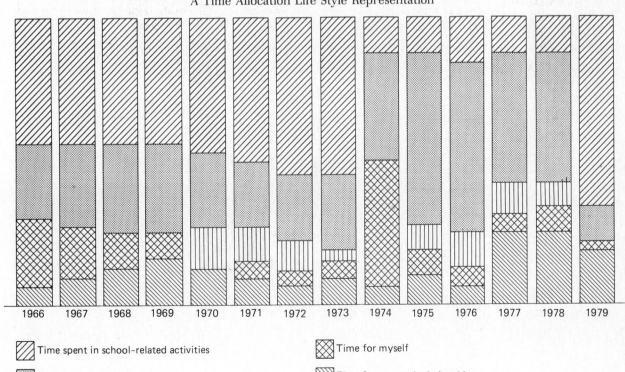

1966 1967 1968 1969 1970 1971 1972 1973 1974 1975 1976 1977 1978 1979

Time spent in school-related activities

Time spent working

Civic/political/organizational activities

Time for myself

Time for personal relationships

Exhibit 8–3

A Chronological Life Style Diagram

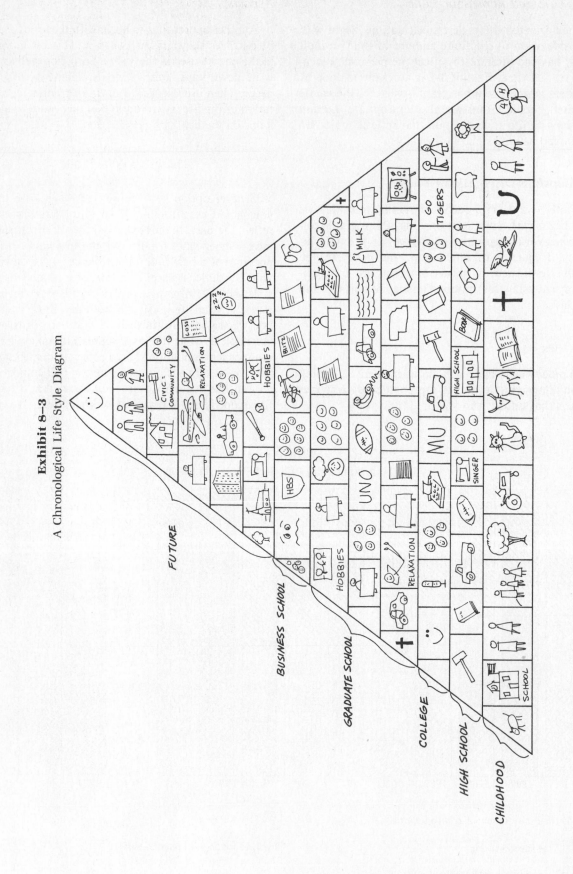

Exhibit 8–4
Aspects of a Person's Life

Physical
Material (possessions)
Financial

Emotional
Spiritual

Professional
Educational
Intellectual
Social
Marital
Parental
Familial

Societal
Political
Cultural

Finally, remember that this is *your* exercise. Be as creative as you like. If you do not feel creative or artistic, relax. We are not expecting a work of art; what we want is a representation that says something about who you were, are, and will be.

When you have completed the Life Style Representation, make an entry in your Feelings Record. What was your reaction to the assignment? Did you enjoy it? Why or why not? What were you thinking about as you made your representation?

Feelings Record: Life Style Diagram

TOM WILSON: LIFE STYLE DIAGRAMS

Analyzing Life Style Representations

You can interpret these data by looking for patterns or relationships between parts of your lives that will provide insight into who you are and what is important to you. Look at Tom Wilson's diagrams (case, pp. 87–88). Note:

1. The relationships between things that appear in the diagrams
2. The strength of those relationships
3. The sources of satisfaction and enjoyment in the diagrams
4. The sources of anxiety and frustration
5. The number of people and how they fit into the diagram

Begin to draw inferences from these observations. Note the specific data that you are looking at as you write down each inference. Again, begin by asking yourself to complete the phrase, "This is a person who. . . ." When you have finished analyzing Tom Wilson's diagrams, go on to your own.

This case was prepared by Kevin E. Sachs, research assistant, under the direction of Associate Professor James G. Clawson, as a basis for class discussion. © 1982 by the Sponsors of the Colgate Darden Graduate School of Business Administration, the University of Virginia, Charlottesville, Virginia. UVA casé OB-196.

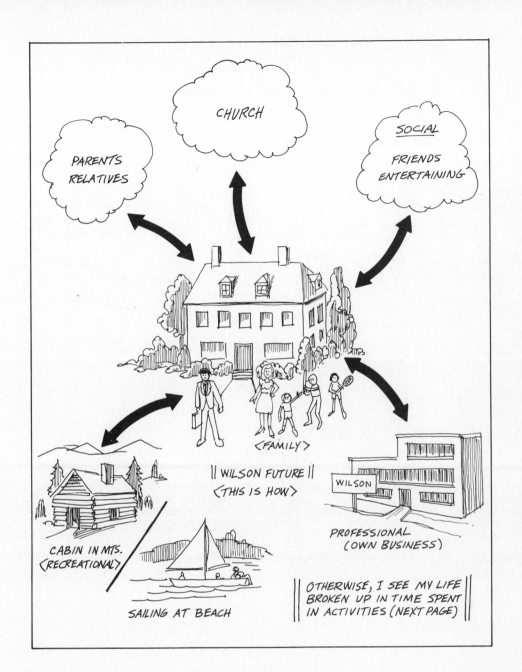

PARENTS RELATIVES

CHURCH

SOCIAL
FRIENDS ENTERTAINING

‹FAMILY›

‖ WILSON FUTURE ‖
‹THIS IS HOW›

WILSON

CABIN IN MTS.
‹RECREATIONAL›

SAILING AT BEACH

PROFESSIONAL
(OWN BUSINESS)

‖ OTHERWISE, I SEE MY LIFE ‖
‖ BROKEN UP IN TIME SPENT ‖
‖ IN ACTIVITIES (NEXT PAGE) ‖

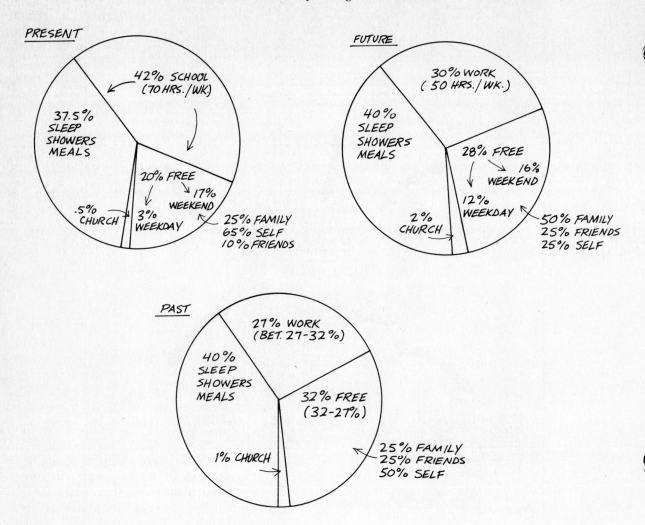

chapter

9   The Strong-Campbell Interest Inventory (SCII)

If you are using this book as a part of a course, your instructor may provide you with a SCII. If you are using this book on your own, you can obtain an SCII and have it scored through any reputable career counseling service (on campus or in a private business), or by sending it to:

Consulting Psychologists Press, Inc.
577 College Avenue
Palo Alto, CA 94306
415-326-4448

The SCII is probably the most widely used vocational interest instrument in the world. It can reflect a lot about the similarities between your interests and the interests of people who are successful in a variety of careers, so we highly recommend that you make the opportunity to take the test.

When you have completed the test, make an entry in your Feelings Record. How did you react to the test? What were your feelings while you were taking it?

The SCII is scored by a computer. There are two options for the scoring—a one-page profile, or a more lengthy analysis. The cost of scoring a single profile was $25 in 1980. Group rates bring the individual costs down considerably.

If you elect to get a profile, this chapter will help you to interpret the results. The more expensive and lengthier analysis tends to be more self-explanatory, but contains little information about the background and development of the instrument. Once you have received your scoring feedback, read the chapter and follow the instructions there.

Interpreting the Strong-Campbell
Interest Inventory

NOTE:
DO NOT READ THIS UNTIL YOU HAVE COMPLETED THE STRONG ASSIGNMENT IN THE WORKBOOK.

The Strong-Campbell Interest Inventory (SCII) is the recently updated version of an enormously respected vocational guidance instrument originally developed over 40 years ago. The output of this instrument, generally called the Strong Profile, provides a great deal of potentially relevant information about a person. Indeed, our students have generally found the SCII to be second only to the written interview in its usefulness as a data-generating device.

To use the Strong Profile for self-assessment purposes, we need, as always, a fairly thorough understanding of the instrument. This chapter has been written to provide you with that understanding.

The Design of the Test

The SCII asks a person over 300 questions that elicit preferences (likes, dislikes, or indifferences) concerning various occupations, school subjects, activities, amusements, and types of people. The test's input, therefore, is data about what we generally call interests or attitudes. The SCII does not elicit information regarding intelligence, aptitudes, or skills.

The instrument uses this information about a person's interests to compute a number of scores generally presented in three parts, as shown in Exhibit 9-1. These parts are the (1) general occupational themes, (2) basic interest scales, and (3) occupational scales. Each of these three sets of scores compares the test taker's interests with either men and women in general, or men and women in specific occupations (bankers, advertising executives). And, as we shall see, these comparisons can be very useful data.

The data presentation in Exhibit 9-1 is organized around six themes, based on the work of J. L. Holland (all occupational scales related to each theme are grouped together).[1] As this book goes to press, the primary scoring license will be held by Consulting Psychologists, Inc., who use the profile shown in Exhibit 9-1. Formerly, different formats were used, but the basic information and data reported remain the same. We will delay a discussion of the themes and focus first on that part of the profile which is most important for our purposes—the occupational scales.

The Occupational Scales

The occupational scales have been created to inform the taker how similar his or her interests are to the interests that are somewhat idiosyncratic to a particular male or female occupational group (such as female bankers or male engineers). Each of the 124 occupational scales was created in the following manner:

1. A group of about 150–450 men or women were identified as being happily employed in an occupation and as having been in that occupation for more than three years (average tenure was usually 10–20 years).

2. These people were asked to answer the 325 questions on the SCII.

3. Whenever these people expressed some particular preference much more or less frequently than a large sample of "people in general," *that alternative was used in creating the scale for that occupational group.*

4. The scale was then normed so that the average person in the occupational group scored 50 on the scale, while two-thirds of the group scored between 40 and 60.[2]

As a result of this scale construction procedure, the more often a person using the SCII expresses preferences that distinguish a particular occupation, the

greater the score he or she will receive on that occupational scale. For example, suppose you indicated in response to question 217 that you liked "living in the city." Suppose also that the criterion group of male architects happened to choose that option much more often than most other people. In that case, your score on the *m architect* scale would go up a notch. If time and time again you chose an option that had been chosen by male architects (liking, disliking, or being indifferent to an item) but not chosen by others, then your final score on the *m architect* scale would probably be high, usually considered to be a score of 45 or above. You and the criterion group of architects are indicating shared attitudes. You have something in common. You express the same preferences they do.

Sharing a large number of preferences with people in an occupation is important because research has linked such commonalities to people's decisions to go into and stay in an occupation.[3] It would appear that, given an appropriate level of ability, those who tend to share the same preferences as other occupational members—those who "talk the same language"—are also more likely to get on, to be readily accepted, to enjoy the work, and to be successful.

To be able to use your scores on the occupational scales effectively, it is sometimes useful to have some supplementary information about the scale's occupation, the criterion group used to construct the scale, or the type of people who tend to score high on the scale. This information is given in Exhibit 9-2, and should be taken into account when examining the profile. For example, in interpreting a high or low score on the male banker scale, it is probably important to recognize that the scale was based on a national sample of bank presidents and vice presidents, many of whom were employed in small commercial banks in small towns. One would suspect that such a group of people is significantly different from, say, a group of New York investment bankers.

---

[1] In *Making Vocational Choices: A Theory of Careers* (Englewood Cliffs, N.J.: Prentice-Hall, 1973), Holland argues that it is useful for career decision-making purposes to conceptualize occupations, job-related-activities, and personality types in terms of the themes, which he labels realistic, investigative, artistic, social, enterprising, and conventional.

[2] One of the consequences of setting the occupational group's average score at 50 is that it is possible to get a negative score on many of the scales.

---

[3] For previous versions of this instrument, Strong verified the predictive values of the occupational scales for the 18 years after the test was taken [E. K. Strong, Jr., *Vocational Interests 18 Years After College* (Minneapolis: University of Minnesota Press, 1955)]; McArthur showed they predicted for 14 years [C. McArthur, "Long-Term Validity of the Strong Vocational Interest Test in Two Subcultures," *Journal of Applied Psychology* (1954), pp. 346–533]. These and other research efforts have found that the odds that the following statements will turn out to be true range from 2 to 1 up to 5 to 1, with 3.5 to 1 being the commonest result.

1. People continuing in occupation X obtained a higher interest score in X than in any other occupation.
2. People continuing in occupation X obtained a higher interest score in X than other people entering other occupations.
3. People continuing in occupation X obtained higher scores in X than people who changed from X to another occupation.
4. People changing from occupation X to occupation Y scored higher in Y prior to the change than in any other occupation, including X.

Exhibit 9-1
Consulting Psychologists Press SCII Scoring Form

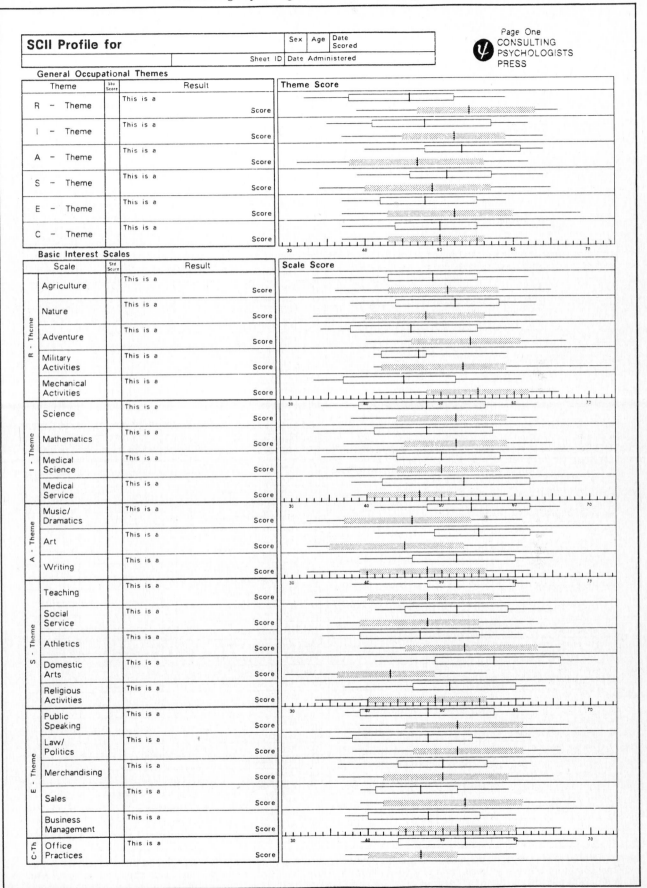

Exhibit 9–1 (*continued*)

Occupational Scales

Code	Scale	Standard Score M	Standard Score F	Very Dissimilar	Dissimilar	Moderately Dissimilar	Mid-Range	Moderately Similar	Similar	Very Similar
RC	Air Force Officer									
RC	Army Officer									
RC	Navy Officer									
RC	Farmer									
RCE	Voc. Agriculture Teacher									
RE	Police Officer									
R	Navy Officer									
R	Farmer									
R	Forester									
R	Skilled Craftsperson									
R	Radiologic Technologist									
RI	Radiologic Technologist									
RI	Forester									
RI	Engineer									
RI	Veterinarian									
RIC	Licensed Practical Nurse									
RAS	Occupational Therapist									
IR	Veterinarian									
IR	Chemist									
IR	Physicist									
IR	Geologist									
IR	Medical Technologist									
IR	Dental Hygienist									
IR	Dentist									
IR	Optometrist									
IR	Physical Therapist									
IR	Physician									
IRS	Registered Nurse									
IRS	Math-Science Teacher									
IRC	Math-Science Teacher									
IRC	Systems Analyst									
IRC	Computer Programmer									
IRE	Chiropractor									
IE	Pharmacist									
I	Pharmacist									
I	Biologist									
I	Geographer									
I	Mathematician									
IA	College Professor									
IA	Sociologist									
IAS	Psychologist									
AIR	Architect									
AI	Lawyer									
AE	Public Relations Director									
AE	Advertising Executive									
AE	Interior Decorator									
A	Musician									
A	Commercial Artist									
A	Fine Artist									
A	Art Teacher									
A	Photographer									

12 21 27 39 45 54 60

Occupational Scales

Code	Scale	Standard Score M	Standard Score F	Very Dissimilar	Dissimilar	Moderately Dissimilar	Mid-Range	Moderately Similar	Similar	Very Similar
A	Librarian									
A	Foreign Language Teacher									
A	Reporter									
A	English Teacher									
AS	English Teacher									
SA	Speech Pathologist									
SA	Social Worker									
SA	Minister									
SIE	Minister									
SI	Registered Nurse									
S	Licensed Practical Nurse									
S	Special Ed. Teacher									
S	Elementary Teacher									
SR	Physical Ed. Teacher									
SRE	Recreation Leader									
SE	YMCA/YWCA Director									
SE	School Administrator									
SCE	Guidance Counselor									
SEC	Guidance Counselor									
SEC	Social Science Teacher									
EA	Flight Attendant									
EA	Beautician									
E	Beautician									
E	Department Store Manager									
E	Realtor									
E	Life Insurance Agent									
E	Elected Public Offical									
E	Public Administrator									
EI	Investment Fund Manager									
EI	Marketing Executive									
E	Personnel Director									
E	Chamber of Comm. Exec.									
E	Restaurant Manager									
EC	Restaurant Manager									
EC	Chamber of Comm. Exec.									
EC	Buyer									
EC	Purchasing Agent									
ERC	Agribusiness Manager									
ES	Home Economics Teacher									
ECS	Nursing Home Admin.									
EC	Nursing Home Admin.									
EC	Dietitian									
ECR	Dietitian									
CER	Executive Housekeeper									
CES	Business Ed. Teacher									
CE	Banker									
CE	Credit Manager									
CE	IRS Agent									
CA	Public Administrator									
C	Accountant									
C	Secretary									
C	Dental Assistant									

12 21 27 39 45 54 60

Exhibit 9–2

Supplemental Data on Occupational Scales

Scale/sample	N	Year tested	Mean age	Mean years education	Mean years experience	Composition and comments
Army Officer (f)	285	1979	32.2	16.8	7.9	57% completed BA degrees, 35% MA. Rank: warrant officer (4%), lieutenant (19%), captain (59%), major (14%), lt. colonel (3%), colonel (1%).
Army Officer (m)	309	1979	36.8	16.9	13.5	See women's sample above. 11% had some college education, 42% completed BA degrees, and 44% MA. Rank: warrant officer (12%), lieutenant (3%), captain (31%), major (23%), lt. colonel (23%), colonel (7%), higher (1%).
Art Teacher (f)	359	1967	46.0	16.6	10.0	From names supplied by the National Art Education Association, plus certified teachers in *Iowa Educational Directory*.
Art Teacher (m)	303	1978	40.2	19.2	14.9	Members, National Art Education Association. 15% completed BA degrees, 64% MA, 19% PhD.
Artist, Commercial (f)	123	1979	35.2	16.1	11.0	Artists working for agencies and studios listed in *The Creative Black Book 1979*, a national directory of art services. 26% had taken art courses not leading to a degree, 50% completed BA degrees, 10% MA. 41% were freelance artists, 22% were employed by a studio, and 17% worked for a combination of employers.
Artist, Commercial (m)	199	1979	38.8	16.2	15.5	See women's sample above. 27% had taken art courses not leading to a degree, 47% completed BA degrees, 6% MA. 39% were freelance artists, 23% were employed by a studio, 10% by an advertising agency, and 15% worked for a combination of employers.
Artist, Fine (f)	247	1979	44.4	17.6	17.0	Names selected from *Who's Who in American Art*, 1978. 18% had taken art courses not leading to a degree, 25% completed BA degrees, 42% MA. 58% were freelance artists, 15% were employed by educational institutions, and 22% worked for a combination of employers.
Artist, Fine (m)	204	1979	43.4	18.0	20.7	Names selected from *Who's Who in American Art*, 1978. 13% had taken art courses not leading to a degree, 15% completed BA degrees, 55% MA. 39% were freelance artists, 39% were employed by educational institutions, and 15% worked for a combination of employers.

(continued)

Exhibit 9-2 (continued)

Scale/sample	N	Year tested	Mean age	Mean years education	Mean years experience	Composition and comments
Banker (f)	271	1968	49.0	13.0	23.0	Members, National Association of Bankwomen. Sampled proportionately by job title from overall roster.
Banker (m)	171	1968	49.0	14.7	24.3	National sample of bank presidents and vice-presidents from a listing of bankers provided in *Martindale-Hubbell Law Directory*, 1968.
Beautician (f)	103	1979	37.7	13.1	14.3	From listings of state licensing boards of Alaska, Georgia, Illinois, Iowa, Michigan, Minnesota, South Dakota, Utah, and Wisconsin. 93% attended cosmetology schools. Major activities included hair dressing (64%), management and supervision (10%), and a combination (22%).
Beautician (m)	186	1975– 1979	37.2	13.8	14.4	See women's sample above. 84%, attended cosmetology school. Major activities included hair dressing (61%), management and supervision (18%), and a combination (14%).
Biologist (f)	207	1975	42.5	21.1	12.7	Members, American Institute of Biological Sciences. 34% were in teaching, 24% in research, and 37% in a combination of activities.
Biologist (m)	209	1975	43.6	21.7	15.5	Members, American Institute of Biological Sciences. 30% were in teaching, 46% in a combination of teaching, research, and administration.
Business Education Teacher (f)	420	1978	38.3	18.0	11.4	Members, National Business Education Association; all were secondary school teachers. 31% completed BA degrees, 66% MA.
Business Education Teacher (m)	232	1978	38.8	18.5	13.2	Members, National Business Education Association; all were secondary school teachers. 15% completed BA degrees, 78% MA, 5% PhD.
Buyer (f)	204	1967	34.0	12.4	13.0	Heads of merchandise departments, nearly all in department stores.
Buyer (m)	176	1969	42.0	14.0	15.8	National sample of department-store buyers listed in *Sheldon's Retail Directory of the United States* (1969).
Chamber of Commerce Executive (f)	211	1979	45.8	13.4	7.4	Members, American Chamber of Commerce Executives (ACCE), and names selected from *Johnson's World Wide Chamber of Commerce Directory*. 67% had high school diplomas, 12% completed BA degrees.

It is also useful when interpreting a profile to recognize that the occupations grouped together in Exhibit 9–1 and marked with a single letter (I, A, S, E, C, or R) all tend to share certain characteristics in common. According to John Holland, the R occupations (such as forester and veterinarian) tend to involve the explicit, ordered, or systematic manipulation of objects, tools, machines, and animals. The I occupations (such as musician and reporter) involve ambiguous, free, unsystematized activities that create art forms or products. The S occupations (such as social worker and personnel director) are chosen generally by people who like to work in groups and prefer to solve problems through feelings and interpersonal relationships. The E occupations (such as realtor and investment fund manager) require strong verbal, achievement, and leadership skills and abilities. These jobs often entail the manipulation of others to attain organizational or self-interest goals. And finally, the C occupations (such as accountant and secretary) usually entail the explicit, ordered, systematic manipulation of data.

The occupational scales on most profiles will have a number of "high" (45 or above) scores in both male and female occupational groups.[4] In addition to accepting at face value what those scores tell you (that you have interests and attitudes much like people in those occupations), it can be useful in interpreting a profile to list those occupations separately, and to try to identify what, if anything, they have in common. The same technique can be profitably used with particularly low scores.

The occupational scales on some profiles will be relatively flat; there will be few if any high scores. The raw datum here indicates that the test taker's values and attitudes have not crystallized around any of the occupational types for which the instrument is scored. The most common reason for this relates to culture. Flat profiles sometimes occur when the test taker was raised in an environment that was different from the white, middle-class, American culture from which virtually all criterion groups come.

The Basic Interest Scales

The basic interest scales, shown in the middle of the Profile in Exhibit 9–1, provide us with less information than the occupational scales. Nevertheless, they can be very helpful.

Your scores on the 23 basic interest scales, in effect, just report back to you what you reported on the SCII. That is, they simply measure the frequency with which you said you liked, disliked, or were indifferent to certain types of activities or subjects. For example, if you said you like art as a school subject (question 136 on the SCII), your score on the art scale would increase. If you said you did not like visiting art galleries (question 234), your score on the art scale would decrease. The only transformation the test makes is to set fifty as the mean score on each scale (with a standard deviation of 10) for a sample of 600 men and women, and to adjust your score accordingly. This allows you to compare your score to people in general.[5]

It is useful to recognize that because of the way these scales are constructed, it is possible for someone to score high or low on most of the scales. The first person simply chose the "like" option very often on the SCII, while the second chose "indifferent" or "dislike" very often. It is also possible for a person to have a high basic interest score (65) on mathematics, and yet have a low score (10) on the occupational scales *m mathematician* or *f mathematician*. In this case, the person has reported on the SCII a high liking for mathematical subjects and activities, but has not reported many of the somewhat unique interests that characterize the people in the mathematics profession (which may have nothing obvious to do with mathematics).

The General Occupational Themes

The third set of scores on the Strong Profile are called general occupational themes (look at the upper middle section of the profile in Exhibit 9–1). These scores are computed in a manner very similar to the basic interest scores;[6] the only major difference is that the scores are related not to fairly narrow activities or subjects, like science or nature, but to the six very broad occupational themes that are based on the research of John Holland (see Exhibit 9–3 for a definition of these themes). There is a second less significant difference for the profile shown in Exhibit 9–1. Instead of giving you male and female averages and

---

[4]The profile shown in Exhibit 9–1 marks, with an asterisk on the line graph, only the male occupation scores or the female occupation scores, depending upon the sex of the test taker. Nevertheless, it presents both scores in the column marked STD score. Some people find it helpful when they work on a profile to fill in by hand the missing asterisks.

[5]As well as to men and women in general. Norms for each sex in Figure 1 are indicated by the bars printed on each scale: the shaded bar gives the norm for men, the unshaded bar for women. The line in the middle of the bar represents the group mean. The thick portion of the bar represents the range of scores for 50% of the sample. The thin lines that extend from the bars show the range for 90% of the sample.

[6]That is, items were identified on the SCII that relate to each theme. Whenever you answer "like" to one of the items, your score goes up on the appropriate theme scale; whenever you answer "dislike," your score goes down. The scales were standardized so that the average person in a general sample of 600 people scored 50 on each scale, with a standard deviation of 10.

Exhibit 9–3
The Six Occupational Themes

R-THEME. People who score very high on this theme tend to be rugged, robust, practical individuals who are physically strong and frequently aggressive in outlook. They often have good physical skills but have trouble expressing themselves in words or communicating these feelings to others. They like to work outdoors and they like to work with tools, especially large, powerful machines. They prefer to deal with things rather than with ideas or with people. They generally have conventional political and economic opinions, and are usually cool to radical new ideas. They enjoy creating things with their hands and prefer occupations such as mechanic, construction work, fish and wildlife management, laboratory technician, some engineering specialties, some military jobs, agriculture, or the skilled trades. Although no single word can capture the broad meaning of the entire theme, the word "realistic" has been used to characterize this pattern, thus the term R-Theme.

I-THEME. This theme tends to center around science and scientific activities. Extremes of this type are task-oriented; they are not particularly interested in working around other people. They enjoy solving abstract problems and have a great need to understand the physical world. They prefer to think through problems rather than act them out. Such people enjoy ambiguous challenges and do not like highly structured situations with many rules. They frequently have unconventional values and attitudes and tend to be original and creative, especially in scientific areas. They prefer occupations such as design engineer, biologist, social scientist, research laboratory worker, physicist, technical writer, or meteorologist. The word "investigative" is used to summarize this pattern, thus I-Theme.

A-THEME. Those scoring high here are artistically oriented and like to work in artistic settings where there are many opportunities for self-expression. Such people have little interest in problems that are highly structured or that require gross physical strength and prefer problems that can be dealt with through self-expression in artistic media. They resemble I-Theme types in preferring to work alone, but have a greater need for individualistic expression, are usually less assertive about their own opinions and capabilities, and are more sensitive and emotional. They score higher on measures of originality than any of the other types. They describe themselves as independent, original, unconventional, expressive, and tense. Vocational choices include artist, author, cartoonist, composer, singer, dramatic coach, poet, actor or actress, and symphony conductor. This is the "artistic" theme, or A-Theme.

S-THEME. People scoring the highest on this theme are sociable, responsible, humanistic, and concerned with the welfare of others. They usually express themselves well and get along well with others. They like attention and see situations that allow them to be at or near the center of the group. They prefer to solve problems by discussions with others or by arranging or rearranging relationships between others, but have little interest in situations that require physical exertion or working with machinery. Such people describe themselves as cheerful, popular, achieving, and good leaders. They prefer occupations such as school superintendent, clinical psychologist, high school teacher, marriage counselor, playground director, speech therapist, or vocational counselor. This is the "social" theme, or S-Theme.

E-THEME. Those who score high here have a great facility with words which they put to effective use in selling, dominating, and leading. These people are frequently in sales work. They see themselves as energetic, enthusiastic, adventurous, self-confident, and dominant, and they prefer social tasks where they can assume leadership. They enjoy persuading others to accept their viewpoints. They are impatient with precise work or work that involves long periods of intellectual effort. They like power, status, and material wealth, and enjoy working in expensive settings. Vocational preferences include business executive, buyer, hotel manager, industrial relations consultant, political campaigner, realtor, many kinds of sales work, sports promoter, and television producer. The word "enterprising" summarizes this pattern, thus E-Theme.

C-THEME. People who score high on this theme prefer the highly ordered activities, both verbal and numerical, that characterize office work. They fit well into large organizations but do not seek leadership since they respond to power and are comfortable working in a well-established chain of command. They dislike ambiguous situations and prefer to know pre-

Exhibit 9–3 *(continued)*

cisely what is expected of them. Such people describe themselves as conventional, stable, well-controlled, and dependable. They have little interest in problems that require physical skills or intense relationships with others and are most effective at well-defined tasks. Like the E-Theme type, they value material possessions and status. Vocational preferences are mostly within the business world and include bank examiner, bank teller, bookkeeper, some accounting jobs, financial analyst, computer operator, inventory controller, tax expert, statistician, and traffic manager. Although one word cannot adequately represent the entire theme, the word "conventional" more or less summarizes the pattern, hence C-Theme.

Source: The SVIB-SCII Profile.

ranges for each theme, as the basic interest scales do with shaded and unshaded bars that are printed on the profile, the general occupational scales tell you how high or low your score is relative to others in your own sex (only). And it does so in English, beside each score, in the column marked "Results."

Because the type of person the R theme describes, for example, often has interests in agriculture, nature, adventure, military activities, and mechanical activities, those five interest areas are put together and marked R on the basic interest scales in Exhibit 9–1. Furthermore, it is because this type of person tends to prefer occupations such as Air Force officer, occupational therapist, army officer, cartographer, veterinarian, etc., that those occupational scales are grouped together and marked R. This same organizing format applies to the other themes, interest scales, and occupational scales. In addition, the secondary themes that are inherent in each occupational scale are noted by the scale names. For example, in Exhibit 9–1, the *occupational therapist f* scale (upper left-hand corner) has RIA printed next to it. This signifies that the main occupational theme inherent in that scale is realistic, and that the investigative and artistic are secondary themes.

In most profiles, scores across the three sets of scales (occupational, basic interest, and general occupational theme) will be roughly similar on the average for those scales related to a single theme. For example, a person whose general occupational theme score for R is very low (25) will probably also score low on most of the basic interest scales associated with the R theme (agriculture, nature, etc.), and will probably also score low on most of the occupational scales associated with R (such as occupational therapist, Air Force officer). Such a pattern simply confirms Holland's thesis and the organizational format used in the latest version of the Strong Profile.

Other Scores

Immediately above the occupational scales shown in Exhibit 9–1 you will find the final pieces of data the instrument provides.

In the center is a box marked total responses. This shows how many answer marks the computer has read from the answer sheet; since there are 325 items, the score on this index should be 325 or close to it. Up to 32 items can be omitted without significantly affecting the results.

A second index, Infrequent Responses, shows the number of rare responses given. It is weighted so that almost everyone scores zero or higher here; if the score is *below zero,* the person has marked an uncommonly high number of rare responses. Usually a negative score indicates some confusion, such as skipping a number on the answer sheet or random marking. You can safely ignore numbers above zero.

The academic comfort scale is a measure of probable persistence in an academic setting. Students graduating with a BA from a liberal arts college average 50, MAs about 55, PhDs about 60. Students seeking advanced degrees who score low (around 40) on this scale inevitably report that they view their education as a necessary hurdle to be cleared and are not usually enchanted with the academic nature of their study. The item content is heavily oriented toward science and the arts (weighed positively) and business and blue-collar activities (weighed negatively).

On the Introversion-Extroversion scale, high scores (50 and above) indicate introversion and low scores (40 and below), extroversion. The item content is concerned almost entirely with working with people in social service, educational, entertainment, or business settings.

The LP/IP/DP indices show the percent of "Like," "Indifferent," and "Dislike" responses selected in each section of the SCII (Occupations, School Subjects, etc.). Although there is some variation from section to section, the average for LP, IP, and DP percentages is about 35, and the average standard deviation is about 16. Most of our students' percentages have been between 5 and 60. Scores in this range are normal and have no effect on the text. Percentages above 60, particularly if they occur in several sections and are consistently in the LP, IP, or DP category, may affect the test results and probably provide helpful information about the test taker in themselves.[7]

Using the Strong

A good assessor can usually learn a considerable amount from a Strong Profile by treating it as we have treated data from all other data-generating instruments: That is, by making sure he or she understands the instrument and then by looking for patterns. The Strong Profile can and should be used both to identify new patterns or ideas, and to test themes and patterns that have emerged from other data.

To facilitate identifying new patterns you may find the following procedures helpful. First, on a separate sheet of paper list all your occupational scores above 45. If you have only one or two scores above 45, list all the scores above 40. Also list all your negative scores; again, if you have only one or two (or none), list all your scores less than 20. Then look for patterns within and across the lists.

Most of the higher and lower occupational scores from two Strongs are shown in Exhibit 9–4 (2 or 3 scores in each case are omitted so that it is easier to see the patterns). In the first profile, the high scores all seem to relate to the relatively high-level management of people. They do not include all the high-level people management scales, but they include most of them. The lowest scores, on the other hand, are almost all blue-collar trades. None are managerial jobs. The latter contrasts sharply in socioeconomic terms with the high-score occupations. And, interestingly, none of the high-score managerial occupations involve su-

Exhibit 9–4

High and Low Occupational Scores from Two Strong Profiles

PROFILE #1			
High Scores		**Low Scores**	
Department Store Manager m	52	Skilled crafts m	10
Sales Manager m	50	Physical Education Teacher f	7
Navy Officer m	48	Vocational Agriculture Teacher m	3
Public Administrator m	48	Instrument Assembler f	−1
Advertising Executive m	43	Farmer m	−3
Department Store Manager m	42		

PROFILE #2			
High Scores		**Low Scores**	
Guidance Counselor m	62	Math Science Teacher	19
Psychologist m	60	Army Officer m	8
Psychologist f	58	Police Officer m	6
Physical Therapist f	57	Department Store Manager m	4
English Teacher f	50	Army Officer f	−1
Social Worker m	48	Agribusiness Manager m	−4
Social Worker f	47		
Life Insurance Agent m	42		

[7]A high LP response style (LP above 60 in several sections) will inflate your scores in the general occupational themes and the basic interest scales. If many (15 or more) basic interest scales are high, only the top three to five scores should be considered. High LP types might be described as overly enthusiastic and vocationally unfocused, particularly if they have none or very few "similar" ratings on occupational scales. They are often very energetic, but in a "ship without rudder" way.

If "dislike" percentages are generally high, the scores on the general occupational themes and basic interest scales will be low, and some information may be gotten from treating the relatively highest scores as "high" regardless of their absolute value. According to Campbell ["Manual for the Strong-Campbell Interest Inventory" (Stanford University Press, 1974)], high DPs tend to fall into two categories: those with such an intense occupational focus that they mark everything "dislike" which falls outside their well-defined realm of interest; and those who have few "likes" in the world and find most of everything repugnant. Those of the first type usually experience few vocational problems, unless a sudden and massive insight or external turn of events shatters their world view, as in the case of many engineers in the late 1960s. The second type, however, can experience serious difficulties in career issues. One way to differentiate the two types is to check if there are at least a few occupational scales in the "similar" range. If so, chances are this is a "type 1" profile of someone with a highly focused sense of direction.

pervising the types of occupations included in the low scores. One might tentatively conclude from these scores that a theme labeled "manager of white-collar and professional people" is appropriate.

In the second profile, the high scores generally seem to be in "helping" professions. That is, they all involve providing another person or persons professional help of some type. The low scores, however, seem to relate to occupations that put a person in the position of having to manage and perhaps discipline other people. In each case, the occupation gives the person formal authority, and expects him or her to use it to accomplish some institutionally set objectives. Possible themes that emerge from these scores might be labeled "helping professions" and "dislikes relations based on formal authority."

Of course, the tentative themes we have identified in these profiles should be checked out both with other Strong data and with data from other devices.

A second way in which one can go about looking for patterns in a Strong Profile is by looking at the high and low scores within each of the theme-related groupings. For example, in the scores in profile 1 in

Exhibit 9–5 all are from the I theme occupations. Yet there is clearly a difference in the higher and lower scores within that theme category. The higher-scored occupations are much more applied, pragmatic, and concrete than the lower-scored ones. This suggests a theme we might label "applied and concrete: not abstract."

The scores from the second profile in Exhibit 9–5 are all from the S theme occupations. But the higher-score occupations are obviously different from the lower ones. The higher are all jobs that require one to organize and manage others. The lower-scored occupations involve giving help to others on a one-on-one basis. The pattern suggests a theme related to the organization and management of others.

Still a third way one can look for patterns in a Strong Profile is to look for high scores on the basic interest scales or the general occupational themes which automatically suggest and label a theme. That is, if the E theme score is very high (67), then "enterprising" is obviously a potential theme. Likewise, if the nature scale has a very high score, then "nature" is a likely candidate for a theme, or for part of a theme.

To test themes or patterns that have emerged in other data with the Strong data, one can simply go over all of the profile, asking questions like these:

1. Is this scale or score relevant to the theme in question?
2. If yes, does its score support or not support the theme?

For example, if "artistic" is a theme that has emerged from the written interview, one would want to examine *at least* the A theme score, the art basic interest scale, and the artist (f, m) occupational scales for support or disconfirmation. Likewise, if "political" was a theme identified in other data, you would definitely want to look at the law/politics basic interest score and the public administrator, school superintendent, and chamber of commerce executive occupational scores.

There are, of course, still other approaches one can take using a Strong Profile. And as long as they include a basic understanding of the instrument and an orientation toward testing and developing themes, they too are appropriate.

Exercise

To help you practice interpreting a Strong, consider Tom Wilson's profile on the next page. Try to do a complete analysis of it. Allow yourself enough time, since interpreting a Strong is much more complex than interpreting a 24-hour diary.

Exhibit 9–5

Examples of Higher and Lower Scores within Theme-Related Grouping of Occupational Scales

PROFILE #1

Higher		Lower	
Engineer f	38	Chemist f	20
Medical Technician f	39	Physical Scientist m	18
Pharmacist f	30	Mathematician f	15
Dentist f	42	Mathematician m	19
Physician m	29	Physicist f	10
Dental Hygienist f	37	Biologist f	12
Physical Therapist f	35	Social Scientist m	19
Medical Technician m	32	College Professor f	18
Optometrist m	38	College Professor m	12
Computer Programmer f	30	Psychologist f	19
Optometrist f	40	Psychologist m	20

PROFILE #2

Higher		Lower	
Personnel Director m	36	Guidance Counselor	13
School Superintendent m	25	Nurse f	14
Public Administrator	41	Social Worker m	19
YWCA Staff f	32	Physical Therapist m	8

TOM WILSON'S: SCII

SCII   Tom Wilson   MALE   DATE SCORED   09/23/81   231624414   065 0009 1

Interpretive Scoring Systems NCS

Division of
National Computer Systems, Inc.
P.O. Box 1294
Minneapolis, MN 55440
Phone 800-328-6116
© 1981 National Computer Systems

I. ADMINISTRATIVE INDICES

A. RESPONSE PERCENTAGES

	L%	I%	D%
1. OCCUPATIONS	34	45	21
2. SCHOOL SUBJECTS	44	42	6
3. ACTIVITIES	45	53	2
4. AMUSEMENTS	46	38	15
5. TYPES OF PEOPLE	38	46	17
PARTS 1-5	39	45	15
6. PREFERENCES	47	13	40
7. CHARACTERISTICS	86	7	7

B. TOTAL RESPONSES = 322
C. INFREQUENT RESPONSES = 11
D. ACADEMIC COMFORT = 53
E. INTROVERSION—EXTROVERSION = 37

II. GENERAL OCCUPATIONAL THEMES

	SCALE	STD. SCR.	VERY LOW 35	LOW INTER. 43	AVERAGE INTEREST 57	HIGH INTER. 65	VERY HIGH
R	REALISTIC	59					
I	INVESTIGATIVE	58					
A	ARTISTIC	51					
S	SOCIAL	58					
E	ENTERPRISING	57					
C	CONVENTIONAL	58					

III. BASIC INTEREST SCALES

	SCALE	STD. SCR.	VERY LOW	LOW INTER. 35	AVERAGE INTEREST 43	HIGH INTER. 57	VERY HIGH 65
R	AGRICULTURE	58					
	NATURE	56					
	ADVENTURE	51					
	MILITARY ACTIVITIES	52					
	MECHANICAL ACTIVITIES	58					
I	SCIENCE	51					
	MATHEMATICS	67					
	MEDICAL SCIENCE	54					
	MEDICAL SERVICE	52					
A	MUSIC/DRAMATICS	47					
	ART	50					
	WRITING	56					
S	TEACHING	57					
	SOCIAL SERVICE	45					
	ATHLETICS	61					
	DOMESTIC ARTS	53					
	RELIGIOUS ACTIVITIES	46					
E	PUBLIC SPEAKING	63					
	LAW/POLITICS	61					
	MERCHANDISING	62					
	SALES	59					
	BUSINESS MANAGEMENT	63					
C	OFFICE PRACTICES	44					

IV. OCCUPATIONAL SCALES

FEM. CODE	MALE CODE	OCCUPATION	FEMALE SCALE	MALE SCALE	VERY DISS. 15	DISSIMILAR 25	AVERAGE 44	SIMILAR 54	VERY SIM.
RC	RC	AIR FORCE OFFICER	47	47					
RC	RC	ARMY OFFICER	52	39					
RI	RI	ENGINEER	50	33					
RC	R	FARMER	34	28					
RI	RI	FORESTER	48	32					
RIC		LICENSED PRAC. NURSE	14						
R	RC	NAVY OFFICER	51	50					
RAS	RAS	OCCUPATIONAL THERAPIST	38	26					
RE	RE	POLICE OFFICER	49	33					
R	RI	RAD. TECH. (X-RAY)	39	17					
N/A	R	SKILLED CRAFTS	N/A	26					
	RI	VETERINARIAN		26					
N/A	RCE	VOC. AGRIC. TEACHER	N/A	24					
I	I	BIOLOGIST	30	14					
IR	IR	CHEMIST	41	21					
IRE	IRE	CHIROPRACTOR	45	35					
IA	IA	COLLEGE PROFESSOR	39	28					
IRC	IRC	COMPUTER PROGRAMMER	51	34					
IR	N/A	DENTAL HYGIENIST	24	N/A					
IR	IR	DENTIST	52	35					
I	I	GEOGRAPHER	49	21					
IR	IR	GEOLOGIST	39	20					
I	I	MATHEMATICIAN	30	18					
IRC	IRS	MATH SCI. TEACHER	38	39					
IR	IR	MEDICAL TECHNOLOGIST	31	21					
IR	IR	OPTOMETRIST	54	44					
I	IE	PHARMACIST	45	36					
IR	IR	PHYSICAL THERAPIST	42	28					
IR	IR	PHYSICIAN	38	36					
IR	IR	PHYSICIST	26	10					
IAS	IAS	PSYCHOLOGIST	30	26					
	IRS	REGISTERED NURSE		28					
IA	IA	SOCIOLOGIST	34	20					
IRC	IRC	SYSTEMS ANALYST	52	42					
IR		VETERINARIAN	38						
AE	AE	ADVERTISING EXECUTIVE	44	43					
AIR	AIR	ARCHITECT	44	31					
A	A	ART TEACHER	34	19					
A	A	ARTIST, COMMERCIAL	32	24					
A	A	ARTIST, FINE	25	10					
A	AS	ENGLISH TEACHER	37	36					
A	A	FOREIGN LANG. TEACHER	23	31					
AE	AE	INTERIOR DECORATOR	34	26					
AI	AI	LAWYER	49	42					
A	A	LIBRARIAN	37	25					
A	A	MUSICIAN	30	28					
A	A	PHOTOGRAPHER	42	34					
AE	AE	PUBLIC RELATIONS DIR.	44	33					
A	A	REPORTER	43	27					
S	S	ELEMENTARY TEACHER	34	33					
SEC	SCE	GUIDANCE COUNSELOR	27	28					
	S	LICENSED PRAC. NURSE		24					
SA	SIE	MINISTER	30	21					
SR	SR	PHYSICAL ED. TEACHER	45	27					
SRE	SRE	RECREATION LEADER	51	39					
SI		REGISTERED NURSE	43						
SE	SE	SCHOOL ADMINISTRATOR	51	41					
SEC	SEC	SOCIAL SCIENCE TEACHER	40	36					
SA	SA	SOCIAL WORKER	38	22					
S	S	SPECIAL ED. TEACHER	29	37					
SA	SA	SPEECH PATHOLOGIST	37	32					
SE	SE	YWCA/YMCA DIRECTOR	53	35					
N/A	ERC	AGRIBUSINESS MANAGER	N/A	22					
E	EA	BEAUTICIAN	31	39					
EC	EC	BUYER	39	40					
EC	E	CHAMBER OF COMM. EXEC.	39	40					
E	E	DEPT. STORE MANAGER	46	43					
EC	ECR	DIETITIAN	49	46					
E	E	ELECT. PUBLIC OFFICIAL	48	46					
EA	EA	FLIGHT ATTENDANT	43	46					
ES	N/A	HOME ECON. TEACHER	27	N/A					
N/A	EI	INVESTMENT FUND MGR.	N/A	40					
E	E	LIFE INSURANCE AGENT	42	37					
EI	EI	MARKETING EXECUTIVE	42	46					
EC	ECS	NURSING HOME ADMIN.	39	44					
E	E	PERSONNEL DIRECTOR	49	44					
E		PUBLIC ADMINISTRATOR	50						
EC	EC	PURCHASING AGENT	57	56					
E	E	REALTOR	43	38					
EC	E	RESTAURANT MANAGER	52	39					
C	C	ACCOUNTANT	47	45					
CE	CE	BANKER	38	39					
CES	CES	BUSINESS ED. TEACHER	28	30					
CE	CE	CREDIT MANAGER	42	48					
C	N/A	DENTAL ASSISTANT	35	N/A					
CER	CER	EXECUTIVE HOUSEKEEPER	35	42					
CE	CE	I.R.S. AGENT	59	47					
	CA	PUBLIC ADMINISTRATOR		40					
C	N/A	SECRETARY	28	N/A					

R
I
A
S
E
C

SCII

STRONG-CAMPBELL INTEREST INVENTORY — FORM T325

Strong-Campbell Interest Inventory
of the Strong Vocational Interest
Blank. Revised and expanded profile
for use with Form T325. Stanford University Press, Stanford, CA.

chapter

10

Analyzing the Written Interview

NOTE:
DO NOT READ THIS UNTIL YOU HAVE COMPLETED THE
WRITTEN INTERVIEW ASSIGNMENT.

Now it's time to come back to your written interview. Most people who engage in individual assessment as a location (such as career counselors) begin data collection with a long interview of the person to be assessed. In one way or another, they say "Tell me about yourself," and then they shut up and take notes, usually intervening only when the interviewee stops talking. Usually this open-ended background interview turns out to be the most important source of information for the assessment.

We began the self-assessment process with a written version of such a background interview. The written interview exercise is very similar to a good introductory counseling interview. And like such an interview, it will be our most important data source.

The Interview Output

To use the responses to the written interview for assessment purposes, we need first to consider what types of information those responses provide. But stop and think for a moment; the most obvious answer is not correct.

If a person claims to have been born March 26, 1948, and to have one sister, it is probably reasonable to assume these assertions are true. That is, they are probably verifiable "facts." But if you examine a typical written interview, you will find that only a small percentage of its content represents clear-cut "facts" about the person's background. More important, if

you examine the interviews of three or four people, you will find considerable variety in the types of "facts" presented. Unlike a more directive interview, in which a person is asked a series of very specific "fact-eliciting" questions, this type of interview allows the interviewee great latitude in deciding what to talk about—which is, of course, the whole idea.

In talking about one's background, any person, given the time, could quite literally write at least one book. (Some autobiographies stretch across three or four volumes.) But because of the context in which the written interview is conducted, one gets instead the equivalent of one or two chapters. And the task of selecting what goes into those chapters is left to the interviewee.

Of course, people being interviewed do not sit down and visualize their history and then develop conscious criteria for editing. They just talk or, in the case of our written equivalent, write. The result, however, is hardly a random selection. Two written interviews produced by the same person a month apart will look remarkably similar (and quite different from most other people's written interviews).

This type of data-generating instrument assumes that, given considerable latitude in responding to questions, a person must consciously or unconsciously choose what and how to answer, and that those choices tell us something important about that individual. What is said, what is not said, how it is said, the order in which it is said—all is potentially useful information about the individual.

Potentially is the key, for some of these data may say more about the manner and the context in which they were generated than they do about the person. Be sure to keep in mind the caveats outlined in Chapter 2 regarding contextual influence (see page 8).

To make sense of this "potentially useful information," to decide what, if anything, the data tell us about the more central aspects of the interviewee, let us return to a more careful consideration of the technique we often use to "interpret" information in our everyday lives: drawing inferences based on patterns we see in the data.

Drawing inferences is something literally everyone engages in almost constantly. We see or hear something, compare, often unconsciously, that perception with our assumptions about the nature of the world and of society, and then draw a conclusion that is to us "logical" or appropriate or consistent with that comparison. This mental process has been recognized for thousands of years. Epictetus, the Greek Stoic philosopher, noted that "Men are not disturbed by things, but by the views which they take of them." In other words, two people may observe the same event and draw entirely different conclusions. This is because of the differences in their assumptions about the way the world operates. Thus, the conclusions people draw reveal something about their assumptions. If we focus on those assumptions, we can learn more clearly what they are and, if they seem unrealistic, perhaps modify them. In self-assessment, this introspective process of examining our own assumptions will help us to draw conclusions or inferences that are more "logical" to others as well as to ourselves.

Consider an example or two. When Mr. Jones arrives at his new boss's home (which he has never seen before) for dinner, he notices that it has a circular driveway, a six-car garage, tennis courts, and a stable. He preconsciously makes a number of assumptions (about the cost of such a home and its upkeep, his boss's salary, his boss's previous work history, and so on) and quickly concludes that his new boss (or his wife) comes from a wealthy family. When Ms. Johnson is introduced to the manager of the Chicago office, she notices that he has a slide-rule tie clasp, a calculator on his desk, and a set of proceedings of an electrical engineering society on his shelf. She infers privately that he has a technical background and orientation.

Although we all are, in some sense, familiar with this technique for making meanings out of data, few people consciously think about the process and about how they tend to engage in it. And most of us often use it in a casual and sloppy manner in dealing with the more inconsequential aspects of our daily activities. For purposes of self-assessment, such casualness is inappropriate. In order to achieve as accurate an assessment as possible, we need to be very careful about how we make inferences.

Exhibits 10–1 and 10–2 display some of the tentative inferences two people independently drew after studying the written interview of a third person (Ms. Jones), along with the data on which those inferences were based. Look at each carefully and see if you can see how they are different.

Most people would agree that the analysis in Exhibit 10–2 seems a lot more sound than that in Exhibit 10–1. That is not to say that the inferences in Exhibit 10–1 are wrong or the inferences in Exhibit 10–2 are correct. We really do not have enough information to make that judgment. But there are a number of differences between Exhibits 10–1 and 10–2 that tend to give one more confidence in Exhibit 10–2.

First of all, the "data" in Exhibit 10–2 are a lot clearer and more specific than those in Exhibit 10–1. Exhibit 10–2 states, with some precision, exactly what it is in Ms. Jones's written interview that has led to such inferences. Exhibit 10–1 is more vague in this regard. One is left wondering how much "a lot" of talk about people is, and what is meant by a "very loose writing style." Is it not possible that Ms. Jones's writing style is fairly typical, but that the person who created the inference in Exhibit 10–1 has a very structured writing style—so what is perhaps typical looks "loose" to such a person?

It is easy to lose sight of the actual data in a written interview and end up analyzing instead your own impressions of the data. We've seen people who, after expressing a strong belief in the validity of a set of inferences, were unable to point to a single specific piece of supporting information in the written interview. They had been performing a reasonably interesting analysis—but it was based mostly on their own impressions, not on the specific information provided

Exhibit 10–1
Some Inferences Made from Written Interview Data

Data	Inferences
Ms. Jones graduated from Stanford with honors.	She is clearly very intelligent.
Ms. Jones's writing style is very loose.	She is probably an unorganized person.
Ms. Jones is an only child.	She is probably achievement-oriented, socially withdrawn, and very tense.
Ms. Jones talks a lot about the people in her life.	She is a very people-oriented and popular person.

Exhibit 10–2
Some Inferences Made from Written Interview Data

Data	Inference
The five periods in Ms. Jones's life which she says were the most "dull and boring" (see page 2, paragraph 2; page 10, paragraph 1; and page 14, paragraph 2) all have one thing in common—she is not in contact with any or many people.	Interacting with people is probably an important source of stimulation for Ms. Jones.
The only "hard" quantitative subject Ms. Jones says she took in high school or college was math, and she says she didn't like it at all (see page 5, paragraph 1; and page 16, paragraph 2).	Ms. Jones does not have strong quantitative skills.
The four people Ms. Jones lists as being "the most influential" in her life are: her father, her tenth-grade teacher, one of her summer job bosses, and her grandmother (page 20).	Ms. Jones probably relates well to authority figures and can be influenced by them.
Ms. Jones grew up in a middle-class family and twice makes references to "not wanting to be poor" (see page 1, paragraphs 3 and 4; and page 30, paragraph 1).	Money is not unimportant to Ms. Jones.

by the other person. So it is important that you have clearly in mind specific data when you are drawing an inference. When you are trying to communicate your logic to another person, it is essential that you reveal not only your conclusions or inferences, but also your data. Otherwise, the other person may not be able to understand how you got from a set of data (which he or she may see very differently) to a set of inferences, and decide that you "have jumped to conclusions."

A second obvious difference between Exhibits 10-1 and 10-2 relates to a number of questionable assumptions. All inferences are based on one or more assumptions than others. Exhibit 10-2's inferences seem more reserved and conservative (and reasona-

ble!) because they assume less. Assumptions are like icebergs, in the sense that at first we may only see the tips of them (in the conclusions we draw). We encourage you in your self-assessment and in your discussions with others to be continually on the alert for iceberg assumptions and to challenge them to make sure the conclusions and inferences you reach are conservatively logical. As you move now into a more intensely inductive phase of the self-assessment process, practice careful consideration of the relationship between data, assumption, and inference.

To get from "Ms. Jones is an only child" to "She is probably achievement-oriented, socially withdrawn, and very tense," one has to assume a great deal. Of course, the inference could be true, but only if a large number of implicit assumptions are also true.[1] Even the first inference in Exhibit 10-1, which assumes a great deal less, is still based on at least the following assumptions:

1. That Ms. Jones really did graduate from Stanford *with* honors.
2. That "intelligence" is a definable, measurable human attribute.
3. That one's "intelligence" is fairly stable over time— it doesn't go up or down drastically in a month, for example.
4. That the "intelligence" one displays does not vary greatly from situation to situation or task to task.

---

[1]Very often when people develop inferences that seem to be based on a lot of assumptions, the reason is that they carry a "model" (often preconsciously) around with them based on their own experiences or something they were taught in school. For example, the person who inferred that because Jones is an only child she is socially withdrawn, tense, and achievement-oriented could have been applying a model of child development learned in school. Such a model might be represented as:

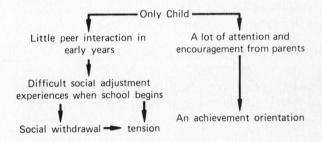

Such a simplified model of a complex phenomenon may be approximately true in some cases, but certainly not in all. Or then again, our data analyst might well have been an only child who had grown up socially withdrawn, tense, and achievement-oriented! That is, the analyst could have been identifying with the data and projecting onto them without even being aware of what was happening. In either case, it would not be unusual for the analyst to believe the inference was "obviously true" and to vigorously defend it until forced to identify the assumptions implicit in the logic that led to the inference.

5. That to graduate with honors from Stanford, one *must be* intelligent. That is, that all the other possible explanations as to why one could graduate with honors (work hard, bribe the dean) are impossible.

People often feel rather uncomfortable when forced to look at the assumptions implicit in their inferences. We often treat our inferences as if the assumptions were known truths, when they seldom are. All five of the assumptions implicit in the inference concerning Ms. Jones's intelligence have some probability of being accurate, but that probability is significantly less than 1.0.

The more assumptions one makes that are not known truths, and the lower the probability that each of those assumptions is correct, the more one engages in what we might call an "inferential leap." Starting with the datum about Ms. Jones graduating from Stanford, inferential leaps of various sizes are shown in Exhibit 10–3.

As the diagram implies, the larger the "leap," the further it takes you from the data. Getting too far away from one's data can be dangerous in self-assessment. Throughout the book, we will remind you to stay close to the data—to let the data do the talking—so that your inferences are clearly connected to the data. We mean "clearly connected" not only to you, but also to another reasonable person who might look at the data you have generated and the inferences you have drawn. In fact, getting someone else whom you trust and respect to look at your data and inferences is an excellent means of checking your own logic and of uncovering large inferential leaps that may be based more on your biases, desires, and "unfounded" assumptions than they are in the data you generated. We will talk more

Exhibit 10–3
Inferential Leaps

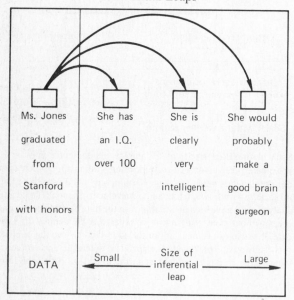

about how to go about getting someone else to look at your data and inferences later.

A third difference between Exhibits 10–1 and 10–2 can be found in the nature of the data used. Exhibit 10–2 never starts with a single "observation" (such as "Ms. Jones is an only child"), but with a number of observations that possibly identify a pattern. And by keeping the patterns relatively simple, the author was able to draw nontrivial inferences without making a large number of questionable assumptions.

Perhaps the single most important part of analyzing a written interview involves looking for relatively simple patterns. Does the author of the interview repeatedly talk about any particular subject or person? Does the author always (or never) quantify things that can be measured? Does the author repeatedly use a certain type of verb or adjective? Does the author always (or never) go into great detail in describing people? objects? events?

Through the identification of patterns, we can start to sort the peripheral and trivial from the more central and important. As any scientist recognizes, an event that occurs once tells us very little. But one that occurs again and again, in some pattern, may well tell us something central about whatever is being studied.

Identifying Patterns

Most people just "see" patterns—that is, the process of identification often occurs unconsciously. However, there are ways in which one can facilitate one's own preconscious processes.[2] Understanding these can be helpful.

Perhaps the easiest technique to facilitate pattern identification is to underline or write on a separate sheet of paper anything that catches your attention when you read through the interview. On a second reading, you can begin to check more systematically whether some pattern is associated with any of those items.

Developing inferences from single bits of data can also help you to identify patterns. If you select a single datum, draw a conservative, tentative inference from it, go on to the next datum, and so on, you can then go back and look at your inferences to see if any of them seem related. If they are, the bits of data from which you generated those inferences may also be related. With a little rewording, you may be able to phrase an inference that captures the essence of several bits of data—and in so doing, identify a pattern. In

---

[2]By "preconscious processes" we mean things which are a part of our mental activity that are not usually in our awareness, but which if focused on with moderate effort can be consciously thought about. We contrast this to "subconscious processes," which are more difficult to bring into awareness.

the end, using a single datum as support for a pattern or theme will be logically weak, but it is a useful way to get started drawing conservative inferences and identifying patterns.

Simple counting can be an important tool. If something seems to occur "a lot," count exactly how many times it does occur. You may find your "sense" was very accurate, or very inaccurate. In a similar vein, if something "seems" never to occur, carefully check that out. Does it really *never* occur?

Very speculative inferences (those based on lots of questionable assumptions), although not very useful as the *product* of an analysis, can occasionally be useful in the *process* of analysis. The major value of a highly speculative inference lies in its occasional capacity to point out an unseen pattern. Having made the inference, for example, that Ms. Jones is socially withdrawn, one might then notice *for the first time* how little she talks about her relationships with people in her written interview, and that she doesn't mention belonging to student organizations of any kind in high school or college. Or you might find just the opposite. In either case, the speculative inference led you to useful data that were previously unseen.

You will undoubtedly develop still other techniques yourself. Just keep in mind that pattern finding, like most good detective work, requires a combination of instinct, disciplined search, and time. And do not be surprised if, at first, you have some difficulty finding patterns. People often feel they don't know what to look for in the data, or that they need a list of "typical patterns" to guide them. But this is not possible. There are literally an infinite variety of patterns that could be developed from a written interview. Because most of us are better versed in deductive than inductive processes, such a response is natural in the beginning.

Guidelines

In analyzing a Written Interview:

1. Stick closely to the data. Make sure you don't end up analyzing something you've manufactured in your own head. Let the data do the talking.
2. Search for patterns. Remember that one datum alone tells you virtually nothing. But be willing to start small and build slowly. Don't leap to conclusions without going back to check the data carefully to be certain that the conclusions are supported.

3. Be careful and explicit with your inferences. Try to be aware of your assumptions.
4. Treat all inferences as "tentative" rather than as hard conclusions.
5. Try to be patient. Good analysis takes time.

Exercise

In the case (pp. 107–13), you will find Tom Wilson's responses to the first four questions of the Written Interview. This interview is typical of most Written Interviews we've seen.

Now, to give you some practice in analyzing this kind of data before you begin work on your own, we would like you to answer the following questions about Wilson's first four responses:

1. What tentative, conservative inferences do you make about Tom?
2. What data do you cite to support your inferences?

As you try to answer these questions, we suggest that you try the following:

1. Read the questions and responses, underlining or making notes of things you think or feel are important as you go along.
2. List several of the data points you identified as potentially important on the Drawing Tentative Inferences Worksheet (next page). Then write down a tentative, conservative inference based on that datum. An example is given on the worksheet.
3. Clarify as well as you can the assumptions you were making that led you to the conclusions/inferences that you drew. An example is given on the worksheet.
4. After you have written a few inferences from single data points, go back through the first four responses and your inferences and attempt to collect evidence related to a single inference. Try to find as much evidence for the inferences you chose as you can.

Finally, stop and consider the strengths and weaknesses of the written interview as a data-generating device. Write these down and note the impact they have on the credibility of the data to you. Be prepared, if you are in a class setting, to discuss these strengths and weaknesses and their implications for your use of the data.

Drawing Tentative Inferences Worksheet
For: Tom Wilson

Paragraph Numbers	Data	My Assumption	Tentative Inference
2	"a girl I can't picture"	People will first mention things that are most important to them.	Tom is a person who is concerned about relationships with women.
9–15	Grandpa . . .	People will describe other people only when they have had a big impact on them.	Tom is a person who respects, perhaps even emulates, his grandfather.

TOM WILSON: WRITTEN INTERVIEW (A)

Reply 1 (Open-Ended Question):

1. Geographically, I can break my life up into 3 areas: Indiana, Virginia, and Georgia. These also follow the early chronological sequence of my life, and then I can add College, Work, and Darden. All of these areas have had profound impacts on my life.

Indiana (Birth to Age 7)

2. I was born in Evansville, Indiana. By most standards I was a little kid and everything was bigger than I was. This seemed to be logical at this age—so I accepted it. I'm thinking back to what first comes to mind:

—Walking home from school in the second grade with a girl I can't picture now.

—All the injuries I had: falling off a split rail fence and getting a split head (I guess that's where the name came from), rolling down driveway slope and running my leg into another bike fender, and hitting Eric in the nose and running like hell over the fence.

3. It's fun to think back on this. I remember several Christmas/Easters in the rec room. I remember the first Frankenstein movie (Frank vs. Werewolf—a big flood at the end engulfs everyone). I have been afraid of wolves since then. I remember my beagle, who was poisoned, probably by the guy down the street. I remember my friends.

4. Susan/Dave: I can picture their house, their Mom. They were both older than I. I remember going to a synagogue once with them. Didn't know the difference between Jews/Catholics. Never understood why they got presents other than at Christmas. They had a pool we used to play in. I remember Dave said he could knock me down by throwing a beachball from ten feet. I said he couldn't. He did—I think I slipped. He was big on the Dave Clark Five—used to play an organ. We had some good birthday parties there. Karen (my sister) and Susan were good friends.

5. Laurie/Eric: Eric was a little obnoxious and got into trouble. Laurie was my age and my sweetheart. I'd like to see how she turned out. We used to play tricks on Karen which I felt guilty about. Karen was a little fat. They had two big poodles that I remember. I can't picture their Mom & Dad though. They had a hammock in the backyard that we played in.

6. Mike/John: Were not close friends but we used to spend the night over there and play basketball/adventures.

7. School was different. I remember Mom taking me to Karen's nursery school and crying all day. First through third grades were OK in our little uniforms. I remember playground /cafeteria. I was a good speller—finished second once.

8. The best memory of this time, which is the strongest because it's always been there, is of my grandparents—really of grandfather.

9. Grandpa had a farm—on which Mom was born. He used to take me for rides in the country through the corn fields. The Metzgers farmed the land and had kids my age. We used to have a great time playing in the barn and pumping water out of the well.

10. We had great fun sitting in the corn bins. There was one stop we'd always make in Dogtown—which is actually the name of the place. Grandpa would buy a beer for himself and Crackerjacks for me. His place is full of memories. Tippy Toes (the dog) would always nip me. Grandpa would get upset at Grandmother all the time; he was fairly calm about it though.

11. My favorite, though, was eating popcorn watching TV with him in his lounge chair.

12. My memories of my cousins are strong in this house. Lisa, Doug, and Dave lived close by. Lisa was my age—Dave/Doug younger. I remember catching lightning bugs behind the house and putting them into jars.

13. Lisa and I would make things to sell on the street. Stuff like Cheerios necklaces—we were real entrepreneurs.

14. Grandpa would make ice cream in the old-style maker. We'd go out to Mac's for barbecue, which was always a big treat. And, we'd sit on

This case was prepared by Kevin E. Sachs, research assistant, under the direction of Associate Professor James G. Clawson, as the basis for class discussion. © 1982 by the Sponsors of the Colgate Darden Graduate School of Business Administration, the University of Virginia, Charlottesville, Virginia. UVA case OB-197.

the front porch which sat on the hill overlooking the Ohio and watch barges come in.

15. I miss Grandpa—he didn't get to see me get married. At his funeral in 1977, I met all of his old farmer buddies who he'd played pool with; I understand he was a good gambler. My last memory of old times of him was of his taking me to Metzger's zoo to see the monkey cage.

16. Other memories at this time were going to swim meets with David. I remember one meet that I was in that I lost. Mom also taught school. Going over there was different because that's where all the big kids were. We moved to Waynesboro, Virginia, in 1962.

Virginia (Age 7–Age 13)

17. We lived there third through first part of seventh grades. We lived first on Rosen Avenue. It was a real house with wood floors that you could slide on in your socks (and also pick up splinters). Mike & David lived across the street with Cindy—their collie.

18. We had a dog—Stuart, an English setter, who liked to roam around. We played with Stuart a lot in the backyard. One time he upset a hornet's nest by barking and almost died from the stings. He was hit by a truck after we moved to Meadowbrook. I remember being very upset that day, and Karen telling me to go ahead and cry and tell people my dog died. It took a while to get over it. I just remembered an incident in Evansville when I was about three. Karen had bunches of cats. Tiger is the one I remember. Anyway, there were a bunch of kittens playing under this table that I was on. It gave way and crushed 2–3 of them. It was difficult to understand what had happened.

19. Most memories of Waynesboro were with friends and school. I remember all of the adventures down the banks of the river (which is no bigger than a large creek) behind Mike & Dave's house. Most time was spent next door with Katie, Tom, Tracy, Mike, and Ted. Katie was my age, and Tom was close. Tom was the "scientist-engineer." He always did the soap box derby stuff. Tracy or "T" was the oldest and the cool guy. Tom and I delivered papers together.

20. Katie was my new "flame," but she didn't know that. I'd go over to see her with the excuse of playing with Tom.

21. Alan was another friend who was fairly crazy. We played a lot of football together and spent the nights at each other's houses. He had older brothers. There was one guy in the neighborhood who was a real turkey that we would abuse all the time. Kids can be mean.

22. These were all neighborhood friends. Katie was the only one I went to school with. School was St. John's. We had our little uniforms again. Sister Jacqueline I remember clearly, and the head sister. The guys (Angelo, Phillip, Thomas, Bailey) had a "Man From Uncle" Club. We were also patrol boys and had the white belts. I remember going to Richmond to visit the capital and having to stop four times on the way back for Phillip to go to the bathroom.

23. I was an altar boy, too, and remember some big times with Father T (never could pronounce his name). I was a real altar boy by the time we moved.

24. Angelo and I worked on a mummy/pyramid project together. I remember the day Kennedy was shot and they announced it and let us go home early.

25. I can remember art classes—Karen was good, I was practical, I drew one figure for everything. My trees looked like my dogs. I painted stuff like houses, dogs, etc., going to the library, a birthday party two guys had for me when they took me to a James Bond double feature, going to Richmond to see "The Sound of Music," driving around town at Christmas time to see the lights, trick or treating, setting up stands of lemonade and candy and having a bus stop by.

26. Seventh grade was a big step up to public schools. I remember fondly Mrs. Dean who was my history teacher. I built Jamestown out of Popsicle sticks which was like big time. I really worked for people I liked. I was elected to home room leader and remember at the school elections voting for my home room nominees even when I had found out another home room had nominated someone else (me). So, I voted against myself.

27. Seventh grade was also chorus. I was the third Wise Man soloist in the Christmas performance. I can picture the flutes we played. I was a small kid and remember that I couldn't do layups for P.E., the only course I ever got a D in because of size. However, I helped a black guy out in health, and he helped me with layups.

28. Sixth and seventh grades were Little League and Midget football.

29. Other memories of Waynesboro are going to Charlottesville for football games. Bob Davis ran around for the last 40 seconds one year to beat Army. Actually, not much has changed (as far as football).

30. We moved to another house in Waynesboro which was across from the golf course. The house was much bigger and not as cozy. We used to camp in the backyard and play football. Mom

would make us wear gear. There was a little area downstairs where Alan, Tom, and I built a "Star Trek" station and had great adventures.

31. Adventures was a big thing then. Make believe. We could spend hours on an adventure playing on the banks of the North Fork and wandering through the parks. I remember one Christmas where it snowed about five feet. When it settled it came up to my chest. I hiked over to Alan's house through the golf course. Mom made me take my walkie-talkie I got for Christmas to check in with her every ten minutes.

32. Waynesboro was also the beginning of Boy Scouts/Cub Scouts and camping. This was with the big guys. I was Crow Patrol, Troop 7. Mr. Showalter was the scoutmaster. Mom was a den mother one year. I remember the Cub Scout meetings and the skit we put on. We also had a lot of meetings at Walter's. We took a tour of the dairy in Waynesboro and had our pictures in the Waynesboro paper. Big times.

33. We used to camp also at Lakes Sherando and Shenandoah. I remember taking the mile swim/canoeing/working on life & star scout. Waking up every morning to "Red Rubber Ball." The guy who taught us canoeing liked to canoe by the cliffs to spot snakes sunning themselves so he could whack them with the paddle. I always thought he was strange and never liked snakes anyway. I remember other guys who had BB guns and would shoot birds. I shot my first when I was about 14 and felt so guilty about it that I've never shot a BB gun since. I'm no hunter and firmly believe that in no way can killing animals/birds be termed "sport."

34. Specific memories of details of camping trips are vague. I remember sitting around camp fires, going on scavenger hunts, walking back to tents in the dark with flashlights. I continued Scouting in Georgia.

35. One fond memory of Waynesboro came to mind when I mentioned Shenandoah. We saw the movie "Shenandoah" with Jimmy Stewart at a drive-in. Parts of that movie are so vivid and moving to me.

36. I just remembered also all the trips we would take on Sunday with Mom & Dad. I usually hated them at the time unless we went to battlefields. I developed an interest in Civil War history and really enjoyed going to Bull Run, Wilderness, Appomattox, Gettysburg, etc. We would also take trips to Skyline Drive. There are three spots I remember clearly: Raven's Roost, Humpback Rocks, and one stretch of road which is all laurel/azalea. When I go to the Drive today, I go to the same spots and appreciate them. Most of the time when I was young, I was bored and resented them. Anyway, we moved to Rome, Georgia next.

Rome, Georgia (1968 to present)

37. My formidable years. Wine, women, song. Sure. This account could fill volumes so I'll try to pick the hotter subjects.

38. I was the new kid on the block. We moved half way into the year so I entered seventh grade in the third quarter. Meeting people was never a problem. I usually got along with most people. I didn't create any lasting friendships at East Rome because I went to a different school the next year—Darlington. My memories of East Rome are being sent home from Bolton's office because I wore shorts one day and playing basketball with one black guy who went on to be pretty good and remembered playing with me. I remember faking, getting fouled a lot.

39. I continued Scouting and camping and went into a troop with guys at East Rome. It was a much smaller outfit. I can remember several camps at Camp Sidney Drew. I received my Eagle and Ad Altare Dei and remember the presentation both in Rome and in Atlanta. I guess I had set these goals because after receiving them I dropped from sight. I was also Senior Patrol Leader for two years. My group of friends had also changed.

40. I was a counselor one year at Sidney Drew with Ricky Marshall. We were in charge of pioneering and built a rope bridge across a river. We charged people a nickel to go over, a dime to get back. After scoutmaster found out, I was demoted to mess tent. I have a lot of memories of camping, hiking, games, Order of the Arrow ceremonies, buying from the camp store, revelry, arts & crafts, canoeing.

41. When I reflect on the Scouting experience, I see it as important in my building as a person. It was both propaganda and value setting. A Scout is kind, courteous, obedient, thrifty, cheerful, clean, brave, reverent, etc. It established an appreciation for the outdoors and doing things on your own and learning on your own as well as learning order and discipline.

42. My formidable years began in the eighth grade—a turning point in growing up. My lasting friends came from relationships established from this point on. Darlington was a prep school and much different. Classrooms were smaller, sports were mandatory—which was good.

43. My highlights of the eighth grade are: the first Bingo party—my first date. I went with Debbie but really wanted to go with Sally. Later Sally and I had a romance through the ninth grade. It was a big time double dating and having Mom & Dad driving you around; those were the days. I wasn't used to dating, didn't kiss a girl until tenth grade, another big time. Also, eighth grade,

scored a goal in soccer game, Coosa vs. Etowah which we won 2–1. Also played Midget football and Little League baseball. I centered punts and played catcher and outfield. My first night game a ball almost hit me on the head because I couldn't see it.

44. I met a lot of people though and was elected ninth-grade president.

45. Another event in the eighth grade was the birth of a boy—Thomas, a brother. I was thirteen at the time and it was overall an uncomprehensible situation. More uncomprehensible was that he died of "crib disease" one month later. I remember getting called from school but didn't understand it. I think back on it now and wish I had a little brother. He would have been eighth-ninth grade now.

46. Ninth and tenth grades sort of blended together until the big awakening in the eleventh grade. I "dated" Sally for months and talked constantly on the phone. The "romance" was abruptly ended one night when I called. Her mother answered and said, "Oh, it's him again!" Then Sally got on the phone and said she never wanted me to call her again. Traumatic experience. I obliged and never called her and didn't speak to her about it until about seven years later, when she said she didn't remember. I don't think I dated anyway until late tenth grade—so it did have a great effect and an effect which I analyzed later as causing me to be cautious in relationships and not open to all situations.

[Left and came back.]

47. Eleventh grade is full of countless stories, things we did and got away with, we thought. I started thinking more towards the future and setting goals. I had always done well in school but really didn't do that well in ninth & tenth grades. I thought that these two years I spent more in getting used to the new environment. I set goals to graduate cum laude—top 10%. I also became active in all kinds of activities—Glee Club, Pep Committee, Dance Committee, Yearbook, Monthly Magazine (Darlingtonian) as well as football, soccer, softball, and other things.

48. My close friends today came out of this time—Andy, Jimmy, and Bob. We experienced a lot of new things together—especially fundamental things like drinking and dating.

49. Andy and I would make liquor runs to Chattanooga where it was 18 and took almost any fake ID's. I don't know how we made it home on some days. There was one time connected with a run that did have an impact. The summer between my eleventh/twelfth grades, Andy and I went on college visitation. During that time my Mom decided to clean out my closet and found

about five rum bottles from a recent trip. I had been working as a YMCA camp counselor that summer. There was one older guy (22) there that Mom immediately connected as a "bootlegger" who was corrupting us youngsters. I remember getting back on a Friday night and coincidentally this guy dropped by our house to invite me to a party. Mom & Dad connected this with a bootlegging transfer and called the police to have his house surrounded. I didn't know any of this at the time. An hour or so later I was informed that they'd found the closet stash and had called the police on the guy. In tears I admitted the story of Andy and my going to Chattanooga and that this guy had nothing to do with it. I really expected severe punishment for this, but my Dad was so taken, he said that since I had told him the truth he would trust me and that I should come to him about things like that. It was probably the best thing he could do—cause I do place a high value on honesty and trust today.

50. Another thing which happened was at that time a big thing. We were walking around one night (Bob and I and three others) when a car stopped and three guys picked a fight with Bob. It happened so fast that Bob was quickly beat up while we pretty much watched. No one else was touched. I felt absolutely helpless and guilty that I had let a friend down. These guys were big so I would have been smashed, too. In a way, I took it as a blow to my masculinity at that time. I swore in a similar situation I wouldn't act that way anymore.

51. I became more achievement-oriented in school and worked hard towards being a top student. To that end I succeeded. I graduated cum laude—was accepted at Virginia and North Carolina (both places my counselor said I didn't have a chance), scored well on SATs and high on Achievement tests, won an award for top student in Algebra II and French III. The French really surprised me. We took a standardized test and I ended up beating the top two students (by accident) and represented the school in Atlanta.

52. The school I went to was a private school—but not as preppy as schools in the North. It was more of a snobbish public school. We had an honor system which worked. I never grew up with much cheating going on.

53. Athletics were a profound experience. I was on the varsity soccer team eleventh/twelfth grades. Eleventh grade we tied for state championship—I pretty much rode bench that year. Twelfth grade I started. We made it to the quarter finals. I remember being very competitive but in a fair, sporting sense. I remember though that the coach said we didn't give 100% one game. I thought about it and concluded that losing wasn't bad if you gave 100% and the other team was simply better. If you gave 100% and lost, there was nothing to be ashamed about. If you didn't give 100% and lost, then you cheated yourself and the team. In remaining games I would ask myself am I really trying as hard as I can at this point in time. You had to constantly push yourself because I didn't want to be ashamed at the end of the game or be disappointed and use an excuse that I didn't try. I wasn't a free rider. The playoff came, we lost. I gave 100%, we lost, it wasn't the end of the world. I was disappointed that the coach gave up on us in the second half.

54. I remember myself being a little different than others in eleventh/twelfth grades. There was also a girls' school in Rome, Thornwood. More often than not guys from Darlington would date girls from Thornwood. I thought that was a little strange, so I dated girls from Coosa High School and East Rome.

55. I went steady with the girl from Coosa in the twelfth grade. My reasons for doing so were mixed. Granted, I liked the girl (Janet), but also everybody has to go steady in high school at one time or another. Janet was a different "counting" kind of girl. She told me that dates would often try to take advantage of her so I was sure in the beginning I wouldn't make such advances. Here I go again. I went steady with her and kept the promise. I was quite naive even for years to come. I got my ring back from her for the reason that I wanted to graduate with it on. This was truly a case of not wanting to hurt anyone and not opening up to the truth. When I finally got around to telling her that I wanted to date other people, I first consumed a bottle of Boone's Farm, then told her. She said she wanted the same, and I wondered why I had spent the money for Boone's Farm. Liquid courage is a joke. We are now friends.

56. I made it through high school in one piece with wild times in college to come. I'm now up to 20 pages and 2/3 of my life—I'll have to stop rambling.

College Days—University of Virginia

57. Now that I think back on it I couldn't have chosen a better place. I have always appreciated tradition and history. An ideal man would be Thomas Jefferson who was impressed by truth, honesty, creativity.

58. College was a continuation of my eleventh-grade awakening. I met people easily even though I really only established two lasting friendships. I have always been an early follower and continued that pattern my first two years. It's

hard for me to say no. Play cards? Sure. Go to parties? Sure. Cut class? Sure. First year was parties, irresponsible, some academic work.

59. I felt, though, that people respected my opinion—that I was sincere and earnest. Some would ask me for advice. I was seen as being cheerful, consistent.

60. During this time I also broke up with a girl I started dating in August before school who had moved to North Carolina. I dated her for a few weeks and I would get tons of mail. I was four years older which when you're first year in school makes a difference. I saw her only occasionally my first year and broke up second year (after I started dating Susan). I once again had trouble explaining the reason and dragged it on. I convinced myself, though, that the reasons weren't just another girl. I learned that she wouldn't date anyone else in high school while I was having a great time in college. I had had a great time in high school and really thought that it wasn't fair. Maybe I watch too many movies. Maybe I have a hangup about being viewed as "honorable" or "gentleman."

61. First and second year I remember taking a lot of strange college-type courses (philosophy, psychology, sociology). A lot of "guy" courses. I'm basically pretty practical and didn't see much use in these and didn't do well. My first four semesters went 2.0, 2.8, 2.4, 2.4. I also would work harder for professors I liked. I remember skipping several classes these years as other social events were more important.

62. Academically I was quite disappointed because I knew I could do better and had to prove it. I set a goal of graduating with a 3.0 and went into the Commerce School, which was supposed to be harder but seemed where the best major was as far as using it once I graduated. Third and fourth years were a lot of work. I became active in school, was elected Pledge Master of Alpha Kappa's Business Fraternity, and ran for offices. I was elected fourth year representative to Commerce Council. I did run for President of the Commerce School, which was also an honor committee position. I feel I ran for the wrong reasons. I wanted to be elected to something. I didn't research the issues and was ill prepared. I did better than I thought, but said to myself that I wouldn't get in that position again of not being prepared before making that kind of commitment.

63. Academically, I achieved my goals with a 3.6, 3.8, 3.6, 3.6, and 3.05 overall. I made Beta Gamma Sigma and graduated with distinction. I also found that I had just as good a time socially if not better and accomplished my other goals, too. I learned I could say "no" and not offend

anyone and was able to schedule my time to accomplish both things.

[Left and came back.]

64. I went through Rush the same as everyone else but did not join a fraternity. I don't think it really fit my personality. I was never good at forced excitement or trying to act excited about whether this is a great house and you're a great guy. My emotional valleys and peaks are minimal at best. I think I'm rather emotionally stable. I really rarely act excited, if you know what I mean.

65. I'm trying to think of all that I can add and even though this was more recent, it seems that I write more and remember more about past events.

66. An event which is important had to do with my first year roommate—Bernie. His parents died third or fourth year. He had actually dropped out of school before third year for personal reasons. I had gotten to know his parents over the last two years. His father was Irish and would bring down half-gallons of Seagrams when he visited. His mother was an alcoholic. The first time I visited his place in D.C., we found bottles hidden under the sofa. His mother died and his father soon afterwards. What troubled me was Bernie didn't tell me about it. I certainly felt bad, but hurt that he didn't come to me. We are now connected in some mutual investments, and I was just in his wedding. We still get together every Christmas for Manhattans—a tradition we started first year at his parent's house.

67. Another thing that happened third year was my car was stolen and driven off a cliff by a 16-year-old black guy. I had left my keys in the car and after it was all over felt like it was just as much my fault as his and was ready to drop charges.

68. Third year was also a great trip to Atlanta to the Virginia-Georgia Tech game. At the Bull Roast I got up on a table, beat some pans together, and made everybody sing for dinner. I was pretty smashed. I got a letter from the University president saying we needed more cheerleaders like myself.

69. Through all of this I never mentioned any religious ties. I'm Catholic and grew up going to church every Sunday plus parochial schools until grade 6. I guess I've mentioned that. I pretty much stopped going to church in college and picked it up again later. My Catholic upbringing has had a great effect on me on establishing values. I was a good kid.

70. I just remembered a time when I was 6. A friend of mine stole some Hershey Kisses from a store. I helped him eat some of them. I was not connected with the theft, but pretty much thought I would go to Hell by eating stolen property. I confessed all of this to a priest.

71. O.K., back to college. I had thought all along that I would go to graduate school immediately after college. So, I only interviewed for a few jobs. What I did which I felt was pretty typical is concern myself with getting current workload done first and then worry about other things—like getting a job. I did this last year at Darden when doing cases that were due the next day and work on that paper or speech the night before.

72. I have always felt though that things usually work out—I have never really been nailed yet. I got a pretty good offer from Control Data and went with them. Graduate schools told me to go get work experience.

73. The summer before going to work I went out west for five weeks with Andy, Jimmy, and Bob. We wondered if we could get along with each other for that long and did remarkably well. We traveled all over and kept a diary of each day's events. Each person would try to outdo each other when it was his day. I'm ready to go back anytime. There are some incredibly beautiful sights. I cooked all the time, and we divided up other chores. We were all incredibly tacky. The first thing we did was to buy cowboy hats and bandanas. We wore these even in San Francisco.

Work—Control Data

74. I worked for Control Data for four years before coming back to school. My work atmosphere was informal and casual. My work style though is to do the very best job no matter how long it takes. I'm a perfectionist to some degree. I like organizing and directing to some extent. I liked by bosses and wanted to improve them. I didn't explicitly seek recognition, but would get amazed if it wasn't there.

75. One thing I don't do is create enemies. I give everyone a chance and try not to pick on others or make fun of others. That's not easy when one guy is a real turkey. But it's pretty unproductive to sit around and talk about others.

76. I was treated well at work and always performed above expectation. I didn't have any particular knowledge about computers and really didn't desire any so long as things worked. I always thought that hard work could surpass being a genius any day. I could figure something out if I had to. I was a "golden boy" to grow for higher positions. My boss liked me.

77. I've been told at work that I was fairly open or frank about situations and would tell people how I felt. Actually I don't see myself as that

frank, but I'll admit how I feel as honestly as possible if asked.

78. We kidded around a lot at work—took advantage of our position at times.

79. I also tended to work by myself rather than in groups. This is true also of Darden last year. I didn't desire groups but preferred individual effort. I usually had female office mates, too. Now that I think about it, most of my friends after high school were females. And, I tend to "hang around" attractive people or associate myself with others who are outgoing, witty, and generally respected.

80. I only worked for one guy the whole time and when he switched divisions I remained loyal and went with him. It was very difficult to tell him I was going back to school. In a way I thought I was hurting him; I delayed the talk as long as I could. I was also trying to finish up a project so I could leave it in good shape. We are friends today and guess always will be.

81. I had a hard time delegating work. I was put more into a management role my last year. I felt that others didn't have the same desire to do the best job. A lot of people tend to be 9–5 only, get the paycheck. I really don't buy into that. I would end up staying late working on something rather than asking someone else, too. I strongly agree with "If you want something right, you have to do it yourself." I'll have to trust others a little more in the future.

82. I was also active at work in other things as well. I was golf commissioner for two years. I liked organizing these things even though it was somewhat of a pain, but I would volunteer. I organized the last two company Christmas parties. I went to Virginia on Career Day to talk about the company.

83. One thing which really bothered me in the work environment is the wife-cheating and all that sort of thing. I thought, "Who are these guys trying to kid?" Being this kind of big wheel stereotype businessman is not for me. I was also amazed at how women were treated in business. I've tried to remain open and actually most of the time I would request a woman to work on one of my projects.

84. That's work in a nutshell. The work was not that exciting or challenging. That's a reason why I came back to school. I could do the work though. When I came back to school I had just received a promotion and been awarded the Outstanding Performance Award—something not many people get. It was a hard decision, but the right one.

[During this time, other things happened too.]

85. I got married in 1977. Susan had gone to work in Norfolk and worked there a year. We traveled a lot back and forth. I won't say that I was madly in love, because I have a hard time with that word.

86. I remember in "Shenandoah" (I think), Jimmy Stewart asks the guy who wants to marry his daughter if he likes her. He responds, I love her. Jimmy says that's not important, the question is do you *like* her!

87. I like Susan a lot and told her that love was something that grows whether it is dependence on one another or thinking alike or enjoying the same things. My unemotionality comes out again.

88. Anyway, we were married in Charlottesville at the chapel and honeymooned in West Virginia. It was fall and why not the mountains? I wasn't going to spend the money and go where everyone else did like to the Bahamas. I like to be a little different.

89. We bought a house in Falls Church with some money I borrowed from Bernie. It didn't look like we'd be able to, but it worked out. I almost feel like Robert Redford in "The Way We Were" when he said things were always easy for him. I feel that way to some extent, that things have always worked out for me. We didn't have many neighborhood friends—they were all pretty strange.

[New train of thought.]

90. Before we got married my grandfather died. I've mentioned that I was close to him, but what I really remember was that when the event happened I didn't feel all that sad. It was expected as he had been sick, and by the time he died it was as if the grief had been rationalized away.

91. Other friends during this time were Mary and George who both went to Virginia. George graduated last year from Darden. Mary was really my last confidential friend. When she got married and I got married, that disappeared. Susan was always jealous of her. Mary and I would talk more then about some things than Susan and I do now. I guess it's personalities that go together.

92. As couples now, they're different types of friends. We do things as couples. We've been meeting each year at Big Meadows as an annual reunion. George and I are closer now, and Susan and Mary are, too. This manuscript would be incomplete without mentioning them.

Final Chapter—Darden to Present

93. Last year was very rewarding to me. I did well in school and became a father, too. The year

was extremely challenging, but I was convinced that hard work could overcome anything. Even though I won one of those academic awards, I feel that I'm no smarter than others who didn't, but I worked harder for it.

94. To some extent I was selfish in how much I gave to that goal because Susan really carried more of other responsibilities. George had also given me an example by being President of the Marketing Club.

95. I looked at my accomplishments in eleventh-twelfth grades and third-fourth years college and saw this as another two year challenge. My style was to become active in school events (Placement Committee, clubs, intramurals) as well as work hard.

96. I regret missing a lot of parties. I saw others growing close to others in a way I couldn't. But that was a tradeoff.

97. Tommy, Jr., really put things into focus. My priorities have really switched or become more focused towards family.

98. We bought a house down here which was worse trouble than it was in Falls Church—but it worked out. I thought a family should have a house.

99. That decision was partially investment and partially family. If we could meet the payments, we wouldn't be throwing our money away in rent payments, but investing it. Other reasons for buying a house in Charlottesville: I wanted to buy a place to rent out. Charlottesville was a better renting town, and I knew it better.

100. I didn't stay in study groups last year par-

tially due to my time commitments with home, and I like to work alone.

101. The classroom situation was fun. Our section kept it at a humorous, friendly competition level which fits me perfectly. I began to think of myself not as the typical MBA who would go to work for a Mickey Mouse outfit.

102. I feel that I created no enemies by nailing anyone on a point, but I really didn't create many real friendships. But then I wonder when I see the type of people here if friendships aren't a result of the convenience of the situation and then "see you later."

103. I don't establish fake relationships for some other purpose.

104. My summer was spent relaxing—I worked at school, played volleyball, put off trying to make career decisions, and planned to take this course.

105. I'm now writing a history of my life. By the way, my favorite movies are "Jeremiah Johnson," "Jaws," and "It's a Wonderful Life." I like walking in the snow. I eat a lot of popcorn and watch TV too much. I'm a great lasagne maker. I hope the Dodgers win the series—Hey, I'm a Libra.

106. I forgot to mention being elected to Placement Office and running for Vice President, which would be a seat on the Honor Committee and Honor Advisor. I didn't win. I had set a goal to become one of the officers—and succeeded. And, I wanted to work on the Honors Committee—I ran for the wrong reasons before, and this time I wanted to make that up.

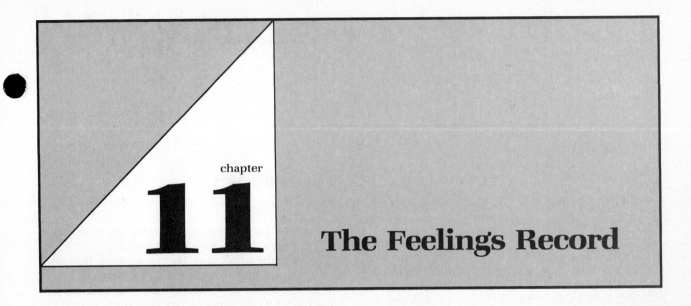

chapter

11

The Feelings Record

After each self-assessment instrument that you have been asked to take, we have asked you to make an entry in your Feelings Record. We asked you to note your mental and emotional reactions to each instrument and to record any other contextual factors that may have affected your scores, the data you generated from each instrument, or your reactions to them. Now, we want to consider how we might go about using that information.

Throughout the self-assessment process, we have used a variety of instruments. Some have been very structured, some have been very unstructured. Some have been very objective in nature, others have been very subjective. Your reactions to the structure, the focus, content, and administration of these various instruments are data that are helpful to you in understanding how you respond to a variety of situations, emotionally and mentally. If, for example, you felt frustrated by the instructions for the Lifestyle Representation, which were very ambiguous you might draw a tentative inference that you do not enjoy unstructured assignments. On the other hand, if you thoroughly enjoyed the highly structured interpersonal style inventory, you might infer that you enjoy structured situations. Both bits of evidence and their related inferences might be drawn together into a theme that might read something like this: "This is a person who prefers to work in structured situations."

The process we will use for analyzing and interpreting the data contained in the Feelings Record is very similar to that which we used in analyzing the written interview. That is, we ask you to consider the data and the context in which it was generated and look for patterns. You may find some new patterns suggested by the Feelings Record data, or you may find

data that will provide support for patterns you have seen in the written interview or in the other instruments.

The written data contained in the Feelings Record provides some insight into your emotional side. Admittedly, it is not a perfectly accurate or detailed description of your emotional side, but it does ask you to consider not only how you think and how you behave, but also how you feel in a variety of situations, and that is an important part of our experiencing of our work and of our ability to function in various jobs.

The Feelings Record also provides information with regard to contextual factors that may have biased or slanted or prejudiced the data you generated at various points along the way. This information will help you to qualify, to modify, and to clarify more accurately the inferences you draw from those various sets of data.

Exercise

To help you gain skill in analzying your own feelings record, we have included a copy of Tom Wilson's Feelings Record (see case, pp. 116–18). Note that Tom used some instruments not in this book. That's okay; it's the feelings we're interested in here, not the content of those other instruments. Consider the following questions in relationship to Tom's Feelings Record:

1. How did Tom respond emotionally to unstructured assignments?

2. How did he respond emotionally to structured assignments?

3. What contextual factors relating to Tom's experi-

encing of the various self-assessment instruments may have affected his responses?

4. How should Tom take all these things into account in interpreting his other data?

5. What new themes, if any, are suggested by Tom's Feelings Record?

TOM WILSON: FEELINGS RECORD

Figure Test

–Fun.

Pictures lend themselves to interpretation using *our* own words. Strong-Campbell asked us to list interests in the form of ranking choices in *their* own words. This test allows you to formulate the words from an impression which it seems would bring out clearer interests on how each of us looks at something.

The pictures are abstract and open-ended but not *confusing* like Rorschach Test.

You are able to put yourself in the figure's posture and respond on what you would be doing in this posture.

Rorschach

–Frustrating.

Most of the figures were meaningless, or I just couldn't see anything. This test is tedious to take or simply *strange.* Most of what I did see were animals and thought that the exercise was similar to looking at clouds and identifying things.

I wonder what the hell this is going to tell me. (More loosed frustration). Is it wrong not to see anything in them?

I was very succinct in my description, so I guess this tells me something.

Learning Style Inventory

I often have trouble with words and meanings. My vocabulary has never been very extensive—so I wonder if comparing these results with others will mean a great deal. I guess I'm trying to qualify the results. We'll see once we get to the interpretation.

The test was short, which for this kind of test is great. I took it without trying to think about it too much. I took it quickly.

It seems to me that styles change over time and getting a trend would be useful.

Overall, not a bad test. But I also took this late at night on a large workload night (I'm tired).

I tend to think of myself as logical/analytical—better with numbers than feelings. Could be a bias.

FIRO-B

The main problem with this test was *It all depends*!

Take for instance, "I try to have people around me." The answer is yes and no. I hope the "occasionally to often" will cover the "depends" range.

Otherwise, it wasn't a bad test to take. I started noticing similar questions and tried not to look back at the way I answered other ones. I tried to take it quickly and not think about it too much.

Later, I looked back to see if my answers differed. If there was a difference in every case it was no more than 1 off. So, I felt a little more comfortable about the test.

I liked the *structure* and *direction.* I don't have any problems with rarely, sometimes questions.

Predisposition

Similar to FIRO-B, some questions are situational. The main disagreement that I thought with the test is that I *rarely strongly* agree or disagree with many things. I'm not too sure what this means—but I'm not too emotional.

The test should have perhaps 6 instead of 4 choices.

The test was easy to take but due to the above disagreements, I wonder how valid it is for me.

This case was prepared by Kevin E. Sachs, research assistant, under the direction of Associate Professor James G. Clawson, as a basis for class discussion. © 1982 by the Sponsors of The Colgate Darden Graduate School of Business, the University of Virginia, Charlottesville, Virginia. UVA case OB-210.

Career Values Card Sort

This was a very difficult assignment that I would like to think about and redo at a later time. I spent about 2 hours on it but still felt rushed. I don't think I've done justice to myself and should spend more time.

I question answers or expected bias: What I really value, vs. what I think I'm expected to value.

Where I am now vs. where I want to be would be appropriate.

I tried (or did) use every aspect card. I didn't really know the meanings of Identity, Physical, Emotional.

If I do it again I want to only select those I understand and like. I was looking for *more direction* on how I should do it and felt *uncomfortable* with the lack of structure.

Interpersonal Style Inventory

I enjoy this kind of feedback because it allows you to see how *consistent* you are with others and compare this view with how you see yourself.

I told acquaintances that all answers would be confidential. I thought that to ensure this I would not use the middleman. Instead, I asked acquaintances to put the sheets back in my mailbox when they were through.

One thing which may be difficult to analyze for me is the difference between desired vs. current self. It seems that I set too high standards for myself which may cause me future problems if unable to meet such goals.

Overall, a very *worthwhile* exercise because it is getting at *actual* feedback and not measuring how we see ourselves or want to (it does this but I see the important part as needed to calibrate some of our other data). If this test shows that there are key differences with how others see us and how we see us, we should really stop and examine the measures and perhaps question prior test results.

24-Hour Diary

I don't think I had representative days because my parents visited from Georgia. However, the time may have been spent in similar activities, except I could have played soccer on Saturday.

I thought it would be a pain to keep track of everything. Actually it wasn't too bad.

I think this type of test is useful because it measures what *actually* is going on. It is simply reporting. If we go back to the axiom we are what we do, there is a lot to be learned from behavior. Also, I get caught up in school activity and don't realize how much time is spent during the day in school activities. This exercise really brought that in focus.

Creative Life Style Diagram

I enjoyed the exercise very much. I like drawing little pictures. I really wasn't too elaborate though. It took me a while to think of how to do it. I like the first exhibit in the note, but didn't really see the diagram answering life style "how" questions. And, I didn't see past, present, and future broken out.

I didn't care for exhibits 2 or 3. So, I drew a picture for "how" and used pie charts to show time allocation. Once I filled in the pie chart, I quickly knew why I didn't have much free time last year. The charts allowed me to show what areas I wanted to increase in the future and at the expense of which items.

The charts don't reflect a difference between quality time and quantity. Four years before Darden working I think back and see that I didn't use my free time effectively. Too much TV.

Creative Life Style—Part II

Even though I thought that the two days weren't representative, the kind of activities they represented would have been substantial for similar activities. So, it is fairly representative.

My current life style is pressured with all the time at school. Work will substitute for it, but the time involved at night for preparation will be substituted for more free personal and family time.

I did a further breakdown of working hours. For total, school activities (which includes studying at home) represent 56% of time; home 31%. Weekly it's (83/11) split, and weekends it's (21/55). I look forward to weekends.

I want to add more time for personal and family, less in school/work related activities. And, add more activities like going out to eat/going to movies/going to a play, etc.

I think the diagram would say more if it was grouped by activity instead of place. I do school work at home but its not the same as other home activities. And, I talk to people at school, which isn't really the same as school activities.

Strong-Campbell

The test was somewhat tedious and long to fill out. What really bothered me was the number of "I" (indifference) I filled in. I did the test late at night and was tired. If given a choice, I would have probably taken most "I's" to "D's". I would like to take the test over again and be forced to make a decision to see if results changed.

I have a feeling though that this test is going to tell me that I can do anything I want. I took similar vocational tests in Atlanta before going to college. These tests said I could do almost anything. I'm trying to narrow down my choices and if this test comes back the same, I'm back at square 1. We'll see.

I'm going to write home and get a copy of my former test results.

Written Interview

I can tell why most theme data comes from the written interview. I wrote almost sixty pages (untyped). This data can be useful if it is complete and parts aren't left out (besides personal, which may be irrelevant) that bias it.

I enjoyed the first 6 questions. I hadn't thought of several things from my past in a while and the memories, though some sad, were good to relive. It took a lot of time, but worthwhile.

Questions 7–11 were frustrating, repetitive, monotonous. I thought they would never end and I really didn't treat them too well. Because I wrote 60 pages in WI, this is all I'm writing here.

Dyad

The exercise was super.

1. My partner did a great job of going through my data and arriving at themes. She spent a lot of time on it.
2. It was useful to go through another person's data. It will greatly help me go through mine.

I was never worried about "here's my life," and being embarrassed about telling sensitive stories. One of my themes is that I don't discuss personal things openly. The instrument was a way I could release these emotions, so I welcomed it.

The exercise will help me be more objective. We both spent a lot of time at it, but it was time well spent (more than I can say for certain parts of the Written Interview!).

Now that you have generated all your data and had a good deal of practice scoring, examining, and drawing inferences from Tom Wilson's data, it is time to begin practicing developing full-blown themes from all the pools of data. In the last two chapters, you began practicing drawing inferences in earnest as you read the first part of Wilson's written interview and his Feelings Record. The critical principles were these:

1. Staying close to the raw data
2. Looking for patterns that were more rather than less common
3. Trying to be aware of your own assumptions
4. Keeping your inferential leaps small and conservatively connected to the data
5. Using more rather than less data to support an inference

In this next exercise, begin in a small way to use all the data by developing a single theme from all of Tom Wilson's self-assessment data (see case, pp. 121–23). Add to the pools you have already examined the rest of his Written Interview, which follows. We encourage you to use the form in Exhibit 12–1 to develop your theme.

You can use the wide right-hand column to collect data that seem connected in some way. Then you can use the narrow left-hand column to note the sources of your data citations. At the bottom there is a place to note evidence that seems contradictory to the underlying thread or theme which seems to hold the mass of your data together.

If you get too much contradictory evidence, you may have to identify another theme or perhaps develop two. How much is too much? Enough that it begins to make you wonder whether you are really identifying a consistent and solid life theme. Some themes may have no contradictory evidence. Others may have three or four items, but if you get more than half as many contradictory bits of data as you do supporting data, we would say that the theme is not clearly established.

Note that there is a place at the top of the form for you to begin framing your theme label. No doubt you will write, erase, rewrite, and rewrite this label many times before you are satisfied with it. As you do, refer to the short note that follows on writing useful theme labels.

Okay, charge ahead. One label from all of Tom Wilson's data. And remember, you are developing your inferential skills as you go, so don't shortchange yourself. You will be glad you didn't when you begin to do the same with your own data.

Exhibit 12–1
Life Theme Development Worksheet

Theme Label: _____

Sources   Data

Contradictory Evidence

TOM WILSON'S: WRITTEN INTERVIEW (B)

Reply 2 (Other Memories?)

107. The only other memories that came to mind are: (1) delivering papers. Getting up at 5:00 A.M. when it was cold and dark and riding around on the bike. A lot of times when it rained or snowed though, Mom would do more delivering than I. (2) When we moved to Meadowbrook Drive in Waynesboro, Dad bought a silver artificial tree with the revolving red, green, yellow lights for Christmas. Pretty tacky.

Reply 3 (Unaccounted for Times?)

108. My first summer job was YMCA counselor. It was outside and easy. The sort of things we would teach were out of Scouting like archery, crafts, and nature. I enjoyed the outdoors. A fun part of camp was making up stories for the kids. My next summer job was working at Fox (furniture manufacturers) where my Dad worked. I worked in the shipping department. Everyone knew who I was, so I was elevated to some degree. I got to see the kind of workers who worked in this sort of industry and the sort of cruel jokes they would play. It wasn't a particularly tough atmosphere though. I worked hard so others didn't think I was cruising because my Dad worked there.

109. During a week when shipping was shut down I went over to the maintenance department. I painted gutters and cleaned boilers. I worked hard and the guy didn't know who I was. He found out on the last day and said that if he had known he wouldn't have made me clean boilers. I didn't want to be treated special, so I'm glad he didn't know.

110. My last summer job (3 summers) during college was at O'Neill's Lumber Company. Jimmy's Dad owned the place. Andy, Jimmy, and I worked there in shipping and the mill. I worked shipping one year and the mill the remaining two years. Once again, I got to see what kind of people worked there. I developed a great respect for the guy who really kept the mill running, Mr. Tanner. He was about 60 and did all the small main-tenance jobs and ran the molding department (3 people). The whole plant only employed 40. I was a "molding man" for two summers which involved making wood molding (like chair rail or window sill). You set up the blades and ran the lumber through the machine. I liked woodworking and got pretty good at running all kinds of machines (except the lathe which I wanted to learn). Mr. Tanner was different from the other "older guys." Some guys had been there for years and would come in, work there 9–5 (actually about 3–4 hours of work) and go home. Tanner made sure the plant worked; it was his life. He would work Saturdays and ask me to come in and help him on occasions. I was his adopted son and worked hard and kidded with him.

111. When I left one summer, I had to teach Elmer how to run the molding machines. What took me about one week, took him all summer.

112. I also worked two jobs one summer. Daytime at O'Neill's and night at a Handy Shop—running the store. I wanted to try doing two jobs and could use the money. I ended up having no free time and was dismissed over a misunderstanding when Susan came down one July 4th, and I didn't show for work. (I had left a message.) I guess I was fired which suited me fine. I remember seeing a kid shoplift some candy and feeling uncomfortable about confronting him. He lied to me but I let him off.

113. Another hobby I haven't included was water skiing. Bob's parents had a cabin at a lake about 45 minutes from Rome. We used to go often in the summertime and ski and have rowdy times. I learned to ski from friends of my Dad's who would take Karen and me. I thought he was obnoxious and quit going with them while Karen continued. That split is similar to others Karen and I have had. We are different in the kinds of people we associate with. In all honesty, I associate more with status, prestige, snobbery. She's opposite. She didn't like Thornwood (girl's prep) where I think she developed a bias against that "sort," and I'm uncomfortable about that. The only girl friend of mine she liked was Janet. She's nonconformist and had violent disagreements with Dad.

This case was prepared by Kevin E. Sachs, research assistant, under the direction of Associate Professor James G. Clawson, as a basis for class discussion. © 1982 by the Sponsors of the Colgate Darden Graduate School of Business Administration, the University of Virginia, Charlottesville, Virginia. UVA case OB-198.

114. One activity which I have failed to mention (or have probably tried to forget) is my involvement in Jaycees for 3 years. I joined in D.C. for the following reasons:

1. I have always felt that service to humanity and community is a "noble" undertaking.
2. I was looking for something to do.
3. My Dad had been a former Jaycee, the President, and had done a lot of work.

115. The Jaycees was a learning experience. After one year I was External Vice President and President the next year. I won a state award for the best project in apple butter—a project to raise money for a mentally retarded camp in Virginia.

116. I knew that I didn't have the best project but I wrote the best report. The problem with being President was that I was never caught up in any excitement. A primary skill of running a volunteer organization is creating excitement. I couldn't get excited. I did the paperwork but didn't give the job the commitment it needed. I tried to do too much and didn't manage the volunteer organizations well. I hadn't been left with much of a foundation though and didn't get much help. I also disagreed with most of the Jaycee philosophies. A lot of people really used the Jaycees to fulfill a missing purpose in life. There was a lot of unnecessary politics plus immature people and lower-middle-class people.

117. It was a learning experience and I myself probably *used* it for that reason and put it on my résumé.

Reply 4 (Jobs)

118. I've covered all the jobs I've had. The characteristics I have liked are: feeling responsible for things, people, recognition from peers, satisfaction of seeing that a good job gets done, feeling important, feeling self-sufficient and independent, impressing others.

119. Dislikes are mainly in jobs that are monotonous. Working with incompetent people. Likes are working with others in a creative environment.

Reply 5 (People, Acquaintances)

120. I do not have many *close* friends; I have several friends. My closest friend would have to be Susan and my best buddy is Tommy, Jr.

121. Susan is similar to myself though she doesn't share my ambitions, and she's neater than I am. She's bright, cheerful, personable, affectionate, sensitive, patient, giving, concerned. She tends to be a little lazy in some things. We like to do the same kind of things. She takes an interest in what I do, to the extent that I tell her about it. She's been a great mother, not as cautious as I am though. I've lived with the person for four years, and it's hard to come up with more descriptions.

122. Tommy, Jr., is a little person. He's 13 months old, runs all over the place, likes to play and laugh, gets into trouble, is happy to see me when I come home. The last 13 months have been a great experience becoming and giving as a father and going through business school.

123. My parents and my sister and I are close in a family sense but we are not a close family. What I'm trying to say is that relationships are on a more casual, friendly plane than on a *close* family basis. When I see other families that are indeed close, I am somewhat jealous. I grew up to be fairly independent and not dependent on the family unit for support. I earned what I received. My mother and I are closer as my sister and father are closer.

124. Let me describe them briefly. My mother is a truly great person. How she has put up with some of the things my Dad has done is beyond me. She runs the house. She is always cheerful. She takes a lot of interest in my friends. She gives me advice in her "stern" way which you can always answer, "Oh, Mom!"

125. Dad's moods are in part due to physical problems in that he just doesn't feel well most of the time. He had half of his stomach removed and just can't eat certain foods and has problems eating most foods so he just doesn't feel well most of the time. He also has bad sinuses.

126. An objective for the future is to get to know him better. I've never really asked him about his work, his early career days, etc.

127. The close friends I've kept since my high school days are Jimmy, Andy, Bob. As I mentioned we traveled out West after graduation from college. Jimmy went to Vanderbilt and the Duke Graduate Business School and now works in San Antonio. Andy graduated from med school last year in pathology and is in Augusta, Georgia, in internship. Bob will graduate from dental school this year. Andy went to Southwestern in Memphis and Bob went to UNC.

128. Andy would probably have to be the closest, with Bob the most similar to me, and Jimmy the funniest. Jimmy and I do a lot of things together though, like parties, so my closest probably switches.

129. We're drawn together because we are so much alike. We all did well in high school. We were on the soccer team together. We like the same things. They are all bright, witty, popular, attractive people. Most of my friends have fit this type.

130. We rarely write each other, though, and see each other only at Christmas unless for some other reason like a wedding. Andy and Bob are married. Bob and Susan just had a baby boy in January. I want to start corresponding more with them so we don't grow apart.

131. My other close friends are Mary and Jed. I have mentioned them before. As a couple we are very similar. We all went to Virginia and share the same kind of feelings about the school. George graduated Darden last year. We go to the mountains every year. George and I would make waffles last year and play golf. Mary and I would play Kismet. I regret not having a gang of friends that I really grew up with. It is probably a reason why I don't have many close friends.

132. Our tastes are a little different from theirs. Susan and I tend to be more down home and practical, where they feel other "higher class" things are important. We will probably have them for friends for the rest of our lives.

Reply 6 (Future, Ending)

133. I do have a happy ending which centers around family, career, and friends.

134. First criteria is *place*—small to medium-size city in the Southeast, close to the water and mountains, say, Charlotte, N.C.

135. Next, is *house.* Colonial style, comfortable, warm, fireplace, open to family and friends. Children—3.

136. Work—challenging but not too time-consuming, and preferably my own business.

137. I want to be close to the water to get away and sail, and close to mountains to have a cabin.

138. At both places would entertain a lot in order to keep friendships, and make it so I can make some new ones. Of course, there's a golf course nearby. I would also be closer to Mom, Dad, Karen.

139. Tradeoffs are how to get there—what path to follow—what do I have to give up now for the future dream?

[No reply was given to questions 7 and 8.]

Reply 9 (Major Changes)

140. The major change that occurred last year was becoming a father. Up until that point I had grown only as an individual. Even through the first years of marriage I continued my independent activities. I made some concessions but not that many. I enjoy all kinds of sports and don't really find the challenge (like tennis) in playing with Susan.

141. Life did take a different direction. My thinking has changed from me to a family. I give up more but it means something, and it's more important. My challenge is to provide for the family. There is a big focus and meaning. I can say "no" to an activity if I have to pick up Tommy somewhere, and I accept it.

142. Other changes were only a matter of adapting. As a person, I grew up last year.

Reply 10 (Disillusionments)

143. I can't really think of any disillusionment. In personal situations when I didn't want to hurt someone and weaseled myself around it, I found out that being open and honest was the best bet.

144. Virginia, CDC, and Darden have been what I expected. My answer to this question is that I am adaptable to a variety of situations.

145. Usually my expectations weren't clearcut, like "At Darden I'll have to work 70 hours a week," etc. Rather, I knew in a more vague way that it would be tough and challenging.

146. One point I didn't mention was the Jaycees. Here I think I did make a mistake in taking the President's job. I knew that my skills were not in motivating volunteers, especially people I really didn't know and who were older. Other factors outweighed this knowledge. I am usually rational, logical, practical in decisions and haven't been too surprised by the outcomes yet.

147. Most decisions have been made on my own. I do value my Dad's influence in the process and try to enlist friends' support when applicable. On joint decisions Susan and I make them with my part being more important.

Reply 11 (Patterns?)

148. The pattern hasn't changed much. There is an altar of planning for the future in what I've done. Future-oriented/goal-oriented may be a theme. Independent in making decisions may be another.

chapter

13

Dyad Exercise

The dyad exercise is an exchange of data between two partners, a thorough, intensive analysis of that data, and a feedback session. It is designed to give you greater skill in inductively analyzing complex data and to give you a second opinion on your own data before you write your self-assessment paper.

Preliminary Considerations

Your chosen partner will read your data and give you a preliminary written analysis of it. You will do the same for him or her. Your partner must be a student in the course. Given the importance of the assignment (many later report it to be one of the key experiences in the course), you should have a clarifying session with your partner before you agree to work with each other to discuss these issues:

1. Confidentiality
2. Level of rigor in analysis and time commitment
3. Format of written feedback
4. Timeliness of feedback
5. Level of candor and care in giving feedback
6. Other concerns you may have

You should allow 8–12 hours of time to work on this assignment. We suggest that you schedule it during your clarifying session.

Schedule some time (1–3 hours) with your partner to conduct the feedback session. In giving your feedback, let one person give *all* of his or her analysis *before* you respond or ask for clarification. The danger

is that you will be so defensive or preset in your own analysis that you won't hear what is being said. Use it to learn and to get another perspective on yourself.

Procedure

1. Select someone who is also taking this course or doing a self-assessment.
2. Exchange notebooks. That is, give the person all your data.
3. Each does an assessment of the other person's data, using the methods outlined in the *Self-Assessment and Career Development* text. That is, identify as many supported themes as you can.
4. You need not write up your assessment formally. Instead, simply prepare some charts or exhibits from which you can talk.
5. Meet with your partner and take turns verbally presenting your assessments. Allow at least 30 minutes for each presentation and 10 or 15 minutes for questions afterward.
6. Insert all the materials, exhibits, and notes from your partner's assessment of you in this section.
7. Remember to record in the Feelings Record at the beginning of your workbook any reactions you may have had.

The written material Tom Wilson received from his dyad partner is shown in the case, p. 126. How will this information help Tom? What different formats can you imagine for giving a person feedback on his or her data?

TOM WILSON: DYAD EXERCISE

Tom's dyad partner, after reviewing his self-assessment notebook developed the following life themes for Tom to consider in writing his self-assessment paper. The numbers in parentheses refer to the number of instruments cited, the number of bits of supporting evidence, and the number of bits of contradictory evidence, respectively.

Life Themes (This is a person who . . .)

1. Needs structure to feel comfortable (7,8,1)
2. Values the presence of women in his life (2,6,0)
3. Is sensitive (4,11,0)
4. Wants to be included in personal interactions (3,5,0)
5. Values his identity and independence (6,12,1)
6. Feels guilty when he falls short of his expectations and standards (3,9,0)
7. Does not express feelings/opinions readily (9,11,0)
8. Goal-oriented (2,3,0)
9. Is hard-working and persistent (2,6,0)
10. Enjoys power and control (3,4,0)
11. Appreciates the out-of-doors (2,7,0)
12. Strives not to hurt others (2,6,0)
13. Proud of his accomplishments (1,4,0)
14. Makes athletics a big part of his life (4,5,0)
15. Has a strong economic orientation (7,11,0)
16. Lives by principles/ideals—sets high standards (3,16,0)
17. Tries to rationalize all aspects of his life (4,7,0)
18. Is concerned with specifics and details (7,10,0)
19. Believes that respect for self and others is important (1,5,0)
20. Is affable (4,5,0)
21. Is controlled and consistent (2,2,0)
22. Discounts importance of mother, father, sister (2,7,0)
23. Seeks approval from significant others (3,4,0)
24. Loves adventure (1,4,0)
25. Establishes priorities and follows through (1,2,0)
26. Is optimistic (1,1,0)

Tom took these themes and, by adding more supporting and contradicting evidence, revised them and added others in developing his own life themes.

This case was prepared by Kevin E. Sachs, MBA 1982, under the direction of Associate Professor James G. Clawson as a basis for class discussion. © 1982 by the Sponsors of The Colgate Darden Graduate School of Business, the University of Virginia, Charlottesville, Virginia. UVA case OB-202.

chapter

14

Other Data-Generating Devices

The 10 data-generating devices contained in the workbook should provide you with enough information to do your self-assessment. Many other possible sources of data, however, might be useful to you. You may wish to use such sources to supplement those you now have. In this chapter we will briefly describe some of those other sources.

We would offer two caveats, however, neither of which should surprise you. First, be sure you understand the nature of other data-generating sources so that you can understand the information they produce. Second, be sure you treat the supplementary data as you have treated those from the 10 devices in this book. Remember that a single datum from a single source proves nothing; look for patterns.

Other Psychological Tests

Various students of ours have at one time or another used the following instruments in their self-assessments:

1. Edwards Personal Preference Schedule
2. Thematic Apperception Test
3. Rorschach Inkblot Test
4. Myers-Briggs Type Indicator
5. FIRO-B

There are numerous other instruments like these.

You may find that you cannot gain access to these tests—especially tests like the Rorschach—except through a properly trained psychologist. And this is probably how it should be. If a psychologist administers a test to you and interprets its output, be sure *you* understand the basis of his or her interpretation.

IQ and Other Aptitude Tests

A number of IQ and so-called aptitude tests exist today. No doubt you have taken at least one of these tests (such as the SAT or GRE tests you took as a part of applying to undergraduate or graduate school). A few of the more popular are these:

1. Wechsler Adult Intelligence Scale
2. Harvard Speed Alphas
3. Skills Inventories
4. Miller Analogies

Be sure to treat these devices as carefully as you do all your data-generating instruments. Sophisticated "tests" such as these look more authoritative to many people than a simple device like a 24-hour diary, and so people may be more passive, less critical, and less demanding in dealing with the output of these tests. Don't be!

Experiential Exercises and Games

In the past decade, a number of exercises and games have been created that simulate some type of real-world activity and can provide interesting data to the participant. An example is the In-Basket test, developed by Educational Testing Service and AT&T, and today available in a variety of versions. In a typical version, an individual is given the role of a manager who has 25 items in his or her in-basket (letters, memos, phone messages, and so on), must catch a plane in three hours, and can reach no one on the phone or in person (it is Sunday). The individual is

127

given three hours to go through the in-basket and take any actions that seem necessary (schedule meetings, write notes, and so on); his or her behavior and decisions become the output of the exercise.

Experiential exercises and games can provide useful data for people of all ages, but we've found them particularly helpful to young people—especially those with no work experience.

The output from these exercises, which can be rather rich, should be treated just like the output of other devices. Again, it is important to understand the data-generating device to avoid misusing its output. The most common misuse of game output is to make huge inferential leaps to grand conclusions, based on the assumption that the game experience was exactly like the real experience it was simulating. (For example, Joe seems to do a much better job than other participants playing a "plant manager" in the in-basket exercise. Joe therefore would probably be a good plant manager.)

The In-Basket exercise can be obtained through Educational Testing Service, Princeton, NJ 08540. Other exercises of this type can be found in *Organizational Psychology: An Experiential Approach,* by Kolb, Rubin, and McIntyre (Englewood Cliffs, NJ: Prentice-Hall, 1974) and in *Management: An Experiential Approach* by Knudson, Woodworth, and Bell (New York: McGraw-Hill, 1973).

Other Personal or Historical Documents

Our students have occasionally used a variety of documents from their pasts as data in their self-assessments. For example, we have asked them to include their graduate school application form, since it requires them to answer a number of interesting essay questions. Some students have also used old diaries, photographs, letters of recommendation, performance appraisals, newspaper clippings, and essays that they wrote. As long as you are sensitive to the circumstances under which these personal or historical documents were generated, they can occasionally be useful additions to your data.

Finally, as you read through Lauren Davis' self-assessment paper (see exercise that follows in Chapter 15), you will see some instruments cited that are not in the book. Do not be alarmed that you are missing something. Recognize that self-assessment is an ongoing, always incomplete process and that you can continue to add to your knowledge of yourself over time through a variety of means.

chapter

15

Assessing the Self-Assessment Exercise

We have outlined a rigorous and multifaceted approach to self-assessment so far in this book. If you have followed along each step of the way, you are ready to begin pulling it all together. Before you do that, we suggest that you read through a self-assessment paper to get an idea of what one might look like.

Given all the time we have spent on Tom Wilson, you may be interested in someone else's self-assessment data and self-assessment paper. We have included both from Lauren Davis (see case, pp. 150–57). Note that she has used some instruments that we did not discuss in this book. You too should feel free to add other data to your information pool.

Using your knowledge of the self-assessment process, the instruments, and the characteristics of useful theme labels, how would you judge Lauren's result? Does her paper seem reasonable? What are its strengths and weaknesses? What do you learn from these materials about writing your own self-assessment?

Alternately, if you are using the book in a course, you might want to read Lauren's data and paper from the viewpoint of an instructor. How would you grade Lauren's paper? Write down the comments you would put on her paper or say to her, and be prepared to present them in class.

LAUREN DAVIS: SELF-ASSESSMENT DATA

This case consists of the complete set of self-assessment data Lauren Davis generated in the career management course she took at the Darden Graduate School of Business, University of Virginia, in the fall of 1981. Note that there are some data/instruments contained in her data which are not in the book. This is a result of copyright law. It should not affect your insights into the process Lauren used in summarizing her data. Most of the other instruments she used are available commercially. If you are taking the

course through a university, your instructor may have already had you use these or other similar instruments.

Lauren Davis: Figure Test

Lauren Davis gave the following responses to the 10 figures. The question she was asked while looking at each figure was: "What might this person be doing?"

This case was prepared by Kevin E. Sachs, MBA 1982, under the direction of Associate Professor James G. Clawson as a basis for class discussion. © 1982 by the Sponsors of The Colgate Darden Graduate School of Business, the University of Virginia, Charlottesville, Virginia. UVA case OB-194.

Responses to Figure 1	Category
• Looking up at clouds on a sunny day	ENV PAS
• Youngster chastised by mother and standing at attention	PEO DEP

Responses to Figure 2

• Giving direction or telling someone to leave via that exit	PEO DIR/ PEO COMM
• Telling someone to leave who has displeased him (arm or hip might mean anger)	PEO AGG

Responses to Figure 3

• Just got in 1st college of choice; jumping for joy	ENV ACT
• Just finished Darden; in jubilation that it's successfully over	ENV ACT

Responses to Figure 4

• Preparing for an attack, defensive position	PEO AGG
• Pulling back a sling shot	PEO AGG
• Nudging his neighbor playfully	PEO AFF

Responses to Figure 5

• Smelling a flower	ENV ACT
• Waving goodbye sadly to a departing friend	PEO COMM
• Waving hello to friend coming up	PEO AFF

Responses to Figure 6

• Leaning on a tree or post	ENV PAS
• Putting his hand on a buddy's shoulder	PEO AFF
• Picking something off a shelf	ENV ACT
• Dancing	PEO DEP

Responses to Figure 7

• Sleeping	ENV PAS
• Diving off a high dive	ENV ACT
• Somersault	ENV ACT
• Exercises	ENV ACT
• Groaning in pain	PEO COMM

Responses to Figure 8

• Shaking hands	PEO AFF
• Jumping exercises	ENV ACT
• Sitting down and taking someone's hand to help get up	PEO DEP

Responses to Figure 9

• Welcoming a group of relatives, friends that haven't been seen for ages	PEO AFF
• Describing something large to someone	PEO COMM

Responses to Figure 10

• Standing with both arms on elbows	ENV PAS/ PEO AGG
• Bending over from waist to touch toes	ENV ACT

Lauren's Scoring of the Figure Test

	Total Tallies	Percentage
Environment		
Active	9	30%
Passive	4	13
Total environment	13	43
People		
Affection	5	17
Aggression	4	13
Communication	4	13
Dependence	3	10
Direction	1	4
Exhibition	0	0
Total people	17	57
Grand total	30	100%

Lauren's Inferences

Highest: ENV ACT (9), PEO AFF (5), ENV PAS (4), PEO AGG (4), PEO COMM (4)

Doing things by myself (sports, emotions)

Doing things with people in which I am expressing an emotion or interest

Lauren Davis: Rorschach Inkblot Test

Lauren Davis made the following replies to four Rorschach cards:

Card Side

I 1. (W) Emblem for the medical profession. Army insignia.
   2. (W) Bird flying (looking down from above). Pig about to chomp on something.
   3. (W) Oriental house, pagoda—Arc de Triomphe.
   4. (W) Boat passing under a bridge.
II 1. (W) Fat ballerina on her tip toes.
   2. (W) Jet flying over dark clouds.
   3. (W) Two elves with tall hats hitting hands and stomping feet.
   4. (W) Same as 2.
III 1. (W) Old guy with hat and beard and overcoat and gray scarf.
   2. (W) Blast shot out of space ship.
   3. (W) Someone being burned at the stake.
   4. (W) Monster sticking out fiery tongue.

IV 1. (W) American eagle emblem.
   2. (D) Alligator head with jaws open.
   3. (W) Showgirl with oriental headpiece, boa around neck and pompoms in her hands.
   4. (W) Race car still moving with clouds of smoke streaming out.

Lauren's Scoring and Analysis

Card:	I	II	III	IV	Total	Percentage
	W	W	W	W		
	W	W	W	D		
	W	W	W	W		
	W	W	W	W		
Total responses	4	4	4	4	16	100%
Total W	4	4	4	3	15	94%
Total D	0	0	0	1	1	6%
Total d	0	0	0	0	0	0%

Lauren's Inferences

94% Ws. Big Picture Person—problems with accounting.

Always wants to be a generalizer—everything reminds person of a concept.

Lauren Davis: Learning Style Inventory

Lauren's Scores

CE 16   RO 7   AC 17   AE 18
AC − CE = 1   AE − RO = 11

Lauren's Inferences

This is how I see myself as a learner:

Active Experimentation: 18 (75%). "Doing" orientation; projects, homework, small group discussions; dislike passive learning situations (lectures), extroverts.

Concrete Experimentation: 16 (63%). Receptive, experience-based approach to learning; relies heavily on feeling-based judgments; empathetic, people-oriented; theoretical approaches unhelpful; treat each situation as unique case; learn best from specific examples in which become involved, oriented more toward peers than authority in approach to learning; benefit most from feedback and discuss with fellow CE learners.

Accommodator

Strengths: Carrying out plans and experiments; involving self in new experiences; more of a risk-taker; excel in situations where one must adapt oneself to specific, immediate circumstances; solves problems with intuitive trial and error; relies on other people for information rather than on one's own analytic ability; at ease with people; impatient and pushy at times; action-oriented jobs—marketing, sales.

Lauren Davis: FIRO-B

Lauren's Scores

	I	C	A	Sum (I + C + A)
e	3	3	4	10
w	0	2	5	7
Sum (e + w)	3	5	9	Total sum 17
Diff (e − w)	3	1	−1	Total diff. 3

Lauren's Inferences

1. Preference for solitude.
2. Desire for considerable amount of giving and receiving affection and interpersonal closeness.
3. Tendency toward active initiation of interpersonal behavior with others.
4. Want others to initiate behavior towards me.
5. Strong preference for considerable amount of interpersonal interaction.
6. Preference for others to initiate inclusion.
7. Preference for taking rather than giving orders.
8. Preference for receiving in contrast to initiating affection.
9. Preference for being the recipient of the initiations of interpersonal activities.

Lauren Davis: Predisposition Test

	Tolerance for Ambiguity	Preference for Autonomy	Predisposition toward Solitary Effort
Lauren Davis	3.0	2.57	2.86
Research organization	2.91	2.83	2.96
Manufacturing organization	2.57	2.17	2.40

1. Very high tolerance for ambiguity: Don't mind a changing set of conditions; less defined work and greater uncertainty of information OK.
2. Preference for autonomy average for age group of HBS; close to my characteristics; closer to research organization than manufacturing; a bit higher preference to define work roles, provide own direction; less inclined to like subordinate relationships with strong authority figures.
3. High disposition toward solitude—prefer to work individually.
4. Scored closer to R&D environmental group: tolerate a bit more ambiguity; have less preference for autonomy; want to work alone a little more.

Lauren Davis: Life and Career Values Card Sort

Most Important Value Cluster

Marital
Tranquility
Changing activities daily
Praised by spouse

Identity
Getting ahead
Being free
Expanding influence
Achieving goals

Very Important Value Cluster

Professional
Run show
Public recognition
Feeling expert
Learning new things
Tackling challenge
Rewarded fairly for efforts
Directing next person
Changing activities weekly
Working on broad issues

Financial/Material
Being independent
Having as much as possible
Planning ahead

Important Value Cluster

Social
Close to others
Part of group
Relaxing
Meeting people

Recreation/Physical
Enjoying activity
Do better than next person
Feeling capable
Moving quickly

Intellectual
Organizing things
Using energy and resources wisely
Finishing task
Working on details

Somewhat Important Value Cluster

Parental
Looking ahead
Teaching
Watching growth
Moving slowly

Familial
Being encouraged
Being praised
Looking back

Other Considerations

Political
Helping people

Emotional
Watching people grow

Spiritual
Admiring beauty of it all

Societal
Involved

Lauren's Inferences

Definite priorities here:
   Personal (Bill & me, me)
   Professional/material
   Extracurricular
   Kids: parents
   Others

Lauren Davis: Interpersonal Style Inventory Data

Item	Acquaintance 1	2	3	4	5	Sum	Mean	S.D.
Takes lead	4	3	2	3	3	15	3.0	.71
Needs support	3	3	3	4	2	15	3.0	.71
Seeks recognition	3	2	2	3	2	12	2.4	.55
Works alone	3	3	4	3	4	17	3.4	.55
Helps others	4	4	3	4	4	19	3.8	.45
Follows rules	3	3	4	4	3	17	3.4	.55
Listens well	5	5	4	4	3	21	4.2	.84
Willing to learn	5	4	4	4	3	20	4.0	.71
Trusts others	4	4	3	3	3	17	3.4	.55
Defensive	2	3	3	4	2	14	2.8	.84
Discusses emotions	4	3	2	3	2	14	2.8	.84
Discusses personal	4	3	2	3	2	14	2.8	.84
Easy to talk to	5	4	2	4	4	19	3.8	1.10
Docile	2	4	4	3	4	17	3.4	.89
Praises	4	4	3	4	3	18	3.6	.55
Is consistent	4	4	4	4	4	20	4.0	0.00
Is conceited	3	2	2	3	1	11	2.2	.84

Lauren Davis: Interpersonal Style Inventory Data (*Continued*)

Item	Acquaintance					Sum	Mean	S.D.
	1	2	3	4	5			
Adapts	4	4	3	4	4	19	3.8	.45
Competitve	3	3	3	3	2	14	2.8	.45
Own decisions	4	3	2	4	3	16	3.2	.84
Calm	5	4	4	4	4	21	4.2	.45
Mechanical	2	2	3	4	2	13	2.6	.89
Tolerant	4	4	3	4	4	19	3.8	.48
Patient	5	5	4	4	3	21	4.2	.84
Keeps promises	4	5	4	4	4	21	4.2	.45
Cheerful	5	4	3	4	5	21	4.2	.84

Lauren Davis: Interpersonal Style Inventory Profiles

Note that the sequence of items has changed. Transcribe the plots carefully!

※ = Current Self,   + = Desired Self,   X = Average of Acquaintances' Reports

ITEM	ACQ. AVG.	S.D.	Never 1	2	3	4	Always 5
Takes lead	3.0	.71					
Seeks recognition	2.4	.55					
Is conceited	2.2	.84					
Is competitive	2.8	.45					
Defensive	2.8	.84					
Works alone	3.4	.55					
Own decisions	3.2	.84					
Mechanical	2.6	.89					
Consistent	4.0	0.0					
Keeps promises	4.2	.45					
Praises	3.6	.55					
Cheerful	4.2	.84					
Calm	4.2	.45					
Patient	4.2	.84					
Listens well	4.2	.84					
Easy to talk to	3.8	1.10					
Tolerant	3.8	.48					
Helps others	3.8	.45					
Trusts others	3.4	.55					
Follows rules	3.4	.55					
Willing to learn	4.0	.71					
Docile	3.4	.89					
Needs support	3.0	.71					
Discusses emotions	2.8	.84					
Discusses personal	2.8	.84					

Lauren Davis: AVL Study of Values

Scale	Lauren's Score	Value Name
50		
49		
48	_____ 48	Social
47		
46		
45		
44		
43		
42		
41	_____ 41	Economics/religious
40		
39		
38	_____ 38	Theoretical
37		
36	_____ 36	Esthetic/political
35		

Lauren's Inferences

1. Social very high: Love of people; prize others as ends in self; kind, sympathetic, unselfish.
2. Economic/religious: Interested in useful, practical; perhaps seeing environment in "totality"—big picture outlook?

Lauren Davis: 24-Hour Diary

Friday

8:00 Got up reluctantly. I'm starting to get a cold, and I feel lousy. No classes today, but plenty to do—have to be at school by 9 A.M. to meet with Advertising Manager group and work on group project. Showered, breakfast, read paper.

9:00 Finally left to get over to school (which means I was going to be 15 minutes late!). When I got to School @ 9:15 only 2 other group members were there—and I thought *I* was irresponsible. I don't like to be kept waiting—so I apologized for being late—however the group member who was supposed to have organized our notes into an outline hadn't arrived, so there was nothing to do yet anyway!

9:30 Bruce and I began calling other group members in order to get going. Every one of them was still at home or in bed.

10:20 Mary brought outline over to school and began reviewing it to clarify any questions we might have.

11:00 Decided how to organize the paper and break it up into sections for four of us to write individually. Planned to work individually until 11:30 and then compare writing styles. Worked on my section until then—also ate lunch in the interim. Didn't eat much because I'm feeling so sick. I wish I could go home and crawl into bed.

11:30 Met with group but no one was very far along. Everyone seemed to be writing in a similar manner (we wanted to make the style as consistent as possible), so we split up again and planned to meet @ 12:30.

12:30 All four read and discussed each other's sections, made some corrections, and broke up again to finish off the writing.

1:30 Met with "final" versions and went through same process again. Began to prepare exhibits, and discussed flaws that had popped up in some of our logic.

2:45 Went to Sponsors seminar on home computers. Wasn't too bad—I would have enjoyed it more if I didn't feel so lousy. I'm dying to learn more about computers. I think that's one of Darden's biggest weaknesses. Everyone should be urged to take a ½–1 semester course on programming and use of computers. We are going to *have* to be able to use and understand computers in most every business-related job. A bit shortsighted on the School's part.

4:00 Back to the group. Winding things down. Rest of members showed up to pick up where we left off. Discussed paper with them.

5:30 Left school for home. What a wasted day. I don't feel like I accomplished much. Plus cold medicines always make me spacey. It's a good feeling if you can lay back and go to sleep, but not if you need to be alert and have to fight off those side effects. Pills like those also affect my mood. I get grouchy and mad at the world.

6:30 Left to go to scuba diving class with Bill. Neither one of us feels up to swimming, so we planned to leave right after the classroom time.

8:15 Came home. Stopped and got subs at the sub shop. Ate subs and watched the World Series. I don't usually like to watch baseball, but I do like to watch the World Series. I guess I like it because something big is at stake. Same goes for the Super Bowl. Those games I can get involved in and enjoy.

9:00 Fell asleep on the couch. Pills made me drowsy. Bill and I finally woke up and went to bed about 1:00 A.M.

Saturday

8:20 Woke up about half an hour ago—don't need to get up early today, but couldn't sleep because of a bad cold and sore throat. Knew I had plenty to do today, so might as well get going. Projects, projects, projects! It's funny how some mornings it's so difficult to get up and others it's so easy. When I'm behind in my work, I'd rather put the pillow over my head and go back to sleep. But if I'm on schedule or ahead in my work, I don't mind jumping out of bed.

8:30 Showered, breakfast, read *Washington Post,* took some cold medicine.

10:00 Drove over to school to get started on school work. Advertising group project was supposed to be in a group member's box so the rest could give it a final review. It wasn't there. It really irritated me. Half the group worked hard on it yesterday and the others were supposed to polish it off last night. Feel a bit put-upon!

10:30 Organizing notebook in order to get started. It's hard to for me to work with a messy notebook. In order to keep the work load organized in my head and in order to make sure I cover everything I need to be organized and neat.

11:00 Talked to Kevin. He's going to the game today even though he has a ton to do, too. I'm a bit envious. I don't mind working when I know everyone else is working too, but it's hard to be disciplined on a sunny football-day.

11:30 Worked in the library until 1:30. Picked up Bill at home and went to Graffiti for lunch. I needed a break. This isn't going to be much of a weekend with all the work I have, so I deserve to take some fun breaks. Bill's working on his SBS, so we both need the break! Found out next World Series game is on at 4, so I'm going to try to work while I watch the game.

3:00 Back to library for more studying.

5:15 Home to see game and watch work on PACS. I wish I had more time, PACS work is beginning to pay off. The themes are really interesting. Watched the Dodgers win. Good for Dodgers, bad for my studying. That means more games on TV to distract me.

6:30 Fixed spaghetti for dinner—made it ahead so it didn't take long. Watched the rest of the game while we ate.

8:00 Went back to work. Am feeling very disorganized because I have lots of half-completed themes.

8:50 Drove to Movie "Rich & Famous." Not bad—some of it was overdone, but it was good, legal entertainment. People around me probably hated me—I blew my nose constantly.

11:10 Home and to bed. I'm sick, so early to bed—getting well!

Lauren Davis: Written Interview

Reply 1 (Open-Ended)

1. I was born in Tacoma, Washington, the daughter of a Lieutenant in the Army. My mother had been raised as an Army brat, married my father at 18, and I arrived when she was 20. Mom didn't work outside the home, so from pictures and what little I remember I had quite a bit of attention as a young child.

2. Kim, my younger sister, was born about 2 years after me in Fort Sill, Oklahoma. From stories, again, I am told that we adored each other. Kim was my shadow and I was her teacher. I have a few recollections about my young life before the age of about 5–6. Our family has lived in four locations over the first 6 years of my life, and when I started kindergarten we lived with my grandparents in Champaign, IL, while my father was in Greenland.

3. I loved school from the beginning. My mom and sister would walk me to the bus each day, and every day Kim would cry because she couldn't come with me. I loved teaching her all the things I'd learned when I came home from school. Whether I was right or wrong or interesting or boring she would listen to every word I said.

4. After kindergarten my dad came back from Greenland and was reassigned to Babenhausen, Germany. My dad went to Germany over the summer, but the rest of our family had to remain in the States for the length of the summer. This was the period of the Berlin Wall Crisis, and President Kennedy had forbidden military dependents from living in Germany temporarily.

5. We finally got clearance to go and after much red tape we flew to Germany. My dad already had an apartment arranged on the Post, so we moved into a neighborhood with lots of families similar to ourselves.

6. The elementary school was just a few blocks from home, so I walked to school each day. Mom became active in outside interests and eventually was elected president of the officer wives club, so she wasn't home everyday when Kim and I got home from school. (Kim was in nursery school.) Because she had to be out a few afternoons a week, Mom hired a part-time keeper who would be at the apartment when she was gone. We had several over the 2-year period we lived in Germany. They were usually middle-aged German women who were very kind to us and taught us German songs and prayers that Kim and I remember to this day.

7. School was enjoyable. I remember very little about it. It was a very structured environment

Lauren Davis: Life Style Diagram

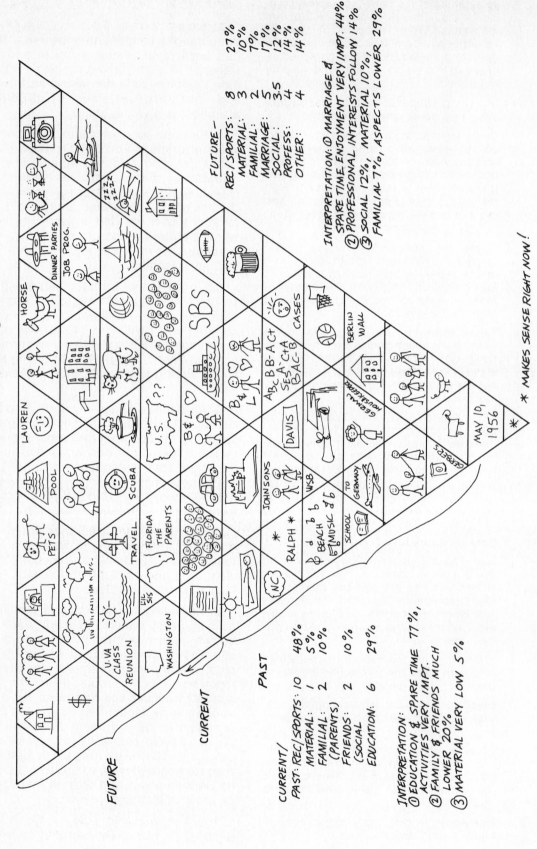

* MAKES SENSE RIGHT NOW !

FUTURE –

REC/SPORTS:	8	27%
MATERIAL:	3	10%
FAMILIAL:	2	7%
MARRIAGE:	5	17%
SOCIAL:	3.5	12%
PROFESS:	4	14%
OTHER:	4	14%

INTERPRETATION: ① MARRIAGE &
SPARE TIME ENJOYMENT VERY IMPT. 44%
② PROFESSIONAL INTERESTS FOLLOW 14%
③ SOCIAL 12%, MATERIAL 10%,
FAMILIAL 7%, ASPECTS LOWER 29%

CURRENT/

PAST:		
REC/SPORTS:	10	48%
MATERIAL:	1	5%
FAMILIAL: (PARENTS)	2	10%
FRIENDS: (SOCIAL	2	10%
EDUCATION:	6	29%

INTERPRETATION:
① EDUCATION & SPARE TIME 77%,
ACTIVITIES VERY IMPT.
② FAMILY & FRIENDS MUCH
LOWER 20%
③ MATERIAL VERY LOW 5%

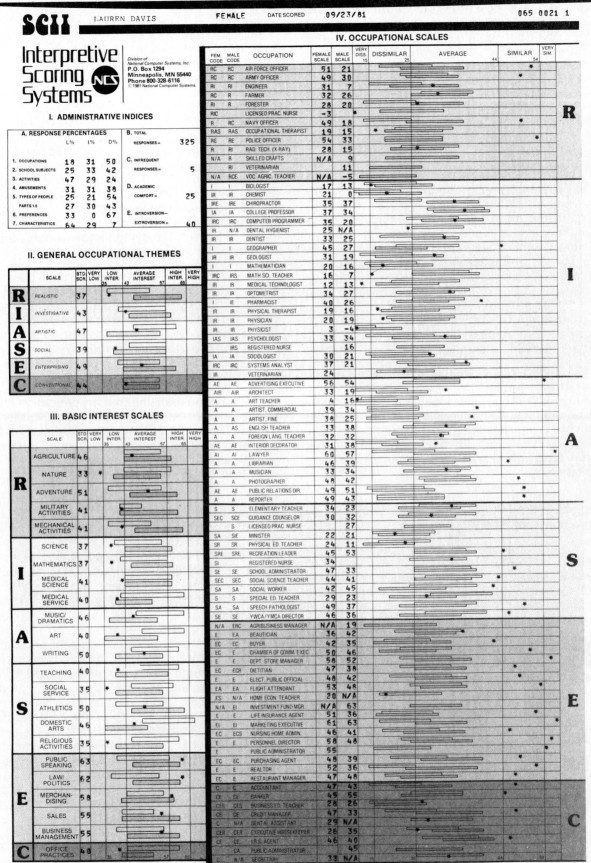

with assigned readings and problems each day. I do remember how frustrated I would get because I could never finish all my work before lunch. We (the class) were competing with one another on a chart, to see who could work the fastest and most efficiently. (You got *stars* depending on your speed.) Well, I couldn't stand it when some (a few) of my classmates were always finishing their work very early. The whole system was based on your *word*, so I claimed to have finished one day before I had and got caught and admonished before the class. I look back and laugh, but what a trauma at 6!

8. I adored my 1st grade teacher, but I remember very little about 2nd grade, except my effort to be in the top reading group. I had one close friend in Germany, and we were inseparable.

After Germany we moved to Cherry, Washington. My dad went back to school to get a masters degree at Eastern Washington State University. I was in 3rd grade in a city school while Kim went to a school affiliated with the university. We lived in a large house across from university dorms, and Kim and I milked the students selling Kool-aid and Girl Scout cookies.

9. I think I was a slightly above average student in school. The teacher liked me this time so I enjoyed being her pet. I was a bit of a tomboy by 3rd grade, and I preferred softball to any other activity. I was the only girl on the "team." My rough activities led to my teacher sitting me down for a talk. I quickly grew out of the tomboyishness.

10. Cherry was fun. We had a big yard and a dog and a cat. Kim and I were just beginning to get on each other's nerves.

11. I was transferred to Kim's school in 4th grade (I had wanted to go there to begin with but my class was full). The school was very progressive in both the style and the content of the teaching. We were at the stage in math where most students go through flash cards and memorization, but our math was concept-oriented "new math." We were told not to worry about the right answers as long as we understood the process. I think that today my math is so weak, but who knows.

12. By 6th grade we changed classes each period and were learning to adapt to the new routine we'd be exposed to in jr. high. My 5th and 6th grade teachers had us learning from TVs before that became more popular. We were observed through a one-way window (it looked black to us). The whole atmosphere was conducive to expanding your learning abilities which normal classroom settings inhibit. We were all told we were smart—that's how we were allowed into the program—and the framework was very positive and I enjoyed it.

13. I took part in two plays that year—which I loved.

14. My father was then transferred to Washington, D.C., for one year. It was difficult to try to establish many friendships in that period of time, and I wasn't sorry to leave for Ft. Leavenworth, Kansas, the next year. We spent 3 years in Kansas, and my memories of Ft. Leavenworth are the best of any of the places I've lived. My parents bought Kim and me a horse, and eventually we bought another. So I learned to ride and entered many horse shows in the area. My closest friend had been riding for several years, so with her help and the many (cheap) lessons available at the stables on Post, I got to be quite good. Leaving riding has been one of the most difficult things to accept; I'm dying to have a horse again and hope to soon in the future.

15. But back to Ft. Leavenworth. I guess in three years you become more attached to friends, and as you grow older friendships mean more—so leaving Kansas was very upsetting. We moved back to D.C. when I was in the 11th grade, so I spent two years in Northern Virginia before proceeding to college.

16. It wasn't a particularly spectacular period of time. I began realizing that my education really was important, so I worked much harder in school. That work got me into UVA in 1974. Virginia was my first choice of colleges, and I was very pleased to get in. I was very ready to get away from my parents and have a little freedom.

17. My first semester grades were a disaster because I was too undisciplined. But my second semester I came back with excellent grades and knew then that I could do it. College was a great life! I majored in English, which was a tough decision—I didn't know what I wanted to do. I didn't think any liberal arts degrees would be best for jobs. I knew I didn't want to go into business.(!!) So I majored in what I liked best and was best at. I thought at the time (and still do from time to time) that I wanted to go to law school. So after living with 5 roommates for the last two years of college in a huge old apartment, I set out to determine if law was the way to go. I took a paralegal course in Philadelphia, Pa., which was reputed (and I believe is) to be the best program around. After 3 months in Philadelphia I returned to D.C. and took a job with a legal document retrieval and publications company as a production assistant for two securities law journals. I moved up quickly in the company and took over my boss's job. (She moved up too.) The company was fairly small so I knew the vice president very well and enjoyed working for the company. It was very people-oriented from the top down. The management's philosophy was very team-oriented.

18. It didn't take long for me to hit the ceiling (as far as challenge goes) again. I knew I couldn't move up fast enough to be challenged or be compensated enough to put up with the lack thereof. So B-School was on the horizon. It didn't just pop up though. After working for a year I became interested in the stock market (I analyzed proxies and registrations all day, so I had enough exposure to know what I was getting into.) After taking 2 business classes at night, I decided it was for me and came.

19. First year was a bitch! I'd hate to think I'd have to go through anything like that again. The pressure was tough. For the first time *ever* I started to realize my capabilities were not endless. In the past I always knew that if I really tried I could do most anything well. The frustration of working hard for hours and accomplishing little was extremely unsettling.

20. Trying to manage (well) a relationship outside of Darden put an extra strain on me. The pressure turned me into a *different person* many times. Darden forced Bill and me to be together in class every morning and we were together for the rest of the day. By December we felt like we'd known each other for a couple of years. The support really helped me get through the year.

21. Over the summer I worked for an industrial manufacturing company in Atlanta. I was disappointed in my project a bit. First it wasn't SBS material and secondly it was not much of an intellectual challenge—but I did a good job and felt good about what I learned about organizational problems and politics from interacting and observing many top managers.

22. By August I was tired of my job, tired of only seeing Bill on weekends and bored with Atlanta. Back to Charlottesville to move 2 apartments into 1 in one week (ha, ha!). And the *wedding*! Then a 2 week honeymoon—which was fantastic and just what I needed in between the job and Darden. I'm very enthusiastic about the coming year!

Reply 2 (Other Memories?)

23. I've always liked getting involved in clubs and organizations, although I always wonder why I got into them after I do because they don't interest me very long.

24. When I was young, I enjoyed Brownies and Girl Scouts—but not for the "fun" things to do— more to be with friends and socialize. I also enjoy sports—particularly swimming, skiing, racquetball and volleyball (at picnics).

25. As I said before I love riding—that sport is by far the most fun for me. I loved competing in horse shows and loved winning ribbons!

Reply 3 (Unaccounted-for times)

26. Going back to Fort Leavenworth—which starts with 8th grade—I got into more trouble during the three years—but I grew up the most then too. My summers were spent at the pool almost every day during those years—after moving back to Virginia in '71 I spent a very boring summer—knowing no one in a rented house while my parents worked and looked for a house.

27. Between 11th and 12th grades I worked as a waitress at a restaurant nearby and hated it. I wasn't very good and got tired of nasty customers—so after graduating I worked in the receiving department of Lord & Taylors and was bored to death putting price tags on merchandise.

28. I'm one year ahead. Between 11th and 12th, I worked in a drugstore as a clerk.

29. Getting back. After my 1st year in college, I worked as a secretary for an attorney to try and see what law was like. Once again, boring. I'm not a very good typist and my OB skills are not the best when I strongly dislike someone (which is not often), but the attorney and I were not sorry to part ways. (I'll bet you're waiting for the good summer to come up. Sorry, the next isn't much better.)

30. Between my third and fourth year in college I worked for the Government as a GS-4 clerk typist at the Federal Employee Appeals Authority. It was a job, and I needed the money. Again I typed and was a conscientious employee so I was well liked by my boss, a lawyer who could give me a recommendation! But I *hate* to type. I hate to take orders from people who are GS-morons. So, it was frustrating. It was also an eye opener to see some of the inefficiencies that are prevalent throughout the Government!

31. The next summer was spent in Philadelphia at the Institute for Paralegal Training. All of the students in the course were bright and close to the same age, so I really enjoyed it.

Reply 4 (Jobs, Likes, Dislikes)

32. The first job I had was in a drugstore. Basically all I did was work the cash register and stock shelves. I didn't find it too bad for a high school student. I worked with some real weirdos, but I was fairly independent. I did a good job. I enjoyed talking to people, although you meet a lot of grouchy people working a cash register.

33. The waitress job I abhorred. I don't like waiting on anyone. I thought the job (along with the secretarial jobs) was demanding. Career waitresses are not the most social creatures.

34. The next job was just plain boring. I hate to sound so negative, but with most summer work you have to take what you can get, and this was all I could find. I worked with a small group of people checking in merchandise and working several machines which print price stickers. I also attached these price tags with plastic "guns" that force plastic strips through material. Neat huh?

35. The secretarial job wasn't a bad job because it was secretarial, but because of the shyster-lawyer I worked for. He ran his own practice and worked out of a small law office. It was interesting, and I did some research for him, corrected his grammar and punctuation and wondered how he ever got as far as he did. My last summer was detailed before.

36. I haven't talked much about my only full-time job. After taking the paralegal course, I worked at the DC Associates. I enjoyed many aspects of the job and clearly detested others. During my first six months I was closely supervised by a woman one year my senior who was a Vassar graduate. Those two criteria alone mean nothing, but I picked up the job quickly and needed little supervision, so I felt very confined and stifled being hovered over.

37. I enjoyed the routine at first. It was the type of work that required a very organized individual. There were a million details involved in getting the information into print. I love organizing, so I enjoyed that part of the job. However organizing materials which you have no time to pursue becomes very dull. So my abilities were recognized, and I moved into the rewriting end of the department. (I had been working with the editor "on the sly" learning the ropes.) The job then required a different kind of detail, reading between the lines. I was working with the latest Securities & Exchange Commission interpretations of the law. I loved the currentness of the job. It was exciting to read in the papers about a case I'd been working on the day before. The thrill wore off, however. A combination of office atmosphere and ceiling bumping (I began to get bored) led me to B-School.

38. I found positive and negative reinforcement to have had more to do with my work at the company than in any other situation. I had two adversaries (for reasons I know not—competition?) who were very difficult to work with and with whom I dealt daily. And I had very good friends and supporters in two vice presidents. The adversaries were not disliked by the VPs—one adversary was very close to a VP—so I don't think rivalry in *that* respect was a factor. It was unsettling, trying to deal with individuals who wouldn't reveal why they disliked you—very

moody individuals. I think I was as neutral as I could be, but it was an eye opener to me. I always thought I could "bring them around" and become friends.

Reply 5 (People in My Life)

39. My closest friend and confidant is Bill, my husband. If I were to arrange the people in my life I'd say Bill and I are closer than any of my other friends. Next to Bill, I value the friendship of my sister most highly. But this is a difficult way to answer this question, so I'll begin again in a more structured way.

40. Who was I closest to? My first very close friend was Joanne Davis. She and I went to two years of jr. high school and one year of high school together. I had friends before Joanne, but we moved around so much I never felt close to any of them. I suppose we were such good friends because we were very similar; we liked to do the same sorts of things. We were inseparable for a long time. We both rode horses, so we rode together after school every day. Leaving Kansas was tough, and I never developed any close friendships with girls again until my second year of college.

41. In college I got to be friends with another girl in my dorm who, again, seemed to have similar interests. Sally and I did a lot of partying together and a lot of activities. It's hard to say why we were close—being around each other a lot, we confided in each other as is natural.

42. I had two other close friends—one boyfriend in high school and one in college. Gordon, the high school boyfriend, was very smart and good natured, so he was a pleasure to be with. Rip, the college friend, was also smart and good natured, but he lacked ambition—which really bugged me. He was lazy in his school work (although he was very capable), so I knew early on that this would be a major stumbling block to any serious relationship. Ambition and self-betterment are important to me, so I couldn't understand Rip's lackadaisical attitude. I always knew Gordon would make it, which was one reason I was attracted to him. He was very capable and intellectual while not being pretentious. (Alas, the chemistry didn't last.)

43. I had trouble getting close to spacey people. They definitely bugged me. Although Joanne wasn't brilliant, I think I was attracted to smart, common-sensible people. Dumb people are no fun to talk to and frustrate me (as friends—that is I have nothing against people less intelligent than myself—I just couldn't be around them a lot and confide in them as close friends).

44. My family consists of Mom, Dad, and Kim, my younger sister. Kim is 2 years younger than I, and we carried on a love/hate relationship while we grew up. Unfortunately I was a bossy sister, which alienated Kim in a lot of ways. All in all, though, I'd say we were good friends and ran in separate circles to stay that way.

45. We have no major changes in our family structure aside from my Dad going to Vietnam for 1 year when I was in 6th grade—and to Laos when I was in 11th grade. My family lived all over, so in some ways our family structure changed every 1–2–3 years. We never lived in one place, except Kansas, for more than 2 years.

46. Marriage—what can I say? I'm hardly an old pro after one month, but it is a comfortable phenomenon. Bill is more patient and less moody (non-moody is a better term) than anyone I know. I grew up in a very up and down household with my parents fighting a lot, so it's important that I get away from that life style. Probably the most influential characteristic about Bill is his confidence and self-assurance that he will be successful.

47. I have neglected to mention many passing friends. I guess I'm not close to many people.

48. My parents are important people in my life in a funny way. I enjoy talking with them from time to time, but they drive me up a wall if I have to be around them for any length of time. Mom is always tired and depressing, and Daddy just can't relate to my life style. He is absorbed (so's Mom) in work, work, work. Hearing about work gets old and makes me mad. They should be doing more avocational and recreational things and try to be happy.

Reply 6 (Future)

49. I'm looking forward to a fun and fulfilling future.

50. I guess my idea in the short run is to move to a comfortable neighborhood in a medium-sized city. I'd want to be able to commute to work in about 15 minutes, but be in an area where I could own a horse again on property behind a house.

51. Work is fabulous at this point, but whatever I end up doing I want it to be in pursuit of developing skills that I can apply in my own business. Challenge is very important. I'd rather be overworked and challenged, than underworked and bored. It's important for me to be growing in a job, so I want to work for a medium-sized company with that philosophy. Success is the key to my happiness, also. I get great satisfaction out of doing a project well—part intrinsic satisfaction but more peer recognition.

52. Part of the happy-ending is also a time for fun. I'd like to travel twice a year on vacations—go to Florida or sunny places often. Vacations with other couples also sound fun at this point. Football games, plays, ACC basketball games, dancing, parties—fun socially.

53. Long run doesn't look much different, except that I hope to establish a business with some partners. I also want to have 2 or 3 kids and a pool, stable, and a fair amount of land. I hope to become active in civic affairs in the area Bill and I buy a house—but not domestic!

54. Housework, cooking and stereotyped women's roles scare me. I don't want to get sucked into those roles so my happy ending would include sharing responsibilities or a maid!

55. I don't need to be rich, but I'd like to be very comfortable, and I'm willing to work hard material comforts. I'd like to have a summer home on a beach that is big enough for lots of friends.

56. A big part of my happy ending is staying in love with my husband. It's really the center of my happy ending, because everything else will be brighter if our relationship continues to be happy.

57. Tradeoffs—where to live—NC? VA? TX? Housework, both of us or neither of us. It won't be *just* me. His career vs. my career? Sacrifices upon promotion? Transfers?

58. It is unclear how these tradeoffs are going to be made. Bill and I are both fairly strong-minded, so a lot of patience is going to be required.

Reply 7 (Points of Change)

59.   0. Lived in Illinois with grandparents from birth to kindergarten
1. Illinois to Germany (1st & 2nd grade)
2. Germany to Washington (3rd, 4th [changed schools] & 5th grade)
3. Washington to Illinois (6th, Dad to Vietnam)
4. Illinois to Va. (7th)
5. Va. to Kansas (8th, 9th, & 10th, started HS)
6. Kansas to Va. (11th, 12th, Dad to Laos in 11th)
7. College (Parents moved to apartment from house)
8. Paralegal course and job hunting
9. DC Associates (work)
10. Graduate school, Bill
11. Marriage

Reply 8 (Options, Pros and Cons, Decisions Made at Turning Points)

60. I guess most of my turning points did not involve personal choice. Since my father was in the military we moved every 1 to 3 years so, although the moves had a major impact on me, I had few options. The only options I can see are whether or not I chose to accept the moves, and how quickly I adapted to new surroundings.

61. It was much more difficult to move from Kansas to Virginia than it was from Illinois to Germany for two reasons: First, the older I was, the more attached I became to friends, and second, the longer I lived in one area, the harder it was to uproot myself. So, my choice in the matter was the speed at which I chose to adapt.

62. The first turning point in which I had options was in my decision about college. The decision to remain in-state was made by my parents because they couldn't afford the out-of-state tuition. I suppose I *chose* not to supplement my parents' tuition payments in order to go to another school, but I had my heart set on UVA anyway. I also applied to VA. Tech and got in but dreaded the thought of having to go there.

63. The pros and cons of the situation: Virginia's academic standing was far and away the most influential factor in any decision. My parents played a minuscule role in the whole process—I was influenced more by my peers. I knew the smart ones that were staying in-state were going to UVA. or to Wm. & Mary, and the air heads were on the road to Tech. I didn't want to be seen as an air head. Or go to a school that was more an extension of high school than college. I think the "cons" in the whole process was that I didn't really look for a school—UVA just fell in my lap, and I was pleased with it.

64. I arrived at my decision long before I started looking for colleges. I just couldn't imagine going anywhere else, so I asked for and got no advice.

65. Turning point 8: What to do when I get out of school? I thought for so long that I wanted to go to law school and then I wasn't sure. I took the boards and did OK, but nothing spectacular. I didn't want to go to a mediocre law school and have to accept a mediocre job after that, so I needed more input into my interests. I took a paralegal course immediately after graduation in order to better find a job in a law firm and then decide whether law was really what I wanted.

66. I had the choice to go out and look for a job right away, but I felt paralegal school would better prepare me (with a skill) since I was coming out of college with an English literature degree.

67. I guess the idea of the course was suggested to me by my boyfriend at that time, but the decision was really mine. My parents financed the venture, so they had some input, but not much.

68. Turning point 9: After the paralegal course I took a waitressing job while I looked for a paralegal job. I had two opportunities to work: (1) for the government as a paralegal or (2) for a legal publishing co. I took the second job, which paid less, but I really didn't want to work for the government.

69. The cons in this decision were: I wouldn't be using my paralegal skills in the manner that I was trained. (The pay was about $2,500 less.) The pros were: the chance of upward mobility was greater, the offices and people were nice, and the employee benefits were great. I think one of the most influential variables in comparing the two jobs was that at DCA those hiring me were impressed with my background and encouraging about my future. Also, it was a team-oriented company. Everyone from the top down contributed in even the smallest project if it was necessary.

70. Turning point 10: Graduate school or boredom were my options—or looking for another job—or confronting my boss. I didn't think my time would be best spent in another job unless I took time off to get an MBA. It's really necessary in order to be taken seriously, quickly. I found that DCA was moving me as quickly as I could hope, but I was tired of waiting. After 4 years in college and 1½ more, I wanted to do something useful. The pros and cons of this: pros—better prospects for jobs after school and taken more seriously without having to start at the *very* bottom.

71. The cons—I saw none then, I was tired of the commuting ratrace, ready for something new. How I arrived at my decision? I became interested in the stock market because my paralegal training was in securities law and my work at DCA involved analyzing proxies and registration statements and the 33 and 34 acts. I took statistics and a finance class at night, liked it, and applied. I only applied to UVA. It's hard to say why. I guess I figured it was the best school I could get into. My boards were good, but my grades were just average. So, again I knew it would be a waste to go to just any B-school. If I couldn't get into VA, I'd just wait and regroup and do something else. (I could stay at DCA.)

72. I didn't talk the idea over with anybody but my roommate—who was also planning to apply to B-school. I guess I always knew I'd get some kind of graduate degree that was important to me. So, it was just a natural progression.

73. Turning point 11: Marriage! That was an enormous turning point. Other options: Call it quits (sure!), wait until after graduation. Pros—it was hard to wait; Cons— interfering with our school work; difficult to plan while in school. How I arrived at the decision? Who knows? Love! No, it wasn't an easy choice, and I didn't talk to anyone before deciding. Just like most other events in my life. It just came along and fell in my lap unexpectedly.

Reply 9 (Differences after Changes, What Stayed the Same)

74. Turning point 7: College: Going to college was one of the *most* exciting times in my life. I was very ready to get away from home. The independence was wonderful. I was ready to plan my own time and not live by my parent's timetable.

75. After college and paralegal school I was again independent in Washington, D.C., but although I enjoyed living alone, I realized what a hermit I was becoming. So, I sought out a roommate. It was a super arrangement, but it wasn't until 6–8 mos. after moving to D.C. that I realized (for the first time) that I really needed friendships. I had become too cut off, too independent in my effort to establish that I could be self-sufficient.

76. DCA: I changed because of the confidence that a couple of the vice presidents showed in me. That kind of positive reinforcement encouraged me to put numerous hours of overtime into my job, which I see as good. I think you have to go the extra mile to get anywhere in this world.

77. Grad school: That has changed me more than anything I can remember. I'd rather not be the person I turned into last year. The pressure turned me into a bitch around Bill. I questioned (regularly) whether I belonged at Darden. But on the other hand it also has helped to make hard work a habit, so I don't (or didn't this summer) mind it as much now.

78. Marriage: I don't feel any different, but I'm happier and more relaxed.

79. I don't understand this question. I can't think of anything that has "withered" away or is "waiting until later"—unless the withering might be my liberalism—which has turned to "conservative liberalism."

Reply 10 (Disillusionments)

80. I'm tired of turning points.

81. College required more studying than I expected. High school had been a breeze, but college was different and it took me a semester to realize that (GPA = 2.4) and one to recover (GPA = 3.6).

82. Tables, Tables*

	Expected Before	Realized After
College	no study freedom friendships	yes study! freedom! yep!
83. Paralegal	work hard meet people	work, but not hard made some very good friends—still in touch
	expect easier getting job	not quite as easy
84. DCA	challenge	developed— but not quite as fast as I wanted
	Education Learned computer stuff	yep yep
85. Grad school	Education Social/fun	yep not ½ as much as I thought
	Extra-curr stuff Time for old school friends	not much nope
86. Marriage	Fun/security	yep

87.	Coll.	Para.	DCA	Grad. Sch.	Marr.*
Right place at right time (Fell into it)	x	x	x	x	x
Independence goal	x		x	x	
Ambition/career	x	x	x	x	
Friendships	x			x	x
Social	x			x	
Friends did it	x				
No outside influence in decision	½x	x	x	x	x
Parents' influence	½x	x	x	x	x

*This doesn't mean ambition/career and independence are not still important—they are, they just don't apply here.

Reply 11 (Patterns)

None given.

Lauren Davis: Feelings Record

Figure Test

Wondered what good my responses would do in telling me something about myself. How did I feel—I didn't enjoy or mind it as I was taking the test. I thought my reactions might have been a bit negative—what I saw in the pictures. It seemed similar to a child's game but I'm sure there must be some value if we have to take it.

Rorschach Test

Again I'm curious what I can interpret from this type of an exercise. I found it difficult to describe the objects differently when they pointed one way or another, although they looked very different when turned upside down.

I also wonder how much my military upbringing is coming out since I saw emblems and insignias and rockets.

Learning Style Inventory

This test is interesting because although I know how I learn best—I don't always apply these rules in class. The active participation of class is most beneficial; however, I do not take advantage of that.

FIRO-B

I enjoyed this test, although it's difficult to answer many of the questions because I feel differently in different circumstances. These questions are hard to answer also because my true answer isn't what I'd always like it to be.

With previous instruments I had some idea where the test was going. I was curious, although I was planning to answer "honestly," what a different answer might mean.

On many of the answers I found myself very much in the center. I like being more specific in my yes-no answers.

After scoring: I have some doubts about the questions regarding autonomy—I would not put myself below average in this category and find some of the numerical values assigned, questionable.

Life and Career Values Card Sort

This is very important in recognizing what makes me happy. By analyzing these criteria I can get a better handle on what I would be most happy doing. These seem to be fairly obvious to me.

Creative Life Style Diagram

An artist I am not—but after "discovering" someone else's form, it was fun. It was kind of a catalog at Christmas—I could draw in all the events and situations that would make me happy in the future.

Getting past that artist block, the rest was fun.

Written Interview

What a chore. I hated it. I wasn't sure how personal to get or how professional/career inputs were more important. I really dislike reviewing my family history—a lot of it was unhappy so I'd rather leave it in the past.

It's also hard to expose yourself when you know someone else will read this. I'm very private about some aspects of my life. It's hard to open up.

I'm glad it's all over.

Lauren Davis: Dyad Exercise

Lauren's dyad partner developed the following themes after reviewing her self-assessment data:

1. I have little tolerance for an environment below my intellectual ability.
2. The people I like most share my values and intellectual ability.
3. I am aspiring to the top and the people and activities I seek out are all avenues to reach that goal.
4. I want to be independent and self-sufficient.
   a. Own decisions.
   b. Marriage, own time.
5. I am competitive, and I want to win.
6. Having friends is important and has become increasingly so over time.
7. One of my life objectives is material rewards.
8. I am often a victim to events in my life, things just fall into my lap.
9. In a supportive environment, I am happier and more productive.
10. I get inspired and then often lose interest.
11. I enjoy routine and organization.

The dyad partner cited the following evidence in support of the themes:

THEME 1, 2, 3 (Grouped because of similarity of themes): Written interview (paragraphs 21, 27, 30, 33, 54, 35, 29, 30, 51, 63, 18)

THEME 4: Written interview (32, 36, 44, 46, 47, 48, 63, 67, 72, 74, 75); Strong-Campbell (highest score 49—enterprising); Life and Career Values (Identity second only to Marital); Predisposition (preference toward solitude 2.86). Disconfirming data cited was only average preference for autonomy in Predisposition Test.

THEME 5: Written interview (7, 8, 25, 9, 17); Learning Style Inventory (75% AE score); Life and Career Values (Professional ranks 3rd)

THEME 6: Written interview (8, 14, 24, 15, 75, 52, 55, 47); Figure Test (57% people—13% affection); Learning Style Inventory (63% CE score); Life and Career Values (Friends/Social ranks 5th)

THEME 7: Written interview (69, 52, 53, 55); Life and Career Values (Financial ranks 4th)

THEME 8: Written interview (34, 60, 64, 71, 73)

THEME 9: Written interview (22, 75, 76, 9, 17, 78, 69); Predisposition Test (average for tolerance for ambiguity)

THEME 10: Written interview (37, 23, 17)

THEME 11: Written interview (37, 39)

16

Writing Your Self-Assessment

We believe that if you take the time to *write down* your self-assessment conclusions, they will be much more useful to you not only now, but also in the future. The writing does several things. First, it forces you to put into words thoughts, impressions, and feelings. This process causes one to think more clearly and carefully about the nuances and meanings of those thoughts, impressions, and feelings. And after all, that is what self-assessment is all about—to make explicit what is already within you in a way that is useful.

Second, once the words are on paper, you can gain some emotional distance from them and view them a bit (not a lot) more objectively than you can in your head or heart. The paper provides a means of detaching the conclusions so that you can consider them.

Third, the paper also provides a greater opportunity for you to check your self-assessment against the views of others. Spouses, partners, family, close friends, and others who know you well may provide interesting confirmations or questions about your life theme conclusions. Those conversations, based on a list of life themes, can stimulate your thinking to further clarify the labels.

Fourth, a written record of your self-assessment will help you to monitor your growth, change, and development over time. It is much easier to see those changes when you can *read* what you concluded in the past rather than try to *remember* the conclusions and then compare them with a current self-assessment.

Finally, writing your self-assessment will sharpen your inductive skill greatly. As humans, we often jump (occasionally, leap) to conclusions that are not well founded in facts. Our minds race ahead so quickly that the weakness of the logical connections may not be considered or even recognized, especially when the topic is charged with emotion, as it is in a self-assess-

ment. Slowing down enough to write out the data and the conclusions you draw from the data forces you to look at the connections between those data and conclusions and to consider their strengths. That mental, analytic skill is one which has application far beyond the self-assessment process. It will help as a person in business, in society, in relationships, in science, wherever.

Procedures and Guidelines

We encourage you to approach writing your self-assessment in two steps. First, develop a *single* theme. Choose one of the many that probably have occurred to you by now and search through the data to see if it is supported. Collect the data on cards or a piece of paper. We have provided another worksheet for you (Exhibit 16–1). If the format appeals to you, use it. If not, devise your own method for developing this theme. Note the contradictory evidence. Phrase the label. Recheck the connections between label and data. Revise the label. Recheck the data pool in light of the revised label.

Then, when you have completed a single theme and written out its name (label) and the related referenced data, show it to someone. Talk about it. Retrace your steps. How did you go about assembling it? How long did it take? How could you be more efficient? Does the label and the process feel right to you? Why or why not? You may wish to discuss this in class if you are in one.

Having completed a single theme and taken some time to debrief that experience, you can then go on to complete your written self-assessment by repeating the process you used and revised to develop your initial theme.

Exhibit 16–1
Life Theme Development Worksheet

Theme Label: _____

Sources   Data

Contradictory Evidence

The Number of Themes

After you have analyzed all available data and found all the themes you can, you may wonder whether the number of themes identified is typical or appropriate—or whether you are still missing something.

Our experience suggests that the number of themes that can be generated depends, to some extent, on the number and type of data-generating instruments used. Using the devices in this book, you normally will find about 15 to 25 themes in a good analysis. Initial analyses based on data from only three or four devices may yield as many as a dozen "tentative" themes that, while not yet convincing, look promising. Good analyses based on more than our devices will generally not produce more than 30 well-supported themes.

Sometimes people are not able to locate more than a dozen convincing themes in their data. Usually they simply haven't looked hard or long enough, but that is not the only reason. Sometimes a person, either consciously or unconsciously, tries to find themes that are completely "independent"—that do not, in a sense, overlap. Similarly, one sometimes looks for themes that fit into a limited number of categories, such as "skills," "values," and "goals." In both cases, the underlying problem is the same: The person is imposing a model or a set of constraints on the data, thereby limiting what the data can say. As we have said before, it is essential to effective thematic development that one let the data speak for themselves.

A different set of factors is often associated with an analysis containing 30 to 40 themes. Often many of these themes say almost the same thing: The degree of overlap is extreme. Or many of the themes may be supported by very few data. In either instance, many similar themes can usually be collapsed into more general and better-supported themes without the loss of any important information.

A good self-assessment does not have to contain a certain quota of themes. But our experience strongly suggests that if you end up with less than 15 or more than 30 themes, it is wise to reexamine them carefully.

Assessing the Accuracy and Importance of Themes

Before you accept a set of themes as final, you have to judge the importance and accuracy of each theme that has been located and labeled. Judgment is required, because no rules, outside of one's own common sense, are available for determining whether the evidence supporting some theme is "enough" to ensure its accuracy, or whether the amount of evidence suggests that a theme is of great importance, moderate importance, or minor importance.

The questions one needs to raise in making this judgment are fairly obvious ones:

1. How many data seem to support the theme? A theme supported by ten data certainly has a greater chance of being accurate and important than one supported by only three.

2. Where do these data come from? Do they all come from just one of the data-generating devices, or do they come from more than one? A theme supported by data from four different instruments seems more likely to be accurate and important than one supported by data from only one source.

3. How many, if any, data contradict the theme? Any contradictory datum raises the question of a theme's validity. But a theme with ten data supporting it and one contradicting it would quite reasonably be handled differently from a theme with four data supporting it and two contradicting it.

One might suppose that, because precise decision rules are lacking, judgments about themes tend to be highly idiosyncratic. However, we have not found this to be the case. Most people, when looking at the same set of themes, tend to make similar judgments regarding the accuracy and importance of each one.

For an example of a final set of themes in a self-assessment, refer to Lauren Davis's self-assessment paper (see case, pp. 150–58). The self-assessment paper assignment that follows is one we have given to our students to guide their efforts; it may be of some help to you.

Self-Assessment Paper Assignment

Purpose

The self-assessment paper (SAP) is designed to help you develop a set of life themes from the data you have generated so that you can use those themes to establish goals and ideas for work and career. The paper is also intended to develop your skills at analyzing large and complex pools of data and at seeing the trends and patterns in that data.

Content

The SAP should stand by itself; that is, a person should be able to read it without the benefit of background information and be able to follow the logic and conclusions easily.

The paper should include the following elements:

1. A brief introduction that establishes the date, the nature of the assignment, and any background you would like to include.

2. A body containing theme labels and related data. Your logic, especially as it connects data and theme labels, should be crystal clear. We suggest putting one

theme per page, with the label at the top and those data and their sources beneath. Separate supporting and contradictory evidence. Number each theme.

Quote data verbatim, then *add* any interpretation if necessary. Citing, for example, paragraph 3 of the written interview but providing *only* interpretation of that paragraph makes it difficult to assess your logic. When you use data from quantitatively scored instruments, cite the scores. Citing the Strong-Campbell without showing scores and your interpretations of those scores does not reveal your logic. Your purpose is in part to demonstrate—to communicate—the logic connecting individual data to the theme label.

Also, remember that *variety* of sources of data lend strength to a theme. A theme supported by data from eight different sources is more believable than one supported by data from two sources. Don't neglect the Feelings Record and other "less formal" instruments. Feel free to include data from sources like journals, other tests, letters, and so on. If you do, include them in your binders.

If the volume of your supporting data for a theme runs on for two pages, feel free to cite only the 10 to 20 *strongest* bits of evidence and then to summarize in one line the volume of additional data not presented.

Be *sure* to recognize and cite contradictory evidence where you find it. If the volume of contradictory evidence is large, perhaps you have two themes rather than one in that pool of data.

3. A description of things that you believe about yourself (preferably in theme label format) which are important to career decisions, but which did not emerge in your data pool.

4. A conclusion that includes a brief description of your level of confidence in the accuracy, comprehensiveness, and importance of the themes. Include a list of your themes (on one page). Include also a consideration of the dilemmas, tradeoffs, or conflicts suggested in your themes.

Format

Your SAP must be typed. *Maximum* length is 35 pages. Put a *copy* of your paper in your blue binder under the blue tab marked Self-Assessment Paper. Then hand in your binder (with *all* of your data and interpretations). Keep the original of your paper. You will need it in class.

Criteria for a Good
Self-Assessment Paper

1. Demonstrates understanding of various instruments.
2. Clear logic between data and theme labels.
3. Sufficient volume of supporting data for themes.
4. Recognizes contradictory evidence.
5. Cites a variety of sources for each theme where possible.
6. Well-written theme labels.
7. Adequate range and volume of themes.
8. Themes grouped where appropriate and ranked.
9. Implications address a variety of dimensions.
10. Readable, easy to follow and check.
11. Reasonable length.

LAUREN DAVIS: SELF-ASSESSMENT PAPER

A little learning is a dangerous thing;
Drink deep or taste not the Pierian spring.
There are shallow draughts intoxicate the brain,
And drinking largely sobers us again.
Fired at first sight with what the muse imparts,
In fearless youth we tempt the heights of arts,
While from the bounded level of our mind
Short views we take, nor see the lengths behind;
But more advanced, behold with strange surprise
New distant scenes of endless science rise!
So pleased at first the towering Alps we try

Mount o'er the vales, and seem to tread the sky,
The eternal snows appear already past,
And the first clouds and mountains seems the last;
But, those attained we tremble to survey
The growing labors of our lengthened way
The increasing prospect tires our wondering eyes,
Hills peep o'er hills, and Alps on Alps arise!

Alexander Pope
From *An Essay on Criticism*

This case was prepared by Kevin E. Sachs, MBA 1982, under the direction of James G. Clawson as a basis for class discussion. © 1983 by the Sponsors of The Colgate Darden Graduate School of Business, University of Virginia, Charlottesville, Virginia. UVA case OB-275.

Introduction

I am approaching an important turning point. The decisions I make in choosing a profession, a job, a company, and a location will have an enormous impact on the direction of my life. This is an exciting time and a frightening time. What if I make a terrible mistake?

The themes that follow are not all-encompassing; however, they do represent many of my values. By compiling these themes, I hope to develop a better picture of myself and sort through the potential consequences of my future choices.

I have divided my themes into four groups, according to their order and magnitude of importance in my life.

1. I work best with positive reinforcement and support.
2. I enjoy being with people.
3. I enjoy change and a fast pace.
4. I am happiest when I am challenged/growing in a job.
5. I do not enjoy taking orders or working for strong authority figures.
6. I learn best by direct experience/involvement.
7. I have very few close friends and confide in few people.
8. The people I like best are smart and strive to better themselves.
9. Material comforts are important to me.
10. Independence is important to me.
11. I prefer a team-oriented environment.
12. Status and prestige are important to me.
13. Owning a horse, riding, and showing are important to me.
14. I enjoy getting organized and work better when I am organized.
15. I place a high value on reliability and honesty.
16. I enjoy teaching and persuading others.
17. I am competitive and like to win.
18. I enjoy athletics.

After each theme title, I have noted in parentheses the number of supporting data, number of disconfirming data, and the number of instruments used.

Instruments

AVL	AVL Study of Values
ESS	Darden Application Essay (2/20/80)—see "Other Data" (not inc.)
EVAL	DC Associates Annual Evaluation (10/14/80) (not included in DATA)
FIRO	FIRO-B

FR	Feelings Record
FT	Figure Test
ISI	Interpersonal Style Inventory
LSI	Learning Style Inventory
LCV	Life and Career Values
LSD	Life Style Diagram
PDT	Predisposition Test
REC	Darden Letter of Recommendation (not included in DATA)
ROR	Rorschach Test
SCI	Strong-Campbell Interest Inventory
24D(X)	Twenty-Four Hour Diary, paragraph (X)
WI (X)	Written interview, paragraph (X)

Themes

1. I Work Best with Positive Reinforcement and Support (14, 0, 4)

CLV	Marital: #4—Praised by spouse.
LCV	Professional: #2—Public recongion. #6—Rewarded fairly for efforts. Familial: #1—Being encouraged/praised.
ISI	Current self—"Needs support": 4-high (mean = 3.5).
LSI	Concrete experience: 63% (second most dominant style). Interpretation: Benefit most from feedback and discussion with fellow CE learners.
WI(9)	The teacher liked me this time, so I enjoyed being her "pet."
WI(12)	The whole atmosphere was conducive to expanding your learning abilities, which normal classroom settings inhibit. We were told we were smart, and that's how we were allowed into the program. The framework was very positive, and I enjoyed it.
WI(17)	My first semester grades were a disaster because I was too undisciplined. But by second semester I came back with excellent grades, and then I knew I could do it.
WI(17)	I enjoyed working for the company. It was very people-oriented from the top down. The management's philosophy was very team-oriented (supportive).
WI(20)	The support (from Bill) really helped me get through the year.
WI(38)	I found positive and negative reinforcement to have more to do with my work at the company than in any other situation. I had two adversaries who were very difficult to work with.
WI(69)	I think one of the most influential variables in comparing the two jobs was that at DCA those hiring me were impressed with my background and encouraging about my future.
WI(76)	I changed because of the confidence that a couple of the vice presidents showed in me— that kind of position reinforcement encour-

aged me to put numerous hours of overtime into my job.

2. I Enjoy Being with People (21, 0, 6)

FIRO Very high (17): Interpretation—Preference for a considerable amount of interpersonal interaction.

FT People: 57%—Slightly more oriented toward people than toward the environment.

LCV Social: #1—Close to others.
#2—Part of group.
Marriage: #3—Praised by spouse.

LSD Friends increased from 10% to 20% from current/past to future.

LSI Active Experimentation: 75% (dominant theme).
Interpretation: Extrovert.

LSI Concrete Experience: 63% (second most dominant theme).
Interpretation: Empathetic, people-oriented.

WI(3) I loved teaching her all the things I'd learned when I came home from school.

WI(4) I guess in three years you become more attached to friends, and as you grow older, friendships mean more—so leaving Kansas was very upsetting.

WI(17) The company was fairly small so I knew the VPs very well and enjoyed working for the company. It was very people-oriented from the top down.

WI(24) When I was young and enjoyed Brownies and Girl Scouts but not for the "fun" things to do—more to be with friends and socialize.

WI(26) After moving back to Virginia in 1971, I spent a very boring summer, knowing no one, in a rented house.

WI(31) All of the students in the course were bright and close to the same age—so I really enjoyed it.

WI(32) The first job I had was in a drugstore . . . I did a good job—I enjoyed talking to people.

WI(33) Career waitresses are not the most social creatures.

WI(56) I would like to have a summer home on a beach that is big enough for lots of friends.

WI(75) Although I enjoyed living alone, I realized what a hermit I was becoming—so I sought out a roommate. It was a super arrangement, but it wasn't until 6–8 months after moving to D.C. that I realized (for the first time) that I really needed friendships.

		Expected Before	Realized Later
WI(82)	College	Friendships	Yep!
WI(83)	Paralegal	Meet people	Made some very good friends Still in touch
WI(84)	Darden	Time for old school friends	Not much

3. I Enjoy Change and a Fast Pace (18, 0, 6)

FT Environmental Active = 30%.
Interpretation: See my environment as a dynamic phenomenon.

LCV Recreation: Moving quickly.
Professional: Learning new things. Changing activities weekly.
Marital: Changing activities daily.

LSI Accommodator
Excel in situations where one must adapt oneself to specific immediate circumstances.
Impatient and pushy at times.
Involving self in new experiences.
Action-oriented jobs.

LSI Active experimentation = 75% (dominant theme).
Interpretation: "Doing" orientation. Dislike passive learning situations.

PDT Very high tolerance for ambiguity.
Interpretation: Don't mind a changing set of conditions.

SCI Enterprising: 49—highest—adventurous—energetic.
Interpretations: Impatient with precise work or work involving long periods of intellectual effort.

WI(17) It didn't take long for me to hit the ceiling again. I knew I couldn't move up fast enough to be challenged.

WI(22) By August I was tired of my job, tired of seeing Bill only once a week, and bored with Atlanta.

WI(23) I have always liked getting involved in clubs and organizations, although I always wonder why I got into them after I do—because they don't interest me very long.

WI(27) I worked in the receiving department of Lord & Taylors and was bored to death putting price tags on merchandise.

WI(37) I enjoyed the routine at first . . . I love organizing, so I enjoyed that part of the job. However, organizing materials which you have no time to peruse soon becomes very dull.

WI(37) I loved the "currentness" of the job. It was exciting to read in the papers about a case I had been working on the day before. The thrill wore off, however . . . I began to get bored.

WI(45) My family lived all over, so in some ways our family structure changed every 1–2–3 years. We never lived in one place for more than 2 years except Kansas.

WI(70) It's (MBA) really necessary to be taken seriously quickly. I found that DCA was moving me as quickly as I could hope, but I was tiring of writing.

WI(71) "The Cons"—I saw none then, I was . . . ready for something new.

WI(80) I'm tired of turning points.

4. I Am Happiest When I Am Challenged/Growing in a Job (12, 0, 2)

CLV   Learning new things #4.
Tackling challenge #5—professional.

WI(18)   It didn't take long for me to hit the ceiling (as far as challenge goes) again. I knew I couldn't move up fast enough to be challenged or be compensated enough to make up for it—so B-School was on the horizon.

WI(21)   I was disappointed in my project a bit. First, it wasn't SBS material, and secondly it was not much of an intellectual challenge.

WI(27)   After graduating, I worked in the receiving department of Lord & Taylors and was bored to death putting price tags on merchandise.

WI(34)   The next job was just plain boring. I hate to sound so negative—but w/most summer work, you have to take what you can get.

WI(37)   I enjoyed the routine at first—it was the type of work that required a very organized individual. There were a million details involved in getting the information into print.

WI(51)   Challenge is very important. I would rather be overworked and challenged than underworked and bored.

WI(51)   Work is nebulous at this point—but whatever I end up doing I want it to be in pursuit of developing skills that I can apply.

WI(51)   It's important to me to be growing in a job.

WI(70)   Grad school or boredom were my options . . . I didn't think my time would be best spent in another job unless I took time off to get an MBA. It's really necessary to be taken seriously, quickly (to be challenged).

WI(70)   The pros and cons of this: pro—better prospects for jobs after school and taken more seriously without having to start at the *very* (boring) bottom.

5. I Do Not Enjoy Taking Orders or Working for Strong Authority Figures (9, 1, 5)

LCV   Run show = #1: Professional.

LSI   Concrete experience 63%—oriented more toward peer than authority in approach to learning.

PDT   2.96 High disposition toward solitude—prefer to work individually.

PDT   2.57 (Closer to research org.): Preference for autonomy.
Less inclined to like subordinate relationships.
Higher percentage to provide own direction.

WI(17)   I enjoyed working for the company . . . The management philosophy was very team-oriented.

WI(30)   I hate to take orders from people who are GS-morons—so it was frustrating.

WI(33)   The waitress job I covered—I don't like waiting on anyone. I thought the job (along w/the secretarial jobs) was demeaning.

WI(36)   During my first six months, I was closely supervised by a woman one year my senior who was a Vassar graduate. Those two criteria alone mean nothing, but I picked up the job quickly and needed little supervision so I felt very confined and stifled being hovered over.

WI(69)   Also, the reason I liked it was that it was a team-oriented company. Everyone from the top down contributed in even the smallest project if it was necessary.

DISCONFIRMING DATA

FIRO   C=5, middle range: I don't prefer to give or take orders, but will do both when appropriate.

6. I Learn Best by Direct Experience/Involvement (14, 0, 5)

AVL   Economic 41/Theoretical 38.
Practical, experience-based orientation stronger than abstract, theoretical orientation.

ESS(2)   Further, the active participation encouraged in the program will enable me to more accurately determine the areas of business which will continue to interest and challenge me.

ESS(3)   Throughout my graduate years, I particularly enjoyed participating in seminars and small classes which required discussion.

FR(3)   I know how I learn best (but) I don't always apply those rules in class. The active participation of class is most beneficial.

LSI   Dominant learning style: Active Experimentation 75%.
Interpretation:
Doing orientation.
Benefit from projects, homework.
Small group discussions.
Dislike passive learning situation.

LSI   Concrete experience: 63%.
Interpretation:
Receptive to experience-based approach to learning.
Theoretical approaches unhelpful.
Learn from specific examples.
Benefit from feedback and discussion.

WI(17)   We were at the stage in math where most students go through flash cards and memorization—but our math was concept–oriented new math! We were told not to worry about the right answer as long as we understood the process. I think that is why my math is so weak.

WI(17)   My first semester grades were a disaster because I was undisciplined. By my second semester I came back w/excellent grades and knew that I could do it.

WI(17) I set out to determine if law school was the way to go. I took a paralegal course in Philadelphia.

WI(18) After working for a year, I became interested in the stock market (I analyzed proxies and registrations all day so I had enough exposure to know what I was getting into). After taking two business classes, I decided it (B-school) was for me.

WI(29) After my first year in college, I worked as a secretary for an attorney to try and see what law was like.

WI(65) I took a paralegal course immediately after graduation in order to better find a job in a law firm and then decide whether law was really what I wanted.

WI(77) But on the other hand, it also helped to make hard work a habit, so I don't mind it (Darden) as much now.

WI(81) College required more studying than I expected. High school had been a breeze, but college was different, and it took me a semester to realize that (GPA 2.4)—and one to recover (GPA 3.6).

7. I Have Very Few Close Friends and Confide in Few People (14, 0, 3)

FR(11) It's also hard to expose yourself when you know someone else will read this. I'm very private about some aspects of my life, and it's hard to open up.

ISI Discusses emotions 2.8. My average and median scores were 3.4. Discusses personal 2.8, so this is fairly low.

WI(8) I had one close friend in Germany, and we were inseparable.

WI(40) My first close friend was Joanne Davis. She and I went to two years of junior high school and one year of high school together. I had friends before Joanne, but we moved around so much I never felt close to any of them.

WI(40) Leaving Kansas was tough, and I never developed any close friendships with girls again until my second year in college.

WI(47) I have neglected to mention many passing friends. I guess I am not close to many people.

WI(63) My parents played a minuscule role in the whole process (choosing a college).

WI(64) I just couldn't imagine going anywhere else (to college) so I asked for and got no advice.

WI(67) I guess the idea of the course was suggested to me by my boyfriend at that time, but the decision was really mine. My parents financed the venture, so they had some input, but not much.

WI(73) No, it (marriage) wasn't an easy choice, and I didn't talk to anyone before deciding.

WI(72) I didn't talk the idea over with anybody but my roommate—who was also planning to apply to B-school. I guess I always knew I'd get

some kind of graduate degree—that was important to me—so it was just a natural progression.

WI(75) Although I enjoyed living alone, I realized what a hermit I was becoming—so I sought out a roommate ... but it wasn't until 6–8 months after moving to D.C. that I realized (for the first time) that I really needed friendships—I had become too cut off.

WI(87) No outside influence in decisions: College, paralegal, DCA, grad school, marriage.

WI(87) Parents' influence: Half college, none in other turning points.

8. The People I Like Best Are Smart and Strive to Better Themselves (11, 0, 2)

AVL Social: 48, Economic: 41 (2 highest scores). Interpretation: Social = love of people, economic = practical, so perhaps love of practical people.

WI(31) All of the students in the course were bright and close to the same age—so I really enjoyed it.

WI(35) The secretarial job wasn't a bad job because it was secretarial—but because of the shyster–lawyer I worked for ... I did some research for him, corrected his grammar and punctuation, and wondered how he ever got as far as he did.

WI(36) I was closely supervised by a woman one year my senior who was a Vassar graduate. (Interpretation: the snob in me is coming out by referring to her school—she wasn't smart, and I had little respect for her.)

WI(42) Rip was also smart and good natured, but he lacked ambition which really bugged me. He was lazy in his school work (although he was very capable) so I knew early on that this would be a stumbling block.

WI(42) Ambition and self-betterment are important to me so I couldn't understand Rip's lackadaisical attitude.

WI(42) I always knew Gordon would make it—which was one reason I was attracted to him. He was very capable and intellectual.

WI(42) Gordon was very smart and good natured, so he was a pleasure to be with.

WI(43) I had trouble getting close to spacey people, they definitely bugged me. I think I was attracted to smart, common–sensical people. Dumb people are no fun to talk to and frustrate me.

WI(46) Probably the most influential characteristic about Bill is his confidence and self-assurance that he will be successful.

WI(63) Virginia's academic standing was far and away the most influential factor in my decision ... I knew the smart ones who were staying in-state were going to Virginia and ... the airheads were on the road to Tech.

9. Material Comforts Are Important to Me (10, 0, 5)

AVL   Economic 2nd highest score.
Interpretation: Interests in satisfaction of bodily needs and the accumulation of tangible wealth.

LCV   Financial/material: #2 having as much as possible.

LSD   Material past/current 5%, future 10%—becoming more important.

SCI   Enterprising: 49 highest occupational theme.
Interpretation:
    Enjoyed working in expensive settings.
    Like power, status, material wealth.

WI(14)   I'm dying to have a horse again.

WI(50)   I would want to be able to commute to work in 15 minutes but be in an area where I could own a horse again—on property behind a house.

WI(52)   I'd like to travel twice a year on vacation—go to Florida or sunny places often.

WI(53)   I also want to have . . . a pool, stable, and a fair amount of land.

WI(55)   I would like to be very comfortable, and I'm willing to work hard for material comforts.

10. Independence Is Very Important to Me (12, 1, 5)

LCV   Run show #1 under professional.
Being free #2 identity.
Independent #1 financial/material.

PDT   Preference for autonomy 2.57.
Closer to research characteristics:
    Higher preference to define work roles, provide own direction.
    Less inclined to like subordinate relationships with strong authority figures.

PDT   Preference for solitude 2.86—high.
Prefer to work individually.

SCI   Artistic 2nd dominant occupational theme.
Interpretation:
    Prefers to work alone.
    Describes self as independent.

24D(5)   Decided how to organize the paper and break it up into series for four of us to write individually.

WI(16)   I was very ready to get away from my parents and have a little freedom.

WI(32)   The first job I had was in a drugstore . . . I didn't find it too bad for a high school student. I worked with some real weirdos, but I was fairly independent. I did a good job.

WI(36)   During my first six months I was closely supervised—so I felt very confined and stifled.

WI(63)   My parents played a minuscule role in the whole process (of choosing a college).

WI(74)   I was ready to get away from town—the independence was wonderful! I was ready to plan my own time and not live by my parents' timetable.

WI(75)   After college and paralegal school, I was again independent in Washington, D.C.

WI(87)   Independence goal: College, DCA, grad school.

DISCONFIRMING DATA

WI(75)   I really needed friendships—I had become too cut off, too independent in my effort to establish that I could be self-sufficient.

11. I Prefer a Team-Oriented Environment (11, 2, 8)

FIRO   C=5, middle range: I don't prefer to give or take orders, but will do both when appropriate.

ISI   Acquaintances reports: (mean = 3.4).
    Keeps promises   4.2
    Patient   4.2
    Competitive   2.8
These attributes would be positive in an environment where teamwork is required.

LSI   Concrete experience: 16 or 63%.
Interpretation:
    Oriented more toward peers than authority in approach to learning.
    Benefit most from feedback and discussions with fellow CE learners.

LSI   Accommodator: "Relies on other people for information rather than one's own analytic ability."

PDT   Preference for autonomy: 2.57—moderate.
Interpretation: Less inclined to like subordinate relationships with strong authority figures.

REC(5)   Her attitude in both positions has been one of . . . cooperation . . . and a strong ability to get along with co-workers.

ROR   W–94%—Interpretation: Look at the *big picture*, in an organization, of a company serving a customer. All employees working as a team to achieve a goal.

WI(17)   I enjoyed working for the company—it was very people-oriented from the top down. The management philosophy was very team-oriented.

WI(54)   Housework, cooking, and stereotyped women's roles scare me. I don't want to get sucked into those roles, so my happy ending would include shared responsibilities or a maid!

WI(57)   Housework: Both of us or neither of us—it won't be just me.

WI(69)   Also, it was a team-oriented company. Everyone from the top down contributed in even the smallest project if it was necessary.

DISCONFIRMING DATA

PDT   Disposition toward solitude: 2.86—high.
Prefer to work individually.

SCI Artistic—47 second highest theme.
Interpretation: prefers to work alone.

12. Status and Prestige Are Important to Me (16, 0, 3)

LCV Professional: "Public recognition" ranked #2.

LCV Identity: Getting ahead #1.
Professional: Run show #1.

SCI Enterprising: 49, highest general occupation theme.
Interpretation: "Like power, status, material wealth."

WI(7) I couldn't stand it when a few of my classmates were always finishing their work very early . . . so I claimed to have finished one day before I had.

WI(8) I remember very little about 2nd grade, except my effort to be in the top reading group.

WI(9) The teacher liked me this time, so I enjoyed being her "pet."

WI(9) I was the only girl on the team!

WI(17) I took a paralegal course in Philadelphia which was reputed (and I believe it is) to be the best course program around.

WI(25) I loved competing in horse shows and loved winning ribbons.

WI(42) I always knew Gordon would "make it"—which was one reason I was attracted to him.

WI(46) Probably the most influential characteristic about Bill is his confidence and self-assurance that he will be successful.

WI(51) I get great satisfaction out of doing a project well—part intrinsic satisfaction, but more peer recognition.

WI(63) Virginia's academic standing was far and away the most influential factor in my decision.

WI(63) I knew the smart ones that were staying in-state were going to Virginia or William and Mary and the airheads were on the road to Virginia Tech. I didn't want to be seen as an airhead.

WI(65) I didn't want to go to a mediocre law school and have to accept a mediocre job after that.

WI)71) Again, I knew it would be a waste to go to just any B-school.

13. Owning a Horse, Riding, and Showing Are Important to Me (7, 0, 2)

LSD My "future" drawings included one block with a horse.

WI(14) We spent three years in Kansas, and my memories of Ft. Leavenworth are the best of any of the places I've lived. My parents bought Kim and me a horse and eventually we bought another.

WI(14) Leaving riding has been one of the most difficult things to accept. I'm dying to have a horse again, and I hope to show in the future.

WI(25) I love riding—that sport is by far the most fun for me. I loved competing in horse shows and loved winning ribbons!

WI(40) We both rode horses, so we rode together after school everyday. Leaving Kansas (and my friend and horse) was tough.

WI(50) I want to . . . be in an area where I could own a horse again.

WI(53) I also want to have . . . a pool, *stable,* and a fair amount of land.

14. I Enjoy "Getting Organized" and Work Better When I Am Organized (12, 0, 8)

AVL Economic: 41—2nd highest score.
Interpretation: Interested in what is useful and practical to accomplish task (being organized helps me perform more efficiently).

EVAL She has a good eye for detail. She has devised production systems (organization) for the SEC NALI and S which have increased the accuracy of our supplement.

LCV Intellectual:
#1—Organizing things.
#2—Using energy and resources wisely.
#3—Working on details.

LSD Interpretation: The format I chose is very organized, with items fitting neatly into a total organized structure.

REC A strong organizational and analytical ability . . . have been clearly evident from her performance in this position.

EVAL She has a good eye for detail, which is invaluable.

ROR 94% whole.
6% large part.
Interpretation: Struggled to "organize" all of the extraneous details so that they fit into one big picture.

24D(5) Decided how to organize the paper and break it up into sections for four of us to write individually.

24D(18) Organizing notebook in order to get started. It's hard for me to work with a messy notebook. In order to keep the workload organized in my head and in order to make sure I cover everything I need to be organized and neat.

WI(37) I enjoyed the routine at first—it was the type of job that required a very organized individual. There were a million details involved in getting the information into print. I love organizing, so I enjoyed that part of the job.

WI(39) But this is a difficult way to answer this question so I will begin again in a more structured (organized) way.

WI(73) Marriage: Cons—interfering with our school work; difficult to plan while in school [Addition: this was a traumatic time in many ways because there were so many school and wedding details to attend to—it drained me because I couldn't deal well with so many constant loose ends. I couldn't even get my "plan of attack" on those loose ends organized.]

15. I Place a High Value on Reliability and Honesty (7, 0, 4)

ISI Acquaintance report: Keeps promises 4.2 (3.4 mean)
Consistent 4
Desired self: Keeps promises 5
Consistent 5

REC Her attitude in both positions has invariably been one of . . . dependability.

24D(2) I was going to be 15 minutes late! When I got to school at 9:15, only two other group members were there—and I thought *I* was irresponsible . . . so I apologized for being late.

24D(17) Advertising group project was supposed to be in a group member's box so the rest could give it a final review. It wasn't there. It really irritated me.

WI(6) . . . so I claimed to have finished before I had and got caught and admonished before the class. I look back and laugh, but what a trauma at six! (*Interpretation:* This incident is one of few that stands out vividly in my memory. I learned a powerful and long-lasting lesson about the importance of honesty.)

WI(30) Again I typed and was a conscientious employee.

WI(38) It was unsettling trying to deal with individuals who won't reveal why they dislike you.

16. I Enjoy Teaching and Persuading Others (9, 1, 6)

APP My present job, which requires that I address short presentations to a sales staff, has extended my appreciation and enjoyment of this type of interaction.

ISI Acquaintance report: "Helps others": 3.8 Relatively high, the mean for all items was 3.4. Current self—takes lead: 4.0, mean is 3.5.

LCV Identity: #3—expanding influence.
Professional: #7—directing next person.
Parental: #3—teaching.
Political: #1—helping people.

REC . . . excellent oral and written communication skills have been evident from her performance in this position.

SCI Basic Interest Scales: Public speaking: 63—highest ranking of all such items.

SCI General occupational theme: Enterprising—49 highest theme.
Facility with words in selling, dominating, leading.
Interpretation:
Prefer social tasks where they can assume leadership.
Enjoy persuading others to my viewpoint.

WI(2) Kim was my shadow, and I was her teacher.

WI(3) I loved teaching her all the things I had learned when I came home from school.

WI(38) It was an eye opener to me—I thought I could "bring them around" and become friends.

DISCONFIRMING DATA

SCI Basic interest scales: Teaching was low (40, mean = 50).

17. I Am Competitive and I Like to Win (9, 1, 4)

LCV Getting ahead #1—Identity.
Achieving goal #3—Identity.
Do better than next person #3—Recreation.

ISI Competitive: Ranked myself 4 (avg = 3.5).

SCI Enterprising 49—my dominant theme.
Interpretation: Prefers social tasks when they can assume leadership.

WI(7) I do remember how frustrated I would get because I could never finish my work before lunch. We (the class) were competing with one another on a chart to see who could work the fastest and most efficiently. (You got stars depending on your speed.) Well, I couldn't stand it when a few of my classmates were always finishing their work very early . . . so I claimed to have finished one day before I had.

WI(8) I remember very little about second grade except my effort to be in the top reading group.

WI(14) So I learned to ride and entered many horse shows in the area. My closest friend had been riding for several years—so with her help and the many cheap lessons available at the stables on Post, I got to be quite good.

WI(25) I love riding—that sport is by far the most fun for me. I loved competing in horse shows and winning ribbons.

WI(38) I had two adversaries (for reasons I know not—competition?) who were difficult to work with.

WI(38) But it was an eye opener to me—I always thought I could "bring them around" and [win] become friends.

DISCONFIRMING DATA

ISI Acquaintance report:
Competitive: 2.8—low (avg = 3.4).

18. I Enjoy Athletics (16,1,8)

24D(23) Watched the Dodgers win—good for Dodgers—bad for my studying—that means more games on TV to distract me.

FT Environment active: 30% Most of my responses in this category dealt with sport activities: dancing, exercises, diving off high dive, somersault.

LCV Recreation/physical: 6th value out of 13.
#1—enjoying activity.
#4—moving quickly.

LSD   Recreation/sports topics:
        Past and current = 48%.
        Future = 27%.
        Large % of total entries.

SCI   Occupational scale: Recreation leader—45
        "similar."

24D(12) Left to go to scuba diving class.

23D(19) It's hard to be disciplined on a sunny foot-
         ball day.

WI(9)   I was a bit of a tomboy in 3rd grade, and I
         preferred softball to any other activity.

WI(24)   I also enjoy sports—particularly swimming,
         skiing, racquetball, and volleyball.

WI(25)   I love riding—that sport is by far the most
         fun for me.

WI(40)   We liked to do the same sorts of
         things . . . we both rode horses, so we rode
         together every day after school.

WI(41)   In college I got to be friends with another girl
         in my dorm who, again, seemed to have sim-
         ilar interests. Jennifer and I did a lot of par-
         tying together and a lot of sports activities.

WI(50)   I want to be in an area where I could own a
         horse again.

WI(52)   Football games, plays, ACC basketball
         games (also sound fun at this time).

DISCONFIRMING DATA

SCI   Basic interest scales: Athletics—50 = av-
        erage.

Conclusion

The process of compiling information about myself was not enjoyable. As a result of the process, however, I have discovered data which provide insights into why the exercise was so difficult. Some of the reasons for my frustration may be found in the following themes:

1. I enjoy change and a fast pace.

   I was very impatient with the written interview because it took so long to write.
2. I have very few friends and confide in few people.

   I had a great deal of difficulty "opening up."
3. I enjoy "getting organized" and work better when I am organized.

With my Rorschach, big picture outlook, I had difficulty envisioning how all the instruments could be consolidated and organized into a useful tool.

I am not satisfied that I have organized the notebook to the best of my ability, or written the assessment to the best of my ability. Time constraints frustrated my efforts at more thorough organization.

Although I have noted only 18 themes, I feel that each is a strong and independent statement about my values. Some may find conflict in the themes:

> "I enjoy being with people."
> "I prefer a team-oriented environment."
>
> vs.
>
> "I have few close friends . . . "
> "Independence is important to me."

However, a team-oriented environment is not necessarily an environment in which one must work together with others. Further, being with people and being very close to people are not necessarily inconsistent themes.

None of the preceding themes contradicts my image of myself. That is not to say that I recognized all of the values in myself before I began the self-assessment process. The dyad exercise was an invaluable exercise in which several aspects of my values were brought to light:

> Theme 5—"I do not enjoy taking orders or working with strong authority figures." The support for this was more emotional and more harsh than I would have anticipated.
>
> Theme 8—"The people I like best are smart and strive to better themselves." This is phrased as a positive theme; however, there is more evidence than I would have imagined which indicated that I actually *dislike* individuals who do not measure up to certain standards.

Finally, I would like to recognize the lack of disconfirming data in several of my themes. It may very well have been an oversight on my part; however, potential themes which were weakened by substantial disconfirming data were eliminated. I attribute the lack of disconfirming data to the selection process.

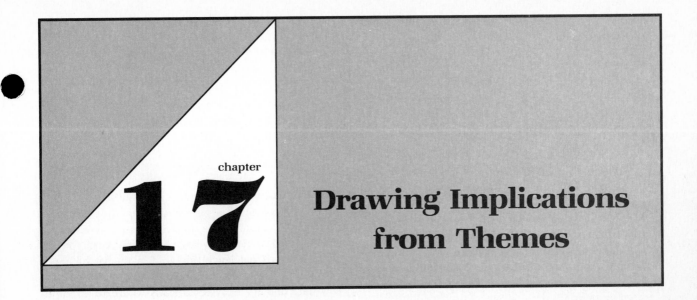

The final step in the self-assessment process involves identifying the career and job implications inherent in a set of themes. The ultimate purpose here is to translate the basic assessment into a more useful form.

It is often possible to identify some job and career implications directly from each theme. If the theme is "short attention span," then one might reasonably conclude that "a job requiring concentrated attention on one task for long periods might prove unpleasant." One could approach this final step in the self-assessment process in just this manner—by taking each theme, one at a time, and looking for what it implies regarding job or career.

Having done that, you should then look for overlaps or connections between and among themes that confirm your preliminary list of implications or add to it.

Procedure

First, group together all the themes that overlap or are strongly related. For example, suppose one had three themes that related to one's way of thinking and approaching problems and tasks: "doesn't like detail," "very systematic," and "future-oriented." These themes would be grouped together. So would the two themes "needs to be number 1" and "needs people contact," which speak to what one wants from life. And so should the three themes "dislikes crowded living," "nature very important," and "strong affiliation with family (who live in Oregon)," which all relate to life style preferences.

Some themes, of course, because they overlap a

Exhibit 17–1
Typical First Grouping of Themes

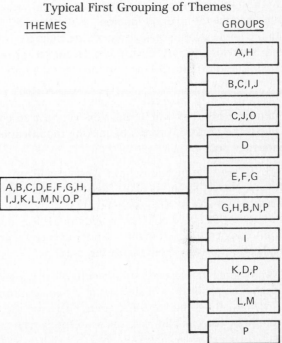

number of other themes in a number of different ways, will end up in more than one grouping. Some themes may not fit into any groups—they seem to be quite independent of the others. The overall grouping shown in Exhibit 17–1 is a sample of the typical kind of result of this process.

You can translate each grouping into an initial set of implications by writing a phrase, sentence, or sentences that seem to capture what is being expressed in the themes. For example:

Drawing Implications from Themes **159**

Themes	Implication
1. Likes immediate feedback. 2. Prefers planning ahead. 3. Pragmatic. 4. Has disciplined responses to uncertainty.	This person should seek work that rewards systematic approaches to practical problems and that does not require initiative or creative responses to a lot of uncertainty.

Guidelines

Some people find the process of grouping themes together and identifying their implications difficult. Here is a step-by-step method that may help such people:

1. Generate an initial set of implications, even if the process seems awkward and uncomfortable.

2. Evaluate your results in light of three criteria: (a) Do the implications overlap to a minimum and yet take into account the overlap inherent in the themes? (b) Do the implications speak about all the characteristics and behavior that are obviously relevant to job and career questions? (c) Do the implications take into account all the information in the themes? If your implications satisfy these criteria, your task is over. More often than not they won't, and you will have to continue in an iterative process of making modifications until they do.

3. If your implications have ignored a theme or themes, correcting this is easy. Take the theme and see if it fits into any of the groupings. If it does, change the implication based on this new addition. If it doesn't fit into any existing grouping, identify and add a new implication directly from the theme itself.

4. If some implications still seem to overlap significantly, the problem probably lies in a poor grouping of themes. By going back and trying different theme groupings, you can eliminate the problem by trial and error.

5. If the implications don't seem to speak to some career and job issues, clearly identify what those issues are and then go back to see if any of the themes speak to them. If you can find one or more relevant themes, group them together and add a new implication.

To aid in assessing whether an initial set of implications speaks to all the basic job and career issues, we have found questions of the following type to be useful:

1. Does this set of implications tell us anything about what types of people (if any) this person likes to be with and work with?

2. Does it say how he or she likes to relate to people?

3. Does it tell us what types of tasks this person prefers to work on?

4. Does it suggest what types of intrinsic and extrinsic rewards he or she prefers?

5. Does it say what types of environments this person strongly likes or dislikes?

Sometimes you will identify an issue that an initial set of implications does not address, and upon checking find that none of the themes addresses it either. If the themes have been developed properly, then you can do nothing except leave this void in the set of implications. It is very important that you not go back to raw data and try unsystematically to create an implication to fill some void.

Finalizing a Set of Implications

One final task should be completed before you stop working on your implications. Insofar as possible, you want to try to differentiate the implications in terms of importance. In a typical self-assessment, some implications are more important than others. The more clearly this is specified, the more the assessment will help you to choose among different "good" job and career options.

To differentiate implication statements by importance, you need only work backward to trace the information each is based on. For example, an implication statement derived from three themes, each based on 15 data from five different data-generating devices, probably is speaking to a more central and important issue than one derived from a single theme based on 8 data from three devices. Your own judgment is crucial here, of course, and it cannot be replaced by mechanical rules.

The best test of whether you are finished writing your self-assessment, or whether it still needs some work, is your own opinion of it. If you feel that your set of implications is sound, accurate, and useful—then your task is done. If you don't feel that way, you need to keep working until you do. *You are the one who will have to use your self-assessment, and if you don't believe it, you won't use it.* We have found that when people really believe in their self-assessment, not only do they use it, but their belief heightens their energy and motivation to overcome job and career obstacles that frustrate and stop many others. Accurate self-knowledge in which one has confidence can be a tremendous source of power for an individual.

Compare the implications Lauren Davis wrote with her list of life themes (see case, pp. 150–58). How well do her implications reflect her themes? Are there other implications you believe she should have included? How would you arrange her implications?

LAUREN DAVIS: THEMES AND IMPLICATIONS

Lauren Davis: Theme List

I am approaching an important turning point. The decisions I make in choosing a profession, a job, a company, and a location will have an enormous impact on the direction of my life. This is an exciting time and a frightening time. What if I make a terrible mistake?

The themes that follow are not all-encompassing; however, they do represent many of my values. By compiling these themes, I hope to develop a better picture of myself and sort through the potential consequences of my future choices.

I have divided my themes into four groups, according to their order and magnitude of importance in my life:

Most Important

1. I work best with positive reinforcement and support.
2. I enjoy being with people.
3. I enjoy change and a fast pace.

Very Important

4. I am happiest when I am challenged/growing in a job.
5. I do not enjoy taking orders or working for strong authority figures.
6. I learn best by direct experience/involvement.
7. I have very few close friends and confide in few people.
8. The people I like best are smart and strive to better themselves.

Important

9. Material comforts are important to me.
10. Independence is important to me.
11. I prefer a team oriented environment.
12. Status and prestige are important to me.

Somewhat Important

13. Owning a horse, riding and showing are important to me.
14. I enjoy getting organized and work better when I am organized.
15. I place a high value on reliability and honesty.
16. I enjoy teaching and persuading others.
17. I am competitive and like to win.
18. I enjoy athletics.

Lauren Davis: Theme Implications

Professional

COGNITIVE:

1. I need to wrap my arms around a project and totally immerse myself rather than reflect or conceptualize (T6, T14).

INTERPERSONAL:

2. I will enjoy a job which requires interaction with other individuals and which requires a strong "team" orientation (T2, T5, T11, T16).
3. The peers with whom I would like to work will have a high degree of commitment and a strong desire to produce superior ouput (T8, T150).

This case was prepared by Kevin E. Sachs, MBA 1982, under the direction of Associate Professor James G. Clawson as a basis of class discussion. © 1982 by the Sponsors of the Colgate Darden Graduate School of Business Administration, the University of Virginia, Charlottesville, Virginia. UVA case OB-212.

ENVIRONMENT:

4. I would not enjoy working in a cluttered or messy setting, or in an office with poorly organized files and research data (T14, T15).

ROUTINES:

5. I will enjoy a job which requires (on a regular basis) no more than 50 hours per week (T2, T3, T13, T18).
6. I would like to spend a maximum of one hour (total) commuting to work each day (T9, T13, T18).

ORGANIZATIONAL STYLE:

7. I will enjoy a position in which frequent feedback is possible (T1).
8. I prefer to work in positions which do not require close supervision (T5, T6, T10).
9. I want to work in an organization which rewards excellence in a timely manner, by increasing my level of responsibility (T3, T4, T17).
10. Recognition by my peers and supervisor that my job, opinions and efforts are valuable to the organization is important to me (T1, T12, T17).

TASKS:

11. I prefer to work on projects which are short term in nature (T1, T3).
12. I will be happiest in a job in which I will be given immediate responsibility (T6, T10, T14).
13. I would enjoy a moderate amount of traveling to visit and work with clients (T2, T3).
14. I would enjoy a position which involved selling or persuading a client or a fellow employee (T1, T16, T17).

Social

15. I want to live in a community in which there is a sizable young professional population (T2, T8).

Physical

16. I would like to live in a city which offers recreational facilities such as racquetball courts, golf courses, and water sports (either lakes or the ocean) (T3, T18).
17. I would like to have enough land to stable a horse or live very close to a stable in the country (T9, T13).

Material

18. I would like to earn a starting salary of at least $30,000 (T9, T17).

Family

19. Bill's support in a new environment will be very important, since he is primary in my support system (T1, T7).

Emotional

SATISFACTION/SELF-ESTEEM:

20. I do not want a job that appears to be a step backward (T4, T12).
21. I am averse to high-risk situations. I do not take failure well (T1, T12, T16, T17).

VARIETY:

22. I would like to live close to a university so that I may have the flexibility to return to school when Bill and I begin to raise a family (T3, T4, T10).

The Career Development Process

Over the past 30 years a fairly large number of people have studied various aspects of career development. One recent review of this literature references well over 500 books and articles.[1] Because many of these writers approached the subject with very different backgrounds and for very different purposes, the literature tends to be split into a number of camps, with little cross-referencing or building. Although there have been several attempts to synthesize these divergent approaches, as yet there is no one generally accepted theory of career development. The different camps may be characterized as having a sociological or a psychological perspective.

Perspectives

The Sociological Approach

The sociological approach tends to look at society as a structure consisting of various occupations. Careers are viewed as movement from one occupational level to another within a structure stratified by status and by the occupational role expectations of a person in a given status. The occupational level achieved in career development is seen as the result of a social process. Membership in a social class (indicated normally by father's occupation status) and socialization—the process by which individuals are trained, their expectations developed, and their values internalized—are seen as the prime determinants of occupational level. In addition, environmental factors (such as personal contacts, available financial backing, and

socioeconomic conditions in society) are also relevant. Any one of these factors may be given major importance as an independent or explanatory variable, depending on the interests of the researcher in question.

The Psychological Approach

The psychological perspective is taken by those who support an individual theory of career development. Some take an intrapsychic approach, seeing unconscious forces as influencing conscious decision making. The shape of these unconscious needs or drives is often postulated to stem from early childhood experiences. Satisfying them then becomes a major determinant in job choice. Others take a rational decision-making approach to career development. Individuals are seen as testing themselves through interaction with their environment, weighing the factors and alternatives, then making conscious career choices. According to some scholars, this all occurs in a developmental process consisting of various stages through which the individual passes.

Scholars in this camp disagree particularly with respect to the relative importance of different variables. Some claim that environmental factors are most important in career development; others make the same claim for intrapsychic factors. Some believe that most career job decisions are made consciously by individuals; others feel they are made unconsciously. Some believe that a person's experiences during the first few years of life are central to career development; others do not. And so on.

For our purposes, these disagreements need not distract us. The basic points on which most of the experts agree are strong enough to provide us with a solid base from which to proceed.

---

[1]S. H. Osipow, *Theories of Career Development* (New York: Appleton-Century-Crofts, 1973).

163

What Is a Career?

The first issue is that of career itself. The term originally referred to the speed with which a defined course was traversed by a wagon or contestant. Two interesting features of this older usage that remain today are those of speed and of defined course. We often think of a *career* as a defined course and of the success of an individual in that career as measured by whether or not the person completed the course (reached the top) and how quickly. But this view is unnecessarily limiting. Consider a broader view.

Scope: Individual, Organizational, Occupational

A person's career lies, in scope, somewhere between life style and job. A life style encompasses all aspects of a person's life. A job is a specific set of interrelated tasks in a particular context. A career may affect most or even all aspects of a person's life, but it is not all of it. Rather, a career is that part of a person's life that pertains to the work they do to sustain their lives physically and psychologically. By *work* we mean that which people do in exchange for the tangible or intangible things that sustain them. A career also consists of more than a job; it is a *series* of jobs that are related in some way.

The means we use to relate that series of jobs determines how we use the term career. We might use individual, job content, or organizational boundaries to relate a series of jobs to one another.

If we use the individual, then we may say that *everyone* has a career. We may or may not be paid for the work we do, but we all do things that are intended to sustain our lives. Homemakers bear and raise children and manage households. In return, they receive things that sustain their lives—food and shelter at a minimum, and optimally, love, support, companionship, and fulfillment. Volunteer workers receive the satisfaction of contributing to society, although volunteer workers must also have some other means of support. For some, this is work; for others, it is heritage. In the latter case, where family wealth provides the support, a person's career may be almost totally in volunteer work. The *individual career* is the most comprehensive view of the term in the sense that it can incorporate the other careers we are about to mention.

Sometimes we say that so-and-so had a fine career at XYZ company. In this instance, we are using organizational boundaries to define a career. The jobs one has in an *organizational career* vary in terms of their content rather than their affiliation. A manager may be promoted or given a new assignment. A wife may have another child, or the family (the organiza-

tion) may move to another location. These examples all represent changes in job content, but not in the career within the organization.

We might have said that so-and-so is pursuing a career in accounting. We then use job content to talk about *occupational careers*. Occupational careers are career courses defined by a particular set of related tasks for which one is compensated. The courses have relatively well-defined career paths. An occupational career in commercial banking, for instance, typically consists of some education in finance and a series of jobs/titles, including financial analyst/credit officer, account responsibilities (assistant vice president), industry responsibilities (vice president), regional responsibilities (senior vice president), and bank responsibilities (president).

Organizations can offer at least a job and at most a career that is both organizational and occupational in nature (in the case of the person who dies while working in the same company in the same occupational area he or she began in). Usually companies offer an organizational career with a varied occupational content or a segment of an occupational career.

Perspective: Internal or External

We also can take either an external or an internal perspective to each of the careers we have discussed.[2] By *external* we mean the observable characteristics of a person's career—the salary, the title, the tasks assigned, the power wielded, the speed of promotion, and so on. When we observe a person's career progress and remark, "That person's going nowhere," we are using the ancient imagery to comment on the person's external career. The internal perspective refers to a person's subjective experiencing of the traversing of the career course. This internal view is distinct from and not necessarily parallel to the external view. A person may, for example, have a "successful" external career by reaching the top (whatever that may be) in good time, but be very dissatisfied with the result. This evaluation grows from a comparison of career-related results with internally held values, beliefs, and aspirations.

For a long time, many employers and researchers ignored the significance of the internal view of the career. You can no doubt see the importance of taking personal reactions to external careers into account in understanding careers. The external measures of our careers occur against the backdrop of our internal experiencing of those measures, and it is the expectations, the hopes, the desires, and the values of the latter

---

[2]See Douglas T. Hall, *Careers in Organizations* (Pacific Palisades, CA: Goodyear, 1976).

that determine in large part the sense of "integration"[3] and satisfaction we experience with the former.

Recently a number of books have been written which recognize this important distinction between the external and the internal career. Their titles are self-explanatory: *Career Success/Personal Failure,* by Abraham Korman (Prentice-Hall, 1980); *Must Success Cost So Much,* by Paul Evans and Fernando Bartolome (Basic, 1981); *The Failure of Success,* edited by Alfred J. Marrow (AMACOM, 1972); *Tradeoffs,* by Barry Greiff and Preston K. Munter (New American Library, 1980); *Work, Family and the Career,* edited by Brooklyn Derr (Praeger Special Studies, 1980); and *Balancing Jobs and Family Life* by Haleyon Bohen and Anamaria Viveros-Long (Temple University Press, 1981). Taken together, these books are saying that it is not fruitful for individuals *or* organizations to think about career management from an external view only. Rather, to avoid potentially high personal and organizational costs, we must look at career management and development from both the external *and* the internal perspectives and understand better the dynamics between the two. Our lives are not so well compartmentalized as we might hope. The activities and events of one sphere will surely affect the other, and we should understand how.

A Conceptual Overview

So far, we have said that:

1. A career is the series of related jobs that a person does to sustain his or her life physically and psychologically.
2. Jobs may be related on at least three different dimensions—the individual, the organization, and the job content.
3. Careers have both an external (or objective) and an internal (or subjective) set of characteristics. Both need to be considered carefully.

Exhibit 18–1 summarizes this conceptual view of careers. It also raises the question of time and how a career changes or "develops" over time.

Career Development

The phrase "career development" is one that has been used extensively and with a wide variety of meanings. Most of the usages of "develop" have to do with growth or progress, and yet there are many situations

---

[3]See Erik Erikson, *Childhood and Society* (New York: Norton, 1950), p. 268.

Exhibit 18–1
The Career

Individual Career
The set and sequence of jobs that sustain life both physically and psychologically. May consist of occupational (related by job content) and/or organizational (related by organization) career segments.

External Characteristics	Internal Characteristics
Title	Self-concept
Salary	Goals
Perquisites	Hopes
Prestige, status	Aspirations
Power	Values
Frequency of changes	Feelings
Location	Satisfaction
Travel	Patience
Influence	Anger
Number of subordinates	Disappointment
Career path traversed	

and cases in which the unfolding of a person's individual career can hardly be described as a progression or growth. We prefer instead the photographic connotation of *develop*—"to render visible"—because it reflects the importance of the internal as well as the external perspective on the career, and it carries with it the notion of a picture gradually taking shape. *Career development* consists of the gradual disclosure of the activities that internally and externally sustain an individual through life. This phrasing permits us to talk about the various careers in a variety of terms—not just progressive ones. We can discuss people who failed in their occupational or organizational careers but are happy in their individual careers, as well as people who succeeded in occupational careers but "failed" in individual careers.

Time is central to the idea of career development. And when one thinks of the passage of time, one wonders about marking its passage and the changes that occur within it in some way. Several researchers have tried to characterize stages through which most people's careers pass. Super[4] and Dalton, Thompson, and Price[5] outlined the two most commonly accepted ones—about which we shall say more later. For the time being, suffice it to say that time is a key dimen-

---

[4]Super, D., J. Crites, R. Hummd, H. Moser, P. Overstreet, and C. Warnath, *Vocational Development: A Framework for Research* (New York: Teachers College Press, 1957).

[5]Dalton, J., P. Thompson, and R. Price, "The Four Stages of Professional Careers," *Organization Dynamics*, Summer 1977.

sion in the consideration of the career development process.

We can add to time a number of other dimensions and begin to sketch out the *shape* of careers over time. Status, income, and learning rate are the most common dimensions used to develop these shapes. Consider the career shapes shown in Exhibit 18–2, which can be generated by using time and status as the defining dimensions. The first four represent common career patterns identified by Professor Michael Driver at USC. These patterns are linear, steady-state, spiral, and transitory, respectively.

The linear pattern reflects the drive of an individual to reach the top of an organization or occupation. The steady-state shape reflects careers that show little change over long periods of time. Many professional occupations fit this pattern. The spiral pattern characterizes the careers of people who for a number of reasons leave an occupational or organizational career every five to ten years to pursue something new. A desire for variety or new learning is often the motivation. Exhibit 18–2D shows the transitory pattern, in which people move from job to job relatively quickly and with no apparent long-term objective in mind.

To these four patterns, we have added two. First, in 2E, is a "plateaued" career; second, in 2F, is a de-clining career. Both are common in occupational and organizational careers.

The notion of a person's career gradually taking shape over time makes us wonder about the factors that affect shape.

Factors That Shape Career Development

The shape a person's career takes over time is a function of several things. Let us consider these factors within the context of the job and career opportunities provided by organizations. Although we will not treat careers that are created by individuals outside organizations, there are many parallels to the organizational context.

When an individual accepts a position in an organization, there are costs and benefits to both parties. Simply put, the individual gives up time and talent and receives compensation and a job focus. The organization gives up financial resources and gains talent and time. In this arrangement, there is an explicit or implicit attempt to match costs and benefits. In reality, these costs and benefits change in various ways over time, and both parties attempt to manage the fit continuously. When changes occur, decisions are made.

Exhibit 18–2
External Career Shapes

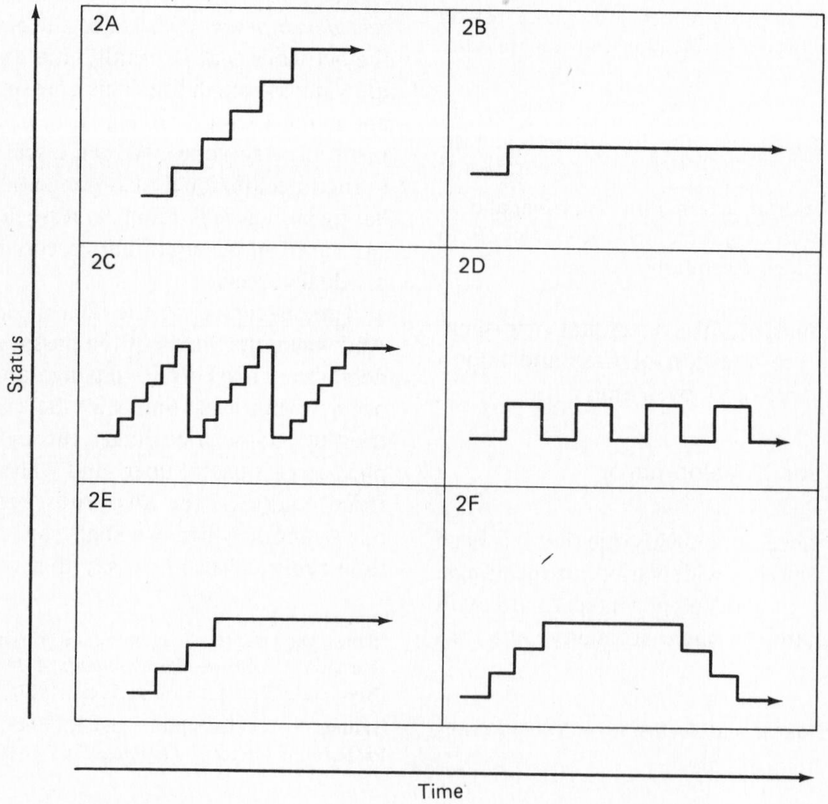

Status

Time

Both parties assess the alternatives and choose one. Thus, the career-related decisions for both sides have a direct impact on the shape of the career development of the individual. The factors that affect the career-related decisions on both sides have an indirect influence on the shape of career development.

A simplified view of this is presented in Exhibit 18–3. The self-assessment process was intended to give you a more accurate picture of your perceptions of yourself. The career development process we are about to consider is intended to help you learn a process so that you can get a more useful picture of the organization, can give the organization a more accurate picture of you, can understand more clearly how the organization sees itself, and can help both the organization and you make more productive decisions.

The Career Development Process

The first step in the individual's side of the career development process is to develop a focus. There are simply too many alternatives in society to examine them all. Next, you must begin to generate options (step 2). This will require that you make contact with organizations in your target focus, and then generate information that both you and the organization can use to assess the fit between you and organization. This assessment will generate career-related decisions based on the criteria both you and the organization deem important. Your experience with those decisions then becomes additional data for your ongoing self-assessment. This process (step 3) continues throughout life, and is summarized in Exhibit 18–4. It is important to note that you have as much responsibility for the accuracy of the decisions as the firm does. Every organization is not right for you. Although many people think of the job search as an exercise in selling, in fact it is also an exercise in buying.

The remainder of this book is organized roughly as follows in Exhibit 18–4. First, we will consider the job search process. The examples we use will relate specifically to people searching for jobs directly out of school, but the process is equally applicable to people about to make job or career transitions. We will help you consider the importance of developing a job search focus using your implications (step 4). Then we will consider ways of getting information about the vast array of opportunities in society (step 5). Having established a focus to your job search, you will then consider how to seek out and generate options that fit your focus. Once you have some options, you will need to assess them and choose one (step 6). We will provide some ways of thinking about and doing that. When you have accepted an offer, your transition to your new job or career will be much more effective and efficient if you manage the joining up process (step 7).

Exhibit 18–3
Factors That Shape Career Development

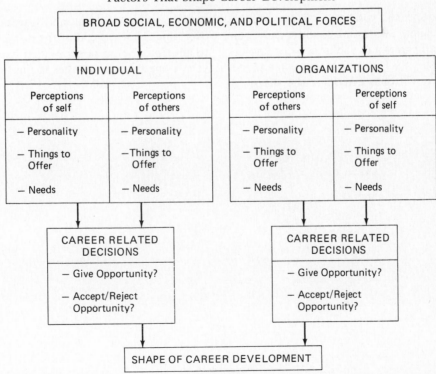

Exhibit 18–4
The Self-Assessment and Career Development Process

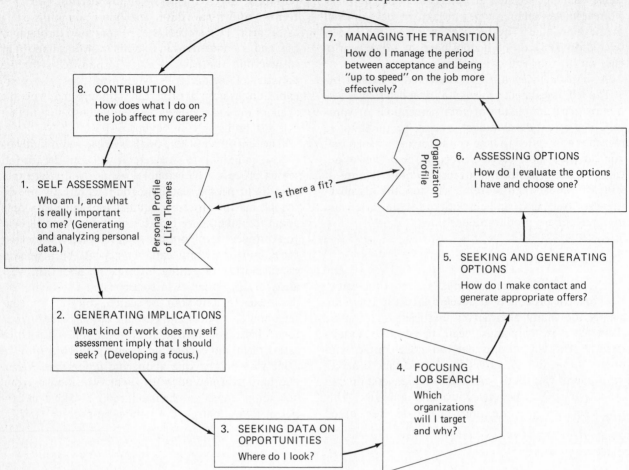

Then, being up to speed in your new job, you will be starting the cycle again, reassessing continuously your fit with the job and career and adding to your knowledge of yourself (step 8). The choices that you and the organization make will then determine the shape of your career development and your satisfaction with it over time. Near the end of the book, we will help you to anticipate some career-related issues that will face you in one form or another in the future.

19

Some Hard Facts about MBA Job Searches

After almost two years of graduate school, John Wainwright was about to receive his MBA from a leading business school. But he was not particularly happy, nor was he looking forward to graduation. John didn't have a job.

Although this situation may seem unusual, every year many MBA graduates discover that their degree does not automatically guarantee them a job. They graduate without an acceptable offer.

General economic conditions certainly contribute to situations like John's, but we find that many job hunters do not plan for the time it takes to conduct an effective and successful job search. Some MBA candidates rely heavily on others, such as the placement office, to conduct the search for them; others merely go through the job search motions, finding false security in published statistics about the placement percentage for graduating classes. Still others, like John, continually postpone the search until, sadly, they are faced with a difficult and trying set of circumstances. Perhaps a little more information about John and his situation will help to illustrate this problem.

John completed his first year of business school without a great amount of difficulty. He was more interested in marketing and consulting courses and, as a result, signed up for several classes in those areas for his second year. While he liked his classes, John was still not sure what he wanted to do. As Christmas approached, conversations with classmates turned more and more toward jobs. Some classmates knew exactly what they wanted, while others were still thinking about different possibilities. John was not particularly worried; others seemed to be in the same stage as he was, and there was still plenty of time before graduation in May. Besides, his attention was better directed toward classes, papers, and finals. After the semester was over, he decided to relax and enjoy vacation. January was soon enough to start his job search.

Interview sign-ups began shortly after vacation ended in January. John felt awkward signing up for interviews because he still didn't know what he wanted to do. Everyone else in the class was securing interview slots, so John decided to sign up for several interviews too. Surely, he thought, at least one of the interviews would work out. Class work at this point was taking most of his time, so he picked firms that were well-known, seemed to be popular with his classmates, and offered above-average salaries. None of the interviews went particularly well, and by the time John realized that he would not get any second interviews, recruiters had stopped coming to the school.

John began to set up appointments with faculty members, hoping that a few words of advice would solve his problem. When that failed, John began to write letters furiously. Much to his dismay, most companies never replied, and those that did were not offering interviews. John's worst fears had come true. He graduated without a job.

What disturbs us most about John and the others that we have observed in his situation is not that they don't have jobs, but that the majority of their problems were unnecessary. Job searching is a personally demanding and time-consuming process. We believe that many of the problems facing MBA job hunters can be foreseen and managed with effective planning.

In order to gather data that might assist MBA candidates in planning their job search, we distributed a questionnaire in the spring of 1981 to the graduating class of the Harvard Business School and to a portion of the graduating class at the Colgate Darden Graduate School of Business, University of Virginia. Approximately 50 percent of the graduating class at Harvard completed and returned the survey. The results therefore reflect the experience of a large portion of the class. The Darden survey was completed by about 30 students who took an elective course on career development in the fall of their second year. We recognize that the results of the surveys may or may not be representative of the MBA community as a whole. Our hope is that the information provides some insights into MBAs and their job searches that you will find useful in planning your own job search.

Key Characteristics of Job Searching

Time

Most MBA candidates encounter difficulties at some time during their job search directly due to lack of time. As we mentioned earlier, job hunting will demand a substantial portion of your time during the second year. The average MBA student in both surveys reported spending 150 to 175 hours on job search activities between September and April of the second year. A few students reported spending no time on job hunting, while others spent as much as 600 hours in job search activities.

Most students spend over 65 percent of this time during a three-month peak period from January to March. During this peak period, the average respondent devoted 10 hours per week to job hunting; this is the equivalent of two full-time courses. Some MBAs even reported spending up to 40 hours per week in March on job search activities. Exhibit 19–1 shows the average hours spent on job search activities by the Harvard respondents. In our experience, most MBAs who fail to plan adequately for this substantial time commitment encounter a variety of problems in their job search.

Career Choice

John Wainwright's uncertainty about the type of career he wanted was not particularly unusual. In fact, most MBAs begin their second year with an unclear idea of what they want to do. Both the Harvard and Darden respondents to the survey reported that in September they were highly uncertain in matters concerning career choice. The average MBA, however, becomes more and more certain as the months progress. This increasing confidence is illustrated in Exhibit 19–2.

In the Harvard survey, only 30 percent of the respondents reported feeling "very certain" of what they wanted to do when school started in September. Twenty-seven percent reported that they were very uncertain. By January, 48 percent felt certain and only 13 percent felt uncertain. By April, 82 percent felt certain that they knew what they wanted to do, while only

Exhibit 19–1
Hours Spent on Job Search Activities
(Harvard Survey)

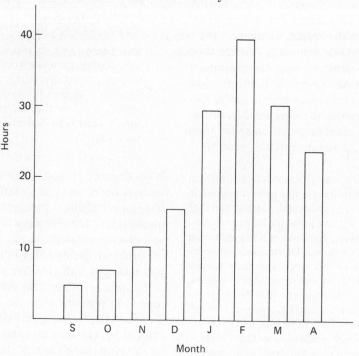

Exhibit 19–2
Student Confidence in What They Want to Do

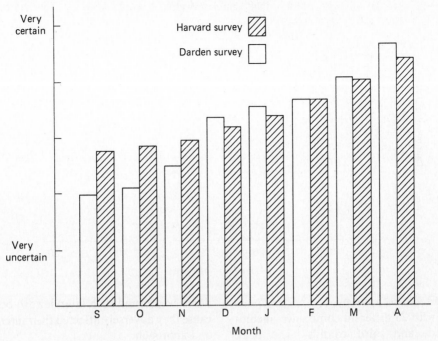

9 percent still felt very uncertain. In our experience in working with MBA students over the years, those students who begin to sort out career choices early in the second year tend to have more productive and satisfying job searches.

Source of Contact

If you are like most MBA candidates, you will rely heavily on the school placement office to identify and contact your future employer. As measured by the sources of contact for accepted job offers, over 43 percent of the Harvard graduates surveyed found employment through the placement office. This was over twice as many as any other source of contact. Summer job experiences and personal contacts accounted for 17 and 15 percent, respectively.

The high percentage of contact made through the placement office is due in part, we feel, to the effectiveness of placement office activities. We also sense, however, that MBAs are increasingly passive in conducting their job searches. John Wainwright, for example, was depending on some unknown factor reflected in placement statistics to conduct much of his job search for him.

Advice

Another indication of the increasing trend toward passivity is illustrated by the ways and stages at which MBAs seek advice. The average respondent talked to 7 people about his or her job choice. A substantial number, 35 percent in the Harvard survey, reported not consulting with *anyone* about their job search. Like John, most MBAs do not seek advice during November, December, and January. During the early stages of the job search, our observations are that MBAs tend to rely on the placement office and to follow the crowd in signing up for interviews.

Many MBAs begin to ask for counsel late in the job hunting process. Most students talk to people about their job search only after they have received some firm offers. Students seem to hope that advisors will somehow guide them toward the "right" offer. The students who do not receive offers often seek advice, hoping that someone else can solve the problem.

Interviews

As John's experience illustrated, having interviews does not necessarily result in having a job. While one must, almost always, have interviews to get a job, there does not appear to be any correlation between the number of interviews and the number of offers. In fact, in our experience, those students with the greatest number of interviews often are below average in the number of offers. Those students with the greatest number of offers often are those who had an average or even slightly below average number of interviews. As illustrated in Exhibit 19–3, there was no correlation between interviews and the number of offers in those surveyed at the Darden School.

Exhibit 19–3
Interviews vs. Offers
(Darden Survey)

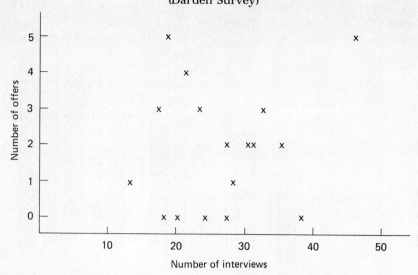

The average MBA in both surveys had about 25 different interviews with 23 different companies, including first, second, and third rounds. The peak interviewing period was between January and March (see Exhibit 19–4). Students have commented to us after the interviewing season that having several "tune-up" or practice interviews was not particularly beneficial, nor did they appear to increase the number of successful interviews as measured by offers. Some stu-

dents even found such interviews to be detrimental because they adversely affected their interviewing attitude and approach.

Offers

The statistics certainly *are* in John Wainwright's favor. Of those we surveyed, over 80 percent had received at least two offers and over 94 percent had

Exhibit 19–4
Average Interviews per Month
(Harvard Survey)

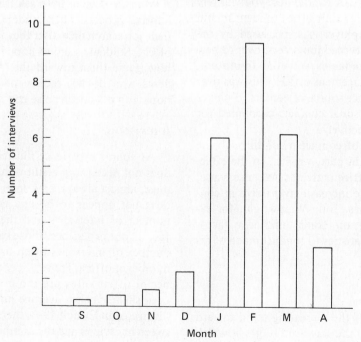

received at least one offer by the end of April. The average MBA in both surveys received between three and four offers as a result of his or her efforts. The statistics show that most MBAs do indeed get jobs.

The statistics also show, however, that some students do not get jobs. Twenty-one students in the Harvard survey reported having no firm offers at the time of the survey. In the Darden survey, four students reported having no firm offers by June. For those students, published aggregate statistics are little comfort.

Job Selection

MBAs we talk to have a fairly clear picture of the factors involved and the relative importance of each factor for their own personal job selection. In the questionnaire, we asked the students to rank 14 various factors in regard to job selection. The MBAs who responded in both surveys did not rank starting salary as particularly important. The most important factors listed by the students were colleagues and work setting, starting function, variety of job content, and geographical location. The least important factors were impact on society, travel demands, prestige of the organization, and starting salary. The ranking of the 14 factors in both surveys is shown in Exhibit 19–5.

Anxiety

Every year we see a new MBA class go through the trauma of looking for jobs. In every class there are some students who have few problems in finding a job.

Exhibit 19–5
Relevant Importance of 14 Factors
in Job Selection

Rank	Harvard Survey	Darden Survey
1	People/work setting	People/work setting
2	Starting function	Geographic location
3	Geographic location	Variety of job
4	Industry	Starting function
5	Nonfinancial prospects	Financial prospects
6	Variety of job	Nonfinancial prospects
7	Financial prospects	Travel demands
8	Independence	Independence
9	Boss/mentor	Industry
10	Starting salary	Spouse's career
11	Prestige of company	Starting salary
12	Travel Demands	Boss/mentor
13	Impact on society	Prestige of company
14	Spouse's career	Impact on society

Some students, like John Wainwright, have severe problems. Most students are somewhere in between. The majority of students that we know experience some type of anxiety during the recruiting process. Feeling some anxiety is natural; choosing a career is an important decision. A significant number of MBAs, however, experience a very high level of anxiety, and high levels of anxiety can interfere with the effectiveness of a job search and with the health of the job hunter. We believe the level of anxiety felt by MBA job hunters is correlated to the way in which students approach the job search process. Those students who plan for the demands and strains of a job search in an MBA setting tend to experience lower levels of anxiety.

The questionnaire we distributed asked students to rate their level of anxiety in recruiting on a month-by-month basis. A 5-point scale was used to measure anxiety, with a 5 being a very high level of anxiety. The average level of anxiety was low during the September to December period, as can be seen in Exhibit 19–6. Anxiety began to build in January and peaked in February and March. In February, 65 percent reported some anxiety; by March, only 30 percent reported a very high level of anxiety.

Summary

Although the outcome of John Wainwright's job search was not typical, we have found that some of the characteristics of John's search were. Many MBA students do not plan for the substantial commitment of time and energy an effective job search entails. Students especially do not plan for the extra 10 hours per week of work. Most MBAs begin their search without a clear picture of what they want to do. Yet despite this, they seek limited, if any, advice from others, especially during the early stages of their job search. Many approach the task passively, preferring to allow others, such as the placement office, to plan much of the job search for them.

Given this lack of a planned approach, it does not surprise us that so many MBAs feel anxiety during their job search. The highest level of anxiety we observed appears to be connected more with the search and the uncertainty of receiving an offer than with the selection of one offer. We believe that you can reduce the level of anxiety in your job search by planning for the extensive process involved in a job hunt. You can also make your experience more pleasant and successful by anticipating this anxiety and developing ways to deal with it. If MBAs planned for their search, perhaps the experience of John Wainwright would become even more unusual.

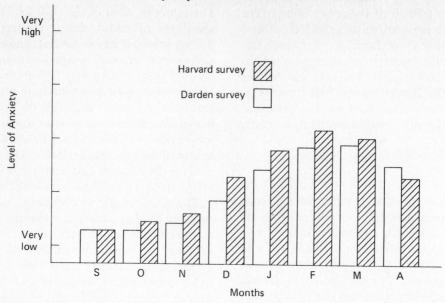

Exhibit 19–6
Level of Anxiety Experienced in Job Search Activities

Assignment

Job Hunting Diary

Because job hunting can be hectic and confusing, some people find that keeping a diary is very useful. Periodically reading back over the last week's or month's entries often helps one put things in their proper perspective and conduct the whole job hunting process more dispassionately.

You might wish to keep a diary yourself and write your entries in this section of the workbook. The following guidelines may be helpful to you:

1. Make entries as often as you can (preferably once a day).
2. When making an entry, ask yourself:
   a. What has happened today of importance with respect to job hunting?
   b. How has this changed my strategy and plans, if at all?
   c. How do I feel about today's events?

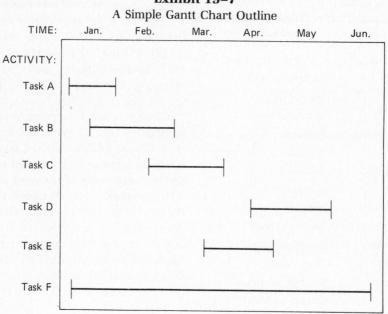

Exhibit 19–7
A Simple Gantt Chart Outline

But before you go on, take time to read Henry Rock's Job Search Diary and Life Themes (pp. 175–89). As you do, develop a Gantt chart of Henry's job search process. A Gantt chart is a chart of the time span covered by specific activities or tasks contained in a process or project. See Exhibit 19–7. This will help you to "see" more clearly the various tasks and lead times related to the job search. Note also the unexpected events Henry encountered. Note the things that Henry managed well and the things that Henry could have managed better in his job search. How, if at all, could Henry have managed his job search more effectively? Finally, note the emotional side of Henry's job search. What is the sequence of *feelings* Henry experienced? What does this tell you about the job search process?

HENRY ROCK: JOB SEARCH DIARY

October

We had our first placement office meeting in Burden. One of the things we spoke about was the writing of our résumés. The "career objective" was stressed as being very important and we were encouraged to be as specific as possible. Since my résumé was due in late October, I agonized over that portion of it for a week or so before realizing that I couldn't honestly be specific. So I put down "initial job in marketing or finance with general management as long-run objective." I hope this general statement isn't harmful.

November

Over Thanksgiving I wrote 11 letters to northern California firms that are either coming to campus this year or who had come in the past. My goal is to work in either San Francisco or Boston. Being a bachelor, I'd hate to be stuck in some dead place.

There was a lot of work involved in getting these letters off. I went through the preliminary lists of companies coming to the school and checked last year's job descriptions for job type and location. The card file (by region) also gave me some additional names. I also looked in *Summitt's* MBA employment guide and got two additional names.

December

The replies to my letters started coming in. By the end of the month I had received replies to 8 of my initial 11 letters. Three of those eight were companies who were signed up at HBS, and they thanked me for my letter and said they looked forward to seeing me when they came to campus. Of the other five, three had come in the past but were not signed up for this year. One said they would be doing no hiring this year. Another said to see them if I came to San Francisco. The third said they planned to sign up soon to interview at the school.

The remaining two letters were from companies who had never come to the B-school. One said they had no needs for someone with my qualifications. The second said to see them when I came to San Francisco. Later in the week, I even got a call from one company that was coming to interview in March.

Before Christmas break, we had to turn in our priority cards. This was easy for me, as I had already researched who was coming to campus. There were four San Francisco firms I was interested in and I assigned priorities to them. For the fifth, I chose a consultant in Los Angeles. I'm not really that interested in number 5, and it made me mildly nervous that I only had four potential interviews that really seemed desirable.

Toward the end of the month, letters from employers started coming in as the result of the résumé book being distributed. These unsolicited letters are really an ego trip. I am especially impressed by the personalized ones.

January 1–7

Received three more replies to my California letters. Two were from companies coming to HBS and were enthusiastic and thanked me in the typical way. The third was from an employer not signed up to interview. They said they couldn't match my qualifications to their needs.

Continued to get unsolicited letters. Also, on January 2, job descriptions began to be posted outside the placement office. I plan to make a daily trip to check the postings.

January 8–14

I continue to make the daily trek to the placement office boards. The office is constantly packed and it's difficult to get near the board. Everyone seems to be looking at each opportunity thoroughly.

January 16

Today I had a new career idea planted in my head. My financial accounting professor spoke of the public accounting profession and its virtues. I enjoy the issues in that class, so my eyes were opened when he said that MBAs often achieve the status of partner in 8–10 years at a salary of over $100,000. In addition, the profession allows initial flexibility in geographical location. I can interview for the San Francisco office with no problem. My interest is aroused!

January 17

I signed up to interview a Chicago firm for a financial position. I was attracted to them by the fact that they sent me a personalized letter and an impressive packet of information. They also have a reputation for paying well and are a growth company. I'm not sure that I could stand to work in Chicago, but I'd like to get an offer, especially one with a high salary, to use as leverage. It's also something to fall back on if all else fails. That seems to be the general psychology here at this time—get an offer as soon as possible. I was one of the last in my neighborhood to sign up for an interview.

January 20

I decided it would be wise to send more letters to West Coast employers, specifically those who aren't coming to school. I spent hours over at Baker Library going through *Moody's* and *Standard and Poor's*. I got a list of about 30 or 40 companies and chose to write to 10 of them based upon my interests and potential compatibility with them. By the time I had sent off these 10 letters, I had invested about 10 hours of research in them. (All were personalized, of course.) To date, I haven't been too concerned about researching Boston firms, as they are right here and can be contacted easily.

January 22

I went out to dinner with my girl friend to celebrate our one-year anniversary of dating. I was

sort of uptight because I had an incredible amount of work for the next day. As we went to say goodnight, she asked me where our relationship was going. She has been pressuring me lately with the end of school in sight, and it has been making me uneasy, especially since I'm uncertain about the relationship anyway. It was a bad time to ask me. I told her that I wasn't sure it was going anywhere and that we both should start to date other people. This completely blew her mind. She sat outside the apartment in her car and cried for 5 hours. I felt really bad, but also felt it was the right thing.

January 23

I signed up to speak with two of the San Francisco companies from my priority list who are coming next month. Also signed up to see a manufacturing company from New York. This is a hedge, also, against failure in San Francisco. However, like the Chicago company, they are an outstanding company and have good opportunities for MBAs. The New York company also seems fairly hot for me. They're taking me out to dinner on the 31st and have me interviewing on a closed list.

January 27

I've been trying to establish some communication with my girl friend. I didn't want to break things off altogether. She's been very hostile toward me, though. This surprises me, as I didn't think our discussion the other night was final. This hassle makes me less interested in staying in Boston. That had seemed to be a possibility before only because of her.

January 30

I had an appointment with my financial accounting professor to further investigate the possibility of working in that area. He turned me on even more and suggested three firms that he thought were the best. I discovered that one of them was interviewing on campus today. I ran home and threw on a suit and ran back, bringing my résumé to a walk-in interview at 4 o'clock. I had to B.S. my way through it, as I had done no research on the company. However, I think I was successful, and the interviewer promised to forward my résumé to the San Francisco office. I was relieved. That half-hour interview had seemed like two hours.

January 31

The dinner with the New York company was a bore. I didn't like the company representatives.

They were awkward and uptight and never seemed to know what to say. Several other HBS students were there and all seemed ill at ease as the result of their bumbling. The food was good, anyway.

February 1

Right after lunch I had my interview with the Chicago company. I had consumed a couple of beers during lunch and was half gassed when I walked into the interview. Luckily, I sat pretty far away from the interviewer so he couldn't smell my breath. The interview went pretty well. I had researched them a lot and asked some good questions. The interviewer seemed tense, though. I wonder if he knew I was gassed.

A couple of hours later I had my third interview of the year with the New York manufacturer. The interviewer, whom I hadn't met, seemed obnoxious and authoritarian. His group was similar to the group I had worked for last summer (although in a different company), so I told him I thought a lot of their work might be busy work and boring. He disagreed and we talked about it, but our interview went downhill. What a disastrous experience. I'll get rejected by them but won't care.

February 2

Signed up to see two more accounting firms and another San Francisco company that I had priority for. The placement office boards remain packed all the time.

February 3–4

Nothing.

February 5–7

Checked all the postings and correspondence opportunities. I read them all, just in case. I have a routine now where I stop by the office every day about the same time.

February 8

Spoke with my second accounting firm. Liked my interviewer a lot. He seemed much sharper than the other people I've spoken with. He promised to send my résumé to San Francisco, although he promised no results. Both accounting firms I've talked with have had about five or six students wanting their résumés sent to San Francisco. They willingly do this, as they are ostensibly national recruiters. However, they are usually partners of the Boston office and would like to attract Harvard people to their own office. So it's a touchy situation. One must tread lightly.

February 9

I have thoroughly researched the San Francisco firm I'm talking to February 12. They are my number one priority. However, they have only one spot available, and my chances of getting it are slim. Perhaps I can get an edge by being well prepared.

February 10–11

This breakup with my girl friend has been continually on my mind. It has affected me in class and in my interviews. It's very upsetting. I'm getting more interested in leaving the area every day.

February 12

After being absent when called on last week, I was well prepared for class today. Directly after my second class I had an interview with my number one priority company. Although my chances of getting the job were never good, I was still very disappointed by the interview. The interviewer was a recent HBS grad, and we just didn't get along. Furthermore, he was 15 minutes late for the interview, so I was annoyed from the beginning. This was definitely one of the best jobs in San Francisco, so it is very disappointing.

However, I felt better when I went home because I had received a letter from accounting firm #1 telling me I was into phase 2 with them. That gave me a lift.

Tomorrow I talk with priority #4 from San Francisco. I am nervous about these West Coast interviews, as I am now sure I want to go to that area.

February 13

I had my interview after my first class today. The interviewer was a young, personable fellow and I liked him. He was also a skillful interviewer. I think he was impressed with me, too, so the interview was a success. Hopefully, they will invite me on a plant trip. Spring break is coming up soon (about 3 weeks), so I mentioned this to the interviewer as a convenient time to visit. I hope they come through.

February 14

I had no interviews today. However, I received two responses to my San Francisco mailings. Most of the replies to these letters have been negative. However, out of the 15 letters I've sent to companies that have no plans to interview at HBS, I've received about one-third favorable responses. I think this is a good yield. I should mention that in the letters I said I'd be in the area soon and asked if they would be interested in seeing me. This removes the barrier of travel expenses. I would guess that this has increased the number of favorable responses. If I get a good job as a result, I think the $305 plane fare is a great investment.

I had a bit of excitement today. At my Creative Marketing Strategy meeting I found out that I will be taking a trip to California. Although this will be a busy trip, I may get an opportunity to call some firms that have responded to my letters.

February 15

Today I spoke with my Starting New Ventures professor about finding a job with a small company in the control area. He got all excited and told me about two jobs he knows of. His enthusiasm is infectious. Now I'm interested in these opportunities.

Right after my appointment I spoke with another New York manufacturing firm. The interviewer was about 32 and was the head of the group I'd be in. He was very aggressive and pushy and made me very tense. He was also an extreme elitist. I knew I wouldn't like working for him.

After that interview, I went to a Pacific Northwest meeting. Only 6–8 people attended, but all spoke of their past and present efforts to get jobs in the West. No one seemed unusually successful, but I did pick up one or two ideas.

February 16

Although this was one of our Fridays off, I had a 10 A.M. interview with the Chicago firm at the Fenway Cambridge. It was my second interview with them and was an hour long. The interviewer was a soft-spoken HBS grad from 1966, whom I liked. He asked a lot of tough questions, such as "What do you consider the biggest potential problem of fit between you and our company right now?" I was very honest in the interview but wondered afterward if I hadn't been somewhat emotional and inarticulate. I sensed that he either was very impressed or very turned off, but I couldn't judge which. I would like to get a job offer from them. They are an impressive company.

February 17–18

This weekend I decided to call up my old girl friend in California. We hadn't talked to each other in about a year but had a great conversation. That evening I went to a party and talked to

a friend who is also moving to San Francisco. She encouraged me to go, too. These conversations really bolstered my determination to go back.

February 19

Nothing.

February 20

Today I got two letters from San Francisco. One was a rejection from a correspondence opportunity. The other was a positive response resulting from my California letters of January 20. Apparently the chairman of the company I originally wrote forwarded my résumé to his management consultant. The consultant said he may have something for me. I became intrigued and went to Baker Library to look for information about the consultant. Found nothing.

I've felt more anxious lately about this job search, particularly with respect to San Francisco. I've heard nothing encouraging or discouraging from any of the people I've spoken with on campus, and it's been about three weeks since I had my first interview.

This nervousness made me decide to take a more aggressive tack. When I came home, I wrote two follow-up letters to companies I'd interviewed in the past week, and one letter to a San Francisco correspondence opportunity from three weeks ago. At the time I hadn't been that turned on about that opportunity, but now I'm beginning to worry about job offers there.

I'm also concerned about the San Francisco companies that haven't replied, because I hope to go to the area over spring break. I'm worried now that I might have to pay for that trip myself, as plant trip invitations are still uncertain. This is compounded by the fact that my research report is sending me to San Francisco and Los Angeles next Monday for a week. Perhaps I should just stay there, as spring break is only one week after I get back. But I'm anxious about missing two weeks of classes. I haven't spoken in any of them at all this term and can't afford to cut, too.

February 21

We had our CMS meeting at 6 P.M. One of the results of this meeting is that our California trip has been pushed back two days. I was really disappointed because I'd really been aiming for Monday. I can still go, though.

At home after the meeting, my day was made, however. I got a call from public accounting firm #2 inviting me out to San Francisco. Since this was my first firm trip offer, it really took a load off my mind. It was magnified an hour later when I got a call from my ex-girl friend in San Francisco who checked on my plans for spring break. She offered me the use of her car and apartment when I come out. That really made me feel good. I appreciate her friendship, especially in light of the recent hostilities between me and my local girl friend.

February 22

I had two interviews today, one with San Francisco priority #3 and one with public accounting firm #3 (first time for each). The first interview was disappointing. The interviewer and I just didn't hit it off and, besides, I found during the interview that the job involved living in Central or South America, and that turned me off.

The second interview was just the opposite. The interviewer and I really hit it off. He was a casual and interesting fellow. (He got his present job by impressing a partner of the Tokyo office during a conversation in a bar in the Philippines.) He appeared to like me, too, and said he'd send my résumé to San Francisco the next day, as I told him about my upcoming trip out West over spring break.

February 23

Today I called two companies in San Francisco and set up appointments for the spring break visit. Both of them were firms that had responded to my letters of November and January. It looks like I'll have about seven interviews when I go out.

At the placement office today the notice went up for my #2 San Francisco priority. It was a week and a half late. I was really glad to see it.

The placement office has been fairly dead. No notices have gone up, because spring break is three weeks away. I continue to drop by every day to check the correspondence opportunities, however.

I still haven't heard from any of the other companies I've interviewed, other than public accounting firm #2. I'm particularly anxious to hear from the Chicago company.

February 24

Some of my questions were answered today. I got two job rejections as the result of interviews, one from priority #1 in San Francisco and one from the second New York company. Neither was a surprise, although I am disappointed that the interview with the San Francisco firm didn't go well. The letter from the New York company was sort of funny because it was curt and uptight just like the interviewer had been (although it was written by a different person). I showed it to my roommates and they got a laugh out of it too.

However, I got a telegram inviting me to visit the Chicago company. This was exciting, as I've been quite interested in them. I was also unsure of my status with them. I'm very encouraged.

Later in the day I got a long distance call from San Francisco priority #2 firm talking about their upcoming visit. I was dismayed to discover that I will miss their visit to campus if I go to California next week for the research report. This, coupled with the need to find time for the Chicago trip, makes me now want to miss the research report trip.

February 25

Our research report team met and changed the California trip to spring break. Since I had a schedule conflict, two new team members were chosen. Strangely enough, I am happy not to be going. Since I'm going for sure over spring break, this trip would have only been a burden.

February 26

I set up a plant trip to Chicago for this Thursday (3 days away). This company is amazingly well prepared. There will be no need for me to send in an expense report, as they sent me a ticket and have arranged for a limousine to meet me at the airport.

At the placement office, a San Francisco company job description that I had been waiting for came in. I signed up for a position as a securities analyst, mainly because the job is in the city. I'm not sure I'm really interested in that type of work, though.

February 27

I called four of the S.F. companies I would like to see over spring break. Two accepted appointments. The conversation with one of them, public accounting firm #1, was disappointing. They were not willing to even split expenses and said they had only a few available positions at that time. In fact, the personnel director flatly told me that they looked toward Stanford for their new hires. However, it's still a visit. Of my other calls, one was lukewarm and said to call again when I got there, and another was enthusiastic and will talk to me more about it tomorrow.

February 28

Today was frantic as I continually tried to call Chicago to tell them what flight I was on. They had asked me to do this, as they were to arrange for a limousine to meet me. However, I couldn't get through, so I had to leave a message. Left the apartment in a rush for the airport. When I got into Chicago, the limousine was there and took me to my home. I was relieved to be there. I immediately called some friends in the area and talked for awhile. Then I stayed up until 1 A.M. reading the company material I'd only skimmed before.

March 1

Got awakened at 6 A.M. by a call from my girl friend in Boston. She wished me well on the interviews. I was glad to hear from her, although our relationship has been upsetting and confusing for the past month.

The same limousine picked me up at 8:30 and got me to the plant by 9:00. There I was met by the personnel man who had originally interviewed me at Harvard. He was extremely friendly and relaxed and seemed completely unlike the tense, businesslike man I'd spoken to at school. We chatted about various subjects and finally got around to discussing who I would talk to that day. It was at this point that I realized that I was being interviewed for a job in the treasurer's office. Until today, there had seemed to be a possibility of entering both the controller's office and marketing directly. Consequently, when he asked me if I had any questions before leaving for the first interview, I mentioned my surprise at being considered for this spot. As he had done at Harvard, the personnel man assured me that they were looking for generalists and not specialists and that this was only an entry point. This reassured me, as I'm not sure how much I would enjoy the type of work done in a treasurer's office.

During the day I spoke with the corporate treasurer, financial vice president, executive vice president, and a first-year employee who had gone to HBS. The talks were very informative, but more importantly, I liked the individuals that I spoke with personally. The style and atmosphere of the company appealed to me very much. The people are very competent, but there is still a casual approach to work. People there were friendly, and the tension level seem low. In addition, since the company is growing so quickly, there seem to be a lot of interesting projects and a lot of appealing positions to rise to.

At the end of the day, I spoke again with the personnel man. He gave me the official company line about getting in touch within two weeks and sooner if they weren't going to make an offer, but then told me that he had heard all good things from the people I'd spoken to. What a relief his final statement was! I left very turned on about the company.

That evening I went out with some old friends from the area. I realized that I was very tense because of the day's experience. I really like the company, but I have a hang-up about returning to Chicago. This conflict was made even worse by my friends' strong encouragement to return. I got sort of depressed thinking about it and got sort of a sick feeling that the potential jobs I will see in California will not match this opportunity.

March 2

My friend took me to the airport this morning. He talked to me again about the virtues of Chicago and how much they'd like to see me come there. I still feel tense about the whole thing.

When I got home there were three letters awaiting me. A shoot-down from New York firm #1 arrived. It was expected and overdue. The other two letters were from S.F. priority #4 and accounting firm #3. Both said they enjoyed the interviews and indicated I would hear from them soon. This is discouraging, as I had hoped both would offer to split expenses on a trip to San Francisco over spring break. I'll have to call them this week and try to rush the decision. This whole interview process goes much slower than I had expected.

March 3–4

I've noticed that I've been very uptight lately. I think it's mostly because of the job situation. I have no interest in doing school work and seem to be thinking either of jobs or dates. Any distraction seems to be enough to keep me from studying. I think this is another source of my tension. Classes are still demanding and I've been behind and haven't even participated in two of them. Although this semester's grades won't mean anything, there remains a certain amount of self-induced pressure to do well and get something out of the classes.

March 5

Today was a hectic day. I was running about constantly. At 7:30 P.M. I went to the meeting arranged by S.F. priority #2. It was to be a two hour lecture and question and answer period about the company. I was really turned off by it. The first hour was devoted to a technical demonstration of the products, complete with blackboard diagrams and technical terms. They certainly made it clear that they were looking for highly technical people. Furthermore, they surprised everyone by announcing that interviews would commence at 10 P.M. after the meeting ended, and would end at midnight. Interviews, all an hour long, would begin again at 7 A.M. the next morning and go until midnight again. Their attitude about interviews bothered me too, obviously.

In spite of this, I signed up for an appointment. Although I was turned off, I feel that I must make a strong effort at every San Francisco job. I don't want to leave any stone unturned.

March 6

Today I called S.F. priority #4 and asked them about seeing me in San Francisco and paying for part of the trip. Their recent letter said that they wouldn't be making decisions for a couple of weeks. The personnel man hesitated at first and didn't make any commitments over the phone, but called back ten minutes later with an invitation. I now have two sponsors for the big trip.

March 7

I called accounting firm #3 in San Francisco today to try to arrange for a spring break interview. I had called them twice before earlier in the week but had no response. Today they told me that the Oakland office would see me. This looks like the third paying customer. I think this is a reasonable portion for each firm to pay.

In the afternoon I had my interview with the San Francisco company that had put on the educational session the other night. True to character, the interview was conducted in a rush on the way to the airport. As we drove a rental car to the airport, the interviewer quizzed me. He was probing, and I must admit that I like him in sort of a perverse way. I took a cab back from the airport. When asked about my plans for spring break, I told the man that I would be in the Virgin Islands, because I was afraid he'd ask me to stop by if he knew I planned to be in the Bay area. I don't have time to talk to them, as I have filled all my days out there with other interviews. However, this problem may never arise, as I don't expect a plant trip invitation from them.

I'm getting excited about my trip tomorrow. Am also apprehensive about it too. It's now or never for my job plans in San Francisco.

March 8

Rushed to catch a 5 P.M. plane. Missed it. First time I've ever missed a plane. I just had too much to do today. I scheduled a direct flight for an hour later which arrived at about the same time.

My old girl friend met me at the airport. I was sort of nervous about seeing her, as I hadn't seen her in over a year. She looked great, and we really were happy to see each other. We drove right over to my ex-roommate's home where a birthday party for him was in progress. I saw several of my old friends. It really was great. I felt very tense though. I've built up this trip in my mind so much that I couldn't adjust to being here.

Went out dancing later and had a great time. I'm really happy to be back.

March 9

I had an interview today with one of the companies I'd written to. Their needs were vague and undefined. The personnel man said they'd let me know more in April, when their plans were more clear. I liked the interviewer, though, and the potential position, which was in the control area, sounded appealing. I'll be in touch with them.

Since the interview lasted only an hour and a half (a surprise to me), I had a lot of free time, so I took a cable car to the wharf and had a crab cocktail. It was a beautiful, warm, clear day. As I hung on the outside of the car, I was really turned on by the smell of the ocean air and the breeze in my face. I love this city. Everything seems alive and exciting here, there is no hustle and bustle atmosphere here, nothing like Boston driving. I must move back here.

March 10

Today my ex-girl friend and I went skiing at Squaw Valley. Really enjoyed that. When we got back, I found that the interviewer from S.F. priority #2, whom I had told I would be in the Virgin Islands, had called the apartment. I thought I was going to have a heart attack. He somehow had discovered that I lied about going to the Virgin Islands and had found out where I was.

March 11

I called home and found out that S.F. priority #2 had called my Cambridge apartment and was told of my whereabouts by one of the roommates. I could strangle him. I decided to call the fellow back as he requested. We set up an appointment starting this Friday noon, possibly going until late Friday evening. I apologized for not having a full day available, but decided not to mention the Virgin Islands lie.

March 12

I interviewed accounting firm #3 in Oakland today. I spent the morning with the managing partner in his plush office overlooking the bay. He seemed like a nice guy, but seemed somewhat awkward and nervous interviewing me. He's a local oldtimer and seems somewhat limited in his abilities. (I later found out that he may have been nervous since he's never hired or dealt with an MBA before.)

The talking lasted until about 2 P.M., when he gave me his card and asked me to call him back Friday after I'd had other interviews to ask questions and give him my impressions about the different firms. This seemed strange to me.

However, I was more concerned by the fact

that I was getting ready to leave and that he'd never mentioned anything about reimbursing me for part of the trip expenses, as they had agreed to do. I asked him about it. He said he'd never heard of the arrangement, but would talk to me about it Friday when I called. All in all, a strange interview.

March 13

Talked with S.F. priority #4 today. I spoke to about eight people, who all explained their area of responsibility to me. Some of the jobs seemed marginally interesting and the flexibility of their program seemed desirable.

I liked the people too. They seemed easy going and appeared to like me, as well. In all, I think that they would do in a pinch. They said I'd hear from them in two weeks. I expect to get an offer from them.

March 14

Today was my day with accounting firm #2. I'm tense about it because I have a terrible cold and am taking all kinds of medicine to suppress it. I'm afraid it will affect my interviews.

As had been true with accounting firm #3, their offices were plush and impressive. I first talked with the personnel man, who was a pleasant and knowledgeable fellow. I was impressed by the fact that they anticipate great growth in their office in the next three years. In fact, they expect to double their size in that time, so they told me they wanted to hire potential managers now. This growth rate really appealed to me.

I was also very impressed with the managers and partners I spoke with. They were all quite young and seemed intelligent and personable. I went to lunch with two staff accountants who were about my age. They seemed OK, but I wasn't as impressed with them as I was with the managers and partners. At the end of the day, I spoke again with the personnel man, who shocked me by offering me a job on the spot. Unfortunately, the salary offer was only $14,000. He seemed embarrassed about this, as I had asked $16,500 on my application, and made all kinds of excuses about why they couldn't offer me more—e.g., cost of living, my lack of experience in accounting, Stanford nearby, etc. However, he did seem very anxious to hire me and said before I left that he would reconsider the offer if I was offered more by another San Francisco accounting firm. My opinion is that they're being cheap because they anticipate hiring 35 people. However, I'm very interested in the company and particularly in this office. This has to be my best prospect, so far.

March 15

I had been dreading this day, as I have two appointments—accounting firm #1 in the morning and a company that I contacted in the afternoon. The first interview was interesting. I didn't feel too comfortable around the people—they seemed stiff and uptight. The personnel man was the exception. He was as loose as a goose. We really liked each other. Although they left things indefinite and said they will call, I believe I will get an offer due to my rapport with the personnel officer. Frankly, though, I didn't think they compared with accounting firm #2.

I had to hustle to get to the second interview and arrived late. However, the personnel man was even later. When we finally saw each other, he was very reserved and seemed to be sizing me up. Finally, he seemed to get enthusiastic when I told him I'd like a line position in the field after some financial staff experience. Apparently that pushed his button. He arranged two interviews with financial officers for an hour later. However, when I met these men, I wasn't too impressed with them and had the impression that finance was not important and, in fact, even looked down upon in the company. Furthermore, the program they had in mind was ill-defined and vague. So, I was turned off, but politely told them that I was interested and would pursue things further at some later date.

I find that I'm becoming weary of all these interviews, and am not worried anymore about getting a good job. Perhaps the offer from public accounting firm #2 took care of that. It doesn't bother me that companies such as the one this afternoon that I aggressively pursued don't seem good at all. There seem to be a lot of good opportunities here. A couple of months ago I wouldn't have believed it.

March 16

This morning I rushed off to my interview with the consultant for one of the firms I had contacted. I was several minutes late but had to wait about an hour to see him. He was an executive search man and a skillful interviewer. I felt that I was inarticulate in the interview, but at the end of the hour he asked me if I wanted to talk to his client (the one I had originally contacted). I was surprised but pleased. The job he described sounded like a high-powered one.

As we left it, I was supposed to call back in the afternoon, and see if he were able to arrange an interview for tomorrow, Saturday, since I was leaving Sunday. This wasn't possible, unfortunately. I told him I would probably return in two or three weeks and could talk to them then.

As the interview ended two hours later than I had anticipated, I drove like a madman for San Francisco priority #2 (the Virgin Islands affair). I was a half-hour late, but ended up waiting another half hour for an interview. The man I had spoken to on the way to the airport back at HBS took me to lunch and then gave me a plant tour and had me meet a few other people. I got way off schedule, as interviews ran over time. Furthermore, I had to take time out to call the two companies that I'd promised to call, accounting firm #3 and the consultant.

When I called the accounting firm, the Oakland partner asked me why I hadn't seen the San Francisco office as planned. Shocked, I told him I never knew of such a plan. He told me to call San Francisco to try and straighten out the mixup. I called them and said I would like to see them, but explained that it would have to be in two to three weeks when I returned, as I was leaving Sunday. They seemed to understand. The personnel man even agreed to pay their portion of my expenses after kidding me about it.

After I hung up, I thought about how badly they had screwed up my interview. They missed connections on my schedule and on my trip reimbursement. At least the reimbursement misunderstanding is straightened out. However, I'm not sure I'll see them again when I come back.

As the result of these phone calls, I missed one interview altogether, and arrived at the last man's office at 5:30 for a 4:30 interview. The fellow was a young guy out of the Stanford Business School for four years, about my age. He was very bright and intense, though personable. He took me directly to his home nearby, and he and his wife took me out to dinner at a really fine French restaurant. Although he quizzed me occasionally, the event was mostly social. The Stanford guy was very noncommittal about my status, so I don't know where I stand. The interview day at their plant was certainly a fiasco, though. I can't see how they could give me an offer. I must say that I'm not too interested in them anyway, although it would be an ego blow to be shot down by a peer.

At 10:30 I left for my friend's place. I felt relieved as I drove back. My interviews here are over. The pace has been hectic, the questions repetitive. (I've spoken with eight companies.) It's tiring to be constantly on your toes trying to impress someone. If I was able to, I'd stay on another week and interview the client of the consultant I spoke with and some of the other companies I wasn't able to see at all. However, I have a midterm Monday and am tired of all this interviewing anyway. I only hope that I can return in a couple of weeks to finish up this interviewing without having to pay for the travel myself.

March 17

I got up early today to see my ex-girl friend. We were planning to spend my last day together. Had a great time. Went into the Santa Cruz mountains for lunch, drove along the coastline and shopped in Sausalito and San Francisco. In the evening, we ate at the Blue Fox restaurant. It really has been great to see her. She's been so nice, lending me her car for the week, cooking for me, and being a great companion. I really enjoyed myself out here.

March 18

Got up early to catch an 8:30 flight to Boston. I was a little depressed to be leaving when I got on the plane, but that passed quickly. In general, I am as high as a kite. I feel very encouraged by my ten days here. I'm more relaxed and happy than I've been in a long time. In fact, my experience out here was such an enjoyable one that I realized that I've been uptight most of the time during my two years at HBS. I really used to be relaxed all of the time.

Seeing my old girl friend was also great for my ego, especially after my experiences with my girl friend in Boston. Finally, I have an offer from the company I like best. I feel great!

When I got to Boston, the scene seemed fitting. It was cold and dark and we were delayed waiting for our baggage. As I was jostled in the MTA, I thought about how much more relaxed people were in San Francisco. I must be psyching myself up to move back.

I couldn't stop talking about the trip when I got back to the apartment. My roommates hadn't gone anywhere over spring break, so they were envious. Studying for my midterm never materialized.

March 19

In the afternoon I spoke with another Bay area firm about financial jobs. I really wasn't too interested, but I hope to get another trip out West to complete all my interviewing. The fellow I spoke with was encouraging.

I felt really loose going into this interview. I'm relaxed and confident from my trip and am not nervous at all anymore. I contrast my feelings now with early in the interview season when I felt I had to get an offer in hand right away. Although I've never been really tense during an interview, every interview seemed critical. Now, some of those that seemed critical no longer seem even desirable.

Also, in contrast to my generally relaxed state of mind, I feel fairly ambitious about school this week. This is probably due to guilt feelings. I've spoken only three times all semester. It is important that I participate pretty soon, particularly if I'm going to miss some class by taking another trip West.

March 20

With my renewed vigor, I went into both classes well prepared for a change (but still didn't speak!). In the afternoon, I had my last on-campus interview of the year. It was for management consulting in Los Angeles. I really liked the interviewer. He was loose as a goose, too, so we got along pretty well. He was very positive about me and indicated an invitation to visit them might be forthcoming.

In the evening, I rushed in expense reports from the recent trip. It really caused a cash flow problem.

March 21

Today I relieved a certain burden from my mind by speaking in New Ventures for the first time. I still have that familiar feeling that I should cover myself in all classes.

The placement office is dead these days, although I continue to stop by daily, partly by habit and partly to check for new correspondence opportunities.

When I got home, I found that I had received a shoot-down letter from San Francisco priority #3, whom I had interviewed about a month ago. At that time they had seemed like a crucial opportunity, but I had forgotten about them completely as these new opportunities have come up. It's amazing how things change.

March 22

Not much happened today. These days I eagerly await the mail, hoping I'll hear something from one of the companies I'm interested in. A part of the excitement, too, is just getting a lot of mail. It's great having so much attention. I'll be sorry when this is all over.

My mood changed drastically in the afternoon when I went to the pub and talked with a friend who has decided he's going to work for an accounting firm. I was angered to find out that none of the firms pay moving expenses for new employees. I was counting on this, as I will have a cash problem in June. It really annoys me and seems really cheap. It shook my interest in accounting firms. I'm willing to pay a salary penalty, but I think this moving expense thing shows something about their attitude. Industrial firms are more generous. These accounting firms are a bit backwards with respect to new employees.

March 23

Had some great spring weather today. It made it hard to work, especially since we have no class on Fridays. Worked on my research report, however. As are most people, we're behind the eight ball with that report. We have a lot to do.

No word from my companies. However, I got an interesting letter from a manufacturer in Ohio. It was the second packet they had sent me, the first being about two months ago. They reminded me that I hadn't seen them and were giving me a second chance, as they were returning to campus for summer job interviews! They must not have had a good yield the first time. I was very flattered though.

This evening I went to a great party and met some interesting new faces. Seems like when it rains it pours. Everything is going right.

March 24

Another beautiful warm day. It puts everyone in a good mood. My roommates are really bubbly. I did some running and spent a lot of time outside.

In the afternoon I was called by accounting firm #1 in San Francisco. They offered me a job as the result of my visit. Although their salary was a guaranteed, set amount (no overtime as with others), it was still low. I'm not really that keen on this firm, but it's nice to get an offer. Besides they offered to split expenses for my trip. I appreciate this, although I think they were kind of cheap for not offering in advance.

March 25

Today I wrote letters to all the companies I visited in San Francisco. I also filled in two application forms for companies out there that I have recently contacted (one via an on-campus interview). This job search takes a lot of time, especially if done aggressively.

In the evening, I was called up by the head of the Los Angeles firm I had interviewed last week. He asked me to meet him at the Fenway, Cambridge this Wednesday. I was disappointed, as I had hoped they would invite me to Los Angeles. However, this may still be in the cards.

March 26–27

Nothing much happened. The wait continues.

March 28

After class ended at 1 o'clock, I rushed over to the Fenway, Cambridge for my second interview with the L.A. firm. At the end of the hour interview, I was startled when told that I would receive an offer in the mail in two days. In addition, they were willing to pay my way to L.A. to visit the company. This put me in a super mood. This offer represents my first definite alternative from accounting and gives me some leverage that I didn't really have before. I will really consider this offer. Just being wanted again has really turned me on.

In the afternoon I had my last on-campus interview with a San Francisco firm. It went pretty well but I won't be able to take the second step for awhile. I'm not really that interested anyway.

March 29

Today I received a packet from accounting firm #2. In it was a description of a course they want me to take this summer if I work for them. We had discussed the content of the course during my visit there, trying to decide whether or not I needed to take it. Their personnel man thought I should, but I don't really want to. The reason is that the course is given only once, starting in mid-June. I had wanted to travel in Europe for a month or so before beginning work. Unfortunately, this course will not allow that. As I read the description, I was depressed to realize that I really need to take it. This really frustrates me. I really like this job the best, but I am faced with paying the price in salary and benefits, and now, in taking vacation. I'm wondering where to draw the line. I've been trading off pleasurable opportunities for career enhancement all my life, and I want to stop it. I look at public accounting as a good learning experience and a stepping stone. I just don't know what to do.

March 30

I've been thinking about who to see on my final trip to the West Coast in the coming weeks. There are a lot of people I could see. However, I sometimes wonder if I'm just making sure I leave no stone unturned, rather than acting out of interest. I doubt if the few jobs I could look into in San Francisco could interest me more than the accounting jobs. And, after all, I really don't have time to spend days interviewing people if the jobs don't have real potential. However, new opportunities are hard to overlook. It's simply hard to say no. The feeling that the next interview might uncover the "dream job" seems to be my attitude.

I'm still disturbed about this summer course I'm faced with taking with accounting firm #2. In the afternoon I spoke with my financial accounting professor about my doubts. He boosted my

spirits a bit by giving me a pep talk about the great experience I'd be getting and how salary, etc., didn't matter. In addition, he told me he strongly felt that accounting firm #2 was the best. I felt better after our talk.

March 31

Today I received a call from the Chicago company I had visited about a month ago. The suspense level with them was high. I had intended to call them in a day or so if I hadn't heard from them. They offered me a job as a profit planner for $18,000. I like them a lot, but I'm not as turned on as I was when I visited them. A lot of good opportunities have unfolded since then.

April 2

Today the mail brought an offer from the L.A. firm that I spoke with last week. It was very flattering and offered a good salary. There was a certain amount of tension in the car going to school, as one of my roommates had just been shot down by them.

In the same mail, I got a rejection letter from S.F. priority #2. Although I hadn't been too excited by them, I nevertheless disliked being rejected. The letter was from the young Stanford fellow who took me to dinner. That was kind of an ego blow.

April 3

I stopped by the placement office, but the place is really dead. I also spent some time chatting with other students who are considering going with public accounting firms. I'm psyching myself up for the offer I have with public accounting firm #2. I still have a lot of questions to ask them about policies, salary, benefits, etc. I've been putting off calling them about these things. They're subjects I'd prefer to avoid.

April 4

I was called in the afternoon by the fellow I'd be working for in the Chicago company. We just chatted about the job I'd start out in. It really sounds sort of boring—one of those paper-generating staff positions.

April 5

I had a very upsetting experience this evening. I ran into another second year student who I've known for years and dislike immensely, and found out that he was thinking of working for accounting firm #2. Two weeks ago he had asked me about my plans, and since he professed no interest in accounting or finance, I told him all the virtues of that job. It turned out that he had a job offer from their New York office and now intends to transfer to San Francisco after a year. His interest is based on what I told him I hoped to do, and he concluded he wants to do the same thing. The idea of having to see this guy all the same really bothers me, and it infuriates me that he weaseled this information out of me. I'm really considering calling the San Francisco office and telling them the situation. If he's going to be there, I'm not sure I want to go.

April 6

I called the L.A. firm that recently offered me a job to arrange for a plant trip during report writing week. The president was very enthusiastic and friendly, but asked me before I hung up what the chance was of me accepting their job offer. I was caught off guard by this question, but babbled that the chances were good, although I was talking with other companies. I feel kind of guilty about making the trip now, as I may have overstated the certainty of my acceptance. I'm really just looking.

April 7

Today I received a rejection letter from S.F. priority #4. This was a surprise, as I had felt that the interviews there had gone well. In fact, this is the first situation I've had during this entire process where I've haven't correctly anticipated the results. However, my other offers in the area have overshadowed this anyway.

April 8

I spent the day in Newport, R.I., today visiting my brother. It was really a relief to get away. Constantly thinking about jobs and the Business School can get very tiresome.

April 9

Today I was utterly unprepared for class and was called on to start Urban Land. My response established an all-time personal low. This put me in sort of a bad mood. I was further annoyed by having to walk over to the Fenway, Cambridge at 4 P.M., for what seemed like the tenth time, to speak with the personnel man from the Chicago firm. However, when I arrived the recruiter bought me a couple of beers and we chatted about the position I was offered. I enjoyed it.

When I got home I called up California to arrange to see the firm I had been in contact with briefly during my spring break visit. I will journey up to San Francisco to see them and accounting firm #3 after my visit in L.A.

April 10

Today I did a thing I've been dreading doing for a long time. I called up accounting firm #2 to talk about benefits, salary, and the summer school class they want to send me to. My strategy was to get them to think I was close to accepting their offer and then ask them about time off before reporting (so I can go to Europe), and a salary increase. I had thought over my exact questions (and wording) and order of asking them for the past two weeks. Naturally, I was nervous about the results, since I would really like to work for them. During the conversation, the personnel man said it was OK to take time off before reporting, but declined to consider raising my salary offer. (My offer is $500 below some others I'd heard of in the area, and he said to tell him of this if it occurred.)

Therefore, the conversation was only marginally successful. However, a half hour after I hung up, he called back and raised my offer by $500. I was ecstatic. He paused and hemmed and hawed around, hoping I'd accept on the spot. However, I repeated to him that I'd be deciding in two weeks. He told me he'd call on the 22nd, which is less than two weeks. Not too subtle a hint. The pressure is on.

April 11

People are continually asking you who you're going to to work for. Until now, I've said I don't know. However, I'm now saying that I'll *probably* work for accounting firm #2. I guess I've pretty much decided that I will work for them, but am holding off to see if a miracle occurs during my trip West next week.

April 12

Had my appointment confirmed in San Francisco with the company I had contacted in the spring. My trip is only next week.

April 13

I can't decide whether to call accounting firm #3 in San Francisco to set up an appointment when I go next week. I told them I'd see them, since my previous meeting was only with the Oakland office. However, I wasn't too impressed by that office and wonder if I'm wasting my time. I'm influenced because several HBS friends are really turned on by accounting firm #3 in San Francisco. I have this dilemma. Will I be missing out if I don't talk to them versus would I really ever work for them anyway based on my experience to date?

April 14–15

Picked up tickets and pressed suit for trip. I'm hustling around working on my research report to justify not being around during report writing week. Luckily our project is not due at the end of the week.

April 16

I left for L.A. this afternoon for my final trip. The day was hectic. I got up at 7 A.M. and worked on my research frantically until 2 P.M. By then I had finished my part so the other fellows could work without me. Then I madly packed and rushed to the airport. I'll be glad when this all ends. On the plane I was still weighing whether I should talk to accounting firm #3 in San Francisco. I just can't decide.

April 17

I was lodged last night in a really luxurious motel. It had a fabulous view and was very impressive. I got up at 6:00 A.M. to meet the president of the company for breakfast at 7:00. However, he called up at 6:30 and said he'd be there at 7:45. Typical. It's really a hang loose company.

I spent the day touring several jobs of theirs with the president. It seemed pretty interesting, although more technically oriented than I would prefer. On the other hand, I really like the people in the company personally. I was also favorably impressed by the location. The recent HBS grad I had interviewed with at school took me to dinner and gave me a semi-hard sell. Later he dropped me off at the airport. I had a really enjoyable day.

Ironically, it bothers me because it further complicates the job choice I must make soon.

I arrived in San Francisco at 9:30. My old girl friend picked me up and we went out dancing again. Had a great time again. I really am looking forward to coming out here.

April 18

I had scheduled no interviews today so I slept late. Unfortunately it was very windy so I couldn't lie by the pool as I had planned. Thwarted, I decided to spend part of the afternoon renewing my California driver's license. Then, having nothing to do, I finally decided to call accounting firm #3 at about 4:00. I got the secretary of the personnel man, who said he had stepped out of the office. She told me that he would call back before he left for the day. He never called. This really annoyed me and I decided to forget about them. It was really rude and typical of my experience with them.

April 19

Drove in a rush to the city this morning for an appointment with the company I'd wanted to speak to last time. Their office was unbelievably plush—oriental rugs and carved wooden doors. I was also quite impressed with the people I interviewed. However, they only had me speak to three people for a total of 1 1/2 hours. This was disappointing. They must not be too serious about hiring anyone.

Since I finished early, I decided to call accounting firm #3 again, although I had sworn I wouldn't. I was finally able to get hold of the personnel man. He said he couldn't meet that afternoon because of meetings and that tomorrow, my last day in San Francisco, was only a half-day for them. He sounded discouraging, but I said I'd come in the next morning for a half-day.

I must still have this "mustn't leave any stone unturned" philosophy. There must be something to this firm, since at least one sharp fellow at HBS is going to work for them. On the basis of my experience with them, though, I'm crazy to pursue it. In any event, I don't have any other plans for tomorrow, so it can't hurt to see them.

I spent the rest of the day visiting friends. The pace of this visit is slower and more relaxed than the last one.

April 20

I showed up at the accounting firm at 9:30. Typically, I had a half hour wait. The personnel guy that I've had so much trouble with brought me to his office at 10:00. He's sort of a crass and arrogant fellow and I didn't enjoy talking to him. To my amazement, he pulled out a letter from the Oakland office, whom I'd spoken with during the last trip, rejecting me. It apparently had been sent after I left for this trip. However, he said the San Francisco office made its own decisions.

He then sent me on my first interview. This lasted about an hour, and I really liked the guy I spoke with. Then he and another fellow took me to lunch. The second fellow, an HBS grad of several years ago, was also a really good guy and very impressive. I spoke with two other people that day and had a similar impression of each. It's a very hang loose group and a friendly atmosphere. Only the personnel man seems like a jerk.

I ended up leaving at 3:00. At the wrap-up interview, I was told I would hear in early May! I had expected that I might get an offer on the spot. Somewhat annoyed, I objected and explained that I had a good deal of pressure to decide by Monday, April 23. He objected at first, but then agreed he would let me know on Monday.

I was so excited by the interview that I drove to accounting firm #2 to talk with them some more about their offer. I wanted to ask them some questions, as my certainty about working for them has been shaken. However, I couldn't remember exactly where their office was and by the time I did, it was too late to see them.

I must say that I am still very upset about the prospect of having the HBS grad that I dislike working at accounting firm #2. Therefore, I feel excited about firm #3, but also frustrated about having the job choice complicated.

April 21

I flew back to Boston this morning. This trip was more enjoyable than the last one. The pace was slower, and I am particularly happy to have seen accounting firm #3 after so much uncertainty. They seemed quite appealing.

When I arrived at my apartment, I gave my research report chairman a call. I was relieved to find that the report was going well and that they hadn't been working all that hard. I had been a little concerned that they would be unhappy about my skipping out during report writing week.

April 22

When I arrived home yesterday, I had received a message that the Chicago firm had called. The personnel man's message was "just tell him I called." In addition, a partner from accounting firm #2 had called. They already are expecting an answer tomorrow and he left a message that he'd call back on the 23rd. So, the pressure is on.

I decided to write letters to accounting firm #1 and the Chicago manufacturer and the L.A. firm rejecting their job offers. I spent a lot of time on them, particularly on the Chicago manufacturer, as I may want to work for them someday. I made copies of the letters for future reference.

I called a number of classmates and talked about accounting firms #2 and #3. I'm trying to get some perspective on the two. I learned a little, but both still look very good to me.

I also talked specifically about the problem of this fellow I dislike working for #2. Most of the people I talked to were surprised that I was so concerned about it. I realize that I'm making too big a deal out of it, but it is a mind-blowing thought. However, I'm beginning to disregard it as a criterion for making a choice.

I also called home and spoke with my parents about the choices. My Dad, who was a personnel man in his company, suggested I make a list of the pros and cons of each job. This seemed to be a good idea, as there seem to be a lot of areas to consider in making a choice. However, I've been sorting things out in my mind. I think one has to choose as much by feeling as by a rational "pros and cons" approach.

April 23

Today I continued to talk to students who are familiar with accounting firms #2 and #3. I'm beginning to feel more positive about #3, although their "loose" approach to everything worries me a bit. It might be excessive.

At 6:00 I called up accounting firm #3 as we had planned. The personnel man told me that I had been liked a lot, but they couldn't give me an offer because they'd had more acceptances on outstanding offers than expected. This was extremely disappointing to me. I really thought I'd get an offer from them.

However, it certainly simplifies my choice. When accounting firm #2 called an hour later, I accepted.

Although I feel bad about not getting an offer from #3, I'm quite happy to have this job business over with. It is fun and an ego trip for a while, but it also is a lot of work, time, and strain.

April 24

Today I spoke with another fellow who had the same experience with accounting firm #3. They had wanted to hire him but couldn't because of having had too many acceptances. This made me feel better, as I had been suspicious that I'd simply been shot down.

I spoke with accounting firm #2 again today. We arranged for my summer school course in accounting. In addition, we agreed that I would not start work until September 17. This will give me about two months off after the end of summer school to travel as I had wanted to. I'm happy about this.

At this point, I feel pleased but not excited about my job choice. I feel that I've done the right thing. I'm going to enjoy this summer and am looking forward to going to work.

April 25–May 2

As people continue to ask me about my job plans, I am becoming more enthusiastic about them myself. While many of my peers consider accounting the ultimate bore (to my frustration), others recognize the same advantages I see. In addition, everyone is envious of my being in San Francisco.

At this point, thinking about the job makes me a little apprehensive, but I'm fairly confident I've made the right move. I think I recognize the bad points as well as the good and feel that I have the total picture in perspective.

Looking back on the last few months I have a number of general observations. First of all, my general job objective did not hurt me at all. A general objective will hurt only in certain professions, such as investment banking, where the recruiters expect you to be interested in only their profession. Banks, consultants, accountants, and most manufacturing firms don't flinch at general objectives.

Secondly, I realized during interviewing just how much some companies value HBS graduates over all others. Whether justified or not, the mystique really seems to exist.

Thirdly, I was interested to note my own tendency to rationalize the experiences that went bad. However, I do feel that bad interviews are usually seen that way by both parties. (I had only one big surprise—S.F. priority #4.) In any event, I think it's not a bad thing to do. Remaining confident and loose is one of the most important things to do during the interview process.

Finally, I compare my job search with that of my two business school roommates. They both sat back, sent no letters and waited for companies to come to them. Their response was poor, and they spent some nervous weeks in April before finally getting jobs. In fact, one roommate panicked and arranged an interview with the placement director, who suggested he write letters expressing continued interest to those companies that had recently rejected him. He finally ended up getting a job with a firm that had earlier rejected him, largely as the result of the interest expressed in his letter.

The Life Themes of Henry Rock

1. Economic considerations influence decisions heavily.
2. Interested in quantitative and technical things.
3. Seeks new experience.
4. Social life and family are important.
5. Monetary rewards are a major motivation.
6. Prefers informal, small work environments.
7. Political considerations influence him strongly.
8. Seeks power.
9. Seeks status recognition—both from self and from others.
10. Resents people who underestimate his abilities.
11. Takes pride in achievement.
12. Works well with others.
13. But can be critical of others.
14. Is not particularly creative or esthetically inclined.
15. But desires to do things with a certain "flair."
16. Likes competition and athletics.
17. Works hard (and long hours).
18. Has a continuing interest in business.

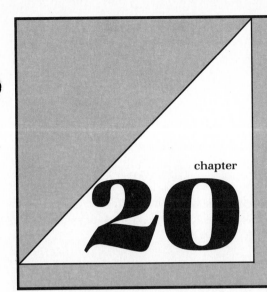

chapter

20

Focusing a Job Campaign

Most people find themselves in the job market, either by choice or necessity, a number of times in their career. At such times, skills in the various aspects of job hunting can play a leading role in career management. In this and the next four chapters, we focus on job hunting and the more effective ways people have found to engage in it.

The Importance of Focus

Considerable evidence suggests that one of the primary reasons some people are much more successful at job hunting than others is that they approach the job market with a clearly defined and reasonably narrow focus.[1] That is, they look not for "opportunities," but for a reasonably specific type of job and career opportunity. Instead of looking for "something exciting" or "a good-paying job," for example, they look for "an entry-level position in a large retailing organization with prospects for promotion to a general management position within seven years" or "a general management consulting job within a moderate to large established firm in the United States."

With a moment's reflection, it is not difficult to understand why a focused approach to job hunting is important. There are over 100 different identifiable major "industries" in the United States (see Exhibit 20–1 for

a partial listing).[2] Each has a large number of different kinds of career opportunities and jobs within it. Indeed, one government publication covering all industries lists 21,741 different types of jobs.[3] And that listing, of course, does not take into account that two jobs with the same title can differ significantly in two different organizations. In the United States alone there are well over 100,000 different organizations that regularly hire people. Operationally this means the number of career and job opportunities that exist at any single point in time, even in a depressed economy, is very large—so large, in fact, that no job hunter could ever hope to pursue more than a mere fraction of the total opportunities. There just aren't enough hours in the day.

A little bit of arithmetic will help clarify this very important point. Let's assume for a moment that you wish to get a job within the next four months. Let's further assume that you can spend, on the average, four hours per day, six days a week, engaged in job hunting activities. This adds up to a total of 24 hours per week, and about 400 hours over the four-month period. To identify a specific job opportunity, to go through a set of employment interviews, and to get to the point where you might get a job offer will require, at a bare minimum, about 10 hours of your time. It will usually require considerably more than 10 hours.

---

[1] For example, in a survey of a sample of the 1974 MBA class at Harvard, we found that those people who reported the highest level of job satisfaction seven months after graduation interviewed fewer employers on campus, wrote fewer unsolicited letters, and pursued a smaller number of different types of organizations while job hunting.

[2] For a more detailed listing, see the *Standard Industrial Classification Manual,* U.S. Office of Management and Budget (Washington, D.C.: U.S. Government Printing Office, 1972).

[3] *Dictionary of Occupational Titles,* Vol. I: *Definitions of Titles,* U.S. Department of Labor (Washington, D.C.: U.S. Government Printing Office, 1965).

Exhibit 20-1
A Partial Listing of Industries

Advertising

Aerospace (airframes, general aircraft, and parts)

Airlines

Appliances

Auditing and consulting

Automotive (autos, trucks, equipment, and parts)

Banks and bank holding companies

Beverages (brewers, distillers, soft drinks)

Building materials (cement, wood, paint, heating and plumbing, roofing, etc.)

Chemicals

Conglomerates

Containers

Drugs (and hospital supplies)

Education

Electrical and electronic

Food processing (baked goods, canned and packaged foods, dairy products, meat, etc.)

Food and lodging

General machinery (machine tools, industrial machinery, metal fabricators, etc.)

Government

Health and medical services

Instruments (controls, measuring devices, photo and optical)

Insurance

Leisure-time industries

Legal service

Metals and mining (nonferrous metals, iron ore, etc.)

Natural resources fuel (crude, oil, coal)

Nonbank financial (brokers, investment bankers, etc.)

Office equipment and computers

Oil service and supply

Paper

Personal care products (cosmetics, soap, etc.)

Publishing (periodicals, books, magazines)

Radio and TV broadcasting

Railroads

Real estate and housing

Retailing—food

Retailing—nonfood (department, discount, mail order, variety, specialty stores)

Savings and loan

Service industries (leasing, vending machines, wholesaling, etc.)

Specialty machinery (farm, construction, materials, handling)

Steel

Textiles and apparel

Tire and rubber

Tobacco

Trucking

Utilities (telephone, electric, gas)

Therefore, at the very most, you can actively pursue about 40 opportunities and stay within your budgeted 400 hours.

Now, if we restrict ourselves to the United States, at any point in time the 100,000 or so organizations that actively hire people will probably have well over a million different job openings (possibly many more). If we take the conservative figure of one million, that means that you will have at most time to pursue about 40 out of one million, or one out of 25,000 job opportunities. Without a clear focus to help identify which one of 25,000 job opportunities to pursue, it is inevitable that a job hunter will waste a great deal of time and energy, and experience considerable frustration. Job hunting without a clear focus is not unlike trying to hit a target the size of a quarter from 50 yards, using a shotgun, while blindfolded.

Without clear criteria to use in screening possibilities, students often find the process of selecting companies to interview on campus frustrating and time-consuming. In their efforts to leave "no rock unturned," they waste time and experience anxiety trying to choose whom to interview, then waste still more time going through two or three times as many interviews as their friends who have a focused job campaign. It is not unusual for job hunters who have a focused campaign to send out 20 letters to a carefully chosen group of potential employers and to receive in return invitations from 10 of them to have an interview. People with an unfocused job campaign sometimes "shotgun" out 100 or 200 standardized letters to a poorly screened group of potential employers and receive in return no favorable replies at all.

We've seen people waste hours aimlessly reading help wanted ads or talking to employment agencies because they didn't have a clear idea what they were looking for. People who tell their friends and acquaintances they are looking for a job are more likely to get useful job leads in return if they specify in some detail exactly what they want.[4] By giving reasonably clear and tight screening criteria to professional friends and acquaintances, for example, you not only increase the chances that they will indeed "keep their eyes open" for you, but you also save yourself the time and effort of following up inappropriate leads that might otherwise be passed on to you.

In job hunting, knowing in advance what you want significantly increases the chances that you will get what you want and significantly reduces the costs associated with the process itself.

Creating an Appropriate Focus

The key to creating a useful focus for job hunting is self-knowledge. Without a clear understanding of who you are, you cannot rationally decide what kind of job and career opportunities you should pursue. A good self-assessment can be enormously helpful in this regard. The decision of whether your self-assessment is adequate probably follows the sequence shown in Exhibit 20–2. There will probably be times when you feel you need more information in order to pursue a particular focus. Gathering more is a waste of time.

Given your self-assessment—that is, your list of life themes and their implications, which describe the kind of work that would seem to fit you—the next step in the process is to use the information you have about the various job opportunities in the world to begin to develop a job search focus.

Your background knowledge of business may be extensive enough to permit you to winnow out a lot of jobs, careers, and industries that look inappropriate. One must be careful here, though, since our experience has been that many students have formed inaccurate stereotypes of jobs they have not experienced. Even students who have held very similar jobs sometimes will have very disparate views of those jobs. So we caution you to test your perceptions of job opportunities before you dismiss them as being entirely inappropriate.

By carefully examining your self-assessment, in light of what you currently know about job and career opportunities, you can identify a number of areas that look promising and a number that don't. For example, if one implication in a self-assessment paper is "hates to travel more than two days a month except for va-

<hr />

[4]Imagine yourself in the position of friend or acquaintance. How would you react if someone said he or she was in the market for a new apartment or home, but didn't specify what kind? You would probably ask for more information. What would you do if the only reply was, "I want something very nice"?

Exhibit 20–2
The Process of Creating a Focus for a Job Campaign
Based on a Self-Assessment

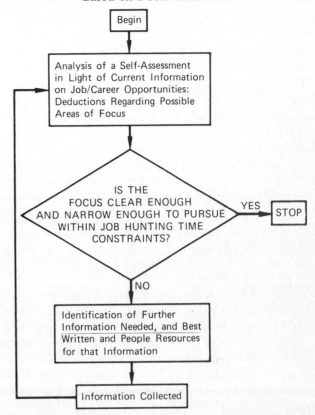

cations," and if you have reliable knowledge that almost all management consultants spend 20 to 75 percent of their time traveling, then management consulting should be given a very low priority, if not tentatively eliminated. By systematically going through all the implications in a self-assessment in this manner, you can usually identify two or three career areas that seem very promising (banking, financial work in large manufacturing firms, auditing for a CPA firm), and a large number of areas that can be tentatively eliminated (such as all production work, all public and nonprofit work). Of course, the more information you have on what job and career opportunities are like, the more focused the output of this exercise will be.

If you do not have a lot of business experience, you may feel at a loss as to how to begin to develop a focus. Many students have expressed a nagging concern that they feel the "perfect job" is out there somewhere, but given the realities we have outlined above, there is no hope of researching all the opportunities before making a decision becomes a necessity. First, we say there are several jobs "out there" that any one person might be well suited for, and that with any job-person match there will be some dimensions that don't fit well. So don't be overly concerned about a perfect fit. Second, there are a number of ways of finding out enough about various opportunities to make a preliminary decision whether to pursue an opportunity further.

Sources of Information

There are three basic sources of information on potential jobs and on the organizations in which the jobs are located: published documents, people, and direct observation. Each is different in the information it can supply and the cost of obtaining that information, but all three can be very useful.

Published Documents

Written sources, such as those listed in Exhibit 20-3, can be especially useful in supplying information on an organization's past financial performance, its current demographic characteristics (size, products/services offered, assets, and so on), its industry, and its major actions (bringing out a new product line, bringing in a new president, and so on). Published sources

Exhibit 20-3
Where to Find Written Information about Companies

A. Directories

There are many published directories of companies. A few are general lists of larger companies, others are specialized, either by location (country, state, or city) or by industry or trade. Some give as much information as the first three below, others merely give address or industry. These first three directories are probably used most often as a starting point for brief information on larger U.S. companies.

- *Poor's Register of Corporations, Directors and Executives*
  Alphabetical list of approximately 33,000 U.S. and Canadian corporations, giving officers, products (if manufacturer), standard industrial classification (SIC), sales range, and number of employees. The latter half consists of brief information on about 75,000 executives and directors. Index of companies by SIC is at front. See also its Geographical Index.

- *Dun & Bradstreet Million Dollar Directory*
  Lists approximately 31,000 U.S. companies with an indicated worth of $1 million or over. Gives officers, products (if manufacturer), standard industrial classification, approximate sales, and number of employees. The yellow pages list companies geographically and the blue pages by SIC industries. The white pages at the end are an alphabetical listing of officers and directors.

- *Dun & Bradstreet Middle Market Directory*
  Lists approximately 33,000 U.S. companies with an indicated worth of $500,000 to $999,999. Coverage and information given are similar to that of the directory above except that officers and directors are not listed.

If your company is a manufacturer, you may find it listed in the following comprehensive directory:

- *Thomas Register of American Manufacturers* (10 vols., annual)
  Volumes 1-6 list manufacturers by specific product.
  Volume 7 is an alphabetical list of companies and includes address, branch offices, subsidiaries, products, estimated capitalization.
  Volume 8 is an "index" to produce categories and also contains a list of leading trade names (pink sheets).
  Volumes 9-10 are a "Catalog of Companies."

1. Regional and State Manufacturers Directories

If your manufacturing company is not in Thomas and you know in which state it is located, try looking for it in a state directory. Examples:

- *California Manufacturers Register*
- *Directory of New England Manufacturers*
- *Greater Boston Directory of Manufacturers*
- Massachusetts Department of Commerce and Development, *Industrial Directory of Massachusetts Manufacturers*
- *New York State Industrial Directory*

2. Directories of Companies in Foreign Countries

Examples:

- *Japan Directory* (2 vols.)
- *Schweizerische Zentrale fur Handelsforderung* [Directory of Swiss Manufacturers and Producers]

Exhibit 20-3 (*continued*)

---

3. Directories for Specific Industries or Trades

Examples:
- American Management Association, *Directory of Consultant Members*
- *Directory of Department Stores*
- *Davison's Textile Blue Book*
- *Franchise Guide: An Encyclopedia of Franchise Opportunities*
- *Lockwood's Directory of the Paper and Allied Trades*
- *Rubber Red Book*
- American Marketing Association, New York Chapter, *International Directory of Marketing Research Houses and Services*
- Money Management Directories, Inc., *Money Market Directory, 1977* (A directory of institutional investors and their portfolio managers)
- Investment Bankers Association of America, *The Blue Book,* 1971
- National Association of Real Estate Investment Funds, *NAREIF Handbook of Member Trusts*
- *Rand McNally International Bankers Directory*
- *Security Dealers of North America*
- *Standard Directory of Advertising Agencies*
- *Venture Capital* (monthly publication)
- *World Space Directory Including Oceanology*

4. Directories of American Firms with Foreign Subsidiaries

- *Directory of American Firms Operating in Foreign Countries,* 8th ed., 1975
- Finance Magazine, *International Almanac of Business and Finance*
- *Who Owns Whom: International Subsidiaries of U.S. Companies*

5. Guides to Directories

If you still do not find a directory for the industry or geographic area you want, look for a bibliography of directories that may list a trade directory your library does not have or a directory issue of a trade journal. One of the best bibliographies is:

- *Guide to American Directories*

B. Financial Information about Companies

The following documents for New York and American Stock Exchange companies can be very useful:
- Annual reports to stockholders
- 10-K reports to the Securities and Exchange Commission
- Listing statements
- Proxy statements
- Registration statements

C. Articles about Companies

- *F & S Index of Corporations & Industries* (weekly, cumulated monthly and annually). Indexes articles on companies and industries that have appeared in selected business and financial publications, and also brokerage house reports.
- *F & S International* (monthly, cumulated annually). An index similar to the one above, for foreign companies.
- *Wall Street Journal Index* (monthly, with annual cumulation). Each issue has two parts: Corporate News and General News. Indexing is based on the final Eastern Edition.
- *Wall Street Transcript* (weekly). A compilation of brokerage house reports on companies and industries. Each issue is indexed, and there is also a periodic cumulated index.

---

have the advantage of relative ease of access. All major libraries will have most of the sources in Exhibit 20-3. You can look over such information at your convenience, as often as you wish; you only need to allocate enough time to this task. People we have observed who have not been very successful at job hunting almost always seem to underutilize published information sources. Their time and their energy get absorbed elsewhere, in less productive activities.

Most large public libraries and university-associated libraries have considerable information about job and career opportunities. In the appendix to this chapter, we have listed the best library sources we know of for information on topics our students have typically researched.

In addition, we have utilized the research energies of our students to generate job research reports. These short reports consist of a two-page summary of vital information about various jobs. The data consist of a job description, including typical responsibilities, tasks, and routines, likely career paths, compensation patterns, and opportunities for advancement; the names of some companies who hire people in those jobs; and sources of additional information. We have found that teams of from two to four people can generate a wealth of useful information on a particular job in less than three days. At present, we have collected over 80 such job descriptions and are planning to publish in the near future a compilation of the findings to help job hunters develop a focus. A copy of the assignment sheet we use appears at the end of this chapter for your reference (see Exhibit 20-4). You may wish to use it as a guide in developing your own portfolio of opportunities to consider in your job search.

People

People, although often less accessible than books, can be enormously useful sources of information on specific job and career issues.[5] Our students have found that by using whatever personal contacts they have to set up meetings (often at lunch) with people who actually work in the industries, companies, types of jobs, or geographic areas in which they think they might be interested, they can get a large amount of useful information very quickly. Armed with specific questions created in conjunction with a self-assessment

paper, a person can sometimes learn more in 30 to 60 minutes from a well-informed source than from 6 hours in a library.

For example, Jerry Jones knows from his self-assessment, among other things, that he does not tend to work well under pressure and that he is very ambitious. In an initial analysis of his self-assessment, he decides he should look more deeply into professional auditing work. So on Tuesday he sets up a lunch with Jim Smith, a partner in a large CPA firm who is also a graduate of Jerry's college. (Jerry got Smith's name from his accounting professor.) Among the questions Jerry asks Smith are the following:

1. Do people in the CPA profession have to work with tight time and/or cost constraints? Or does it vary from firm to firm or job to job?

2. Do you feel much pressure in your job? What about most new employees you have observed—do they feel a lot of pressure?

3. How much does the average employee in your firm make after 5, 10, or 15 years?

4. Is your firm growing? How fast? Is the industry growing? How fast?

5. Out of every 20 people hired each year, how many will probably become partners? How long will that take most people?

Contrast that scenario with this one. Phil Roy has a "gut feel" he may enjoy being a CPA. He spends his lunch hour on Tuesday asking the people who are sitting at his table in one of the university's cafeterias whether they think being an auditor is a good job. He gets two unqualified yesses, two qualified yesses, three maybes, one noncommittal response, two qualified nos, and a piece of paper thrown at him (possibly an unqualified no).

It is very easy, while job hunting, to end up in Phil Roy's position—wasting his own and other people's time in endless dialogues about careers and job opportunities that do not help him focus on a limited number of rational opportunities out of the many possibilities. And the reason it is easy is because most people do not begin job hunting with a good, accurate, up-to-date assessment of themselves.

There are two types of human information sources about potential jobs: current employees of the organizations with the job openings, and others. These others might be former employees, consultants who have worked with the organization, financial analysts who have studied the organization for their own firms, and so on. A job hunter automatically gains access to some of the organization's employees while interviewing. For moderate-sized to large organizations, our students have almost always been able to find a few people who fall into that "other" category. It is a rare case, for

---

[5]We've noticed that some of our students resist this strategy of identifying and using people because they feel they don't know any such people or because they think it would just be too cumbersome to try to find such people and convince them to talk. Once prodded into action, however, virtually all our students have found that: (a) they do know someone who in turn knows the type of person they are looking for; and (b) when contacted, people are usually more than willing to talk.

Exhibit 20–4
Career Development Job Research Report

Job Description (Activities, Routines, Life Styles, Key Required Skills):

Compensation (Salary Range, Usual Benefits):

Career Paths (Future Potential, Transferability, Likely Advancement Routes):

Employers (Some Companies Likely to Hire, Sources for Finding Others):

Additional Data:

example, in which no faculty member has ever had dealings with such an organization and no student has worked for it (if only for a summer).

In brief conversations with informed nonemployees, one can usually get reasonably candid and unbiased information of a type that doesn't tend to appear in print and that is awkward to obtain from the organization's current employees. What kind of problems does the organization have? How does it treat employees? Is it really going to be able to grow as fast as it says? If you previously worked for this organization, did you enjoy it? Why?

Inside sources can supply slightly different types of data. They can give you first-hand information on what it is currently like to work for that organization, what the potential job is really like, what the career path associated with it is really like, and what the people you would be working with are like. And possibly the easiest way to get that information is to ask these people about themselves. How long have you been working here? Why did you join up? What job did you

start in? Specifically, what did you do? Whom did you work with? What did you like and dislike about that job? What job did you move to next? When did the move occur? Why did it occur? What did you do in your next job? And so on. People generally enjoy talking about themselves. When describing their own careers and jobs, they also generally give much more accurate and useful information than when they try to generalize about careers or jobs in their organization.

The third means of gathering data about job opportunities is direct observation, which we will come back to in the chapter on company visits.

The Key: Self-Assessment

By systematically going back and forth from analyzing one's self-assessment, to gathering some more information, to reanalyzing the self-assessment, one can create in a practical amount of time a rational focus for a job campaign. Hundreds of students have done

Exhibit 20–5
The Narrowing Job Search Focus
Number of Organizations of Interest

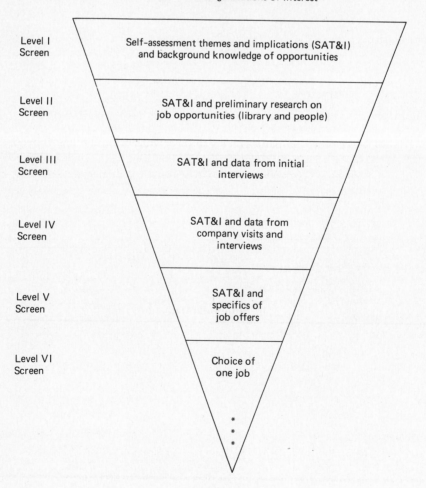

Level I Screen	Self-assessment themes and implications (SAT&I) and background knowledge of opportunities
Level II Screen	SAT&I and preliminary research on job opportunities (library and people)
Level III Screen	SAT&I and data from initial interviews
Level IV Screen	SAT&I and data from company visits and interviews
Level V Screen	SAT&I and specifics of job offers
Level VI Screen	Choice of one job

just that. And the competitive advantage this has given them over those classmates who behave more like Phil Roy while job hunting is very significant.

The important things to remember here are these:

1. The importance of developing a focus so as not to dilute your job hunting efforts unnecessarily
2. To use your self-assessment as a set of criteria for making a decision on whether or not to pursue a particular opportunity

The latter point is extremely important. It would not make much sense to generate a careful self-assessment and then abandon it in favor of momentary excitement as you generate a job search focus. Consequently, we urge you to *use* your self-assessment by considering each theme and each implication to check the fit with a potential career opportunity. This process will also help you to discard with confidence opportunities that on one dimension may seem attractive, even glamorous, but that are not good fits with you.

This process of focusing is a progressive one. Your breadth of focus probably will be much wider at the beginning of your job search than it will be at the end. As you move through the job search, your focus will gradually narrow until you have accepted a single offer. Exhibit 20–5 represents this narrowing focus and the screens you will use as time goes by.

Assignment

We have included Tom Wilson's life themes lists and their implications (see case, pp. 199–203). Consider them along with Lauren Davis's themes lists and implications (Chapter 17, pp. 161–62) and develop a job search focus for each person. Use your own background knowledge of career opportunities to develop these focuses. Be prepared to explain your rationale, based on Tom's and Lauren's themes and implications, for the focuses you have developed. More specifically, try to answer the following three questions for each person:

1. What job and career areas seem promising for this person? Why?
2. What areas can be eliminated? Why?
3. What areas might be promising, although you're not sure because you don't have enough information? What extra information would you like to have?

TOM WILSON: THEMES AND IMPLICATIONS

Tom Wilson: Theme List

Theme Labels

1. I see my family as the foundation of my current and future life.
2. I value being independent in thought and action.
3. I value my identity and being "different."
4. I value a few close, lasting friends.
5. I see friendships as being important in my life in a social, active sense.
6. I set goals and plan for the future.
7. I like to be in control and influence others.
8. I value living by set principles/ideals where honesty is paramount.
9. I am hard working and persistent.
10. I am motivated by a challenge.
11. I see respect for self and others as important, and often work harder for those I respect/like.
12. I strive not to hurt others' feelings.
13. I want to be included in personal interaction.
14. I do not express feelings/opinions readily.
15. I am an achiever who is proud of his accomplishments.
16. I feel guilty when I fall short of my expectations/standards.
17. I allocate much of my time to athletic activity (participating and observing).
18. I appreciate the out-of-doors and like outdoor activity.
19. I value imaginative, adventurous activities.
20. I apply reason and logic in analyzing situations.

This case was prepared by Kevin E. Sachs, research assistant, under the direction of Associate Professor James G. Clawson, as a basis for class discussion. © 1982 by the Sponsors of The Colgate Darden Graduate School of Business, the University of Virginia, Charlottesville, Virginia. UVA case OB-209.

21. I am often motivated by practical reasons.
22. I have a strong economic orientation.
23. I am often concerned with specifics and details.
24. I need structure in work, school environment to feel comfortable.
25. I value my own and others' sense of humor.
26. I am sensitive (inwardly emotional) to past events.
27. I value the presence of women in my life.

Tom Wilson: Theme Priority

Most Important

1. I see my family as the foundation of my current and future life.
2. I value being independent in thought and action.
3. I value my identity and being "different."
4. I value a few close, lasting friends.
5. I see friendships as being important in my life in a social, active sense.

Very Important

6. I set goals and plan for the future.
7. I like to be in control and influence others.
8. I value living by set principles/ideals where honesty is paramount.
9. I am hard working and persistent.
10. I am motivated by a challenge.

11. I see respect for self and others as important, and often work harder for those I respect/like.

Important

12. I strive not to hurt others' feelings.
13. I want to be included in personal interaction.
14. I do not express feelings/opinions readily.
15. I am an achiever who is proud of his accomplishments.
16. I feel guilty when I fall short of my expectations/standards.
17. I allocate much of my time to athletic activity (participating and observing).
18. I appreciate the out-of-doors and like outdoor activity.
19. I value imaginative, adventurous activities.

Somewhat Important

20. I apply reason and logic in analyzing situations.
21. I am often motivated by practical reasons.
22. I have a strong economic orientation.
23. I am often concerned with specifics and details.
24. I need structure in work, school environment to feel comfortable.
25. I value my own and others' sense of humor.
26. I am sensitive (inwardly emotional) to past events.
27. I value the presence of women in my life.

Tom Wilson: Theme Implications

Implication 1: I Need Structured Tasks in the Work Environment to Feel Comfortable

In the early stages of a career, I would be more comfortable in a structured environment. Later, as one becomes accustomed to the environment, self-initiated tasks take on more importance.

The process is similar to 1st and 2nd year at the Business School. This implication comes directly from data gathered in the self-assessment paper in creating T24 (Structure—I need structure in work, school environment to feel comfortable). Other themes supporting this implication are: T6 (Plan—Setting goals and planning implies structure) and T16 (Guilty—Expectations are probably easier to define in a structured environment).

Items which I will have to manage in a structured environment are: T14 (Express Feelings). And, I will be able to make the transition to a self-initiated task because of these theme implications: T2 (Independent) and T9 (Persistent).

Implication 2: I Seek Work Which Would Allow Flexible Hours

I would be able to schedule family activities and outdoor activities better with flexible hours.

This case was edited by James G. Clawson. © Copyright 1983 by the Sponsors of The Colgate Darden Graduate School of Business Administration, University of Virginia, Charlottesville, Virginia. UVA case OB-226.

The dominant themes are: T1 (Family), T17 (Athletics), and T18 (Out-Of-Doors).

Implication 3: I Seek to Work in an Informal Atmosphere

I would fit much better into an informal organization structure. The dimensions to which this implication applies are social activities and interpersonal style. The dominant themes are:

- T2 (Independent)—Informality allows more independence.
- T3 (Different)—Informality allows one's identity and personal style to come out.
- T5 (Social Friends)—I value friendly interaction and kidding around and would desire work friendships to take on this tone.
- T13 (Included)—Informal structures allow personal interaction.
- T17 (Athletics)—Informal structures may place more emphasis on company recreational activities.
- T25 (Humor)—Formality tends to stifle one's sense of humor.

Implication 4: I Prefer to Work in a Small to Medium-Size Firm

A small to medium-size firm may be more conducive to flexible times and informal structures and allow my personality to come out. Themes which imply a small to medium-size firm are:

- T2 (Independent)—Smaller size allows more independence.
- T3 (Different)—Smaller size allows personality to come out. I feel lost in a large organization.
- T4 (Close Friends)—Having a few close, lasting friends implies not requiring a large organization around as a support system.

I have no desire to become CEO of a billion-dollar multinational corporation or become involved in the political infighting that large bureaucracies tend to breed.

Implication 5: I Prefer Individual Work over Group Effort

I would feel more comfortable in a work setting if a greater proportion of work was individual work rather than group effort. The theme which especially related to this is: T2 (Independence). My experience with groups shows that the main reason why groups fail is differences in work style of the participants. Some themes which may conflict with others' styles and would imply individual work are: T9 (Persistent—I have

a tendency to overwork certain areas), and T23 (Specifics—I tend to be a perfectionist). I also have a preference for flexible hours, which makes scheduling group meetings more difficult.

Implication 6: I Seek Work That Would Average 55–60 Hours per Week or Less

The major constraint on the amount of time I can allocate to work is time spent for family. Consulting with a large firm or investment banking which demands 60–70 hours per week is simply out of the question. Also, companies which require a lot of travel (1–2 days per week) are out of the question too. The dominant theme is: T1 (Family). Also, I am hard working and persistent (T9) and am motivated by a challenge (T10). I do not want just a 40-hour per week job.

Implication 7: I Need to Respect Those I Work For

This implication is taken directly from the theme developed in the SAP: T11 (Respect—I see respect for self and others as important and often work harder for those I respect/like). What also ties in with this implication is T8 (Ideals). I would not be being very honest with myself if I worked for someone I did not respect.

Implication 8: I Desire Variety and Creativity in Tasks Rather Than Routines

Data which supports this implication is my high tolerance for ambiguity (2.86). The primary theme supporting this implication is T19 (Imaginative). Also, T10 (Challenge) implies variety of tasks may be more challenging. Included in this theme is the desire to find work that allows skills from all functional areas to be used.

Implication 9: I Seek Work That Is Challenging

This implication was also taken directly from the SAP: T10 (Challenge)—I am motivated by a challenge. The implication ties in directly with my definition of success, which is presented later. A job which is not challenging would be boring and would cause unhappiness.

Implication 10: I Seek Work Where Loyalty Is Important

Inherent in this implication is the idea that I also do not like to move. Family considerations: T1 (Family), would make this important. However, the main theme which fits is T8 (Ideals).

Loyalty implies respect, trust, mutual openness and honesty. An organization which breeds this is one I want to work for. And, if the job is interesting and challenging, I would have no desire to leave.

Implication 11: I Prefer My Own Office

As far as physical setting in the office goes, my experience shows that I can be more productive if I have my own office. T2 (Independent), T7 (Control), T14 (Express Feelings) fit this implication. T5 (Social Friends), T13 (Included), and the desire for an informal setting seem to contradict, but these themes can be satisfied in other ways than physical setting. I would not consider a partitioned room as my own office and would also prefer a window, thank you.

Implication 12: I Need Work Where I'm Responsible, Trusted

The implication fosters a feeling of importance in the firm to where I'm a person, not just another worker. The theme which first jumps out is T8 (Ideals). Trust is a valued principle based on honesty. Also, T2 (Independent) may be prerequisite for the superior to give one responsibility. T7 (Control) fits the implication in the sense that one who is trusted and responsible is more likely to be in control. And, T11 (Respect) fits because being trusted would create a feeling of mutual respect where I would work hard and achieve.

Implication 13: I Desire Work That Is Line Oriented vs. Staff

A reason why I decided not to pursue a finance career is that for the most part, financial analysts are perched somewhere in the corporate ivory tower in staff positions. One becomes a professional percher, who becomes alienated from the specifics of what the company does. I do not think that that sort of job makes a contribution. I would feel insignificant. Themes which support this are: T23 (Specifics), T19 (Imaginative), T7 (Control), T2 (Independent), and T15 (Achiever).

Implication 14: I Seek Work Where I Can Make a Contribution

I do not want to be just another spoke on the wheel. It is the reason why I would prefer a small to medium-size firm. Themes which fit are T2 (Independent), T7 (Control), and especially T15 (Achiever). One who is an achiever and is proud of his accomplishments strives toward making a contribution.

Implication 15: I Desire Work That Is More Analytical Than Qualitative

I frankly feel more comfortable with numbers and have consistently performed better in quantitative, analytical exercises. Data supporting the implication is derived directly from the SAP: T20 (Logic—I apply reason and logic in analyzing situations.) T26 (Analytical—I perform better in an analytical, quantitative environment.)

Implication 16: I Seek Work Where Achievement Is Recognized

The theme supporting this implication is directly from the SAP: T15 (Achiever—I am an achiever who is proud of his accomplishments.)

Implication 17: I Prefer Work That Emphasizes Recreational Activities

This implication would fit with a desire for informal structure. The themes that fit this implication are: T17 (Athletics), T18 (Out-Of-Doors), and T19 (Imaginative). Also, it would permit friendships as being important in life in a social, active sense—T5 (Social Friends).

Implication 18: I Desire Work That Provides Regular Feedback on How You're Doing

The only way to plan or that a goal can be reassessed or adjusted is to find out where you are. One piece of knowledge required is whether or not your expectations meet the company's. Themes which fit this implication are: T16 (Guilty), T6 (Plan), T8 (Ideals), T13 (Included), T15 (Achiever), T23 (Specifics).

Implication 19: I Seek Work in a Location That Satisfies Family, Friends, and Recreational Goals

Location is a key decision variable in the job search process. It has important implications for future life style. Location must take into account housing costs and school systems. We also want to move geographically closer to our close friends and renew these friendships. The dominant themes are: T1 (Family), T4 (Close Friends), T17 (Athletics), and T18 (Out-Of-Doors).

Specific Career Implications

When I was a junior in high school, my father decided it was time that I undergo rigorous tests to determine what my strengths and weaknesses were in order to highlight career opportunities. I went to a guidance center and took about eight tests which determined that I could be anything I wanted. (The results of the tests were included in my SAP.) This caused some problems. To solve them though, I attended a liberal arts college.

Ten years later, I took the Strong-Campbell Interest Inventory test in a career management course to help determine if my interests matched certain careers. On 23 Basic Interest Scales, 9 were high or very high, 14 were average, and zero were low or very low. The results showed that I have a variety of interests and simply do not dislike many occupations.

Appendix to Chapter 20

Sources of Information
on Selected Industries
and Career Opportunities

The references listed here represent a selected set of useful information that is readily available to you. Each reference can be located in any major library.

Titles are listed first according to industry or profession and then by type, e.g., Directory, Book, Periodical, etc.

Advertising and Consumer Marketing

Encyclopedias and Dictionaries

1. *Ayer Glossary of Advertising and Related Terms.* Philadelphia: N. W. Ayer & Son, 1972.

2. *Encyclopedia of Advertising,* 2d ed. New York: Fairchild Publications, 1969.

3. Shapiro, Irving J. *Marketing Terms: Definition, Explanations and/or Aspects,* 3d ed. West Long Branch, N.J.: S-M-C Publishing Co., 1973.

Handbooks and Manuals

4. Barton, Roger, ed. *Handbook of Advertising Management.* New York: McGraw-Hill, 1970.

5. *Do's and Don'ts in Advertising Copy: A Looseleaf Service of Advertisers, Advertising Agencies, Broadcasters and Printed Media.* New York: Council of Better Business Bureaus, 1975. Successor to "A Guide to National Advertising."

6. *Handbook of Independent Advertising and Marketing Services.* New York: Executive Communications, 1974.

7. Stansfield, Richard H. *The Dartnell Advertising Manager's Handbook.* Chicago: Dartnell Corp., 1969.

8. Worcester, Robert M., ed. *Consumer Market Research Handbook.* New York: McGraw-Hill, 1972.

Bibliographies

9. Culley, James D., et al. *Current Sources of Marketing Information: An Annotated Bibliography of Major Data Sources.* Newark, Delaware: Bureau of Economic and Business Research, 1974.

10. *A Basic Bibliography on Marketing Research,* 3d ed. American Marketing Association, 1974. Includes material in the social sciences and other disciplines that have direct applicability to marketing research. Coverage is up to the end of 1973.

11. *Marketing Information Guide.* Monthly. Washington, D.C. Marketing Information.

12. "Marketing Abstracts," *Journal of Marketing.* Quarterly. Each issue contains an annotated bibliography covering selected articles of interest to marketers. It is arranged in 22 broad subject headings.

13. Steilen, Charles, and Roley Altizier. *Guide to Marketing/Advertising Information.* Atlanta: Admar Books, 1972. An annotated bibliography covering general as well as specific secondary sources of marketing and advertising information.

14. Thompson, Ralph B. *A Selected and Annotated Bibliography of Marketing Theory.* Austin, Texas: Bureau of Business Research, 1970.

15. Crissy, W. J. E., and Robert M. Kaplan. *Salesmanship: The Personal Force in Marketing.* New York: Wiley, 1969. Written primarily for students enrolled in courses in salesmanship, the majority of whom have career aspirations in business and particularly in marketing.

16. Dirksen, Charles J., and Arthur Kroeger. *Advertising Principles and Problems,* 4th ed. Homewood, Ill.: Irwin, 1973.

17. Dunn, S. Watson, and Arnold M. Barba. *Advertising: Its Role in Modern Marketing,* 3d ed. New York: Dryden Press, 1974. An up-to-date introduction to the world of advertising for students.

18. Haas, Kenneth B., and John W. Ernest. *Creative Salesmanship: Understanding Essentials,* 2d ed. Riverside, N.J.: Glencoe Press, 1974. Includes chapters on "Opportunities in Selling" and "Selling as a Career."

19. Mandell, Maurice I. *Advertising,* 2d ed. Englewood Cliffs, N.J.: Prentice-Hall, 1974. An up-to-date source that includes chapter-length examples and good illustrations. It is an introductory overview of advertising intended for those who are interested in careers in advertising.

20. Zober, Martin. *Principles of Marketing.* Boston: Allyn and Bacon, 1971.

Periodicals

21. *Academy of Marketing Science Journal.* Monthly.

22. *Advertising Age.* Weekly. This journal publishes five annual surveys of special interest to advertisers: (1) Marketing Profiles of 125 Leading National Advertisers; (2) 100 Leading National Advertisers; (3) AA's Yang Estimates—annual summary of the economy and estimates of advertising expenditures; (4) U.S. Agency Billings; and (5) New Market Data.

23. *Journal of Advertising.* Quarterly.

24. *Journal of Advertising Research.* Bimonthly.

25. *Journal of Marketing.* Quarterly. Features: book reviews, legal developments, and marketing abstracts.

26. *Marketing News.* Bimonthly.

27. *Marketing Times.* Bimonthly. Issues usually focus on one topic, e.g., "Women in Selling" and "How to Sell in a Recession/Inflation Era."

28. Special Libraries Association. Advertising and Marketing Division. *What's New in Advertising and Marketing.* Monthly.

Directories

30. American Business Press, Inc. *Leading Advertisers in Business Publications.* Annual. Ranks about 600 leading advertisers in business journals. Includes an alphabetical list of over 2,400 companies that spend $35,000 or more in business publications.

31. Bradford, Ernest S. *Bradford's Directory of Marketing Research Agencies and Management Consultants in the United States and the World.* Biennial. A list and description of reliable market research agencies in the U.S. and abroad.

32. *Commercial Atlas and Marketing Guide.* Skokie, Ill.: Rand McNally & Company. Lists of railroads, airlines, colleges, and universities (by state). Lists of top 50 (largest) corporations: advertising agencies, commercial banks, life insurance companies, retailing companies, transportation, utilities, and industrial corporations.

33. Marketing Economics Key Plants. *Guide to Industrial Purchasing Power.* New York: Marketing Economics Institute, Ltd., 1973. Directory of 40,000 plants with 100 or more employees. Useful as a statistical research tool, as a prospect list, and as a geographic guide to sales territories.

34. *Standard Directory of Advertisers.* Directory of 17,000 companies that advertise nationally, arranged by industry groupings, with alphabetical index. Gives officers, products, agency, advertising appropriations, media used, etc. Includes a "Trademark Index."

35. *Standard Directory of Advertising Agencies.* Skokie, Ill.: National Register Publishing Co., 1975. Covers 4,400 agency establishments, both national (4,000) and foreign (400). Issued three times a year in February, June, and October. Supplements called "Agency News" are issued in the months between publications.

36. *Who's Who in Advertising,* 2d ed. New York: Derna V. Morgan, 1972. Index to company names. Limited to United States and Canada.

Statistics

37. *A Guide to Consumer Markets.* New York: The Conference Board, Inc., 1974/1975. Published annually since 1960. A standard source of statistical information concerning the consumer—his demographic and social profile and his economic behavior.

38. *Measuring Markets: A Guide to the Use of Federal and State Statistical Data.* Washington, D.C.: U.S. Dept. Of Commerce, August 1974. Brings together in one convenient and concise package those materials published by the federal and state governments that would be useful in marketing research, especially consumer market research.

Career Information and Opportunities

39. Catalyst. *Advertising Career Opportunities.* Series C2. Prepared by Catalyst, the national nonprofit organization dedicated to expanding employment opportunities for college-educated women who wish to combine career and family responsibilities. A concise and simple overview of what advertising is and what opportunities are available. Good source of information for both women and men.

40. Gamble, Frederic R. *What Advertising Agencies Are: What They Do and How They Do It.* New York: American Association of Advertising Agencies, 1963. This pamphlet is also available from the AAAA at no charge.

41. Heidrick & Struggles, Inc. *Profiles of a Chief Marketing Executive: Findings of a Study of the Chief Marketing Executives of America's Largest Companies.* New York: H & S, Inc., 1971.

Aerospace and Air Transportation

Reports

42. *Frost and Sullivan Reports: Transportation in the U.S.A. to 1990,* No. 315. A profile and projection of the aviation industry.

43. National Petroleum Council. *U.S. Energy Outlook: An Initial Appraisal, 1971–1985.* 2 vols. Includes projections and task force reports.

44. U.S. President. *Aeronautics and Space Report of the President.*

Abstracts and Indexes

45. *Air University Library Index to Military Periodicals.* Quarterly. See "Aerospace Industry" and "Aeronautical Research." See "Airlines" for articles on companies.

46. *Applied Science and Technology Index.* Monthly.

47. *Government Report Index.* Biweekly.

48. *International Aerospace Abstracts.*

49. *Scientific and Technical Aerospace Reports.* For NASA contractors, ongoing research projects and reports issued by the government.

Guides to Sources

50. Metcalf, Kenneth N. *Transportation Information Services.* Detroit: Gale Research, 1966.

51. Flood, Kenneth U. *Research in Transportation: Legal/Legislative and Economic Sources and Procedure.* Detroit: Gale Research, 1970.

52. Wasserman, Paul, Ed. *Encyclopedia of Business Information Sources.* Detroit: Gale Research, 1970.

Statistical Sources

53. *Aerospace Facts and Figures.* Annual. Aerospace Industries Association of America.

54. *Air Shippers Manual.* Annual. Import Publications.

55. *Air Transport Facts and Figures.* Annual. Air Transport Association of America.

56. *Air Transport World,* "Market Development Issue." Annual. May issue.

57. Aviation Daily. *Aviation Daily's Airline Statistical Annual.* Washington, D.C.: Ziff-Davis.

58. *Aviation Week and Space Technology,* "Forecast and Inventory Issue." Annual.

59. *Business Flying.* Quarterly. National Business Aircraft Association.

60. U.S. Civil Aeronautics Board. *Handbook of Airline Statistics.* Biennial. Updated by *Air Carrier Traffic Statistics,* monthly; and *Air Carrier Financial Statistics,* quarterly.

61. U.S. Federal Aviation Administration. *FAA Statistical Handbook of Aviation.* Annual.

Books

62. Aerospace Industries Association of America, Inc. *Aerospace and the U.S. Economy: Its Role, Contributions, and Critical Problems.* 1971.

63. Hoyt, Edwin Palmer. *The Space Dealers: A Hard Look at the Role of American Business in Our Space Effort.* New York: John Day, 1971.

64. Kane, Robert M., and Allan D. Vose. *Air Transportation.* Dubuque, Iowa: Kendall/Hunt, 1974.

65. Stekler, Herman O. *The Structure and Performance of the Aerospace Industry.* Berkeley: University of California Press, 1965.

66. Stratford, Alan H. *Air Transport Economics in the Supersonic Era.* New York: St. Martin's Press, 1967.

Directories

67. *World Aviation Directory.* Washington, D.C.: American Aviation Associates, Inc. Semiannual. Aviation/aerospace companies and officials.

68. *World Space Directory Including Oceanography.* Biannual.

General Investment Services

69. *Forbes.* "Annual Report on American Industry." First issue in January each year. Has section on aerospace.

70. Standard & Poor's Corporation. *Industry Surveys.* Coverage is separate for aerospace and air transportation; latest issue is in a separate folder.

Census Publications

71. *Census of Transportation.* Washington, D.C.: U.S. Bureau of the Census, Government Printing Office, 1972.

72. *Current Industrial Reports.* U.S. Bureau of the Census. Washington, D.C. Irregular. Contains pamphlets that are arranged alphabetically.

73. Harvard University Graduate School of Business Administration, Baker Library. *Energy Information Sources.* 1976, Mini-list #14.

74. Harvard University Graduate School of Business Administration, Baker Library. *Sources of Information for Industry Analysis*. 1977, Mini-list #15.

75. Harvard University Graduate School of Business Administration, Baker Library. *U.S. Transportation Statistical Sources*. 1976, Mini-list #8.

Arts Management

Bibliographies

77. Georgi, Charlotte. *The Arts and the Art of Administration: A Selected Bibliography*. Los Angeles: UCLA Graduate School of Business Administration, Division of Research, 1970.

78. Georgi, Charlotte. *The Arts and the World of Business: A Selected Bibliography*. Metuchen, N.J.: Scarecrow Press, 1973. Supplement I. Los Angeles: UCLA Graduate School of Management, 1974.

79. Georgi, Charlotte. *Management and the Arts: A Selected Bibliography*. Los Angeles: UCLA Graduate School of Management, Division of Research, 1972.

80. Prieve, E. Arthur, and Ira W. Allen. *Administration in the Arts: An Annotated Bibliography of Selected References*. Madison: University of Wisconsin Graduate School of Business, 1973.

81. Quint, Barbara, and Lois Newman. *Performing Arts Centers and Economic Aspects of the Performing Arts: A Selective Bibliography*. Santa Monica, Calif.: Rand Corporation, 1969.

82. Reich, Ann S. *Bibliography for Arts Administration*. n.p.: 1972. This paper is a master's thesis.

Directories

83. *American Art Directory*. New York: R. R. Bowker, 1974. Museums, art schools, and art associations in the United States; includes lists of art magazines, fellowships, and scholarships, art schools abroad, and other art resources.

84. *Annual Register of Grant Support*. Orange, N.J.: Academic Media. Annual. Architecture and Fine Arts, p. 100; Performing Arts, p. 162.

85. *Art Direction Buyer's Guide of Art and Photography*. Annual. New York: Art Direction. Lists approximately 2,500 suppliers of art for advertising, illustrations, design, photography, and graphic art services; includes classified listings, representatives, and studio listings, each giving address, telephone number, and services performed.

86. Associated Councils of the Arts. *Directory of National Arts Organizations: Membership Associations Serving the Arts*. New York: Associated Councils of the Arts, 1972.

87. *Fine Arts Market Place*. Annual. New York: R. R. Bowker. See Organizations and Associations.

88. *The Foundation Directory*. New York: Columbia University Press for the Foundation Center, 1971. Arranged by state; check subject index in back for various fields of interest—i.e., Performing Arts, Dance, etc.

89. *Who's Who in American Art*. New York: R. R. Bowker, 1973.

Indexes

90. *Art Index*. Quarterly. New York: H. W. Wilson. For relevant articles check under subject headings such as Museums and Art Galleries—Administration, Art Patronage, Art and State, Art and Society, Business Committee for the Arts, National Endowment for the Arts, etc.

91. *Business Periodicals Index*. Monthly. New York: H. W. Wilson. For relevant articles check under subject headings such as Art and State, Museums, Performing Arts, The Arts, Art and Industry, Art Patronage, Theater, Opera, etc.

92. *PAIS*. Weekly. New York: Public Affairs Information Service. For relevant articles check under subject headings such as Arts Market, Museums, Theater, Opera, Art and Industry, Art and State, Art and Society, Performing Arts, Art Patronage, etc.

93. *Reader's Guide to Periodical Literature*. Semi-monthly. New York: H. W. Wilson. For relevant articles check under subject headings such as Art and Industry, The Arts, The Arts—Finance, The Arts—Federal Aid, Museums, Museum Directors, Theaters, Dance, Opera, Orchestras, etc.

Books

94. Baumol, William J., and William G. Bowen. *Performing Arts: The Economic Dilemma*. New York: Twentieth Century Fund, 1966.

95. Chagy, Gideon. *Business in the Arts '70*. New York: P. S. Eriksson, 1970.

96. Chagy, Gideon. *The New Patrons of the Arts*. New York: Abrams, 1972.

97. *Cultural Policy and Arts Administration*. Cambridge, Mass.: Harvard Summer School in Arts Administration, 1973.

98. Easton, Allan. *Community Support of the Performing Arts: Selected Problems of Local and National Interest*. Hempstead, N.Y.: Hofstra University, 1970.

99. Eells, Richard Sedric Fox. *The Corporation and the Arts*. New York: Macmillan, 1967.

Annual

76. *The Aerospace Year Book*. This contains information on all phases of the aerospace industry.

100. *The Finances of the Performing Arts.* New York: Ford Foundation, 1974.

101. Gingrich, Arnold. *Business and the Arts: An Answer to Tomorrow.* New York: P. S. Eriksson, 1969.

102. Henry, Austin H., and E. Arthur Prieve. *Improved Financial Management of Smaller Performing Arts Organizations.* Madison: University of Wisconsin, 1973.

103. Kaderlan, Norman S. *The Role of the Arts Administrator.* Madison: University of Wisconsin, Graduate School of Business, Center for Arts Administration, 1973.

104. Moore, Thomas Gale. *The Economics of the American Theatre.* Durham, N.C.: Duke University Press, 1968.

105. National Endowment for the Arts. *National Endowment for the Arts: Our Programs.* Washington, D.C.: U.S. Government Printing Office, 1972.

106. National Endowment for the Arts. *New Dimensions for the Arts, 1971–1972.* Washington, D.C.: U.S. Government Printing Office, 1973.

107. Osborne, Alan. *Patron: Industry Supports the Arts.* London: Connoisseur, 1966.

108. Raymond, Thomas Cicchino, Stephen A. Greyser, and Douglas Schwalbe. *Cases in Arts Administration.* Cambridge, Mass.: Institute of Arts Administration, 1971.

109. Reiss, Alvin H. *The Arts Management Handbook,* rev. 2d ed. New York: Law-Art Pub., 1974.

110. Reiss, Alvin H. *Culture and Company.* New York: Twayne Publishers, 1972.

Newsletters

Though no periodicals focus on this topic, many general art periodicals and business periodicals contain information on arts management. These are accessible through the indexes as mentioned above.

111. *Arts Business.* Quarterly. New York: Business Committee for the Arts.

112. *Arts Management.* 5 a year. New York: Radius Group. This newsletter is edited by Alvin H. Reiss.

113. *BCA News.* Quarterly. New York: Business Committee for the Arts. The editor and publisher of this newsletter is Gideon Chagy.

114. *Management in the Arts Program: Newsletter.* Irregular. Los Angeles: UCLA Graduate School of Management in cooperation with the College of Fine Arts.

Communications

Directories

115. *Broadcasting Yearbook.* Washington. Broadcast Publications. List of all TV stations and AM-FM radio stations in the United States and Canada, including addresses and telephone numbers, licenses and owner, representatives. Lists names and addresses of radio and TV commercial and program producers, news service distributors, network executives, and research services.

116. Weber, Olga S. *Audiovisual Market Place,* 3rd ed. New York: R. R. Bowker. Company names, addresses, key personnel, and product lines for all active producers, distributors, and other sources of audiovisual learning materials. Includes national, professional, and trade organizations, educational, radio, and TV stations.

117. Weiner, Richard. *Professional Guide to Public Relations.* Englewood Cliffs, N.J.: Prentice-Hall. Lists 500 public relations services with names, addresses, phone numbers of firms, and key personnel. Services include: clipping bureaus; literary, mailing, radio, and TV public relations services; media directories, motion picture distributors; fine art and rare photo services.

The Computer Industry

Statistical Sources

118. *Computer Review.* Lists significant features of virtually all digital computers and related peripheral devices and indicates comparative prices. Updated every four months to include specifications of new equipment.

119. Lee, Wayne J., ed. *The International Computer Industry.* Washington, D.C.: Applied Library Resources, 1971. Surveys nations that are leading users of computer equipment and systems and provides information concerning the market, duties and trade restrictions, and technical requirements.

120. *Predicasts.* Provides forecast data by SIC number. Sources for each forecast are given.

121. *U.S. Industrial Outlook.* Annual. Pertinent forecast and statistical data in Chapter 29: "Computing and Calculating Equipment."

Investment Services

122. Smith, Barney & Company. *Subscription Research Service.* Provides financial data for specific companies within the industry; pertinent information listed in "Data Processing" section.

123. Standard & Poor's Corporation. *Industry Surveys.* Provides basic data with current updating. Check under "Computers" in index.

124. *Value Line Investment Survey.* Provides stock evaluation for specific companies.

Directories, Encyclopedias, and Yearbooks

125. *Computer Yearbook*. Triennial. Provides overview of the industry. Includes sections on state of the art, computer applications, and a computer language summary.

126. *Computers and People: Computer Directory and Buyer's Guide*. Annual. In addition to organizational listings, includes information on the industry as a whole: a world computer census, a comprehensive list of computer applications, and a roster of college and university computer facilities.

127. *Directory of the Computer Industry*. Washington, D.C.: Applied Library Resources, Inc. A list of over 25,000 computer organizations and computer users, their names and addresses and other information.

128. *International Directory of Computer and Information System Services*. Detroit: Gale Research. Alphabetical listing and addresses of all types of electronic data processing agencies.

129. Jordain, Philip B., ed. *Condensed Computer Encyclopedia*. New York: McGraw-Hill, 1969.

130. *Worldwide Directory of Computer Companies*. Four indexes provide extensive coverage of material included. Presents full financial profile of public, private, and nonprofit companies, when available.

Dictionaries

131. Berkeley, Edmund C., and Linda L. Lovett. *Glossary of Terms in Computers and Data Processing*. Newtonville, Mass.: Berkeley Enterprises, 1960.

132. Committee on Computers and Information Processing. *American National Standard Vocabulary for Information Processing*. New York: American National Standards Institute, 1970. Includes list of references used in compilation.

133. Sippl, Charles J. *Computer Dictionary and Handbook*. Indianapolis: Bobbs-Merrill, 1966. The several appendices provide general introductory information on the industry. Two specialized appendices provide mathematics and statistics definitions.

134. U.S. Bureau of the Budget. *Automatic Data Processing*. Washington, D.C.: U.S. Government Printing Office, 1972.

135. Weik, Martin H. *Standard Dictionary of Computers and Information Processing*. New York: Hayden Book Companies, 1969. Extensively illustrated.

Bibliographies and Guides to the Literature

136. Carter, Ciel. *Guide to Reference Sources in the Computer Sciences*. New York: Macmillan, 1974. Provides detailed annotations for industry information sources.

137. *Computing Reviews*. Monthly. A journal of reviews and abstracts of current publications in areas of the computing sciences.

138. *International Computer Bibliography*. Manchester, England: National Computing Centre, 1969.

139. *New Literature on Automation*. Monthly. A journal of abstracts of recent industry literature: books, reports, articles, works of reference, proceedings, standards.

140. Pritchard, Alan. *A Guide to Computer Literature*, 2d ed. Hamden, Conn.: Shoe String Press, 1972.

141. *Quarterly Bibliography of Computers and Data Processing*. Phoenix, Arizona: Applied Computer Research. Selection designed for use by those actively engaged in profession; highly research-oriented material not included.

142. U.S. Bureau of Domestic Commerce. *Data Communications: Market Information Sources*. 1972.

Trade Journals

143. *Communications of the ACM* (Association for Computing Machinery). Monthly.

144. *Computer Decisions*. Monthly.

145. *Computerworld*. Weekly.

146. *Data Processing Digest*. Monthly. "Alerting" service with summaries of selected articles.

147. *Datamation*. Monthly.

Access to information in trade journals is provided by periodical indexes such as *Applied Sciences and Technology Index, Business Periodicals Index, F & S Index of Corporations and Industries* (by SIC code number), and *Public Affairs Information Service Bulletin*. Appropriate headings to check are: Computer Industry, Computers, Electronic Data Processing, Information Processing Systems.

Books

148. Bassler, Richard A., and Edward O. Joslin. *An Introduction to Computer Systems,* 2d ed. Arlington, Va.: College Readings, Inc., 1972. Selected articles divided into three sections: background, technology, applications.

149. Billings, Thomas H., and Richard C. Hogan. *A Study of the Computer Manufacturing Industry in the U.S.* Springfield, Va.: National Technical Information Service, 1970. Presents history of the industry with emphasis on economic importance of its present structure. Bibliographical References, pp. 211–213.

150. Gruenberger, Fred, ed. *Expanding Use of Computers in the 70's: Markets, Needs, Technology*. Englewood Cliffs, N.J.: Prentice-Hall, 1971. Treats industry from viewpoint of market needs. Bibliographical references at end of some chapters.

151. *Frost and Sullivan Reports*. Reports provide detailed industry analysis.

152. Stern, Robert A., and Nancy B. Stern. *Principles of Data Processing*. New York: Wiley, 1973. Presents overview of data processing as it specifically relates to the business world. Numerous illustrative aids.

153. Turn, Rein. *Computers in the 1980's*. New York: Columbia University Press, 1974. Discussion of industry potential with specific forecasts concerning hardware and software. Bibliographical references at end of each chapter.

Conservation and Environment

Directories

154. *Conservation Directory*. Annual. Washington, D.C.: National Wildlife Federation. Lists organizations and agencies concerned with the conservation, management, and use of this country's national resources.

155. *Directory of Organizations Concerned with Environmental Research*. State University College at Fredonia.

Geographic and subject listing of organizations (governmental, university, and private) throughout the world involved in environmental research.

156. *Pollution Control Directory*. Volume 4, No. 11, of Environmental Science and Technology, American Chemical Society. Lists manufacturers and suppliers of pollution control equipment, products, and services.

Consulting

Bibliographies

157. Association of Consulting Management Engineers, Inc. *Selected References on Management Consultation*. New York: 1974. Excellent entry point to the current and retrospective literature in the field. Includes speeches, articles, pamphlets, books. etc.

158. Hollander, Stanley C. *Management Consultants and Clients*. Michigan State University Business Studies, 1972. An annotated bibliography of books and monographs.

Guides

159. Angel, Juvenal L., compiler. *International Marketing Guide for Technical, Management and Other Consultants*. 1971. Deals with the international aspects of consulting including management consulting.

160. Wasserman, Paul, and Janice McLean. *Who's Who in Consulting: A Reference Guide to Professional Personnel Engaged in Consultation for Business, Industry, and Government*, 2d ed. 1973. Biographical information on over 7,500 individuals engaged in consulting. Listed alphabetically with cross-reference through the subject index.

Directories

161. American Management Association. *Directory of Consultant Members*. Annual.

162. American Management Association. *Directory of Membership and Services*. Annual.

163. American Society for Training and Development. *ASTD Consultant Directory*. Madison, Wis., 1967.

164. Association of Consulting Management Engineers. *Directory of Membership and Services*. Annual. New York.

165. Association of Management Consultants. *Directory of Membership and Services*. Updated annually. Milwaukee.

166. *Directory of Management Consultants and Industrial Services*. Los Angeles Chamber of Commerce. Lists consulting firms, business and industrial services.

167. *Engineering Careers with Consulting Firms*. Resource Publications, D. R. Goldenson and Company. Page profiles describing the activities of the firm and the nature of engineering services, requirements for positions. Information arranged by specialty and geographic location.

168. *European Directory of Economic and Corporate Planning 1973-1974*. Penelope Lloyd, ed. Eppine, Essex, U.K.: Gower, 1974. Lists European management consultants among others. Use the unit index as an access point.

169. *Industrial Research Laboratories of the U.S.*, rev. ed. William Buchanan, ed. Washington: Bowker Associations. Irregular.

170. Institute of Management Consultants. *Directory of Members—Institute of Management Consultants*. New York: 1974. Contains Supplement I, August 19, 1974.

171. *National Roster of Minority Professional Firms*. U.S. Department of Commerce. February, 1973. Not limited to management consultants.

172. *New Consultants: A Periodic Supplement to Consultants and Consulting Organizations*. June 1973–January 1975.

173. Smith, Robert, ed. *Register of Management Consultants and Advisory Services to Industry*. Eppine, Essex, U.K.: Gower, 1972. Contains over 1,000 entries as well as many useful chapters such as "How to Select and Use a Management Consultant" and "Presentation and Layout of a Consultant's Report."

174. Wasserman, Paul, and Janice McLean, eds. *Consultants and Consulting Organizations: A Reference Guide to Concerns and Individuals Engaged in Consultation for Business and Industry*, 2d ed. Detroit: Gale Research, 1973. Lists over 5,000 individuals and firms. Contains a subject index and lists both U.S. and foreign firms.

Monographs and Conference Reports

Works dealing with various aspects of business or management consulting may be found by consulting the card catalog at a library under the subject heading "Business Consulting." A few examples are listed below.

175. Amon, Richard R., et al. *Management Consulting.* Management Consulting Report Associates, 1958. Although somewhat dated, this does contain a good history of consulting.

176. *Management Consulting in the 1970's: Proceedings North American Conference of Management Consultants,* January 25, 1972.

Periodicals

Articles on consulting appear in many different periodicals, but they can usually be located by using one of the various indexes such as *ANBAR Management Services, Business Periodicals Index, F & S Index to Corporations and Industries, Public Affairs Information Services Index,* and *Readers' Guide.*

177. *American Institute of Certified Public Accountants Management Advisory Services Guidelines Series.* Irregular. New York.

178. Association of Consulting Management Engineers. *ACME Survey on Compensation for Professional Staff in Management Consulting Firms.* Triennial. New York. Excludes partners, officers, directors, and owners.

179. Association of Consulting Management Engineers. *Management Consultant.* New York. Irregular.

Books

180. Wasserman, Paul, and W. R. Greer, Jr. *Consultants and Consulting Organizations.* Ithaca, N.Y.: Graduate School of Business and Public Administration, Cornell University.

Educational and Library Administration

Indexes to Educational Information

181. Wasserman, Paul, ed. *Encyclopedia of Business Information Sources.* Detroit: Gale Research, 1970. Volume I. Includes references for educational information under the topic "Schools."

Directories

182. *A Directory of Educational Programs for the Gifted,* 1st ed. Lavonne B. Axford, ed. Metuchen, N.J.: Scarecrow Press.

183. *A Summary of Paraprofressional Training in Colleges and Universities.* Office of New Careers. Washington, D.C.: U.S. Government Printing Office. Geographical listing of opportunities for "new careers for the poor."

184. *Accredited Institutions of Postsecondary Education, and Programs and Candidates.* Washington, D.C. American Council on Education. Annual.

185. *American Junior Colleges,* 8th ed. Edmund J. Gleaser, Jr., ed. Washington, D.C.: American Council on Education.

186. *American Library Directory,* Helaine MacKeigan, ed. Biennial. New York: R. R. Bowker. Lists public libraries, county and regional systems, college and university libraries, and private libraries. Information includes names of key personnel and addresses.

187. *American Universities and Colleges,* 10th ed. Otis A. Singletary, ed. Washington, D.C.: American Council on Education.

188. *Barron's Guide to the Two-Year Colleges.* R. William Graham, ed. Woodbury, N.Y.: Barron's Educational Series.

189. *Barron's Profiles of American Colleges.* Benjamin Fine, ed. Woodbury, N.Y.: Barron's Educational Series. Detailed profiles on 1,350 colleges. Competitive ratings listed.

190. *Comparative Guide to American Colleges.* James Cass and Max Biernbaum, eds. New York: Harper & Row. Descriptions of U.S. four-year colleges, with indexes by state, religious affiliation, selectivity, and number of degrees granted in selected fields.

191. *Comparative Guide to Two-Year Colleges and Four-Year Specialized Schools and Programs.* James Cass and Max Biernbaum, eds. New York: Harper & Row.

192. *Directory of National Association of Schools of Music.* Washington, D.C.: National Association of Schools of Music.

193. *Directory of Accredited Institutions.* Washington, D.C.: United Business Schools Associations. Alphabetical and geographic listing of accredited business schools.

194. *Directory of Accredited Private Home Study Schools.* Washington, D.C.: National Home Study Council.

195. *Directory of Approved Counseling Agencies.* Washington, D.C.: American Board on Counseling Service, Inc., APGA.

196. *Directory of Catholic Special Facilities and Programs in the U.S. for Handicapped Children and Adults.* Washington, D.C. National Catholic Educational Association.

197. *Directory of Computer Education and Research.* Washington, D.C.: Science and Technology Press, Inc. In two volumes; offers information on over 1,400 institutions in the U.S. offering educational programs in

computer and computer-related fields; their courses and research activities.

198. *Directory of Educational Statistics, A Guide to Sources.* Malcolm C. Hamilton, ed. Ann Arbor, Mich.: Piernan Press, 1974.

199. *Directory of Exceptional Children, A Listing of Educational and Training Facilities,* 7th ed. E. R. Young and Porter Sargent, eds. Boston: Porter Sargent. Annual. Lists private residential and day schools and treatment centers for the emotionally disturbed and socially maladjusted.

200. *Directory of Experimental Schools, Issue No. 57.* Pettigrew, Arkansas: New Schools Exchange.

201. *Directory of Free Schools.* Sebastopol, Calif.: Alternatives Foundation.

202. *Directory of Full-Year Head Start Programs.* Washington, D.C.: Office of Child Development, Project Head Start, U.S. Department of HEW. Geographic listing with key personnel of all the programs. Addresses of regional offices.

203. *Directory of Library Consultants.* John Berry III, ed. New York: R. R. Bowker. Lists qualified consultants in the United States and Canada and in every area of librarianship. Names, addresses, backgrounds. Listed alphabetically and by specialty.

204. *Directory of Member Colleges.* Washington, D.C. Council for the Advancement of Small Colleges.

205. *Directory of National Association of Trade and Technical Schools.* Washington, D.C.: Accrediting Commission of National Association of Trade and Technical Schools. Schools listed under subject headings, alphabetically, by state. Includes course descriptions and use of the school by public and private agencies.

206. *Directory of Predominantly Black Colleges and Universities in the U.S.A.* Washington, D.C.: National Alliance of Businessmen. Geographic directory, including enrollment, curricula, degrees offered, and description of each institution.

207. *The Academic Underachiever.* Triennially. Boston: Porter Sargent. Selective information on the classification and description of over 700 sources of help for the able student who needs special assistance in planning his educational career.

208. *Directory of Special Libraries and Information Centers.* Anthony Kruzas, ed. Detroit: Gale Research. Volume I lists information facilities in the United States and Canada: special libraries in colleges and universities, branches of public library concentrating on one group of subjects, company, government, and non-profit-sponsored libraries; Volume II gives geographic and personnel listings.

209. *Directory of State and Local Resources for the Mentally Retarded.* Washington, D.C.: U.S. Department of HEW. List of state and local agencies, facilities, and other resources that serve the mentally retarded. Includes clinical programs and residential facilities, special rehabilitation facilities, and type of client served.

210. *The Directory of Traditional Black Colleges and Universities in U.S.* Detroit: Ford Motor Company & U.S. Plywood Champion Paper, Inc.

211. *Early Childhood Education Directory.* New York: R. R. Bowker. Guide to approximately 2,000 schools devoted to the educational interests of preschool children.

212. *Education Directory. Education Associations.* Annual. U.S. Office of Education. Washington, D.C.: U.S. Government Printing Office. Includes association's publications and frequency of issue.

213. *Education Directory—Higher Education.* Washington, D.C.: U.S. Department of HEW, National Center for Educational Statistics. Lists accredited institutions (alphabetically by state) in United States and its outlying areas.

214. *Education Directory. Public School Systems 1973–74.* Washington, D.C.: U.S. Government Printing Office, 1971.

215. *Education Directory—State Governments.* Washington, D.C.: U.S. Department of HEW. Lists principal officers of state agencies responsible for elementary and secondary education and vocational-technical education in United States.

216. *Encyclopedia of Associations.* Volumes 1, 3. Detroit: Gale Research. Volume 1 is an annual compilation of names and addresses for all types of national organizations arranged by broad index to provide easy access. Volume 3 is published quarterly and lists "new associations and projects." Section 5 of Volume 1 is "Educational Organizations."

217. *Directory of Facilities for the Learning Disabled and Catalog of Tests.* San Rafael, Calif.: Academic Therapy Publications; New York: Harper & Row. Geographic listing of schools, learning centers, and clinics.

218. *Guide to Master of Arts in Teaching Program.* Anne M. Scott, ed. State University of New York at Binghamton. Programs, by state, described by level of specialization available; program length; intern and salary information.

219. *Hand Book of Private Schools.* Boston: Porter Sargent Publications. Schools and academies listed by geographical districts; leading private schools classified; summer academic and camp programs.

220. *Encyclopedia of Library and Information Science.* New York: Marcel Dekker, Inc. Lists alphabetically all information related to library and information science. Includes organizations, individuals, conferences, countries, libraries, systems, codes, copyright information, etc.

221. *Index of Opportunity in the Teaching Profession.* Employer profiles. Princeton, N.J.: Princeton University Press, 1970.

222. *Guide to the Two-Year Colleges.* Woodbury, N.Y.: Barron's Educational Series.

223. *Lovejoy's Career and Vocational School Guide.* Clarence Lovejoy, ed. New York: Simon and Schuster. Private and public vocational school programs.

224. *Lovejoy's College Guide.* Clarence Lovejoy, ed. Annual. New York: Simon and Schuster. Entries for more than 3,368 American colleges, universities, junior colleges, and technical institutes; 500 programs geared to specific careers and discussion of new college board program.

225. *Private Independent Schools, The American Private Schools for Boys and Girls.* Annual. Wallingford, Conn.: Bunting and Lyon, Inc. Lists by state, summer programs.

226. *Requirements for Certification for Elementary, Secondary Schools and Junior Colleges.* Elizabeth Woellner and Maurilla Woods, eds. Chicago: University of Chicago Press. Listed for each state are classifications of certificates and requirements for elementary and secondary, including special subject areas, guidance, supervisory, and junior college.

227. *Scholarship Program, Education of Handicapped Children.* Washington, D.C.: U.S. Office of Education.

228. *The Counselor Education Directory 1971,* 1st ed. Muncie, Ind.: Ball State University. Counselor education programs; lists institutions and the degrees, majors, and certificates available; lists 2,500 counselor educators, and state directors of counseling and guidance.

229. *Who's Who in American College and University Administration Annual.* New York: Crowell-Collier Educational Corporation. Presents biographical information on "11,000 administrators including presidents, deans, librarians, bursars and others."

Bibliographies and Guides

230. *Comparative Guide to American Colleges.* James Cass and Max Biernbaum, eds. New York: Harper & Row. Descriptions of U.S. four-year colleges, with indexes by state, religious affiliation, selectivity, and number of degrees granted in selected fields.

231. *Comparative Guide to Two-Year Colleges and Four-Year Specialized Schools and Programs.* James Cass and Max Biernbaum, eds. New York: Harper & Row.

232. Forrester, Gertrude. *Occupational Literature—An Annotated Bibliography.* New York: H. W. Wilson, 1971, p. 432. Information found under "School Administrator."

233. Pierce, Milo C. *Administration and Planning in Higher Education: A Bibliography of Books and Reports.* Monticello, Ill.: Council of Planning Librarians, 1972. Encompasses five aspects of administration and planning in higher education: Policymaking, Legal, Financial, Physical Plant, and Academic.

234. *School Executive's Guide.* Englewood Cliffs, N.J.: Prentice-Hall, 1965. A practical compendium for administering public schools in the United States.

Statistics

235. College and University Personnel Association. *Administration Compensation Survey.* Biennial. Washington, D.C.: C.U.P.A. Excellent survey including both fringe-benefit and salary analysis.

236. Harris, Seymour E. *A Statistical Portrait of Higher Education.* New York: McGraw-Hill, 1972.

237. National Education Association, Research Division. *Salaries Paid and Salary-Related Practices in Higher Education.* Washington, D.C.: NEA. Biennial. Includes salary and fringe benefits.

238. *Predicasts.* This publication gives forecast data by Standard Industrial Classification number. Education SIC number is 8200. Sources for each forecast are given. It is suggested that you check the original source for the most complete forecast information.

239. *Standard Education Almanac.* John S. Greene, ed. Indianapolis, Ind.: Academic Media, 1972.

240. U.S. Department of Commerce. *U.S. Industrial Outlook for 1975.* Washington, D.C.: U.S. Government Printing Office, 1975. "Educational Services," pp. 413–415 with projections to 1980.

241. U.S. Office of Education. *Digest of Educational Statistics.* Annual. Washington, D.C.: U.S. Government Printing Office.

242. U.S. Office of Education. *Projections of Educational Statistics to 1982–83.* 1973 edition. Washington, D.C.: U.S. Government Printing Office, 1974.

Books and Pamphlets

243. Biegeleisen, J. I. *Careers and Opportunities in Teaching.* New York: E. P. Dutton, 1972. Considerations about teaching at various levels or in related orientations; suggestions and list of accredited colleges with teacher education programs.

244. Bolin, James F., ed. *Management Information for College Administrators.* Atlanta: University of Georgia, 1971.

245. Carnegie Commission on Higher Education. *The More Effective Use of Resources: An Imperative for Higher Education.* New York: McGraw-Hill, 1972. A report and recommendations.

246. Committee for Economic Development, Research and Policy Committee. *The Management and Financing of Colleges.* New York: C.E.D., 1973.

247. Eisen, Irving. *Careers in Teaching and Education.* Washington, D.C.: B'nai B'rith Vocational Service, 1972. Descriptions of wide variety of professional jobs of a teaching nature within the school, college, or vocational school settings.

248. Getzels, Jacob W., James M. Lipham, and Roald F. Campbell. *Educational Administration as a Social Process—Theory, Research, Practice.* New York: Harper & Row, 1968.

249. Hefferlin, J. B. Lon, and Ellis L. Phillips, Jr. *Information Services for Academic Administration.* San Francisco: Jossey-Bass, 1971.

250. Hungate, Thad L. *Management in Higher Education.*

New York: Bureau of Publications, Teachers College, Columbia University, 1964.

251. Lahti, Robert E. *Innovative College Management*. San Francisco: Jossey-Bass, 1973. Includes annotated bibliography.

252. Minter, John, and Ben Lawrence, eds. *Management Information Systems: Their Development and Use in the Administration of Higher Education*. Boulder, Colo.: Western Interstate Commission for Higher Education, 1969. Seminar on the Advanced State-of-the-Art/The Sterling Institute, Washington, D.C.

253. Organization for Economic Cooperation and Development. *Institutional Management in Higher Education*. Paris: O.E.C.D. Publications, 1972. Four-day conference report; 21 countries and 83 institutions of higher education represented.

254. Richman, Barry M., and Richard N. Farmer. *Leadership Goals, and Power in Higher Education*. San Francisco: Jossey-Bass, 1974.

255. Wingfield, Clyde J., Ed. *The American University, A Public Administration Perspective*. Dallas: Southern Methodist University, 1970. Symposium on administration of higher education and presidential perspectives.

Indexes to Periodicals

256. *Business Periodicals Index*. New York: H. W. Wilson. Monthly except July (Cumulative).

257. *Current Index to Journals on Education* (CIJE).

258. *Educational Administration Abstracts*. Published three times a year by the University Council for Education Administration, Columbus, Ohio. Abstracts approximately 100 journals.

259. *Educational Administration Quarterly*. Published three quarters a year by the University Council for Education Administration, Columbus, Ohio.

260. *Education Index*. New York: H. W. Wilson.

261. *Educational Resources Information Center* (ERIC). ERIC is a national information system established by the U.S. Office of Education in 1964. Its purpose is to collect, process, and make available a wide range of educational documents. These are four major parts to the ERIC system: (1) Thesaurus of ERIC Descriptors, (2) educational documents on microfiche, (3) abstract indices to microfiche—ex. RIE (Research in Education), and (4) machinery to read and reproduce microfiche. Initially, use the topic "Educational Administration"; for more in-depth research, check with Thesaurus of ERIC Descriptors.

Electronics and Engineering

Directories

262. *Electronic News Financial Fact Book and Directory*. New York: Fairchild Publishers. Annual. Lists officers and directors, products, and sales for electronic companies.

263. *Electronic Industries Association, Membership List, Trade Directory*. Annual. Washington, D.C.

264. *Science, Engineering, Research and Development Directory*. Annual. Small Business Administration (Regional Offices). Issued separately for each of the nine SBA regions.

Periodicals

265. *Electronics. Top 100*. A listing published each year in the July issue of *Electronics News* magazine.

Financial—Banking

Bibliographies

266. American Bankers Association. *Stonier Graduate School of Banking, Cumulative Catalog of Theses, Supplement*. New York. Annotated. Annual.

267. Federal Reserve Bank of Philadelphia. *The Fed in Print*. Quarterly. Current information on Federal Reserve publications.

Directories

268. *Who Owns What in World Banking*. London: Banker Research Unit. Annual. A guide to the subsidiary and affiliated interests of the world's major banks.

269. *Banking*. "A Bankers Guide to Washington." Annual. New York: Banking. Gives names, addresses, phone numbers of all federal agencies affecting banking, as well as key politicians, committees, and trade associations in the area.

270. *Banks of the World*. Frankfurt-am-Main:Fritz Knopp Verlag.

271. *Directory of American Savings and Loan Associations*. Baltimore: T. K. Sanderson Organization. Annual. Listing of 5,000 U.S. associations, with branches, key officials, officials, affiliations, etc.

272. *Financial Market Place*. New York: R. R. Bowker. Lists names and addresses (some foreign firms) of companies grouped by industry—such as banks, investment organizations, capital firms, credit and collection services, stock and commodity, and so on.

273. *International Bankers Directory*. Skokie, Ill.: Rand McNally & Company.

274. *Major Independent Finance Companies*. A listing pub-

lished each year in the April issue of *Bankers Monthly* magazine.

275. *Polk's World Bank Directory*. Nashville, Tenn.: R. L. Polk and Company. Lists banks and information.

276. *Rand-McNally International Bankers Directory. Bankers Blue Book*. Biannual. Skokie, Ill.: Rand McNally & Company.

277. *Who's Who in Banking: The Directory of the Banking Profession*. New York: Business Press, Inc. Irregular.

Investment Services

278. *Frost and Sullivan Reports: Markets for Specialized Financial Services,* No. 221. Includes data on the banking industry.

279. Investors Management Sciences, Inc. *Financial Dynamics.* Gives financial analysis and comparisons, quarterly and annually, of individual industries, including banking and savings and loan associations.

280. Smith, Barney & Co. *Subscription Research Service.* Contains finance and research reports analyzing facts about banking.

281. Standard and Poor's Corporation. *Industry Surveys.* Includes current and basic analyses of the banking and savings and loan industries, with financial comparisons and outlook.

282. *Standard and Poor's Stock Reports.* Usually found in loose-leaf binder. Single page for each company listed on the New York, American, and over-the-counter stock exchanges. Each report gives fundamental position, recent developments, and so on, for companies.

283. *Value Line Investment Survey.* Includes ratings and reports on the banking industry, with special situation analysis.

284. *World Who's Who in Finance and Industry.* Career sketches of leading businessmen and others noteworthy in the fields of finance and industry. A selected index by company is at the front.

Additional Statistical Sources

285. Bank Administration Institute. *A Biennial Survey of Bank Officer Salaries.*

286. Federal Home Loan Board. *Savings and Home Financing Source Book.* Annual. Statistics on loans held, mortgages.

287. National Association of Supervisors of State Banks. *Profile of State-Chartered Banking.* Biennial. Includes statistics on state banking departments, number of banks, assets and liabilities, as well as operations, competition, etc.

288. *Predicasts.* Abstracts forecast statistics by SIC number, gives original sources of data.

289. Standard and Poor's Corporation. *Standard and Poor's Trade and Securities: Statistics.* "Banking and Finance." Current and basic statistical source.

290. U.S. Bureau of Domestic Commerce. *The U.S. Indus-*

trial Outlook. Annual. Recent trends, with a brief outlook on commercial banking.

291. U.S. Bureau of the Census. *Statistical Abstract of the United States.* Annual. Includes government data on the banking industry, and a "Guide to Sources of Statistics."

292. U.S. Dept. of Commerce. *Survey of Current Business* (annual) with its biennial supplement, *Business Statistics.*

293. United States League of Savings Associations. *Savings and Loan Fact Book.* Annual.

Statistics on banking are published mainly by the various federal agencies: The Federal Reserve System (assets and liabilities of all commercial banks in the United States, etc.); The Federal Deposit Insurance Corporation; The Comptroller of the Currency of the Treasury Dept.; The Federal Home Loan Bank Board. The U.S. Savings and Loan League, the American Bankers Association, and various others also publish current material. For statistics in banking journals, see below. (Individual FRS banks also publish journals.)

Encyclopedias and Manuals

294. Bank Administration Institute. *Bank Administration Manual.* Park Ridge, Ill.: Bank Administration Institute, 1970. An aid in solving problems likely to arise in banking.

295. Ritter, Lawrence S. *Principles of Money, Banking, and Financial Markets.* New York: Basic Books, 1974.

296. Munn, G. G. *Glenn G. Munn's Encyclopedia of Banking and Finance,* 7th ed., revised by F. L. Garcia. Boston: Bankers Publishing Co., 1973.

Journals and Magazines

297. *American Banker.* Daily.

298. *The Banker.* Monthly. London.

299. *The Banker's Magazine.* Quarterly. Includes a book review section.

300. *Banker's Monthly.* Monthly. National banking magazine.

301. *Banking.* Monthly. Journal of the American Banking Association.

302. *Burrough's Clearing House.* Monthly. Reports much S & L news, including annual meetings.

303. *Federal Reserve Bulletin.* Monthly. U.S. Board of Governors of the Federal Reserve Systems. Includes the FRS Directory, current events; one of the best sources of national and international banking statistics.

304. *Journal of Bank Research.* Quarterly. Bank Administration Institute.

305. *Journal of Commerce Bank Lending.* Monthly. Robert Morris Associates.

306. *Magazine of Bank Administration.* Monthly.

307. *Savings and Loan News.* Monthly. United States Sav-

ings and Loan League. Features a "Current Trends" section.

308. *United States Federal Home Loan Board Journal.* Monthly. Contains current statistics on savings and loan associations; annual reports in the April issue.

For recent articles in journals, magazines, and newspapers, see *Business Periodicals Index, Funk and Scott Index of Corporations and Industries, Funk and Scott Index International, New York Times Index, Public Affairs Information Service Bulletin, Wall Street Journal Index.*

Guides

309. Andriot, John L. *Guide to U.S. Government Serials and Periodicals.* McLean, Virginia: Documents Index.

310. Andriot, John L. *Guide to U.S. Government Statistics.* McLean, Virginia: Documents Index. Contains valuable sources of banking statistics published by the various federal agencies.

Lists of Largest Banks

311. *American Banker.* "500 Largest Banks in the Free World"; "300 Largest Banks in the U.S.," in last July issue each year; also "300 Largest Commercial Banks in the U.S.," each year in late January or early February; "300 Top Savings and Loans," in the late February issue.

312. *The Banker.* "The Top 300 World Banks." Annual, June issue.

313. *Fortune.* "Directory of Largest Corporations." Annual, 4 parts. Part 3 (July) lists 50 largest commercial banks; part 4 (August) lists the 50 largest commercial banks outside the U.S.

314. *Moody's Bank and Financial Manual.* Annual, with biweekly supplements. Center blue pages include 300 largest banks in U.S. (by deposits), 50 largest banks (by amount of permanent capital funds), 100 largest savings and loan associations.

315. *Savings and Loan News.* "The Top 200 Associations." Annual, February issue.

Annual Surveys and Special Reports

316. *The Banker.* "International Banking Annual Review." August 1974, p. 891 ff.

317. *Business Week.* "A Close-up of How the 200 Top Banks Are Performing," "Annual Survey of Bank Performance." Mid-September issues.

318. *Business Week.* "New Banking," Special Report, Sept. 15, 1973, pp. 86–166. Tells of changes in the banking world, new operations and businesses.

319. *Forbes.* "Annual Report on American Industry." Includes section on Finance—Banks. Always 1/1 issue.

320. *Journal of Bank Research.* "The Changing Dimensions of Banking Structure." Autumn 1974, pp. 145–155.

321. *Management Controls.* Special Issue: "Bank Management," June 1974. Discusses issues, trends, and systems involved in improving organizational and operational efficiency; information on the computer process.

322. *World Banking Survey.* Annual. Includes list of the world's leading banks.

Recent Publications

323. Mayer, Martin. *The Bankers.* New York: Weybright and Talley, 1974. Report on the revolution in American banking and its possible consequences; examines most facets of banks today.

324. Prochnow, Herbert V., and Herbert V. Prochnow, Jr., eds. *The Changing World of Banking.* New York: Harper & Row, 1974. Survey of American banking; articulates numerous aspects of modern banking developments by authorities; includes bibliographical references.

Financial—Nonbanking

Directories

325. *Best's Digest of Insurance Stocks.* Morristown, N.J.: A. M. Best Company.

326. *Best's Life Insurance Reports.* Morristown, N.J.: A. M. Best Company.

Food Processing and Distributing

Directories

327. *Frozen Food Fact Book and Directory.* New York: National Frozen Food Association. Lists members of association by state. Lists are broken down into several different divisions (packers, brokers, warehouses).

328. *Grocery Distribution Guide.* Greenwich, Conn.: Metro Market Studies, Inc. Grocers listed by city and state.

329. *Supermarket Grocery and Convenience Store Chains.* New York: Business Guides, Inc. Chain Store Guide. Lists of supermarkets by city and state.

330. *Thomas Grocery Register.* New York: Thomas Publishing Company. Lists supermarket chains by states; exporters, importers, brokers; canners; frozen foods; packers; warehouse; trade associations.

Bibliographies

331. Davis, Morris E. *Planning Medical Care: Assessment of Distribution and Costs of Physician Services.* Monticello, Ill.: Council of Planning Librarians, Exchange Bibliography No. 475, November 1973.

332. Harrison, Fernande P. *Planning Health Care Facilities: A Bibliography.* Monticello, Ill.: Council of Planning Librarians, Exchange Bibliography No. 369, February 1973.

333. Sharma, Prakash C. *Health Services: A Selected Research Bibliography.* Monticello, Ill.: Council of Planning Librarians, Exchange Bibliography No. 586, June 1974.

334. Williamson, John W. *Health Services Research Bibliography.* Washington, D.C.: U.S. Department of HEW, 1972.

335. DMS, Inc. *Health Care Systems, 1972–1976.* New York: McGraw-Hill, 1971. Excellent basic source for cost estimates and outlook; division breakdowns with charts and tables, market outlook; directory of manufacturers of health industry equipment with description and use of instruments; directory of hospitals and of consultant assistance available in specialized clinical areas.

336. "1974 Salary Scoreboard." In *Modern Healthcare,* August 1974, pp. 19–24. Comparison charts and graphs of salary ranges in the field.

337. *Reference Data on Socioeconomic Issues in Health.* Annual. Chicago: American Medical Association. Statistics and graphs on hospitals and nursing homes, health insurance, and personal and national health care expenditures.

338. Stewart, Paula A. *Health Manpower: A County and Metropolitan Area Data Book.* Washington, D.C.: U.S. Department of HEW, 1971.

339. Troy, Leo. *Almanac of Business and Industrial Financial Ratios.* Annual. Englewood Cliffs, N.J.: Prentice-Hall. Detailed listing of financial ratios for medical industry services operation; same for medical industry manufacturing.

340. U.S. Bureau of the Census. *Census of Manufacturers—Preliminary Reports.* 1972. Quinquennial. Uses Standard Industrial Classification (SIC). See Report Nos. 3841–42 for preliminary statistics on employment, payrolls, cost of materials, value added by manufacturer, and value of shipment.

341. U.S. Bureau of the Census. "Industry Series," *Census of Manufacturers.* 1972. Quinquennial. For operating ratios as well as an elaboration of *Preliminary Reports,* see SIC Industry Groups, pp. 384–387.

342. U.S. Social Security Administration. *Medical Care Expenditures, Prices and Costs: Background Book.* 1973. Overall view of operating costs and projections of hospital and nursing facilities.

Industry Information

343. DeSalvo, Robert J. "Medical Marketing Mixture." In *Medical Marketing and Media,* February 1974, p. 18. Structure of health care industry viewed.

344. Fritz, Eli. "Overview of the Hospital Marketing." In *Medical Marketing and Media,* November 1971, pp. 11–16. Comparisons of hospital expenditures in the years between 1946 and 1970.

345. Frost and Sullivan, Inc. *The Hospital Drugs, Supplies, Services, Equipment and Building Materials,* Report No. 333. New York, February 1975. Covers community hospital industry with projections to 1984.

346. Frost and Sullivan, Inc. *Markets for Health Care Equipment Leasing,* Report No. 264. New York. Covers present market, future trends with 10-year projections, opportunities, etc.

347. Gallop, Renee. "Health and Medical Services." In *U.S. Industrial Outlook, 1975, with Projections to 1980,* pp. 399–404. U.S. Bureau of Domestic Commerce, 1975. Annual. Broad-scoped article on the growing needs in health care industry as well as graphic depiction of present and projected costs. Brief explanation of health maintenance organizations.

348. *Health Care Facilities, Existing and Needed.* Washington, D.C.: Department of HEW, 1969. Dated but valuable, as projections of that year can be compared to actual current progress. Discussion of the Hill-Burton plan.

349. Industry File. *File I-80, Health Organizations.* For specific information on a number of hospitals and health service programs.

350. *Medical Marketing and Media.* Monthly. Stamford, Conn.: Navillus Publishing Corp. Up-to-date reports on advances in medical industry and manufacturing. Indexed in *F & S.*

351. *Nursing Home Fact Book, 1970–71.* Washington, D.C.: American Nursing Home Association, 1971.

352. Schiffman, Leon G., and Vincent Gaccione. "Opinion Leaders in Institutional Markets." In *Journal of Marketing,* 38(2):49, 1974. Impact of opinion leaders in health care institutional market.

353. *Sources of Medical Information.* New York: Exceptional Books, Inc.

354. Standard and Poor's Corporation. *Trade and Securities.* Monthly with annual cumulations. Industrial surveys on many aspects of health care industry. Reports accessible through subject index under "Medical Care" at the beginning of each year cumulation.

Administration/Management

355. *Comprehensive Health Care Centers Including HMO's.* Report No. 271. New York: Frost and Sullivan, Inc.,

June 1974. In-depth view of health care industry manpower resources, and supplies as well as the economics
of health care including health care plans and HMOs.

356. DMS, Inc. *Health Care Systems, 1972–1976.* New
York: McGraw-Hill, 1971.

357. Durbin, Richard L., and W. Herbert Springall. *Organization and Administration of Health Care: Theory,
Practice, Environment,* 2d ed. St. Louis: C. V. Mosby,
1974.

358. Forsyth, G. C., and D. Glyn Thomas. "Models for Financially Healthy Hospitals." In *Harvard Business Review,* July/August 1971, pp. 106–117.

359. Griffith, John R., Walton M. Hancock, and Fred C.
Munson. "Practical Ways to Contain Hospital Costs."
In *Harvard Business Review,* November/December
1973, pp. 131–139.

360. Hepner, James O., and Donna M. Hepner. *The Health
Strategy Game: A Challenge for Reorganization and
Management.* Saint Louis: C. V. Mosby, 1973.

361. *Hospital Financial Management.* Monthly. Chicago:
Hospital Financial Management Association. Current
issues in hospital and health services management.

362. *International Journal of Health Services.* Quarterly.
Westport, Conn.: Baywood Publishing. Covers policy,
planning, administration, and evaluation of health services.

363. Weber, James B., and Martha A. Dula. "Effective
Planning of Committees for Hospitals." In *Harvard
Business Review,* May/June 1964, pp. 113–142.

364. Wren, George R. *Modern Health Administration.* Ath-
ens: University of Georgia Press, 1974.

Indexes and Abstracts

365. *Business Periodicals Index.* Articles on health services
industry accessible through author and subject index.
See subject heading "Medical Care" and its related
subheadings and cross-references. Particularly good for
articles on health maintenance organizations.

366. *F & S Index of Corporations and Industries.* Article
citations accessible through numerically sequential
Standard Industrial Classification (SIC) numbers; for
"Health Services Manufacturing Industry," see SIC
No. 3840; for "Health Services," see SIC No. 8000.

367. *Medical Care Review.* 11 per year. Ann Arbor, Michigan: Bureau of Public Health Economics. Includes abstracts of books, articles, and conferences.

368. Public Affairs Information Service (PAIS). Accessible
through author and subject index.

369. Smithsonian Institution. Science Information Exchange. *Catalog of Health Services Research: Abstracts of Public and Private Projects, 1967–70.*
Washington, D.C.: U.S. Department of HEW, 1971.
Abstracts of 1,226 funded projects in all aspects of
health care including hospital and nursing home
administration.

Directories

370. *Directory of Member Services.* Washington, D.C.:
American Association of Psychiatric Services for Children. Geographic directory including names of key personnel, listing of approved training centers and
programs in career child psychiatry.

371. DMS, Inc. *Health Care Systems, 1972–1976.* New
York: McGraw-Hill, 1971.

372. *Guide to the Health Care Field.* Annual. Chicago:
American Hospital Association. Directory of health
care institutions, AJA membership, health organizations, agencies and educational programs; includes
guide for hospital buyers.

373. *Health Organizations of the United States and Canada.*
Ithaca, N.Y.: Graduate School of Business and Public
Administration, Cornell University. Lists national, regional, and state organizations involved with health and
related fields in the United States and Canada.

374. *Hospitals.* Guide issue of the *Journal of the American
Hospital Association,* Parts 1 and 2. Chicago: American Hospital Association. Lists hospitals.

Leisure—Hotel
and Motel Ventures; Entertainment

Bibliographies

375. Barsenik, Frank D. *Literature of the Lodging Market:
An Annotated Bibliography.* East Lansing: Michigan
State University, 1966.

376. Bootle, Valerie, and Philip Nailon. *A Bibliography of
Hotel and Catering Operation.* London: New University Education, 1970. A guide to books on operations,
including some annotations.

377. Spinney, Katherine, and Blanche Fickle. "Bibliography Prepared for Hotel and Restaurant Related Subjects," in *Cornell Hotel and Restaurant Administra-

tion,* August issues. A list of books, pamphlets, and
articles related to hotel administration.

378. Wasserman, Paul, et al. *Encyclopedia of Business Information Sources.* 2 vols. Detroit: Gale Research,
1970. Lists handbooks, manuals, bibliographies, periodicals, directories, statistics sources, financial ratios.

Books

379. Dukas, Peter. *Hotel Front Office Management and
Operation.* Dubuque, Iowa: William C. Brown, 1970.
An account of daily procedures and how to operate.

380. Gunn, Clare A., and Robert W. McIntosh. *Motel Planning and Business Management*. Dubuque, Iowa: William C. Brown, 1964.

381. Keister, Douglas Carlyle. *Selected Readings, for an Introduction to Hotel and Restaurant Management*. Berkeley, Calif.: McCutchen, 1971.

382. Lattin, Gerald W. *Careers in Hotels and Restaurants*. New York: Henry Z. Walch, 1967.

383. Lattin, Gerald W. *Modern Hotel and Motel Management*. San Francisco: W. H. Freeman, 1968. Tells about the industry, organization, career opportunities, future, and where to get training.

384. Lundberg, Donald Emil, and James P. Armatas. *The Management of People in Hotels, Restaurants, and Clubs*. Dubuque, Iowa: William C. Brown, 1974. Deals with screening, interviewing, managing, training; emphasizes the human aspect.

385. Lundberg, Donald E. *The Hotel and Restaurant Business*. Chicago: Institutions/Volume Feeding Management Magazine, 1971.

386. Pickering, J. F., J. A. Greenwood, and Diana Hunt. *The Small Firm in the Hotel and Catering Industry*. London: Her Majesty's Stationery Office, 1971. Covers structure, economics, changes, labor, and management of the industry.

387. Podd, George O., and John D. Lesure. *Planning and Operating Motels and Motor Hotels*. New York: Ahrens Publishing Co., 1964.

388. Scholz, William. *Profitable Hotel/Motel Management*. Englewood Cliffs, N.J.: Prentice-Hall, 1975. Techniques, employee relations, customer service, economy, hotel rules and laws.

389. Sonnabend, Roger P. *Your Future in Hotel Management*. New York: Richard Rosen, 1964.

390. Witzky, Herbert K. *Modern Hotel-Motel Management Methods*. New York: Hayden Book Companies, 1964.

Directories

391. *Celebrity Service International Contact Book*. Earl Blackwell, ed. International trade directory of the entertainment industry. Lists names, addresses, and telephone numbers in New York, Hollywood, London, Paris, and Rome. Stage, screen, radio, TV, dance, music agents.

392. *Directory of Hotel and Motel Systems*. Annual. New York: American Hotel Association Directory Corp. Hotel and motels and chain hotel and motel organizations owning or operating three or more properties.

393. *Hotel and Motel Red Book*. Annual. New York: American Hotel and Motel Association. Hotels in the United States, Canada, Central and South America, by state, size, cost and owner.

394. *Hotel and Travel Index*. Hollywood: Elwood M. Ingledue. Lists over 7,000 hotels and resorts throughout the world, travel agents, and other travel information.

395. *Hotel-Motel Buyers' Directory*. Annual. New York:

American Hotel and Motel Association. Products and services used by hotel-motel industry.

396. *Leahy's Hotel-Motel Guide and Travel Atlas*. Annual. Chicago: American Hotel Register Co. Geographical list of inns, hotels and motels with locational sites for use with atlas, part 2.

Industry Statistic Sources

397. *Canada Bureau of Statistics, Hotels*. Annual. Ottawa: 1949–1968. Superseded by *Traveller Accommodation Statistics*.

398. *Hotels, Motels and Tourist Courts*. U.S. Bureau of the Census. Washington, D.C.: U.S. Government Printing Office, 1966.

399. *Investment Policy Review: Strategy Phase II*. Quarterly. Dean Witter and Co. Includes a section for the lodging industry.

400. Laventhol, Krekstein, Horwath, and Horwath. *Lodging Industry: Annual Report on Hotel and Motor Hotel Operations*. Annual. Trends, statistics, analysis.

401. Smith, Barney & Company. *Research Service*. Economic outlooks, statistics.

402. *Traveller Accommodation Statistics. Statistique de l'hebergement de Voyageurs*. Annual. Ottawa: Statistics Canada.

403. *Trends in the Hotel-Motel Business*. Annual. New York: Harris, Kerr, Forster and Company.

404. *U.S. Industrial Outlook*. Annual. U.S. Bureau of Domestic Commerce. Recent trends and ten-year outlook.

405. *Worldwide Operating Statistics of the Hotel Industry*. Annual. New York.

Periodicals

406. *Cornell Hotel and Restaurant Administration Quarterly*. Quarterly. Ithaca, N.Y.: School of Hotel Administration, Cornell University.

407. *Food and Lodging Hospitality*. Monthly. Chicago: Patterson Publishing Co.

408. *Horwath Accountant*. Monthly. New York: Horwath and Horwath, Public Accountants. Traces trends in the hotel business in various sections of the country and presents numerous statistics on hotel operations.

409. *Hospitality Magazines Lodging Combination*. Monthly. Chicago: Patterson Publishing.

410. *Hotel and Motel Management*. Monthly. Chicago: Clissold Publications.

411. *Hotel and Travel Index*. Quarterly. Hollywood: Elwood M. Ingledue.

412. *Hotel Bulletin*. Monthly. New York: Hotel Bulletin, Inc.

413. *Hotel Bulletin*. Bimonthly. New York: International Geneva Association.

414. *Hotel Management Review*. Monthly. New York: Ahrens Publishing.

415. *Hotel-Motel Greeter*. Monthly. Denver: Allen Bell.

416. *Innkeeping*. Monthly. Chicago: Clissold Publishing.

417. *Motel News*. Semimonthly. Washington, D.C.: Motel Association of America.

418. *Tourist Court Journal*. Monthly. Temple, Tex.: Tourist Court Journal Co.

419. *Transcript*. Monthly. New York: Harris, Kerr, Forster and Co.

Trade Associations and Professional Societies

420. American Hotel and Motel Association. 221 West 57th Street, New York, N.Y. 10019.

421. Inter-American Hotel Association, P.O. Box 730, Harrisburg, Pa. 17108.

422. International Hotel Association, 89 rue du Faubourg Saint-Honore, Paris 8ᵉ, France.

Manufacturing

Directories

423. *Directory of Key Plants*. 2 vols. New York: Market Statistics, Inc. A directory of 41,000 plants with 100 or more employees. Volume I is by state and county and within each county, by SIC and employment size; Volume II is by SIC and then by state and country.

424. *Kelley's Manufacturers and Merchants Directory*. 2 vols. London: Kelley's Directories. Annual. World directory of merchants and manufacturers with comprehensive coverage for British Isles, and sections listing companies by major product for other countries. Includes a "Trade & Services Index."

425. *Thomas Register of American Manufacturers*. 10 vols. New York: Thomas Publishing Co. Annual. Volumes 1–6 list manufacturers by specific product; Vol. 7 is alphabetical list of companies, giving address, branch offices, subsidiaries, products, estimated capitalization, and occasionally, principal officers. Volume 9 is "Index" to product classifications and includes a list of leading trade names (pink), boards of trade, chambers of commerce. Volumes 9–10 are "Catalogs of Companies."

Multinational Companies and International Business

Bibliographies

426. Lall, Sanjaya. *Foreign Private Manufacturing Investments and Multinational Companies*. New York: Praeger, 1975. An annotated bibliography.

427. Public Library of Newark. *Business Literature*. Irregular. Newark, N.J. Includes articles and books and has a section on job hunting.

428. Raine, John S. *Multinational Companies and Overseas Direct Investment*. Aberystwyth, Dyfed, U.K.: Business Information Press, 1975. A selected bibliography and books and reports.

Directories

429. *American Agencies Interested in International Affairs*. New York: Council on International Affairs. Lists approximately 300 organizations; gives the names of officers, purposes, founding dates, and other pertinent data.

430. *American Firms, Subsidiaries, and Affiliates*. Washington, D.C.: U.S. Bureau of International Commerce, 1972. Alphabetical by country list of 4,000 American corporations that operate foreign business enterprises.

431. *American Register of Exporters and Importers, Inc.* New York: American Register of Exporters/Importers Corporation. Directory of over 30,000 manufacturers, export/import buying agencies, by product class. Also foreign offices of chamber of commerce and U.S. buying agencies.

432. *Bureau of International Commerce Trade Lists* (of every country). Annual. Washington, D.C.: United States Department of Commerce. Lists American firms, subsidiaries, and affiliates in country with brief descriptions and address.

433. *California International Business Directory*. Center for Advanced Studies in International Business, Los Angeles. Lists California companies in alphabetical order (description, imports, exports, addresses).

434. *Current European Directories*. G. P. Henderson, ed. Beckenham, Kent, England: CBD Research, Ltd. Section 1 is an annotated guide, arranged by country in Europe, to general directories of associations, research organizations, biographical dictionaries, gazetteers, city directories. Section 2 is an alphabetical list of more specialized industry directories, incorporating title references to directories in Section 1.

435. *Directory of American Firms Operating in Foreign Countries*, 7th ed. Compiled by Juvenal L. Angel. New York: World Trade Academy Press. Section 1 lists companies alphabetically, giving name of officer in charge of foreign operations, and countries of operation; Section 2 lists companies by county of operation; Section 3 classifies the firms by product or industry.

436. *Directory of Corporate Affiliations*. Skokie, Ill.: National Register Publishing Co., 1976. Who owns whom—the family tree of every major corporation in America including foreign subsidiaries and affiliates.

437. *Directory of Foreign Firms Operating in the United*

States. Compiled by Juvenal L. Angel. New York: World Trade Academy Press, 1971. Lists American companies that are affiliated or divisions of foreign countries.

438. *Directory of International Engineering and Construction Services.* Washington: National Construction Association. Information about each member company in the association and description of their particular interests in the construction industry.

439. *Directory of Opportunities for Graduates.* Annually in October. London: Cornmarket Press, Ltd. Reference book for undergraduates and their advisers for work in Great Britain.

440. *Directory of Overseas Summer Jobs.* Charles James, ed. Cincinnati, Ohio: National Directory Service. Vacation work.

441. *Directory of United States Firms Operating in Latin America.* Washington, D.C.: Pan American Union. Company listings (including the name of each manager) arranged by country.

442. Dun and Bradstreet. *Principal International Business.* New York. A world marketing directory by country, by product classification, and alphabetically by business.

443. *Europe's 5000 Largest Companies.* New York: R. R. Bowker, 1975. Information on the top 4,000 industrials and the top 750 trading companies, ranked in terms of their latest declared annual sales.

444. *Federal Jobs Overseas.* Pamphlet No. 29. Washington, D.C.: U.S. Civil Service Commission. Describes overseas jobs in nine departments of the federal government. Included are Departments of Agriculture, Air Force, Army, Navy, Commerce, Interior, State, and the Agency for International Development, Panama Canal Company, Peace Corps, and the U.S. Information Agency.

445. *Foreign Direct Investors in the United States.* Washington, D.C.: U.S. Department of Commerce, Bureau of International Commerce, Oct. 1973, Mar. 1974, and Jan. 1975. Information on the parent company, American subsidiary, location, and product is given.

446. *Forbes.* "Annual Directory Issue," May 15 issue each year. The 500 largest corporations are ranked by revenues, assets, market value, and net profit. Each year the first January issue ranks companies by profitability, growth, and stock price gain.

447. *The Fortune Double 500 Directory.* Reprint of the annual May to August issues of *Fortune* Magazine. The May issue lists the 500 largest U.S. industrial corporations; June, the second 500 largest; July, the 50 largest banks, life insurance companies, diversified—financial, retailing, transportation, and utility companies; and August, the 300 largest foreign industrial corporations and the 50 largest foreign banks.

448. *Guide to Foreign Information Sources.* Semiannual. Washington, D.C.: Chamber of Commerce of the United States. Contains sources of information on foreign nations, addresses of foreign embassies, organizations and services offering information, and annotated bibliography.

449. *International Almanac of Business and Finance.* Annual. *Finance* magazine. A list, by country, of U.S. corporations operating in that country, of U.S. banks, leading banks of the country, and of U.S. brokerage firms. Gives address and name of manager.

450. *Jaeger's Europa-Register: Teleurope.* Darmstadt: Deutscher Addressbach-Verlag. Addresses of European firms, in two parts: alphabetical list by country; classified trades section.

451. *Rand McNally International Bankers Directory.* Annual. Skokie, Ill.: Rand McNally & Company. Officers, directors, and balance sheet data for United States and principal foreign banks.

452. *Social Work Opportunities Abroad.* New York: National Association of Social Workers. A directory of over 100 organizations offering social work opportunities in foreign countries. Identifies the type of social work engaged in by the organization.

453. *Trade Directories of the World.* Compiled by U. H. E. Croner. New York: Croner Publications. This annotated list of business and trade directories is arranged by continent and then by country. Includes an index to "trades and professions" and a country index.

454. *U.S. Non-Profit Organizations in Development Assistance Abroad.* New York: Technical Assistance Information Clearing House. Comprehensive directory of information on over 400 nonprofit organizations, agencies, missions, and foundations and their work in 124 countries in Africa, East Asia and Pacific, Latin America, and Near East-South Asia. Alphabetical listing giving programs and objectives with cross-reference by region, country, and organization.

455. *Walker's Manual of Far Western Corporations and Securities.* Annual. Berkeley, Calif.: Walker's Manual, Inc. Lists corporations by city, state, and industry. A description of each is available. Aerospace, chemicals, computers, construction, merchandising, financial, food, utilities, real estate, entertainment.

456. *Who Owns Whom, Australia and the Far East.* Compiled by O. W. Roskill and Co., Ltd. London: 1976. A directory of parent, associate, and subsidiary companies for Australia and the Far East.

457. *Who Owns Whom, Continental Edition.* 2 vols. Compiled by O. W. Roskill and Co., Ltd. London: 1974. A directory of parent, associate, and subsidiary companies for the Continent.

458. *Who Owns Whom, North America.* Compiled by O. W. Roskill and Co., Ltd. London: 1974. A directory of parent, associate, and subsidiary companies for the United States, Mexico, and Canada.

Handbooks and Yearbooks

459. Angel, Juvenal L. *Looking for Employment in Foreign Countries Reference Handbook,* 5th ed. New York: World Trade Academy Press, 1972. Discussion of a va-

riety of topics in looking for foreign employment including markets, government work, and compensation.

460. Angel, Juvenal L. *Résumés for Overseas Employment.* New York: World Trade Academy Press, 1974. Offers sample résumés.

461. *The Financial Times International Business Yearbook.* London: Financial Times, Ltd., 1975. General information on countries around the world, and specific information on subsidiaries, officers, and capital of many industries.

462. *Informations Internationales.* Paris: DAFSA, 1975. Eight volumes and an index in French, English, and German on specific companies giving background information, activity of the company, subsidiaries, and capital.

Indexes

463. Business International, *Master Key Index.* Quarterly. New York. Current information on international business concerning management techniques, country, and company.

464. *Business Periodicals Index.* Monthly. New York: H. W. Wilson. Look under "Corporations—Foreign Business" and "Corporations, International" and "Corporations—Subsidiaries."

465. *F & S Index International.* Monthly. Cleveland: Predicasts. Look under "International Groups" or by specific company.

466. *Index to Foreign Market Reports.* Monthly. Washington, D.C.: U.S. Department of Commerce, Bureau of International Commerce. Foreign market surveys on unclassified commodity, industry, and economic reports, including market research summaries and market surveys.

467. *Index to International Business Publications.* Washington, D.C.: U.S. Department of Commerce, Bureau of International Commerce, June 1975. Indexes *Overseas Business Reports* and *Foreign Economic Trends.*

468. *Public Affairs Information Service Bulletin.* Quarterly. New York. Under "International Business Enterprises."

469. *Public Affairs Information Service Foreign Language Index.* Cumulated annually. New York.

Investment Information

470. *Financial Dynamics.* 14 vols., loose-leaf. Denver: Investors Management Sciences. Detailed quarterly and annual analyses of major companies by industry.

471. *Jane's Major Companies of Europe.* Lionel F. Gray, ed. New York: Franklin Watts, 1975. Detailed financial and general information on major European companies.

472. *Standard and Poor's International Stock Report.* Monthly. Stock reports from major companies around the world.

Monographs

473. Brooke, Michael Z., and Lee Remmer. The Multinational Company in Europe. Ann Arbor: University of Michigan, 1972. Experts from five countries discuss the management problems of multinational corporations.

474. Haner, F. T. *Multinational Management.* Columbus: Charles E. Merrill Books, 1973. An overall picture of the problems of managing multinational companies due to differences in culture, attitudes, etc.

Books

475. Robbins, Sidney. *Money in the Multinational Enterprise.* New York: Basic Books, 1973.

476. Stopford, John M. *Managing the Multinational Enterprise.* New York: Basic Books, 1972.

477. Wortzel, Louis H. *Scientists and Salesmen.* New York: Basic Books, forthcoming.

Periodicals

478. *The International Executive.* Irregular—about 5 a year. Hastings-on-Hudson, N.Y. A bibliography of books and periodicals as well as a summarization of selected books.

479. *Mergers and Acquisitions.* Quarterly. Washington. General information on mergers and acquisitions and who is planning what. Also includes a roster of joint ventures and foreign acquisitions.

480. *Multinational Business.* London. Quarterly. A review of news and analysis on multinational business.

Reports and Articles

481. *The Conference Board Record.* "International Economic Trends to Watch in 1976," Alfred F. Miosi, XII (11):37, November 1975. General article on multinational business.

482. *The Conference Board Record.* "Mini-Multinationals," John M. Roach, XI(2):27, February 1974. Fifty smaller companies report their experience in operating overseas.

483. *Forbes.* "Annual Report on American Industry," January issue. Measuring the management performance of the biggest public companies, with articles on major industries.

Printing and Publishing Industry

Introductory Reading

484. Blum, Eleanor. *Basic Books in the Mass Media.* Urbana: University of Illinois Press, 1972. An annotated bibliography covering source material about communications, including sections on book publishing, newspapers, advertising, indexes, etc.

485. Dessauer, John. *Book Publishing: What It Is; What It Does*. New York: R. R. Bowker, 1974. A general introduction to book publishing, with chapters on the creation of books, the history of the book trade, the manufacturing, marketing, storing, and delivering of books, and the general management theories of the industry.

486. Strauss, Victor. *The Printing Industry*. Washington: R. R. Bowker, 1967. A general introduction to the printing industry, with chapters on the printing process, theories of printing, and technical services (presses, inks, binding, graphics). Includes a selective bibliography.

Outlook for the Industry: Forecasts and Trends

487. *Census of Manufacturers*. 1972 Preliminary Report (Series MC 72). Washington, D.C.: U.S. Government Printing Office, 1975. SIC 2700 includes statistical information on the trends in growth of newspapers, periodicals, book publishing, book printing, miscellaneous publishing, commercial printing, etc. Data given for time span (1958–1972); geographic area; the value of receipts of products, of materials consumed; the number of employees; costs, etc.

488. J. S. Eliezer Associates. *The New Dynamics of Book Publishing: An Analysis of Trends 1967–1980*. New York: Eliezer Associates, 1973. Includes chapters on the economic trends affecting book sales, external forces affecting the industry, trends in book clubs and mail order sales, the future outlook for juvenile, trade, text, professional and reference books.

489. Frost and Sullivan. *Graphic Art Supply Market*, Report No. 265. New York: Frost and Sullivan. August 1974. Forecast data for the printing and publishing market as it relates to the graphic arts.

490. Smith, Barney & Company. *Subscription Research Reports*. Volume 5. Under "Publishing and Broadcasting," includes current and selective research reports about trends and forecasts of specific companies within the industry. Data given on growth trends, current assets of the company, analysis of revenues, etc. Special features include "Reviews and Outlook Analysis" and a discussion of the factors affecting stock market activity.

491. *U.S. Industrial Outlook*. Annual. Washington, D.C.: U.S. Government Printing Office. Under "Printing and Publishing" gives the recent developments and projections for the industry, with a brief outlook for newspapers, periodicals, book publishing, commercial printing, graphics, etc. Projections to 1980.

492. *Union Wages and Hours: Printing Industry*. Washington, D.C.: U.S. Government Printing Office. July 1, 1972. Cites the average salary scales of employees in the printing industry as of July 1, 1972. Data broken down by specific job function, age of employee, city and population statistics, etc. for 68 selected cities. Overall analysis given for the nation as a whole. Abbreviated version in *Printing and Publishing*, January 1974, pp. 7–13.

Investment Advisory Services

493. Investment Management Sciences, Inc. *Financial Dynamics*. Quarterly, with annual cumulations. Quarterly and annual financial analyses of selected leading publishing companies, with annual industry comparisons. Tab indexed under "Publishing." Includes information on income, expenses, invested capital, market data, assets, marketability, etc., for each company listed.

494. Standard and Poor's Corporation. *Industry Surveys: Communication*. Gives the latest current and basic analyses of the industry, with brief information on the industry and financial comparisons of leading companies. Includes a comparative stock analysis for selected companies. Offers a brief outlook, choices of favored issues, statistical comparisons of stocks. Also general information about industrywide trends and individual trends (e.g., newspapers, magazines, etc.)

495. *Value Line Investment Survey*. Weekly. Under "Publishing and Advertising Industry" has analysis of the publishing industry for newspapers, with information for specific publishers on their financial outlook, and their current assets and liabilities. Also, an analysis of their monthly situation, and fortnightly commentaries appraising the political and economic conditions affecting the industry.

Ratios for the Industry

496. Printing Industry of America. *Ratios for the Use of Printing Management*. Arlington, Virginia. Annual.

Directories

497. *American Book Trade Directory*. Biennial. New York: R. R. Bowker. List of 4,000 publishers and booksellers with addresses and areas of interest, affiliated companies, subsidiaries, special distributions, mergers, foreign representatives, etc. Includes mainly American firms, with British and Canadian publishers and their American representatives. No personnel information.

498. *Ayer Directory: Newspapers, Magazines and Trade Publications*. Philadelphia: N. W. Ayer & Son. Firm, newspaper advertising agents.

499. *Ayer's Directory of Newspapers and Periodicals*. Philadelphia: N. W. Ayer & Son.

500. *Directory of Scholarly and Research Publishing Opportunities*. Indianapolis, Ind.: Academic Media. Lists magazines and other publishing concerns by subject category.

501. *Editor and Publisher International Yearbook*. Annual. New York: Editor and Publisher. "The Encyclopedia of the Newspaper Industry." Worldwide data on newspapers with information on dailies, association and club papers, supplies, equipment, awards, foreign language papers, Negro news in the U.S., listing of journalism schools and standards of education, etc. Statistical information includes a brief summary of circulation trends, a review of the British newspaper year, etc.

502. *Literary Market Place.* Annual. New York: R. R. Bowker. "The Bible of American Book Publishing." Directory of American book publishers and personnel. Subject arrangement by book publishers, associations, trade events, services and suppliers, free-lance editors, book manufacturers, magazine publishers, U.S. publishers' imprints, etc. Includes addresses and personnel information. See also the *International Literary Market Place* (annual) for similar information about European publishers.

503. *Names and Numbers.* 21st ed. New York: R. R. Bowker. Provides an alphabetical index to over 17,000 names of publishers with phone number, street address, city, zone. Companion to *Literary Market Place.*

504. *Newspaper International.* Published annually in January, plus updating supplements. Skokie, Illinois: National Register Publishing Company. Lists newspapers and newsweeklies in over 90 countries.

505. *Publisher's International Directory.* 4th ed. New York: R. R. Bowker. Directory gives names and addresses of 20,000 active publishers in 144 countries.

506. *Standard Periodical Directory.* Annual. New York: Oxbridge Communications. A subject listing of 53,000 U.S. and Canadian periodicals, giving address, scope, year founded, frequency, subscription rate, circulation, and one basic advertising rate. Alphabetical index at end.

507. *Who's Who in Publishing—An International Biographical Guide.* Quinquennial. New York: R. R. Bowker. Contains detailed biographical data of 3,500 leading persons in the publishing field.

508. *Writer's Market.* Annual. Cincinnati: F & W Publishing Corp. Lists over 3,000 possible markets for writers, photographers, and artists. Requirements and other pertinent information are included.

Professional Associations

509. *Encyclopedia of Associations.* Volume 1, *National Organizations of the United States.* Volume 3, *Supplement.* Irregular. Alphabetical and keyword indexes provide access to all types of national associations under "Print" and "Publishers." Provides the name of the chief officers, a brief statement of activities, committees, number of members, and names of publications.

510. *Encyclopedia of Business Information Sources.* Volume 1 under "Printing" and "Publishing Industry" provides a selective list of professional associations, as well as suggested sources for statistics, periodicals, directories, financial ratios, price sources, and general readings.

Journals

511. *Book Production Industry.* Bimonthly. General news and articles of interest to book manufacturers and publishers. Includes book reviews, concentrating on the format and textual quality of the book.

512. *Editor and Publisher.* Weekly. General news and articles in the newspaper medium. Special features include reprints of statistical studies done by Media Records, Inc.

513. *Folio: The Magazine for Magazine Management.* Monthly. General management articles for the publishing industry.

514. *Inland Printer/American Lithographer.* Monthly. General articles of interest to the printing industry. Emphasis is on changing trends and technology within the industry. Special feature appearing semiannually is "Forecast."

515. *Knowledge Industry Report.* Semimonthly. Newsletter with tidbits of information and gossip on the publishing world. Acts as a source of current awareness information.

516. *Printing and Publishing.* Quarterly. Offers miscellaneous articles on the printing and publishing industries. Its regular feature is a Statistical Series, with comparisons of principal markets, imports and exports of books and other printed matter, economic indicators, percentage changes on a quarterly and yearly basis, etc.

517. *Printing Management.* Monthly. Articles about printing management, with an emphasis on forecasts and changes in technology. Special feature: "Forecast."

Public Administration in City Government

Almanacs and Handbooks

518. *Directory of Urban Corps Programs.* Washington, D.C.: National Development Office. Alphabetical and state listing of urban corps programs.

519. *Municipal Yearbook.* Annual. Chicago: International City Management Association. An authoritative résumé of activities and statistical data on American cities. It is also the source for annual reviews for all significant developments, problems, and conflicts in the field of local government.

Bibliographies

520. Government Affairs Foundation, Inc. *Metropolitan Communities: A Bibliography with Special Emphasis upon Government and Politics.* Chicago: Public Administration Service, 1956–1972. A series of 5 volumes containing listing of books, periodical articles, and government reports dealing with (1) the functions, problems, and the organization of metropolitan governments, and (2) the socioeconomic background of metropolitan areas.

521. Holler, Frederick L. *The Information Sources of Political Science.* Santa Barbara, Calif.: ABC-Clio, Inc., 1975. Consult the local government section of Vol. 3 of the 5-volume set.

522. Joint Reference Library. *Recent Publications on Governmental Problems.* Semimonthly. Chicago. References are listed under the heading "Municipal Government" in some issues.

523. McCurdy, Howard E. *Public Administration: A Bibliography.* Washington, D.C.: College of Public Affairs, The American University, 1972.

Indexes and Abstracts

524. *Index to Current Urban Documents.* Westport, Conn.: Greenwood Periodicals Co. A quarterly and annual publication that indexes official documents on urban affairs issued in 154 cities and 24 counties. All documents cited in the index are made available by the publisher either individually or in regional sets.

525. *Sage Public Administration Abstracts.* Beverly Hills: Sage Publications.

Journals

526. *Public Administration Review.* Bimonthly.

527. *Public Personnel Management.* Bimonthly.

528. *Urban Research News.* Bimonthly.

529. *Urban Affairs Quarterly.* Quarterly.

Books

530. Banovetz, James M. *Managing the Modern City.* Washington, D.C.: International City Management Association, 1971.

531. Bish, Robert L., and Vincent Ostrom. *Understanding Urban Government: Metropolitan Reform Reconsidered.* Washington, D.C.: American Enterprise Institute for Public Policy Research, 1973.

532. Bollens, John C. *The Metropolis: Its People, Politics, and Economic Life,* 2d ed. New York: Harper & Row, 1970.

533. David, Stephen M., and Paul E. Peterson. *Urban Politics and Public Policy: The City in Crisis.* New York: Praeger, 1973.

534. DeTorres, Juan. *Government Services in Major Metropolitan Areas; Functions, Centers, Efficiency.* New York: The Conference Board, 1972.

535. Drake, Alvin W. *Analysis of Public Systems.* Cambridge, Mass.: MIT Press, 1972.

536. Goodman, Jay S. *The Dynamics of Urban Government and Politics.* New York: Macmillan, 1975.

537. Hawley, Willis D. *Improving the Quality of Urban Management.* Beverly Hills: Sage Publications, 1974.

538. Kotter, John P., and Paul R. Lawrence. *Mayors in Action: Five Approaches to Urban Governance.* New York: Wiley, 1974.

539. Martin, Michael. *Management Science and Urban Problems.* Lexington, Mass.: Lexington Books, 1974.

540. Rosenbloom, Richard S. *New Tools for Urban Management: Studies in Systems and Organizational Management.* Boston: Graduate School of Business Administration, Harvard University, 1971.

541. Russell, John R. *Cases in Urban Management.* Cambridge, Mass.: MIT Press, 1974.

542. Stillman, Richard J. *The Rise of the City Manager: A Public Professional in Local Government.* Albuquerque: University of New Mexico Press, 1974.

543. Sweeney, Stephen B. *Governing Urban Society: New Scientific Approaches.* Philadelphia: American Academy of Political and Social Science, 1967.

Public Administration in Federal and State Government

Directories

544. *A Directory of Public Management Organizations.* Washington, D.C.: U.S. Government Printing Office. National organizations of state and local governments and associations of public officials with an interest in public employee-management relations.

545. *Directory of Government Agencies.* Littleton, Colorado: Libraries Unlimited, Inc. Lists department and description.

546. *Directory of Information Resources in the United States: Federal Government.* Rev. ed., 1974. Washington, D.C.: Library of Congress. Lists information offices and information analysis centers for various agencies and programs.

547. U.S. Civil Service Commission. *Federal Career Directory.* Annual. "Specific information about federal careers and the agencies that employ college graduates for these positions."

548. U.S. Civil Service Commission. *Guide to Federal Career Literature.* Annual. Note chart, "The Federal Job System," explaining how to apply for a federal job.

549. U.S. Civil Service Commission. *Summer Jobs in Federal Agencies.* Annual.

550. *United States Government Manual.* Annual. Describes federal agencies and programs. Provides listings of key personnel, regional offices, and organization charts.

Books

551. Adrian, Charles R. *Governing Our Fifty States and Their Communities,* 3d ed. New York: McGraw-Hill, 1972.

552. Smoot, Dan. *Business End of Government.* Belmont, Mass.: Western Islands, 1973.

553. Steiss, Alan W. *Public Budgeting and Management.* Lexington, Mass.: Lexington Books, 1972. First 6 chapters deal with public management.

554. Van Dersal, William R. *The Successful Manager in Government and Business.* New York: Harper & Row, 1974.

555. Wamsley, Gary L. *Political Economy of Public Organizations: A Critique and Approach to the Study of Public Administration.* Boston: D.C. Heath, 1973.

Magazines and Journals

556. *CG Weekly Report.* Weekly. Weekly coverage of government and congressional activities.

557. *Government Executive.* Monthly.

558. *Public Administration Review.* Bimonthly.

559. *Public Personnel Management.* Bimonthly.

560. *Public Policy.* Quarterly.

561. *Trends in Federal Hiring.* Quarterly. U.S. Civil Service Commission.

Articles

562. Bowman, James S., and David L. Norman, Jr. "Attitudes Towards the Public Service: A Survey of University Students." In *Public Personnel Management,* March–April 1975, pp. 113–121.

563. Buchanan, Bruce II. "Government Managers, Business Executives, and Organizational Equipment," In *Public Administration Review,* July/August 1974, pp. 339–347.

564. Graham, G. A. "Ethical Guidelines for Public Administrators: Observations on the Rules of the Game." In *Public Administration Review,* January–February 1974, pp. 90–92.

565. Imundo, Louis V., Jr. "Ineffectiveness and Inefficiency in Government Management." In *Public Personnel Management,* March–April 1975, pp. 90–95.

566. Malek, Frederic C. "Managing for Results in the Federal Government. . . ." In *Business Horizons,* April 1974, pp. 23–28.

Bibliographies and Guides

567. Andriot, John. *Guide to U.S. Government Publications.* Mclean, Va.: Documents Index 1972 and supplements. Lists publications by issuing agency.

568. Joint Reference Library. *Recent Publications on Governmental Problems.* Semimonthly. Chicago.

569. U.S. Superintendent of Documents. *United States Government Publications, Monthly Catalog.* Monthly. Indexes government publications by author, title, and subject.

Public Utilities

Directories

570. *Brown's Directory of North American Gas Companies.* Annual. Philadelphia: Harcourt, Brace, Jovanovich. Provides lists of gas utilities by state plus extensive company information. Also includes information on state public utility commissions.

571. *Electric World Directory of Electric Utilities.* Annual. New York: McGraw Hill. Lists of electric utilities by state and company information, including officers and major department heads, etc.

572. *Moody's Public Utilities Manual.* Annual. New York: Moody's Investors Service, Inc. Extensive company and financial information, including historical financial tables for the industry. City index lists names of utilities serving different areas. Updated by *Moody's Public Utilities News Reports.*

Periodicals

573. *American Gas Association Monthly.* Monthly. Reports the activities of the various sections of AGA in sales promotion, research, and public relations. January issue provides a 25-year industry forecast.

574. *Bell Journal of Economics.* Biannual. Scholarly articles on public utility economics and management.

575. *Bell Telephone Magazine.* Quarterly. Articles of interest to Bell management.

576. *Edison Electric Institute Bulletin.* Monthly. Reports EEI activities in research, sales promotion, accounting, and public relations.

577. *Electrical World.* Weekly. Technical and business articles on the electric power industry. Regular statistical review issues.

578. *Land Economics.* Quarterly. Includes scholarly articles on public utility economics.

579. *Public Power.* Monthly. January issue has a directory of publicly owned electric utilities. Includes articles of interest to the management personnel of municipal and federal power agencies.

580. *Public Utilities Fortnightly.* Biweekly. Feature articles on current news and issues in public utilities. Regular columns on government regulations, financial analysis of selected utility companies, and industrial progress. First January issue contains "Washington Outlook for Utilities," which projects current government regulation and ratemaking trends.

581. *Telephony.* Weekly. Telephone industry news, management information, and regulation news. Regular statistical reviews.

Conference Proceedings

582. *AGA-EEI Accounting Conference Proceedings.* Annual. Arlington, Virginia: American Gas Association and Edison Electric Institute. Papers on various aspects of public utility accounting and related areas.

583. *National Association of Regulatory Utility Commissioners Convention Proceedings.* Annual. Washington, D.C.: Papers on different topics relating to public utilities. Also includes brief biographical sketches of attending public utility commissioners.

584. *New Challenges to Public Utility Management: Proceedings of the Sixth Annual Conference 24–25 April 1973.* East Lansing: Michigan State University, Institute of Public Utilities, 1974.

585. *Now, a New Generation in Utility Marketing: Proceedings of the 17th Public Utilities Marketing Seminar.* Denver, 1971. Colorado Springs: Colorado Interstate Gas Co.

586. *Today's Challenge, Tomorrow's Opportunity: Proceedings of the 18th Public Utilities Marketing Seminar.* New Orleans: 1972.

Books

587. Farris, Martin T. *Public Utilities: Regulation, Management, and Ownership.* Boston: Houghton Mifflin, 1973.

588. Garfield, Paul J. *Public Utility Economics.* Englewood Cliffs, N.J.: Prentice-Hall, 1964.

589. Haring, Joseph E., and Joseph F. Humphrey, eds. *Utility Regulation During Inflation.* Los Angeles: Occidental College, Economics Research Center, 1971.

590. Hayden, Howard R., ed. *Risk and Regulated Firms.* East Lansing: Michigan State University, Graduate School of Business Administration, 1973.

591. Phillips, Charles F. *The Economics of Regulation.* Homewood, Ill.: Richard D. Irwin, 1969.

592. Samuels, Warren J., and Harry M. Trebling, eds. *A Critique of Administrative Regulation of Public Utilities.* Ann Arbor: Michigan State University, Graduate School of Business Administration, 1972.

593. Shepherd, William G., and Thomas G. Gies. *Regulation in Further Perspective: The Little Engine That Might.* Cambridge, Mass.: Ballinger, 1974.

594. Shepherd, William G., and Thomas G. Gies. *Utility Regulation: New Directions in Theory and Practice.* New York: Random House, 1966.

595. Sichel, Werner, and Thomas G. Gies, eds. *Public Utility Regulation: Change and Scope.* Lexington, Mass.: Lexington Books, 1975.

596. Turvey, Ralph. *Public Enterprise.* Baltimore: Penguin Books, 1968.

Rates and Regulations

597. *A.G.A. Rate Service.* Loose-leaf. American Gas Association. Rates for various types of service by state, updated periodically.

598. *Federal and State Commission Jurisdiction and Regulation of Electric, Gas and Telephone Utilities,* 6th ed. U.S. Federal Power Commission, 1973. Comprehensive information on government regulation of utility rates, accounting forms and requirements, financial and corporate regulation, licenses and permits, etc.

599. *National Electric Rate Book.* Loose-leaf. U.S. Federal Power Commission. Rate schedules for electrical service by state, updated periodically.

600. *Public Utilities Reports.* Issued periodically. Opinions of commissions and courts on public utility cases.

601. *Typical Electric Bills for Residential, Commercial, and Industrial Services.* Annual. Washington, D.C.: U.S. Federal Power Commission. Consumer costs for representative amounts of electricity for different types of service and for different areas in the country.

602. *Uniform System of Accounts Prescribed for Public Utilities and Licensees Subject to the Provisions of the Federal Power Act.* Loose-leaf.

Statistics

603. *Electric Power Statistics.* Monthly. U.S. Federal Power Commission. Various statistics, including monthly operating and income statements of privately owned electric utilities.

604. *Electric Utility in New England Statistical Bulletin.* Annual. Electric Council of New England. Industry statistics on supply, uses, sales and revenues, finances, operations, etc.

605. *Gas Facts: A Statistical Record of the Gas Utility Industry.* Annual. American Gas Association. Contains statistical data on energy reserves, production, transmission, distribution, storage, sales labor, and finance.

606. *Historical Statistics of the Electric Utility Industry.* Decennial. Edison Electric Institute. Information on electrical utility generating capacity; sales, customers and revenues; financial and operating data and ratios, etc.

607. *LP-Gas Market Industry Facts.* Annual. LP-Gas Association. Industry statistics on production, transportation, storage, sales, etc.

608. *Statistical Yearbook of the Electric Utility Industry.* Annual. Edison Electric Institute. Annual updates of the information contained in the *Historical Statistics of the Electric Utility Industry.*

609. *Statistics of Communications, Common Carriers.* Annual. U.S. Federal Communications Commission. Includes financial and operating data for telephone and telegraph companies.

610. *Statistics of Privately Owned Electric Utilities in the United States,* annual, and *Statistics of Publicly Owned Electric Utilities in the United States,* annual.

611. *Statistics of the Telephone Industry.* Annual. U.S. Independent Telephone Association.

612. *U.S. Federal Power Commission Annual Report.* Annual. Industry statistics. Also reviews electric power and natural gas developments for the year, including regulation and legislation.

613. *World's Telephones.* Annual. American Telephone and Telegraph Co. Statistics on number of telephones and types of calls made in the world.

Industry Outlook/Investment Advisory Services

614. *A.G.A. Report of Gas Industry Operations.* Quarterly. New York: American Gas Association. Various information on the gas industry: income statements, operating trends, customers, sales and revenues, etc.

615. *Business Week.* Weekly. Quarterly covers sales and profitability of large public utility companies.

616. *Financial Dynamics.* Loose-leaf. Investor's Management Services, Inc. Comparative company financial analyses in Vol. 10 for telephone companies and in Vol. 13 for electric utilities.

617. *Forbes.* Weekly. January 1 issue contains information on the industry outlook and on the growth and profitability of major public utility companies.

618. *Fortune.* Monthly. August issue contains "The Fifty Largest Utilities Ranked by Assets."

619. *Gas Utility Industry Projections.* Annual. American Gas Association. Industry sales outlook, projected 15 years, by various regions in the U.S.

620. *Industry Surveys.* 3 times a year. Standard and Poor's Corporation. Industry outlook and comparative company appraisals listed under "Telephone," "Utilities—Gas," and "Utilities—Electric."

621. *Quarterly Survey of Utility Appropriations.* Quarterly. Conference Board. Capital appropriations and expenditures of investor-owned gas and electric utilities.

622. *Subscription Research Service.* Periodically updated. Smith, Barney & Co. Volume 5 contains industry and individual company information for gas and electric utilities.

623. *Value Line Investment Survey.* Loose-leaf. Arnold Bernhard & Co. Industry analysis and company data for electric utilities and telecommunications.

Career Information

624. Bowman, Dean O. "Executive Development for Public Utilities," *Public Utilities Fortnightly* 89:39–43, March 16, 1972. Results of a survey on participants in the Public Utility Executive Program.

625. Byars, Lloyd L. "What Others Think: Management Training in Public Utilities," *Public Utilities Fortnightly* 88:58–60, December 9, 1971. Outlines some in-house management development programs within public utilities.

626. Easlick, D. K. "The New Face to the World of Work," *Public Utilities Fortnightly* 90:24–26, October 12, 1972. Examines equal opportunity in the Bell System.

627. Garlinghouse, F. Mark. "Employment Discrimination Law and Equal Employment in Public Utilities," *Public Utilities Fortnightly* 92:83–84, September 13, 1973.

628. Holmberg, Stevan R. "Integrating Manpower and Corporate Strategic Plans," *Public Utilities Fortnightly* 94:31–35, November 21, 1974. Survey of manpower planning systems in public utilities.

629. King, Sandra L. "Occupational Pay Benefits in Electric and Gas Utilities," *Monthly Labor Review* 97:53–54, November 1974. Survey of wages and benefits for hourly employees.

630. Smith, Chesterfield H. "Management Responsibility—Past, Present and Future," *Public Utilities Fortnightly* 91:32–35, June 21, 1973. Discusses the general concept of public utilities serving the public interest.

631. *Encyclopedia of Business Information Sources.* Volume 1. Detroit: Gale Research, 1970.

632. Hunt, Florine E. *Public Utilities Information Sources.* Detroit: Gale Research, 1965. "An annotated guide to literature and bodies concerned with rates, economics, accounting, regulation, history, and statistics of electric, gas, telephone, and water companies."

633. Lapinsky, M. "Guide to the Sources of the Economics of Regulation Literature," *Public Utilities Fortnightly* 96:21–29, July 17, 1975.

Retail Trade Industry

Directories

634. Aspley, J. C. *The Dartnell Sales Manager's Handbook,* Ovid Riso, ed. 11th ed. Chicago: Dartnell Corp., 1968. A list of directories, by key word, is in each edition of this handbook.

635. *Directory of Department Stores.* Annual. New York: Chain Store Guide.

636. *Directory of Franchising Organizations.* New York: Pilot Books. Lists franchise opportunities with concise descriptions and required investment. Includes a franchise evaluation checklist.

637. *Directory of National Trade and Professional Associations of the United States.* Washington, D.C.: Columbia Books, Inc. Alphabetical list of 4,300 national trade and professional associations, with key word and executive indexes. Gives chief officer, number of members, annual budget, publications.

638. *Encyclopedia of Associations,* 9th ed. M. Fisk, ed. Detroit: Gale Research, 1975. See items 2380–2389, p. 200.

639. *Fairchild's Financial Manual of Retail Stores.* Annual. New York. Lists names of officers and directors. Includes basic financial information about each store.

640. *Retailer Owned Cooperative Chains; Wholesale Grocers; Wholesaler Sponsored Voluntary Chains.* Business Guides, Inc. Lists companies by country and state.

641. *Sheldon's Retail Directory of the United States and Canada,* 88th ed. New York: Phelon, Sheldon & Marsar, Inc. Annual. Formerly *Sheldon's Retail Trade of*

the United States. Includes chain, independent, department, junior department and specialty stores. Lists executives, general and divisional managers, department buyers.

642. *Shopping Center Directory (United States and Canada).* Burlington, Iowa: National Research Bureau, Inc. Lists shopping centers by city and state.

643. *Stores of the World Directory.* Biennial. London. Includes list of retail trade journals with addresses.

644. U.S. Department of Commerce. *Franchise Opportunities Handbook, 1973.* Complete guide to franchises. Bibliography.

Retail Trade Statistics

645. *A Guide to Consumer Markets 1974/75.* New York: The Conference Board. A standard source of statistical intelligence concerning the consumer and his relation to retail trade. Of special interest are the sections "Expenditures," pp. 158–206, and "Production and Distribution," pp. 207–232.

646. Marketing Economics Institute. *Marketing Economics Guide, 1973–74.* New York. In three sections. Includes SMSA rankings, population estimates, households, incomes for 1,500 cities, metropolitan areas, and retail sales data for nine retail store groups.

647. *Sales Management.* "1974 Survey of Buying Power," October 28, 1974. Includes market rankings as well as national, regional, and metropolitan area market data. Projections are made up to 1978.

648. U.S. Bureau of the Census. *Annual Retail Trade Report.* Statistics include per capita sales of five basic types of retail stores by geographic division as well as total annual sales.

649. U.S. Bureau of the Census. *Monthly Retail Trade Reports.* Has estimates of retail sales and accounts receivable listed by type of business. Firms with 11 or more retail stores are listed individually. These reports include data on department store sales, all retail stores, and major types of businesses such as furniture, lumber, and auto retailers.

650. U.S. Bureau of the Census. *Weekly Retail Sales Reports.* Estimates volume of sales, but considered less reliable than *Monthly Retail Trade Reports,* since they are made on a small sample and on estimated (vs. actual) sales.

651. U.S. Dept. of Commerce. *U.S. Industrial Outlook.* Annual. Describes recent developments and gives a 10-year projection.

Operating Ratios

652. *Department and Specialty Store Merchandising and Operating Results.* 4 vols. Annual. New York: National Retail Merchants Association, Financial Executives Division.

653. *Financial and Operating Results of Department and Specialty Stores.* Annual. New York: National Retail Merchants Association, Financial Executives Division.

654. National Cash Register. *Expenses in Retail Business.* Dayton, Ohio. Annual. Operating ratios for 50 lines of retail business.

655. *Operating Results of Self-Service Department Stores.* Annual. Ithaca, N.Y.: New York State College of Agriculture and Life Sciences, Cornell University, in cooperation with the Mass Merchandising Research Foundation. Provides financial history and performance indicators for 47 self-service department store companies.

656. Urban Land Institute. *The Dollars and Cents of Shopping Centers.* Washington, D.C. Triennial. Provides benchmark figures against which operating results for individual shopping centers can be compared with those that are typical for the industry on a uniform basis.

Investment Services for Retail Trade

657. Investors Management Sciences, Inc. *Financial Dynamics.* Multivolume set giving financial analysis of leading companies in major industries. For retail trade see Vols. 8 and 9.

658. Smith, Barney & Company. *Subscription Research Service.* Research reports about trends and outlook in the retail trade industry as a whole with analysis of selected large companies.

659. Standard and Poor's Corporation. *Industry Surveys.* Current analysis of retail trade market, with specific company stock analysis.

Journals

660. *Discount Merchandiser.* Monthly. Issues annual *Discount Merchandiser: True Look at the Discount Industry,* June. Includes operating ratios.

661. *Economics Priorities Report,* Vol. 5, No. 3, 1974. Council on Economic Priorities. "Minorities and Women in Retail Industry." Entire issue devoted to analysis of employment opportunities in five major retail chains: Sears Roebuck, J. C. Penney, Ward's, Kresge, and Grant's.

662. *Footwear News.* Weekly. Issues annual *Footwear News Fact Book.* Includes statistics concerning marketing information as well as consumer market data.

663. *International Association of Department Stores—Retail News Letter.* Monthly. Covers trends in international department stores.

664. *Jewelers' Circular Keystone.* Monthly. Each issue includes statistical indicators for imports, exports, monthly sales trends.

665. *Journal of Retailing.* Quarterly. New York: New York University Institute of Retailing Management. Book reviews.

666. *Mass Retailing Merchandiser.* Monthly. Special reports include: "How Much Do You Earn? An Industrywide Salary Survey of Mass Retailing," December 1974, pp. 10–16, and "General Merchandise Share of the Market Report," January 1975, pp. 8–15.

667. *Men's Wear.* Semimonthly. Special report: "Who's Gaining Share of the Men's Wear Market?" February 14, 1975, pp. 59–88.

668. *Modern Retailer.* Monthly. Concerned with consumer goods market, marketing and management and distribution in the United Kingdom. Special issue: March 1975, "Annual Review of Retailing," pp. 5–18.

669. *Shopping Center World.* Monthly. Special issues include January 1975 "State of the Industry," pp. 19–30. Includes statistics for United States (by state) and Canada—update of 1972 survey; and February 1975 "Annual 1975 Regional Roundup."

670. *Stores.* Monthly. International coverage of department, chain, variety, mass merchandising, and specialty stores. August issue annually has special report, "100 Top Volume Department Stores."

Books

671. Boone, Louis E., and James C. Johnson. *Marketing Channels.* Morristown, N.J.: General Learning Press, 1973. Includes bibliography.

672. Duncan, Delbert J., and C. Phillips. *Modern Retailing Management: Basic Concepts and Practices,* 8th ed. Homewood, Ill.: Richard D. Irwin, 1972. Includes annotated bibliography.

673. Harvey, Reed A. *Managerial Need Satisfaction in the Retailing Environment.* New York: National Retail Merchants Association, 1971. Retail trade as a profession. Includes bibliography.

674. Rachman, David J. *Retail Strategy and Structure: A Management Approach,* 2d ed. Englewood Cliffs, N.J.: Prentice-Hall, 1975. Includes annotated bibliography.

675. Walter, Bruce, and J. B. Haynes, ed. *Marketing Channels and Institutions.* Columbus, Ohio: Grid, Inc., 1973.

Small Business and Entrepreneurial Prospects

Bibliographies

676. Center for Venture Management. *The Entrepreneur and New Enterprise Formation: A Resource Guide.* Compiled by James W. Schreier and John L. Komives. Milwaukee: Center for Venture Management, 1973.

677. Dun & Bradstreet. *Management Source Publications for Small Business.* New York: 1972.

678. "Resources." An annotated bibliography that appears in each issue of the *Journal of Small Business Management.* Quarterly.

679. U.S. Small Business Administration. *Small Business Bibliographies.* A series of pamphlets that list sources of information on the management of specific types of small businesses.

General Books

680. Baty, Gordon B. *Entrepreneurship: Playing to Win.* Reston, Va.: Reston Publishing Co., 1974.

681. Baumback, Clifford M., comp. *Entrepreneurship and Venture Management.* Englewood Cliffs, N.J.: Prentice-Hall, 1975.

682. Baumback, Clifford M., et al. *How to Organize and Operate a Small Business,* 5th ed. Englewood Cliffs, N.J.: Prentice-Hall, 1973.

683. Broom, H. N., and J. G. Longenecker. *Small Business Management,* 4th ed. Cincinnati: South-Western Publishing Company, 1975.

684. Cohn, Theodore, and R. A. Lindberg. *Survival and Growth: Management Strategies for the Small Firm.* New York: AMACOM, 1974.

685. Dible, Donald M. *Up Your Own Organization. A Handbook for the Employed, the Underemployed, and the Self-Employed on How to Start and Finance a New Business.* Santa Clara, Calif.: The Entrepreneur Press, 1971. Includes a list of seminars on small business management, Small Business Administration office locations, and business and financial periodicals. Also includes "Recommended Reading" at end of each chapter.

686. Goodman, Sam R. *Financial Manager's Manual and Guide.* Englewood Cliffs, N.J.: Prentice-Hall, 1973. Includes a section on "Cash Management for Small and Medium-Sized Companies."

687. Greene, Gardiner G. *How to Start and Manage Your Own Business.* New York: McGraw-Hill, 1975.

688. Griffen, Barbara C. *A Successful Business of Your Own.* Los Angeles: Shelbourne Press, 1974.

689. Klatt, Laurence. *Small Business Management: Essentials of Entrepreneurship.* Belmont, Calif.: Wadsworth, 1973.

690. Klein, Howard J. *Stop! You're Killing the Business.* New York: Mason & Lipscomb, 1974.

691. Lasser (J. K.) Institute. *How to Run a Small Business,* 4th ed. New York: McGraw-Hill, 1974.

692. Lilies, Patrick. *New Business Ventures and the Entrepreneur.* Homewood, Ill.: Richard D. Irwin, 1974. Contains a note on the legal forms of business.

693. Markstein, David L. *Money Raising and Planning for the Small Business.* Chicago: Henry Regnery, 1974.

694. Nicholas, Ted. *How to Form Your Own Corporation Without a Lawyer for Under $50.00.* Wilmington, Del.: Enterprise Publishing Co., 1972.

695. Petrof, John W., P. S. Carusone, and J. E. McDavid. *Small Business Management: Concepts and Techniques for Improving Decisions.* New York: McGraw-Hill, 1972.

696. Roberts, E. Wilson. *How, When and Where to Go Public with a Small Company.* New York: Exposition Press, 1973.

697. Small, Samuel. *Starting a Business after Fifty.* New York: Pilot Books, 1974.

698. Steinhoff, Dan. *Small Business Fundamentals.* New York: McGraw-Hill, 1974.

699. Tate, Curtis E., et al. *Successful Small Business Management.* Dallas: Business Publications, 1975.

700. U.S. Internal Revenue Service. *Tax Guide for Small Business.* Annual.

Venture Capital and Small Business Investment Companies

701. Dominquez, John R. *Venture Capital.* Lexington, Mass.: Lexington Books, 1974. Includes a list of venture capital firms by investment limit.

702. Kelley, Albert J., F. F. Campanella, and J. Mc-Kiernan. *Venture Capital: A Guidebook for New Enterprises.* Chestnut Hill, Mass.: School of Management, Boston College, July 1971. Includes a selected list of venture capital sources.

703. New Enterprise Systems, Inc. *Venture Capital in the U.S.: An Analysis.* Wellesley, Mass., 1972.

704. Noone, Charles M., and S. M. Rubel. *SBIC's: Pioneers in Organized Venture Capital.* Chicago: Capital Publishing Co., 1970. Background on the development of the SBIC industry and a directory of a few firms.

705. Rubel, Stanley M. *Guide to Venture Capital Sources,* 3d ed. Chicago: Capital Publishing Co., 1974. Biennial. Presents an analysis of the venture capital industry and includes a directory of venture capital companies in the U.S., Canada, Puerto Rico, France, United Kingdom, and South Africa.

706. Rubel, Stanley M., and E. G. Novotny. *How to Raise and Invest Venture Capital.* New York: Presidents Publishing House, 1971.

707. U.S. Small Business Administration. *List of Small Business Investment Companies.* Irregular.

708. *Venture Capital.* Chicago: S. M. Rubel & Co. Monthly.

Presents news of new venture groups and financial performance of venture capital firms.

709. Western Association of Venture Capitalists. *Directory of Members.* San Francisco, 1974/75.

Management Guides

710. *How to Start Your Own Small Business.* New York: Drake Publishers. Volumes 1–3, 1973–1975. Information is given on starting specific types of small businesses.

711. *Small Business Reporter.* Issued periodically. San Francisco: Bank of America. A collection of reports on starting and managing specific types of small businesses. Also booklets on specific management problems in small business management.

Publications of the Small Business Administration

712. 115A *Free Management Assistance Publications.* Lists titles in the following series: *Management Aids and Small Business Bibliographies.*

713. 115B *For-Sale Booklets.* Lists the contents of the *Small Business Management* and *Starting and Managing Series* as well as the annual issues of *Management Aids for Small Manufacturers* and *Small Marketers Aids.*

714. *Management Aids for Small Manufacturers.*

715. *Small Business Management Series.* Irregular.

716. *Small Marketers Aids.*

717. *Starting and Managing Series.* Irregular.

Journals and Magazines

718. *Journal of Small Business Management.* Quarterly. West Virginia University: Bureau of Business Research, College of Business and Economics.

719. *NASBIC News.* Washington, D.C.: National Association of Small Business Investment Companies.

720. *Quarterly Economic Report for Small Business.* San Mateo, Calif.: National Federation of Independent Business. A series of quarterly economic reports based on survey data from members of the National Federation of Independent Business.

721. *Small Business News.* Monthly. Waltham, Mass.: Small Business Administration of New England.

Social Service

Directories

722. *Community Action Agency Atlas.* Washington, D.C., Office of Economic Opportunity. Geographic listing of all agency offices, regional, state, local, and those in Indian land areas.

723. *Conservation Directory.* Annual. Washington, D.C.:

National Wildlife Federation. Governmental and private organizations concerned with natural resource use and management.

724. *Directory of Agencies Serving Blind Persons.* Revised biennially. New York: American Foundation for the Blind. Lists 500 American agencies and schools serving blind.

725. *Directory of Approved Counseling Agencies.* Washington, D.C.: American Board on Counseling Services, Inc., American Personnel and Guidance Association. Directory of counseling agencies that have been evaluated and approved. Includes sponsor, clientele, fees, and professional staff. Arranged geographically for the United States and Canada.

726. *Directory of Full-Year Head Start Programs.* Washington, D.C.: Office of Child Development, U.S. Department of HEW. Geographic listing of the programs including the names of directors.

727. *Directory of Spanish Speaking Community Organizations.* Washington, D.C.: U.S. Government Printing Office. Listing of national, state, and city organizations.

728. *Directory of State and Local Resources for the Mentally Retarded.* Washington, D.C.: U.S. Department of HEW. List of state and local agencies, facilities, and other resources that render services to the mentally retarded.

729. *Directory—United Way of America.* Alexandria, Va.: United Way of America. Listing of United Funds, Community Chests, and Community Health and Welfare Councils that are members of United Way of America. Address and name of executive included.

730. *Encyclopedia of Social Work.* Quinquennial. New York: National Association of Social Workers. International indexed directory of social welfare agencies.

731. *JWB Personnel Reporter.* Biannual. New York: National Jewish Welfare Board. Listing of current job openings in Jewish community centers and other personnel and training information.

732. *Public Welfare Directory.* Washington, D.C.: American Public Welfare Association. Lists all federal, state, local, and territorial public welfare agencies throughout the United States and Canada. Lists other related public agencies—federal and state level.

The last chapter was intended to help you develop a job search focus based on your self-assessment. At this stage you should have identified one or more areas of interest to which you will apply your energies. The next step in the process is to generate options—that is, job offers from which you can choose.

The process of obtaining job offers typically includes a number of key activities: getting job leads, interviewing, and follow-up. In this chapter we'll explore the first of these activities, getting job leads.

Sources of Job Leads

There are five primary sources of job leads: college-associated placement offices, unsolicited direct-mail campaigns, friends and acquaintances, ads in newspapers and journals, and profit-making placement firms (such as personnel agencies and executive search firms). A typical successful job hunter relies on one, two, or three of these sources, depending on his or her particular needs.

School Placement Offices

The placement offices of colleges and universities are generally designed to help graduating students get together with moderate to large prospective employers from the local area. (The more prestigious the school, the larger the area.) Most placement offices are very good at that limited objective. They are generally not particularly helpful if one is looking for a job in a small company, or in another part of the world, or in any type of organization that hires few of the school's graduates (e.g., few hospitals interview at business schools). In addition, most placement offices are not organized to help alumni or students seeking summer jobs.

Virtually all undergraduates and most graduate students use their placement office as a source of job leads. From our own observations, we suspect that few people who should use the placement office as their primary source fail to do so, while a considerable number who should be relying primarily on other sources instead rely exclusively on placement offices, simply because it's easier that way.

To decide how much to rely on a placement office for job leads (or whether to rely on it at all), a student needs to learn, well in advance of the recruiting season, which organizations with what types of job tend to recruit on campus. (Lists of organizations, along with job descriptions from the previous year's recruitment activities, are usually available at placement offices.) If the types of companies and jobs on which you are focusing don't usually recruit on your campus, you will need to rely on other sources for job leads. We have known many graduate students who obtained very satisfying jobs without ever using their placement offices.

Personal Solicitation

Most of our students who have not relied primarily on our placement office have gotten their job leads through direct personal solicitation.[1] That is, they have written unsolicited letters to potential employers ask-

---

[1]In a 1973 survey, 45 percent of the entire graduating class at Harvard Business School said they learned of the job they eventually accepted through placement-office activities. Twenty-seven percent learned of their job through personal solicitation. Fourteen percent learned of it through summer or previous employment.

ing if they have any job openings. In a typical case, a student will send out 10, 20, or 30 one- or two-page letters to carefully chosen targets.[2] The letter, in one way or another, asks that the writer be considered for a job, and encloses a résumé. If the letter and résumé are well written, and if the targets are well chosen, the person may expect to receive from 10 to 50 percent "positive responses" (usually an invitation for an interview). Poorly written letters and résumés sent out to inadequately screened targets often net no positive responses. We've seen people send out 100 letters and receive mimeographed rejection letters from 20 organizations, personal rejection letters from another 3, and no response from the remaining 77.

Personal solicitation can be time-consuming and very frustrating. It takes a reasonably strong ego to withstand getting rejections in the mail day after day after day. It's both easier and less ego-deflating to look over ads in the newspaper or lists of employers at the placement office—a process in which *you* reject (screen) *them*. As a result, most job hunters probably underutilize personal solicitation as a source of leads.

Personal Contacts

The single most important source of job leads for nonstudent professional, technical, and managerial workers is their own personal contacts. In a study of such people who had changed jobs in the past five years in one geographical area, Mark Granovetter found that about 55 to 60 percent of them had identified their new job using a personal contact source. (The percentage was even higher for managers and people earning over $25,000 per year.) Furthermore, these people expressed a higher level of satisfaction with the jobs they obtained that way than people who relied on other sources.[3]

The most useful personal sources of leads include people who are looking for a similar job, former work associates, and professional acquaintances made through professional organizations.[4] People inside an organization often know of, or can easily find out about, job possibilities that are never advertised externally. Professional associations often actively solicit job-possibility information from all their members and then make that information available to their members or to anyone who requests it. The tactic of trading leads with another similar job hunter often can net a large number of previously unknown possibilities.

Some successful job hunters spend virtually all their effort in the first month of job hunting setting up a network of contacts who are aware of their new job-hunting status as well as the exact focus of their job campaign. They then use that network as a radar screen to identify job leads.

Advertisements

A fourth source of leads job hunters often use is advertisements. Newspapers carry job ads on a daily basis for the area they serve. Professional journals and magazines sometimes include a help wanted section. Access to these sources is relatively easy, by subscription or through a library.

Almost all job seekers who are out of school use this source of leads to some degree, probably because it is easy and doesn't require much personal initiative. And ads are the most visible source of job leads. However, very few students seem to actually find jobs through this source, and a relatively small percentage of nonstudent professionals (managerial or technical) actually gain their jobs through ads.

However, job advertisements may serve a useful function beyond being a source of job leads. For the same reason that advertising in general is often useful to people who are not currently looking for a specific product, job advertisements probably help some people get a useful "feel" for the job market. That is, they can sometimes supply information to a job hunter regarding what types of jobs, at what salaries, exist in what numbers, and where. Particularly at the start of a job hunt, such information could be very useful.

Profit-Making Organizations

A final source of leads commonly used by job hunters is profit-making organizations such as executive search firms and personnel agencies. We know of no student at all who has found a job as a result of a lead from these sources. And although we have known many nonstudents who have used this source of leads, very few have actually found jobs that way.

We have personally heard many more bad stories than good about people's interactions with personnel agencies. One gets the sense that they can be helpful to nonstudents, but that there are plenty of risks involved, due to the large number of marginally competent people in those agencies.

Many of the established and larger executive search firms have a reputation of doing a competent job for their market. But that market is fairly small—managers in the $30,000-and-up bracket.[5]

---

[2]Chapter 22 will have more to say on exactly how one "carefully chooses" such targets.

[3]Mark Granovetter, *Getting a Job* (Cambridge, Mass.: Harvard University Press, 1974).

[4]Granovetter found that most of the contacts people used successfully were work and educational acquaintances, not social friends.

---

[5]For an interesting discussion of executive search firms, see Jacquelin A. Thompson, "The MBA Guide to Executive Recruiters: Who They Are and How They Work," *MBA,* May 1976.

Exhibit 21–1

Summary Chart: Sources of Job Leads

Sources	Comments
1. College placement office	By far the most widely used source for students. Probably overused.
2. Unsolicited direct-mail campaigns	Number-two source for all job hunters.
3. Personal contacts	By far the most widely used source for nonstudents.
4. Advertisements	Useful for job-market data. Not terribly useful for specific leads.
5. Personnel agencies and executive search firms	Best for people earning $30,000 a year or more.

Exhibit 21–1 summarizes this discussion. The number-one job-lead source for students is the placement office. For nonstudents, the number-one source is personal contacts. Unsolicited letter campaigns and other forms of direct application are the second most-used source for both groups.

Before you make an initial contact with an organization (through one of the five sources outlined above), we suggest that you do a little preliminary research to develop an informed first impression as to whether or not the organization seems to offer a good fit with your self-assessment. If the results of this research are completely contradictory to your self-assessment, you may decide not to waste any time on making the contact. Moderately contradictory impressions, however, probably should be followed up (especially if the company fits your focus), since your first impressions may not be completely accurate. Your research, along with your self-assessment, will arm you with specific questions that you can carry to the interview (see the next chapter.)

Annual Reports

One of the most common sources of information on job opportunities is the annual report. If you are able to develop a framework for reading annual reports, it will help you immensely in your attempt to focus your job search and to wade through large volumes of data relatively quickly and efficiently.

We will not pay attention to financial analysis related to the balance sheets, income statements, and other financial reports contained in an annual report, since much has been written about that elsewhere. And we assume that you will use that kind of analysis in your preparation for interviews. Rather, we will ask you to focus on the nonfinancial aspects of the annual report—its composition, the photographs, the prose, the company's products, and so on.

Looking for a Fit between Organization and You

As you read through an annual report to decide whether or not to make contact, you should remember that, in a focused job search, you are looking for a fit between yourself, a particular job, and the organization in which that job is embedded. In this sense, you are looking for a fit between your personality and the organizational culture of the organization that will be employing you. The annual report can provide a number of clues and signals to help you assess the fit. As was the case in the self-assessment process, no single signal or datum is sufficient to give you an accurate, reliable view of an organization. And so our philosophy here is the same as that expressed earlier; namely, that if you can generate a variety of pools of information about potential employers, you will have a better perspective on the goodness of fit between you and the organization. The annual report will provide several signals that will contribute to that multifaceted pool of data about an organization.

Corporations are spending increasingly large volumes of money, energy, and time in preparing their annual reports. In one study of 27 large corporations, it was estimated that top management spent well over a thousand hours in planning, editing, and approving the annual report. The range was from 112 to 5,760 hours. If one values senior management time at an average of $275 per hour, the average cost for management time spent on the development of those 27 annual reports comes to $61,750. You can see that, from the corporation's point of view, the impression that is left by an annual report is an important one. In the same way that you as a job candidate will be trying to create an impression with your résumé and cover letter, the organization is trying to create an impression with the annual report that will be both accurate and favorable (see the alternate exercise on p. 237). When you read an annual report, the signals and characteristics we identify below will no doubt do much to create the impression that you have of that organization. We want to make those signals explicit to you so that you can use them more efficiently and effectively in assessing the fit between you and the organization.

The Cover and the President's Letter

One fundamental issue in reading an annual report is a consideration of who wrote the president's letter and the other explanatory prose contained throughout the report. In many cases, the letter and the explanatory prose are written by corporate staff people who may or may not be accurately reflecting the philosophies and ideas of top management. In most cases, we assume that annual reports have been approved by top management people. Ask yourself if the president's letter seems to have been written by him or her individually or by a staff member. What does that tell you about the organization and its management? The question of authorship introduces a question of validity into your reading of an annual report. It should also caution you not to either accept or reject what is contained in an annual report as fact without further investigation.

Consider the cover. What is on the cover? Why do you think that particular cover (in many cases a photograph) was chosen? What was the company trying to say about itself by choosing that cover? What does the cover say about what is important to the company?

Next, consider the relationship of the president's letter to the financial results of the corporation. If the results were bad, who gets the blame? Does the corporation look to outside factors to explain its business results, or is the organization willing to look internally as well? What does this tell you about the management of the organization and about what it might be like to work with? If the results were good, to whom does the credit go? Are the senior managers willing to disperse credit throughout the organization, or is it again attributed to factors over which management feels it has little control?

People

Look for the attention given to people. How many people are mentioned in the annual report? In what ways? Are they described in personal or impersonal ways? How many people are there in the organization? Is the number of people growing? What does this tell you about the industry the organization is in? What is the ratio of sales to employees? What does this tell you about the efficiency of the organization? What does this tell you about what it would be like to work in this organizational culture? What about turnover in the organization? Are the reasons for turnover mentioned? If not, why? If they are mentioned, what do the reasons tell you about what it would be like to work for this organization?

What about changes in senior management? Who has gone and who has come in the past year? Where did they go? From where did they come? Outside the organization? If inside, from what areas? What does this tell you about the standards and criteria for advancement within the organization? Are senior management all of a particular age or ethnic background? What does this tell you?

Try flipping through the annual report without reading anything. Look only at the pictures. What do you see? People? Products? Neither? If you see people, what can you learn from them? Are they all the same age, same sex, same race? What are they doing? Why do you think those pictures were chosen?

Problems and Plans

Note the problems identified in the various prose descriptions of the organization's business. What kinds of problems does the company face? Are these problems you would find interesting to work on? Are they the same ones you would expect the company to be facing?

You might also look for plans for dealing with those problems. Are there any? Do they seem realistic? Are they reasonable given your knowledge of the economy and the industry? Do they seem attainable, given the resources the organization has at its command?

Consider the organization of the company. Is this outlined in the annual report? What is it? What does that imply about what it would be like to work for that company? Will there be a lot of transfers? Where are the facilities? Which parts of the organization report to whom?

Look for signals about how decisions are made in this corporation. Are many people involved, or do decisions seem to be made by a single individual? What does this tell you about what it would be like to work for this company?

You may not be able to glean answers to all these questions from any particular annual report. That in itself is data and can provide you with questions for an interview.

Exercises

Comparing Annual Reports

Choose annual reports for two companies in each of two different industries. Then read the president's letter from each and compare and contrast the tone and content of the letters. You might, for instance, get the latest General Electric, GTE, General Mills, and General Foods annual reports. Ask yourself:

What tentative inferences can be drawn about what it would be like to work for each of these companies?

How are the annual reports similar?

How are they different?

Do you see any common characteristics in the two companies in the same industry? (This will give you some insight into industry characteristics that might be true regardless of the company you interview with in a particular industry.)

How do these reports differ from others you have read?

What seems to be most important to each company?

What can you infer about the management style of each company?

This assignment will help you to calibrate the amount of variation you can expect in recruiting within and among industries. It will also sharpen your insight into the realities of corporate cultures and the ways they influence corporations and the people who work in them. This skill will be very useful to you later on when you begin interviewing and making company visits.

Alternate Exercise: Gaining Insight
into the Accuracy of Written
Promotional Materials

An interesting exercise that will help you see more clearly how well written promotional materials reflect the experience of living in an organization is to examine a situation in which you have both personal and written experience. Consider your school if you are taking this material in a course. It might be interesting to have the class review promotional material (brochures) published and distributed by the school. Read the brochures in advance of the class and be prepared to discuss how well the brochures match or do not match your experience and view of the school. Then consider the differences you found with the kind of differences you might expect to find between an annual report and working for a company. This may help you to calibrate the information you will glean from reading annual reports.

If you are working through this book on your own, you may wish to compare the annual report or descriptive brochure of an organization you have worked with in the past with your own experience.

22

Making Contact

Once you have decided to make contact with an organization, you must decide how to do it in a way that will make the organization receptive to you. Of the sources of job leads outlined in the previous chapter, unsolicited direct-mail campaigns and answering advertisements present the greatest difficulty, since usually the only introductions one has in those two cases are one's cover letter and résumé. In order to get an interview in which the employer is receptive to you, you must pass through an initial screening process.

Most employers have no more desire to waste their time in the labor market than you do. So they too set up some type of screening process. The key to success is to differentiate yourself from the masses and convince the decision maker that the time taken to interview you probably isn't going to be wasted.

It is not unusual for an organization to receive 20 to 50 inquiries for a job opening. Some jobs will attract hundreds of inquiries. Since simply hiring a single managerial or professional person can cost an organization as much as $20,000, employers have a strong financial incentive to try to keep costs down. Interviewing everyone who inquires about a job opening can significantly increase costs.

Convincing some decision maker to take the time to interview you is not just an exercise, as many people seem to think, in making yourself look "impressive" in some ill-defined, abstract sense. What is "impressive," like beauty, is in the eye of the beholder. The beholder is an employer with particular goals, values, problems, and needs. And here lies the key not just to getting an initial interview, but to getting job offers.

The more you can put yourself in the position of the potential employer and understand that person's (or those people's) point of view, the more successful you will be in getting job offers. With respect to getting an initial interview, this means that it helps enormously to know something about the potential employer before you make your initial contact. Any person who has gone through the process of creating a rational focus for a job campaign, and who has done the little additional research necessary to screen leads, has probably learned enough about potential employers to make the type of initial contact that gets an interview. It doesn't require hours and hours of additional effort. Since so many job hunters do almost no research, doing just a little can be a real competitive advantage. Then, if you can somehow communicate to those making the screening decision that you may have the potential of meeting *their needs,* you will certainly get the interview.

You should not attempt to do this, of course, if it means ignoring parts of your self-assessment that are central to who you are. Remember that "fit" from both your and the employer's points of view is the essential factor. The point here is that what you say and how you say it will be more effective if you consider carefully the person who will be reading or listening to what you say than if you are concerned only about satisfying some personal needs.

Résumés

Consider, for example, your résumé. Most people, even those with no full-time job experience, could write a several-page résumé if coached. They could elaborate at length on their schooling, their part-time jobs, their hobbies, their health, their job objectives, and so on. Most people don't, of course. Instead, they ask

239

someone what a résumé is supposed to look like, or for a sample résumé, and then semiconsciously select things to put into that format. The end result is seldom a great résumé.

A good résumé is nothing more than a tool that can convince employers you will be able to meet their particular needs, help with their problems, and share enough in common with them to "fit in." Creating a good résumé therefore depends on your understanding of what an employer's needs are, what the problems are, what the values are, and what you can contribute. Since books and volumes of articles have been written on how to prepare and compose résumés, we will not spend much time on the mechanics of this process. Rather, we refer you to the appendix at the end of the chapter. However, we would like to make a few comments with regard to the philosophy behind résumés and then give you a brief exercise to help you translate those philosophical comments into practical applications.

Format

Résumés have two fundamental dimensions—format and content. One might believe that the format of the résumé is unimportant. We have not found that to be the case. One recruiter, looking at a professionally composed and typeset résumé, remarked enthusiastically to the job candidate: "It really is nice to see such a well-done résumé. I could tell from the moment I saw it that you believed in high standards of professionalism in your work. We get so many résumés here that are poorly typed and photocopied or mimeographed, that it really is refreshing and reassuring to get one like this." That recruiter was responding to the format of the résumé he was looking at.

A résumé that looks as if it was typed on a cheap typewriter by a nontypist communicates a number of things about you. It says that you are a sloppy person (and who wants to hire a sloppy person?), or that you really don't care much about getting a job (and who wants to hire someone who doesn't want to work?), or that you don't really care much about the person you sent the résumé to. It's worth the time and money to *look* professional and interested.

The way your résumé is laid out on a sheet of paper is extremely important in leaving an impression with the person who reads it. We encourage you to experiment with a variety of formats and to choose the one that leaves an impression consistent with who you are and what you are looking for in a corporation. You may have a terrific résumé in substance, but if the format is poor it may leave a poor impression.

There are several aspects to format we would en-

courage you to keep in mind. The first is the spacing on the page. Résumés with very small margins leave the impression of a great deal of activity. But they also leave the impression of disorganization. Although it is general practice to have résumés limited to one page, crowded margins may undo whatever benefit you may get from increasing the volume. One alternative if you have too much to put on one page is to type it on a longer page with wider margins and have the entire page photoreproduced and then duplicated on an 8 1/2 by 11 sheet.

Another item is the question of parallelism in format. Recruiters read hundreds, perhaps thousands of résumés in the recruiting season. They get in a rhythm as they read, using whatever framework they have personally developed to help them quickly get the pertinent information. Some of this is conscious; some of this is subconscious. Every time a résumé format interrupts or jars that rhythm, the recruiter's impression is also interrupted or jarred. An effective résumé will pique the recruiter's attention at the places *you* want to emphasize and not at unintended or inappropriate places.

A lack of parallel construction is one way to jar or interrupt a recruiter's reading rhythm. Most résumés, for instance, begin paragraphs with a noun describing the previous job title and then the activities that it included in the lines that follow. However, a lot of people under the "Education" sections of their résumés begin those paragraphs with verbs like "Graduated" or "Received." It is our preference to maintain parallel construction by beginning the descriptive paragraphs under each job or educational experience in the same way. If, for example, you wanted to begin each paragraph with a noun, you could begin your educational paragraphs with the word "Graduate" followed by your degree and the honors and activities associated with your experience there.

Content

Format alone, of course, will not ensure a good impression. Content is also extremely important. A well laid out format that has no substance will not get you very far. As you think about the content of your résumé, keep in mind that résumés are very much like short stories. They are designed to leave a particular impression with the reader in a minimum of space. Because of their brevity, every word or phrase in a short story and a résumé counts. You cannot afford to waste space or words when you are trying to create a favorable impression on one page.

Remember that you are creating an impression. The impression must be an accurate one; it must reflect who you are and what you've done, but it is indeed an impression. The words you choose, the sentences you frame, and the format in which you package this content will create impressions in the minds of the people who read the résumé. Try to create the impression that *you want* to leave; one that accurately reflects the results of your self-assessment.

Perhaps the major feature of the content part of a résumé is the repetition with which patterns or themes appear in the material. A person who writes a résumé that includes a degree in education, teaching in an elementary school, teaching in a secondary school, a masters degree in higher education, and work for an education foundation has created a pattern that sends the signal they have selected a career in education. Applying for jobs in noneducational areas will require some additional impression-creating and selling.

In some cases, students who have not developed a focus in their job search have attempted to list all their activities and in some cases to fluff up or expand their résumés by including activities and memberships that were only marginal experiences. We find this to be more harmful than helpful. If, for instance, in the business educational section of your résumé you list membership in the Management Consultant Club, the General Management Club, the Small Business Club, the International Finance Club, and the Marketing Club, in the belief that the range and diversity of your interests will be an attractive feature to a recruiter, we believe you are mistaken. A person with a focused job search who wants a job in marketing would eliminate the other club activities from the résumé so that the impression left is that of a person who knows what he or she wants to do. Recruiters in marketing-oriented companies who read the résumé are more likely to be left with the impression that here is a person whose interests seem to match our own.

Another common characteristic of poorly written résumés is that their writers tend to use very general words to describe the activities and responsibilities of each experience or position. A well-written resume will always contain nouns, verbs, adjectives, and adverbs which pinpoint the job focus that person is trying to create. Again, a person seeking a position in marketing will look for the words that accurately describe his or her activities and experience but that also have immediate and relevant application to careers and positions in marketing.

Summary

The point of what we have been trying to say is that like a short story, a résumé is basically an impression-creating document. When you write your résumé, you should be sensitive to this feature. Be careful with every word you use. Ask yourself if it helps to create the kind of impression you want to leave and if it is relevant to the kind of recruiter who will be reading your résumé. If you are uncertain about the impression that is being left or of how it will be received, leave the word out.

Assignment 1

Consider Kathleen Johnson's résumé (case, p. 242). What impressions does it leave with you? What do you think Kathleen's job search focus is? What inferences can you draw about Kathleen?

Cover Letters

The cover letter is a means of contacting an organization, presenting your résumé and your job focus, and of asking for a response. You may in fact write several different kinds of cover letters if you are deciding to pursue more than one focus in a particular job search. Most people write cover letters with the idea that they must sell themselves to the reader. While this is an important part of the cover letter's purpose, a more effective cover letter is one that also provides the writer with an opportunity to learn from the responses it generates.

Assignment 2

Jim Lydon, for example, after going through an extensive self-assessment process, decided to focus his job search on real estate and banking. He signed up for 12 interviews offered by his campus placement office, and in addition decided to write to 13 banks and 12 real estate firms.

Assume that you are Jim Lydon's roommate and that before sending out his letters, he has asked you to critique his cover letter (see case, p. 243). What is the paragraph by paragraph structure he has used? How would you respond to Jim? What suggestions would you make? What predictions would you make?

Chase Hall B-11
Harvard Business School
Boston, MA 02163
Phone: (617) 498-0000

Home Address:
33 Upland Road
Summit, N.J. 07901
Phone (201) 273-0000

education
1978–1980   HARVARD GRADUATE SCHOOL OF BUSINESS ADMINISTRATION

Candidate for the degree of Master in Business Administration in June, 1980. General management curriculum with emphasis on marketing and production. Member of Management Consulting, Marketing and Real Estate Clubs.

1977   AMERICAN MANAGEMENT ASSOCIATION   NEW YORK, NEW YORK

Seminars in sales management.

1969–1973   FAIRLEIGH DICKINSON UNIVERSITY   RUTHERFORD, NEW JERSEY

Received Bachelor of Science degree in Experimental Psychology, January 1973. Dean's List. New Jersey Scholar and Travelli Grant recipient. University Administrative Intern, Residential Advisor, and Counselor at a medium security prison. Extracurricular activities in sports and music.

work
experience
summer
1979   NEW JERSEY BANK & TRUST   NEWARK, NEW JERSEY

Credit Analyst. Analyzed financial position of potential corporate customers and made loan development calls.

1973–1978
1977–1978   BABBITT PHARMACEUTICAL CORPORATION   WHITE PLAINS, NEW YORK

Midwest Regional Sales Manager. Brought region from last to first place with respect to quota attainment while reducing the proportion of selling expense to sales by 25%. Developed and implemented a management by objectives plan and supervised field work for a major test market. Handled all recruitment, conducted sales seminars, trained sales representatives, provided expense budgets, coordinated cooperative advertising programs, and developed key accounts for a 9 state area.

1973–1977   Sales Representative. Sales and service of a vitamin and health care product line to pharmacies. Designated 1975 "Sales Representative of the Year" for highest attainment of quota.

1973   PUBLISHERS GUILD   MORRISTOWN, NEW JERSEY

Sales Representative. Personal contact sales of dictionaries and magazines.

other
experience   United States Representative to a Swiss Girl Guide International Conference. Financed college education through various part-time and summer jobs.

references   Personal references available upon request.

JIM LYDON: COVER LETTER

Dear Mr. _____:

   I shall receive an M.B.A. in June 1978 and plan a career in the real
estate field with a leading properties firm. My survey of the industry
indicates that your firm has established an outstanding record and, therefore,
it would be advantageous for me to learn more about the specific opportunities
it offers and to discuss with you my objectives and capabilities.

   My highest priority is to find a challenging, fulfilling environment
in which to learn and work. Pursuant to this objective, I seek a firm which:
(1) recognizes the need for professional management of M.B.A. caliber in this
rapidly growing field, (2) gives a broad exposure to real estate and discourages
overspecialization, (3) operates in an informal structure with close personal
relationships among employees, (4) allows new M.B.A.'s to contribute immediately
and to assume early responsibilities, and (5) measures performance and
allocates compensation and advancement accordingly without regard for
senority. I would like to know more about your firm with respect to these
criteria.

   The enclosed resume gives you a brief outline of my background but
does not deal with relevant personal qualities. I have an entrepreneurial
spirit, the ability to coordinate several projects simultaneously with proven
results, and a "knack" for working successfully with diverse groups of people
eliciting their trust and confidence. I am performance-oriented, mature,
willing to travel, able to communicate effectively, and confident that the
pattern of success that has characterized my past will lead me to greater
achievements in the near future.

   Mr. _____, if you feel that my objectives and qualifications may
be compatible with your firm's opportunities and needs, please contact me to
arrange a meeting that could be to our mutual benefit. I shall hope to hear
from you soon.

                              Sincerely,

                              James L. Lydon

JLL/lmm

Enclosure

Appendix to Chapter 22

Sources of Information
on Developing Job Opportunities

- Résumé writing, cover letters, and follow-up
- Interviewing
- Executive recruiting search firms
- Salaries in different industries and jobs

- Job opportunities: geographic sources
- Life style information in specific geographical areas
- Geographic relocations outside the U.S.
- Dual career families

The references listed here represent a selected set of useful information that is readily available to you. Each reference can be located in any major library.

Titles are listed under subject headings and then by type of publication where appropriate.

Résumé Writing, Cover Letters, and Follow-up

Books

1. Alumni Advisory Center, Inc. *How to Write Your Résumé.* New York: 1970.

2. Angel, Juvenal L. *Specialized Résumés for Executives and Professionals.* New York: Regents Publishing Co., 1967.

3. Angel, Juvenal L. *Why and How to Prepare an Effective Job Résumé,* 5th ed. rev. and enl. New York: World Trade Academy Press; distributed by Simon and Schuster, 1972.

4. Biegeleisen, Jacob I. *Job Résumés: How to Write Them, How to Present Them.* New York: Grosset & Dunlap, 1969.

5. Boll, Carl. *Executive Jobs Unlimited.* New York: Macmillan, 1965.

6. Bolles, Richard Nelson. *What Color Is Your Parachute?* Berkeley, Calif.: Ten Speed Press, 1972.

7. Black, James Menzies, and Edith M. Lynch. *How to Move in Management.* New York: McGraw-Hill, 1967.

8. Brennan, Lawrence David, Stanley Strand, and Edward C. Gruber. *Résumés for Better Jobs.* New York: Simon and Schuster, 1973.

9. Cass, Frank. *Recruitment Advertising.* New York: American Management Association, 1968.

10. Dickhut, Harold W. *Professional Résumé/Job Search Guide,* 3rd ed. Chicago: Management Counselors, 1975.

11. Greco, Benedetto. *How to Get the Job That's Right for You.* Homewood, Ill.: Dow Jones/Irwin, 1975.

12. Gruber, Edward C. *Résumés That Get Jobs.* New York: Arco, 1963.

13. Irish, Richard K. *Go Hire Yourself an Employer.* Garden City, N.Y.: Anchor Books, 1973.

14. Johnson, Gil. *How to Prepare Your Job Résumé,* 2nd ed. Monrovia, Calif.: Association Writers, 1971.

15. Mandell, Milton. *The Selection Process: Choosing the Right Man for the Job.* New York: American Management Association, 1964.

16. Schrameck, Carolyn F. Nutter. *The Résumé Workbook. A Personal Career File for Job Applications.* Cranston, R.I.: Carroll Press, 1970.

17. Uris, Auren. *The Executive Job Market.* New York: McGraw-Hill, 1965.

18. Vogel, Erwin. *How to Write your Job-Getting Résumé and Covering Letter.* Brooklyn, N.Y.: Copy-Write Creations, 1971.

Guides and Handbooks

19. Angel, Juvenal L. *Looking for Employment in Foreign Countries Reference Handbook,* 6th ed. Volume 7 of *Encyclopedia of International Information.* New York: World Trade Academy Press, 1972.

20. Employment Management Association. *Job Hunting Guide.* John D. Erdlen, ed. Boston: Herman Publishing, Inc., 1975.

Periodicals

21. Dortch, R. N. "What Businessmen Look for in the Résumé." *Personnel Journal,* 54:516, October 1975.

22. Hayden, R. L., and J. H. Jackson. "Behavioral Research and Computer Methods Applied to Managerial Résumé Design." *Personnel Journal,* 51:728–732ff, October 1972.

23. Perham, J. C. "What's Wrong with Executive Résumés?" *Duns Review,* 105:50–52ff, May 1975.

24. Smith, L. "Notes from the Job Underground," *Duns Review,* 106:46–48, August 1975.

Interviewing

Popular Works

25. Boll, Carl. *Executive Jobs Unlimited.* New York: Macmillan, 1965. See Chapter 6. Very basic, introductory source. Material is sometimes dated but still useful. Good for beginners.

26. Bolles, Richard N. *What Color Is Your Parachute?* Berkeley, Calif.: Ten Speed Press, 1973. Emphasis is on self-analysis as preparation for job search. Information on interviewing is scattered throughout.

27. Crystal, John C., and Richard N. Bolles. *Where Do I Go from Here with My Life?* New York: Seabury Press, 1974. See Chapter 14. Stresses self-evaluation and analysis. Contains brief but unusual approach to interviewing.

28. Dauw, Dean C. *Up Your Career.* Prospect Heights, Ill.: Waveland Press, 1975. See Chap. 7. Mainly a list of questions most frequently asked by interviewers as well as a sample of questions that are illegal.

29. Dickhut, Harold W., and Marvel J. Davis. *Profes-*

sional Resume/Job Search Guide. Chicago: Management Counselors, 1975. See Section 12. Brief discussion of interview preparation, types of questions asked, conduct, and follow-up.

30. Djeddah, Eli. *Moving Up: How to Get High-Salaried Jobs*. Philadelphia: Lippincott, 1971. See Chapters 7, 9, and 10. A popular work, easy reading, many helpful hints.

31. Erdlen, John D., ed. *Job-Hunting Guide: Official Manual of the Employment Management Association*. Boston: Herman Publishers, 1975. See Chapter 6, Very brief section that includes crucial points in interviewing and follow-up evaluation.

32. German, Donald R., and Joan W. German. *Successful Job Hunting for Executives*. Chicago: Henry Regnery, 1974. See Chapter 13. Informative chapter designed for individuals in management. Includes information on planning and analysis of interviews.

33. Greco, Benedetto. *How to Get the Job That's Right for You*. Homewood, Ill.: Dow Jones/Irwin, 1975. See Chapter 9. Includes discussion of handling job interview, selling yourself, and sample of tough questions.

34. Hopke, William E., ed. *Encyclopedia of Careers and Vocational Guidance*. Chicago: J. G. Ferguson, 1972.

35. Irish, Richard K. *Go Hire Yourself an Employer*. Garden City, N.Y.: Anchor Press, 1973. See Chapter 4. Very readable, popular book offering a variety of hints for the job search.

36. Jameson, Robert H. *The Professional Job Hunting System: World's Fastest Way to Get a Better Job*. Verona, N.J.: Performance Dynamics, 1972.

37. Kent, Malcolm. *Successful Executive Job Hunting*. New York: Laddin Press, 1967. See Chapter 5. Aimed at business professionals; seems to be on a higher level than some of the other popular works. Discusses stress interviewing, executive search firms, and psychological testing along with preparing for and conducting interview.

38. Powell, C. Randall. *Career Planning and Placement for the College Graduate of the '70s*. Dubuque, Iowa: Kendall/Hunt, 1974. See Chapters 4 and 5. Discusses all aspects of job search. Very good introductory source. Includes information on screening, preparation, first interviews, frequently asked questions, illegal questions, and how to handle job offers.

39. Snelling, Robert O., Sr. *The Opportunity Explosion*. New York: Macmillan, 1969. See Chapter 10. Written by executive of well-known placement firm. Heavy emphasis on appearance and luck in interviewing. Author presents different approach to topic.

Especially for Women

40. Bird, Caroline. *Everything a Woman Needs to Know to Get Paid What She's Worth*. New York: David McKay, 1973. Questions and answers, some dealing with topic.

41. Higgenson, Margaret V., and Thomas L. Quick. *The Ambitious Woman's Guide to a Successful Career*. New York: American Management Association, 1975. Deals primarily with career development. Contains chapter on job hunting with subsection on interviewing. Helpful for men as well as women.

42. Krohn, Miriam. *Your Job Campaign*. New York: Catalyst. A workbook in the Catalyst Self-Guidance Campaign Series, 1974. See Chapter 7. Designed to address the "unique problems of adult women." Very helpful section on preparing, conducting, and evaluating the interview. Definitely useful to men as well.

Periodicals

43. Clarke, John R. "Landing that Right Executive Job." *Management Review,* August 1975, pp. 31–36. Contains small section on interviewing within article about job searching.

44. Costello, John. "Executive Trends: Playing the Interview Game." *Nation's Business,* September 1974, p. 6. Very brief discussion of stereotypes who interview and tips on avoiding becoming one.

45. "Finding a Job in the Recession." *Business Week,* January 11, 1975, pp. 101–106. A supplement to the regularly featured Personal Business section. Contains several paragraphs on interviewing as well as information on other aspects of job search. Includes bibliography.

46. Flanagan, William, ed. "How to Keep Bias Out of Job Interviews," *Business Week,* May 26, 1975, p. 77. Discusses what an interviewer may not ask.

47. Keyser, Marshall. "How to Apply for a Job." *Journal of College Placement,* Fall 1974, pp. 63–65. Discusses qualifications most often desired by employers as expressed in a survey of Los Angeles businessmen.

48. Kohn, Mervin. "What Off-Campus Interviewers Look for in Young Job Seekers." *S.A.M. Advanced Management Journal,* 40, pp. 59–62. Lists qualities considered important by campus recruiters. Moderately helpful to MBA students.

49. Luk, Henry. "Interviewing: A Statistical Look at Columbia '74." *MBA,* November 1974, pp. 43–45. Investigates and records statistics resulting from a study of aggressiveness in interviewing using students from Columbia.

50. Lumsden, Howard, and James C. Sharf. "Behavioral Dimensions of the Job Interview." *Journal of College Placement,* Spring 1974, pp. 63–66. Types of behavior influence job interviews. Could be a helpful list to use in preparation.

51. Shaw, Edward A. "Behavior Modification and the Interview." *Journal of College Placement,* October/November 1973, pp. 52–57. Designed mainly for counselors, but students would find it quite helpful. Discusses pros and cons of being coached or even acting natural at interviews.

52. Welch, William F. "A Professional Approach to Job Hunting." *Public Relations Journal,* October 1972, pp.

22–24. Section on interviewing has helpful hints. Aimed at those in public relations but so general as to be useful to anyone.

Several periodicals frequently offer information related to this topic, and new issues should be checked:

53. *Business Week.* Personal Business section.

54. *Journal of College Placement.*

55. *MBA.* Career Tactics column—new in January 1976.

56. *Nation's Business.* Executive Trends column.

Miscellaneous Sources

57. Amsden, Forrest M., and Noel D. White. *How to Be Successful: Step by Step Approach for the Candidate.* Cheney, Wa.: Interviewing Dynamics, 1974. Recom-

mended for beginners as a practical reference book in interviewing by *Journal of College Placement,* Fall 1975.

58. McDonald, Stanleigh. *Ten Weeks to a Better Job.* Garden City, N.Y.: Doubleday & Company, 1972. See Chapter 4. Popular but thorough work that includes sample questions from interviews.

59. Noer, David. *How to Beat the Employment Game.* Radnor, Pa.: Chilton Company—Book Division, 1975. Discusses use and misuse of interview. Author believes it is much overrated. Has innovative viewpoint.

60. "The Interview Game." University Park: Career Development and Placement Center, Pennsylvania State University. Color videotape cassette. Teaching aid to interview process; uses game-show technique to introduce humor. Material discussed is helpful.

Executive Recruiting Search Firms

These selected sources provide information about executive recruiting search firms, commonly called recruiters or headhunters. They are frequently retained and paid by employers. Their job is to find qualified candidates for specific positions their clients have available. Recruiters do not hire people; they only recommend them to their clients. The two professional associations to which recruiters belong are:

Association of Executive Recruiting Consultants (AERC)

347 Madison Avenue, New York, N.Y. 10017. Phone: (212) 686–7194.

Association of Consulting Management Engineers (ACME)

347 Madison Avenue, New York, N.Y. 10017. Phone: (212) 686–7338.

Guides and Directories

61. American Management Association. *Executive Employment Guide.* New York: AMA, 1975. Excellent directory also including a guide indicating 150 firms' positions, salary levels, résumé and interview policies. Bibliography.

62. Consultant News. *Directory of Executive Recruiters.* Fitzwilliams, N.H., 1976. Lists over 1,000 firms retained by management to locate executives.

63. Erdlen, John D. *Job Hunting Guide: Official Manual of the Employment Management Association.* Boston: Herman Publishing Co., 1975. Contains a directory section, by states, of both employment agencies and executive search consultants.

64. Executive Selection Institute. *Handbook of Executive Recruiters, 1967–68.* Detroit, 1967. An alphabetical list of firms practicing executive recruitment.

65. National Survey Information Co. *The National Service Directory of Executive Employment Research, 1972–*

73. Lake Bluff, Ill., 1972. Lists, geographically by state, firms and individuals participating in recruiting.

International Reference Sources

66. Angel, Juvenal L. *Looking for Employment in Foreign Countries Reference Handbook,* 6th ed. Volume 7 of *Encyclopedia of International Information.* New York: World Trade Academy Press. Provides guidelines for overseas employment, employment agencies, and sources of employment abroad.

67. *European Executive Position Information Guide.* Geneva. Enables the user to assess the job market. A source of information for those who may be looking for a chance to live and work in another country; lists executive recruiters, alphabetically, by country.

68. Jameson, Robert J. *Worldwide Directory of Employment Recruiters.* Verona, N.J.: Performance Dynamics, 1975. Executive search firms listed geographically by state and country; covers 3,000 recruiters.

Books

69. Bolles, Richard N. *What Color Is Your Parachute?* Berkeley, Calif.: Ten Speed Press, 1972. Contains a discussion and bibliography of periodical literature on the pros and cons of using executive job counselors.

70. Cox, Allan J. *Confessions of a Corporate Headhunter.* New York: Trident Press, 1973. Personal reminiscences.

71. Jameson, Robert J. *Professional Job Changing System: World's Fastest Way to Get a Better Job.* Verona, N.J.: Performance Dynamics, 1975. Helpful hints.

72. Johnson, Miriam. *Counterpoint: The Changing Employment Service.* Salt Lake City: Olympus, 1973. Background notes.

73. Ruttenberg, Stanley H. *Federal-State Employment Ser-*

vice. Baltimore: Johns Hopkins Press, 1970. An overview.

74. Sweet, Donald H. *Modern Employment Function.* Reading, Mass.: Addison-Wesley, 1973. "How-to" for the recruiter.

75. Uris, Auren. *Executive Job Market.* New York: McGraw-Hill, 1965. A guide for executive job seekers and employers.

76. Williams, Roger K. *How to Evaluate, Select, and Work with Executive Recruiters.* Boston: Cahners, 1974. An overview.

Periodicals

77. Browdy, J. D. "The Personnel Man and the Headhunter." *Personnel Journal,* November 1974, pp. 46–52.

78. "Executive Recruiting: A Growth." *Business Week,* January 26, 1973, pp. 58–59.

79. Kleinschrod, W. A. "What You Always Wanted to Know About Executive Recruiters . . . But Were Afraid to Ask." *Administrative Management,* February 1972, pp. 24–26 ff.

80. Newman, Barry, "The Rite of Spring: Recruiting of MBAs by Firm Is a Game with Strange Rules," *Wall Street Journal,* April 9, 1974.

81. Pfeffer, J. "Executive Recruitment and the Development of Interfirm Organizations." *Administrative Science Quarterly,* November 4, 1973, pp. 46–52.

82. "A Peek at the Money in Headhunting." *Business Week,* July 29, 1972, pp. 22–23.

83. Porter, K. "He Finds Jobs for Executives." *Duns Review,* June 1974, pp. 78–81.

Salaries in Different Industries and Jobs

Bibliographies

84. Mohn, N. Carroll. *Compensation of Professionals: A Selected and Annotated Bibliography.* Austin: Bureau of Business Research, Graduate School of Business, University of Texas, 1972. Mostly reference materials pertaining to theory of compensation.

Statistical Surveys

85. Crystal, Graef S. *Compensating U.S. Executives Abroad.* 1972. Based on a survey of 28 companies in 14 industries.

86. Dartnell Corporation. *Dartnell Survey of Executive Compensation.* Biennial. Chicago. Extensive Statistics, charts, graphs, comparisons of compensation components by functional areas. Includes a section on Salary Administration.

87. *1970 Census of Population: Earnings by Occupation and Education.* Subject Report PC (2)-8B. Extensive Census Bureau report on wages, earnings, and income, classified by various demographic, social, and economic statistics.

88. Powell, C. Randall. *MBA Career Performance 10 Years after Graduation.* St. Paul, Minn.: Midwest College Placement Association, 1974. Includes tables giving salary statistics.

89. Powers, Janet T. *Executive Compensation in Retailing.* New York: National Retail Merchants Association, 1973. Excellent survey of salary and compensation trends in retailing.

90. *Report on Executive Compensation.* Prepared by the Executive Compensation Office of Wage Stabilization, Cost of Living Council, May 1974. Mostly textual, includes tables, graphs, etc. Also includes detailed analysis of changes and trends. Covers manufacturing and nonmanufacturing companies.

91. *Salary Survey of Business Economists.* Washington, D.C.: National Association of Business Economists. Quadrenniel. 1972 report includes tables, statistics, charts and graphs for Business Economists, salary comparisons by industry, functions, size of firm, years of experience, education, etc.

92. Teague, Burton W. *Compensating Key Personnel Overseas.* New York: The Conference Board, 1972. Analysis of compensation structure of 267 of the largest U.S.-based international companies.

Job Opportunities: Geographic Sources

Directories

93. *Career Opportunity Index.* Huntington Beach, Calif.: Career Research Systems, Inc. Professional edition, biannually with weekly supplements. California. Alphabetical listing of companies with job openings—descriptions of openings.

94. Los Angeles Times. *California's Leading Companies.* 1974. Directory listing.

95. *Organization Members of Chamber of Commerce of*

the U.S. Directory of local and state Chambers by state. Chambers sometimes publish listings of job opportunities.

96. *Standard and Poor's Register.* Volume 3, *Indexes.* 1975. Yellow pages list companies by major cities within states.

97. State Industrial Directories. Consult *CPP*—blue-edged pages for specific titles. Listings of companies within the state, mostly manufacturing or industrial.

Bibliographies

98. *Encyclopedia of Business Information Sources.* Volume 2, Geographical Sources. Detroit: Gale Research. Pages 652–684 list bibliographic references to consult for life style and business information by state.

Directories

99. *Almanac of American Politics.* Boston: Gambit. Biennial. State-by-state listing of senators and representatives, their records, states, and districts. Includes political background, census data, economic base, and voter statistics.

100. *Commercial Atlas and Market Guide.* Annual. New York; Chicago: Rand McNally. Useful for checking map locations and gives useful geographic, social, and economic synopses.

101. *Ayer Directory of Publications.* Annual. Philadelphia: Ayer Press. City within state listing of newspapers and magazines (consumer, business, technical, trade, and farm).

102. *Organization Members of Chamber of Commerce of the U.S.* Annual. Washington. Alphabetical listing of state and local organizations, arranged by state. Many of these organizations will be quite happy to furnish life style information to prospective residents.

103. *Sales Management.* "Survey of Buyer Power." Annual. Chicago. Features population, income, retail sales, and merchandise line sales of all U.S. markets. Section D gives county-city data by states.

Geographic Relocations Outside the U.S.

This list provides material helpful to a family or individual making a geographic relocation outside of the U.S. Information is given about those aspects of relocation, such as taxation, adaptation, etc., that would be common to all moves, regardless of country. Attention is also given to the process of finding a job abroad.

General Background

104. Prendergast, Curtis. "If You're Transferred Abroad," *Money,* December 1975, pp. 91–98. This is an excellent source for weighing the pros and cons of living abroad in terms of taxation, family life style, family considerations, etc. A graphic cost-of-living chart indicates the relative expensiveness of various cities around the world, and the author cites the personal experience of his family and friends.

Encyclopedias

105. Angel, Juvenal L. *Looking for Employment in Foreign Countries.* New York: World Trade Academy Press, 1972. Volume 7 of *Encyclopedia of International Information.* This is an excellent source of information about passports, visas, work contracts, and specific information about various countries. Some warnings about cultural acclimatization are given, and a list of American firms operating overseas is provided. Types of compensation policies are detailed.

106. Wasserman, Paul, ed. *Encyclopedia of Business Information Sources.* Detroit: Gale Research, 1970. This is a useful reference tool for books, government documents, and periodicals about international business and specific places, although the emphasis is on corporate rather than individual situations. Most useful as a guide to getting a job overseas.

Guides and Directories

107. *Directory: Public Elementary and Secondary Day Schools.* Vol. IV. Office of Education. Washington, D.C.: U.S. Government Printing Office. At the end of the directory is a list of schools in various countries with a brief reference to grade spans and types of programs.

108. *Europa Yearbook,* 1975. London: Europa Publications, Ltd. The emphasis is on the various organizations of the UN and different countries. Economic, historical, and cultural information is given, and there is a directory section regarding newspapers, periodicals, publications, trade associations, etc., for each country.

109. *Fodor's Modern Guides.* New York: David McKay Company. Although geared to tourists, these guides to various countries are excellent for explicit details about various countries, highlighting cultural and entertainment opportunities.

110. *Schools Abroad.* Anne Maher, ed. Boston: Porter Sargent Publishing, 1975.

111. *The World of Learning.* London: European Publications, 1975.

Journals

112. Krause, David, and Patrick Stewart. "International Executive Compensation—Unmanaged or Unmanageable?" *Business Horizons,* December 1974, pp. 45–55. Although the tax structure has changed somewhat since this was written, the article gives an excellent outline of the various complexities of company compensation polities and their hazards and recommends lump-sum inducements to executives being considered for overseas transfers.

Books

113. Casewit, Curtis W. *Overseas Jobs: The Ten Best Countries*. New York: Warner Paperback Library, 1972. Aside from detailed information about ten selected countries, this book covers issues including visas and entry permits, life styles, salaries, opportunities, and employment leads.

114. Hopkins, Robert. *I've Had It—A Practical Guide to Moving Abroad*. New York: Holt, Rinehart and Winston, 1972. This book covers the many aspects of moving abroad and also serves as an excellent bibliography. Chapters on such topics as climate and maps give numerous references to other materials published on the topics. Twelve countries are selected for more detailed treatment.

115. Winfield, Louise. *Living Overseas*. Washington, D.C.: Public Affairs Press, 1962. Although dated, this well-written book by the wife of a Foreign Aid official is highly informative on the daily details of establishing a home in a foreign country. Everyday realities such as medical treatment, marketing, what to bring and what to leave behind are treated in detail and with humor. An excellent source from the housewife point of view.

Government Publications and Company Documents

116. Arthur Anderson and Co. *U.S. Taxation and Its Citizens Overseas*. Chicago: Arthur Anderson and Co.

117. Price Waterhouse Company. *Information Guide for Citizens Abroad*. New York: Price Waterhouse Company, 1975.

118. U.S. Department of Labor. *U.S. Department of State Indexes of Living Costs Abroad and Living Quarters Allowances*. Quarterly. Washington, D.C.: U.S. Government Printing Office.

119. U.S. Department of State, International Development Agency. "Helpful Information Excerpted from *Living Abroad,*" by Eleanor B. Pierce, March 1969.

Dual Career Families

Dual career families are a growing trend. The references cited here represent the major studies and findings of recent years.

Books and Excerpts

120. Fogarty, Michael. *Sex, Career and Family*. London: George Allen and Unwin, 1974. See especially Chapter 9, "The Reconciliation of Work and Family Life—The Dual-Career Family."

121. Hoffman, Lois, and F. Ivan Nye. *Working Mothers: An Evaluative Review of the Consequences for Wife, Husband, and Child*. San Francisco: Jossey-Bass, 1974. Jossey-Bass Behavioral Science Series.

122. Holmstrom, Lynda Lytle. *The Two-Career Family*. Cambridge, Mass.: Schenkman Publications, 1972.

123. Morgan, James N., and Gred J. Duncan, eds. *Five Thousand American Families—Patterns of Economic Progress*. Volume 3, Dynamics. Ann Arbor: Survey Research Center, Institute for Social Research, University of Michigan, 1974.

124. Ohio State University, Columbus, Center for Human Resources Research. *Dual Careers: A Longitudinal Study of Labor Market Experience of Women*. Washington, D.C.: U.S. Department of Labor, Manpower Administration, 1970.

125. Rapoport, Rhona, and Robert Rapoport. *Dual-Career Families*. Baltimore: Penguin, 1971. Case studies done in England.

A professional person will virtually always be asked to interview with from 1 to 25 or more different members of a hiring organization. Many people look forward to these interviews, especially initial "screening" interviews, with the same ambivalence that precedes an operation—and with good reason. Interviewing, for many people, is an anxiety-arousing, painful experience in which they display little skill or common sense. Exhibit 23-1 outlines some of the common problems that arise in interviews.

The archetype of the poor interviewee is the young student. Such a person goes into an interview, especially at the beginning of the recruiting season, with an awkward feeling that is usually reinforced by his or her friends ("Hey, Jerry, is that really you underneath that suit and without any hair?"). Sometimes people have a gnawing feeling, which they know is silly, that they are basically unemployable (born in the wrong century). At some level, these young people often see the interviewer as someone with life-or-death power over them (which frightens some and enrages others). The fright, anger, and awkwardness are made even worse in the interview when the interviewer doesn't behave as the interviewee somehow expects. Trembling or hostile, interviewees exhibit defensive behaviors that even they usually recognize are not in their own best interests. As a result, some people have real difficulty getting job offers—even people who eventually go on to have splendid careers.

Much of the anxiety that accompanies a person into an interview can be reduced or eliminated by following the procedures outlined previously in this book. People who are confident in knowing who they are and what they want invariably feel more relaxed going into interviews than people who don't. Even people who spend just a half-hour or so before an interview (or a set of interviews) doing some research on the employer tend to be more confident and relaxed.

In addition, we have found that anxiety can be significantly reduced if you have a realistic understanding of the context of the job interview, the different types of job interviews, and the situation the interviewer is in. A surprisingly large number of people go into interviewing situations with very unrealistic assumptions.

For example, most job interviews are 30 to 60 minutes long. As any successful salesperson knows, it's extremely difficult to sell an expensive and complex product (and let's face it, you are an expensive and complex product) within a short time constraint without excellent preparation. Yet many interviewees do not prepare adequately.

Being prepared in a job interview has two elements: (1) anticipating what the interviewer will want from you and being ready to supply it; (2) knowing what you want from the interviewer and being ready to ask for it.

Exhibits 23-2 and 23-3 supply data on what interviewers want from an interview. When 236 recruiters were asked what behavior on the part of the interviewees led to the "best" interviews, they responded as shown in Exhibit 23-2. Interviews seem generally to like interviewees who have "done their homework"— who know what they want, and who know something about the organization they are interviewing. In another survey of well-known business and industrial concerns, college recruiters were asked what types of questions they typically ask in an interview (see Exhibit 23-3). Exhibit 23-4 lists some common questions by interviewers with different styles. Well-prepared students take the time to create short (1- to 5-minute), articulate answers to these kinds of questions before

Exhibit 23–1
Common Problems in Recruiting Interviewing

Common Problems for Interviewees	Common Causes	Appropriate Action
Is unable to present self and ask questions within short time.	Does not recognize implications of *30*-minute interview.	Prepare. Polished answers to usual questions and a set of key questions to ask.
Tries to do too much in on-campus interview.	Does not recognize screening purpose of first interview.	Recognize purpose of first interview.
Behaves in calculated, guarded way. Appears to be insincere.	Assumes goals of both parties are in conflict.	Recognize *mutual* desire to find a good "fit."
Gets angry at interviewer for not conducting good interview. Anger makes it worse.	Assumes interviewer will be competent.	Understand the interviewer's frame of reference. Be prepared to make his/her job easier.
Gets angry at what appears to be incompetence. Creates poor impression.	Is unaware of organizational and situational constraints on interviewer.	Assume interviewer wants to do a good job, but is operating within unknown constraints.
Stresses wrong things in interview.	Incorrect assumptions about interviewer's criteria.	Try to get some idea in advance about screening criteria.
Highly anxious in interview. Creates poor impression.	Bad history in interviews, assumes stakes are gigantic.	Being prepared tends to relieve anxiety, as do realistic expectations. Know the company, self.
Judges and rejects interviewer quickly.	Fear of rejection.	Be aware of fear, be realistic about process.
Interview ends without discussion of relevant issues.	Interviewee either misunderstands interviewer's purpose and method or is unwilling or unable to take initiative.	Assess the interviewer's skill. If purposeful, realize importance of "fit." If unskilled, gently ask appropriate questions.
Learns nothing from interview.	Assumes the interviewer is the only one who has purpose.	Recognize your purpose to gather information. Prepare questions based on implications and be prepared to seek answers at the appropriate time.

they begin interviewing prospective employers. These students seem to be much more successful.

Types of Interviews

When preparing for interviews and while interviewing, it is important to remember that there are a number of different kinds of job interviews.

Screening Interviews

The primary purpose of the screening interview is to save an organization and its managers time and money by limiting the number of job applications they will have to examine. The interviewer has a very limited number of more or less specific criteria that constitute the rough screen. The question he or she is addressing is simply: Does the interviewee make it through the screen or not? The campus interview is typically a screening interview. So are many of the interviews in large companies with a person from "personnel."

The most common mistake made by job applicants in screening interviews is to try to get into too much depth. In many cases, especially with larger corporations, the responsibility of the individual doing the screening stops at selecting from among the interviewees the most appropriate candidates to be invited for a second interview, usually on the company's premises. The interviewer in such cases is seldom the final decision maker regarding a job offer and may not even know the specific requirements of the jobs to be filled. Consequently, an interviewee who attempts to tell an interviewer everything about him or herself, and who tries to learn everything about the company and job, as if both parties had to make a final decision regard-

Exhibit 23-2
What Made the Best Interviews?*

1. *Interviewee knew about company*
   ("had done homework," "knows
   the field")   66% (174)

2. *Interviewee had specific career
   goals*
   ("knew what he/she wanted,"
   "good fit between our needs
   and his/hers," "well-thought-out
   career interests")   41% (108)

3. *Interviewee knowledgeable*
   ("asked good questions,"
   "knew what to ask")   29% (76)

4. *Interviewee socially adept*
   ("rapport," "in tune with me,"
   "outgoing and expressive")   28% (74)

5. *Interviewee articulate*
   ("able to express ideas,"
   "spoke well," "good with tricky
   questions")   19% (50)

* Based on questionnaire responses from 236 people
who recruited at Harvard Business School in 1973;
more than one response allowed.

Exhibit 23-3
The Most Commonly Asked Questions*:
General Classification

1. Goals and purposes—Life purposes—
   Career objectives

2. Type of work desired—Kind of job—Job
   expectations

3. Reasons for selection of company—Knowledge of company.

4. Personal qualifications—Strengths and
   weaknesses

5. Career choice—Reasons for decisions

6. Qualifications for the job—How college
   education has prepared the candidate

7. Educational choices and plans—Choice of
   college—Choice of major

8. Geographical preferences—Willingness to
   relocate

9. Major achievements and accomplishments

* From the *29th Annual Endicott Report,* by Frank S.
Endicott, Director of Placement Emeritus, North-
western University, Copyright 1974 by Northwestern
University.

ing employment on the spot, seriously undermines a
screening interview.

Decision Interviews

A second type of interview is with the person (or
one of the persons) whose responsibility it is actually
to make the hiring decision. These interviews sometimes conclude with the interviewer making a job offer. The question that guides the interviewer's behavior
is this: Do I want to hire this person? In this type of
interview, you want to make your full "sales presentation." Forgetting or not having time to tell all the
major messages you have—about what you want in a
job and career, why you want that, and why you think
you can help the company with its needs and problems—can diminish your possibilities of getting a job
offer. At this stage, it is important to go into detail.

Data-Gathering Interviews

A third type of interview is with people who will
have only an input into the hiring decision, and who
often will end up working with the person who is hired.
Because they have less at stake in the hiring decision,
they often are more casual and less prepared for the
interview. The key question that tends to go through
their minds is this: What's it going to be like around
here if this person is hired?

Interviewees often treat this third type of interview
just like the second one; this is a mistake that can create problems. It's important in this third type of interview just to establish some rapport with the person,
and not to try to make the big sale. Coming on too
strong with potential peers might hurt an interviewee
(few people like the idea of too much competition
around them). Because the stakes are somewhat lower
in this type of interview than in the second type, one
can also safely allocate more time to gathering information from the interviewer (more on that in the next
chapter).

Although the objectives of these three types of interviews are different, they are seldom in direct conflict with the objectives of the interviewee. Both parties
want very much to find someone who can meet their
needs. A job decision never works out really well unless both sets of needs are met. (If only one set is met,
the employee will typically quit or be fired before too
long.) For these reasons it is in the best interests of
both parties to see if they have compatible resources
and needs. Yet interviewees sometimes assume an adversary relationship, taking the interviewer's objectives to be in conflict with their own. They behave in
a somewhat guarded and competitive way. No only
does that behavior undermine the interview, but it usu-

Exhibit 23-4
Questions Frequently Asked by Interviewers with Different Styles

Stress Interview Questions:

Given your background, you don't seem to be qualified for this job.

People like you (on whatever dimension) have never done well in our firm. Why do you think you will?

We aren't hiring this year, just keeping in touch.

We only take the best people. What makes you think you measure up?

I think you're wrong. (To whatever you might say.)

Specialized Knowledge or Skill Questions:

How do you calculate ROI?

What is PIMS and how would you use it in this job?

What is the corporation's liability under Title IX?

What would OSHA (or other related regulatory agency) say about that?

How would you assess the future of this industry given the current situation?

Open-Ended Questions:

Tell me about yourself.

What do you know about our company?

What is important for us to talk about today?

What do you plan to do in this industry?

What else would you like to know? Or talk about?

What questions do you have?

Person-Job Fit Questions:

This job demands assertiveness. Are you assertive? What are your strengths and weaknesses?

What kind of person do you think would succeed in our company? Could you?

---

ally gives the interviewer a poor impression of the interviewee.[1]

An Interviewer's Perspective

I spend nearly all my time between January and March interviewing at universities. It's a tough three months. I'm almost always on the road and away from home. The pace can be very hectic.

Yesterday is a beautiful example of the difficulties involved in this job. I got in late two nights ago. Yesterday morning during breakfast I briefly looked over the résumés of the 15 people I was supposed to see that day. Three of them looked like a mistake; I couldn't imagine why they wanted an interview with us. Because I was running late I walked three blocks in the rain to flag down a cab. I managed to get to the campus a few minutes before my first interview—who didn't show up. I got some coffee and then had a good interview at 9:30. When I asked the 10:00 interviewee, shortly after we started talking, if he had worked full time before coming to school, he gave this annoyed look and said, "I sent you my résumé two months ago—haven't you read it yet?" The interview went downhill from there. My schedule had no break in it until 12:30, and for that last half-hour I thought more about my bladder than about the student I was interviewing. I think my 2:30 interviewee was just trying to kill a half-hour between the naps he takes in his classes. He didn't even know what business we were in and had no conception of what he wanted to do. What a waste of time. My 4:00 interviewee was a very impressive young man, but I can't get over the feeling that I was conned. Some of these kids are more skilled at interviewing than I am. When I got back to my hotel at 5:45, I immediately started reviewing the day and my notes. Already the interviews were beginning to blur together. You know, you end up thinking, now which one was the guy who said such and such.

---

[1]Interviewers usually react negatively if they think the interviewee isn't being honest. This happens surprisingly often. In a 1973 survey of interviewers at Harvard Business School, 60 percent said they felt they were being more honest than the interviewees, while only 9 percent said they felt less honest than the interviewees. An interviewee who assumes an adversary stance often comes across as being not very honest.

Last week I came up against one of the parts of the job that really annoys me. I interviewed a young woman that I think could turn out to be a very important addition to one of our divisions. But I decided against recommending her because it was too risky. You see, in evaluating my contribution it can take years and years to determine whether the people I recommended (who eventually join the company) are a real success. But it only takes 12 months or less to determine if they are a disaster. So I tend to be evaluated more on not producing disasters. And that, of course, discourages risk taking. And hiring that woman would, I'm afraid, be risky.

I hired seven people for my department last year. I must have interviewed around 50 people. Of all the parts of my job, I feel in many ways least sure about this one. I keep thinking, there must be a better way.

Interviewing is often an intrusion on other parts of my job. As a result, I'm sure that at least some of the time when I'm interviewing someone my mind and heart are elsewhere. And I can't believe I do an effective job under those circumstances. I often wish I could spend a lot more time with interviewees, but that's just not possible.

I've read a few things on the subject of how to interview, but they haven't been terribly useful. I still wonder if I'm asking the right questions or correctly interpreting the interviewee's remarks.

I just don't know what to do with the person who doesn't really know much about us or our industry, or the one who isn't sure what he or she wants. You could spend hours talking to that kind of person trying to sort things out.

On some days when I'm tired and hassled, I wish the interviewee would run the interview. I've actually seen a few who did just that.

Some of the most common mistakes interviewees make stem from their own inaccurate assumptions regarding the interviewer and the position such a person is in. Job hunters, for example, often behave as if the responsibility for the success of failure of the interview were solely the interviewer's. They themselves assume no responsibility. They further behave as if they expect the interviewer to be extremely competent and working under ideal conditions. When the interviewer subsequently doesn't behave as he or she "should," these people get angry or annoyed, and that feeling further undermines the interview. Less-than-ideal conditions, a less-than-perfect interviewer, and an interviewee who is prepared to tolerate neither systematically produce bad interviews.

The best interviewees not only have realistic expectations regarding the interviewer, they even try to empathize with him or her. Such activity helps them develop a rapport that leaves a favorable impression, as well as helping promote the kind of information exchange that is needed to meet the objectives of the interview.

Interview Structure

Interviews occur in a variety of ways. Sometimes the candidate does all the talking; sometimes the recruiter does all of the talking. Given our basic premise that recruiting is an attempt on the part of *both* the organization and the individual to find a good fit, we believe that a balanced approach is most effective. By that we mean that since the fit is important to both parties, *both* parties in essence have a screen and need to collect data to see if the other passes the screen.

Thus, it is as important for you, the job candidate, to collect information as it is to give it. The company has to sell itself as well as you having to sell yourself. With this mutuality of purpose in mind, you will be able to approach interviews with less anxiety (since the evaluation process is two-way rather than one-way) and with greater clarity about *your* objectives for the interview. Your self-assessment provides the base from which you can develop a list of questions specifically designed to gather information related to your most prominent themes.

Given this dual purpose to a recruiting interview, a common 30-minute interview structure looks like this:

Greetings and introductions	1–3 minutes
Recruiter's questions and candidate's responses	5–10 minutes
Recruiter's summary question or comment	1–3 minutes
Argreement on the nature and timing of the next step	1–3 minutes
Goodbyes	1 minute

Some recruiters may have so many questions to ask that they may not allow you the time to ask questions (see Exhibit 23–4). You should remember that *you* bear part of the responsibility for the success of the interview. All recruiters are not professional interviewers. Hence, you must decide how you will meet your objectives for the interview. Will you interrupt or divert the recruiter? Will you save your questions for a later interview?

Getting a Commitment

Always get a commitment from the employer before leaving an interview (or a set of interviews) regarding what will happen next, and when you will hear from them next.

Some of the uncertainty that accompanies this period in job hunting can be eliminated simply by asking the employer to clarify the process. When will you make a decision as to whether a job offer will be made? How is that decision reached? When will I hear from you next? Most employers will expect better, more confident job applicants to ask these questions.

In addition, by getting a specific date when you can expect to hear next, you put yourself in a less dependent position. The knowledge of that date allows you more accurately to plan the other aspects of your own job campaign so that you don't suddenly find yourself caught in a timing conflict. If you find that date is too far away—after, for example, you are expected to accept or decline someone else's offer—you can tell the employer so and often get it changed. And when you interview with other employers and are asked when you can reply to their offer, you can respond knowing that it will be after you hear from the places you have already interviewed.

Getting a commitment regarding the time of an employer's reply also reduces the chances that you will be strung along. Without a date, some job hunters wait for weeks or months, often afraid to call or write the employer because it will make them look impatient or desperate. The job applicant who has a commitment to a specific date can legitimately call at once if the employer doesn't respond as promised.

After the Interview

It is a good idea to record your reactions to each interview after it is over. These data will be very useful to you later during the decision-making process. When you have written your observations down, file them in the folder for that firm.

Your log of the interview may include the data, name of the organization, the name and a description of the recruiter, a list of the questions he/she asked, and an outline of your responses. Note which answers you need to think about and prepare better. Note too the data you collected and how it relates to your self-assessment. Are there still large unanswered portions of your themes and implications? What additional data will you want to get next time? Ask yourself too if you accomplished *your* objectives for the interview. Did you present yourself well?

An Interviewing Exercise

It is probably a good idea for most people to do some practice interviewing before undertaking any serious job interviews. There are any number of ways in which you can practice, (including the one we have just given you based on the Martin Taylor case), but let us also suggest the following exercise.

PARTICIPANTS: 4 people.
TIME: 3 hours.
PREPARATION:

1. Each participant should give a résumé, a brief description of a type of job he or she would like to interview for, and a description of the interviewer and the interview location to one of the other three people.
2. To prepare for being an interviewee, each participant should think about the kinds of questions that may be asked (see Chapter in the textbook) and the kinds of questions he or she may wish to ask in return. (It may be useful to write out some of these questions and answers.)
3. To prepare for being an interviewer, each participant should look over the résumé and job description he or she has been given and consider how to conduct the interview.

THE EXERCISE: The exercise will consist of four 30-minute interviews (each involving an interviewer, an interviewee, and two observers), each followed by a 15-minute debriefing.

1. The interviewer should start and stop the interviews.
2. The observers should use the forms on the following pages to record their observations.
3. At the conclusion of each interview the observers should share their observations with the others, and everyone should discuss them.

You may find it useful to enter in this notebook any feedback you receive plus answers to common questions.

Assignment

Read the Martin Taylor case that follows and the On Campus Recruiting Interview Forms that follow it. Try to take the perspective of Martin Taylor about to interview Kathleen Johnson (see page 242 for her résumé) for a position as a commercial banker. What questions would you ask her? Why?

If you had a choice, which of the five recruiting forms would you use? Why? What do you learn from these forms about the variety of criteria used in screening interviews? If you were Kathleen Johnson, what questions would you ask of Martin Taylor? (See page 261 for a copy of Kathleen's theme list.)

Note: If you are taking this material as part of a course, you may want to use a classmate's résumé rather than Kathleen Johnson's to role play the interview. If so, ask the interviewee (job candidate) to give you a copy of his or her résumé before class so you can prepare your questions.

OBSERVER FORM

Interviewer: _____

Interviewee: _____

Observer: _____

Date: _____

Brief description of
interview situation and
job opening: _____

_____

_____

_____

Observations: Record here any specific behavior on the part of the interviewee that you think helped or hurt the interview	Comments: Note here whether the behavior helped or hurt and (very briefly) why

OBSERVER FORM

Interviewer: _____   Brief description of

Interviewee: _____   interview situation and

Observer: _____   job opening: _____

Date: _____   _____

_____

_____

Observations: Record here any specific behavior on the part of the interviewee that you think helped or hurt the interview	Comments: Note here whether the behavior helped or hurt and (very briefly) why

KATHLEEN JOHNSON: THEME LIST

Theme Labels

1. Needs to be close to "family."
2. Needs a group of friends and time to spend with them.
3. Enjoys meeting new people.
4. Wants a job with a lot of interaction with people.
5. But doesn't want to have to get involved with social service or counseling activities.
6. Has a need for constant attention and support.
7. Will buck strict social or organizational norms but then reacts poorly to estrangement.
8. Wants things to be fair and just.
9. Enjoys roles involving leadership and responsibility.
10. Needs a standard or goal to measure myself against.
11. Needs to be a success, preferably number one.
12. Prestige is important.
13. Often needs to be motivated, needs encouragement from authority figures.
14. Is indecisive when confronted with too many options.
15. Disorganized.
16. Practical orientation.
17. Wants activity and variety.
18. Doesn't like situations that require long periods of intellectual effort or theoretical or academic approaches.
19. Uncomfortable with situations requiring creativity.

This case was prepared by Ellen Porter Honnet, research assistant, under the direction of Assistant Professor James G. Clawson for class discussion. Copyright © 1980 by the President and Fellows of Harvard College. Harvard Business School case 9-481-040.

MARTIN TAYLOR

Martin Taylor, a corporate account manager for one of the largest commercial banks west of the Mississippi, had been asked by the bank's headquarters to make a two-day recruiting trip to the East Coast to interview second-year MBA students at a large Eastern business school. This was to be the second year in a row that he would be recruiting, a task he had performed conscientiously the previous year. He was not a full-time recruiter, but looked forward to speaking with MBA graduates-to-be from his alma mater. Martin knew that, as much as he tried to plan ahead, the two days of interviewing would be an intense, energy-consuming process and that at the end of it he would be more exhausted than after two days at his regular job at the bank.

Taylor's Background and Preparation for Employment

Martin Taylor grew up in Ann Arbor, Michigan, and had a fair amount of freedom to travel and to choose his own summer activities. His mother had been the first person on either side of the family ever to go to college.

This case was prepared by Mark P. Kriger, research assistant, under the supervision of Assistant Professor James G. Clawson as a basis for class discussion rather than to illustrate either effective or ineffective handling of an administrative situation. Copyright © 1979 by the President and Fellows of Harvard College. Harvard Business School case 9-480-035.

During the summer of his junior year in high school, Martin made a trip east. Upon seeing Amherst, Massachusetts, he knew that Amherst College, with its rural setting and relatively small student body, was for him. He ended up attending Amherst and doing, in his words, "reasonably well." He majored in economics which he felt was "a pretty marketless degree."

Upon graduation, Martin went to work for the government as a bank examiner in Detroit, Michigan, for which he received an occupational deferment from the draft. Although his job with the government was relatively comfortable and his pay was better than it would have been in private industry, Martin was concerned that he might get stuck working for the government. So, two years after receiving his BA he applied to three business schools and was accepted into all three.

After Martin Taylor's first year in the MBA program of his first-choice school, Martin went back in the summer to his job as a bank examiner in Michigan because he "could live at home and earn a good salary." In addition, Martin liked what he had been doing, so he did not really try to find another summer job. In the back of his mind he could see himself directing the efforts of a small bank. However, Martin felt that he had to start out in a large bank because, as he put it, "You could go from a big bank to a small bank, but you can't go the other way around."

During the fall of his second year in the MBA program, Martin began his job search process by visiting the placement office and doing some reading. Martin mentioned to Jim Davis, one of the staff members of the placement office, that he had worked as a bank examiner. Davis, in response, made a passing reference to one of the major banks west of the Mississippi River and stated that more people always signed up for their interviews than the allotted interview slots. Martin said to himself, "Well, if everybody wants it that bad, it must be worth looking into." So he examined the material available on the bank, including the annual report, and signed up for an interview with a high rank on his preference card.

Over Christmas vacation he set up several interviews with banks in Detroit, mostly as practice for future interviews with firms that were among his top choices. He quickly concluded that his choice had to be in a large bank in a major city with a corporate banking orientation. Martin ended up flying out during spring vacation to the bank first mentioned when he was in the placement office, and eventually accepted the offer he was given.

Martin's New Job

When Martin arrived for work there was no formal training program at the bank. He was temporarily assigned to Bill Johnson, who was willing to take him on as a special projects assistant. Martin was then given a number of different tasks designed to give him exposure to a number of areas in the bank. In his words, he "spent a lot of long hours in the evening just trying to get the overall picture without a great deal of help from anyone else."

One of the line people who worked for Mr. Johnson as head of the western region in the corporate bank got a position in another part of the bank. As a result, the western territory opened up and was assigned to Martin. After just one previous business trip, Martin Taylor found himself responsible for servicing corporate customers ranging in size from about $20 million to $3.5 billion in sales. His territory expanded and shrank over the next year and a half, but generally it covered the Southwest, including the Rocky Mountains, New Mexico, and Texas. In order to service his customers Martin spent an average of one week per month on the road. Several weeks of additional travel time were required each year for special bank meetings and seminars, but since he was single he rather enjoyed the chance to move about.

Martin's Selection as a Recruiter and Preparations for Interviewing

In 1975 the corporate bank took over its own recruiting from central personnel. That year there was a graduate from Martin's alma mater who had more seniority, so he did the recruiting. However, when this person left the bank in 1976, Martin went to the corporate personnel manager and asked, "Who are you sending back this year?"

The response was, "I'm going to try to go, but I don't know if I'll have the time. Would you be interested?"

Martin was glad to have the opportunity to go back to visit his former school. He also hoped to develop some faculty connections and establish some continuity in relations that he felt had not existed in the past between the bank and his school.

The first year that he went recruiting, he had ample time to prepare. When the résumés arrived at the bank in early December, he took time out to familiarize himself with all 800. He then wrote letters in advance of Christmas to some of the people inviting them to come to the bank during the holidays if they were available. He also wrote a second set of letters in advance of his interviewing trip in February.

The next year Martin was asked to recruit once again. He was to interview only at his alma mater, even though the bank made recruiting visits to about fifteen schools. This time Martin was very busy with business obligations during the latter part of November and most of December.

It suddenly occurred to him on December 20 that he had not looked at the résumés yet and the recruiting trip was only a few weeks away. He did manage to screen the résumé book with the help of the preselected list the students put their names on. Martin wrote letters to eleven people who impressed him as having more than just passing interest in the bank for which he worked. He had chosen these people by virtue of their record and their interest in locating in the West.

The Recruiting Trip

Martin's plane arrived two hours later than expected due to a snowstorm. As a result, Martin had less sleep than he would have liked. In addition, he had only a doughnut and a glass of orange juice for breakfast, since he wanted at least a half hour for reading the résumés for the day's interviews. Despite the relatively short sleep and quick breakfast, Martin was looking forward to the interviews with enthusiasm.

When Martin arrived at the Office of Career Development at 8:20 A.M. to pick up his schedule for the day and the stack of résumés, he found the place in tumult. Three additional recruiters, each from other divisions of the bank, were to have arrived. However, the snowstorm had prevented one of the members of the four-person team from coming. Martin, looking at his schedule, noticed that he had received a couple of shift-overs from the absent man's schedules. This further crowded his schedule.

Martin arrived at the interview carrel at 8:30 to spend a half hour reading over and familiarizing himself with the résumés. To his surprise Martin found the carrel without any chairs and had to go and borrow some from a classroom. He then organized the company literature and brochures he had brought with him and finally turned to reviewing the student résumés.

A few minutes before 9 A.M., Martin was smoking a cigarette while finishing reviewing the résumés of the people on his list. He wondered why some of the people were interested in interviewing with a bank since their résumés revealed no banking experience whatsoever. He felt that the preferences listed in the résumés book probably had little correlation with the positions people finally accepted. Upon reading one résumé his interest was piqued by the phrase "presented findings to management." Martin reflected, "That's relevant to us in our loan review committee work. I'll ask him about that, for sure."

Martin's objective in recruiting was to spot from the 25 interviews four or five people who would be invited west to the bank's headquarters for further interviewing. Martin would have to decide who was going to be advanced to the next step in the recruiting process based on a 25-minute interview plus a résumé. Each person invited

back to headquarters would cost the bank approximately $500 to $600 in expenses.

Taylor's 9 A.M. appointment did not show up. At twenty past the hour, he was not angry but he felt he would write to the person later, saying that he missed them at the interview and hoped that they would stop by and visit the bank if they were in the area. Martin believed in offering the person the benefit of the doubt. The student for the 9:30 interview showed up on time.

For each of the interviews Martin followed pretty much the same tactics and timing. He would begin the interview by asking a few questions to try to get a feel for how interested the person was in banking. Martin would use the résumé to spot key experiences and interests. If the person had some banking experience he might ask, "What is it about banking that you like?" On the other hand, if the person had a lot of varied experience, but none in banking, he might ask, "Could you tell me how your interest in banking developed?" The second question after that often would be, "How did you learn about our bank?" or, "As you reviewed the many banks that interview here, why did you choose us?" A tougher version of this last question might be, "Could you give me your impressions or notions about what made our bank different from the other banks you have looked at and, therefore, why are you talking to me now?" After the first eight to ten minutes Martin would let the person being interviewed come back at him with some questions for about ten minutes. Next, he would go back at them for another five minutes, leaving time for one final question.

He used this strategy of alternately questioning the student and then allowing the student to ask questions because he wanted to meet two objectives: first, to see how the interviewee conducted himself in response to focused questioning, and, second, to give the interviewee a chance to get some basic questions answered. Furthermore, the quality of the questions asked gave him considerable insight into how well prepared the person was, as well as how seriously they were considering working for the bank. Finally, it would take two to five minutes to say good-bye, leaving Martin from three to five minutes to fill out his interview form. After each interview, Martin filled out his impressions of the candidate on the company interview form. His company had separate forms for campus recruiting and for home-office recruiting.

At noon Martin received a letter from Peter Carlson, the person who was to have been Martin's 9 A.M. appointment. The letter, which was poorly typed with a number of words crossed out, stated that the people in charge of interviews had told him that since one of the interviewers on the bank's team had not arrived, all the interviews were cancelled. The letter seemed to be sincere to Martin, and he appreciated that the student had gone out of his way to let him know what had transpired. Martin planned to get in touch with Carlson as soon as possible.

The remaining interviews Martin conducted in the morning went relatively smoothly, with Martin feeling enthusiastic and on top of the interviewing process. "For me, the best time for interviews is early in the day. But I can't remember them all. I have to rely on my brief notes."

Martin's luncheon discussion with his colleagues ran on so late that when Martin returned to his carrel, his next appointment was already waiting. Although Martin needed to visit the men's room, he did not want to keep the student waiting.

As Martin was about to go into the carrel another MBA student approached him and said, "I'm not on your list, but I'm supposed to be. Can I see you sometime? Here's my résumé."

Martin doubted that the student had done his homework because the appointment office had made no mention of any slip-up. As a result, he shunted the student off to one of the other interviewers from his bank who had had a cancellation. Martin conjectured, "Maybe he'll get in, maybe not."

After his 2 P.M. interview, Martin remarked to the casewriter, "That was a big disappointment. His résumé looked the best to me—my most promising candidate. But he was the most nervous, shy and unaggressive of all. It may be under there, but it wasn't showing today."

Martin was filling out the form from his previous interview when the next interviewee popped his head into the carrel and asked, "Do you want me to give you a minute or two?" Martin replied, "Yes, just a minute, 'til I finish filling this out." Meanwhile, Martin's colleague in the next cubicle could not get the sliding door unlocked. He and the person he had been interviewing were working on the door from the inside,

while the next appointment was banging on it from the outside. After five minutes of banging, shoving, and exchanging suggestions back and forth, the door finally snapped open.

At 3 P.M. Martin was due for a half-hour break, and by this time, much needed, but Peter Carlson came by. Since Martin had been favorably impressed by Peter's effort and honesty, Martin broke his rule of not conducting interviews during the break. Breaks were important, he felt, as a chance to refresh himself mentally and physically. Martin agreed to see Peter and had no break.

Fortunately, however, the 3:30 appointment did not show up. Martin was finally able to take a break. As he and the casewriter walked down the hall, Martin commented on his interviews:

> The people don't seem so well prepared now. When I was interviewing as a student, I read every issue of *American Banker* to be up on the latest. I don't see it in these people. They're not aware of the major news in the industry. If they're sincerely interested in banking, they should be on top of all that stuff.

By 4:30 P.M. Martin had interviewed ten people (see Exhibit 23–5) and was beginning to get rather tired. He felt he was starting to fumble. With less than six hours of sleep, he thought that he was starting to lose the advantage in the interview process. He wanted to give each person interviewed an equal chance, but his mind was just not as sharp as it had been at 9 A.M. and had begun, in his words, "to turn to mush." Martin's thoughts drifted to his plans for that evening: to see an old friend, drink a couple of beers, and get some badly needed sleep before another day of the same thing. In this state of mind, Martin Taylor finished filling out the interview form, and rose to meet his last interview of the day.

Exhibit 23–5
Martin Taylor's Schedule

Arrival (Monday evening)

11:30 P.M.	Snowstorm caused delay in airplane schedule; Martin's flight arrives 2 hours later than expected.
12:30 A.M.	Martin arrives in hotel room.
12:45 A.M.	Goes to bed.

First Day of Interviews (Tuesday)

6:30 A.M.	Wakes up.
7:00 A.M.	Leaves hotel without having had breakfast.
8:00 A.M.	Martin has a doughnut and a glass of orange juice on campus.
8:20 A.M.	Picks up résumés and schedule for the day.
8:30 A.M.	Has a half hour to read résumés.
9:00 A.M.	First interview does not show. Continues reviewing résumés.
9:30 A.M.	Interview.
10:00 A.M.	Interview.
10:30 A.M.	Coffee break at a coffee machine in the hallway near the interview carrel.
11:00 A.M.	Interview.
11:30 A.M.	Interview.
12:00 noon	Interview.
12:30 P.M.	Lunch. Discussion with two other colleagues.
1:30 P.M.	Interview.
2:00 P.M.	Interview.
2:30 P.M.	Interview.
3:00 P.M.	Scheduled coffee break, but 9 A.M. appointment comes by for interview.
3:30 P.M.	Appointment does not show. Takes a break.
4:00 P.M.	Interview.
4:30 P.M.	Interview.
6:00 P.M.	Plans to meet an old friend for dinner and drinks.

Second Day of Interviews (Wednesday)

6:30 A.M.–5:00 P.M.	Similar schedule expected for the second day.
6:00 P.M.	Plane flight west, shortly after last interview.

ON-CAMPUS RECRUITING INTERVIEW FORMS

This case consists entirely of interview forms used by five companies for on-campus MBA recruiting. It is intended to give you a perspective of the range of complexity of forms used and a sample of the criteria used by recruiters in evaluating on-campus interviews.

Company A

One major company that interviews on campus has no recruiting interview form. Recruiters are free to make notes as they please.

This case was written by Mark P. Kriger, research assistant, under the direction of Assistant Professor James G. Clawson, as a basis for class discussion. Copyright © 1979 by the President and Fellows of Harvard College. Harvard Business School case 9-480-023.

Candidate		Previous Interview Data	
Position			
Interviewer			
Today's Schedule			

1. Please briefly summarize the major topics covered in your conversation with the candidate, including both his/her major questions about us and the major topics you raised.

2. Based on your interview, do you believe that this candidate would make a positive contribution to the morale and internal work environment of the firm? Would you enjoy working with the candidate on a project team? Why?

3. What are the candidate's major career alternatives? How does he/she currently rank them? If   should eventually extend an employment offer, what do you think the probability of acceptance is? Timing of decision?

4. What major topics should we pursue or follow up on with the candidate in subsequent interviews?

5. Please use this space for general comment and to expand on your answers to the other questions if you need to:

Signature: _____

CANDIDATE:_____ INTERVIEWER:_____

POSITION:_____ DATE:_____

The purpose of this form is to aid you in your assessment of the candidate's strengths in each of the key areas listed. Consider the candidate's academic background, work and/or military experience, extra-curricular activities and personal interests. Be sure to cite the evidence behind your assessments. Also, please check one of the three symbols located to the right of each key area.

+ = Good
o = Acceptable
? = Questionable

1. ACHIEVEMENT/ACCOMPLISHMENT
   (Is there a solid, consistent record of achievement? Is there evidence of clear objectives, personal initiative, perseverance, and growth?)

   Supporting evidence:

   + _____
   o _____
   ? _____

2. LEADERSHIP
   (Has the candidate been an effective leader? Has he/she actively sought leadership roles? Was this candidate able to instill confidence in his/her peers and subordinates?)

   Supporting evidence:

   + _____
   o _____
   ? _____

3. THOUGHT PROCESS
   (Did the candidate appear to be alert and attentive? Did he/she proceed logically from premises to conclusions? Was the candidate insightful in his/her questions?)

   Supporting evidence:

   + _____
   o _____
   ? _____

4. INNOVATIVE ABILITY
   (Has he/she demonstrated an ability to think and act creatively?)
   Supporting evidence:

   + _____
   o _____
   ? _____

5. COMMUNICATION SKILLS
   (Did the candidate provide clear, concise, logical answers to questions?
   Is the candidate direct and persuasive? Did he/she listen well?)

   Supporting evidence:

   + _____
   o _____
   ? _____

6. SELF-CONFIDENCE
   (Did the candidate present himself/herself in a mature and professional
   manner? How has the candidate reacted to pressure situations?)

   Supporting evidence:

   + _____
   o _____
   ? _____

7. CAREER DIRECTION
   (Is the candidate's record consistent with his/her stated objectives? Is
   the candidate genuinely committed to this position?)

   Supporting evidence:

   + _____
   o _____
   ? _____

8. POTENTIAL
   (Does this candidate have the ability to grow and accept increasing
   responsibility?)

   Supporting evidence:

   + _____
   o _____
   ? _____

DECISION
   Do you recommend this candidate for a second interview? _____ Yes _____ No

WHY?

Company D

PRIMARY EVALUATION
for
CORPORATE ACCOUNT OFFICER

CANDIDATE'S NAME: _____

INTERVIEWER'S NAME: _____

INTERVIEW DATE: _____

SCHOOL: _____

1. Rate each skill or trait in one of the following categories:

SKILLS AND TRAITS	BELOW AVERAGE	AVERAGE	ABOVE AVERAGE	EXCESSIVE
Demonstrated Initiative:				N/A
Priority-Setting Ability:				N/A
Conceptual Ability:				N/A
Analytical Ability:				
Perceptiveness:				N/A
Enthusiastic Demeanor:				
Verbal Communication:				N/A
Pressure-Handling Ability:				N/A
Aggressiveness:				

NOTE: In questions #2 – #4, please check only one answer per question:

2. Rate the candidate's composure in the interview:

☐ a. Very poised and personable.

☐ b. Somewhat nervous but could be developed.

☐ c. Poor.

3. If you were a corporate client, what would your initial impression be of this individual as a calling officer?

☐ STANDS OUT   ☐ AVERAGE   ☐ NEGATIVE

4. Given background and experience, how insightful was the candidate about this job?

A. AMOUNT OF BACKGROUND AND EXPERIENCE:

☐ Summer only   ☐ Bank or bank-related

☐ 0 to 2 years   ☐ Non-bank

☐ Greater than 2 years

B. INSIGHTFULNESS:

☐ Superficial understanding

☐ Some research and understanding

☐ Realisitic understanding

5. How do you rate the candidate's knowledge of our bank or the banking industry?

☐ Superficial knowledge

☐ Some research and knowledge

☐ Very good knowledge

6. Is there anything about the candidate that you feel might distinguish this person as a calling officer?

_____

_____

_____

_____

_____

7. In which group will this person fit best? _____

8. Do you feel that this candidate should be invited back for the second interview?

☐ YES   ☐ NO

INTERVIEW EVALUATION GUIDE

PURPOSE

This guide is designed to:
- Help you obtain the information you'll need to make a good selection decision.
- Be consistent with   s commitment to equal employment opportunity and compliance with Federal and State EEO laws.

SELECTION CHARACTERISTICS

- The Selection Characteristics listed on the following page were judged most important by   Managers surveyed.
- All characteristics listed should be scored. The most relevant to the position under consideration should have the most influence in the final decision.
- The questions provided should be viewed as aids to the interviewers. Alternative questions which help interviewers to focus on relevant experience information can be substituted.
- If a special technical or professional skill is required, use the blank space provided to describe the relevant characteristic following the guideline format.

INTERVIEW GUIDELINES

NOTE:
An Interview Evaluation Guide must be completed for each external candidate interviewed for a   position.

This guide can be used most effectively if before interviewing you familiarize yourself with the questions and rating scales. In addition, you should keep in mind the following basic principles:
- Avoid questions that can be answered with a yes or no.
- Try to obtain clear and detailed responses about the applicant's experiences — what has been done.
- Satisfy yourself that the applicant's descriptions are consistent and generally accurate.
- Concentrate only on those areas that are relevant for evaluating applicants on the Selection Characteristics.
- Complete this form as soon as possible after the interview, and definitely before interviewing any other applicants.

SELECTION CHARACTERISTIC	CONSIDER	SUGGESTED PROBES/QUESTIONS
EXPERIENCE/CAREER/SKILLS SCHOOL EXPERIENCE	• Applicability of courses, studies to position • Ability to apply skills and knowledge in solving problems	• What was your major course of study in school? • What parts of your course work are most applicable to a (position) at _____?
WORK EXPERIENCE	• Applicability of prior work to current position	• What were (are) the major responsibilities (activities) of your last (current) job? What did you do? • What was your most outstanding achievement in your last (current) job? What impact did it have on the organization? • What responsibilities have you had supervising others? How many? What did you do?
CAREER ASPIRATIONS	• Clarity and specificity of career goals and plans • Ability to assess own strengths and weaknesses in relation to career in	• What did you accomplish in your last job that was most related to your career goals? • How did you decide on your career? What characteristics do you feel you have that are most (least) suited toward a career in _____?
TECHNICAL/PROFESSIONAL (Please complete prior to interview)		
PERSONAL CHARACTERISTICS ASSERTIVENESS	• Forcefulness, ability to persist in accomplishing goals • Ability to overcome obstacles and problems in attaining goals	• What was the most challenging task/activity you've ever attempted? Why was it difficult? What happened? • Why did you try to accomplish (complete) that task/goal/activity? Who set the goal? Why?
COMMUNICATION SKILLS	• Ability to present ideas in a clear, interesting and persuasive manner — orally and in writing • Ability to sell self; persuade	• What would you consider your most outstanding success in persuading someone to do something? What did you do? What happened? • To what extent are you (have you been) involved in public speaking, debating or dramatic presentations? What did you do? What happened?
DECISIVENESS	• Appropriateness of the time and information needed to make a decision • Uncertainty about decisions; frequency with which decisions change • Ability to accurately assess risks	• What was the most challenging decision you were ever asked to make? What happened? What did you do? What effect did this have on your organization? • What was the worst decision (best decision) you ever made? What happened? What did you do? Why?
ENERGY	• Ability to work hard over extended period of time • High activity level	• Have you ever been in a situation that required long and hard work for a period of time? What was this due to? What happened? Were others in this situation required to work under the same conditions? • How often do you find yourself in this type of situation?
FLEXIBILITY	• Ability to adapt to changing situations • Alertness and sensitivity to the environment in which one is working	• Were you ever faced with a situation where you had to change the direction (nature) of your activities? (change direction on a project)? What happened? What did you do? • How did you feel about having to change direction in the middle of an activity?
INTERPERSONAL SKILLS	• Ability to establish and maintain effective working relationships • Tact, sensitivity to the feelings of others	• What was your most challenging personal encounter with someone? How did you deal with him/her? • Consider a project where you had to work with other individuals to complete some task. What happened? What was your role?
MATURITY	• Acceptance of responsibility • Ability to avoid impulsive or confusing actions • Calmness under pressure	• Tell me about an occasion when you were responsible for some major activity. What impact did this activity have on your organization? What did you do? What happened? • What was the most frustrating experience you've ever had? How did you handle it? • Have you ever worked under pressure? What happened? What did you do?
REASONING/JUDGMENT	• Ability to abstract the essential elements of a problem and develop/find an appropriate solution	• What was the most challenging (work/technical) problem you've ever encountered? What happened? What did you do? • Given the following situation . . . what would you do? Why?

	COMMENTS	EVALUATION				

SCHOOL EXPERIENCE

Not ascertained; Don't know

1	2	3	4	5
Course of study not relevant to position			Major course of study directly relevant to position	

Not ascertained; Don't know

1	2	3	4	5
Academic knowledge; shows little understanding of problems involved in applying skills and knowledge			Has practical experience applying skills and knowledge; understands and able to handle problems applying knowledge	

WORK EXPERIENCE

Not ascertained; Don't know

1	2	3	4	5
Prior work experience not relevant to skills and knowledge required			Prior work experience directly relevant to skills and knowledge required	

Not ascertained; Don't know

1	2	3	4	5
Little or no supervisory responsibilities; experience mostly as an individual contributor			Has had broad management responsibilities; experience in coordinating and integrating functions	

CAREER ASPIRATIONS

Not ascertained; Don't know

1	2	3	4	5
Career goals vague and poorly articulated; low agreement between personal qualities and career			Career goals clear and well articulated; high agreement between personal qualities and career requirements	

TECHNICAL/ PROFESSIONAL

Not ascertained; Don't know

1	2	3	4	5

ASSERTIVENESS

Not ascertained; Don't know

1	2	3	4	5
Easily discouraged; passive; tends to react to events; avoids challenging situations			Initiates activities; continues at tasks despite problems and setbacks; confident, seeks new and challenging situations	

COMMUNICATION SKILLS

Not ascertained; Don't know

1	2	3	4	5
Hesitant and uncertain; has difficulty presenting ideas clearly and logically			Poised, confident and convincing; can present complex ideas in a clear and interesting manner	

DECISIVENESS

Not ascertained; Don't know

1	2	3	4	5
Uncertain, ill-at-ease about decisions; frequently changes mind; takes excessive time to make decisions			Confident about decisions; accurately assesses risks and implications; makes decisions within appropriate time frame	

ENERGY

Not ascertained; Don't know

1	2	3	4	5
Rarely works hard; appears to have difficulty maintaining a heavy workload and performing efficiently			Frequently works hard; capable of maintaining a heavy workload while remaining efficient	

FLEXIBILITY

Not ascertained; Don't know

1	2	3	4	5
Unaware, oblivious of changing situations; has difficulty adapting and changing goals, directions, etc.			Sensitive to changing situations; capable of adapting to changing demands, goals, requirements, etc.	

INTERPERSONAL SKILLS

Not ascertained; Don't know

1	2	3	4	5
Has difficulty maintaining relationships; insensitive; lacks tact			Capable of working effectively with others; sensitive to the feelings of others; tactful	

MATURITY

Not ascertained; Don't know

1	2	3	4	5
Responds carelessly and impulsively; avoids assuming responsibility for own actions; panics under pressure			Carefully considers effects of potential actions; reliable; willingly accepts responsibility for handling difficult problems; calm under pressure	

REASONING/ JUDGMENT

Not ascertained; Don't know

1	2	3	4	5
Doesn't seek enough information; misses essentials of problem; solutions are superficial			Identifies need for and seeks relevant information; solutions have been innovative and effective	

Company E (continued)

	RETURN COMPLETED FORM WITH RESUME TO		

MANAGEMENT RECRUITING / COLLEGE
INTERVIEW SUMMARY FORM

CANDIDATE'S NAME	SCHOOL	DEGREE / YEAR	DATE OF INTERVIEW / /

SOURCE (CHECK ONE)

☐ INTERVIEWED ON CAMPUS   ☐ REFERRAL   ☐ WALK IN / WRITE IN   ☐ CAREER DEVELOPMENT

☐ SUMMER INTERN   ☐ INTERNAL TRANSFER (OTHER THAN CAREER DEVELOPMENT)

OVERALL IMPRESSION

TAKING INTO ACCOUNT ALL OF THE RELEVANT INFORMATION YOU HAVE OBTAINED IN THIS INTERVIEW, WHAT IS YOUR OVERALL IMPRESSION OF THIS CANDIDATE?

1	2	3	4	5
VERY WEAK	WEAK	CAPABLE	STRONG	EXCEPTIONAL

COMMENTS

PLEASE COMPLETE EXPLORATORY <u>OR</u> FULL DAY SECTION

EXPLORATORY INTERVIEW (ON CAMPUS OR IN HOUSE)

I N T E R V I E W   D E C I S I O N

☐ INVITE FOR FURTHER ASSESSMENT AND EVALUATION BY YOUR GROUP

GROUP: _____

SUGGESTED AREA: (IF APPLICABLE)

☐ REFER RESUME AND EVALUATION TO OTHER GROUP FOR INVITE OR TURNDOWN DECISION

RECOMMENDED GROUP

☐ TURNDOWN

C O R R E S P O N D E N C E   I N F O R M A T I O N

SALUTATION: DEAR _____

☐ NO   INDICATE WHETHER YOU WOULD LIKE TURNDOWN
☐ YES   LETTER SIGNED BY A PROFESSIONAL RECRUITER

FULL DAY INTERVIEW

RECOMMENDATION TO HIRE

NO   YES
☐   ☐

DO NOT WRITE IN THIS BOX – FOR CRU USE ONLY		
NO LETTER ☐	TYPE OF LETTER A B C D E F G H I #9 #12	DATE OF LETTER / /

INTERVIEWER'S NAME TITLE (PLEASE PRINT OR USE STAMP)	INTERVIEWER'S SIGNATURE	DATE / /

A major source of information on jobs is direct observation. Most professionals are invited to visit the organization itself before any job offer is extended, even if that means a long trip (at the organization's expense). The 4 to 20 hours that are spent in the organization itself can provide an enormous amount of information beyond that obtained in interviews. All you have to do is keep your eyes and ears open.

Visual Clues

Job hunters tend to underuse direct observation for a number of reasons (chief among them is that most well-educated people do not seem to be very visually oriented). Yet this information source is very attractive in two ways. First, it doesn't require the use of the job hunter's most precious resource—time. If you visit a company for a day, you get 8 hours of visual data at no extra cost. Second, it can be an incredibly rich source of impressionistic data, which you can use in checking out your conclusions about the company and its people derived primarily from what people were saying.

Ignoring visual data, or not being alert to cues provided by direct observation, can get a job hunter into trouble. The following story, related by a very bright and capable young man, illustrates the point rather clearly:

> While job hunting, I found this small firm that built the most beautiful modern lighting that money can buy. I spent a full day there and yet I just didn't pay attention to all the visual clues that suggested I might not get along with the boss. I was so enchanted by the job, and by what he said, that I didn't see the obvious signs.

You see, I recognize that I have a fairly large need for autonomy, and a fairly large need for an aesthetic environment. The job opening was for a director of marketing (reporting to the president), which was exactly what I wanted. When I talked to the company president, he assured me that I would be able to run my own show without interference. Since he did not have a background in marketing, nor any great interest in it, I believed him.

Most of the time I spent visiting the company was with him at his home and at a restaurant, but we did meet for about two hours in his office. His office is quite large—about 40 by 40 feet. It has very functional furniture in it, and it's usually a mess. Outside his office is a smaller office area, 20 by 20 feet, that has five desks in it (yes, five people share that office!). It has the same functional furniture and it's slightly less messy. Off of that area are three other small offices, 9 by 9 feet, each with a functional desk, chair, and grey filing cabinet.

So here we have a setup where his space is clearly dominant, and where his tastes (he was an engineering/manufacturing background) dominate also. I sat in the middle of that for two hours and yet didn't really see it.

When I came on board, I was given one of the 9 by 9 offices, and for the first month everything was OK. Then the dreary office area began to bug me and when I asked my boss about getting some nice office furniture, he just effectively ignored the request. Each month thereafter, especially as I started to initiate some new marketing programs, we began to clash. After five months it became clear he was not about to give me the autonomy he promised. I quit after six months.

So we encourage you to be alert when you make company visits and to pick out signals that tell you something about the firm.

Bosses and Insiders

Of course, visual signals are not the only data you will be collecting on a company visit. The people you interview with will be a major source of information. It's useful to distinguish between two types of inside information sources: those who would be your superiors and those who would be peers. The former are better equipped to give you data on careers in the company and the company itself. The latter are usually the best sources of information about the job itself.

Do not underestimate the helpfulness of talking to someone who is in a job exactly like, or similar to, the one you have been (or might be) offered. Talking to such a person about what he or she actually does on a daily basis can be enormously useful. We have seen people actually accept job offers based on an image they have developed that unfortunately has nothing to do with what the job actually demands. At the extreme this produces mild tragedies. One young man we knew took a job, as he put it, as a "California banker," no doubt with great images of sun, surf, and doling out money behind a large mahogany desk. When he arrived in L.A. he discovered that being a California banker in his case meant spending 2 1/2 hours a day driving to and from work, and 8 hours a day in a small branch many miles from the ocean performing clerical functions as a part of a 12-month "training program."

We have also learned from our students that one should not underestimate the importance of meeting and talking to the person you will be reporting to (your boss) if you accept the job. We have seen a number of people accept what seemed to be excellent jobs, only to discover after starting work that they could not get along with the boss they hadn't met while job hunting.

And finally, don't underestimate the usefulness of talking to more than just two or three insiders. In a sample of MBA students from the Harvard Business School class of 1974, those who reported high job satisfaction seven months after graduation had spent more time talking to more people at their future employer's during job hunting than had those people who reported lower job satisfaction. By talking to a number of employees while interviewing, most people can begin to get a "feel" for an organization that is difficult to develop from other sources.

If an employer does not take the initiative in scheduling interviews for you with your potential boss, with a person occupying a job similar to the one that is open, and with a number of peers and superiors, then you must do so. Most employers will respond favorably to that kind of initiative. And even if they don't respond positively, you learn something very important about them in the process.

To prevent losing the information that one gets verbally and visually from a visit to a prospective employer, it's a good idea to sit down and write out a debriefing as soon as possible after you leave the organization. If, for example, you are flying home on a plane, spend some of that time *writing* out answers to the following types of questions:

1. To whom did you talk today?
2. What did you learn from each person?
3. What do you think of each of them?
4. What did you notice about the architecture and the physical setting that might be important?
5. What did you notice about the people in general, and how they interacted with each other?
6. How do you feel right now about the possibility of working there?
7. How does all this data compare with your themes and implications?

It is important not only to write out your answers, but to do so soon after the visit. Time clouds a memory.

Assignment

In the case that follows, (pp. 279–87), we have simulated a visit to the New York investment firm of Goldman, Sachs and Co. Look at the pictures carefully and draw what inferences you can from your observations about what it would be like to work there.

Goldman Sachs

The accompanying pictures were taken by a visitor to Goldman Sachs' main offices (55 Broad Street in New York City) in December of 1972. The visitor was given a quick (unannounced) tour of the type a job applicant might receive.

55 Broad Street

The ground floor

The reception area on the fourth (main) floor

The Board Room, also on the fourth (main) floor

Goldman Sachs International (fourth floor)

New York Institutional Sales (fourth floor)

The Order Room (fourth floor)

Convertible Bond and Listed Block Trading
(fourth floor)

Sales Administration (fourth floor)

A salesman who sells to individuals (fourth floor)

Stairway between the fourth and fifth floors

Commercial Paper Sales (fifth floor)

Fixed Income Trading (fifth floor)

Sales and Trading of Short Run Instruments
(fifth floor)

Sixth-floor reception area

Library (sixth floor)

Research Department (sixth floor)

An analyst—specializes in the broadcasting industry
(sixth floor)

The Research Department (sixth floor)

The Research Department (*continued*)

Tenth-floor reception area

The Corporate Finance Department

Managing Your Life during the Job Search

After interviewing for a job, and before a job offer is made (or not made), an interviewee often feels helpless; there is nothing to do but wait and hope. While it's easy to understand why people feel this way—the ball, so to speak, is in the employer's court—passive behavior is not in an interviewee's best interests.

Follow-up Techniques

Systematic follow-up after interviewing can be an important part of successful job hunting.

Keeping in Contact

Keep in contact with potential employers during the waiting period(s). After an initial screening interview, and after a final set of interviews, many successful job hunters will write a letter (or letters) to those with whom they spoke. The letter can communicate your appreciation of the way in which you were treated, your interest, your initiative, and the reasons why you think there may be a good match between your abilities and desires and the job. It can also help keep you visible, even though you're not there.

When visiting a potential employer, if you find that you share some professional interests with someone you meet, you may wish to follow up on that after leaving. Successful job hunters will sometimes stay in contact by letter or in person (if the employer is geographically close by) with a few of the people they met at a particularly interesting potential employer. Such contacts can help produce job offers.

Persisting and Persevering

Recognize that the key to getting what you really want—not your second, or third, or tenth choice—often depends upon your own perseverance. Some people would argue that the key to the whole process of getting job offers is persistence. The following story, while not at all typical, is instructive in this regard.

Jim Howard began job hunting with a major focus on consumer product management jobs and a minor focus on advertising jobs. Primarily because he had a good understanding of product management jobs, of himself, and of why he would probably make a good product manager, he was enormously successful in his initial interviews with consumer product companies. He contacted 10 such companies, got initial interviews with each, and was invited for a second set of interviews at all but one place. His understanding of advertising jobs and how he might fit in, as well as his commitment to an advertising career, was much lower. He contacted six ad agencies, was invited to interview with two, and was invited back to only one. All this occurred in January and February.

During March, while Jim was going through the second round of on-site interviews, he began to learn more about advertising through a course and his own research, and as he did he grew more and more excited about it. It became clearer and clearer to him that he could be really good at account management and derive a lot of satisfaction from it.

In April Jim found himself in a rather unusual position. He was the envy of all of his friends—for he had seven attractive job offers. Unfortunately, all seven offers were in product management, which he was no longer convinced that he wanted. Worse yet, he had fallen in love with the ad firm in which he had a set of second interviews. And the attraction was not just emotional infatuation. The job and company sounded almost perfect in light of his self-assessment paper.

On April 15, five days before he had promised some employers that he would respond to their job offers, Jim tentatively decided to accept a particular product management job. But it didn't feel right to him. He kept thinking to himself—if you know what you want, why take anything else unless you have to?

The next day he called the one person at the ad firm who had seemed to respond the most favorably toward him when he had visited them six weeks earlier. He invited that person to lunch, saying he needed some advice. At lunch he presented his dilemma, including his detailed analysis of why he would probably do a very good job at that ad firm. He effectively ended by saying that unless he heard very convincing evidence to the contrary, he was going to turn down his offers and pursue the ad firm until it offered him a job. The man he spoke with was visibly impressed.

At 8:30 the next morning his luncheon partner from the previous day called an invited him to come down to the agency that afternoon. Jim spent the afternoon talking to other employees of the firm, much as he did with the first person the day before.

On April 19, one day before he was to respond to his other offers, the ad firm called and offered him a job. He accepted, and when last heard from was doing very well and was extremely pleased with his job and company.

This brief description of Jim's job search, especially his management of his life during the process, illustrates the importance of persevering. But it is difficult to portray in print the emotional ups and downs that one can experience during the job search process. Even more difficult is trying to prepare for the sometimes lengthy periods of anxiety caused by the uncertainty of waiting.

Keeping Things in Control

Managing Anxiety

There are many reasons why people find job hunting anxiety-producing. Serious young students, in particular, often overestimate the stakes involved and then worry about making errors. Many people, who find rejection in any kind of social situation unpleasant, live in daily fear of being rejected by some employer they are beginning to like. The stream of ambiguous information a job hunter receives from potential employers drives some people to despair. The relative success experienced by other job hunters leave some people feeling like the "ugly child at the orphanage." And the

stream of first positive (an invitation to a second set of interviews), then negative (a rejection), then positive (a job offer) stimuli can turn one's life into an emotional roller coaster.

It has been our observation that many of the poor judgments people make while job hunting are due to their own anxiety, or more broadly, to an emotional state that is increasingly out of control. An individual's success at managing his or her own emotional state can be a very important factor while job hunting.

Just knowing that it is not unusual to feel anxious, and knowing the typical events that create anxiety, can help you to reduce and manage your anxiety while job hunting. People become "out of control" when they are surprised and frightened by their own anxiety. When typical human anxiety becomes predictable, it becomes manageable.

A technique our students have found useful in putting the hectic events of job hunting in a rational perspective is to keep a diary. By spending just a few minutes almost every day to summarize job-hunting events, your own thoughts and strategies, and your current feelings, you create a "monitoring system" that can be very useful in keeping things under control. By periodically rereading the entries for the last few weeks or months, one is able to make current decisions based on a more accurate understanding of what has really been happening. Rereading the diary helps put things in perspective. An example of such a diary is the Henry Rock case you encountered earlier (pp. 175).

Managing Time

It should be apparent from our discussion in the past few chapters that job hunting can be a very time-consuming activity. People who have not recently had to search for a job seem invariably to underestimate the time involved. It is not at all unusual for a non-student to spend half to all his or her time for three or four months looking for a job. Even students will often spend about a quarter of their time for four months. Some individuals, in both cases, spend up to five times as long.

Because job hunting is time-consuming, it seldom fits very neatly into an already busy life. It causes conflicts with school, work, family, and leisure time. Unless one is prepared for these conflicts and prepared to manage them, they can create a continuing sense of crisis.

Individuals who normally have a busy schedule, and who normally manage it well, tend to be quite successful at managing their time while job hunting. People who do not typically have a busy schedule, or who do not usually manage their time well, often run into problems while job hunting.

For the person who has problems managing time or

who normally has an unbusy schedule, we offer two specific recommendations that can help to manage time while job hunting. First, get an appointment book (if you don't already have one). By recording in it all your time commitments (not just appointments) while job hunting, you can make it serve as an effective time-management tool. Second, every time you undertake a task, stop and ask yourself a few questions. Do I really need to do this? Can someone else do it instead? Do I have to do this now? Or is something else a higher priority? What is the most efficient way to get this done? And so on.

Managing the Scope of the Search

As we mentioned earlier, people who are more successful in finding a very satisfying job tend to keep a narrower focus during job hunting. Among other things, a clearer and more structured focus helps one keep one's time demands within reasonable bounds.

Despite its importance and usefulness, however, maintaining a restricted scope while job hunting can be very difficult. Forces exist that push toward a widening of one's focus. For a variety of reasons, people sometimes do succumb to these forces, and they end up facing all the problems associated with an unfocused job search.

For example, most job hunters, at one point or another, begin to worry that maybe they just won't get any job offers. Some try to reduce that possibility by broadening the scope of their search. We've seen students who, after receiving their first rejection letter, panic and discard any and all focus in their job campaign. Many people, once they have spread the word that they are looking for a job, receive a few unsolicited leads that are not even close to what they are looking for. But if they are attractive in some way, some job hunters will take the bait.

We've seen companies send telegrams to students telling them what wonderful things the company has heard about them and asking them to please sign up to interview with the company when it is on campus. Students who have no interest whatsoever in the firm or its jobs will often sign up for an interview. Maintaining a rational focus in a job search is also difficult when one is around other job hunters whose enthusiasm for a different kind of job can be infectious. Some students seem to change the focus of their search almost daily to whatever the last excited friend they talked to was describing. The "grass-is-greener" phenomenon is very much at work here. Finally, some people expand the scope of their job search after they receive their first job offer. They seem to find their first "valentine" very exciting, want more, and so they go out and collect lots and lots of job offers.

If you feel yourself wanting to broaden your focus

while job hunting, don't do it immediately. Examine the idea carefully over a period of time. You will probably decide it is not a good idea.

Managing Pressure

Most job hunters get more than enough advice regarding what they "should" do from friends, professors, parents, spouses—even from a little voice inside them. While this advice is sometimes helpful, often it is not. One of the challenges of job hunting is not to succumb to well-intentioned but inappropriate advice and pressure.

When Fran Kelly's parents learned that she was not looking for a job in banking, they let her know (almost on a daily basis) how terribly disappointed they were that she wasn't following in the family tradition. When John Allen decided he would not interview anyone on campus or even look for a job until after he graduated and moved to the city he wanted to make his home, his peers gave him blank stares and an occasional, "Boy, does that sound like a dumb idea." When Frank Lenaro decided to change his career field after working for 10 years, his friends made it a habit of saying (while Frank was present), "Frank's decided to throw out everything he has built up over the past 10 years." When Kim Evans decided that she wanted to look for a job in an area seldom entered by graduates from her school, she was greeted constantly with puzzled looks and questions such as, "Why don't you want any of the good jobs?"

The more highly one is integrated into a network of friends, relatives, and acquaintances, the more pressure one is likely to feel from others while job hunting. This short-run pressure can, and sometimes does, push people away from a rational course of action.

Differentiating between inappropriate pressure and good advice can be difficult, especially if you are already out of control, and letting events and feelings direct your behavior. Periodically reviewing your themes and their implications from your self-assessment can be invaluable at this point. So can keeping a job-search diary. Both can help you keep on the right track.

Assignment

Read the vignettes that follow. Then carefully outline how you would handle each situation. Be specific. Outline what you would do, what you would say, where you would go, and what the impact of your actions would likely be.

1. REJECTION After a long and particularly grueling week of classes during which you have been eagerly

...ticipating a response from your number one company choice, you receive a letter in the mail informing you that, while the company appreciated your interest, it is unable to offer you a position at this time. You still have not heard from the other two companies who have expressed interest, but they are not particularly attractive openings anyway.

2. FATIGUE AND OVERLOAD   It is Sunday evening about 7 P.M. You have just returned from a cross-continent recruiting trip and are exhausted from the flight. You have a major paper due the following morning that needs some polishing and one or two additional exhibits. You also have two very stimulating classes scheduled for the following morning in subjects you feel are important to your education, but you have not yet read the cases. The phone rings. An old, close friend from out of town who is here for one day wants to go out to dinner.

3. RESPONSIBILITY   Your field project team has scheduled a very important meeting to pull together the data and analysis for your term project for Thursday night. Today is Wednesday, and you have just received a telephone call from your number-one recruiting choice asking you to fly to its city on Thursday evening to be there for Friday morning interviews.

4. LATE   You are walking out of class with two of your friends who are excitedly chattering about the job offers they have received, the benefits associated with them, the high salaries offered, and the thrill of being wanted by companies of such prestige. You, however, have not yet received any job offers, and in fact have not yet received any strong expressions of interest.

5. DATA   You receive a telephone call from your number one choice. The personnel director on the other end of the line thanks you for your recent company visit and expresses to you how interested they are in you. Then he says that, of course, in the recruiting process they have been interviewing a number of students from the business school, and wonders if you have any observations that may be of help to them on the following three people.

6. LOCATION   You have received two job offers, one that seems to fit your career objectives, personality, and skills perfectly, and the second which is less well matched. The first, however, happens to be in a rural community in the Midwest, and the second is located in a major urban center with all its attendant opportunities. While you are eager to accept the position in the Midwest, your partner feels very strongly that he/she would rather live in the urban location.

7. PARENTS   You have received three offers from firms in different industries, one of which is clearly more prestigious in the eyes of the world than the other two. Nevertheless, the second option seems to match up more closely with your personal interests and career objectives. When you describe the three options to your parents over the telephone, it is clear that they hope and expect you will accept the most prestigious offer.

8. SALARY   You are sitting in the Pub having a snack and a drink with several of your classmates. The talk naturally turns to the job recruiting process, and several of them start talking about the salary offers they have received. The only offer you have received at this point is more than $5,000 less than the lowest offer the others have mentioned.

9. FRIENDSHIPS   Your parents are coming for a short visit on Sunday, and you have blocked the day off. You have a major paper due on Monday, and have scheduled Saturday to do the final analysis and writing. On Saturday morning, as you are sitting down to write, your roommate and close friend at the business school calls from a city two hours away to say that his car was stolen with his wallet in it. He wants you to come down, pick him up, and bring him home.

10. HOLDING OUT   Your number two choice has made you a reasonable offer and asked for a reply next week. Your number one choice has just called to say that they enjoyed your visit. They also report that since some people are going on vacation, you will not be notified one way or the other for two weeks.

11. CHOOSING   You have received two job offers, both of which, although in different parts of the country and with different job descriptions, seem to fit very closely the goals and objectives you had had for a first job. The more you analyze the two alternatives, the more equal they seem. You have promised one of the firms that you would let it know the following morning.

12. PRIORITIES   You have received two offers. One includes a salary that is well above last year's class's mean salary, but is in a location that you find distasteful. The other offer has a salary that is slightly below last year's mean salary, but is in a location that meets your life style objectives well.

13. OTHER SITUATIONS   There may be other situations that you could imagine or have heard about that take place during job search and that tend to disrupt one's routine or one's emotional equanimity. Describe one such situation, how you would feel, and devise a response to it.

chapter

26

Analyzing and Choosing a Job Offer

At some point in the job search process, usually in March or April for business school candidates, you will receive some offers for employment. You are then faced with the task of assessing these offers.

To assess job offers rationally, a job hunter needs a considerable amount of information. Although some people would argue that you can't know much about a company or job until you have actually worked in it for six months, evidence from our students suggests otherwise. Clearly, there is a limit to what you can "know" about a job without directly experiencing it, but many people stop far short of that limit during job hunting. Often, because they are so worried about being rejected by potential employers or so flattered by all the attention and offers they are getting, some job hunters neglect to assess their job offers and potential offers seriously and rationally. By neglecting to use all available sources of information, by failing to understand how to utilize their sources properly, and by relying on inappropriate methods to analyze the data they obtain, they consistently make poorly informed decisions on which potential offers to pursue, which to eliminate, and finally which offer to accept.

Job-offer decision making can usefully be thought of as made up of two parts: (1) analysis and (2) choice. To understand this type of decision making, one needs to understand both of these very different parts of the overall process. By avoiding or doing a poor job in either part, job hunters can create serious problems for themselves.

Analysis

The analytical part of decision-making processes is characterized by words such as *cognitive, conscious,*
rational, and *objective.* With regard to job selection, it involves the systematic assessment of an individual, the systematic assessment of a number of job options, and the deduction of a set of most probable future events for each option if that option were selected by that individual. Virtually the entire book, up to this point, has been directed at helping you become more aware of this process and more skilled at using it.

Engaging effectively in analysis helps a job hunter more accurately predict the future consequences of accepting each of the available options. It provides a more realistic understanding of the rewards one might receive, and the problems one might encounter, with different options.

For a number of reasons, job hunters sometimes engage in analysis in a superficial and ineffective manner. Many people simply do not have the information, the expertise, or the training to analyze job offers effectively. Others are just not analytically oriented; they neglect serious analysis in almost all their decision making. Still others avoid analysis in this particular case because, at some level, they don't want to have to face the objective reality of their own personal limitations, or the limited future possibilities their current options offer them.

The person who fails to engage effectively in the analysis of a job decision may end up in a situation where he or she simply cannot do what is being demanded and expected, and is constantly and unpleasantly surprised by obstacles and problems. Typically, the individual who does a poor job of analysis while selecting a job offer will either quit or be asked to leave the job in 4 to 12 months. The employer will often be disappointed in the person's performance, and the employee will often be disappointed in his or her lack of satisfaction in the job.

Most job hunters we have observed do a fair or good job of analysis before selecting a job offer. A small number do an excellent job of analysis, and an equally small number do a very poor job.

Using the Self-Assessment

We have been developing the means for a job choice analysis all along. You now have a set of life themes and their implications for work. Since these are the criteria that will determine your satisfaction at work, they should also be the criteria that govern your choice of that work. We have been surprised on occasion by students who have diligently and enthusiastically developed a careful self-assessment, but who in the throes of choosing a job have ignored their themes and implications. In those cases, we ask the students to bring their self-assessment to our next meeting. There, we go through each theme and implication one by one to see how each option measures up. That discussion often makes it clear that one or maybe two of the offers they are considering are better than the rest.

Sometimes a student will say, "Yeah, but that theme is not what is *really* important. This [other criterion] is." If you feel this way during your decision-making process, you need to ask yourself two questions. First, ask yourself again (see "Writing Your Self-Assessment") if your self-assessment is accurate. It is intended to be systematic *and* accurate. If your thinking about choosing tells you that something else needs to be added to your self-assessment, do it.

But before you do, ask yourself another question: What forces are influencing you to think the way you are thinking now? Your self-assessment was generated systematically over two or three months of time and utilized a wide variety of tools in the data generation. Are you sure that your desire to change that assessment now is based on something more than impulse or peer pressure or some other transient phenomenon? Only when you have thought about it carefully and convinced yourself that the potential change to your self-assessment is an enduring part of you would we recommend that you go ahead and make the change.

The important, central point is that insofar as your self-assessment is complete and accurate, it reflects the criteria on which you will judge your life and your career. As such, your self-assessment should be used explicitly—theme by theme and implication by implication—in your job offer analysis.

This careful approach will do two things for you. First, it will help to clarify how well each opportunity matches up with the things that are most important to you. Second, it will clarify those dimensions on which the fit is not so good. Rarely does one find a job that is perfect in every way. Almost always there are as-

pects of a job that one finds less than ideal or even downright irritating. Your themes and implications can help you identify these areas in advance and, in so doing, help you think about how you will manage those aspects of the job so as to reduce the negative impact on you or your work. This will reduce the number of shattered expectations you will experience on the job after the "honeymoon" period is over.

Utilizing Other Information Sources

In addition to using your self-assessment as the basis for assessing the information you have about an opportunity, you may wish to consider the questions in Exhibit 26–1 as a means of stimulating your thinking about the job and the organization and the ways they will affect you.

To recap the previous chapters on written sources, interviewing, and company visits, there are a variety of ways of collecting data that will be useful to you. These are summarized in Exhibit 26–2.

People we have known who have been very successful at job hunting tend to rely extensively on all the information sources we've mentioned. Their less successful peers, on the other hand, do not. And if asked why they do not, they will often complain that they just didn't have the time. The *management of one's time is a very real problem for the job hunter*. In the case of assessing job offers, the dimensions of the problem can be understood if we consider how much time a professional (consultant or financial analyst) will typically spend just assessing a single company (not including an assessment of a specific job in it). Forty to 100 hours is typical. If job hunters tried to do a thorough, professional job of assessing each job and organization they were interested in, it would require literally thousands of hours. Since that is impractical, many job hunters simply give up and do a very random and superficial job.

The keys to an effective strategy to assess potential job offers are: (1) *utilizing all information sources,* but systematically emphasizing different ones at different times, depending upon how many organizations and jobs are under examination at the time; (2) *accurate self-knowledge.*

Choice

The process of choice is often much more nonrational, emotional, subjective, and unconscious than the analytic job assessment process. We don't know a great deal about the actual dynamics of job choice, but we do know the function it seems to serve and the consequences of not engaging in it.

Regarding the Job Itself

1. What major tasks are involved, and what are their key characteristics?

2. What skills are needed to perform each task?

3. Approximately what percent of the time will the job holder spend on each task? How does this vary (if at all) over time?

4. What time and resource constraints does the job holder have to work within?

5. How many hours per week do people holding similar jobs work?

6. What percent of the time will the job holder be working alone?

7. Who else will the job holder interact with? What are these people like? What percent of the time will the job holder be with them?

8. How much discretion will the job holder have in deciding how to perform the job?

9. How many people and how much money or equipment will the job holder be responsible for?

10. How many people will report to the job holder?

11. Who will be the job holder's boss? What is this person like? How good a coach is he or she?

12. How is performance measured in this job?

13. What type of salary and other rewards are available given what level of performance?

14. Specifically what type of advancement opportunities are available to the job holder?

15. Who makes decisions and how regarding promotions?

Regarding the Organization

16. How large is the organization's industry (employment, number of competitors), and what are its prospects for future growth?

17. Specifically what parts of the industry will probably grow (or decline) at what rates over the next few decades?

18. What are the industry's most important characteristics? (Is business seasonal? What type of organizations do well or poorly?)

19. How is the industry changing now?

20. How old is the organization? What are the big events in its history?

21. How large is the organization (people, assets, sales volume, net income)?

22. What goods and services does it produce?

23. How does it produce these goods and services?

24. Where does it have plants or offices?

25. Does the organization have any particularly important suppliers, customers, or regulators? If yes, who are they, what are they like, and what is their relationship to the organization?

26. What important technologies does the organization use?

27. What are the major parts of the organization, and how are they structured?

28. What are the organization's compensation policies? Performance appraisal practices? Training and development practices? Other important personnel policies?

29. What type of people work for the organization?

30. What do they generally like about the organization? Dislike about it?

31. Does the organization have any important traditions?

32. How are the people and the way in which they interact different from people in other organizations you have known?

33. What are the company's plans for the future?

Exhibit 26-2
Information Sources and Their Uses

	Library	Informed Nonemployees	Potential Boss and Superiors	Potential Peers and Others	Direct Observation
Industry Characteristics	***	**	*	*	
Major organizational characteristics (what it does, where, etc.)	***	**	*	*	
How the organization functions		***	**	*	**
What it's like to work for the organization		**	*	***	***
Job characteristics			*	***	*
Career possibilities	*	*	***	*	

*** Best source.
** Good source.
* A source.

In the only systematic examination of the job-offer decision-making process we are aware of, Peer Soelberg studied 32 graduate students at the Sloan School of Management (MIT) while they were job hunting.[1] He was surprised to find that the process these students engaged in, especially near the end, was much less rational and analytic than he expected. Among other things, he found that:

1. The students tended to reduce their options to two (precisely two in almost every case) using a pragmatic, although not very elegant, analytical process.

2. They would then often agonize while deciding which of the two options to take.

3. Significantly, before the average student would announce that he had reached a decision, Soelberg found he could predict which option would eventually be chosen.

4. Upon announcing a decision, the average student could then provide an elaborate "justification" for his choice, the details of which sometimes clashed with what he had said earlier.

These findings are entirely consistent with what we have observed less systematically over the past few years. Even people who have done an excellent job at analytically assessing themselves and their options typ-

ically go through an emotional phase of varying lengths and intensity during which they seem unconsciously to: (1) create a situation of choice (usually between two options); (2) emotionally try to come to grips with the implications of each option; (3) choose one of the options; and (4) find some rationale for rejecting the option not chosen.

The Importance of Choosing

No matter what the exact dynamic of this process is, it seems to be important, or needed, because it serves two important functions. It helps the decision maker develop an emotional commitment to one of the options. It also helps the decision maker cope with feelings of loss associated with cutting off the other option.

To follow through on a major life decision with the energy and vigor needed to ensure its successful implementation, people seem to need some emotional commitment to the direction the decision will take them. Among other things, that commitment seems to help them overcome obstacles when they encounter them. But the very process of choosing, and emotionally committing oneself to one option, means that another must be cut off. The feeling of loss associated with such cutting off can be very powerful and troublesome to people. To help cope with these feelings, people tend to find some "rational" reason that minimizes the loss.

People sometimes avoid choosing or engage in it only minimally. They allow others, or "fate," to

[1]See Peer Soelberg, "A Study of Decision Making: Job Choice" (dissertation, Sloan School, 1967), and "Conclusion from a Study of Decision Making" (MIT Working Paper 173-66).

choose for them. Or they simply deny that they have a choice. (How often have you heard someone say, "I had no choice"?) Some people always behave this way in their decision making, just as some others always avoid serious analysis. Sometimes it seems they just can't accept the responsibility of cutting off what might be a "good" option. The loss of what "could be" is too painful for them.

The Consequences of Not Choosing

The consequences of not engaging in choice can be as serious as the consequences of not engaging in analysis. Without the emotional commitment to a particular direction, it is often very difficult to mobilize one's energies and overcome the inevitable obstacles. Without effectively dismissing the other options, and suffering the loss, one can often be plagued by thoughts of their continuing availability. These thoughts can paralyze a person.

One student we observed, a very bright and highly analytic young man, devised an elaborate mathematical formula to help him select one among four job offers. He announced that he did so to help him make a rational decision, "not an emotional one like so many people seem to." The formula gave option 1, 110 points; option 2, 85 points; option 3, 118 points; and option 4, 96 points. He aggressively defended his formula against occasional jokes from friends. ("What does an 8-point difference mean, Larry? One less ulcer every 8.0 years?") He accepted option 3, even though he didn't feel entirely sure it was right.

After eight months on the job, a downturn in company sales and layoff of personnel put everyone in Larry's division under some pressure. He thought there must be better opportunities elsewhere and quit. Five months later, he started to work in another job. When his boss was promoted six months after that and the person who replaced his boss was not "as easy to work with," Larry quit again. He was also to get still another job within three months. When we talked to him last, he expressed concern that his career did not seem to be progressing as well as those of some of his less able classmates. We are left wondering whether his seeming inability to really choose an option, and to commit himself to it, might not underlie his lack of career progress.

Assignment

The Mike Downer case which follows raises several of the issues introduced in this chapter. Read the case and prepare your answers to the following questions.

1. What tools did Mike Downer use to evaluate and analyze his choices? Do you think they were useful or effective? Why or why not?

2. As Mr. Reese, what, if anything, would you say to Mike?

3. As Mike Downer, what would you do? Why?

4. How would *you* go about making the decision between two job offers?

MIKE DOWNER

I feel lousy. I can't sleep. I can't eat. I can't concentrate on my classes. My whole life is being affected. This is the fourth and last semester of business school and I have two good, firm offers. Most people would welcome either offer. I should be enjoying myself, but I still feel lousy.

Mike Downer, a second-year MBA student, sat and stared out the window. He was tired and emotionally drained. His job search had been a long and exhausting process, especially when considering his efforts were in addition to normal classroom work. In an attempt to sort out his

thoughts, Mike had sought the advice of his organizational behavior professor, Mr. Reese.

Mr. Reese was attentive as he listened. Mike appeared to be confused and bewildered as he searched for words to express himself. Mr. Reese watched and waited. Still gazing out the window, Mike began to speak again.

I've got to make a decision. I promised Mammoth Foods a decision by Friday. That gives me just four days to make up my mind.

What infuriates me is that this should be the easy part. The hard part is all done. The preparation,

This case was prepared by Kent Guichard under the direction of Associate Professor James G. Clawson. All names have been disguised. © 1982 by the Sponsors of the Colgate Darden Graduate School of Business Administration, University of Virginia, Charlottesville, Virginia. UVA case OB-227.

the interviews, and the waiting for offers is all·behind me. All I have to do is choose one of two offers. Both offers are good opportunities with excellent firms. Both offers have advantages, both have disadvantages. It's so hard to choose.

I'm in trouble. I haven't smiled in four days. I'm in the deepest depression I have ever experienced during two years of business school. At this point, I'm not very popular with too many people. Even my friends tell me that I'm a mess. I feel lousy. Is this normal? What should I do?

Background

In preparation for his job search, Mike Downer had enrolled in the fall elective on career management. Mike felt that he came out of the course with a good view of himself and with a solid plan of action for his job search. While he knew that the job search would be strenuous, Mike felt that he was well prepared for the challenge.

As a course requirement, Mike made a list of life themes (see Exhibit 26–3). He felt the themes were a strong and accurate assessment of what he considered important. Mike expanded the themes into 21 career implications (see Exhibit 26–4). These implications described the characteristics of the type of job he wanted. It was from these implications that he developed his action plan. Mike briefly outlined his plan as follows:

The main focus of my job campaign was people oriented (selling/persuading) positions within the financial services industry. At one time, I believe that my choice would have been very segmentable along the lines of Investment Banks, Commercial Banks, Insurance Companies, and Real Estate Firms. However, the distinctions between these industries are diminishing, creating the opportunities I was seeking among all four.

One of my toughest assignments in my job search was to determine whether I wanted to be on the selling side (Institutional Sales, Loan Officer) or client side (Investment Management) of the financial services industry. However, I viewed the job hunt as a unique opportunity to gain valuable insight into the industry.

In determining which companies I contacted, I used two main vehicles as the focus of my efforts: the placement office and firms which I contacted on my own initiative. The following is the method I used to select companies through the placement office:

1. Read the placement job descriptions for each position that was interviewed for on campus.
2. Check each position against my themes and implications for suitable fit.
3. Rank each position on a scale of 0 (no interest) to 5 (high interest). Allocate my interviewing time to firms ranked 5 to 1 in descending order.

By using this method, I felt that I would be focused, but at the same time would have a sufficient number of interviews to satisfy my job search goals.

Outside contacts were the other source of my interview prospects. Whenever possible, I contacted an alumnus or key contact in a firm by telephone to introduce myself and express my interest in a company. When I was unable to make contact by telephone, I contacted the company in writing. I developed my letters along the following format:

1. Who I was, why I was writing
2. What I wanted
3. What I could offer
4. Asked for a specific action

I enclosed in each letter a copy of my résumé (see Exhibit 26–5).

Exhibit 26–3
Mike Downer's Life Themes

Most Important

1. Meeting people is important/people-oriented
2. High value placed on variety/diversity/change
3. Enjoy leadership/controlling positions
4. Want to be in on what's going on/dislike isolation
5. Motivated by money as a reward for work
6. Place a high value on self-reliance/independence
7. Achievement-oriented
8. High value on learning new things
9. High value on being recognized for efforts

Very Important

10. Dislike of detailed work/repetitive tasks
11. Action-oriented/like to be doing a lot
12. High value on receiving guidance and support
13. Emphasis on the practical
14. Enjoy politics
15. Enjoy persuading/selling
16. High value on tackling a challenge
17. Like physically demanding activities/keeping in shape

Important

18. Self-starter/entrepreneurial
19. Want to have time for my own benefit
20. Desire to be close to people
21. Strong sense of likes/dislikes/priorities
22. Enjoy traveling
23. Active/passive involvement with sports activities

Important Minor Theme

24. Underlying sense of ethics/fairness

Exhibit 26–4
Implications of Life Themes

Implications	Theme Support
1. A job that offers a high degree of people interaction	1,4,12,20
2. A job that offers an opportunity to experience a changing environment with a minimum of detailed and repetitive tasks.	2,8,10,16,22
3. A job that offers some flexibility as far as being able to leave the office when desired (not chained to a desk from 9 to 5).	6,17,18,21
4. A job that offers the independence to take an idea, design its implementation, and implement it.	3,6,15,18
5. A job that offers a tangible feeling of accomplishment.	5,7,9,13,15,16
6. A job that offers visibility, quick feedback on and support for efforts.	4,9,12
7. A job that keeps me busy—where I don't have to wait for work.	11,16
8. A job that relies on some understanding and interest in the political process.	13
9. A job that offers the opportunity to persuade others to my viewpoint.	3,15
10. A job that offers enough free time for me to pursue outside interests like keeping fit.	17,23
11. A job that offers the opportunity to become financially independent.	5,6,18
12. A job that deals with a subject matter I truly enjoy (i.e. investments, politics, real estate).	21
13. A job that offers the opportunity for travel within the work setting and time to travel on my own during leisure hours.	2,8,19,22
14. A firm that keeps its promises to its employees and also requires employees to practice high ethical standards.	24
15. A firm that places a high value on employees' physical well being.	17,23
16. A firm that rewards performance with good monetary increases.	5
17. A firm that has the resources available for me to draw on in order to constantly improve my professional abilities.	6,8,12,13,16,18
18. A city that offers a lot to do.	2,8,11,23
19. A place that offers facilities so that the opportunity to keep in shape is available.	17,23
20. A place where the local political scene is active.	14
21. A place that has an open social system to get to know people.	1,20

My planned approach to interviewing was simple. I was prepared. I looked at company reports, talked to classmates, explored alumni contacts, and scanned the business press. I also planned to be ready for some standard questions.

To assist me in my final choice, I developed an evaluation form (see Exhibit 26–6). The evaluation went into a notebook that I kept on each company. The notebook contained all the pertinent information about the company.

I realize my choice is not all rational. Therefore, after all is analyzed, I am also trying to choose a job I can build the most emotional commitment to.

The Job Search

Mike went through the interviewing process almost exactly according to his action plan. He saw every firm he wanted to see. Most of his interviews were in three areas: banking, institutional sales of stocks and bonds, and investment management. In addition, Mike also interviewed for product management positions with three large consumer goods packaging companies. Mike explained the reasoning behind the product management interviews to Mr. Reese:

The three interviews with consumer goods packaging companies were out of my original plan. I had made a change in my job focus sometime during the fall semester. Originally, my job objective was for a position in marketing in consumer goods and/or financial services.

The first brief contacts with the investment banks caused me to do some thinking about my objective. They reacted very negatively to the consumer goods part of my résumé. In fact, the inclusion of consumer goods would probably have eliminated me in the first round weeding-out process. So, I decided to narrow my focus in the plan to just financial services.

But, I still wanted to talk to some consumer goods companies. I received excellent grades in marketing courses and wanted to find out what it was

Exhibit 26–5
Mike Downer's Résumé

Michael Downer
P.O. Box 000
Central States, USA
Phone: (100)234–5678

Employment Objective	Seek position in marketing of financial services leading to general management responsibilities.
Education	Candidate for MBA degree in May 1982, The Graduate School of Business.
	Bachelor Degree Magna Cum Laude, East Coast College. Outstanding Young Men of America, Dean's List, President of the local chapter of the National Business Society, Vice President of Sigma Chow Fraternity.
Experience	**NEW YORK BANK** Summer 1981. Full-time summer intern responsible for a project in the marketing department on how to serve small business customers better.
	MIDATLANTIC BANK 1979 to 1980. Marketing Representative responsible for marketing checking and savings accounts, cash management services, investments, and loans to businesses and individuals.
	NATIONAL SAVINGS AND LOAN ASSOCIATION 1978 to 1979. Business Development Representative marketing a pilot program for investment and retirement plans to both individuals and businesses.
	U.S. STOCK BROKERS, INC. 1978. Account Executive involved in the marketing of financial instruments. Successfully completed the New York Stock Exchange examination.

really like outside the classroom environment. I tried to select three companies that had a reputation of being good teaching firms. One company, Mammoth Foods, I picked out because of a good fall presentation at school.

Mike experienced a very high success rate in his first-round interviews. All his interviews went smoothly. In fact, Mike almost had too many callbacks. There wasn't enough time to get back to all the firms that had invited him for a second interview. The commercial banks were all very impressed with Mike and felt even more comfortable with him because of his previous banking experience. The investment banks were equally impressed; Mike received four callbacks out of five companies. In the product manage-

ment area, he received one callback, from Mammoth Foods.

Mike had a total of nine job offers. Five offers were in commercial banking. These positions were mostly in business development and credit management. One offer was in commercial banking product management. Two more offers were in sales and trading with two investment banks. And finally, Mike received an offer from Mammoth Foods.

From Nine Down to Two

After the offers started coming in, Mike continued to follow his plan. With each company visit,

Exhibit 26-6
Company Evaluation Form

Company Name_____   Interviewer_____

Address_____   Date _____

Phone _____

Implication   Rank (1 to 5)   Comments

People-oriented
Changing environment
Detail/repetition
Office flexibility
Tangible accomplishment
Visibility
Feedback/support
Workload
Politics
Selling/persuading
Free time
Financial independence
Subject matter
Travel
Fairness/ethics
Physical well-being
Monetary incentives
Training
City attributes
Recreational facilities
Political scene
Open social system   _____
                              Total

Overall impressions:

Office appearance (visual data):

Things to remember:

---

he wrote down his impressions and compared them to the criteria listed in his life themes and job implications. Then he compared and rated the companies against each other.

Mike managed to eliminate six of the nine offers fairly quickly. He narrowed it down to three choices from three different areas: First Commercial Bank in business development; Madison and Monroe, an investment bank, in stock and bond sales; and Mammoth Foods in product management. Two of the offers, First Commer-

cial Bank and Madison and Monroe, were in areas of Mike's original plan. The Mammoth Foods offer was not in the plan, but Mike considered the company unique and wanted to pursue the opportunity.

First Commercial eventually began to drop out of the picture. Part of the reason was that Mike had left commercial banking to get his MBA. Returning to basically the same type of position and doing much of the same type of work would, in a way, be almost like saying that his MBA was not worth the effort it took to get it. Mike gave some additional reasons to Mr. Reese for eliminating First Commercial:

> The job content itself looked questionable. The office was great. The perks associated with the position were fine. But the work looked terrible. I would go through company after company after company doing the same thing over and over again. After a while, they would all look the same.

> I also began to wonder about my fit with the "banking" mentality. The people I met were cynical people. They were also very, very risk adverse. If a company was highly successful, they were always trying to find out how it was going to fail and fall. I just didn't like that atmosphere.

Mike eliminated First Commercial in his selection process. Now there were only two left: Mammoth Foods, and Madison and Monroe.

Mammoth Foods

Mammoth Foods is one of the largest consumer goods packaging companies in the world. The company is headquartered in Kansas City, Missouri. Mike and Mr. Reese discussed the recruiting trips to Kansas City:

> My first visit is what really made me start to seriously consider joining the company. I had pretty much ruled out product management because of the amount of detailed work involved and because of my dislikes for the electives that I had taken in the MBA program. The visit changed my view.

> I liked what I saw. I had six interviews in all levels of the organization. I liked the people. They were truly professional. It seemed like a healthy work atmosphere.

> There were some negatives. The company places people in product areas almost at random. You have very little to say as to where your first job assignments are. Where they need you is where you go. Also, the management style of the company is to provide a limited number of positive strokes for a job well done. Finally, I talked to several "East Coast" people who said that they went through a tough adjustment period living in the Midwest.

> Thinking back, the positives of my first visit outweighed the negatives. They made me an offer on the spot and that was good. I knew where I stood.

> My second trip to Kansas City continued to increase my evaluation of the Mammoth Foods opportunity. My reservations about the city, the people, and the job content were all effectively reduced.

> I really like the city. I am surprised at how much there is to do. The city has sports and culture. The entire area has a positive feeling.

> I was also reassured about the people. I was especially impressed with many of my peers. There is a lot of positioning and image building during the first six months. The organization is so large that you want the management to notice you right from the start. My peers are competitive as a result, but not cutthroat. There is a mentality that everyone is working through the system together. It is like an extension of the business school environment.

> The job content is still a stumbling block. There is detail upon detail. The initial year is full of detailed work, but it does get less and less as time goes on.

> After two visits to Kansas City and Mammoth Foods, I had two overall impressions. First, I had a good feeling that said I would fit in. Second, it seemed like a very nice place to live and work.

Madison and Monroe

Madison and Monroe is one of the leading investment banking firms on Wall Street. The firm is engaged in a wide variety of financial services for a broad range of clients. Mike had a very different experience at Madison and Monroe than he had at Mammoth Foods.

> The first round visit at Madison and Monroe was a little on the impersonal side. Impersonal in the sense that the process dictated events. They set aside eight Fridays for the partners to interview MBAs who had received callbacks. Each Friday they had six or seven people come in. We all went through six one-on-one interviews on the Friday we visited.

> The interviews were not typical investment banking interviews. There was not as much stress and I considered most of the questions to be better than average. I enjoyed the interviews.

> I also enjoyed the people. They were serious, but fun. They were competitive, but not cutthroat. The firm had an air of competence about it. The people were top-notch and their personalities blended together well.

> After the first visit to Madison and Monroe, I felt that it would be a good fit if I decided to go into investment banking. At this point, I felt Madison was convinced that I could handle the job content. The remaining question was one of fit.

> My second visit to Madison and Monroe gave me a real flavor of investment banking. I spent most of the day with three people. The first was a Graduate School of Business alumnus from last year. I don't know how well he was doing, but I don't think that he was very happy. He answered my questions for over an hour and I think I got some valuable insights.

> The second guy was an equity sales trader who had an MBA. I didn't like his attitude. It was like,

"I'm here and you're not" and "I'm bigger on this block than you are." He sat back and made me force the conversation. The exposure to him was marginally helpful.

The third guy was in equity research sales and had been with Madison for about three years. He was extremely helpful and I was lucky enough to spend two hours with him. We discussed what he did, how he felt about the firm, and the pros and cons of the whole investment banking situation.

After visiting Madison and Monroe twice, I continued to be impressed. The whole operation is first class. They are a top firm, and I believe I would fit in.

Which One?

At this point, Mike had managed to narrow down his choice between two strong opportunities. He had visited each company twice and had spoken to several people in each firm. Mike set out systematically to evaluate the two alternatives.

Both offers were firm. Madison and Monroe had offered Mike $33,000 a year plus unspecified, but negotiable, extras. Mammoth Foods was offering $31,000 and a nice, neat package of attractive benefits. Neither firm had put a time restriction on Mike, but he had promised Mammoth Foods a decision by the coming Friday.

Mike explained his process up to this point in evaluating the offers:

> I started by listing the pros and cons of each offer. I went through different career paths, flexibility, job content, people and the rest of the criteria that I had set up in the beginning. I ended up with a whole set of reasons for and against each offer (see Exhibit 26–7).

> I looked at the lists and found that they weren't much help. The idea was good and the list looked good, but it really wasn't much help.

> I went back and reread my original plan. I had pretty much executed it exactly, with the exception being that one of my final two choices was in product management. My original negative feelings about product management weren't that strong now that I think about it.

> After my first attempt to evaluate the offers, I was leaning towards Mammoth Foods. It was a nice situation. I already had the selling experience that was the primary function in the Madison position.

Exhibit 26–7
First Evaluation of the Alternatives

Mammoth Foods

Pros:	Cons:
1. Good fit with people	1. Structured work atmosphere
2. Exposure to the other side of marketing	2. Time-oriented promotions and raises
3. Career flexibility	3. Less financial independence
4. Flexible start time	4. Team play (I'm a doer)
5. Pleasant city to live in	5. Grunt work
6. Fair amount of variety	6. City is out of the way
7. Some travel	7. Slow-moving organization
	8. Confined to desk
	9. Past work experience with this type of work was less than satisfactory

Madison and Monroe

Pros:	Cons:
1. Money potential	1. Limited management support
2. Capitalize on existing selling skills	2. Nontransferable skills
3. Job variety	3. Heavy rejection factor
4. Relies on doer skills	4. Will be doing the same thing for at least 5 years
5. Would lead to a career in financial planning	5. Everyone is fairly cynical
6. Immediate satisfaction from work	6. Alcoholism is an occupational hazard
7. East Coast location	7. Confined to desk
8. Some travel	8. Past experience in this atmosphere was not enjoyable
9. Working with investments	9. Limited chances to be a consultant to clients

Exhibit 26–8
Second Evaluation of the Alternatives

Mammoth Foods		vs.		Madison and Monroe
Promotion on time		vs	**	Promotion on merit
Strengthen weaker skills	**	vs		Use existing skills
Skills to run my own business	**	vs		Money to start my own business
Structured atmosphere	**	vs		Little management support
Less interesting work		vs	**	Work in investments
Delayed feedback		vs	**	Immediate feedback
Midwest location		vs	**	New York location
Career flexibility	**	vs		Specialization
Good fit with people	**	vs		Intimidated by people
Group work		vs	**	Doer role
Number crunching at first		vs	**	Verbal skills
Minimum control of destiny		vs	**	Major control of destiny

Note: ** indicates the stronger offer.

Scorecard: Mammoth Foods: 5
Madison and Monroe: 7

Exhibit 26–9
Third Evaluation of the Alternatives
(RANKED 1 = WORST TO 5 = BEST.)

Implication	Mammoth Foods	Madison and Monroe
People orientation	4	4
Environment	3	4
Detail/repetition	2	3
Flexibility	2	2
Tangible accomplishment	3	4
Visibility	3	3
Feedback	3	2
Workload	2	3
Selling	3	4
Free time	3	3
Financial independence	2	4
Nature of work	2	4
Travel	3	3
Ethics	4	2
Monetary incentive	2	4
Training	4	2
Social system	4	2
City attributes	3	4
Recreational facilities	3	3
Physical well-being	4	2
Total	59	62

Mammoth Foods would give me the planning and policy side of marketing. Put that together with my selling, and in five years you've got a full marketing executive.

My second attempt to evaluate the offers was also on a pro and con basis. But this time, I positioned Mammoth Foods against Madison and Monroe. This time Madison came out on top, but the two were still so close (see Exhibit 26–8). As far as I was concerned, I had gotten absolutely nowhere.

Yesterday morning I sat myself down and said, "Look Mike, this is ridiculous. Look at both offers. Evaluate them. Make a decision." Simple as that. So I read over all my notes. I read "Confessions of a Brand Manager" again. And I rescored the two jobs. This time I used my evaluation sheet. Madison won again, barely. Well, call it even (see Exhibit 26–9).

I feel that there is a war raging inside me. When I sit down and analyze the situation, Madison seems to come out ahead "on points." Yet, emotionally I am still drawn to Mammoth Foods. I like the people. I enjoy Kansas City. My salary would go further.

Product management is new and unknown. But then, I didn't know much about sales and I loved it once I tried it.

I feel lousy.

Mike needed to make up his mind. He felt that his whole life was being consumed by the decision. It almost haunted him. Mike recognized that he was tired and confused, that he needed new information. Information from a different perspective. It was for this reason that Mike sought out Mr. Reese.

What Now?

Mike Downer sat and stared out the window. Mr. Reese had been listening for over an hour now. Mike was almost through.

What is wrong with me? This is simple. I've got this nice, neat package from Mammoth Foods and I can get to be a marketing director or I can go with Madison and Monroe and cash in on a competent sales skill, make a lot of money, and go from there.

It should be simple, but I just can't decide. Both offers are equal. What should I do?

chapter

27

Negotiating and Accepting a Job Offer

Sometime in the later stages of your choosing process or perhaps even after you have chosen your favorite firm and before advising the firm that you have accepted the offer, you will be considering and assessing the various job-related characteristics of the offer. In some cases, you may be satisfied with the offer; in other cases, you may not be satisfied. These situations bring the need to negotiate the terms of employment. A number of dimensions may be the object of your negotiations. (See Exhibit 27–1 for a sample list).

While the characteristics of a job offer may or may not change as a result of negotiations, we believe it is important in the process of selecting a job that matches your self-assessment as well as possible that you take into consideration each of these characteristics and in so doing reduce the number of surprises you will have on the job. It is important to negotiate or to discuss the specifics of these various characteristics before you accept an offer. Some corporations have policies for various of these characteristics that cannot be negotiated; generally, when you raise the question, they will advise you of this. Other corporations may be much more willing to meet your needs. In either case, before accepting a position, it is important that you understand clearly the details of the offer. Again, this will reduce the likelihood of both positive and negative surprises after you have already committed yourself.

Gentlemanly Agreements

The first thorny issue around receiving and accepting a job offer relates to the desire of everyone not to be rejected. This is also true of organizations. Many firms will not make a job offer until they are reasonably sure that it will be accepted. This motivation will become

Exhibit 27–1
Negotiable Characteristics of Job Offers

Job content and activities

Supervisor

Title and its review period and likely next steps

Location and office space

Salary level, bonuses, and additional compensatory perquisites like stock options

Starting time—that is, beginning work

Vacations, holidays, sick leave

Travel

Overtime work

Flexibility of working hours

Moving expenses

House hunting expenses

Medical, life, and other forms of insurance

Maternity leaves

Educational participation programs

Pensions

Company expectations for performance in the first year of employment

apparent to you in your conversations with interviewers at the company. In fact, in some cases they may say: If you received an offer, would you accept it? This kind of approach puts the candidate in an uncomfortable position, and in reality may create additional problems for the recruiting organization because people who otherwise might have accepted offers later on might not be given the opportunity.

One student, after a day of interviews at her first-choice company, felt very confident that she was about to receive an offer. In the last interview of the day with the person charged with the responsibility for making offers, she was asked if she were to receive an offer, would she accept it. She had not yet learned all the details of that position, nor had she heard from her number two and number three choices. She did not know how the specifics of those offers might stack up against what appeared to be her primary interest. Her response was that she liked the company, but wanted to hear what a couple of other alternatives would have to say before she made her decision. She sensed an immediate change in the attitude of the recruiter and felt as though she could almost see the offer being withdrawn.

In that case, this person, if made a firm offer, probably would have in the longer run accepted the company's offer. But the company's reluctance to extend that offer with anything less than 100 percent certainty made it difficult for the individual to make a commitment on the spot.

One way to deal with this problem is to express to the corporation your sincere and genuine interest in the company and in the position you have been discussing. Then go on to say that many of the details, not only of the job but of the life style, associated with the job require further investigation in your mind, and that a real decision is only possible once all the details have been collected. Nevertheless, from all current indications, your interest in that company is extremely strong and the probability is very high that if extended an offer, you would accept it. This approach expresses sincere interest in the corporation and yet leaves the candidate the option of choosing another alternative if in some unforeseen way it should be more attractive.

Buying Time

During the course of your analysis and choosing process, you may have looked at the details of job offers and know exactly what it is that you want. In many cases this will not be true, so that when you receive an offer you will need to buy yourself some time to consider the details. One response to a telephone offer is to say that it is very attractive and that you are appreciative of the company's expression of confidence, but that you would like to take one or two days to consider some detailed questions relating to the offer and get back to the individual to talk about some of those additional characteristics. You may at this point say that in principle the offer seems satisfactory, and you are very likely to accept it.

Then you can refer to Exhibit 27-1 and your self-assessment to develop specific questions about your

activities, compensation, and the parameters that will constrain you when you join the organization. The question of how much to ask for depends upon the importance of the money criterion to you in your experiencing of the work and to the urgency of gaining employment. If you're low on funds and need work immediately, you may be more willing to sacrifice some of the details than if you are determined and have the means to wait for a more attractive and better-matching alternative.

Most employers will leave a job offer open for a particular period of time. Frequently this period is two weeks, but it may extend up to several months. On occasion, companies will demand an immediate response. This they do in part because they want to feel that they are in the candidate's first choice and are reluctant to hire people who would accept them as their second or third choice. Unless you are very sure that the company which has extended you an offer is the right fit and that the details of job offers have been considered carefully, we do not recommend that you allow yourself to be pressured into making a commitment in the same moment that you receive an offer.

Again, the strategy employed above seems to provide an acceptable and usually effective alternative approach. That is, to express your appreciation at the offer and to say that although it is extremely likely that you will accept it, you want a day or two to consider it carefully before responding. In many cases, a day or two is insufficient time, and you may ask for a week to two weeks to consider the offer. This is not unusual in industry, and you should not feel embarrassed or unique for asking for this time. You might also make a point to the recruiter that it is in their best interest as well as your own that both parties have the opportunity to consider the match carefully.

Assignment

Read the vignettes that follow. For each one, write down your specific plans for dealing with each of the situations. What would you say? What would you do? Where would you go? With whom would you talk?

1. Salary Differentials

You have just received an offer from Company XYZ, which is high on your priority list. During the day you discover from friends that other people have been given offers $5,000 above yours. Knowing the people and the jobs they would be taking in the company, you do not understand the difference in salary, since you are at least as well qualified as they and the position you are being offered is at least as responsible as theirs.

2. Moving Expenses

You have just been offered a position in a distant city but do not have a lot of excess funds in savings and personal bank accounts. You have learned from other people who have been given offers by the company that the company does not pay moving expenses.

3. House Search Expenses

You have a house, but have just been offered a position with a company in another city. You are to leave within the month. You are concerned about the time and expense of selling your own home and the time and expense involved in purchasing a new one in the city to which you're moving.

4. Starting Work

You feel mentally, emotionally, and physically exhausted by the rigors of your academic program. Although the job you have chosen is exciting and stimulating, you are concerned about starting work immediately. You have sufficient money in your savings to spend a month or two on vacation, and even though you've heard the company needs you immediately, you are thinking about negotiating for a later starting date.

chapter

28

Decision Making for Couples

In a situation where a job hunter is not a relatively independent individual, but is highly interdependent with another person—such as a spouse or a fiancé—any decisions made will directly affect not just one, but two people. The job selection decision-making process, which we have already seen is complex for an individual, becomes even more complex when the decision maker is a part of a couple. But exactly how much more complex it becomes, and in what ways, will vary depending upon the nature of the couple's relationship.

The Spectrum of Relationships

Exhibit 28-1 presents a spectrum of relationships for couples. At the extreme left of the spectrum is the traditional relationship: The husband is the breadwinner and the wife is the homemaker and child-raiser. As one moves from left to right across the spectrum, male and female roles change toward more equal participation in family and career. At the right extreme, both people essentially assume the same role, in terms of careers and homes.

Exhibit 28-1
A Spectrum of Relationships for Couples

THE TRADITIONAL COUPLE	THE SEMI-TRADITIONAL COUPLE	THE TYPICAL DUAL CAREER COUPLE	THE EGALITARIAN COUPLE
HE is the breadwinner SHE is the homemaker and child-raiser HE competes and succeeds for both SHE provides child care, social, and maintenance for both	HE is the breadwinner (with some involvement in family and home) SHE is the homemaker and child-raiser but she also works, usually for a specific purpose (such as better vacations for the family, college tuition, braces for someone's teeth, her own personal satisfaction) HE has the dominant career but acknowledges her contribution to their quality of life, and her need for some kind of outside activity SHE works, but neither of them thinks of her as having a "career"	HE is committed to a professional career SHE is committed to a professional career The couple think of themselves as being a dual career family BUT, one of them (almost always the woman) takes on more than 50 percent of the responsibility for housekeeping and child-raising, and provides less than 50 percent of the income	HIS and HER roles vis-à-vis career and home are essentially the same. BOTH work; they have an equal commitment to their jobs. BOTH do 50 percent of the housework. BOTH do 50 percent of the child-raising.

Note: Couples can change their relationships on the continuum. Perhaps the most typical example we see of this today is the couple who in their twenties assume a traditional couple role. In their thirties, after their children are in school, they shift to the semi-traditional role. And in their forties, after the children have left home, they become a dual career couple.

In the case of the traditional couple, the job selection decision-making process usually comes the closest to what we have already seen for individuals. The only additional complication is that the decision maker typically adds to his selection criteria a few constraints related to his perception of his spouse's needs (e.g., "She will never move outside the United States, so I won't bother to pursue non-U.S. jobs").

As we move to the right on the spectrum, the job selection decision-making process tends to become more complex. The further right we are, the more we are likely to find not one, but two decision makers, both involved in analysis and choice. The additional complexity derives from the need to somehow coordinate two different cognitive *and* emotional processes—which may be very difficult and time-consuming.

Today, most couple relationships are still traditional, or semi-traditional. But the trend over the past decade has been movement from left to right in Exhibit 28–1. And for our purposes, that means movement toward additional complexity in job-related decision making. One might reasonably wonder how well prepared most people are for the increased complexity.

Assignment

The Bradshaw case (starting below) is of a young couple involved in a job decision. Consider these questions when you study the case:

1. How is the decision being reached?
2. What are the key forces that affected the manner in which they went about reaching a decision?
3. What job do you think Jim accepted? Why?
4. How well do you think subsequent events will work out for the Bradshaws?
5. What generalizations, if any, might you draw from this case regarding job decision making for couples?

THE BRADSHAWS

Jim and Helen Bradshaw, both in their late twenties, looked tired and somewhat tense as they sat down in the apartment of a close friend on the afternoon of April thirtieth. They had felt the need to talk over their current problems with someone whom they knew to be a good listener. Jim, a second-year MBA student, had promised one company that he would let them know by May first whether he would accept their offer for full-time employment. He and Helen had spent the last few nights talking nonstop about the merits and drawbacks of the two offers they were considering. After lighting a cigarette, Jim launched into the subject.

Jim: A lot of things have been happening lately and it seems like it is happening a little bit too quickly. We have been on the merry-go-round here the last two years with Helen out working and me totally involved in school work. Now all of a sudden we're being confronted with issues that we didn't really spend enough time thinking about or discussing.

The way I see it, there are really two dilemmas. One is the personal dilemma I have regarding job choice, and that can't really be separated from the other dilemma, which is my relationship with Helen.

Helen: I think it would be helpful if we explained to Doug what the two jobs are and the difference between them, since he doesn't really know.

Jim: Well, there are two companies. One is Davidson Manufacturing Company, which is located in St. Joseph, Missouri, and . . .

Helen: Small town—30,000 people.

Jim: . . . on a continuum that would be at one extreme according to my viewpoint, as far as its being the typical MBA opportunity. It has a lot of responsibility and a lot of exposure to top-level management. They have a lot of Harvard MBAs and they push them ahead and give them many opportunities to move around. The big negative is the location. St. Joseph, Missouri, is just out in farm country and it's a small town.

Helen: It's not near a big city and it doesn't have in its immediate vicinity all the nice things about a city that we very much like; theatre, museums, galleries, restaurants, etc.

Jim: On a rational level I can say that as an MBA going to work for them I would be on the fast track and it would just be very stimulating professionally, but socially it would leave just an awful lot to be de-

Helen: Which *we* have no interest in doing and everybody there does!

Jim: The other extreme is working for Browning Corporation in San Francisco. I would start out as an auditor—an internal consultant type. I would be on my own or working with another person—which really appeals to me—but I would have to travel at least 50 percent of the time. I would be going to all their subsidiaries and operations to find out what their problems are and to make some recommendations. There would be a lot of, I guess what people would term, mechanical work to that as well. A lot of number crunching.

And yet that's a location we both like. We lived there before we came here. We enjoyed the life style out west. Our friends are out west. If we ever wanted to settle in a place, that would be it.

The reason I've said this option is toward the other end of the spectrum is that there aren't many MBAs in the company. There is some uncertainty at this point concerning what I might be doing in the future. It's not clear that in one and a half years I would get this or that type of job. The potential is certainly there, because they are growing at the same rate Davidson is. They are a larger company to begin with, which means that it might be a little faster moving, but it is so difficult to tell based on one visit. The reason Davidson is so attractive is that I worked for them last summer, or rather for one of their distributors (which is an independent business). Anyway I got to meet a lot of the people, and they got to know me and I performed very well and I guess they all liked me.

Helen: Jim's got a couple of friends here at the school who worked with them, and so when we are with them it is very easy to get carried away and become very excited about the possibilities of working for that company.

Jim: There are so many little minor pluses and minuses. You can live very well in St. Joseph, Missouri. It is very inexpensive. You can get a house comparable to something in Boston at half the price. Yet the wages there are higher or equal to Boston and New York. On the other hand, this offer on the West Coast is substantially lower in salary. Now money is not my top priority. I don't think money is that important in the short run or even in the long run. There has to be enough so we can live comfortably, but I don't think I would make a job decision based solely on that. I would make a decision based on the elements of the job.

Helen: If you were just making a decision on money, then the decision would very easily be made.

Jim: Right. I have talked to two firms in New York and one in Boston that I'll probably get offers from at higher salaries. (*Turning to Helen*) Perhaps this is a good time for you to get into the aspect of what you'd like to be doing, and I can talk about those other jobs and the cloudiness as far as my decision goes a little later.

Helen: My problem is I don't know what I want to do. I want to work and I feel a very urgent need to work but I don't have any professional expertise. I don't have any credentials. I went to college and was then married and I have worked as a secretary ever since.

Jim: And part of the reason that took place is we were moving every two years.

Helen: We were never in one place long enough for me to get into anything.

Jim: And there's always been that certainty. We knew when we got to a location that we would only be there as short as six months or as long as two years. That's been part of the problem, I guess.

Helen: But I do want to work. I don't know what I want to do, as I said. In St. Joseph, Missouri, I don't see very many alternatives. I see none in the town itself. It's all unionized and there have been layoffs left and right, and it is not a good time for someone from outside the area to come in and expect to be able to get a job. It is located about 30 miles from Greensville, which is where the University is. I suppose if I wanted to commute, I would look there for either employment at the University or consider going back to school. Neither of those options has an enormous amount of appeal to me right now. In San Francisco there are lots of options. I know several people who are in various businesses that I have some interest in. I see a couple of choices for myself out there. Some things I would like to try. I don't see any in Missouri.

Jim: Another thing about Davidson is that if you survive and do very well with the company, opportunities are pretty much in St. Joseph, Missouri. Certainly there are field operations and international operations, which would be a sidelight for a few years, but if you thought in terms of the long term, that's where we would be. The thought of that kind of scares me, because the things we like to do socially and even athleticwise just don't happen to be in the Midwest. They happen to be on the coasts. The life style itself is something we have always taken for granted because we have always lived in good places. In Georgia we lived not too far from Atlanta. We lived overseas for a couple of years in Japan, when I was in the Navy, and then the West Coast, and then Washington, D.C. These are all places we were very comfortable with—big cities, metropolitan areas, lots of activity. Of course Boston has a lot more to offer also.

Helen: I think that the closest I have ever come to living in what I would call a small-town environment is when we were in the military overseas. The American community was very close-knit and I didn't particularly like that. My idea of living in a foreign country is not spending your life on the base. So I had very few American friends over there and I had many Japanese friends. The thing I disliked about the ugly-American syndrome which went on over there was that U.S. people had nothing better to do than talk about other U.S. people, and I don't like—I am not comfortable in—an environment where everybody knows me, everybody knows when I come and go. I like the city. I have a need for that kind of privacy.

Jim: Because we have always had a lot of the good things that a big city has to offer, it's hard to decide what it is exactly that really attracts us. I did receive what I considered good professional offers in New York City, but the jungle aspect of the city just sort of overwhelmed me.

There's another company which I guess would be a compromise between the two companies we talked about earlier, and that was Johnson Comapny. It's in Chicago, which is a big city and not a bad place. The company happens to be located in the suburbs. It's not San Francisco, certainly, but it takes away the disadvantages that Davidson has, being in a small town in Missouri, because it has the restaurants, the museums, and what have you. I was really expecting to get an offer from them, and had I received an offer from them, that would have been the best of both worlds. It would have been a professional challenge on one hand, and also it wouldn't have been such a bad place to live. We have never lived in Chicago before, so it would have been an adventure for us, and we probably would have really enjoyed it. The program that they had for MBAs was very flexible. You could almost name the area you wanted to start in, and they would guarantee that you have a different job after about 6 to 12 months. There was a lot of mobility, top-management exposure, and good salaries. It just really seemed to be sort of an ideal situation. Unfortunately, I didn't quite make the final cut, and I know why—I had a good set of interviews with the exception of one person and he happened to be the person that they were looking for an MBA

to work with. He was a little bit older than everyone else, and I knew he wasn't totally impressed with me. I wasn't totally impressed with him .either. I have one trait which sometimes turns out to be a weakness. I am honest. After the day was over, someone asked me what my impression was, and I told them exactly what my impression was. I felt that at that point in the job search I fool myself when I try to fool anyone else, because it can come back and bite me in the ass. I also value very highly a person's honesty and straightforwardness, and that's why I discuss everything the way I see it. I think that's probably the way I cut my throat, although they waited until the very end until they rejected me. I suspect that I wasn't unacceptable, but there were other people that were more acceptable, so they had to wait until they had everything in.

There was another factor that added to the confusion of the job search. The company I worked for last summer was in Los Angeles and, as I said, was an independent distributor for Davidson Manufacturing. They have on the order of $15 million in sales. When the summer was over I was told by my employer, who was an HBS alumni, that he would be in a position to offer me a job. He was president of a company by the age of 36 or something like that. He was 32 when he got out of the B-School, so he didn't waste much time in going through the hierarchy. He went in as a divisional manager and a year later he was a vice-president and two years later he had his own business. He was in Boston last week, and unfortunately I didn't get to see him. I just talked to him on the phone. He saw Helen before he saw me.

Helen: And so he told me that he couldn't offer Jim a job. . . .

Jim: . . . because of the economy. He said the last nine months had been slow. So he told Helen. I was on an interview trip out in Denver. She called me up on the phone that night before I had my interview with Browning (that's where their headquarters is). . . .

Helen: I thought you'd like to know.

Jim: I'm glad you told me, because prior to that I wasn't too serious about Browning. I got rejected from Johnson at the beginning of the same week, which was last week. Johnson rejected me on Monday morning and on Thursday afternoon I found out that I wouldn't have an offer from the place in L.A. Then—this is the same day—I called Davidson because I hadn't heard from them in a month, and they told me the job I was being considered for initially at Davidson, which was assistant to this Executive Vice-President, and which I was really excited about, was being filled by someone else. So now they had something else in mind for me but they didn't know exactly what it was. I found out just last night when this other vice-president called that essentially it would be a sales rep. I would do that for six months just to learn the product, and that appeals to me. I think that would be the best way to find out about the nature of the business and their customers and deal with the people.

Helen: Well, it's almost a kick in the teeth from them, isn't it?

Jim: Well, in a sense. But then again, when I asked them last night on the phone if they didn't hire me for this job would they hire someone else, they said no, they wouldn't hire anyone. So that sort of re-built my ego a little bit by saying that they are interested in me as a long-term investment as a person. The fact that I got rejected from Johnson and the guy I worked for last summer in the same week and I didn't know what my status was has sort of weighed a little bit heavy on me. Now I am getting a little concerned that while the job in San Francisco has so many pluses, there are a lot of question marks.

Helen: Long-term question marks you mean.

Jim: Right. I must admit that the organization and the people I have met in Davidson by and large really impressed me. I got along with them, and it's just a great working environment. But then there is St. Joseph. There would always be other options—I could take no job and just pack up and go out to the West Coast or any other place.

Helen: I don't really see that as beyond the realm of possibility.

Jim: At the same time it is not something that one would like to do.

Helen: It's the riskiest option.

Jim: Right. There's enough uncertainty in our lives already. It costs a lot of money to move, so financially it would be a hardship in the short run. Of course in the long run I am sure we are talking about nickels and dimes. On the other hand, if we did go out to San Francisco, say, no matter what company I would go with, unless it was a small business, chances are that I wouldn't stay in one place.

Helen: To get ahead and have the kind of professional future that we would like, we must move. That's always been our assumption.

Jim: I think I've always enjoyed moving. I love being on the go, and adventure, and new experiences, and new challenges and not doing the same thing year after year.

That's been in my blood, but needless to say, that might change. I try to keep an open mind even now.

Helen: In me that is starting to change now. The idea of settling down and staying in one place has more appeal to me today than it used to. Maybe that's because I'm tired out—I'm moved out.

Jim: But the reason that appeals to you is that you were in a place, the San Francisco Bay area, that you really enjoyed. Since you're a little more uncertain about your professional future than I am, you feel that you have to be in a location for longer than just a year so that you can get into a job and get some experience and maybe find out some of the things you'd like to do. I don't think you could say with certainty that a profession you might get into would require that you would stay in one place forever and ever.

Helen: It might not, I'm just saying that, professional considerations aside, I think what I want to do more and more is settle down, have a house, live in a neighborhood.

Jim: That definitely has appeal, but one of my problems is that I'm not ready to say that's what I want to do. (*Pause*).

Going to San Francisco if nothing else has some very good short-term considerations from our point of view, and it could or could not have some good long-term possibilities. But when you look at Missouri, you think that it wouldn't be so bad for a couple of years. Professionally I could do very well, and yet the thought of spending 20 or 30 years in a place like that just leaves us both very cold.

Helen: I keep thinking, well you know it might only be for a year and a half and then we would move someplace else, but the fear that keeps jumping into my head is that someday I am going to wake up 40 and be in the same damn spot that I am right now and I really don't want that to happen.

Jim: I could always say, well a company like Davidson would be a great challenge and give me much more than I could handle, which would push me along and help me. Then after a couple of years if I found I didn't really like St. Joseph, Missouri, I could go somewhere else. It's a good place for corporate headhunters, so there is a lot of visibility there. Yet making a decision to do that scares me a little bit, too, because I have never done anything like that.

When I was in the military for four years, I always got my first choice and I had independent jobs so that people were not pressing their thumbs down on me all the time. I had a lot of flexibility and latitude. I was allowed to become an expert in some areas that nobody else had any detailed knowledge of. It was very rewarding and satisfying. Yet at the B-School here it has been a very painful experience. Certainly there's more work here than any place I have been before, although I am not averse to work. Most of my classmates say they view it the same way. I must admit, it's a real chore to get up in the morning at times.

Two years is a short amount of time, however. I certainly don't regret the decision, and it will be worth it to me. I probably won't realize the benefits fully until I have been gone for several years, because many of the things we acquire at the B-School are intangible. After having been here, I say maybe I'm ready to quit postponing my pleasure.

I don't mind paying my dues. I realize that whatever company I go to work for will have services I'm not totally knowledgeable about, and it will take a little bit of effort in burning some midnight oil to come up to speed and learn the politics of the organization and learn how everything flows. I think that is normal wherever one goes. I think I can be very happy in a place if I have an unpalatable job or if there are some painful things to do for a few months like working late or working on weekends. But when you put together a bad environment with bad working conditions, well, I'd rather dig ditches, I really would.

Helen: You just answered the question then.

Jim: I say that now, but my gut will be gnawing away at me when I go home tonight. I'll be thinking, now wait a minute, am I giving up an opportunity. . . . If I say no I don't want to go to Missouri, am I giving up an opportunity that I might have had otherwise?

Helen: If it were such a great opportunity, it wouldn't be this hard to make a decision, would it?

Jim: Well, probably not.

Helen: (*Looking at Doug and shaking her head.*) We seem to be going back and forth just day in and day out.

Jim: We're very happy about Davidson and that offer, and then not so happy about the other. Then the next day we'll think of San Francisco and some of the possibilities with Browning, and I guess when we do this we rationalize whichever decision we seem to be leaning toward. For instance, the other day we were looking through the St. Joseph local newspaper and looking at the houses. There were some fantastic prices and just really far-out things. We were, I don't know, trying to come up with some good things we could do there that we couldn't do elsewhere. You could play golf cheaply and play it every weekend, for example.

Helen: Somehow all of those very nice little things don't add up to having enough weight to really swing us that way.

Jim: And yet the anxiety about going the other way is that. . . .

Helen: Maybe part of the problem with the Browning job is that you don't have a clear enough picture in your mind as to where you could go with that company, whereas you do have somewhat of a clearer idea of where you would go in Davidson.

Jim: Well, that's part of it. But I'm not averse to that kind of uncertainty—that's what life's all about.

Helen: It's not just a question of uncertainty. You don't even know what options there are.

Jim: Well, I know a little bit about the options. They have a computer subsidiary and they have a leasing subsidiary which leases anything. It is a financial institution. They have many service operations like food service, catering, transportation, and things along that line. While their total sales aren't growing at the same rate that some companies' sales are going, some of their businesses are growing quite a bit. I'm certain that at some point in the future, if I decided I liked the company, I'd be given the advantage of these vacant slots. But there aren't a lot of MBAs in the company and so they look upon this institution as, you know, one of those Ivy League schools which turns out arrogant people. It demands exorbitant salaries for people who don't like to get their hands dirty. Some of it's true. They do hire MBAs, though; in fact what they call an internal audit staff is composed of 26 people evenly divided between career people and MBAs—young guys like myself who come in and go out and see all the businesses and give them a lot of ideas and yet rely on experience that the older guys have. So there is a constant turnover and the average guy maybe takes three years before he goes into a line job. The best guy probably gets out in about 18 months. Now I would consider myself as good as the rest of the competition. I could get out of some of the mundane tasks within two years. That doesn't bother me. I think I could learn an awful lot about their business and a lot about just going in and evaluating businesses.

Helen: Now you see, my impression all along has been that that was the part of the offer that you found most unpalatable. I have been thinking all along that you would just be unhappy for the first 18 months and wouldn't like what you were doing. (*Directed to Doug.*) I don't want to ask him to do that.

Jim: Well, if I was with Davidson, my dues-paying period would be shorter, probably about six months. As long as I was learning, that Browning deal wouldn't bother me at all. There is travel involved in the Browning job which would involve a month or two months in one location, where I'd be by myself. That's a little bit of a headache. On the other hand, I don't mind personally at this point in my life traveling around. I think the MBA program really prepares one to adjust to situations like that very rapidly.

We're still not addressing the problem that we as a couple, as a married couple, face. We've avoided the issue very conveniently in the past—realizing that what Helen wants to do and what is best for her growth and what is best for me might not be in the same place. We don't have any children, so that's not a factor, and we don't have aspirations of starting a family now. I still suspect that in a couple of years from now, at most, when I do well, I will be offered an opportunity and it probably won't be in San Francisco. It will probably be somewhere else. It could be in Denver, could be Boston, could be anywhere. Someone will come to me or I will go to them and say, "Hey, I want to get my teeth into a little bigger responsibility," and there will be an offer made. We have no idea what Helen will be into at that point.

Helen: And that's a problem. I don't know how to find answers short of trying a bunch of things, but I have to be in an environment where the possibilities are open so I can try them.

Jim: I realize that it would be unfair for me to expect Helen just to pack up and move wherever the company says they want to send me.

Helen: That's what we call the tag-along syndrome.

Jim: Well, we have been married six years and Helen has had to move along wherever I have gone up until now. I guess there was some hesitancy in the past. You didn't really want to come to Boston because you liked San Francisco. You even applied to Stanford, and in fact I didn't apply to Stanford, even though it probably would have been the easy way out. I probably could have found it a bit easier to get a job on the West Coast when I graduated had I been there. Harvard was unquestionably the best opportunity for me as far as graduate education, and it was really Helen who pushed me toward it.

Helen: That's what I've done all along, encouraged Jim to go after the *best* opportunity available.

Jim: And yet, up to now I haven't pushed her into anything. That is the basic difference in our personalities.

Helen: It's a big difference. It's just the whole way I was raised. I wasn't taught to think. I was always pushed—told I would do this and I would do that. I would go to college. It didn't matter where I went. Nothing mattered but that after a certain number of years the sheepskin. My parents expected that I would then get married and be a housewife just like my mother, and I didn't really quite question that or start thinking about it until the last few years. Now I'm really in a fix because I don't know what to do or how to go about finding out what I'm good at.

Jim: Well, there are two problems in that regard. The first being that I don't have that much confidence in my ability to be objective and to help Helen find out what she wants to do. I certainly don't have any training or experience. By nature, I just don't like to impose my standards or my ideals consciously on someone else, and my perception is that's what I'd be doing if I tried to suggest what Helen should do and. . . .

Helen: And I don't quite see it the same way.

Jim: In fact you see it very differently.

Helen: In fact, I would like to think that Jim would say, you know, well here's the way I see you, here's what I think you are good at, why not check out these possibilities. I want to hear something from him. I want some advice.

Jim: Based on our conversation the other day, I suspect you would also like a little bit of firmness from me, like saying, "Hey, get off your ass and go do this."

Helen: That wouldn't hurt. But that's not what I need. I know full well that nobody can make any decisions for me; I just feel that I'm not aware enough of what sorts of jobs are out there. It sounds incredibly naive, but I don't feel that I have the knowledge of what sorts of positions I could go after and I want some help in trying to find out what they are.

Jim: And since I don't go ahead and fulfill the expectations that she has for help, she looks upon me as being unconcerned, or less concerned, which isn't true.

Helen: Well yes, but you see that's the biggest difference between Jim and me. He's an extremely analytical person and I operate intuitively, almost exclusively. So you can see how he's trying at this level and I'm at another level—and it gets in the way.

Jim: In the past when I have tried to explain things to Helen, it has become very frustrating for me because on my terms she won't understand it. If I can be aware that

I should relate to her on her level then perhaps I can be persuasive, but that takes a lot of awareness and a lot of energy as well.

Helen: See, because I am such an intuitive person, I am greatly affected by my environment. If I'm not going to feel happy there, I'm not going to be happy there. I'm not going to feel comfortable or at ease. I'm not going to like it. I mean that's the only way to say it.

Jim: Why, Helen?

Helen: Well, you know when one is talking about intuitive feelings it is very difficult to say why I am not going to like it.

Jim: Since we both make decisions at a very different level, one of the things we know that happens between us is that Helen often has a tendency to overreact or to imagine bad situations as being worse than they really turn out to be, and I on the other hand tend to underestimate the badness. Many times unconsciously and unknowingly we can both make totally different assumptions in a situation. I'm trying to think of a good example that has happened recently. Well, we made a different assumption the other day and we both got upset and started arguing and there was no cause for that.

Helen: We had a conversation and I came away perfectly satisfied that I knew what was supposed to take place. Jim came away satisfied that he knew exactly what was going to take place, but we were thinking different things.

Jim: So in the case of this job decision I made a lot of assumptions about Helen that are just very far off base compared to her assumptions, especially with respect to this job search for her and this uncertainty she has about what she might be doing. So I guess Helen doesn't want to feel that her needs are being imposed on me by saying, "Well, we have to go to San Francisco because that's where I can do my thing." She doesn't want to feel guilty or responsible if I take a job that I don't consider to be the best job for me just to make her happy. Yet I don't want to say, "Hey, Helen you have to go to St. Joseph, Missouri, and live there for a while," because that would be forcing my structure on her.

So I guess there's another option. She can go to San Francisco, and I can go to St. Joseph, Missouri, which probably creates more problems in the long run than it would solve. Although we certainly have an element of independence. Last summer I spent three months on the West Coast and she stayed here most of the time because that was the best job opportunity. Now I could have stayed here and had a job that I didn't enjoy. After spending nine months at HBS

doing work I didn't enjoy I wasn't about to do that. She really couldn't have quit her job because part of the condition of her employment was that she would stay here during the summer.

Helen: Well, I accepted that job and I felt I didn't want to give it up for what was in my mind a ridiculous reason. I have a sense of responsibility about wherever I work even though it might not be the most glamorous job in the world. It was my choice to stay at work.

Jim: In that case, it was a simple decision for both of us. While I was in the Navy I was always away, so it was not a new experience to be separated. Living under the same roof 365 days a year tends to make one nonobjective at times. We all need a rest and a change of pace.

The way we come out is we don't mind sacrificing for the other person, but if you're in that other person's role the knowledge that the other one is giving up something just for you is just not acceptable. That's why if we had another job offer. . . .

Helen: Well, we don't, so that's not another possibility—two jobs or none.

Jim: Well, we can just pack up and start driving around and I can extend my job search for a while longer. (*He pauses and stares at the floor, and then lifts his head suddenly.*) The other thing that is frustrating from my point of view is that I haven't fully thought this out and it's sort of catching up to me. The circumstances are sort of forcing me to think about it. Yet to compare all our awareness of this dilemma we're in now versus what it was two months ago—is just a totally different situation. We've really sort of been complacent, I guess for too long. We can't undo that, of course, so we won't sit here and be anxious about it, but . . .

Helen: I have no doubt that I will eventually find some work which is meaningful to me and satisfying to me and that's not my real problem. My real problem. . . . Six months ago if anyone had said, "What are you going to do in June?" my answer would have been, "Well, we'll go where Jim gets a job." But I took an Interpersonal Behavior course this spring and I began to really think about me and Jim, and now I don't like the implications of simply following Jim around. But now we get down to what's more important. . . . Is it more important for me to be Jim's wife or for me to be an employed member of the work force? Since I'm only just beginning to think about the implications of both, I don't know which direction I am going in. (*Long pause.*) Work is not so important to me that I would do that at the risk of our relationship, however. . . . (*Long pause.*)

Jim:	Well, you've already said that you don't want to go to Missouri. So if I said I want to take that job because that's the best job for me, we have a problem?
Helen:	Right.
Jim:	Whereas if I take the other job, which I may be a little more anxious about myself because there is not quite as much certainty as to how or where I'll progress, then I'm giving in a little bit to you. But, I.... (*Pause.*)
Helen:	Well, I can't make the decision for you.

Jim:	(*Pause.*) I realize that . . .

On the following day, Doug stopped by Helen's office at noontime to find out what they had decided to do.

Doug:	Well?
Helen:	Jim is supposed to phone both companies at 1:00.
Doug:	And . . . ?
Helen:	(*Long pause.*) I don't know for sure. . . .

An Exercise for Couples Making Career Decisions

We hope that your analysis of the Bradshaws' decision process may have given you additional anticipatory insight into your (plural) own decision-making processes. That case may also have helped you to see another of the recurring themes of this book—namely, that all our decisions are interconnected, just as the various aspects of our lives are interconnected. Career decisions for both the Bradshaws had a significant impact on their personal lives.

If we have accomplished our goals in this chapter, you feel ready to look more carefully at your own decision-making processes. The following exercise can help you do that. Make a copy of the exercise for each of you. The instructions are self-explanatory. Work through it individually first. Then, as outlined in the exercise, meet to discuss your responses together.

You may not get all the answers or resolutions you would like from an exercise like this, but you can begin to work toward those answers and resolutions. To ignore the implications of your career or personal decisions on the lives of those around you, especially your partner, can create bitter experiences later on.

COUPLES' CAREER AND LIFE STYLE EXERCISE*

SESSION I - INDIVIDUAL PREFERENCES AND NEEDS

Each individual in a "partnership" should find a quiet period in which to sit down alone and assess his/her own preferences and needs for the future. The following form might be helpful although you should use a different format if you prefer. Assess in terms of High, Moderate or Low importance to you.

	Next 12 months			Next 3-5 yrs.		
	High	Mod.	Low	High	Mod.	Low

A. CAREER

Education or training

Work experience

Geographical location

Geographical mobility (frequency of changes, new locations)

Amount of the time traveling on assignments

Amount of time working at home (evenings, weekends)

Other — list specifics

B. LIFE STYLE

Location: Urban___ Suburban___
Rural___
Geographic locations

Residence: Rent ___ Buy___
House___ Apt. ___
Condominium___
Other___

	Next 12 months			Next 3-5 yrs.		
	High	Mod.	Low	High	Mod.	Low

Time with partner:
Activities _____

Time with family:
Having children ___
How many___
Relationship with parents

Time with friends:
Activities _____

Time for personal activities:
_____

Community involvement:
Religious group_____
Politics_____
P.T.A. _____
Cultural _____
Other (specify)_____

Vacations:
Together ___
Separately ___
Location _____
Activities_____
(e.g. mountains, beaches)

Financial arrangements:
Separate accounts
Joint accounts
Budget responsibility
Me___ Partner___ Joint ___

Children's special needs:
_____

Other, specifically:
_____

COMMENTS:

COMMENTS:

* From "Teacher's Manual," Victor A. Faux; Self-Assessment and Career Development, John P. Kotter, Victor A. Faux, Charles C. McArthur, Prentice-Hall, Inc., Englewood Cliffs, 1977, pp. 134-141. Reprinted by permission of Prentice-Hall, Inc.

Now, still working alone, fill out the same form and predict where you think your partner will come out on all of these issues. When you have finished, make a copy of your own preferences and needs and give it to your partner. DO NOT DISCUSS IT AT THIS TIME.

A. CAREER

	Next 12 months			Next 3-5 yrs.		
	High	Mod.	Low	High	Mod.	Low
Education or training						
Work experience						
Geographical location						
Geographical mobility (frequency of changes, new locations)						
Amount of the traveling on assignments						
Amount of time working at home (evenings, weekends)						
Other—list specifics						

COMMENTS:

B. LIFE STYLE

	Next 12 months			Next 3-5 yrs.		
	High	Mod.	Low	High	Mod.	Low
Location: Urban____ Suburban____ Rural____ Geographic locations						
Residence: Rent ____ Buy____ House ____ Apt. ____ Condominium ____ Other____						
Time with partner: Activities _____						
Time with family: Having children ____ How many ____ Relationship with parents						
Time with friends: Activities_____						
Time for personal activities:						
Community involvement: Religious group____ Politics____ P.T.A. ____ Cultural ____ Other (specify)____						
Vacations: Together____ Separately ____ Location____ Activities____ (e.g. mountains, beaches)						
Financial arrangements: Separate accounts Joint accounts Budget responsibility Me____ Partner____ Joint ____						
Children's special needs:						
Other, specifically:						

COMMENTS:

Session II. Examination of Partner's Needs and Preferences

Still working alone:

1. Privately study your partner's sheet and compare it with your predictions. Where were your predictions accurate? Where were you off and why? Where were you surprised, irritated, hurt, delighted? What other feelings did you experience? What does this tell you about your partner? About yourself?

2. Now put your own list beside your partner's. Where are the similarities? Where are the differences? When you come to the differences, try to be aware of what you feel about them too. (Feelings of disappointment when differences look as though they might create problems; feelings of pleasure when your needs run the same way? What else?) The intensity of your feeling reaction will give you some ideas of how important each item is to you.

3. Now go through the two sets of needs and preferences. List the differences in order of their importance to you. For instance, you want to live in the city and your partner in the suburbs. That may be much more important a choice to you because of commuting time than another difference you have about wanting to rent or buy. Or you may find that regular vacations together are less important than being sure there is one day each weekend when neither of you brings home work.

NOW PLAN A TIME WHEN YOU CAN BOTH SIT DOWN AND LOOK AT YOUR LISTS TOGETHER FOR A COUPLE OF HOURS WITHOUT INTERRUPTIONS.

Session III. Sharing Preferences and Needs

Working together:

1. Toss a coin to see who starts.

2. One of you runs through his/her list of preferences. Describe them in ways that your partner understands. If necessary, give details or explain underlying reasons. Do this *without* discussion between you. The presenter's job is to *explain*. The listener's job is to *listen* (and ask questions when they don't understand; or ask the other partner to move ahead when they have understood).

The most important thing is for each partner to refrain from telling the other what he or she *should* want!

3. Now exchange roles. (You might want to take a short break or a walk before continuing—but prefer-

ably not a martini! The pause can last an hour or a day but *not* a week—that's too long.)

The second partner now explains his/her list in the same way. What you have done so far is to surface things that are important to each of you, and explain them to each other without being interrupted (or at least not very often!). It won't be easy, because some of the things you talk about may have been lurking in the corners of your lives together for quite a while. You may have been brushing some of them under the rug in order to get to school on time, or to get that paper prepared before 2 A.M.

After each of you has shared your needs and preferences, go back and share anything relevant about your prediction of what your partner would need; and your reactions when you saw his/her list. Do this in the same presenting and listening manner as you used to describe your own list.

Session IV. Discussion and Negotiation of Preferences and Needs

Working together:

1. Now comes the time to put your prioritized list of differences together. What do each of you think is the most serious difference? Can you agree on an order in which to tackle differences? If you can't, don't let the discussion founder here. Toss a coin. Then discuss the winner's top priority item. Then move to the top item from the other partner's list. And so on.

2. If you get stuck on something and absolutely can't agree, go on to another item and come back to it later when you've each had some time to think it over.

Remember that at bottom this is a negotiating process between two independent people. If your differences have any real substance it won't be completed in a few hours. It may take quite a while to understand what some of your partner's needs and priorities mean to you; to accept that Atlanta isn't such a bad place to live, or that it really is time to decide whether or not to try for that first baby. What you will be evolving in these conversations is the next piece of your life together. Some of it will depend on things that haven't happened yet—for instance, who will invite your partner for interviews; or what you feel when your partner is offered a promotion in Boston at the very moment you've both decided to move to San Francisco. But a good deal of it you will be able to lay out together. Start soon, so that you don't find yourselves in the same dilemma as the Bradshaws at the same time that a decision needs to be made.

The process outlined here is one way to go. It has

been designed to encourage both partners to think independently and carefully about what they want and need; and to make sure that each has a chance to hear what the other has to say. Most people are able to take it from there. However, if you happen to be a couple who somehow get really deadlocked on an issue, remember that there are professionals who have had a lot of experience in working with couples who want to sort out their goals and choices more carefully.

This stage may go on for the rest of your life together!

Good Luck!

chapter

29

The Career Development Paper

Purpose

Once a person has developed a job search focus, and anticipated the job search process by working through the previous chapters, we have found it very useful to develop a document that will guide one through the actual process. We outline here a career development paper (CDP) which our students have found very useful as a guide during recruiting. The career development paper works similarly to an annual budget in a corporation, so the skills of developing it, using it, modifying it, and finishing what it outlines are very relevant to necessary organizational skills.

The career development paper is designed to help you to use your self-assessment paper—that is, to think through and to manage in an active, rigorous way the implications of that paper.

The career development paper is a nuts and bolts strategy paper that asks you to outline a job search program and to lay *specific* plans for implementing it. Our experience has been that students who carefully consider and execute the assignment and then implement its components during their job search find that process to be much less difficult than it otherwise could have been (and often is for their peers). The notebooks are *not* to be handed in with the papers. You should hand in a *copy* of your typed paper, *keeping* the original.

Content

The CDP should contain the following elements:

1. A copy of the themes list developed in your self-assessment paper. If, upon reexamination, you wish to

refine those thematic labels, you are encouraged to do so. The themes should be listed on one page and *numbered for easy reference*. Whereas the raw data from the various data-generating devices was your data base for the self-assessment paper, your themes will be your basic data base for the career development paper.

2. Implications of your themes for work and career. These implications should (1) be specific; (2) address a variety of dimensions of work; and (3) be referenced to specific themes (again to demonstrate the logic you used to construct them). Some dimensions you might wish to consider would be physical environment, interpersonal requirements, location, tasks and routines, organizational style, rewards. The logic connecting implications to themes should be clear.

3. An analysis rigorously based on your themes and implications of what career opportunities you have elected to pursue in your job search and *why*. Be sure that your assumptions are explicit and that your focus is clearly defined. Note briefly how each alternative could fit into a long term career path.

4. A statement describing the kind of life style you intend to live next year, including a justification, based on themes and implications, for that plan. I encourage you to push yourself here to think through the variety of life style issues we have raised throughout the course and at the same time to be realistic. You may wish to include your personal definition of ''success,'' a typical intended weekly schedule, and expected financial allocations.

5. A *detailed* action plan for your job search for the coming year. *What* will you do? Calendar *whom* you will visit, contact. *When*? *Where* will you go? *What* will you want to learn? *How* will you learn it?

What is your time frame/schedule? How will you manage your personal life and school work? These issues (and others) should be addressed carefully. The action plan should be justified clearly by your themes and implications and should consider the topics raised in the career development half of the course. We encourage you to review this plan several times asking yourself these questions: "What am I assuming or taking for granted? Is that reasonable?" and then to be very explicit about the answers.

If you have a job or are not looking this spring. Some of you have already accepted jobs for next year or are in joint programs that will keep you off the job market next spring. Those of you deferring your entry to the job market for a year should write the paper as assigned. For those who have already accepted a job, the content of the paper is altered slightly.

A. Write section 3 as a *detailed* justification of your job next year in light of your themes and implications. How well does it fit? What difficulties do you expect to encounter? Specifically, (who, what, how, when, where) how will you manage the joining up process?

B. Substitute for section 5 a discussion of your long-term career strategy (based on themes and implications) and of how the job you have accepted fits into that plan.

Format

Your CDP must be typed. *Maximum* length is 25 pages. Hand in *two copies. Keep the original* for yourself. Do *not* hand your notebook in. Do not put your papers in a notebook or cover. Staple in the upper left corner.

Criteria for a Good Career Development Paper

1. Logic of connections between themes and implications

2. Logic of connections between themes/implications and jobs to pursue

3. Logic of connections between themes/implications and intended life style

4. Detailed and specific action plan with attention given to the issues raised in the CD half of course (focus, correspondence, interviewing, support systems, company visits, coping, choosing, and joining up)

5. Reasonable length

6. Clarity of communication

7. You may wish to include various forms you will use to help you organize your job search [contact log, interview questions (tied closely to and referenced to themes and implications), company research form (again, based on themes and implications), list of target companies, a linking chart (a matrix with themes and implications down one side, life style aspects or job demands across the top and comments in the cells), and/or a typical weekly schedule during the second-semester job search (have you realistically allocated enough time to implement your action plan?)].

Assignment

We have included here a copy of Lauren Davis' career development paper so you can see what one might look like and be able to see its strengths and weaknesses. Read through it and be able to identify what it does well and what could be improved. How will you improve on this design when you write yours? What feedback would you give to Lauren? Are there any cautions you would pass on to her?

LAUREN DAVIS: CAREER DEVELOPMENT PAPER

"It is a capital mistake to theorize before one has data."

"These are much deeper waters than I had thought."

Self-Assessment Themes

1. I work best with positive reinforcement and support.
2. I enjoy being with people.
3. I enjoy change and a fast pace.
4. I am happiest when I am challenged/growing in a job.
5. I do not enjoy taking orders or working for strong authority figures.
6. I learn best by direct experience/involvement.
7. I have very few close friends and confide in few people.
8. The people I like best are smart and strive to better themselves.
9. Material comforts are important to me.
10. Independence is important to me.
11. I prefer a team-oriented environment.
12. Status and prestige are important to me.
13. Owning a horse, riding, and showing are important to me.
14. I enjoy getting organized and work better when I am organized.
15. I place a high value on reliability and honesty.
16. I enjoy teaching and persuading others.
17. I am competitive and like to win.
18. I enjoy athletics.

Implications of Self-Assessment Themes

Professional Aspect

Cognitive:

1. I need to wrap my arms around a project and totally immerse myself rather than reflect or conceptualize (6,14).

Interpersonal:

2. I will enjoy a job which requires interaction with other individuals and which requires a strong "team" orientation (2,5,11,16).
3. The peers with whom I would like to work will have a high degree of commitment and a strong desire to produce superior output (8,15).

Environment:

4. I would not enjoy working in a cluttered or messy setting, or in an office with poorly organized files and research data (14,15).

Routines:

5. I will enjoy a job which requires (on a regular basis) no more than 50 hours per week (2,3,13,18).
6. I would like to spend a maximum of one hour (total) commuting to work each day (9,13,18).

Organizational Style:

7. I will enjoy a position in which frequent feedback is possible (1).
8. I prefer to work in positions which do not require close supervision (5,6,10).
9. I want to work in an organization which rewards excellence in a timely manner, by increasing my level of responsibility (3,4,17).
10. Recognition by my peers and supervisor that my job, opinions and efforts are valuable to the organization is important to me (1,12,17).

Tasks:

11. I prefer to work on projects which are short term in nature (1,3).
12. I will be happiest in a job in which I will be given immediate responsibility (6,10,14).
13. I would enjoy a moderate amount of traveling to visit and work with clients (2,3).
14. I would enjoy a position which involved selling or persuading a client or a fellow employee (1,16,17).

(continued)

Implications of Self-Assessment Themes (*continued*)

Social Aspect

15. I want to live in a community in which there is a sizable young professional population (2,8).

16. I would like to live in a city which offers recreational facilities such as racquetball courts, golf courses, and water sports (either lakes or the ocean) (3,18).

17. I would like to have enough land to stable a horse or live very close to a stable in the country (13,18).

Material Aspect

18. I would like to earn a starting salary of at least $30,000 (9,17).

Family Aspect

19. Bill's support in a new environment will be very important since he is primary in my support system (1,7).

Emotional Aspect

Satisfaction/Self-Esteem:

20. I do not want a job that appears to be a step backward (4,12).

21. I am averse to high-risk situations. I do not take failure well (1,12,16,17).

Variety:

22. I would like to live close to a university so that I may have the flexibility to return to school when Bill and I begin to raise a family (3,4,10).

Note: Numbers in parentheses refer to supporting themes.

Careers I Intend to Pursue

I. *Advertising*
I am interested in a consumer goods-oriented agency.

A. *Why?*

1. *Link with Themes and Implications*

(i) Account executives are involved in an account's total marketing mix and must become totally immersed in information relating to the product (1).*

(ii) Advertising management requires a lot of interaction with clients, account team, creative staff (2).

(iii) Since this field is very competitive, the peers with whom I would work would likely be top-notch thinkers (3).

(iv) Advertising agencies actively compete for accounts, which fosters loyalty and a team concept within the firm (2).

(v) In order to "get inside" the reams of demographics, psychographics, media statistics and media models associated with a product, an account executive must have superior organizational skills (4).

(vi) Account executives do not as a rule put in excessive hours of overtime (5).

(vii) Traveling is often involved in order to meet with a client (13).

(viii) "Winning" an account is an immediate form of feedback which would be satisfying to me (1).

(ix) Constant interaction with several levels of managers within an agency and a client firm provides continual feedback to the account executive (7).

(x) Advertising agencies, very much like consulting firms, have an "up or out" attitude. This assures the superior performer of commensurate recognition and reward (9,10).

(xi) Profit margins are small for advertising agencies, so marginal performers are not permitted to remain. I would infer that the opinions of advertising executives are highly regarded, as each individual must "carry their weight" in order for the firm to keep costs in control (10).

(continued)

(xii) While many accounts are long-term clients, advertising campaigns are continually dissected and altered. Working on an account consists of tailoring various pieces of the marketing mix to the constantly changing objectives and goals of a client (11).

(xiii) Most agencies assign a new assistant account executive to a small account immediately (12).

(xiv) Agencies must compete with other firms for an account by "selling" or persuading via an advertising presentation. After winning the account, the executive must continue to be effective in persuading the client to accept an advertising plan (14).

2. *Other Influences*

  (i) Enjoyed advertising management course 2nd year. Excelled in advertising projects assigned during the semester. (B + , A)

  (ii) First-year marketing was my favorite course.

  (iii) Exceptionally high score on Strong-Campbell Interest inventory for advertising executive.

  (iv) Believe I have the personality to work well with a client. I am flexible, open to suggestions, and I am a good speaker in front of a group.

B. *Why Not?*

1. *Link with Themes and Implications*

  (i) Mean salary offers for Darden students: 1980: $20,666: 1981: $23,000. These do not meet my salary expectations (18).

  (ii) Advertising agencies are not recession-proof. Job security is only moderate (21).

  (iii) The "up or out" policy could be quite serious if my performance was rated unacceptable. (This is unlikely, however, as I have exceeded company expectations in every previous job.) (21)

  (iv) Since I do not enjoy losing, the loss of an account with which I was involved would be disturbing (21).

2. *Other Influences*

  (i) Only two students were hired from Darden last year by advertising agencies.

  (ii) Due to the economy there may be a limited amount of hiring this year by advertising agencies.

C. *Long-Term Career Pattern*

Beginning as an assistant account executive and moving up in an advertising agency provides one with the opportunity to get "hands-on experience," eventually manage other employees (as the Account Executive), and finally manage the client and the success of the agency. An advertising agency partner is the kind of general manager I would like to be. I would like to work in a *service*-oriented (people) organization which provides a service or product I thoroughly understand and enjoy.

II. *Consulting*

I am interested in a small to medium-sized regional consulting firm.

A. *Why?*

1. *Link with Themes and Implications*

  (i) I enjoy working on short to medium run projects that have definite beginning points.

  (ii) A large amount of interaction with the client is necessary, which I would enjoy (2,14).

  (iii) The individuals employed by consulting firms are usually top notch. Small firms cannot afford mediocrity (3).

  (iv) Consulting requires systems. Organizing data in a useful format, which may be duplicated in order to prevent reinventing the wheel (4).

  (v) Since consulting jobs are relatively short-term in nature and require interaction with the client and your peers, my need for feedback would be served (7).

  (vi) Independence and responsibility are important in a consulting firm. Employees are expected to take the ball and run with it—which I would like (8,12).

  (vii) Regional consulting firms have an up and out policy, just like the big boys—which is a positive feature (9,10).

  (viii) Regional firms also look for a longer-term commitment from their employees, so the long hours are not so long and the traveling not so intense as the larger firms (5,13,21).

  (ix) I have traveled all my life and enjoy it. I can see a significant tradeoff in my life involving travel. While I want to live in a community for an extended period of time (finally), traveling in my work would help to alleviate my ingrained desire to move every few years (13).

  (x) I enjoy analyzing problems, and persuading and presenting my viewpoints, which consulting requires (14).

(continued)

The Career Development Paper **329**

(xi) A regional firm would allow Bill and me to satisfy our desires to live in a moderate-sized city (see city analysis).

(xii) Consulting is a lucrative profession. This, while not a priority, is important to me. There is also prestige associated with this profession; another plus (18,20).

2. *Other Influences*

(i) Excelled in A & C in both writing and speaking.

(ii) Scored extremely high on Campbell Interest Inventory in the category of public speaking.

(iii) As an undergraduate English major and a professional editor, my writing abilities are excellent. Since reports are a necessary and important part of consulting, I would be able to capitalize on my writing skills.

B. *Why Not?*

1. *Link with Themes and Implications*

(i) I am frequently frustrated by my inability, due to time constraints, to produce the quality of work which I would like. Consulting jobs do not end when it is convenient for the consultant, but when it is convenient for the client (1,21).

(ii) Consulting may require more time than I would like to invest in my career. It may also require more traveling than I would be willing to accept. It is important that my marriage not be disrupted by my career (5,13,19).

(iii) Having a horse is important to me. Consulting may require irregular hours which would not allow me to pay proper attention to a horse.

2. *Other Influences*

(i) It was very difficult to join a regional consulting firm without more experience than I have and without an area of specialization.

C. *Long-Term Career Pattern*

Consulting is not necessarily an end in itself to me. I am very interested in learning more about a variety of industries to which I have never been truly exposed. I would enjoy establishing my own consulting firm in the future in a marketing-related field. I believe experience in an established firm is essential before I even think about undertaking such a venture. The two long-run directions that I see consulting leading to are as follows:

Initial Consulting

Gain expertise in one or more fields.
Gain experience with clients and the organizational framework.

Marketing Function

Experience provides steppingstone to interesting marketing position.

Experience value in establishing direct-mail venture.

Private Consulting

Establish private practice.

---

*Numbers in parentheses refer to implications.

Life Style 1982–1983

A. Location

Factors I have taken into consideration:

1. Background:

Since this is a joint decision, I believe that Bill's life style is significant.

Lauren	*Bill*
Lived in 11 cities in 7 states and in Germany.	Lived in small town in NC (population 5,000) for 18 years, 24 years in all in NC.
Moderate family bond in Florida.	*Very* close family bond.
No strong attachment to any one area.	Strong attachments to North Carolina.

2. My Preferences: Evaluation of Three Cities in Which I Have Lived

Likes	*Dislikes*

Washington, D.C., & Surrounding Area (1972–1974, 1978–1980)

Likes	*Dislikes*
Theaters, cultural events	Crime rate
Shopping malls	2-hour commute
Museums, historical attractions	High cost of living
Aesthetics (in certain areas)	Traffic
Washington *Post*	Cold atmosphere of people
Superior local TV news	Small apartment
	Difficult to meet friends
	Poor quality of pools
	Size

Charlottesville, VA: (1974–1978, 1980–1982)

Likes	*Dislikes*
Sports facilities	Limited shopping availability
ACC basketball	
People my age	
Size	
Little traffic	
Landscape	
Chris Greene Lake	
Monticello, Law, Rotunda	

Atlanta, GA (Summer 1981)

Likes	*Dislikes*
River rafting	Traffic
Shopping malls	Stark landscape
Friends there	Crime rate
	Difficult to meet people

3. Decisions

Based on the previous data I believe I would be happiest in a moderate-sized city, no smaller than Charlottesville and not as large as Atlanta or Washington, D.C. Since Bill has strong ties to North Carolina, and I have enjoyed the mid-Atlantic region, we plan to focus on moderate-sized cities in North Carolina as well as Virginia, South Carolina, Florida, and Texas. The following chart represents the method by which I plan to rate cities, according to the characteristics that are important to me. A factor of 1 to 10 has been assigned to each value item in order to weigh those criteria that are most important to me.

(continued)

Analysis of Cities

Criteria: Rank criteria from .1 to 1.0. Multiply factor x ranking = total.

City: _____ _____ _____ _____

Cultural events (5)
Shopping availability (6)
Museums, historical sites (3)
Sports facilities (7)
ACC basketball (4)

Water sports (8)
Aesthetics (6)
Media (news) (2)
Friends (1)
Low crime rate (9)

Moderate COL index (8)
Minimal commuting (9)
Moderate traffic (8)
Friendly atmosphere (10)
Young professional segment (6)

Appropriate size (7)
University in area (4)

Total Weighted Score: _____ _____ _____

B. Home

I would like to live in a community in which Bill and I could become friends with neighbors our own age and with similar interests.

I hope to live outside the city close to a stable or in an area where I could board a horse near our house.

I am hoping that Bill and I can afford to buy a house so that we won't be required to move again for some time. (I am tired of moving.)

I would like to invest in new living room furniture also, along with a few other furnishings to fill out our home.

C. Recreation

I would like to join a racquetball club and a country club so that Bill and I can play racquetball and golf, and meet friends.

I would also like to resume riding lessons and enter a show within a year. Owning a horse will require a lot of my spare time, but I think that I want a horse enough to schedule my time suitably.

D. Vacations

I would like to take two vacations a year (short), in the summertime and at Christmas.

Within the next 4 to 5 years I would like for Bill and I to travel to Europe for an extended vacation.

I would also like to charter a boat & sail in the Carribbean with one or two other couples.

E. New Experiences

In the future I would like to learn to fly.

I would also like to learn to water ski and sail.

When Bill and I have children (5 years), I believe that I will want to stop working for a short period of time. I may wish to return to school (Law School perhaps).

Hurdles I Recognize, and That I Plan to Work on Consciously in the Joining up Process

Themes and Implications	Hurdles
T8,3	I have trouble working for individuals less capable than myself.
T2,10	I am affected by the "joining up blues" and wish to minimize anxiety.
T3	Getting "up to speed" is a frustrating and slow process which I must recognize from the outset.
4	I may become frustrated at the lack of organization in the office.
Writ In	I have difficulty asking secretaries to perform their function due to:
	Guilt. Reflected in my self-assessment that I felt the position was demeaning.
	My effort to "do it all."
	Inexperience. I have never had a secretary work for me directly.

Questions to Ask Interviewers

Implications	Job Information
5	1. How many hours do people holding similar jobs work?
2	2. How much time is spent working alone? in groups?
11	3. Are the tasks involved long-term or short-term in nature?
3, 10	4. What are the backgrounds of the people with whom I'll be working?
8, 12	5. How much independence and responsibility will I receive?
9	6. Who will I be reporting to? How did that individual reach that position and how long did it take?
1	7. How will my performance be measured? How often? Possible results?
9	8. What type of advancement opportunities are available in the short run and long run?
1	9. How much information will be at my disposal in order to perform effectively?
T3	10. Will any travel be involved?
9, 10, 11	11. How long do individuals normally remain in this position before being promoted?

	Company Information
2, 3	1. Is there any reorganization impending which may change the nature of my responsibilities or the individual for whom and with whom I will work?
3	2. What are the backgrounds of the people with whom I'll be working? How many MBAs?
9, 10	3. Where does the company, SBU, division see itself headed in the next year? 5 years and beyond?
2	4. Do employees socialize outside of work?

	Community
6	1. How long does it take the average employee to commute to work? What are the ranges?
13	2. What portion of the population in this community is between 25 and 40?
15	3. How long is the commute to the countryside?
14	4. How are the recreational facilities (golf, racquet clubs)?
2, 13, 14	5. Are individuals in the company active in community events?

Schedule

Dec. 22–Jan.

Write to Chambers of Commerce of selected cities requesting information on housing, demographics, community events, civic events.

Examine geographic index, Standard & Poors *Register of Corporations,* Dun & Bradstreet, to determine what firms within my career interests are located in those cities.

Research advertising agencies in the *Standard Directory of Advertising Agencies.*

Use the *Business Readers Guide* to read extensively about advertising and consulting.

Compile listing of regional consulting firms and advertising & consulting firms.

Compose letters to those in geographic areas of interest asking many of the questions I have listed to ask recruiters (see list later in paper).

February

Narrow choices based on criteria outlined in paper based on research, discussions with AH and SH (both worked in advertising agencies), phone calls to alumni who may be of help, responses from targeted alumni whom I wrote letters to.

Compose and mail letters (early in Feb.) to targeted regional consulting firms expressing interest in employment.

Follow-up letters with calls and visits.

March

Visit cities of interest.

Follow up on contacts with regional consulting firms.

Arrange to visit firms of interest; continue with interviews; keep up log on research, interviews, evaluations.

April

Request organization chart.

Request background materials on the job I will be performing.

Research on type of product or account I will be working on.

Contact a real estate agent to send information and begin search process for a house.

Obtain a copy of a phone book to become familiar with recreational facilities, shopping facilities, stables, parks.

Obtain city map to determine prime areas in which Bill and I would like to live based upon our social and recreational interest and our wish to minimize commuting time.

May

Wrap things up—RELAX!

COMPANY RESEARCH

COMPANY: _____

TYPE OF BUSINESS: _____

SIZE ($): _____

CORPORATE HQ: _____

BRANCHES: _____

(locations) _____

ORGANIZATIONAL _____

STRUCTURE: _____

(centralized,particip.) _____

_____

GENERAL INFORMATION: _____

(continue on back) _____

_____

_____

_____

_____

_____

_____

_____

_____

_____

_____

_____

_____

_____

RECENT CHANGES/PROBLEMS: _____

_____

_____

FURTHER RESEARCH _____

NECESSARY: _____

_____

_____

```
CONTACTS

DATE:
COMPANY:
CONTACT:
DISCUSSED: _____
_____
_____
_____
_____
_____
_____
_____
_____
_____
_____
_____
_____
_____
_____
_____
_____
_____

FOLLOW-UP: _____
_____
_____
_____
_____
_____
_____

DATE FOLLOW-UP
COMPLETED:
```

POST – INTERVIEW

DATE: _____   FIRST INTERVIEW: _____
COMPANY: _____   SECOND INTERVIEW: _____
COMMENTS: _____
_____
_____
_____
_____
_____
_____
_____
_____
_____
_____
_____
_____
_____
_____
_____

INTENDED FOLLOW UP: _____
_____
_____
_____
_____
_____
_____
_____
_____
_____
_____
_____

CALL BACK-EXPECTED?
DATE EXPECTED?

30

Managing the Joining Up Process

The change from student to employee is, in most instances, a great one. Many people, especially those with little or no full-time work experience, tend to underestimate the size and nature of this change. They enter the job with very unrealistic expectations, based mostly on their student experiences. This leads to inappropriate behavior, which sometimes alienates others or is just ineffective at accomplishing given tasks. The end result for the individual is frustration and disappointment.

The Differences between Student and Employee

Consider for a moment a few of the major ways in which the environment of a student and that of a full-time employee differ:

1. *Bosses.* A student at any one point in time will have four, five, or six "bosses" (teachers), who usually change every four months, and who are often selected by the student. An employee usually has one boss, sometimes for years, with little if any influence over the choice of that superior. These different situations make for very different superior-subordinate dynamics. New workers sometimes continue to behave as if their boss were a professor whom they can ignore, or at worst, get rid of in a few months. Such behavior causes obvious problems.

2. *Feedback from superiors.* A student learns to expect brief, quantitative performance evaluations (grades) on numerous specific occasions throughout the year. Such a person will often get written feedback on his or her work also. An employee, on the other

hand, may *never* get any concrete feedback from superiors outside of pay raises or promotions. It is not unusual for new workers to feel that they are working in a vacuum and that the organization is at fault for not giving them more feedback.

3. *Time span.* A student learns to think in terms of time cycles of one or two hours (a class), one week (after which a sequence of classes repeats itself), and four months (a semester, when classes change). The time span of an employee can be as short as a few hours (in some production/operating jobs) or as long as many years (in some planning jobs). More important, the time cycle can change on the job, often leaving the new employee confused and disoriented.

4. *Magnitude of decisions.* A business student often gets used to making a number of major decisions (hypothetically) every day. At least at first, the new employee will rarely make any major decisions in his or her job. This often leads to feelings of being underused or ignored.

5. *Speed of change.* Because of the pace of academic life and the number of major innovations and changes students are encouraged to consider, they often develop highly unrealistic expectations concerning the ease and quickness of making changes in the real world. Discovery of the realities is often quite frustrating and depressing.

6. *Promotion.* A student with a master's degree and no full-time work experience has lived in an environment where promotion occurred once every 12 months—19 promotions in 19 years. It is no wonder that when a student takes a job five levels below the president, others often complain that "the young hotshot seems to want to be president in just a few years.''

7. *The nature of problems.* Schools often carefully select problems that can be solved in a short period of time using some method or theory that is being taught. Such a process is "efficient" by many educational standards. New workers often find it incredibly frustrating when the problems they are given are not as neat and solvable and the information needed for a decision is not available.

We could go on, but the point should be clear by now.

Unrealistic Expectations

Individuals also create a slightly different kind of unrealistic expectation through a poor assessment of themselves and the job while job hunting. The benefits of the assessment processes described in this book go far beyond the job decision. The very process of systematically assessing yourself, your future organization, and your job helps create more realistic expectations about what your initial experiences will be like in that job. More realistic expectations lead to fewer disappointing surprises and to more intelligent, adaptive, problem-solving decisions on your part.

Phil Hammer, for example, learned through his self-assessment how much he tended to overlook detail. He learned through his job assessment that his new job would require some (not a lot of) attention to certain types of detail. When he started work, he took specific actions to avoid a potential problem. First, he managed to rearrange his secretarial assignment so that he was assigned a person who was very detail-oriented. Second, he explained his "problem" to his secretary, and requested her as a major aspect of her responsibility to keep track of details for him. Finally, he made it a habit to carry a note pad with him at all times and forced himself to make himself notes so that he wouldn't overlook things. After 12 months on the job, Phil had not created one single significant problem because of his personal "weakness."

Regardless of the source, inaccurate expectations cause problems for recent graduates. They cause poor performance, disappointment, frustration, and low morale. In some cases, the organization concludes that the inappropriate behavior reflects a poor employee selection on their part, and the person is let go. In some cases, feeling "had" by the organization for not being warned about what was to come, the employee quits. In still other cases the problems are overcome, but seldom without leaving some bad feelings all around.

Managing One's Own Joining Up

Perhaps one of the most lethal expectations of recent graduates is that, in effect, "It is the organization's responsibility to make sure that the new employee gets the orientation and training needed to be able to do his or her job." Some organizations do try systematically and quickly to help all new employees get "up to speed." They have "orientation programs," "training programs," and "special first assignments." But very few companies do even a fair job of making sure that all new people get the specific orientation, training, and help they need to get "up to speed" quickly and efficiently.

Most people who have an effective, relatively trouble-free year after leaving school explicitly or implicitly take responsibility for their own "joining up." Regardless of whether or not their organization has programs for new people, these people systematically take actions to help themselves get "on board." They recognize that if they don't take the initiative and something goes wrong, they will probably have to suffer the consequences.

In assuming responsibility for their own joining up, people typically take a variety of actions both before

Exhibit 30–1
Actions That Can Help a Person
Get Up to Speed in a New Job

BEFORE STARTING WORK

1. Get on the organization's mailing list.
2. Get your new boss's secretary to send you copies of memos, etc., that you would receive if you had already started work.
3. Request an organization chart and a book of pictures of employees (if one exists) and start learning names and faces.
4. Subscribe to the local paper in the town or city where you will be working.
5. Write to the Chamber of Commerce and real estate agents for information on housing, schools, etc.
6. Open a local bank account.

AFTER STARTING WORK

1. Invite people to lunch to get to know them.
2. Get to know the secretaries (great sources of information).
3. If athletically inclined, join some of the organization's teams (a good way to form relationships informally).
4. Sit down and have a long talk with your boss regarding what he or she expects of you.

---

they start work and immediately afterward (see Exhibit 30-1). While most students do virtually nothing between the day they accept a job offer and the day they show up for work to help their period of adjustment from school to work, others do a number of useful and practical things. By requesting an organization chart and a book of employee pictures (if available), for example, you can start to learn the names and faces of people you will be working with. Knowing who's who, of course, can be enormously helpful to a new employee. It's much easier to do this in a leisurely way over a two- or three-month period instead of trying to learn names and faces in the first few weeks of work, when you are trying to learn so many other things too. As a general rule, the more that you can do before starting work to relieve the burden of your first few weeks on the job, the fewer problems you will face in your first year out.

A variety of actions that people sometimes take once they start work are designed primarily to assist their joining up. By sitting down and having a fairly long and detailed talk with one's boss regarding what he or she expects, for example, you can help minimize the probability that you will inadvertently violate those expectations. Disappointing, surprising, or annoying your new boss during your first few months on the job can prove to be a major impediment, since your boss is usually the key person who can help you during that period or block your way.

Different people will no doubt prefer different specific tactics to help them manage the joining up process. We encourage you to prepare as much as you can for work *before* you walk through the front door on your first day on the job.

Assignment

Read Cyrus Walker: "Making the Transition" (starting below). Develop from it a list of the things you think you will have to deal with in making the transition from school to work. How will you deal with them?

CYRUS WALKER: MAKING THE TRANSITION

In the spring of 1982, Cyrus Walker graduated from the Darden Graduate School of Business at the University of Virginia. A year later, Cyrus reflected on what it was like for him to move from school to work.

Being in School after Accepting a Job Offer

This is just to give you a feel of some of the things that occur after making a decision, some more practical things that may appear very basic to some people, but which become very relevant.

For instance, the man I was negotiating with called me up one Friday and said he'd get back to me on Monday. I got a call from my alumnus contact on Sunday telling me that my negotiating contact had been fired and that now he, the alumnus, would be doing the negotiating. I found that very uncomfortable. So my contact within

the firm was down to an alumnus from the school, who said a senior manager would call me on Monday. He didn't. More anxious moments. He finally called me late Tuesday, explained what had happened with the other guy, and that the offer that he had made would stand and stand alone without any further negotiation. Any ambiguous things like benefits, vacation, moving expenses, starting date, etc., would be handled by the Personnel Department. My response was, I would prove to him that I was worth what I had been asking for, and that I was happy to be joining such a fine firm. The Personnel Department sent down an information package later explaining what was going to happen and that helped.

I made my decision by mid-April, and a ton of bricks came off my shoulders. I felt good. I had done all I could to make the right decision, and I got real determined that I was going to implement it. And it's a good thing I did because not all things were going to go my way. Some may

This case was prepared by Associate Professor James G. Clawson as a basis for class discussion rather than to illustrate effective or ineffective handling of a career situation. © 1983 by the Sponsors of the Colgate Darden Graduate School of Business Administration, the University of Virginia, Charlottesville, Virginia. UVA case OB-255.

have a difficult transition from school to work, but even if you have an easy transition, there are going to be adjustments along the way. Without a mental attitude that you are going to make this thing work, you know, it will be hard.

The basic question was, "Okay, I've made the decision and I'm going to do it. Now what?" The first thing that came to my mind was to enjoy the rest of the year at school. All my friends were there. I had been around these people for two years, and we only had four to six weeks remaining. It was a unique period to just take time to go out, to have the parties, to go to the mountains, whatever. I realized it was going to be very difficult to get these people back together again.

Finals were approaching; I had a few group projects to finish, but I had finished my term project early. I remember being very busy during that time. There were a lot of things to do. At the same time, I was comfortable. I think you reach the point that the pressure has been resolved, and you really have a chance to enjoy. It was a real golden time for us to do all of the things we hadn't been doing for the past two years. After this year, after this season, you realize that you won't be able to see Monticello, or the Blue Ridge, or Ralph Sampson dunk for UVA. Believe me, it takes a lot more time and energy to do those things and keep up, but that's what I did, and I really looked at it as a big plus.

We had a lot of parties. We had the softball game with the sales class. We got together as a group and went out to the lake and just had a lot of cook-outs. There are moments you get depressed. You are trying to enjoy the groups of people that you have gone through this experience with and all of a sudden the realization is that you won't be seeing them anymore.

The B-Bar Ball

I got engaged the night of the "B-Bar Ball" two weeks before graduation. My girlfriend had been in on the job search and choice process all along, so that my job selection was not a surprise to her. Anyway, we had to wait until October to set a date for the wedding because of my training program and the fact that my permanent assignment wasn't going to be made until then.

So, that led to something else. With a significant other involved, as soon as the decision is made, if they're going to work, things should start rolling right then and there. They should make their contacts in that city. I had one employer offer to help out in any way they could to find a job offer for my fiancee. Your significant other needs to contact friends in the area, firms to work for, maybe even use some of the resources in the school to get the job search rolling. It is a virtual

time bomb sitting there waiting to go off if nothing is done. You come home from being all hepped up about your job, and they are still struggling to find a job. That is a difficult transition to handle, and it can really try your personal relationships.

As an example, I had a friend whose wife was a teacher. If she hadn't gotten her applications in early, right after he had made his decision, she would not have been considered for employment. These are the deadlines that can pass that you never think about. You've made your decision, but now there are other deadlines that people have to look at. This is a very individualized process. You can't rely on your classmates' timetables or you can run out of time.

So we were at the "B-Bar Ball." Someone had been up in New York the week before and was telling about the apartment crunch: "Hey, it's going to take a lot longer than you think, there is a very tough real-estate market up there." I'm sitting there and all of a sudden I realized, Hey, you better get on the stick! I was having a good time with school over, but I realized I had to go to New York.

We had plans to go to the beach for the week between the B-Bar Ball and graduation. There were three or four people who were getting a house, and we were going to go and relax. We canceled our plans, although without this jolt we probably would've gone. That was what REALLY started the transition period for me. It was like, BOOM, you better get a roof over your head.

So, I got REAL determined to make the transition work. It had been a long process, putting a lot of work into the job search, and I'd made my decision. Then it was time to move on and DO it. I had to get myself psyched up while I was still at school that I was going to MAKE this thing work. It's getting the attitude built up that you've made a decision, and you're going to MAKE it work so that when times get tough, you'll know you've thought about it and you'll know why you're there. Without that attitude, and I've talked to a lot of people who graduated the same time I did, it becomes very difficult and you have a lot of second thoughts.

For me, the first test came in my search for an apartment in New York. I spent the week between the B-Bar Ball and graduation in New York, and that was a tremendous eye-opening experience. I realized that it wasn't as easy in New York as it was in Charlottesville, where you came for the day and looked at three or four vacant apartments, picked one based on what you liked and what you could afford, and decided. In New York, there is a very tight real estate market. And there are all different kinds of neighborhoods and all different kinds of price ranges and all kinds of conveniences and things to be weighed. And, it is very difficult. At the end of the first week, nothing was resolved and I came back to Virginia for graduation.

Right after graduation, I went back to New York. I tried to settle this thing, and finally it got to be the end of the second week and on the last day I decided I had to find SOMETHING, so I took a furnished summer sublet. Even then it wasn't resolved because it wasn't permanent. But it was a good way to look at the situation, actually. Especially in a city like New York where there are a lot of different neighborhoods, and they offer different things, different commutes, different stores, different people. If you don't know the city, you learn quickly, but it also is good to just live up there on a three-month sublet deal and get a feel for where you want to live.

After School before Joining

The funny thing is that there was a great contrast within the school. Some people were going to take off the whole summer, going to go to Europe; they don't worry about moving. Others might start the day after graduation, and boom, they have to be up in the City. If you are in that circle of friends who are going to Europe, moving out and starting in late August, then there you are, watching them pack to go off. . . .

I returned to Charlottesville after lining up the New York sublet on a Tuesday. On a Wednesday, one of my friends said that the air fares to the West Coast were the cheapest they were ever going to be. Thursday, we were on a plane to the West Coast planning a twelve-day vacation.

It was the first time we had been to the West Coast. It was a fantastic trip; it met and exceeded all expectations that I ever had. I had never been to the West Coast, but knew two or three other couples from Darden who were going cross country, all doing the same routine. The people who did that seemed to have a much healthier attitude toward work when they finally started. I have pictures of, unbelievable pictures of, five or six rolls, 200 pictures, of the trip that are sitting there on the mantel. It was a nice transition from school back to the city and starting a job. So . . . I took a two-week vacation, you might say, on the spur of the moment.

We only had about $1,000 free cash in my checking account. We didn't have the money—did it on plastic. I'm still paying for the trip; I will be paying for the trip for a long time. When I came out of school, I was heavily in debt. I was as leveraged as I ever want to be. I was on loans; I had stretched financially even to be able to come back to school. I figured it out that, overall, I have, including undergraduate school loans, $19,000 or so to pay back. And I had no cash, very little cash. The trip to California cost us about $1,000. I usually do not use my credit cards. I'm a guy that charges on them and then pays them off, but I used them then. However, the trip was worth it.

There were some financial surprises. First, there was the brokerage fee. If you go through a broker to find an apartment in New York the buyer pays a fee of usually 15% of the annual rent. The company should pick that up; you've got to negotiate hard to make sure that the firm picks that up. You've also got to put down a month's rent for a security deposit, if you're lucky, possibly two months if you're not, and then you've got to have your first month's rent. So, you're looking at about $3,000 on day one in a city like New York. Now, I don't know how many people have $3,000 laying around, but I sure as hell didn't. I was fortunate the firm picked up the broker's fee, but I still had to do the embarrassing thing which was to borrow from my parents. I increased the lines on my credit cards when I got back from the West Coast, so I would have some slack. For the first time in a while, I was very, very concerned about cash flow.

I still do daily and weekly cash flow statements to see where my money's going. Maybe people who move into a non-New York atmosphere don't have to consider it as much. Another thing, you move into an apartment, and you've got to furnish it, draperies, rugs. Even if you've got some stuff, you've still got to buy some things for the apartment. Maybe you got by the interviewing season with one or two suits, and now you're not going to be able to do that, so you've got to go out and buy suits, shoes, shirts, etc. These are some things that hit me a little unexpectedly.

A funny thing looking back: you make a decision in a group environment at the Darden School. You make a decision with their help and advice, but when you make your decision, that support group is gone, and you're living with that decision, and your friends are in Chicago or Atlanta or wherever, and suddenly, it's you all alone. And, you've got to make it work now. You can't call "time-out" and say well, let's meet and talk about it. Those people are GONE. Now, you've got to make it work. It's a subtle thing. Some people don't believe in this positive mental attitude toward it, but you get tested real early.

So, we had about a week before work to settle into the apartment. Then, one day, you wake up and you go to work. It's a funny feeling that first day: Even after all the preparation you're not exactly sure what is going to happen when you walk in the door.

Going to Work

I was part of a training program with 21 other people. I had been in touch with the firm several times: once to nail down moving expenses, another time to nail down what the real starting date was going to be, another time to find out what the training program was like, how it had changed people. I walked in the front door, and here's where I got a break that I'm not sure other people got. They said, Day One, we are going to begin a general introduction to the firm that will last the first week. So many weeks of analytic training, eight weeks of rotation, and you'll see in your booklet that you're going to be at this desk on this day, etc. You will be evaluated every day, and at the end of this we're going to have a draft pick. The firm delivered. The training program was extremely organized. Fifteen weeks. He spelled everything out which was phenomenal. I got a folder, and I knew where I was going to be, to the desk, on a day by day basis.

They spelled out the expectations for the training program right then and there. You see, I came off a 90-day game plan that we did in business policy. I knew that I had three goals in mind because I had been through similar situations. One, I needed to differentiate myself from the rest of the pack. I wanted to be considered among the top people. And two, I wanted to get to know the people who were in my training program very well, because they were a good resource. The third thing is that I wanted to get to know as many people in the firm as I could because this was a once-in-a-lifetime shot to circulate around the whole firm with no job to worry about and just talk with them about what they thought about the firm, what they didn't like, etc. Those were the three goals I took in, and I did get off to a good start.

We had a classroom part of the training in which we had some tests. I scored no. 1 in those. I kept studying and made sure that I came out no. 1. That gave me respect with my peers and the training people. Then the word started to get out that this guy can do the work which later helped out in the draft pick. And it built my leverage around some things were that were surprising later on. I had some leverage.

After the first week of training, there were three weeks of classroom work where they give you three volumes of material to study. You had classes during the day and three volumes to review at night and were tested every day or at least at the end of the week on each major volume. It was straight memory work, back to undergraduate days. That's my ballgame. I knew it was my ballgame. I just basically studied the material very hard.

I was working in the evenings, too. There was a Darden student who was in New York for the summer as well, not at my firm, though. He graduated with me, and was spending the summer in New York with his wife. I would come home bas-

ically around 4:30 or 5:00 and have a little bit of dinner, study for a couple of hours, and maybe give them a call and meet them somewhere to just get out and walk around. The sublet was in Greenwich Village, and there is always entertainment on the streets in the summer. Then back and study maybe another hour or two, and hit the sack around 11:30. Then on Friday we would have an exam. We did a fair amount of booking it in those three weeks. I was making sure that I was memorizing the material that would help me through the registered representative exam, and I knew that it was a way to differentiate myself from the start.

We went out as a group a lot of times, going out to bars after the exams, you know, finding out where the people are from and what they are like, what their past experience has been. I made an effort to do that. It was a great way to get to know those people. If you're generally interested in getting to know them, then they become interested in you, and you get along very well, and that was important to me.

Plus all this time I was trying to find a permanent apartment. The person that I had talked with in Personnel had agreed to pay my moving expenses on a U-Haul basis. He agreed to fly me back home when I found a permanent place to pick up some stuff I had stored. I had stored some of my stuff at my fiancee's place and some at home. So, he said I could go back down and get it. It was a long, drawn out process. I didn't find a place until late in the summer. The actual move into my own room didn't take place until the Labor Day weekend. On Labor Day I flew back down home, picked up all my stuff, drove back up, unloaded the trailer.

Then we began our rotation. We were on a schedule, so we sat with the same group of trainees. There were four major areas: Equity, Corporate Finance, Municipal Bonds, and Money Market Securities. We spent about two weeks in each area. Each Monday would usually be a lecture day where someone from that area would come in and teach a class and give us the product knowledge. At the end of each day, they evaluated you on such things as interest, attentiveness, and ability to learn. They sat there, and you asked questions. You had to go home and think about what you were going to ask these people. At the same time everybody else was rotating through different parts of the firm. Here's where the contacts that you had made in the first three or four weks of the classroom session became very helpful because you knew this guy would treat people like dirt, he wouldn't answer questions, or this guy was great, ask him anything you want, he's a good resource. We swapped all of these stories.

We were getting closer to this giant draft pick

for final assignment. People, very similar to Darden, were very cooperative, but there is a little competition and as that begins to shape up, people begin to express some preferences. Then the mass of politics starts going, certain people make sure they get known in certain areas. This is what they really want, they try to nail down some kind of commitment for a final assignment.

You have to express three preference areas within the firm, and then you have some time to rearrange those, communicate those to the management in those areas, and they give you feedback whether they liked you or didn't like you in kind of a general way. All through the training area trainees start communicating bits and pieces about their needs and likes.

All this time there are contacts within the firm. All this time you are finding out who you want to work for, what they are like, things you need to do to be good, what the firm likes, the people. It's just a whole socialization process that they use to get to know you.

Then management sits down one day and has a giant draft pick. Like the NFL, I guess. They've got the performance on the classroom part. They've got your evaluation sheets which were all quantified: People skills—one, two, three, four, five, excellent, good, whatever. And then the four heads of the departments sit down, and they deal. They have their political interplay. They all want the best people, and certain people do emerge as top candidates. Then a little swapping goes on here and there, and then you are assigned to that area.

Joining Up Again

Then you get your permanent assignment. October 16th. I emerged as one of the top three out of the 21 in the training process. I had expressed some preferences in corporate bond sales and told them that I had wanted to do that. I have to say, there were a lot of interesting positions across the floor; there were a lot of things that I could have done and would have enjoyed very much. Anyway, apparently, I was bid for in all four major areas, they were bidding for my services, and I ended up assigned to an area that I hadn't put on my preference sheet at all.

And here's where I cashed in some chips. I had been a top performer in the training program, everybody had liked me. It just so happened that in the political situation in the wrangling, corporate bonds had ended up with one of the other top three people in the training class. So, then they said they wanted a salesman. All of the other people sort of said, well, okay now you've

just got a trader, so you're not going to get one of the top people to be a salesman. So, I ended up assigned to an area I had not chosen. It was a great opportunity as a start-up position, and a great job, a challenging job, a sales job that I liked, but I had ignored the department.

I was called in by the partner of that area and he told me that I had been assigned to that particular job, and I cashed in my chips. I told the person that I had realized what had happened. Then I said in a not-so-controlled voice, "One, I want accounts and I want them early, I don't want to wait. I want to get on with it and perform." He assured me that that would happen, that my immediate manager who reported to him would convey that and that that would happen. "Two, if I produce, I want to be paid." As it worked out, having gone on record for that, it was a smart thing to do.

All along I was making sure that I met those three criteria that I brought in for the first 90 days: (1) try to shape myself as one of the top performers, (2) know the people in the training program very well which has turned out to be great, and (3) make sure a lot of people in the firm, top management, etc., get an exposure to me.

Becoming a Colleague

Now, once I got into the department, I also did something else. I went home the evening of my first day on the job and did some scratch sheet analysis on some bonds. The reason I did that was I said "This is Day #1, and I don't want to be treated just like another person. I am going to go home and do this." The World Series is playing, and I'm punching out on my calculator. I was just doing some averages and some standard deviations which is helpful information. Now, believe me I am not a mathematics buff—I know zippo, just the bears about quantitative analysis, but I worked up some standard deviation numbers on these averages.

They absolutely loved it. All of a sudden, my boss tells me that my name has come up with management and senior management and the president of the company, and my boss is telling the president about this standard deviation analysis, that it was a way that they had not looked at a particular thing before.

I had to explain it to the entire department at a meeting and say this is what is available to you, and I will help you in any way I can. So, now I have positioned myself within the department as somebody. And they're thinking, Okay, this guy knows what he is doing. I am going to respect him. He has a little bit more on the ball than somebody else who has just come on. He is above the average bear.

They said that I would get my accounts around the first of December. On Friday, December 4th, I received my accounts, on schedule and in half the time it took the people in the department from the training class before me. And so far, all indications are that the money will flow if the production is there. I have a very challenging position.

chapter

31

The First Year Out

For many people the first year of work after graduating from school is a period of great challenge and excitement. It is a time characterized by considerable changes—a new job, new work associates, a new dwelling, a new city.

The first year out can also be a difficult period. In a recent survey of MBAs six months after graduation, 62 percent reported that they were less than happy with either job, employer, career progress, or life style. Only 5 percent of those sampled reported no real problems since graduation.

Those who have studied the experiences of recent graduates have concluded that people who have a relatively trouble-free first year out tend to be systemically different from those who experience some difficulty. Specifically, those students who make more personally appropriate job choices, who start work with realistic expectations concerning what will follow, and who take an active role in managing their own joining up process, seem to experience significantly fewer problems during their first year out than those students who don't.

The Impact of Job Choice
(and Related Decisions)

As one might expect, many of the problems reported by people during their first year out can be traced directly to an inappropriate job selection. For a variety of reasons, some people make job decisions based on an incomplete or inaccurate understanding of themselves, the job, or both. These kinds of decisions invariably lead to problems and often to a change of jobs within a year of graduation.

The same underlying causes that lead people to poor job decisions often lead them to poor decisions in other important areas of their lives. Recent graduates sometimes make inappropriate decisions regarding how to approach a new job, where to live, how to allocate their income, and so on. Again, an incomplete or inaccurate understanding of themselves, the option they are choosing, or both, creates first-year-out problems for them.

Some Examples

Underestimating how much he depends on the proximity of friends for relaxation and support, Bill Jones takes an apartment by himself in an area where he knows no one. Within three months his loneliness seriously affects his work. Helen Johnson, who never commuted more than a few miles to work or school before, finds exactly what she wants in a house about 25 miles from work. After moving in, she finds that it takes one hour to drive to or from work. The 10 hours-a-week commute eats into both her work and nonwork activities, creating a variety of problems for her. Herb Palmer is not really aware of how slowly he gets up to speed in a new situation, so he bases his decision to "not even think about work" after accepting the job offer on other considerations. The same is the case with his decision to take a six-week vacation and start work on August 1. When October 1 comes, all of Herb's contemporaries are well settled in their jobs and Herb's continuing awkwardness stands out like a sore thumb to him and others, including his boss.

As the above examples suggest, virtually none of the important individual decisions made just before or during one's first year of work are independent of the other decisions. Each decision tends to affect other parts of one's life in small and large ways, now and in the future. Insensitivity to the interdependence among decisions and their consequences inevitably leads to problems for many recent graduates.

Pete and Pam Marsh, for example, really wanted to return to a less urban part of the Midwest after graduation. Their families and many of their old friends were still there. Peter carefully looked for jobs in that area but found nothing really appealing. Bit by bit, he began to search in a wider area. Eventually he landed a job, enviously considered by his friends to be "a find." The starting salary was good and the company would allow a long vacation period and pay moving expenses—to New York City! After a tense and anxiety-producing process, the Marshes agreed to accept the job. They found a decent apartment and put their 6-year-old in school. Pam made some friends and so did their 4-year-old. Pete threw himself into the job. Next came another "find"—a great house, close to the apartment, and at a good price. They moved. But after

8 months Pete became increasingly frustrated. The job was not developing, and the company seemed less than supportive as time wore on. After 10 months he left. He wanted once again to look for jobs in the less urban part of the Midwest. But what of the child in school, the other child's friends, Pam's attempts to dig in, and the house? He ended up taking another job in the city. Their big-city life style in a short time quite subtly had become the constraint affecting Pete's job choice. It didn't start out that way.

Taking a Life System into Account

Operationally, this means that in making important job and nonjob decisions, one needs to take into account all aspects of one's life. The relevant system to analyze when making a job decision or a life style decision is one's entire life system (see Exhibit 31-1). The critical thing to realize here is that each of the areas

Exhibit 31–1
A Life System

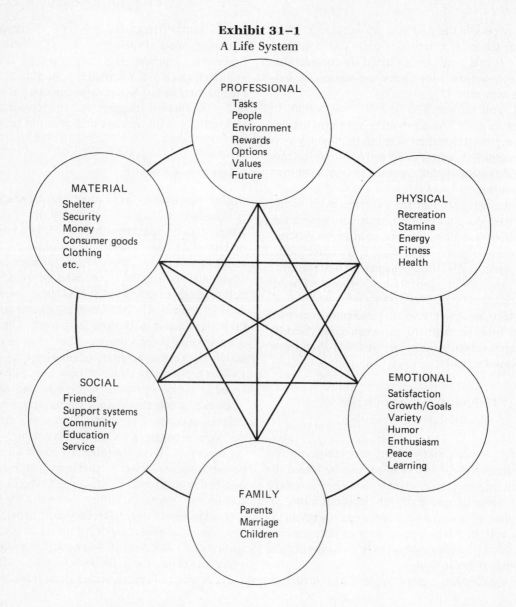

of a person's life—job/career, family, psychological and physiological selves, and life style, including where they live, their movement patterns, their use of money, their social life, their recreation, and so on—are affected, inexorably, by career-related decisions.

People occasionally like to deny that these decisions are interdependent. They want to believe that what they do at work and what they do out of work can be totally separated. They want that "freedom." As they soon learn, the world as we experience it today is one big interdependent mass, and the interdependencies are growing, not shrinking. And those who do not understand that, or who refuse to accept it, are in for a tough time.

Exhibit 31-2 presents a list of the issues commonly mentioned by graduates of major business schools when they return to campus a year after graduation to talk with students. The list reveals that many graduates experienced some surprises in their first year of work. Work, and especially work embedded in a particular organizational culture, was not exactly what they ex-

pected. Sometimes the work was too fast, sometimes too slow. Often they were surprised by the vagaries of dealing with people—people who moved within or left the organization, people who had different values from theirs, people who weren't as talented as they, people who didn't communicate well, people who sought power, and so on.

One of the major tasks associated with the first year of work is the tentative exploration and establishment of a life style. People test the ways that the four major components of a life system (see Exhibit 31-1) are going to fit together for them.

Assignment

Read the Jewel Savadelis case (pp. 350–56). What should she do, and why? How are the issues she is facing similar or dissimilar to ones you may face? What seems typical or unusual about her first year out?

Exhibit 31–2
Issues Faced by MBA Graduates in the First Year

1. How do I manage my marriage *and* my career? Especially if my spouse is also working—and maybe in a different city?

2. How do I manage the frustration of dealing with a hierarchy? Decisions seem to take so long and to be made as much for political reasons as for analytic conclusions.

3. How do I manage my time and priorities? What should I do next? (These questions were particularly poignant for entrepreneurs.)

4. How little sleep can I get by with?

5. There have been a lot of changes in bosses and colleagues. How do I manage *that* uncertainty?

6. How do I learn about corporate culture, and how much will I have to conform?

7. Where should I live? Where will I find my (our) social life?

8. How long and in what ways will I have to pay my dues? How long will it take until I have established credibility? How long will I have to do junk work?

9. How do I deal with the big changes in seasonal workloads?

10. I am getting virtually no feedback on my performance. How do I find out how I'm doing or learn to live with the lack of feedback?

11. I had the joining up blues. No one wanted to bother with me. Everyone was busy doing their work and I was the low man on the totem pole.

12. How do I find a mentor? Do I need one?

13. Things were more disorganized than I expected.

14. Authority is not always clearly linked to responsibility. People don't respond just because you have a title. Managing relationships is a bigger part of it than I thought. People have their own hidden, but powerful and often irrational, agendas.

15. How do I work for someone who is less capable than I am?

16. Timing goes in fits and starts. Sometimes things move very fast, faster than seems wise. Other times it seems to take forever to accomplish the simplest things.

17. How long can I go on with this pace? It's okay now, but I don't want to be working this hard in five years.

18. I just got married. That took a lot of my time. But now that I've got my social life buttoned up, I can focus on my career.

JEWEL SAVADELIS

On Friday, September 25, Jewel Savadelis pulled slowly out of the parking lot of Atari, Inc., and headed south on Mathilda Avenue toward her home in Sunnyvale, California. Jewel was oblivious to the rush hour traffic. An offer she had received from her boss kept rolling over and over in her mind. Mr. Moon, the president of Atari's Consumer Division, had asked Jewel to be the director of the Software Development Department. The offer presented an exciting opportunity for Jewel at an early stage in her career, but she wondered if it was the right move to make and, if so, under what circumstances.

Atari, Inc.

Atari operated three main lines of business. Coin-operated video games stood in game arcades and high-traffic areas in bowling alleys, supermarkets, and restaurants. Home video games were attached to consumer televisions. Personal computers were designed not only for games, but also for personal data processing applications. Atari was the only company which operated in both the coin-operated and home segments of the growing video game market. By 1980, Atari was generating an estimated $415 million in sales revenues and earning an estimated $77 million in operating profits. Company analysts expected these figures to more than double in 1981.

Atari was founded in 1972 by Nolan Bushnell, a young engineer graduate of the University of Utah. Mr. Bushnell had written a computer game later named "Pong" while working as a research engineer in the area between Palo Alto and San Jose, California, known as Silicon Valley. Mr. Bushnell formed his own corporation, Atari, Inc., to produce and market the game in the coin-operated arcade market, and it became an instant hit.

Mr. Bushnell's love of games and creative, flamboyant style encouraged other Atari engineer/managers to imagine and to create new, increasingly more exciting games. Groups of managers and engineers would go off to local resorts for two- and three-day brainstorming sessions that included "plenty of marijuana and beer."[1] The video games required weeks and sometimes months of painstaking and careful programming. Then the problems of mass producing the programmed chips that were the heart of the video game hardware had to be overcome before attacking the common production and assembling tasks associated with a video game console.

Some games were developed specifically for either the arcade or home video markets, but the company generally tried to apply the considerable development costs to products in both segments. In 1975, the company produced over 100,000 copies of a home version of Pong which was sold out before it reached the Sears, Roebuck outlets. Sears had had to help Atari finance the buildup of the Pong inventory, and it became apparent to the management of Atari that the company would need additional funds in order to pursue its high-growth strategy. In 1976, Mr. Bushnell agreed to sell the company to Warner Communications for $28 million.

With the infusion of cash from Warner, Atari continued to develop and distribute new products. Officials at Atari had realized from their experience during the early years that video games often became repetitive to players and had concluded therefore that the future growth of the industry in both the home and arcade markets would rely on a continuous stream of new and ever more interesting products. Evidence to support this conclusion was found in the arcade market where the Space Invaders game, imported from Japan and produced in the United States by Bally Corporation, had become extremely popular. Space Invaders added variations of color, sound, control, and skill development to the relatively simple Pong video game experience. Atari was able to capitalize on the arcade popularity of Space Invaders by introducing to the consumer market in 1977 the Video Computer System, a flexible device that would accept cartridges each programmed with a different game. By 1981, the Atari cartridge version of Space Invaders introduced in 1980 had sold over one million copies. In 1980, Atari also intro-

---

[1]Peter W. Bernstein, "Atari and the Video-Game Explosion," *Fortune,* July 27, 1981.

This case was written by Associate Professor James G. Clawson as a basis for classroom discussion rather than to illustrate either effective or ineffective handling of an administrative situation. © 1981 by the Sponsors of the Colgate Darden Graduate School of Business Administration, University of Virginia, Charlottesville, Virginia. UVA case OB-190.

duced the coin-operated Asteroids. The game quickly became another major seller. Over 70,000 units were sold by the end of the year.

The architect of much of Atari's success in the late seventies and the man who did much to change the operating culture at Atari was Raymond Kassar, who had worked for Burlington Industries for 25 years before coming to Atari. In many ways, Mr. Kassar was a sharp contrast to Atari's founder. Mr. Kassar had been steeped in corporate management philosophy and techniques over the course of his career. When he was made the chief executive officer in 1978, he immediately set about establishing formal control and reporting systems. He expected people to be to work on time and to dress in more formal attire rather than the T-shirts and jeans that were commonplace at Atari and in the industry. Mr. Kassar also proved to the industry that video games were not just a seasonally oriented toy business. His introduction of four new game cartridges in late January created a run on retail outlets and a year-around demand for Atari products. Mr. Kassar's considerable marketing skill and the fact that only 3.5% of American homes had video game players augured well for Atari in 1981.

Jewel Savadelis

These were the fascinating and compelling highlights of Jewel Savadelis's investigation of Atari as she searched for an appropriate position during her last semester in the Harvard Business School MBA program in the spring of 1981. The previous fall, Jewel had taken an intensive course on career management in which she had developed a well-supported list of personal life themes (see Exhibit 31–3) and implications for work (see Exhibit 31–4) that she thought would help guide her in her job search. After careful consideration of her knowledge of herself, of Atari, and of its industry, Jewel had accepted the product manager position, which would play a large role in the marketing activities of the Consumer Division of the company, which produced and sold the home video games.

After graduation, Jewel and her husband took a much-needed vacation, returning in time for Jewel to begin work August 3. As the new product manager for home video games, Jewel had no set job description, no subordinates, and an open mandate to structure the position in light of the company's growing portfolio of video games. Jewel spent the first eight weeks on the job familiarizing herself with the company's products and meeting most of the key people whom she would be dealing with in the years ahead. On several occasions during this two-month period, Jewel's boss, Mr. Stringari, had expressed his satisfaction with Jewel's recommendations and work. By the third week in September, Jewel was settling in. That week, Jewel went on a trip to New York with Mr. Edward Jones, director of software development, Mr. Stringari, vice president of marketing, and several other executives. During that trip, Jewel learned that Howard Sels, the last manager in the Software Development Department other than Mr. Jones, had received a job offer from a competitor and had left on one day's notice.

Exhibit 31–3
Life Themes

To facilitate a clearer understanding of the links between my life themes and their implications for work, I'd like to summarize the rationale behind each theme.

Dominant Themes

1. Likes control.
   Likes control over self and work situation. Prefers autonomy and nonauthoritarian boss. Solicits added responsibility. Likes control over others; seeks leadership. Is decisive, enterprising, self-motivated. Enjoys persuading people; is manipulative.

2. Has self-confidence.
   Confident in most work-related situations and of ability to deal well with most people. Lacks confidence in technical, quantitative areas.

3. Likes dealing with people.
   Enjoys dealing with people rather than things. Social activities, even if business-related, are relaxing and recharging. Enjoy acting as teacher or mentor. Enjoy diverse types of people.

4. Needs Chuck's support (husband).
   Chuck has always been central to my stability and well being. Experienced conflict between strong feelings of affection for Chuck and lack of time spent with him.

(continued)

Exhibit 31–3 (*continued*)

Major Themes

---

5. Deals well with people.
    Is successful with superiors, peers, subordinates, and clients by understanding motivations. Able to influence and persuade, inspire, handle difficult people, form cohesive group. Varies style with different people. Sometimes, too domineering.

6. Wants to achieve significant ends and to improve self.
    Requires challenging work to feel accomplishment. Driven to accomplish many tasks. Continually seeking personal growth, self-improvement. Perseveres in accomplishing tasks.

7. Is creative and appreciates esthetics.
    Solves problems creatively. Has characteristics of the artist: expressive, original, intuitive, nonconforming, independent.

8. Is risk-loving.
    Has no fear of taking manageable risks. Has ability to move confidently in totally new situation. Has need for constant stimulation in environment. Shows courage.

9. Needs praise and recognition.
    Driving force behind need for achievement is need for recognition.

10. Can get things accomplished.
    Delivers on promises. Attends to details. Handles variety of tasks simultaneously and efficiently. Builds teams and accomplishes tasks through others.

11. Needs self-respect.
    Must stand up for issue I believe in. Demands integrity in others.

12. Likes variety.
    Self-explanatory.

13. Is emotional.
    Exudes enthusiasm. Is not objective in opinions. Has mood swings. Likes periods of extreme activity followed by periods of relative calm.

Intermediate Themes

---

14. Is flexible.
    Willing to experiment with new approaches. Sees relationships in unrelated fields. Willing to change mind in light of fresh evidence. Ability to improvise (particularly in crisis).

15. Has high material needs.
    Self-explanatory.

16. Needs support of friends and family.
    Support systems permit risk-taking because they provide a secure base.

17. Lacks stamina.
    Self-explanatory.

18. Is self-reliant.
    Tied to need for control (Th 1), confidence in own ability (Th 2), ability to accomplish tasks (Th 10). Depends on self rather than others to get things started (relies on others to carry through, under my direction).

19. Concerned about women's position in life.
    Fights loss of control and dependence on men fostered by discriminatory practices. Interested in promoting equal rights for self and for other women as humanitarian gesture.

20. Is organized.
    Systematically sets goals, uses effective criteria for projects, attends to details.

21. Is intuitive.
    Self-explanatory.

Subordinate Themes

---

22. Is unconventional.
    Self-explanatory.

23. Is impatient.
    Self-explanatory.

24. Is practical.
    Self-explanatory.

Exhibit 31–4
Summary of Implications

Company Implications

C1	Renegade
C2	Sufficient leisure time
C3	Personal growth & advancement
C4	Open access to executives
C5	Ethical leadership
C6	Company values employees
C7	Pleasant surroundings
C8	Mainstream industry

Life Style Implications

LS1	Time for leisure activities
LS2	Preferred geographic location
LS3	Satisfy high material needs

Task Preference Implications

T1	Low structure & supervision
T2	High variety
T3	Minimum quantitative & technical tasks
T4	Central importance of task
T5	New learning
T6	Use many HBS skills
T7	Deal with people often
T8	High creativity
T9	High risk
T10	Measurable outcome
T11	Organization required

Co-Workers (People) Implications

P1	Diverse co-workers, few similar to me
P2	Nonauthoritarian supportive boss
P3	Open, informal atmosphere
P4	Co-workers have integrity
P5	Make unique contribution

Leadership Style Implications

L1	Challenge subordinates and be fair
L2	High expectations of self and others
L3	Achieve organizational goals

Approach to Tasks Implications

AT1	Use unusual approach & intuition

Meeting with Mr. Moon

On Thursday, September 24, shortly after returning from New York, Jewel was called into Mr. Moon's office. The president began by recalling that while Jewel was in New York three of the programmers had gone to Mr. Moon and expressed their dissatisfaction with their supervisor, Mr. Jones. Mr. Moon had already discussed their complaints with Mr. Stringari and Mr. Ebertin, vice president engineering, and had decided to replace Mr. Jones immediately. Mr. Moon said he had advised Mr. Jones that he was to relinquish his position as director of software development and to become the director of special projects. (See Exhibit 31–5 for an organization chart of the division at that time.) He had then called a meeting with the programmers in the software development department. At that meeting, Mr. Moon, knowing that the programmers were a headstrong group, had tested their reaction to his idea that Jewel would make a good director of product development. The programmers had agreed. He asked if Jewel would take the job.

Jewel ended the meeting by asking for a couple of days to think it over. The next morning, Friday the 25th, she went to see the three senior programmers. Her knowledge of the characteristics of that group made her wonder if she would be effective in trying to manage their efforts.

The Programmers

There were 16 video game programmers working for Atari in the Consumer Division's engineering software department. Fifteen of these were men, and they ranged, in Jewel's estimation, from normal to temperamental. Most of them were single, recent college graduates with degrees in computer science. In school, they had been dedicated computer enthusiasts accustomed to working when, where, and how they wanted.

This preference for control over their work habits extended from their appearance to their schedules and activities. Programmers usually wore sandals or sneakers, jeans, and T-shirts to work. Many of them wore longish hair and on occasion would smoke marijuana on the job. They knew little about business, much less about corporate procedures. When disgruntled or dissatisfied, as evidenced by their previous actions, they were used to going "straight to the top" to get satisfaction.

The compensation system in the group called for individual bonuses to be based on the sales of video games created and programmed. If a programmer conceived and produced a game that was successful, he or she could earn large bonuses. Several of the programmers would soon be earning an annual income, including bonuses, well into six figures—more than three times Jewel's salary. This system and the high visibility of the programming department's prod-

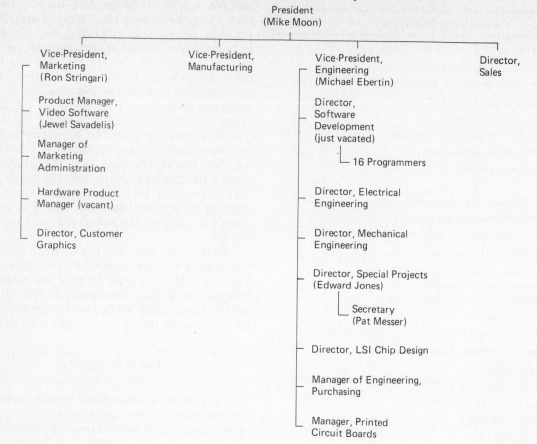

ucts gave the programmers a clear sense of their importance to the company's future. Turnover among the programmers was low in comparison to industry standards. The group had lost only four people in the last two years to budding competitors.

Meeting the Senior Programmers

Jewel's meeting with the three senior programmers reconfirmed her concerns. They told her that they would be willing to accept her as their new manager, but that she should understand a few things at the outset. First, they would retain hiring, firing, time allocation responsibilities, and monetary sanctions. Second, they would work three-day weeks only. Third, they were to be permitted to do the cartridges they wanted and to smoke pot on the job. Fourth, they would tolerate no creative suggestions on their cartridges from Jewel. Jewel's responsibilities would consist of filling out the paperwork required of their department by the corporation and to buffering them from other corporate interference. They said that their complaint with the previous man-

ager had been that he was not supporting them enough to senior management when management wanted them to program games that did not fit their current interests. The director's responsibility, they said, was to maintain the freedom of the programmers to work on projects of personal interest. Finally, while they did admit that none of them was prepared yet to assume the position of director of the department, they wondered out loud if Jewel's marketing background did not disqualify her at the start. Programmers simply did not trust the marketing types.

Jewel thanked them for their candor and confidence and said that she was going to think about the offer over the weekend.

Meeting the Former Director and His Secretary

After meeting with the programmers, Jewel went to see Mr. Jones. Edward received her in a restrained way, and said that he would have resigned had it not been Jewel who was being tapped to replace him. He offered to help her in whatever way he could and even drew up a list of things needing attention in the department (Exhibit 31-6). Mr. Jones indicated that he wanted to stay in his current office, which was in the middle of the programming area, and that his secretary would be staying with him. Jewel could take a small office down the hall.

Upon leaving Mr. Jones's office, Jewel went next door to see his secretary, Pat Messer. Pat was Jewel's age and had been with Atari for six months. Pat knew extremely well the systems and procedures that were in place in the programming department. When Jewel asked if she would be interested in working for her, Pat gave a cautious answer.

Jewel's Deliberations

As Jewel walked back to her office, collected her things, and drove home, she pondered some other considerations connected with the offer.

She would be doing two full-time jobs working for two different bosses. Ron Stringari, the vice president of marketing and her current boss, had proven in eight short weeks to be a powerful ally and a helpful guide. At 38, he was only ten years older than Jewel. Michel Ebertin, on the other hand, the vice president of engineering, was 45, had numerous years of experience as an engineer at National Semiconductor, and from afar, seemed to be much more "businesslike" and demanding. It was generally known that Mr. Ebertin had high standards and if disappointed would reprimand the offending employee in public meetings. Since Jewel had no programming background and knew virtually nothing of the technical side of the programmers' work, she was concerned about her ability to run the operation to Mr. Ebertin's satisfaction.

Jewel also wondered if she would get the support she would need to succeed in the proposed dual position. The programmers tended to be autonomous and freewheeling, and they had all the technical knowledge needed to monitor progress in the department. Mr. Jones seemed supportive, but he was still sitting in the same office with the same secretary, overlooking the software development group. And Mr. Ebertin's style contrasted with that of her current boss, Mr. Stringari.

Finally, although the appointment could clearly be a major expansion of responsibility and therefore a promotion, no one had said anything to Jewel about a change of title or salary. Mr. Jones, as the director of the software department, had been earning much more than Jewel's current salary.

All in all, the opportunity was an exciting one for Jewel, coming as it did so early in her career. She felt that her decision would be an important one. If she accepted it and succeeded (and she

Exhibit 31-6
Mr. Jones's List

1. Fix "bug" in already released cartridge.
2. Customer Week preparations.
3. Find assistant.
4. Coordinate requests for carts in development (200 cart requests per month).
5. Devise schedule for carts and their completion dates.
6. Coordinate marketing research projects.
7. Coordinate instruction manual writing.
8. Determine standards for final game design approval.
9. Initiate title selection procedures.
10. Handle personal problems of staff.
11. Coordinate technical support interface.
12. Coordinate activities contracted for interior decoration.
13. Devise de-bug standards.
14. Devise game standards.
15. Define programmer reporting relationships.
16. Devise/initiate on-the-job training for new programmers.
17. Write technical manuals and documentation of operating system.
18. Study manpower/hiring requirements.
19. Fill out copyright information sheets to legal department.
20. Provide legal support for pending lawsuits against competitors.
21. Coordinate interface with hardware department to get correct controllers for new hardware.
22. Do 1982 budget.
23. Customer service interface.
24. Attend Michel Ebertin's meetings: staff—every Tuesday; project review—every Thursday.
25. Address issue of software security.
26. Address issue of programmers unhappy with current cartridges.
27. Pursue job reclassification for tester.
28. Initiate request for fireproofing system for computer room.
29. Engineering—status reports required twice monthly.
30. Set up room with competitors' products.
31. Order coin op games for research.
32. Schedule and announce department meetings.
33. Address design of next generation of video systems.
34. Joint venture with DC Comics on new cartridge.
35. Extended offers in the mill to new programmers—2 are due to arrive within 3 days.
36. Hire department secretary.
37. Order office equipment for new hires.
38-45. Assorted confidential projects.

was not sure what that meant), she would surely have learned a lot about another critical part of the company, expanded her general managerial skills, and built her reputation with senior management. If she accepted and failed, she would have a major black mark on her record in the first year of employment. If she declined the offer, management might see her as less capable than they had calculated and her reputation—and future career opportunities—might suffer.

Developmental Relationships

In recent years there has been a significant increase in the interest of employers and employees alike in understanding and developing mentor-protégé relationships. Many articles and books have left people with the impression that in order to get ahead in business it is necessary—even critical—to have a mentor. The current research on this question is not so clear. In one study (Roche, 1979), it was determined that over 66 percent of the people claimed that they had had a mentor, but the definition was so broad that it left one wondering just what a mentor or a mentor-protégé relationship was. Further, the article did little to help one understand whether or not one has a mentor-protégé relationship, much less how to develop one. What we need is an idea of what a good mentor-protégé relationship (MPR) looks like, and then, more important, an idea of how to go about developing our relationships so that they become more and more like that ideal MPR.

Exhibit 32–1 outlines the characteristics of a full blown mentor-protégé relationship as described in a wide body of literature. As you read the characteristics, you will probably conclude that a "true" mentor-protégé relationship is a relatively rare phenomenon. Most researchers presently conclude that there are a variety of "developmental relationships" which vary along several dimensions in terms of their impact on the development of the younger person. These may involve "coaches," "quasi-mentors" or "partial mentors" or "career mentors," or just plain supervisors."

Exhibit 32–2 presents a grid on which these various relationships can be categorized. The important thing to note is that people learn from a variety of relationships, not just the relatively rare mentor-protégé relationship. "Quasi" or "partial" mentors are senior people who take an interest in a portion of the younger person's life and have a significant influence on them, but who do not have the comprehensive and intimate impact on a protégé's life that Mentor did on Ulysses' son, Telemachus, or that the medieval guild masters did on their apprentices.

Consequently, a much better way to think about developmental issues in relationships on the job is to think about the developmental aspects of the relationships that form naturally. The most common one, of course, is the superior-subordinate relationship. As you begin your career you will no doubt have several superiors who will be charged with the responsibility of supervising, monitoring, and perhaps developing your activities.

As Exhibit 32–3 shows, superior-subordinate relationships take place primarily in the context of an organization, which constrains the relationship in many ways. Organization structure, personnel policies, hiring, promotion, and compensation practices like the history of relationships within the organization and the philosophy of the current senior management all tend to affect what superiors and subordinates can do in managing the developmental aspects of their relationship. In addition, the organization and, in part, the relationship take place within a broader environmental context. Alternatives for both individuals at other organizations in the environment, the economic demands of the current environment, the supply and characteristics of co-workers coming from the environment, and the set of societal and cultural norms and values supported by the environment all contribute to the set of forces which will affect the growth of the developmental relationship on the job. We can reconstruct this model, as shown in Exhibit 32–4, to indicate the cause and effect relationships among these

Exhibit 32-1

An Eclectic Profile
of Mentor-Protégé Relationships

1. Mentor-protégé relationships (MPRs) grow out of personal willingness to enter the relationships and not necessarily out of formal assignments. Thus, MPRs may not coincide with formal hierarchies.

2. MPRs pass through a series of developmental stages characterized as formative, duration, and fruition. Each stage has a characteristic set of activities and tasks.

3. Mentors are generative—that is, interested in passing on their wisdom and experience to others.

4. Mentors try to understand, shape, and encourage the dreams of their protégés. Mentors often give their blessings to dreams and goals of their protégés.

5. Mentors guide their protégés both technically and professionally; that is, they teach things about the technical content of a career and things about the social organization and patterns of advancement of a career.

6. Mentors plan their protégés' learning experiences so that they will be stretching but not overwhelming, and successful. Protégés are encouraged to accept responsibility, but are not permitted to make large mistakes.

7. Mentors provide opportunities for their protégés to observe and participate in their work by inviting their protégés to work with them.

8. Protégés learn in MPRs primarily by identification, trial and error, and observation.

9. Both mentors and protégés have high levels of respect for each other.

10. Mentors sponsor their protégés organizationally and professionally.

11. MPRs have levels of affection similar to parent-child relationships.

12. MPRs end in a variety of ways, often either with continuing amiability or with anger and bitterness.

five elements that produce a series of outcomes from the relationship. Obviously, there are many outcomes, only some of which have to do with development.

In one study of a major insurance company (Clawson, 1979), 51 managers involved in 38 different superior-subordinate relationships were examined in regard to the amount of learning perceived by both the superior and the subordinate to have taken place in the subordinate on three different dimensions. Those relationships that were most effective in terms of developing the subordinates were then compared with those that were least effective and the sets of criteria that appear in Exhibits 32-5, 32-6, and 32-7 were developed.

Characteristics of Effective Coaches

As shown in Exhibit 32-5, the coaches whose subordinates learned more tended to be people-oriented and even-tempered. Their subordinates knew how they were going to respond because of the consistency in their behavior. They also had somewhat higher tolerance for ambiguity than their less effective counterparts. This meant that they were able to assign projects and tasks to their subordinates without feeling the need to watch over their shoulders every step of the way. A fourth psychological predisposition that characterized effective coaches was the value they placed on working at and advancing in their organization. This was important because it reflected a sense of loyalty which they passed on to their subordinates.

The effective coaches saw their subordinates as being capable, intelligent, and likable people. They also saw themselves as teachers and accepted as part of their managerial jobs the responsibility for developing and instructing and coaching their subordinates.

These psychological predispositions and perceptions were played out in the behavior of the effective coaches in several ways. They took a lot of time to stay in touch with their subordinates. They walked around the office, maintaining a real and not just symbolic open door policy. Their communications were characterized by an informal style. They tended to use first names and to be excellent listeners, trying as best they could to understand their subordinate's points of view. They carried out their instructional responsibilities by trying to broaden the perspective of their subordinates. This meant sharing information with regard to their own jobs, setting high but obtainable standards, and giving their own opinions about the way things were accomplished within the confines of the organization. In a sense, this was teaching their subordinates the organization politics of their particular company. Finally, they were willing to sponsor their subordinates to other members of senior management.

Characteristics of Subordinates Who Learned

The subordinates who learned more in the study also had a higher orientation toward people and were somewhat more independent than the subordinates who learned less. This is consistent with the notion introduced earlier that subordinates who took more responsibility for their own learning and for their own joining up tended to do better and to learn more than

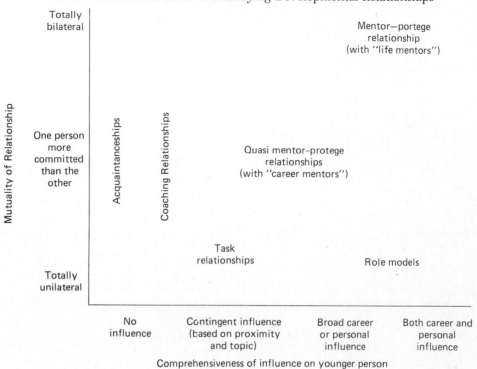

Exhibit 32–2
Two Essential Dimensions in Classifying Developmental Relationships

Mutuality of Relationship

- Totally bilateral
- One person more committed than the other
- Totally unilateral

Mentor–portege relationship (with "life mentors")

Acquaintanceships

Coaching Relationships

Quasi mentor-protege relationships (with "career mentors")

Task relationships

Role models

Comprehensiveness of influence on younger person

- No influence
- Contingent influence (based on proximity and topic)
- Broad career or personal influence
- Both career and personal influence

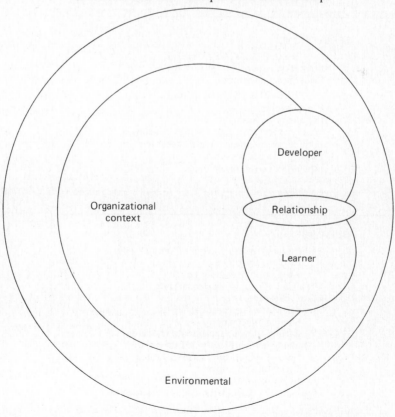

Exhibit 32–3
Basic Elements in Developmental Relationships

- Organizational context
- Developer
- Relationship
- Learner
- Environmental

Exhibit 32–4
A Casual Model of Developmental Relationships

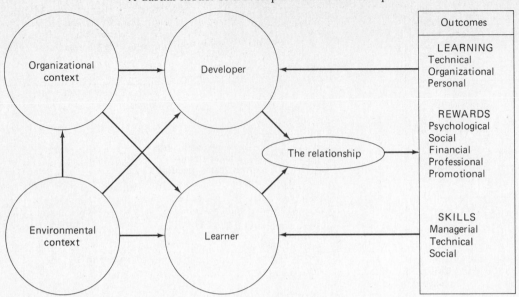

Exhibit 32–5
Characteristics of Effective Superiors

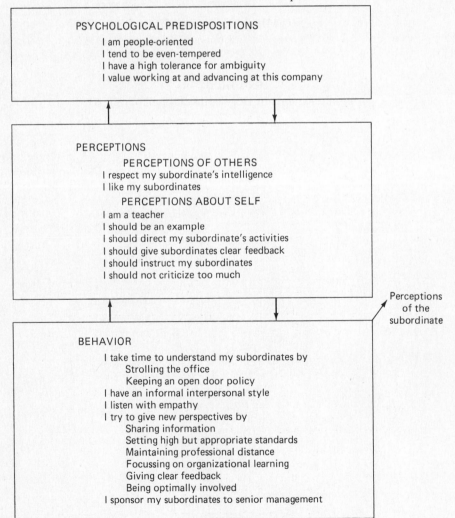

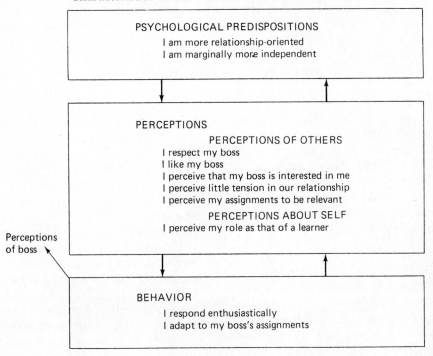

Exhibit 32–6

Characteristics of Subordinates Who Learned More

PSYCHOLOGICAL PREDISPOSITIONS
I am more relationship-oriented
I am marginally more independent

PERCEPTIONS

PERCEPTIONS OF OTHERS
I respect my boss
I like my boss
I perceive that my boss is interested in me
I perceive little tension in our relationship
I perceive my assignments to be relevant

PERCEPTIONS ABOUT SELF
I perceive my role as that of a learner

Perceptions of boss

BEHAVIOR
I respond enthusiastically
I adapt to my boss's assignments

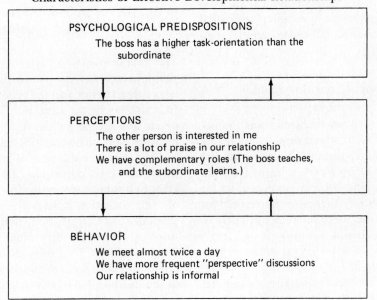

Exhibit 32–7

Characteristics of Effective Developmental Relationships

PSYCHOLOGICAL PREDISPOSITIONS
The boss has a higher task-orientation than the subordinate

PERCEPTIONS
The other person is interested in me
There is a lot of praise in our relationship
We have complementary roles (The boss teaches, and the subordinate learns.)

BEHAVIOR
We meet almost twice a day
We have more frequent "perspective" discussions
Our relationship is informal

those who expected managers and bosses to teach them what they needed to know.

The subordinates who learned more liked and respected their bosses, and had perceptions that were consistent with their bosses' high levels of regard for them. They felt appreciated, and they felt liked. Not only that, they saw themselves as learners and were willing to accept that role, particularly in the early stages of their career.

The learning subordinates were also willing to adjust their schedules in order to accept invitations by their bosses to work on particularly important or time-constrained projects. This enthusiastic response to their bosses' requests signaled to their bosses the level of commitment and loyalty they had to their work and to the organization and in turn encouraged the bosses to provide them with additional responsibilities.

Characteristics of Effective Developmental Relationships

Taking these characteristics of the two individuals in developmental relationships together, the characteristics of an effective developmental relationship are in many ways complementary. The superior takes an educational role and the subordinate takes a learning role. There is a great deal of mutuality of trust and respect in the relationship. The effective developmental relationships had a higher frequency of interaction than those which were ineffective. They also had a higher number of "perspective discussions," discussions in which the superior asked open-ended questions about the subordinate's view of the world and in turn shared his or her own. These discussions considered many topics that were not work-related. And finally, the relationships were much less formal than those which were ineffective: The two individuals could talk as people on a first-name basis about important personal as well as technical and organizational matters.

The Interpersonal Learning Ladder

One thing that emerged from this study was the importance of mutuality of trust and respect in a highly effective developmental relationship. Consider the diagram in Exhibit 32–8. When a person learns from another person, that learning is based upon respect for the first person's expertise. If there is no respect for the coach's expertise, the subordinate is not likely to be open to what that superior has to say.

The respect may be in a variety of areas. It may relate to technical parts of the job, to organizational parts of the job, to personal characteristics, or to other specialized areas of expertise. The broader the subor-

dinate's respect for the superior's expertise, the more likely the superior is to have a broad influence on the subordinate's life and career. Unless the respected areas are ones the trainee wants to develop, however, the respect will play a passive role. If the area of respected expertise is one the younger person wants to develop, he or she is likely to be motivated to act on that respect by emulating the coach's behavior in that area, by listening to the coach talk about that area, and by striving to become involved in the coach's activity in that area.

The third and fourth rungs in this ladder of learning revolve around the question of safety for the subordinate when he is in relationship with the superior. If the superior has two characteristics—first a concern for the general well-being of the subordinate, and second a consistency in behavior—the subordinate will begin to develop trust for the superior. The first trust is a "defensive trust" in the sense that the subordinate can rest assured that the boss will not do anything to harm the subordinate intentionally. If one adds to that a "protective trust" for the superior's interpersonal skills—that is, a reassurance that the boss will not only not intentionally harm the subordinate, but also is skilled enough to avoid unintentionally harming the subordinate, then the subordinate is likely to lower his defense mechanisms and be open to the influence of the superior.

This takes us to the fifth rung of the interpersonal learning ladder, where the superior exerts some positive teaching influence on the subordinate who, because of the respect for his expertise and his trust in the superior's motivations and interpersonal skills, responds to those activities and is now most able to learn from what the superior has to offer.

Developing the Characteristics of Effective Developmental Relationships

The characteristics of effective developmental relationships are not necessarily natural ones. In cases where the superior and the subordinate have a natural fit, this may be the case. But there is much a subordinate and a superior can do to manage the development of these characteristics and their relationship.

Let's consider the case of the subordinate. Many new employees, particularly those with graduate degrees in business administration, feel that the strength of their education is wasted in the early months and years of their careers. Sometimes they see themselves working for people they judge to be less competent than themselves. They often do not hide their opinions and evaluations well. What they fail to realize is that in the history of business management careers in the United States and in the history of the people working

Exhibit 32–8
Interpersonal Learning Ladder

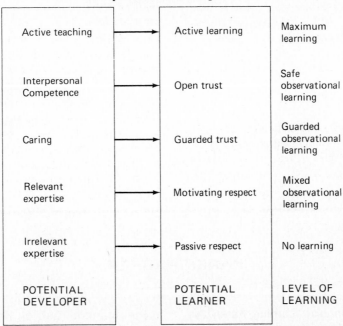

POTENTIAL DEVELOPER	POTENTIAL LEARNER	LEVEL OF LEARNING
Active teaching	→ Active learning	Maximum learning
Interpersonal Competence	→ Open trust	Safe observational learning
Caring	→ Guarded trust	Guarded observational learning
Relevant expertise	→ Motivating respect	Mixed observational learning
Irrelevant expertise	→ Passive respect	No learning

above them in the organization are embedded values based on experience and proven track records that relate to credibility. In order for a senior manager to strive to develop a subordinate by giving him or her additional responsibility and instruction, the superior must first have confidence in the subordinate's capacities and abilities. In some cases, as we have mentioned above, this confidence comes naturally to the superior. In other cases it may not be so, and the subordinate bears much of the responsibility for building that confidence.

Perhaps the first and most important step in building this confidence is communicating to your boss that you have his or her best interests at heart. Letting your superior know that in any way that you are capable, you will strive to make the superior look good and to be successful will go a long way toward reassuring the superior as to your basic motivations and attitudes.

The next step is to demonstrate your own expertise and ability at doing this. A fundamental guideline here is avoiding surprises. Few managers enjoy surprises, even if they are positive ones. A key in business management is being able to anticipate results and to manage one's activities accordingly. In the same way that a boss's dependability and consistency in dealing with a subordinate fosters the relationship, your consistency and dependability in dealing with your superior goes a long way toward developing your superior's respect for you and sense of safety in dealing with you.

If you can add to that the excellent discharge of your current duties, even though they may be "dues-paying" responsibilities, and an additional perspective on

the demands facing your boss's position, he or she will be reassured as to the commitment you have for making him or her look good. If your analysis and comments regarding the problems and decisions facing your boss's office are accurate and consistent with his or her own thinking, you probably will be invited to participate more in the formulation of those problems and their solutions.

Summary

Subordinates can do a great deal to manage their learning in the early stages of their careers. They would do well to consider the managing of developmental aspects of their current relationships, rather than constantly seeking for some mentor or sponsor elsewhere in the organization.

Developmental relationships are characterized by high degrees of learning, trust, and respect, and the subordinate can do much to develop those characteristics by accepting the role of a learner, by being as dependable and consistent and concerned about his superior as he would like his superior to be about him, and by looking for ways to demonstrate expertise in areas that are relevant to the superior and his job. This process requires a multifaceted assessment of the subordinate, of the superior, and of their relationship. It requires the subordinate to refrain from making snap judgments, and to consider all the reasons why a superior might be in the position he or she is in in the first place, and to accept the possibility there is much to learn from that experience and background.

Assignment

Read the Karen Harper case (starting below). What should Karen do? Why? What are the pitfalls she should avoid? What are the potential consequences of your recommendations?

Bibliography

Clawson, James G. "Superior–Subordinate Relationships in Managerial Development." Unpublished doctoral thesis, Harvard Business School, 1979.

Clawson, James G. "Mentoring in Managerial Careers," in *Work, Family and the Career,* ed. Brooke Derr, Praeger Special Studies, 1980.

Gabarro, John J., and John P. Kotter. "Managing Your Boss," *Harvard Business Review,* January–February 1980.

Hill, Norman C., and Paul H. Thompson. "Managing Your Manager," *Exchange Magazine,* Fall–Winter 1978.

Roche, Gerard R. "Much Ado about Mentors," *Harvard Business Review,* January–February 1979, pp. 14–24.

Smith, Roy C. "How to Be a Good Subordinate," *The New York Times,* November 25, 1979.

KAREN HARPER

I've got to know by tomorrow morning, Karen. I've got two MBAs from Harvard bugging me every ten minutes on the phone about whether or not they're going to get the job. If you say no, it goes to one of them. Besides, I'm beginning to feel a little uncomfortable around Harry when I see him in the hall—if you leave Fund Management to come work in Investment Advisory, he'll be all over me. I can handle that, but I'd like to get things settled.

Those had been Steve Ackerman's words to Karen Harper this afternoon. As she rode home on the train she began to once again make a list of pros and cons.

The Last Six Years

Karen was 28 years old and had spent the last six years in the Fund Management Group at Hingham Investment Co. Like so many other English Lit grads, she had graduated from college with absolutely no career preparation. She moved from New England to Chicago without a job and into a crowded apartment with three roommates.

On the first day of her job search she registered with a personnel agency as a junior secretary. Right now all she wanted was a job that promised a paycheck every week—she would think about a career or graduate school later. All that mattered was that she survive in Chicago. The agency sent her to Hingham Investment Co., a large, well-known investment management firm whose offices occupied a 20-story older building in the financial district. Karen was well-dressed, attractive, and articulate and didn't think she'd have any trouble getting a job fast.

Her interview took 20 minutes. She was offered an entry-level marketing slot in the Retail Marketing Department. Her boss (and interviewer) was Harry Rosenberg, the vice president and manager of the department. Harry, who had been with Hingham for the past five years, was a modishly dressed man in his early fifties. He had started the Retail Marketing Department at Hingham, which was a departure from Hingham's traditional business of investment advisory services for large institutional and retail clients.

Karen and Harry liked each other right away. Karen saw Harry as a father-type figure who was very interested in her, both professionally and personally. He told her that she was selling herself short as a secretary and that the marketing slot was a great opportunity to learn the business. He was very concerned about her adjustment to Chicago and invited her to join him for dinner that evening. Karen was flattered and grateful. After pinching pennies for so long, it was great to go out in style. Harry talked a lot about the business and treated Karen like an old friend. Harry's general philosophy seemed to be that hard work really pays off, and since Karen was bright and willing, the sky was the limit.

The next six years seemed to prove Harry's theory. Karen worked hard, often until nine in the evening. After two years in marketing, Harry promoted her to the most prestigious and highly paid area—securities acquisition. Until Karen

---

This case was prepared by John P. Kotter as a basis for classroom discussion. Copyright © 1980 by the President and Fellows of Harvard College. Harvard Business School case 481-054.

assumed this role, Harry had done it himself. Karen was viewed by the other members of the department as Harry's favorite. This was undoubtedly true, since no one else spent as much time with Harry, nor did he brag to outsiders about anyone else. When Karen decided to get an MBA and was considering applying to Harvard and Stanford, Harry convinced her to remain in her job and get her MBA by doing evening course work at Northwestern which the firm paid for. Karen's salary increased from $8,000 at her time of hiring to $40,000 plus a sizeable bonus six years later. Harry told her she had it made.

At times Karen believed him. She made plenty of money to support herself in a comfortable apartment. No more roommates. Her job was lots of fun and was coveted by others in the department. Harry allowed her considerable fringe benefits—expense account, free cabs home after a late night at work, after a big project she was free to take a day off. But still she always felt vaguely uneasy—why was Harry doing all this for her? Was it all in her best interests? What did the rest of the firm think? Now she had an MBA—why weren't any other MBAs attracted to Retail Marketing? There were plenty of them in Investment Advisory.

Karen knew the answer to this last question—it was because of Harry. General opinion in Hingham was that Harry was a real eccentric. Karen had to agree that Harry had a rather unorthodox management style and didn't know the first thing about delegating authority. Harry had started Retail Marketing at Hingham and could do all the functions better than anyone else in the department. He loved his work and had to get his hands in everything. Subsequently, no one in the department had much autonomy and the general feeling was that Harry was "on everybody's back" all the time. Karen found that her working relationship with Harry was smoothest when she didn't try to take over things, but instead checked every so often with Harry to keep him informed and ask his advice. Usually she didn't mind this, since it made for the most tranquil atmosphere, but sometimes she felt angry about having to ask Harry's advice on something she felt perfectly able to handle herself. Waiting to see Harry slowed things down considerably and often created problem situations.

The real zinger about Harry was that in spite of all his yelling and meddling, he paid his people exceedingly well and always gave them a sizeable bonus at the end of the year—much bigger than those given out in Investment Advisory to nonpartners. He was always ready to help out an employee in an emergency or problem situation—with either money or time off or whatever. Those who worked for him often said that "just as they were feeling real good about hating Harry for being such a tyrant, he'd go and do something really great out of the blue and totally screw up their heads."

The Investment Advisory Division

Karen's opportunity was to start out as an associate in the Investment Advisory Division. Providing investment management advisory services to clients had always been Hingham's main business. The associate position had been created in order to give young, talented individuals an introduction to money management by working closely with a variety of senior investment managers. Associates were considered to be part of a "resource pool" that was available for work on different projects as they came up. If a large pension fund, for example, requested Hingham to make a presentation on fixed income management, a senior manager in the Fixed Income area of Investment Advisory would select a group of Fixed Income specialists and an associate from the "pool" to work on the presentation. Senior managers also called on associates to assist on day-to-day work with existing clients, which could involve gathering research on a particular industry or providing market information. After a year or so of being in the "pool," the associate has the opportunity to indicate his/her preference for where he/she would like to be placed—whether it be Fixed Income, Equities, Foreign Currency, Research, etc. If this preference coincides with the firm's needs, the associate moves into the desired area. After initial placement, an individual often decides that he/she would like to try another area. If he/she has developed a strong reputation, this movement is usually easy to accomplish.

At the present time, nearly all the associates in the "pool" were recent graduates of top business schools. Investment management was generally regarded as a prestigious field, and the possibility of being made a partner lured many MBAs who were eager to earn big dollars over a period of time. Hingham had recruited at the top business schools for many years for the Investment Advisory Division. No MBA had ever been hired to enter any other area of the firm, including Fund Management.

Associates were expected to work long hours in the first few years. Most associates stayed until early evening at least and were often in the office on weekends. The hours one put in were viewed with a certain degree of pride and indicated how committed one was to the firm and to getting ahead. Associates were often called upon to travel with senior managers to clients' offices. Often this travel was on very short notice. You never really knew where you were going to be the next day.

The Retail Marketing Department

Retail Marketing seemed to be viewed as an amusing curiosity by the rest of Hingham and the investment community. The product was portfolios of securities which were assembled and sold through a broker network to small individual investors and were subsequently not managed. They were sold on the basis of providing steady income and safety through diversification. Its very nature was in contrast to Hingham's traditional business, which was to provide expert advisory service to very wealthy clients and institutions on managing their investment portfolios. By its design, Retail Marketing was a very profitable department for Hingham. Although other firms had tried to imitate the Hingham product, none had been as successful. Most observers attributed Hingham's success to their high-quality and long-standing reputation in the investment community and access to extensive brokerage sales networks. But Harry Rosenberg, the partner in charge of Retail Marketing, insisted that it was his genius that was responsible for the success and that he could do the same at several other firms.

Only about 40 people worked in the Fund Management Department—of these about 10 could be considered to be professionals, either in buying, marketing, or research. The majority of the staff had been there for several years—several had come to Hingham with Harry about 11 years ago when he had joined the firm. Hingham employed close to 500 people, of whom about 100 were professionals and 28 were partners.

The major part of Karen's job was selecting securities for the "packaged pools" of securities Hingham marketed. The purpose of the "pools" was to allow small investors to participate in the attractive yields offered to institutional investors without having to select their own individual portfolios. The product was very successful—popular with both investors and securities brokers and very profitable for Hingham. In fact, during the bad times of 1974–75, it was Retail Marketing which kept Hingham in the black.

Due to the Fund's popularity, there was an almost constant need to accumulate more securities for the pools. Karen bought about $50 million each week. The process of buying securities involved following credit market rates, checking with the department's research team on the current creditworthiness of individual issuers, maintaining a balance of different types of issues in the portfolio, and most important, trying to get the best price on every security purchased. Karen bought stocks and bonds from a wide variety of brokerage firms—she had direct phone lines to eight of the largest firms. Every day involved taking phone calls from about 20 different bond salespeople—mostly aggressive,

smooth-talking salesmen. These people worked on commission and had a vested interest in keeping Karen happy, since she was such an important customer. They were continually offering theater tickets, dinners on the town, party invitations, etc. Although they could be a nuisance, Karen enjoyed this part of her job a lot—most of them were reasonably bright and funny. She had to keep reminding herself, however, that their attentiveness was due solely to her buying power, not her personal charms.

Because of her close relationship with Harry, Karen was involved in all the strategic decisions of the department—something which was not a strict function of her job. In the past Karen had helped develop new concepts for pools to expand on the theme. Harry valued Karen's opinions very highly and often designated her as his spokesperson at meetings both inside and outside the company.

When Karen tried to analyze her feelings about the job, it boiled down to the old joke about "not wanting to join any club that would have me as a member." She suspected this might be silly, but she had learned this job almost five years ago without any MBA or financial background—how difficult could it be? Harry made such a big deal about it—in moments of hyperbole he called her the "most important woman on Wall Street." She really enjoyed the job itself, but she didn't feel that she was really "growing" any more, and wasn't growth supposed to be essential? Karen's doubts were exacerbated by the fact that Hingham was practically unique in both the size and the activity of its Retail Marketing Department—no other firm offered a position similar to hers, so there was no way of comparing herself with others. She got a lot of attention from salesmen, but nobody else really knew anything about the pools—it wasn't a well-known glamour position like investment advisory or investment banking. She was worried that she would become a high-priced but "illiquid" commodity. If something went really wrong with the department, where would she go? To sum up, she felt like a very large fish in a very small pond.

The atmosphere in Retail Marketing could best be described as "chaotic." Harry Rosenberg's personality definitely contributed to this situation. His moods seemed to determine the group mood. He involved himself in all areas of the department and delegated very little authority but much responsibility.

Harry Rosenberg

Harry usually arrived in the office at ten or eleven in the morning after calling his secretary and key people at least once by phone from home. Everyone knew when he arrived and there was always a "mood check"—is he in a good or bad mood?—which would be relayed verbally throughout the department. Harry spent most of the day in meetings and on the phone and always left the office at one o'clock for a two-hour lunch. Since so little authority was delegated, workers in the department had to consult Harry before making important decisions and this resulted in a line of people outside his office all day. Once you did get in to see him there were constant interruptions—phone calls, secretaries (three of them) walking in and out to extricate papers from his jumbled desk, urgent questions from underlings who didn't know what Harry wanted done about this or that. Harry liked to stay in the office late—often until eight or so, and several people regularly stayed late in order to get to talk to him without the constant interruptions. Often Harry would take an employee out to dinner to continue these discussions. He expressed great disdain for "nine-to-five-ers" and commented that they would "never get ahead in his department."

Harry had a very controversial management style. If something or someone displeased him, he would let the offender know exactly how he felt. He had a violent temper which didn't last very long. He seemed to explode only with those workers from whom he expected a lot and had disappointed him. In spite of all his noise, he had never fired anyone. There was a continual rumbling in Retail Marketing that Harry was "absolutely nuts" and that he was "driving everybody crazy." Key people would threaten to leave from time to time, but actual turnover was very low.

Harry gave the impression of having absolute authority in his department and gave little indication that he was concerned about any hierarchy at Hingham that was above him. The partnership structure at Hingham was actually quite stratified, and Harry was several rungs down from the top of the partnership group. He found this structure exceedingly frustrating and was very critical of top management. The senior partners tended to stay away from Retail Marketing—it was not the mainstream of the firm's traditional business and, though it was extremely profitable, was not fully understood by many of the older partners. Most of the professional staff in Retail Marketing had had limited, if any, exposure to the partners above Harry's level.

Most sources attributed Harry's managerial autonomy to the profitability of the product. General sentiment was that "as long as Harry brings in the dollars, nobody's going to tell him what to do." Harry enjoyed running the department as a little profit center and did many things which were not "standard Hingham policy."

I like to think of Retail Marketing as my little family and I'd do anything for my people. I pay them much more than they'd get anywhere else and they feel they're working for me, not Hingham and Company. Yeah, I know I don't do things by the book but I don't want this place to be just a regular department of a stuffy, impersonal firm where everybody gives 50% of their energy and ability and gets a raise every year and a vacation. People here know that if they put out the maximum effort, they'll get rewarded—and that any job in the department, including mine, is open to anyone who shows me they can do it.

Karen's Dilemma

I know Investment Advisory *seems* to be appealing to Karen, but it's dead wrong for her. She's got it made here if she'd just wise up and realize it. That's the trouble with young people in business today—they think they've got to keep moving all the time—get titles, etc. If they'd just plug away at something and be patient they'd be a lot better off. Look, I've been in business for 30-odd years and I've seen just about all there is to see. If Karen just sticks with me and accepts the fact that I've got her best interests at heart and have the experience to know what's the best course for her, she'll be fine. She's a bright kid, but when she gets all this MBA rhetoric in her head, she's dangerous. What happens if she goes to Investment Advisory? She'll be just one MBA in a sea of them— and they're all after the same thing—to be a partner. Well, the existing partners would have to be hit by the plague for spots to open up fast enough to please these kids. She'd be working her ass off for a whole bunch of people, none of whom would be able to give her the kind of close direction and support I can. I'm not going to be alive forever; I'm 57 years old—somebody's got to take my spot— and Karen's the obvious choice if she doesn't lose her head and do something stupid.

Karen had heard Harry's thinking a million times. She thought he was sincere, but seriously doubted that if she stayed in Retail Marketing a senior partnership would ever open up for her. The rumor mill had it that the senior partners were concerned about Harry's management style and were just waiting until he retired to put someone into that spot who was "one of them"— someone who could integrate Retail Marketing better into the Hingham mainstream. Karen felt sure that no matter how competent a manager she was, she would always be viewed as "Harry's girl" and would be considered suspect. She thought a lot about how she could stay in Retail Marketing and get more visibility with top management, but was at a loss as to how to accomplish this. Day-to-day business did not put her in much contact with the rest of the firm and it was Harry who met with the partners at the weekly luncheon and planning sessions. She knew that he always spoke highly of her but didn't know if that was a positive or negative fact, given the partners' general reaction to Harry.

Maybe she should grab at the associate's spot while it was available. She had known Steve Ackerman, the junior partner in charge of the training program, for several years and they had always been cordial. After a particularly frustrating day last week, she had called him on an impulse and asked to meet him for lunch. She had guardedly confided her frustration in working with Harry to Steve. He seemed to understand completely and said that he himself could never work for someone like Harry. This made Karen wonder if there was something wrong with her—why was she putting up with this situation? The more she thought, the madder she got. Before lunch was over, Steve had offered her the chance to enter Investment Advisory as an associate. He warned her that initially it might seem like a step down—taking orders from everyone and doing grunt work after she had been largely on her own, not counting Harry's influence, for the past few years. The move would mean an initial pay cut of $5,000, which would still make her the most highly paid associate. Steve explained that this was the best he could do, since he didn't want the newly hired MBAs to think that someone doing the same job, although experienced in another area, was being paid $10,000 more than they. Besides, Steve had explained, the salary would increase over time and her chances of making a partnership were definitely enhanced.

Karen felt depressed and confused. The idea of entering the competitive world of an associate in Investment Advisory really didn't appeal to her. She felt she had proven her ability and didn't want to go through the initial stages of having to make a big impression again. Besides, Harry was her mentor, wasn't he? And from all she'd read about women in business, wasn't the mentor system supposed to be an essential ingredient in helping women move to the top? Was she looking a gift horse in the mouth and just being a spoiled brat? After all, without Harry's guidance and support, she might be still typing somewhere.

The flip side of this argument was that Karen felt that she was getting too old to be involved in the paternalistic relationship with Harry. If she didn't stand on her own now, when would she? She knew that some of the partners had definite opinions as to the nature of Harry and Karen's relationship. Even though Karen knew that their insinuations were unfounded, she still felt a little embarrassed. The rumor mill also postulated that the reason why Harry was so supportive of Karen was that she was a woman—and in Harry's macho mind that meant "nonthreatening." Why had Harry never taken a bright young *male* under his wing and pushed him along?

Karen knew she had to decide tonight. She didn't want to throw a great thing away—but she didn't want to get trapped in a childlike relationship either.

chapter

33

The Early Career

In the early phase of a career, usually between ages 20 and 35, people make and deepen initial commitments to a type of work, an organization, and a nonwork life style. Professionals, in particular, expend considerable energy to become competent (and recognized as such by others) in their chosen trade. It is usually an exciting period, in which one begins to try to fulfill expectations about the "professional me" that have been developing (through education) for two decades.

Four general sets of issues seem to be particularly important if one is to try to understand this early phase, the obstacles encountered, and the methods typically used to deal with them. One set of issues relates to adapting to being an employee in a complex human organization. A second has to do with getting established in one's work or organization and achieving some initial success. A third has to do with establishing some type of a workable relationship between one's career and the nonwork aspects of life. The fourth relates to a period of questioning of initial career and noncareer choices, which most people go through around age 30.

Adapting to the Realities of Complex Organizations

Most professionals start their careers within an established organization. Having been students in an educational setting for anywhere from 16 to 22 years, they suddenly become employees inside what are usually noneducational organizations. This change can create some serious problems for people in their first year of work. Beyond that, the ability to grasp quickly the more subtle realities associated with human organi-

zations often makes the difference between a very successful and an ordinary early career. Some of the more important of these realities are discussed below.

Distribution of Rewards

Simply doing what you think is a good job, or even a very good job, is no guarantee that you will receive the rewards you desire.

For a number of complex reasons, most established organizations do not have performance evaluation systems that (1) completely define what "good performance" is for each job, (2) make sure that employees are aware of those performance criteria, (3) systematically collect data on employees' performance, (4) feed those data back to employees so they can monitor how they are doing, and (5) use those data as the basis for distributing rewards (such as interesting assignments, promotions, money, discretion).

Considerable evidence exists that such a system would be very beneficial for employees, especially during the early career. But because "good" performance is often difficult and expensive to define and measure, and because creating such systems where they don't exist is expensive and time-consuming, good performance appraisal systems are very seldom found in organizations.

Instead, rewards are distributed in most organizations based on the "judgments" of a number of people (a person's immediate superior is usually the key judge), some of whom may have only secondhand information on many of the people they are asked to judge.

People who are successful in their initial careers are those who perform well on the criteria used by the judges, and whose performance record is known by the judges. It is for these reasons that the better "how to" books on building a successful career stress (a) learning what your bosses' expectations are concerning your work and (b) getting involved in some highly visible projects.

Development of Potential

Most organizations have no coherent system to make sure that people, in their early careers, get the experience, training, and human contacts needed to really develop their potential for their own benefit and the organization's.

Although the development of people is an important goal for most organizations, it is a *long-range goal*. In most organizations, long-run objectives receive a priority lower than short-run concerns. For this and other reasons, employee development is seldom given anything close to the resources needed to do a uniformly good job. Even in companies where resources have been allocated to employee development, and where training programs and job rotation systems have been created, numerous individuals seem to end up coping with short-run demands at the expense of their future development.

We have seen many former students who seem to learn more in their first five years of work than others learn in 15 years or more. The fast-learning group appear to be different from others in that they proactively take responsibility for their own learning. They seek out role models and mentors, recognizing that one relationship with a highly talented and successful senior person can be enormously instructive. They don't stay in any one job for more than a few years, taking advantage of the fact that almost all the learning associated with most jobs comes in the first two years. They don't wait to be assigned to new projects and jobs by others; they nominate themselves. In this and other ways, they actively manage their own careers.

Dependency on Others

Most professional jobs in organizations, especially managerial jobs, make an individual dependent on numerous others, who often have different or conflicting objectives. Complex interdependencies and conflict are facts of life in most organizations. Individuals who cannot (or will not) find a way to manage their own dependencies are in for a hard time.

Younger people in particular often feel their dependence on others who know more than they do about the job, the organization, the people, and how to get things done. Young managers will often find themselves dependent on the cooperation of subordinates, a boss, other senior officials, various service departments, and possibly even outside suppliers, customers, and regulators. All these individuals and groups have limited time and talent, and their objectives sometimes clash with cooperation. Students are seldom if ever trained in how to manage this type of dependence network.

Managers use a wide variety of techniques to cope with their complex dependencies. Their techniques are sometimes aimed at reducing dependence, sometimes at influencing those on whom they are dependent to cooperate in certain ways, and sometimes at gaining power over the dependencies (which makes influencing them much easier). The faster a young employee learns to use these techniques effectively, the more successful he or she will generally be in the early career.

The larger and more complex the organization, the more time people end up having to spend managing interdependencies. For example, the following is excerpted from a 29-year-old manager's description of what he does in a typical day at a moderately large manufacturing company:

When I arrive in the morning I normally read the paper for 15 minutes or a half hour to catch up on the latest news. Randomly throughout the month I will call my boss before working hours actually begin, to let him know that I'm there and on the job, and he can reach me whenever he wants me. This is an important game to play in my situation, because he is located in a different building eight miles away, and sometimes he feels a little insecure as to whether all of his people are working full time and are doing the kinds of things he would like to have done.

I spend about one-fourth of the day actually here in my office. The table in the center of the office is the major working area, and it's round. I don't have a standard desk. This was something that I designed when I was promoted six months ago. The average age of my direct reports was about 47–48 years old, and I felt that it would be very difficult for me, being only 28 at the time, to sit behind a big desk and give these guys orders. They had 20 years of experience and knew the company backward and forward. There wasn't any way I could effectively tell them what to do. So I decided to get in a round table and to make sure that all the chairs around the table were of the same type and description so there wouldn't be any overt status difference between anyone in the office, so that we could build a teamwork relationship among all members of the group.

After reading the morning paper I would normally attend several meetings. I spend almost 70 percent of my normal day in meetings. By the way, that drives a lot of people nuts, and it bothers me too, but most of our meetings really are necessary. My peers and I have got to know what each other and top management are doing or we trip all over each other. Meetings are often the best way to get the information across. Meetings are also useful when I need the commitment from other divisions for some action, and when we have a problem but not all the expertise to solve it.

This would take me normally till about 10:30 or 10:45, at which point I would come back to the office and handle the mail. The mail comes in a stack of about 4 to 6 inches each day. I would quickly sort it and deliver messages to my staff to work on the projects and various assignments that came through the mail. I would delegate all the assignments with the exception of *politically* sensitive issues. Those I would discuss with the appropriate manager and handle them together with him. Normally it would take me 10 to 15 minutes to sort the mail and another 15 to 20 discussing the various sensitive issues.

This would bring me to around 11:30–11:45, where I would work on my personal mail, which includes salary and merit reviews, expense accounts, purchase requisitions, etc. This would take me right up to lunch.

After lunch, the schedule of activities changes, depending on what part of the year it is. During the first half of the year the work load is not as heavy as during the last half. During the first half of the year I would spend most of the afternoon in meetings of the type described earlier. In the latter part of the year I spend a great deal of time working on the annual long-range plan. This is a very extensive effort and requires hundreds and hundreds of man-hours of work to put together the details, schedules, and plans that support the strategies of this division. One of the reasons that this effort takes such a great deal of my personal time is that my boss' incentive salary depends on the achievement of many specific goals.

Parenthetically, this young man has had a very successful and satisfying early career.

Achieving

For most professionals, the early career is a period directed toward personal achievement. Considerable time and energy are invested in work and in establishing themselves as credible professionals with proven "track records."

In most of the cases we have observed personally, or heard others report, those people who achieved the most professionally in their early careers were people who were able to generate what Doug Hall has called a "success syndrome."[1] As we have observed it, this process can be described as follows:

1. The new employee does not usually have a traumatic first year and is able to adjust rather quickly to organizational realities. As a result of careful selection or luck, the individual fits well with the organization and its work.

2. The individual gets some challenging initial assignments which, because of the lack of adjustment problem and the generally good fit, he or she performs well on.

3. This initial success bolsters the individual's self-confidence and helps him or her get challenging, more important (and visible) assignments.

4. The person's self-confidence, on top of everything else, helps him or her to do well in these next assignments.

5. These successes continue to bolster the individual's self-confidence and provide access to additional human and technical resources that are needed to continue to quickly grow and handle more important work.

6. The cycle continues, more or less dramatically, throughout the early career period. Success continues to breed success.

The "high flyers"—those who achieve more success in less time than 95 percent of their peers—seem to be people who position themselves to have opportunities come their way, and then take advantage of most of these opportunities. Eugene Jennings had studied this process in managerial careers,[2] which he calls developing mobility, and has identified the types of underlying rules associated with it. Those rules are:

1. Never become overspecialized. Get broad experience in a number of areas and always maintain your options.

2. Become a "crucial" subordinate to a very mobile and successful boss. If you find yourself working for an immobile superior, move.

3. Make yourself highly visible. Make sure your superiors know about your accomplishments and your ambitions.

4. If you are blocked and can't find a way out, leave the organization, but do it in a way that allows you to part as friends. Never allow a showdown to occur, and don't quit work with an emotional parting shot.

Both moderately and very successful people seem to reach a point late in the early career period where continued growth in their achievements requires that they be put "in charge." It is not unusual for professionals around age 35 to abandon their mentors and begin to feel frustrated because they don't have the power to continue producing even larger achievements. For many, this period doesn't last long, because they are soon put "in charge."

---

[1]Douglas T. Hall, *Careers in Organizations* (Pacific Palisades, Calif.: Goodyear, 1976).

[2]Eugene Jennings, *The Mobile Manager* (New York: McGraw-Hill, 1967).

Establishing a Workable Relationship Between a Job and Other Aspects of One's Life

Most professionals develop two key commitments during their twenties—a commitment to get a job (or organization) and a commitment to an off-the-job life style (with or without a spouse, with or without children). The demands made on an individual by these two commitments periodically change in ways that conflict and put strain on the individual.

The following example, reported by a 28-year-old man who had established a successful initial career at a bank, is not atypical:

> I usually get home by 6:00 P.M. My wife and I have got until at least 7:30 P.M. before we really have any time to exchange more than a ''Hi, how are you?'' By 7:30 we get the kids to bed. Sometimes we eat with Bobby, sometimes we don't. After dinner we do get some time together, even though we're both a little bit tired. Alice complains, with some reason, that I read magazines and newspapers during the little free time that we have together. We find that time is more precious than it was before. Ever since the baby came, we haven't been able to go to bed before 11 P.M. because that's when Alice completes her last nursing. Normally, we would try to get to bed earlier than that. We hope to resume our normal schedule as soon as the baby starts sleeping through the night.

> We're thinking of moving out to the suburbs soon. There's not much for kids to do in the city. There are a lot of other reasons, though. One of our biggest problems is that it is just too damn expensive to live in the city. So we might buy a house—we're really looking into it now—but with a lot of mixed feelings.

> Kids, I don't know, we didn't realize until after we had them how much time they require of you. They are just so damn dependent upon you. There's so much work involved with younger children that you've just got to reorder your life a bit. We found the change from being young marrieds without kids to being young marrieds with kids to be something more than we expected.

> We have no real desire to go to the suburbs. It's just that it costs so much less to live in the suburbs than in the city. We can own a house, save money, and build up equity at the same time. But in the suburbs I would have a 45-minute commute. I don't like the thought of that very much. On the other hand, I should get to play a little more tennis out there. I have let myself go; I've gotten a little soft. The extra commuting will make time even more precious than it was before though. It's a rough choice . . .

Young professionals whose spouses also are pursuing careers often find it even more difficult to establish and maintain a workable relationship between their two jobs and an off-the-job style. ''Dual career'' couples who also have children usually find that their time and energy are very scarce resources.

The work vs. off-the-job strains that develop during the early part of a career are not confined to married couples or couples with children. Single people often run into difficulties, too. Witness the comments of these two young men:

> We're having a meeting next week out at St. Georges. This is the fifth week out of the last eight that I have been at one of these conventions. Many of these conventions are executive oriented, and many of the executives bring their wives. This creates an interesting situation for a bachelor like myself, particularly when most of the women are middle-aged and older. You see, they don't appreciate seeing me show up at each convention with a different attractive young woman.

> I'm in a rather tough situation right now, and I don't see any relief in sight. I was given a promotion six months ago, and at 31 I am now the company's youngest plant manager—which, of course, is terrific. But, the promotion moved me from Chicago to Panto Flats, Texas, which has a population of about 6000. I would like very much to establish a permanent relationship with a woman, but unlike in Chicago, there just aren't many unmarried women around here. My nonwork life style, at this point, is very unsatisfactory.

There are three ways in which people generally deal with a work-nonwork conflict. Some people make changes in their nonwork lives that, in effect, reduce their commitment there. Many successful young executives take this option. One *New Yorker* cartoon captures this response well. A 30- to 35-year-old manager in a posh office holds a phone in his hand and displays a very annoyed expression. The caption reads: ''Martha, how many times have I told you not to bother me while I'm on the way up?''

A second option some people choose is to take actions that reduce their commitment to work. Individuals who receive a great deal of satisfaction from their nonwork lives, and individuals who are disppointed in the amount of satisfaction they are getting from their work, both often select this option.

A third option people sometimes choose attempts not to reduce the commitment to either work or other activities, but simply to allow the conflict to exist and to absorb the strain personally. The young plant manager from Panto Flats ''solved'' his problem by jetting to Houston and back an average of two or three nights per week, where he eventually did meet a young woman and got engaged. In the interim, he lived with less sleep and a special variety of jet lag.

Pace

People in the early career stages are working hard even without the special demands faced by this young

Exhibit 33-1
Symptoms of Burnout

Low morale	Exhaustion/chronic fatigue
Depression	Frequent headaches
Absenteeism	Nervous stomach
Increased anxiety	Ulcers/colitis
Overly critical	Weight loss
Disenchantment	Rapid, irregular heartbeat
Mental rigidity	Poor appetite
Loss of sense of humor	Loss of sexual interest
Easily discouraged	Change viewed as a threat
Bored	Not enjoying time off
Easily angered	Feeling out of control
Negative attitude	Overuse of alcohol
Withdrawn from people	Making everything a problem
Cynicism	Postponing decisions
Difficulty in concentrating	Not recognizing limitations
Unwillingness to ask for help	Perfectionism

Adapted from "Burn Out" by Marvin Fogel, *DM* Magazine, August 1979, and "Burn Out in Academia" by Gib Akin, *Exchange: The Journal of the Organizational Behavior Teaching Society,* Vol. V, no. 2, 1980, p. 5.

plant manager. In the early stages of a career, people are experimenting with, among other things, the *pace* of their lives. Pace is a widely variable and individually specific feature of life style. Some people work and live faster than others. Although many organizations value efficiency (speed) in their employees, faster is not always better. Sometimes doing more faster can mean doing more in a mediocre fashion.

Another potential pitfall of rapid pace is burnout. Exhibit 33-1 highlights the commonly observed symptoms of burnout. These symptoms can arise from very rapid-paced life styles in which the person comes to one of two conclusions. The first is, "Is that all there is?" Here, the emotional sense is one of disappointment—that I've worked too hard and achieved so much, but somehow it's not satisfying. The second conclusion that can lead to burnout is resignation. This is the sense of having worked so hard and still not having been able to keep up. Effort is no longer seen to produce rewards and so much energy has already been expended in the search for those rewards that there is none left. One becomes exhausted.

In her book, *Living with Stress,* Nancy Gross makes the following statement:

> . . . You owe yourself the indulgence of a sense of humour through which you can cut . . . annoyances down to size. You owe yourself the indulgence of the patience that permits you to ignore pressures and delays. . . . You owe yourself the indulgence of vacations, of

aspirin when you are coming down with a cold, of hours of peaceful privacy, of relaxation, of occasional bursts of the extravagance . . . that give[s] color to life. You owe yourself the responsibility of using your body and your mind in the interests of the constructive realities and aspirations that mean the most to you. You owe yourself a pace . . . which meets your temperamental needs, which neither hurries you nor holds you back.

We believe this is true and encourage you to find the pace that fits you and that will sustain you and your enthusiasm for life throughout your career and lifetime. Indeed, part of the individual-organization matching process involves matching the paces at which each desire to operate.

Balance

Another characteristic of early career work-nonwork experimentation is balance—that is the proportion of time and energy to be allocated to each aspect of a person's life. Balance does *not* imply, in this case, equal proportions; rather, it simply refers to the proportion of time and energy chosen by an individual. One person's "balanced" life may seem "out of balance" to another.

A common such phenomenon in the business world is the workaholic's life style. Workaholics balance their lives heavily in favor of their careers. They typically exhibit the characteristics outlined in Exhibit 33-2. To

Exhibit 33–2
Characteristics of Workaholics

Spend most of their time working

Seldom take vacations

Get up early regardless of how late they go to bed

Read or work while they eat

Make lists of things to do each day

Have a hard time doing nothing

Are fiercely competitive

Work on weekends and holidays

Dread retirement

Really enjoy working

Have strong self-doubts and fear their own inadequacy

Strive to get the most out of their time

Make little distinction between work and play

Pursue everything with vigor, enthusiasm, and intensity

Adapted from *Workaholics* by Marilyn Machlowitz, Addison-Wesley, Reading, MA, 1980.

many people, a workaholic's life is out of balance. To the workaholic, says Marilyn Machlowitz, author of the book *Workaholics,* life is as it should be. Whether or not workaholics *choose* their life styles or are *driven* to them, many seem to enjoy and thrive on them. Regardless of the workaholic's predispositions, though, living and working with workaholics creates some special problems that need to be managed carefully. We refer you to Machlowitz's book for a detailed discussion of these. The important point for our purposes here is that regardless of the particular balance between work, family, self, and life style you choose, you should try to consider the short-run and long-run consequences of that balance in each component and for the people in it. If you are able to do this, you are less likely to be surprised or disappointed by your choices later on.

Not everyone, of course, experiences the same amount of work-nonwork conflict during the early career. The people we have observed who have experienced the most conflict, and who tend to "solve" this problem in ways that eventually create even more conflicts and problems, make decisions in one aspect of their lives without considering the implications for the other parts. That is, they ignore, to some degree, the interdependence that exists between the various aspects of a life. We have even seen people who tend to be planning-oriented create problems for themselves by planning only *within* their careers. People who behave this way are often able to survive during their early career, but the lack of total life planning and decision making eventually catches up with most of them—often in the midlife period between 35 and 45.

There are at least four ways to characterize different approaches to balance in one's life. These are shown in Exhibit 33–3 and are a career focus, a family focus, a pendulum focus, and a do-it-all-now composite focus. The exhibit lists the basic dominant values, the critical demands, the potential rewards, and the potential consequences for each focus. We encourage you to stop and think a moment about your balance, to identify which of these four seems closest to yours, and then to write down your feelings and observations about the values, demands, rewards, and consequences as they might apply to you. How will you manage the consequences? Will the rewards be sufficient? Do you have the skills to meet the critical demands?

Questioning Initial Choices

Most professionals seem to go through a period of questioning their initial work, organization, family, and life style choices after about five to ten years. For some this is a mild period, while for others it can be fairly difficult and traumatic. As a result, some people abandon their initial commitments and make new ones; they sometimes change organizations, go back to school, start over in a new line of work in a new city, or get married or divorced.

People who make poor initial decisions—who start work with very unrealistic expectations, who have serious problems adapting to their new environments, or who have trouble creating a workable arrangement between their work and nonwork lives—often find around age 30 that the satisfaction they are getting from the various aspects of their lives is less than they expected or desired. This leads them to a period of reexamination. A few are forced into reexamination and change. Some are fired. Others lose a key promotion they expected. The spouses of a few walk out on them. Even people who are fundamentally satisfied with their lives seem at least to pause and ponder their life situation around age 30. Is this what life is really all about? Have I really made the right choices? Am I responding too much to what I think I "should" do?

Those who actually make major changes as a result of this period of questioning are a minority, no doubt partly because of the difficulties associated with change. Unless one is in a highly unsatisfying position, change usually increases the pain one feels in the short run. Finding a new job or breaking off a marriage relationship can be a traumatic experience.

After the period of questioning is over, or after a change has been made, people generally plunge back into their careers with increased dedication and energy. For five to ten years, they focus again on achievement in their chosen profession.

Exhibit 33–3
Approaches to Balance in Life

	Career Person	Family Person	Pendulum Person	Composite Person
Basic Values	Success is getting ahead.	Success is love at home.	Success is getting ahead and then having love at home.	Success is having it all at once.
Critical Demands	Singular focus. Large amounts of time on the job. Political skill. Suppression of "softer" desires. Supportive partner.	Large amounts of time at home. Suppression of "harder" desires. Sharing partner.	Ability to reconstruct from neglect. Ability to change habits. Sense of timing. Patient partner.	Large amounts of time. Ability to plan time, not projects. Ability to manage stress. Sense of timing. Ability to shift focus and to learn quickly. Supportive partner.
Potential Rewards	Power. Money. Prestige. Satisfaction.	Peace. Love. Friendships. Satisfaction.	Sense of quick growth (career). Changing satisfactions.	Power, money, prestige, and love at home. Peace, fulfillment, and satisfaction.
Potential Consequences	Loss of love at home. Sense of hollowness of rewards. Desensitization. Stressful life.	Loss of power, money, and prestige. Loss of impact, sense of contribution.	Loss of love at home. Loss of pinnacle achievements (in order to deal with other focus). Desensitization.	Mediocrity. Sense of being out of control. Stressful life.

Assignment

Read the Ben Jerrow case (starting below). Be prepared to describe Ben's life style and the events which caused him to review his life style. What kind of events would (will) cause you to reexamine your life style? What are Ben's options? What do you think Ben should do? Why? What would *you* do? Why?

BEN JERROW

At age 36, Ben Jerrow was the youngest full partner in C. B. Kline and Company, one of the world's most prestigious management consulting firms. Jerrow, his wife, and three children led a very comfortable life on his $65,000 salary.

Except for a slight cold, May 12 (1974) was in many ways a very typical day for Jerrow. He left his Westchester home at 6:30 A.M. and arrived at his office in Manhattan at 8:00. At 3:00 in the afternoon he took a cab to La Guardia, then flew to Pittsburgh for what was scheduled to be a short planning meeting with one of his clients. Instead of ending at 8:00, however, the discussion dragged on until 12:30, at which point Jerrow headed back toward the airport in his rented car. At 1:15 A.M., about three miles from the airport, Jerrow fell asleep at the wheel and drove his car at 50 miles per hour into the back of a truck parked on the side of the road. At 2:12 A.M. Nancy Jerrow received a call from the Woodlands Community Hospital informing her that her husband was in critical condition in their emergency room.

*   *   *

Benjamin Jerrow was born and raised in Chicago, the second son of a behavioral science professor at a local college. His father served as a consultant to a number of organizations in the Chicago area, and Ben actually worked with him during his summers while going to school at Northwestern. After getting his BS in economics, Ben attended a midwestern business school, getting both an MBA and a doctorate. While in graduate school he married Nancy McKenzie. They had their first child soon after he began work at Kline in the Chicago office.

"I started work at Kline," Ben had said to others, "thinking I'd transform the place in a couple of years into something more competent and exciting. I suppose almost everyone who is attracted to Kline is that way: the five letter men, the superstars, who just look at a problem and it gets solved. Which is to say, they are all very egocentric."

> I remember my first assignment well. The old Buttersworth College was taken over by the Board of Regents for higher education in Illinois. They were going to transform a 3,500-student technical school into a 30,000-student university in the course of five years, and ours was the mission to figure out how the hell to do it; how should you organize, how should you staff, and on and on and on. I remember thinking, well that looks easy enough.

> What I didn't know at the time was that the study was badly negotiated, and even more poorly managed.

> Jim Welch was the study manager. He's about 5'6" and had a mind that went about 400 miles an hour and a mouth that went about 500. Unfortunately they weren't quite in sync. Jim was very very bright, but he could piss off the Good Humor Man. He was just unbelievable. We'd go up to Jim and say, "Here are the five different organizational alternatives we've got," all laid out on charts. He'd say, "Where's the date." "What do you mean, where's the date?" "Well, there's no date on the organization chart." Half an hour later after a lecture as to why dates are important, you grab the thing and say, "All right Jim, I'll put a fuckin date on it." It was just interchange after interchange like that. In all fairness, every time he'd come up with things like that, there would be a message in it. You just had to pull the skin over your head to make sure it didn't absolutely destroy you.

> About halfway through the study, or what we thought was halfway through it, Jim ended up crossing irons with the head of the Board of Regents commissioned by the governor to get this college going. We had laid out the economic analyses and what the organizational and staffing al-

ternatives were, etc. In that meeting, the chairman said, "No, no, that isn't what I really want. I want to know what the University of Illinois, the University of Chicago, Northwestern and a half a dozen other universities are organized like and I'll decide which type of organization we want." That isn't the way Kline operates. To make a long story short, it ended up Jim pissing off the chairman and we got pulled off the study. It just ended right there. An absolute disaster.

Jerrow's second assignment at Kline was not a disaster, but his performance, as rated by the project manager, was close to being unsatisfactory.

> I didn't know what the hell I was doing and I wasn't thinking very clearly. That was a phenomenal ego blow. It isn't that it hadn't happened previously in sports or whatever. Part of my game has always been that of the street fighter—I may not start out winning but by the time the thing is over I will. And it was clear at that point in time that I not only wasn't winning, but it wasn't all that clear that I ever would. I had serious doubts about whether I was smart enough to be able to do it. I knew I worked hard enough to be able to get it done. I began to wonder whether I fit with them from a personal chemistry point of view, and so forth. In fact, I started looking a little for a job. I figured, screw this, I just gotta do something else. I got a couple of offers, none of which really seemed very exciting, but they did help my wounded feelings at that point in time.

Six months after joining Kline, Jerrow began his third assignment. He ended up traveling five days a week for the next six months with almost no break. His performance, as judged by more senior employees, rose to "average" during this period.

> It was then I got my first little view of political infighting. I found ideas on this or that which we traded over cocktails or dinner circling back and being presented to the engagement director and the engagement manager by some people as their own neat new idea. I found that happened two or three times and it ended up pissin me off a little bit. So I decided at that point in time, all right, I'll set you up with one that will give you 80% of the answer and when you get shot out of the saddle I'll come in with the other 20% and make it clear who the hell's idea it was anyway. Well, one guy got cut up pretty badly on that one. It was good clean fun.

After one year with Kline, Jerrow decided he probably wasn't ever going to "make it" there. He seriously considered taking a job offer as a VP for a $80 million a year industrial firm. The offer, however, came from a longstanding client of his Dad, and it wasn't ever clear to Jerrow whether the offer was made because of that relationship or because of his demonstrated abilities. He turned it down.

> It got to the point where I didn't really give a damn whether I stayed at Kline or not. And that really helped in a way, because I started to be a bit more bold. I decided to take a number of calculated risks.

In July on a plane from Montreal to Chicago, John Michaels (the head of the Chicago office) asked Ben if the project teams that he had seen since joining the company were different in any ways from what he had expected. Ben said yes, that they were about one-half as effective as he would have expected. A month later, Michaels sent Ben a note asking him to take on the administrative assignment of looking into the effectiveness of their project teams. In September Jerrow put together an effort that included a questionnaire survey of all people in the Chicago office concerning the effectiveness of project teams and the methods by which they usually operated. He analyzed the results, gave them to Michaels, along with suggestions for corrective action. Michaels agreed with Jerrow's report and told him to go ahead with his improvement program. By December, almost everyone in the office agreed that the working climate had changed considerably for the better. Michaels was clearly impressed.

> By early December, while I was far from being out of trouble, the bleeding had stopped and it looked like I was at least not going to be fired. By January this was virtually assured.

In February, Jerrow was asked to come and do a similar survey in the San Francisco office. In April, he was asked by the New York office (headquarters) to work with virtually every Kline office to evaluate and improve their effectiveness. By April, Jerrow was beginning to establish a positive reputation throughout the firm.

Kline had been anxious to make headway into the market for organization, manpower planning, and compensation studies, but had been relatively unsuccessful for the previous three years. With Jerrow's new visibility and reputation, principals in New York began to solicit and then listen to his ideas about how to get into these areas. They also began to ask his advice regarding the two or three cases in that area which they did have.

On May 10, Jerrow received a call from the managing director in New York asking him to take a look at a questionnaire they had developed as a part of a large manpower planning project they were doing for one of the 10 largest industrial companies in the United States.

A couple of weeks later, I finally got the questionnaire. I looked at it, called them back and said it's dog meat. It's just not going to work. It's poorly designed. I don't understand really what you're trying to do, and so on. To make a long story short, they asked me to come to New York to help. I went, and found the way they were trying to go about the case didn't make any sense at all. I ended up spending five days a week there for the next two months—the Monday morning special going out and Friday night or Saturday morning coming back. We ended up completely changing the thrust of the study from one in which we were going to provide answers to one where we were going to provide questions. It served as the first real personnel diagnostic I think the firm had done.

With great effort, we finished just before we were scheduled to present the findings. Our presentation wasn't going to give the chairman the answers he was looking for. In fact it was going to raise questions that would make him as well as the whole personnel function, look awfully bad. And I probably was a little overly aggressive on that one. I showed the presentation to the managing partner on the case (Bob Jordan) the day before the meeting, and he turned white. He said, "Oh, shit, we're dead. The chairman isn't going to like this even a little." But he didn't have time to change the presentation and he didn't really want to cancel the meeting or postpone it, so he made one of the other guys (George Elms) give the presentation with me there. It was one of those things where you figure, "That's it baby. I better get the résumé polished up." The chairman sat there for 45 minutes or so just stone-faced. There wasn't a word that came out of anyone in this whole entourage of his. About three-quarters of the way through the presentation there was one specific piece of data that a personnel guy picked up on and started to blast. Elms couldn't answer the question and immediately passed it to me. I came up with one quick fact that put it all back into perspective again while the personnel guy sat there smoking. He started to interrupt one other time and the chairman told him to shut up and quit trying to cover his ass and that he wanted to hear the whole story. That was when I knew we were in pretty good shape.

I pulled one other coup on that one which was unbeknownst to either Bob or George. I suspected the question that was going to come out of it was, "All right, what do we do from here? You've pointed out that things are in total disarray, how do we fix them?" I had half a dozen slides prepared the day before showing how to proceed from there. The chairman asked the question at the end of the session, Bob turned white and George turned red. We took a five minute break and I gave the slides to George and—bang—we were right in for another 200,000 bucks or so with a new project.

In June, Jerrow was asked to come permanently to the New York office, with a healthy increase in pay. They moved in July, to the chagrin of his wife.

Nancy was thoroughly pissed off with me for being away too much and moving to New York didn't really help any.

Kline began getting more contracts in the areas of Jerrow's interests, and he succeeded in developing a few techniques that were considered technical breakthroughs. One of his clients offered a VP job at a 75% increase in pay, but he turned it down on the basis that he was having a good time and learning a lot at Kline. When the annual spring announcement of new partners at Kline came, Jerrow expected to be named one. He wasn't.

It was a legitimate decision. The screw is that I had been led to believe I was going to be made a partner that year. And one other person made it whose track record wasn't as good as mine. I was clearly disappointed, and went out looking for job offers. I got two or three attractive ones, but each had some fatal flaw. And I began to think it would be smarter to wait a year and leave after being elected partner so there would be no questions at all about whether I cut it or not.

I learned later that Jerry York, a very influential partner in the New York office, had real trouble supporting my candidacy. Jerry is a silver-spoon type of guy, very bright, very good. I managed to finagle my way into doing a project with him, which was the first study we had ever done for this fairly complex client organization. The chairman was an old school buddy of Jerry's. It turned out to be a very interesting study and the beginning of a long-standing relationship—five years now—with the firm. Jerry was directing it and I was managing it. (For all intents and purposes, I was directing it too.) I got very close with the president of their major subsidiary as a result of our compensation work. It was clear that there were sticky problems of communications, trust, and direction between New York, which is where the headquarters were, and Los Angeles, where the sub-headquarters were. This subsidiary represented 60% of their sales and about 90% of their growth potential.

The chairman of the corporation (Ted Young) knew there were problems but wasn't really fully aware of the magnitude. We had an intriguing session with him. I guess I had met with him twice prior to that meeting. The last item on a four or five point agenda was something innocuously worded like "closing the gap between Los Angeles and New York." I went through a brief academic description of what I saw were some of their problems, communications-wise, without really suggesting what the source of the problem was. Jerry began to get a little uncomfortable. Ted has a style of listening in which he will give you his undivided attention while you're talking and won't think about the thing until you stop. Then there will be a massive pregnant pause as he considers a reply. And he has a complete poker face all the time. You'd get absolutely no response—no laughter, nod, shake of the head. I was convinced that I wasn't getting through to him, and Jerry meanwhile didn't know what the hell was going on. He kept confusing the issue with general management platitudes about this, that and the other thing. About ten minutes into it, I said, "Let me try and put it as crisply and clearly as I can in terms of this last specific event we were talking about. You fucked up." Jesus, I thought Jerry was going to crawl under the table. He started talking about 84 different things at 100 miles an hour.

Ted is sitting there with an absolute poker face. Five minutes later Jerry stops. Ted just sat there. There had to be what felt like a 10-minute pause, although it was probably 30 seconds or so. Jerry couldn't stand it any longer, so he started back into it again. When he stopped, another 30-second pause and he started again. Ted broke in and said, "Jerry, you're covering old ground. Ben, why did you tell me I fucked up?" I said, "Two reasons: one, you did, and two, I didn't know any other way to get your attention." And then we started into it. Jerry was obviously sweating armpits through the whole thing. We made some major strides in terms of helping Ted understand what the problem was, and what he could be doing about it.

Jerry and I have been good friends ever since. That was the turning point in my relationship with a number of the powers that be at Kline. If it was still a bit unclear whether I was going to make it at Kline, after that it wasn't.

Within six months Jerrow was elected a partner.

*   *   *

The 12-room Westchester home owned by the Jerrows sits on 3 acres of land overlooking a small valley. Approaching it from the road, all one sees at first is a large driveway bordered by woods on one side, and by grass and flower gardens on the other.

A friend of Ben's from Harvard Business School stopped by on July 2, 1974, to see how well he was recovering. He found Jerrow in very good spirits, despite still being confined to a bed or a wheelchair. The doctors had concluded a week earlier that there would be no permanent damage, but that he still needed a few more months of rest.

Nancy's been an absolute savior the last two months—especially just after the accident. She got in touch with Kline the day after the accident and gave my secretary the 48-item agenda I had planned for the next day and worked with her to notify people, and so on. She made it VERY clear that "No conversation with him is allowed. I don't care what your problem is, he just is not available." Two or three days after the accident, when I could see that projects were going down the tubes, my reaction would have been to start calling people from the hospital and setting up shop by the bed.

Three or four days after I got home, as we were getting ready for a medical progress review, about a dozen guys from Kline showed up. And I can remember just sitting out there thinking, "Well, you son of a bitch, I guess you're really going to have to die before you are going to get these guys off your back."

That started me thinking. All right, if you're going to stay with Kline for any extended period of time, you're just going to have to do some things to cut down on the workload, especially the physical demands. My average workday had been 10 or 12 hours, and then I'd have a 3½ hour commute on top of that. I'd spend some time with Nancy and yet have very little time with the three kids. So it would mean I'd get four or five, or if I was lucky six, hours of sleep.

I suppose if Nancy was less effective and less strong then this thing may well have been precipitated a lot earlier. She's doing a super job raising the kids. We've always assumed that, you know, her job is to raise the kids and my job is to go out and raise the money. Now we're beginning to realize that really wasn't the way to operate.

Anyway, in the past week I've been trying to think out what my alternatives are. So far I've identified six.

I could try to cut back my responsibilities at Kline. Right now I'm responsible for all training activities for our U.S. offices, for secretarial and support services for the New York office, for three firm research projects, as well as a full client load. And that's insane. If I could just cut off a few things, to get the 65-hour work week down to say 45–50 hours, I think I could manage.

I'm unquestionably in a good position right now to go to the people at Kline and get them to take some of these things off me. What I'm afraid of is that because of the way Kline is, they won't stay off. Other things will come up and I guess I'm afraid that in a place where: (1) there is an unending amount of work to be done, and (2) the norm is for everyone, or at least all the young stars, to work until they drop, that it might not be possible to work a 50-hour week.

A second obvious option is to try cutting down the commute time. There are seven of us from the New York office that live within a 5-mile radius of here, so why not open an office up here. It would be a working office—not for clients. Even if we still had to go into the city two days a week, that would save 10½ hours. And it would be so nice to be able to drive home for lunch.

This idea just might not be practical. Economically it's no problem. And I talked to two of the Kline people who live nearby and they think it's a good idea. But I don't know.

Of course, I could leave Kline. The thought has crossed my mind before. I've got one offer and two potential offers floating around right now. All three are for VP jobs in very large companies. The money in all three cases is very nice, as much as

double what I get now. All three of them have the major drawback of being in New York City, which brings us back to the problems of the commute. In two of these there is substantially less travel involved. In the other there is about as much travel. I think in all three cases I could cut the work week back considerably. But I'm not sure. I've always had itchy fingers to run something and all three offer that. But I'd frankly just as soon not get bogged down in a bunch of administrative trivia. It's all I can do to screw up my courage to pay our personal household bills; and, the fewer administrative things I have to worry about, the better I feel about it. In terms of types of people to interact with, it's one of the real negatives in leaving Kline. They are very bright, talented, creative kinds of people. You look at any of the corporate alternatives and, boy, they get very thin on talent very quickly in terms of stimulating your own thinking.

The final obvious option is to leave Kline and start my own consulting company. I really do think I've got some concepts and ideas that are unique and for which there is a huge market. And I've only begun to develop this business at Kline.

We can afford a lower income while I get started. I could set up an office somewhere here near the house.

Unlike the other situations, I'd be in control. One of the beauties about consulting on your own is that if you get cross wired with a client, or you don't like what he's doing or whatever, you can say screw you. You can afford a hell of a lot more risk. So I take a 10 or 15 or 20% cut in pay—big deal. Once you get to a certain level, an extra buck doesn't mean that much. Yet, if I do well, I could make a bundle at consulting.

One of the problems in sorting out these options is that I'm still not sure how important money is to me. Our family really never had a hell of a lot of money, but we were always reasonably well off. I can still remember selling Christmas cards and cutting lawns, caddying and working in the local gas station and all of that sort of thing. I guess I was 10 when I started selling Christmas cards. I sold vegetables around the neighborhood. The next-door neighbor had a big garden and I would go out and pick his vegetables. He knew that I was picking part of them. I don't know if he knew I was picking all of them. I would just go peddle them to all the neighbors. It was always one of those jokes—what's Ben going to be selling next? I got a job working in a gas station in the summers when I was 13 and 14. The summer when I was 15 years old my dad got me a job as a laborer in a plant. I did the playboy kind of thing between 16 and 17, starting as a lifeguard at the country club swimming pool and ending up as manager of the pool. And there was always, you know, one kind of outside extracurricular deal or another like getting the flower concession and hamburger truck at college. I often say to myself that money isn't really important, but then, I look at my behavior pattern and I say—who are you kidding?

When I first joined Kline, Nancy and I sat down and tried to specify what an idealized life style would be in terms of how we would like to live. Then we translated that into dollars and totaled it up. And then we made an estimate of what that meant in terms of yearly income. We passed that figure three or four years ago. I'm doing everything I want to do. I'm not driving a Ferrari and no, I don't have an airplane, but shit I don't have enough time to fly one anyway. No, I don't have a yacht, but I decided I don't like sailing that well either. I'd rather play golf. So maybe the money doesn't really mean a hell of a lot other than as a scorekeeping thing.

There's one other factor that's probably important here. Nancy is the only child of a guy that runs one of the largest privately held real estate development companies in the world. So, she and the kids are going to come out all right financially. Her dad and I have never really talked about it, other than to say that they are in pretty good shape, and I don't really need to worry a hell of a lot about that.

Jerrow paused and stared out the living room window at the valley below.

I don't know. I wish one of the options looked very good and clearly better than the rest.

chapter

34

Managing a Career over Time

A professional is called on to make decisions related to job and career throughout his or her life. From the time we leave school until the time we retire, we are faced with a continuous string of questions:

- How should I approach my new assignment?
- Should I try to get the marketing research job when it becomes available next year?
- Am I spending sufficient time on my job now, or am I spending too much?
- Should I quit my job soon and go into business for myself?
- If the vice president asks me to go to Europe to open up a new plant, should I accept?

The career of Ben Jerrow rather clearly illustrates that the quality of the answers to these questions is directly related to the quality of our lives.

The approach to making these job and career decisions so far is summarized graphically in Exhibit 34–1. The alternative life style systems shown in the exhibit are extensions over time of the snapshot model introduced earlier in Exhibit 31–1 (p. 348). The elements in the system are, clockwise from the top, professional (P), physical (Ph), emotional (E), family (F), social (S), and material (M). In this final chapter we will discuss how this approach can be used not only to make one or two important initial career decisions, but to manage a career effectively over time.

The Decision-Making Model

The approach to job or career decision making shown in Exhibit 34–1 begins with a self-assessment process characterized by:

1. The use of multiple sources of data which have been carefully selected
2. Thematic analysis, based on explicit logic

This type of process can generate the accurate self-awareness that is the cornerstone to our whole approach. Self-understanding makes systematic and effective opportunity assessment, option generation, and option analysis possible.

The approach to identifying, securing, and understanding opportunities shown in Exhibit 34–1 can be characterized as highly proactive and based on a reasonable understanding of the realities of job hunting, career development over time (career stages, adult development), and your own character. These processes can generate options that you will find attractive, and that you will understand.

The approach to the actual decision-making process shown in Exhibit 34–1 is made up of two components—analysis and choice. The analytical process is characterized by the rational examination of each option in terms of its impact on the various interdependent parts of one's life, and the projection of the most probable events into the future for each option.

The choice process is characterized by coming to grips emotionally with each of the options and then choosing one and building emotional commitments toward it. Together these processes lead to a rational decision that one is prepared to implement.

With one modification, this systematic approach to making job- and career-related decisions can be used throughout your career. And that modification relates to the self-assessment and opportunity-assessment processes.

It obviously is not necessary, every time you wish to make a job- or career-related decision, to do the

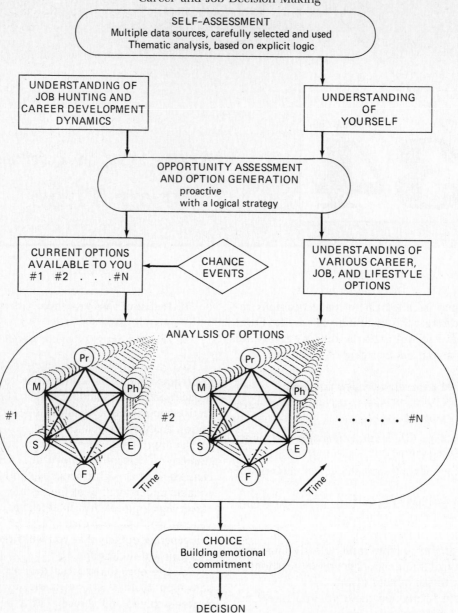

Exhibit 34–1
Career and Job Decision Making

type of self-assessment outlined in Part One of this book or the type of opportunity assessment and option generation described at the beginning of Part Two. Those processes are designed to give you self-awareness and understanding of opportunities in general that can support decision making over a period of time. Only when those understandings grow to be out of date do the processes need to be repeated, in whole or in part.

Reassessment

Keeping an up-to-date assessment of yourself and your opportunities requires periodic reassessment. Our ob-servations of people who seem to manage their careers effectively suggest that at least three different types of reassessments are needed (see Exhibit 34–2).

At least once a year it seems useful to sit down to review your performance, the satisfaction gained from work and other parts of your life, and any indications of problems that are not being addressed. This one- or two-day review might usefully be scheduled soon after a formal job performance review if your organization has a performance appraisal and feedback system. If it does not, then the ball is squarely in your court to seek out this information.

Once every three to four years, a more detailed analysis of how you and the world around you are

Exhibit 34–2

Activity	Intensity	Frequency	Sources of Input and Help
General evaluation of year's performance and of satisfaction with various aspects of life. Any problems?	One or two days' worth of work.	Once a year.	Organization-initiated formal performance appraisal. Conversations with important others in your life.
Analysis of changes in you and your opportunities. Are changes needed?	Up to a week's worth of work, at one time or spread out over a few months.	Every three or four years.	Three- to seven-day career planning seminars.
Major reassessment of self and opportunities.	Of the magnitude described in this book.	Once every seven to ten years.	Assessment centers. Career counselors. Three- to four-month university programs.

changing can be very useful. The questions you address here are: Do any of the assumptions about myself and my opportunities used in my last complete reassessment need to be altered because of changes in the last few years? If yes, what are the changes? Do they call for some type of change in my current career or life situation?

This type of assessment takes more than a day. In structuring it, three-day to one-week career planning seminars that are offered by some companies to employees and by some consulting firms to the general public can be very helpful.

Finally, about every seven to ten years, one needs to take the time to do a complete reassessment of the magnitude described in this book. Setting aside the time to do any of these reassessments and structuring them is extremely difficult, but this one is probably the most difficult of all. Assessment centers of the type some companies are now developing can be helpful. So can professional career counselors and structured sabbaticals (such as to a three- to four-month program at a university).

The Challenge

Many professionals get on a track during their twenties as a result of carefully made choices or of chance events and then chug along that track for a lifetime, never looking to the left or right or up. They don't ever stop the train to reevaluate their situation, even if they recognize that the ride is not as much fun as it used to be. Some people go through life this way. Others, like Ben Jerrow, have their trains derailed by a sudden boulder from the sky and are forced to do some reassessment. As you might expect, being forced into a major reassessment and change during one's mid or late career can be a very painful experience.

It's amazing how many excuses people can invent to avoid reassessment exercises. And this tendency is exacerbated by most professions and organizations, which provide people with little or no help or encouragement for reassessment. Often both individuals and organizations avoid the subject of individual career reassessment out of uneasiness—let well enough alone, don't open up Pandora's box.

One of the biggest challenges you face in your career is to use the tools and knowledge you now have regarding career management and not to let yourself slip into a self-induced career coma. Dealing with the challenge requires awareness and self-discipline on your part, because while you may receive some help from elsewhere (more and more organizations are providing career planning workshops, assessment centers, and counselors each year, but the total amount of such services is very low), the burden rests mostly with you.

Although the amount of available support for career management is not as great as we might like it from the point of view of society, it does make career planning in one sense even more attractive for the proactive individual. Today a person who is willing and able to use the ideas presented in this book to manage his or her career has a real competitive advantage. In a world that currently supplies considerably less money and fewer interesting jobs than people would like, competitive advantage is very important. The ideas here can give you an edge. Use them!

Assignment

Read the case material that follows, "About Life and Career Stages," pp. 384–90. Then read "The Life and Career of a Chief Executive Officer," pp. 391–401. Which career and/or adult life stage model or pieces of models helps you to best understand Harold Clawson? Pick one model and, using it, be prepared to describe Harold's life. How would you summarize Harold's career and its impact on him, his family, and his life style? What do you learn from the case about managing your own career development?

ADULT CAREER AND LIFE STAGES

We all have many sides to our lives. The most obvious are the physical, the emotional, and the mental. But we also have social, familial, marital, recreational, and spiritual sides as well. Exhibit 34–3 outlines a starting list of our many facets. Each of these aspects develop and evolve over time. In some of these areas, the development seems to follow fairly consistent patterns; in other areas, it does not. Research conducted over the past three decades, for instance, shows that people's careers tend to follow predictable patterns of development. Various researchers have characterized the stages in this development in different terms, but there are a lot of similarities. On the other hand, although there is still much to learn about it, emotional development seems to be much less predictable. We don't have time to discuss all the current knowledge about the developmental processes observed in each of life's aspects, but we can consider the more common ones.

As we do, keep in mind the two-dimensional framework of the various aspects on the vertical scale and the developmental stages outlined below on the horizontal one. The image, then, is like a musical score, with each melody line representing an aspect of our lives and each bar representing a developmental stage. From bar to bar, some are in crescendo, others diminishing. But whether the melodies are salient or not, they are there and together comprise the symphony of one's life.

We will first present three of the major theories on adult life development and then turn to the professional aspect of our lives and the development of identifiable career stages.

Adult Life Stages

Although the changes in activity, interest, ability, and tasks that humans experience over a lifetime have been the subject of literary pieces

Exhibit 34–3
Aspects of Our Lives

Physical
Emotional
Mental/intellectual
Spiritual/philosophical
Recreational

Social
Familial
Marital
Parental

Professional
Educational
Financial
Organizational

Political
Societal

for millennia, modern social scientists have not paid much attention to the topic until relatively recently.

Erikson's Theory

The most influential early adult life stage theoretician was Erik Erikson. In his book, *Childhood and Society,* published in 1950, he identified stages of human development in terms of several psychological dilemmas that confront all individuals. The dilemmas common to young people built on the work of Sigmund Freud, the first person to begin to describe human development in terms of predictable stages. Freud left off before addressing adult development; Erikson continued to hypothesize. He believed that:

1. From early adolescence to early middle age, the key psychological task a person faced was one of *intimacy vs. isolation.* One had to learn to care for and be concerned for another person

This note was written by James G. Clawson to provide a basis for class discussion. © 1982 by the Sponsors of the Colgate Darden Graduate School of Business Administration, University of Virginia, Charlottesville, Virginia. UVA case OB-224.

without fear of losing one's self. If one did not learn to do this, then life became a series of experiences in which the individual felt isolated from the rest of society.

2. In middle age, the key issue was *generativity* vs. *self-absorption*. In this dilemma, the individual had to choose between developing concern for individuals beyond one's own family, including colleagues at work and people in society, and remaining absorbed in self. Failure to develop a generative approach to life would, he said, leave one feeling stagnated and bitter.

3. Finally, in old age, Erikson saw a battle between *integrity* and *despair*. Integrity was the sense that life and all its choices and experiences had "come together," become whole and integrated. Despair was the feeling that things had not turned out as one would have liked, that one had missed a lot of opportunities—and that it was too late to do anything about it.

Again, not much was done in the field of adult development for many years. Then in the late 1970s several social scientists began publishing the results of their observations from clinical practice and formal research projects.

Gould's Theory

Roger Gould was a California psychologist who began to notice common patterns in the issues clients of similar age groups would bring to him. In his book, *Transformations,* he presents a series of assumptions which people learned in their formative years and which must be reconciled in later life, typically at predictable stages. He outlines the following adult life development themes:

16–22   *Leaving the parents' world.* False assumption: "I'll always belong to my parents and believe in their world." During this period young people move from a set of beliefs that revolves around their parents' teachings and support to developing confidence in their own ability to care for themselves and to make decisions that will affect their lives. They feel half in, half out of the family. They wrestle with learning about their independence, their own opinions, their own ability to provide, and relying on people other than family members.

23–28   *I'm nobody's baby now.* False assumption: "Doing things my parent's way, with willpower and perseverance, will bring results. But if I become too frustrated, confused or tired or am simply unable to cope, they will step in and show me the right way." Although people in this period are feeling their autonomy, they are still learning what "works" in the world, and confront the notions that people who play the game by the rules do not always get rewarded, that there is no one best way to do things, that others cannot do for us what we cannot do, and that rationality does not always win. They also are learning about commitment to spouses, to children, to work—and the responsibilities that all these carry—and in so doing, are learning many new roles they will play in society.

29–34   *Opening up to what's inside.* False assumption: "Life is simple and controllable. There are no significant coexisting contradictory forces within me." Having spent nearly a decade establishing oneself in a family and work, an individual now begins to look internally and to question whether or not the commitments and responsibilities assumed were really independently chosen or were mere extensions of parental guidance. People in this period typically begin to confront the difference between the intellectual (rational) and the emotional; they realize that in some ways that they did not want to be like their parents; they learn that others are not so neatly understood as they once thought; and they realize more fully than before that their security depends upon them alone. Marriage and career lives are established. Children are growing.

35–43   *Midlife decade.* False assumption: "There is no evil or death in the world. The sinister has been destroyed." Gould believes that this period is centered on the question of vulnerability. In it, he says, we work to come to grips with the reality of our own mortality and with the illusion that safety can last forever. We also, he says, work to face the notion that we are not "innocent," but that we, like others, invite others to play complementary roles to the ones we assume. That occurs most obviously in marriage, and in this period we examine these "unhealthy conspiracies" to make our own roles and our relationships more comfortable. Gould notes: "It is always unhealthy to sacrifice our identity for the stability of the relationship" (p. 280).

44–50   *Post-midlife period.* Realization: "That's the way it is, world. Here I am." In this period, finite time is resigned to as reality; one feels that "the die is cast." We become more actively involved with young adult children. We depend on our spouses for sympathy and affection. We may regret "mistakes" we made in raising our children. Money becomes less important. We attempt to reconcile what is with what might have been. Life settles down, becomes even. We accept the new ordering of things.

50+   *Meaning making.* The false assumptions of childhood have been encountered, if not all proved false. It is a period of mellowing, of making within us sense of the things that have happened both within and without. Children are seen as potential sources of comfort and satisfaction. We value spouses more. We have greater self-acceptance. There is little concern for past or future; the present is emphasized. We renew our questioning of the meaningfulness of life. And as we are concerned about our health, we hunger for personal relationships. We realize that we cannot do things as well as we once did.

Levinson's Theory

Daniel Levinson, a psychiatrist at Yale University Medical School, and his colleagues studied the lives of 50 men from five different walks of life. His theory concludes that there are a series of transitions and periods of relative stability in adult life. Each transition examines the life structure that preceded it and evaluates its appropriateness for the next era. Transitions are often times of turmoil and stress. The stable periods are often ones of renewed commitment and focus. Levinson's cyclical stages look like this:

17–22   *Early adult transition (EDT).* This is a critical transition in which the young man is half in and half out of his parental family. He is faced with necessity of leaving his family, but is not yet sure how to enter the adult world before him. His choices in this transition begin to form his adult self, both as he and as others will see it.

22–28   *Entering the adult world (EAW).* In this period, the young man attempts to establish a link between his view of himself and adult society. He seeks assistance, often, in doing this and may become a protégé. He begins to engage in adult relationships and explores what that means to him. He attempts to establish a life structure that will at the same time be flexible, leaving him options to change, and sufficiently stable to allow him to get on with his initial choice of means for making something of himself.

28–33   *Age thirty transition (ATT).* The young male adult now feels that if changes are to be made, he had better begin, for time is passing. The life structure initiated in the twenties is reevaluated. Once fondly held dreams are reassessed in the light of several years of adult experience. Some continue on rather smoothly, but for many it is a time of stress—one struggles with how to make the changes one desires. These three periods—EDT, EAW, and ATT—together form the early adulthood or novice stage.

33–40   *Settling down (SD).* In this period, the male adult attempts to consolidate his experience and efforts to build a life structure that will allow him to invest heavily in the things most central to him. Becoming an expert and a valued member of society are key objectives. He is no longer a novice, but is now a full adult determined to "make it." At the end of this period, he looks for a sense of becoming his own man—a male adult with seniority and respect. As one becomes more of one's own man, the need for active mentors begins to wane.

40–45   *Midlife transition (MLT).* Now the reexamination focuses not on where one is going, but where one has been. One becomes concerned about his accomplishments and whether or not they have fulfilled his dreams and ambitions or been less significant diversions. Aspects that have been suppressed during the early adulthood period bubble up for reassessment. One wonders if the path taken thus far is really the one that is right for him. One begins to sense physical declines and being no longer young. For some, these questions bring reconfirmation, for others great turmoil and perhaps drastic changes—in career, in relationships, in activities, in the attempt to resurrect long-neglected but valued parts of the self.

45–50   *Beginning of middle adulthood (BMA).* This is a period of consolidating the reassessments conducted during the MLT. Old relationships receive new attention, and new ones are developed more consciously. One settles into his new or reconfirmed view of himself and savors it. Some sense that a middle adulthood of decline and constriction have arrived; others begin to feel a deep sense of fulfillment in their lives and a mature sense of creative ability. For some, this is the most satisfying season of life.

50–55   *Age fifty transition (AFT).* In this period, the issues which were brushed over or not fully treated in the ATT and MLT are brought forcefully to the fore. Levinson does not believe that is it possible to escape at least a moderate transition crisis in either the MLT or the AFT.

55–60   *Second middle adult structure (SMAS).* Similar to SD, this period is one of the completion and settling into. One must prepare for the next transition from middle adulthood into late adulthood. For some this is a time of rejuvenation and realization, filling out the structure outlined in the AFT.

60–65   *Late adult transition (LAT).* This transition anticipates the change in structure from SMAS to late adulthood in which career changes are likely to have a significant effect on one's self and relationships. It is often a period of deep reflection. For some, this is a particularly painful change which they try to avoid.

65+ *Late adult era (LAE).* One must now decide not only the meaning to one's previous existence, but also begin to establish the new structure formulated in LAT. Much more needs to be learned about this period.

Career Stages

Four very useful and comprehensive theories of career stage development were identified by Miller and Form; Super; Schein; and Dalton, Thompson, and Price. We will outline these theories and then ask you to consider them in the life of a person who has lived through them all.

Miller and Form

In 1951 these two pioneering researchers identified five career stages and attempted to describe career development patterns throughout a person's lifetime. They found it useful to think of career development in these terms:

0–15 *Preparatory work period:* From the time we are born, we are socialized by our parents, by our schools, and by the experiences we are exposed to in our immediate environment into a set of views about the world of work. These views and values tend to follow us into our adult working careers. Young people develop their attitudes as they do their first work (chores and homework) in limited doses. Not only do parents and teachers affect this formation, but so do one's peers and social cliques. One of the main features of this preparatory socialization was the American cultural injunction to "make good." They note that most young people were socialized with what they call the four main values of Puritanism: (1) It is man's duty to know how to work and how to work hard; (2) success in work is evidence of God's favor; (3) the measure of success is money and property; and (4) the way to success is through industry and thrift.

15–18 *Initial work period:* This period is a temporary one consisting of the time when one gets the first part-time job until one accepts full-time, year-round employment. One knows that the initial jobs are temporary and therefore there is a lack of commitment to each position. The common goals are to make "spending money" and to "prepare oneself" for something else. Psychologically, they note, the common agendas are to manage the transition from school to work, to

gain independence, to demonstrate an ability to work hard, to learn how to get along with people, to get money as a symbol of independence, and to get a good track record. Most of the occupational frustration comes from work values held as a result of social class membership, expectations of reward based on educational achievement, a decline in the generally accepted intrinsic value of work (see Puritan value 1 above), and expectations of specific monetary rewards for work.

18–34 *Trial work period:* The trial period begins when one takes the first "permanent" job—and yet the period is marked often by considerable changing of jobs. Finally, after trying several different jobs, one "finds himself," "steadies himself," or perhaps just "resigns himself" to a more long-term position. Miller and Form characterize six distinct types of career orientation that begin to form in this period: (1) the ambitious worker who has confidence he can move up; (2) the responsive worker who fulfills the career expected of him by others; (3) the fulfilled worker who has attained his occupational goal; (4) the confused worker who is uncertain about past and future decisions and whose career pattern is erratic; (5) the frustrated worker who feels thwarted; and (6) the defeated worker who views himself as a failure. Common to all these is the cultural imperative they call the "American career stereotype" of a young, ambitious man who with average intelligence, but high character, unbounded determination, initiative, and hard work climbs from the "lowliest jobs" to higher income levels which signify "success."

25–65 *Stable work period:* This period is characterized by long-term commitment to "the kind of work that I've always wanted" or to the resignation that one will not find it. Not everyone, Miller and Form state, will continue in one stable work period throughout the rest of their careers. There are many reasons why one stabilizes in one company or job: (1) realization or rationalization of the trial period goal, (2) advantages gained by seniority; (3) age; (4) higher levels of income; (5) family responsibilities; (6) home ownership; (7) friendship ties; (8) institutional ties; (9) identifying with the company and community. The emotional tasks faced in this period relate to redefining occupational goals that may have been achieved or will never be achieved, to waiting for promotions in informal seniority systems, to doing work for which one is overqualified which no longer is stimulating, and to changing personal and family interests which may no longer fit the job. Some will enter another trial period, although Miller and Form say little about why.

65+   *Retirement period:* Anthropologists claim that the elderly have four common psychological goals: (1) to live as long as possible until the troubles of old age exceed the benefits of living; (2) to remain active in personal and group affairs; (3) to protect the privileges accumulated over the career; (4) to withdraw from life honorably with high prospects for the next life. Some do not accept the withdrawal in the fourth goal and hence develop a negative attitude toward retirement.

Super's Theory

Six years later, in 1957, Donald Super and his colleagues published an expanded career theory that built on the earlier work of Eli Ginzberg, his colleagues, and of several other researchers and psychologists. Eli Ginzberg and his colleagues had outlined an ooccupational choice sequence they felt was an irreversible process. Each stage in this process was influenced, they said, by four factors: (1) the reality of the occupational environment, (2) a person's educational experience, (3) certain personal and emotional characteristics, and (4) a person's values. These four factors, especially the tradeoffs between the first two factors and the last two, shaped the decisions a person would make in the *fantasy, tentative,* and *reality* stages of career development. Super expanded Ginzberg's theory as follows:

0–14   *Growth stage:*
Fantasy substage (4–10): fantasy, role-playing
Interests substage (11–12): emphasizes likes
Capacity substage (13–14): emphasizes abilities

15–24   *Exploration stage:*
Tentative substage (15–17): makes tentative choices
Transaction (18–21): enters labor market
Trial (22–24): begins working

25–44   *Establishment stage:*
Trial substage (25–30): may change occupation
Stabilization substage (31–44): tries to settle down

45–66   *Maintenance stage:*
Holding on to what one has

65+   *Decline stage:*
Deceleration (65–70): beginning to retreat from work
Retirement (71–): moves out of career

Super's theory outlined activities characteristic of periods covering one's entire lifetime, but most of his work and focus was on the exploration stage.

Schein's Theory

Ed Schein of MIT finds the following theoretical framework most useful:

1. *Preentry and entry:* The person prepares for work by exploring the possibilities and making a choice.
2. *Basic training and initiation:* One is socialized by the people in the organization into the formal and informal rules and norms of behavior in the organization.
3. *First assignment and promotion:* One establishes one's reputation as probable managerial material or as one who will "level off."
4. *Second assignment:* One either continues toward further advancement or continues to level off.
5. *Granting tenure:* One is admitted to the inner circles of the organization as a permanent member.
6. *Termination and exit:* One withdraws from the organization.
7. *Postexit:* One tries to come to grips with a life style in which the career plays a very reduced or very different role.

Perhaps the most distinctive characteristic of Schein's scheme is the conical view of organization structure which he takes to describe the movement of individual careers within organizations. There are, he says, three directions of movement: (1) *up,* which approximates the conventional notion of promotion up a heirarchical ladder; (2) *in,* which describes the movement of a person from the outer circles at entry to the inner circles later on; and (3) *around,* in which person moves from one functional area to another in job rotation assignments. Each promotion, of course, may involve one, two, or all three of these kinds of movement.

Dalton's, Thompson's, and Price's Theory

These three researchers from Brigham Young University have studied the careers of thousands of people, many of them engineers, and report the following typical pattern:

Stage One: Apprentice. The individual must learn how to make the transition from school to organizational life, how to be an effective subordinate, and how to live within the informal and formal social system of the organization. This stage is critical because the novice learns values, beliefs, and habits of organizational and interpersonal life that he will use throughout his career.

Stage Two: Independent specialist. One begins to work without supervision. In order to develop one's abilities to contribute and one's reputation, one works hard to build competence, often by specializing. One of the main tasks of this stage is to take the initiative for one's own work so that one is no longer dependent upon supervision for decisions about what needs to be done.

Stage Three: Mentor. One becomes concerned not only about one's own work, but also about the work of those who follow. One of the main tasks here is to move from a frame of mind that focuses on doing to one which focuses on managing the work and development of others—to coaching and directing rather than producing.

Stage Four: Sponsor. One becomes involved not only with the objectives and activities of face-to-face subordinates, but also with the goals and work of large groups or systems of groups of people. Sponsors begin to ask about the goals of the organization or how the organization fits into the rest of society—and to take initiative for answering those questions.

One way to summarize the work of Dalton and his colleagues is to note that each stage in their theory describes an increasingly broad perspective of the work that needs to be done and of the people involved in doing it. In stage one, for instance, the apprentice focuses on his boss and the demands he places on the new employee. In stage two the full-fledged employee is now interested primarily in his own work. In stage three, his view expands to include the activities of those immediately around him. And in stage four, the sponsor is concerned about the work of hundreds, thousands, perhaps hundreds of thousands of people.

These researchers also note that individuals do not necessarily move through all the stages. Some people (probably Driver's steady-state types) prefer to remain in the independent specialist stage, and others may not move from the mentor to the sponsor stage.

Summary

This case has introduced very briefly the main points of several major adult life stage and career development theories. You may have noticed similarities in them (see Exhibit 34–4). We would expect this of theories that attempt to describe similar phenomena. For instance, Erikson's generativity vs. self-absorption dilemma may be viewed as a psychological task facing a person near the end of the Dalton independent specialist stage. The individual who opts for "generativity" is likely to move on to Dalton's mentor stage, while the person who chooses "self-absorption" is likely to remain an independent specialist. Similarly, Levinson's EAW stage has

Exhibit 34–4
A Brief Comparative View of Selected Major Adult Stage Theories

Theorist	Age						
	10	20	30	40	50	60	70
Adult Life Stages							
Erikson		Intimacy vs. isolation			Generativity vs. self-absorption		Integrity vs. despair
Gould		Break away	Mastery Questions		Resigned	Mellowing	
Levinson (Stable)			EAW	SD/BHOM	BMA	SMAS	LAE
(Transitions)		EAT		ATT	MLT	AFT	LAT
Career Stages							
Miller and Form		Preparation	Trial Initial	Stable		→	Retirement
Super		Growth Exploration	Establishment		Maintenance		Decline
Schein		Preentry	Entry Initiation	Promotion Watershed (Up or level)	Tenure	Termination	Postexit
Dalton et al.		Apprentice		Independent specialist	Mentor	Sponsor	

many of the same characteristics of Super's establishment trial period stage.

One relatively common feature of the theories we have reviewed is a cyclical pattern. Levinson, for instance, holds that adults experience alternating periods of stability and transition. Miller and Form agree that many careers are characterized by alternating trial and stable work periods.

We believe that people have a basic internal tension between stability and variety. Although we all vary in our personal preferences for a balance between these two psychological states, we all tend to reexamine the current state (whether it be variety or stability) with an eye toward moving toward the other one. Thus, if our lives and/or careers have been stable and orderly for a while, we begin to get bored and to think about introducing some change or variety. If our lives have been filled with change, we may seek periods of stability to consolidate our perspectives and feelings. Perhaps you can identify additional steps in a cyclical pattern of adult life and career stage development. We encourage you to do this, and to note how they relate to the development of the various human aspects outlined in Exhibit 34–3.

References

Davis, John. "Theories of Adult Life Stages and Their Relevance for the Management of Human Resources." Unpublished subfield examination, Harvard Business School, 1980.

Erikson, E. H. *Childhood and Society,* 2d ed. (New York: Norton, 1963).

Ginzberg, E., J. W. Ginsberg, S. Axelrod, and J. L. Herma. *Occupational Choice* (New York: Columbia University Press, 1951).

Levinson, Daniel J. *The Seasons of a Man's Life* (New York: Knopf, 1978).

Miller, D. C., and W. H. Form. *Industrial Sociology* (New York: Harper and Row, 1951).

Osipow, S. H. *Theories of Career Development* (New York: Appleton-Century-Crofts, 1973).

Super, D., J. Crites, R. Hummd, H. Moser, P. Overstreet, and C. Warnath. *Vocational Development: A Framework for Research* (New York: Teachers College Press, 1957).

THE LIFE AND CAREER OF A CHIEF EXECUTIVE OFFICER

My first goal was to be a school teacher. There were very few jobs in Cache Valley, and Salt Lake City wasn't much better. Ninety percent of the people were engaged in agriculture or manual labor. If one didn't have land that meant he worked as a farmhand for somebody else. Without capital, one couldn't own land.

There were ten children and fifteen acres in my family, so what was I to do? I had to prepare for something. The most lucrative job in those days, other than farming, was school teaching, unless one could get to the very rare jobs in a bank. The banks seldom had turnover. School teaching, while it was not lucrative, really, was a white collar job and it had something more in it than muscle work. The best job I could hope for at teaching was $65 a month.

So began James Harold Clawson as he reflected at age 80 on his life and career as an auditor, manager, and chief executive officer of one of the United States' major private utilities. That statement was perhaps the best simple summary of the motivation that propelled Jack Clawson from a modest and isolated farm community to the paneled boardrooms of corporate America. His story is neither unique nor common; it reflects the imprints of great individual drive and of serendipitous luck. It also reflects the subtle and intricate ways in which career can become life and life become career. Mr. Clawson's family knew him as Harold; his business associates called him Jack. Yet in spite of this superficial separation of roles, whenever he was asked about his life, the dilemmas he faced, or the emotions he felt, Mr. Clawson always began to explain by describing what was happening at the company. He was loyal yet independent; demanding yet understanding, intense yet calm. By almost any standard, he was successful.

The Early Years

Harold Clawson was born in 1899 in Providence, near Logan in the northern, mountainous part of Utah. Automobiles were still in their infancy; airplanes were yet to fly. William McKinley was president, the Spanish-American War barely ended. Harold was the second in what was to be a family of ten children—eight boys and two girls. His father had 15 acres of land, but could not make a living out of them alone. So he worked at a variety of odd jobs, working now as freighter hauling stone by wagon team from the local quarry, then as laborer, always doing his farming on the side. His mother was hardly educated at all, but worked hard and had a great love for her children.

Harold grew up farming, milking cows, and attending a small rural school. In the summer of his twelfth year he contracted an unusual fever that refused to go away. He felt weak and lethargic; he could not walk more than a half-mile without resting. When the Scouts went off hiking, they took a horse for Harold to ride. From that summer on, he did not feel physically strong. He did not grow so tall as his brothers and tired more quickly at physical labor. Some foods did not sit well in his stomach, and he began to have abdominal pains.

Consequently, Harold began to spend more time reading and thinking. His favorite uncle, Leo, attended Utah State University and then became a local school teacher. He brought books home from the school library for Harold to read— a new book each week.

> I was under his influence for about five years. He got me started in seeking an education and in doing well in my studies. He was a teacher for awhile in the school to which I went, and so that he wouldn't show any favoritism, he really held me to a higher standard than the others. When I was 15 he unfortunately died from the bad effects of sickness contracted during his youth.

In his local high school (an academy that included two years of college work), Harold did very well. He was outgoing and popular. He took up tennis, and in his junior year won an oratorical contest. His senior year, he defeated the high-status and well-to-do candidate from Logan in the student body presidential election by talking quietly to all the students from the various small farming towns that surrounded Logan, collecting their support for a rural ticket.

Harold worked during his summer vacations as a laborer at the local sugar factory. He re-

This case was written by Assistant Professor James G. Clawson as a basis for class discussion rather than to illustrate effective or ineffective handling of an administrative situation. Copyright © 1979 by the President and Fellows of Harvard College. Harvard Business School case 9-480-036.

membered clearly the advice of Mr. Campbell, the foreman:

> He came up to me where I was working, sweating it out—I wasn't too strong physically—and he said, "Harold, my boy, it's a lot easier pushing a pencil than it is pushing these shovels. It pays better, too!" That impressed and encouraged me quite deeply.

While Harold was at the academy, the nation entered World War I. Expecting to be drafted, he enlisted voluntarily and was sent to Officer's Training School in Waco, Texas, in the fall of 1918. He took correspondence courses at the academy to add to his credits while he was gone. The war ended a few months later, and Harold returned to school. By virtue of his earlier work and the correspondence courses, he was able to complete the six-year course for teacher certification in five years.

He no longer intended to teach, but thought it wise to have the training and credential just in case. In the meantime, his thoughts had turned to law so much that the academy yearbook predicted he would become a judge.

> In the fall I enrolled at Utah State. There I met Parley Peterson and George B. Hendricks (professors of accounting and finance). Both of them were very strong on postgraduate work. I was in a formative stage as to what I was going to do. I didn't have any money and thought mostly of getting a job. If somebody had offered me a hundred dollars a month I probably would've postponed or given up going off to Harvard.

Peterson and Hendricks dissuaded young Clawson from going into law ("there were too many starving lawyers") and encouraged him to think about the Harvard Business School. Harold's older brother Charles had gone there that year, so the idea was not altogether new. He applied and was accepted. About that time, Harold also applied for a Rhodes scholarship, but did not receive the appointment.

After finishing his college program at Utah State in June 1920, Harold went to southern Idaho to work on a dry farm and to prepare for Harvard. He took with him the accounting and finance texts (acquired from his brother) written and used by Business School faculty and read them line by line, underlining as he went.

> I spent the summer growing and harvesting wheat on a big farm. All my spare time I spent reading these first-year books and some of the reports that had been written by students for the management classes. I went to HBS well prepared. I figured I had to dig because Utah State at that time was not rated too high academically.

The Harvard Business School and First Job

Harold Clawson went to the Harvard Business School in the fall of 1920, and having read many of the texts used at the school, he did well his first year. He was often able to quote and argue the professor's point of view, since the texts he had read the previous summer were written by the same faculty that he had as instructors. No particular professor was influential in Jack's development, though he had very high respect for all of them.

Jack did not have a lot of time for extracurricular activities at the Business School. He focused his studies on finance, accounting, and auditing and was consistently at the top of his classes in these areas. Jack dated only occasionally (usually a girl from the New England Conservatory of Music) and took trips to Marblehead beach, the theater, or the symphony. One of Harold's classmates noticed that Harold's initials were J.H. and took to calling Harold "John Harvard." Another friend shortened that to "John" and later "Jack," the nickname that stayed with him throughout his professional life.

Jack financed his degree with a mixture of funds—summer jobs, part-time work at Widener Library, and borrowing from his father and other sources. The library work was ideal for him because he was able to study at work and was also able to see what books his classmates were checking out and later read them. During the summer between his first and second years, Jack lived in the campus dorms for about $6 per month. He earned his living expenses and savings by working first in a packing house and then as the editor for the Camp Devens Citizens Military Training Camp newspaper. When he finished school, Jack had about $2,000 in education debts.

Jack began his job search with the usual campus recruiters. He interviewed with one of the Big Eight public accounting firms that came, and it first appeared that he would go to work for them, but they delayed their decisions until after graduation. So Jack followed up on interest expressed by the engineering, management, and investment firm of Stone and Webster of Boston. Jack had a great interest in traveling, so when Stone and Webster recruiters described the company's far-flung holdings and the job of a traveling auditor, Jack accepted their offer. He went home for a month and then reported to his senior traveling auditor in Houston, Texas, to begin work.

Jack and his senior companion traveled the country auditing the company's electric, gas, and street car system holdings. He learned "the ABCs" of these businesses in those early assignments, but he felt that his performance reviews were mixed:

> One senior man I went out with said I wasn't much good, but another said I was a humdinger. So I went to the head of the department and asked which one of these men was right. He said I was doing just fine, excellent in fact. So I was okay.

On the auditing circuit, Jack occasionally dated women in the towns where he was working. In one midwestern city he met a banker's daughter who was eager to get married, but their religious backgrounds were so different that Jack decided not to pursue the relationship in spite of his fondness for the lady.

After two years of heavy traveling and extremely long hours, Jack was exhausted. He told the company he was going home for the summer to regain his health. Harold spent a month in Logan chopping wood and farming. By then, he felt renewed enough to return to work on the auditing circuit. He established a regular program of exercise and health care which he followed rigorously thereafter.

> After a year and a half I got a call which said that our team of auditors out in Seattle needed another man, would I leave the circuit I was working on and go to Seattle? So in January 1924, I left Columbus, Georgia (where I was working), crossed the snow-covered plains and mountains and came down into Seattle, where the roses were still blooming.

Leora Gibbs

On his way to Seattle, Harold stopped off in Logan and had his first date with Leora Gibbs. Leora was the second of three daughters of a struggling family in Cache Valley. She was very outgoing and full of spunk—qualities which Harold liked and felt complemented his own quietness and reserved manner. Leora was teaching school near Logan at the time.

Harold came to see her during his summer vacation the following year, and they were engaged. The next year, 1925, Harold was reassigned to Boston. On his way east, he stopped in Logan and married Leora. They honeymooned across the country.

Harold spent one week in Boston, found his wife an apartment, enrolled her in a finishing school, and went to Florida and Texas on a three-month auditing trip. He had become a senior auditor himself, and his new circuits included the entire United States, Nova Scotia, and Puerto Rico.

I left her alone. I told her she was just a young girl and needed to learn more about the world and to get a little Boston culture. So she went to a finishing school. It was a choice experience and she learned a great deal, including expression, oratory, and social graces. She mixed with some very fine people.

Having gone to college and studied to be a teacher with the idea of helping people to learn and to excel in all things, and having been through fine colleges and a good education, I had a high sense of the responsibility and the opportunity to help my wife to excel in those things. I got her interested in going to school in Boston, and later in Seattle I encouraged her to take a class here at the University of Washington from an excellent professor in child training. She took copious notes, and we both read them and studied them together. I wanted my wife to be able and capable in all things. I wanted her to have her own personality, to do the things in life that *she'd* like to do. She sometimes feels like she's been treated *too* independently, but I think that the woman *should* have a real degree of independence. I believe that couples can help each other and be useful to one another.

In the fall of 1926, Jack (in Boston) was about to begin a six-month tour of companies in the southern states. Their first child was soon to be born. Leora felt that six months was too long to be alone, so she decided to return to Utah. They were packed and scheduled to leave on diverging trains in the early afternoon. At eleven o'clock the phone rang. A man for whom Jack had worked in the South was now in Seattle, needed help, and wanted Jack to come out. Sudden though it was, the change in plans was more than appealing to both Jack and Leora, so they changed his tickets and headed west.

> In Seattle they had an audit force of five men and needed another senior man to work with the other senior man for about six months. So, in an hour we were on the same train and headed in the same direction. Instead of a sad parting, it was a celebration traveling west together.

Moving to Seattle

Jack's first boss in Seattle left shortly thereafter and was replaced by a man who was unfamiliar with the work. Jack was in the uncomfortable position of having to work for a man who knew less than he. Jack was asked to stay beyond his six-month assignment. Then in 1928, Stone and Webster put Jack in charge of that small but permanent auditing operation. He was responsible to the company for all the audits of the West Coast holdings including the principal one, Puget Sound Power and Light Company (PSPL).

That (auditing work) was very interesting, because it included innovative processes of suggesting improvements. It was not merely seeing if everything was in order and that all the money was accounted for. It was more finding shortcuts, things that were taking up too much time or wasting money and that sort of thing. The reports were all, "what can be done to better performance, reduce costs and improve profits?"

When we came to Seattle I had reached a point where being away from home for long periods of time, two or three months at a time, was distasteful. I didn't intend to stay with the traveling when I got married. I had figured I would continue traveling for two or three years. Leora and I had agreed on that. I missed her terribly. It makes me almost weep to think about it, some of those long weeks away from her. (*Tears.*) I don't want to think about it. It wasn't easy.

It was hard on our marriage. Lorie had to take care of the boys, but she was good about it. We used to talk about it. When we came to Seattle, I traveled some, but seldom on weekends.

We recognized, looking ahead, that there were many people in the accounting department, but that there were only a few people in the auditing department of which I was head. Both roads led to the top of the company. In auditing, one had only a few competitors. Plus the work was a fine learning process. Those people in the accounting office had their daily routine work, and seldom saw the whole picture as the auditors did. I highly recommend the auditing approach for an ambitious person.

The public library was very close to my office. At five o'clock when work was over, instead of going home I would go right over to the library and stay there until ten o'clock when the library closed, then take a street car home. I'd leave the house about seven (A.M.) and get home after ten. I did this every weekday for about two years. I went through *every* accounting book and auditing book in the Seattle Public Library. I also obtained the questions on every Washington State CPA examination for the previous ten years, and without reference to the answers (which were available in other books) I worked the answers to all the questions and compared my work with the suggested answers.

At one time, I signed up in a coaching class for CPA examinations. After listening to two lessons and the students who didn't know very much what it was all about—asking simple questions about things that I knew backwards and forwards—wasting my time, I just gave up the fee I'd paid to join the class and went back to the library. By the time I sat for the examination I had it cold.

The big depression of the 1930s caused a heavy (20%) reduction in staff, but that did not have a debilitating effect on PSPL. The Holding Company Act of 1935, however, had a much greater impact on Stone and Webster. As a result of that act, the company had to divest itself of most of its holdings. The reduction in holdings meant the elimination of the auditing department to which Jack Clawson was attached.

The man who was the head of the department was one whom I liked very much, a Mr. Bissell. He was a high-type individual who encouraged improvement and growth. The other men in the department, who were my seniors, were rather ordinary people. I had realized that I was every bit as capable as any of the thirty of them and perhaps more so. I was a CPA and had a Harvard Business School background, which none of them had.

It looked like I would shortly be out of a job, so I went to Mr. Bissell and said: "You have a highly qualified auditing force here. Why don't we set up a public accounting firm specializing in auditing public utilities around the United States?" He was not a CPA, and couldn't quite see hanging his hat on a single CPA to put up a firm as I had proposed. I wanted to go out and take a swing at it because I knew we were really good at auditing public utilities.

In the meantime, however, the treasurer of PSPL argued successfully with his management, over the course of three or four months, that they needed a senior auditor, and so Jack became an employee of Puget Sound Power and Light Company.

Opportunities for Career Advancement

One year later, the treasurer of PSPL instructed his head accountant to draft a plan to centralize the accounting systems for all its companies. The accountant spent about four months on the project, but when he brought in his report the treasurer felt that it was inadequate. Furthermore, he disagreed with its recommendations. He handed the assignment to Jack. The other man failed, Jack believed, because he did not have an overall perspective of the company. Jack knew that his Stone and Webster experience had given him that perspective. He wrote up the plans in one month, including the use and assignment of various personnel, and took it in to the treasurer's office. The treasurer thought the plans and proposals were "just great," and then asked Jack to go ahead and implement them. Jack, at 37, was made the assistant treasurer, in charge of the Auditing Department.

It was that little knowhow from auditing that helped me. There's a little saying, "An expert is a man eighty miles from his home." When one goes out and audits companies one after another all over the country, he is keeping up on all the latest procedures and practices. I saw a little benefit here, or a little better way there.

Pretty soon one can say in an office, "Well, you could be doing this." And they say, "Well, you're sure smart to think of that." You're just learning and copying from the places you've been. Pretty soon I came to know all of the best practices in the utility industry, and had become an "expert" in the judgment of others.

That operation focused the attention of the company on me. First, there had been the dilemma whether or not to keep me. Then when I put this reorganization together, the president and the treasurer both were very pleased. I took over the whole financial system then, making a big jump from just being kind of an "outsider" into head of all the departments underneath the treasurer. I had about 150 people working for me.

That same year a Public Utility District (PUD) law was passed granting any county the power to condemn private utility companies and to take over their operations. Almost immediately, about two-thirds of the counties in the northwestern part of Washington formed PUDs and initiated a struggle for the electric power business that was to last over 25 years. During the course of that struggle, PSPL lost about a third of its holdings to municipal and various PUDs, but was able to forestall the complete dismantling of the company and a proposed merger with another Washington company. During this struggle there was a competition with the City of Seattle during which services were duplicated—power lines and poles ran down both sides of the streets. In Jack's words, "It was really a mess."

When World War II began, Jack, an officer in the Naval Reserve, received a "critical industry" deferral from serving and continued working. In 1942 he was approached by a CPA friend on behalf of Boeing, then a fast-growing airframe manufacturer, with a proposal to become a special assistant to the president. The job held the allure of being a steppingstone to any number of positions at Boeing.

I was at that time third or fourth from the top at Puget and with all of the comdemnation suits (by the PUDs), it looked like the company was hanging by a thread. One local newspaper had been running cartoons with the company depicted as a big corpse being hacked to pieces. It looked like I was going to be out of a job. I was invited to dinner with the president of Boeing, his financial vice president, and my CPA friend. We had a nice discussion and the president was all for employing me. Later, I talked further with my friend who was the go-between about terms. It was about double the salary I was getting, but the war was just starting and I told him, "I don't like to leave a job I've had for twenty years to work for two to three years in an industry that will decline drastically after the war." I told him I'd take it, but that I would need

some assurance that I would be continued on with Boeing in some capacity after the war. The president of the company didn't like that and chose the other candidate. It was a big setback for me, and I could hardly live for about a week. It looked like my company was going out of business and I had insisted on something hard and sure. I should have taken my chances on my own abilities rather than ask for assurances.

However, it wasn't too long after that that another individual came to me and wondered if I'd be interested in taking a high financial position in Weyerhaeuser, about the largest timber company in the world. I said, "And how!" even though it would have meant moving to another city and it was a family company. Everything was being set up and then all of a sudden I got word that the deal had died cold. I feel sure that Weyerhaeuser decided not to disturb their close relationships with Puget.

I had missed both jobs, and it looked like Puget was going out of business for sure. I felt very low. I didn't have much appetite for about three months. I thought I'd made a big mistake, especially in fouling up the Boeing offer.

Another inquiry came from Seattle-based General Insurance Company looking for a potential top executive. In this case, the president of PSPL called me in and told me that General Insurance had inquired of him about me, and he had dissuaded them from making me an offer. So I settled down to work it out with and for Puget.

In about a year, the man in line to succeed the treasurer of PSPL died suddenly of a heart attack and I moved into second place. Only two years later the treasurer retired because of illness. I took over as treasurer, working with the president of the company.

The affairs of the company began to brighten. The PUDs had failed to take over and I was happy that the Boeing deal had not worked out. The war was over and Boeing was having a rough time adjusting to drastic reductions and cutbacks.

Financial Strategy

Jack had saved vigorously throughout his life. When he was traveling, he lived on an expense account and so was able to pay off his education debts within two years. He established his financial strategy early:

1. Save enough cash to cover unforeseen emergencies.
2. Carry as much life insurance as possible.
3. Protect wife and family with trusts as fast as possible.
4. Save enough to invest in income assets to cover retirement without relying on pensions.

I set goals for myself and made plans on which I was always working, revising and extending them from time to time, and by preparation, training and fortuitious circumstances succeeded considerably beyond my expectations. The main hope and goal in my occupation was to become the chief financial officer of a major corporation. I achieved it and went considerably beyond it to become the top executive of such a corporation, as well as a director in two other large corporations.

My personal financial goal was to earn and save sufficient that by wisely investing I could build up a personal estate to protect my family financially and to provide well for the time when I would no longer be employed. I continually studied and looked for promising investments with these essentials:

1. A basic, sound, noncyclical industry
2. Young, capable, aggressive management
3. Good growth prospects
4. High earnings on investment mostly retained in the business (little or no dividends, but compounding investment value)

In an unspectacular way I worked at this over my early years with a fair modicum of success. Some of my investments were good, a few were rather sorry. In fact, I almost lost my "shirt" on three really bad ones. They could have been disastrous except for special diligence on my part.

About 1950, a close, relatively young friend for whom I had done some favors and who had been an outstanding, successful businessman was asked to take over the management of a relatively small, struggling drugstore chain. He discussed the matter with me and a couple of other friends and subsequently agreed to take over the business, provided he and (we) his associates would acquire a controlling interest. The plan was to plow back all the earnings into the opening of new stores. It appeared to have all the elements for success and be very much in line with my investment purposes. I liquidated all of my investments, borrowed 25% more than that, and put it all into the business.

From the modest beginning of three small stores in the Seattle area, the company has grown to over 200 stores (in all the far western states including Alaska and Hawaii), generating over a half billion in annual sales. The original stores required an investment of around $50,000 each; present stores, which now include not only a drug division but hardware, soft goods, nurseries, sporting goods, require an investment of over $500,000 each. No dividends were paid for about the first ten years. However, expansion became so great that it became necessary to go public and begin to pay dividends—which at first were only stock dividends. The result of this compounded reinvestment of earnings plus inflation has produced a remarkable—not to say fantastic—increase in the market price of the original stock over the 30 years. The stock, allowing for splits, is now selling for about 75 times its original cost. Cash dividends, which are a payout of only about 20% of earnings, are annually 200% of the cost of the *original* stock;

that is, an *original* stockholder now gets back in cash *double* the cost of his investment *every year*. Of course, there were only a few in that position, but subsequent investors have done very well.

In 1965, when I was approaching retirement in PSPL (I remained on the board of directors for some years thereafter), I realized that I was building up a rather large estate which would be subject to very heavy state and federal inheritance taxes. I therefore began an orderly divestment of my holdings by liberal donations to educational, religious, civic and other organizations and to hard-pressed relatives, but principally by gift to my three sons to permit them to establish businesses or other investment pursuits, and also educational trust funds for each of our 21 grandchildren and a few other needy and worthy young relatives, retaining sufficient to assure taking care of all of our own possible needs, including such travel (mostly to our scattered family) as we may enjoy, as well as further modest contributions to family, relatives, and worthy causes.

Family Strategy

When asked about his children, Jack said: "Just ask Leora what you want to know, and she'll tell you." But when pressed gently, he continued:

I have had some rather basic principles for guiding, inspiring, and helping my children make the most of their talents and get all the education and training they possibly could. The country needed it, the church needed it, and the children needed it to have a fulfilling life. They needed knowledge and understanding and wisdom. The way to get that, of course, is to pursue a logical course of training and education and to give their best to it. However, you just don't push them into it.

Leora: And he worked with his boys on this *all the way along,* and I may say, very successfully.

Jack: You have to *lead* them so that they want to do it. Nothing is more sorry than pounding on the backs of children to get them to do this or that. The better way is to set before them patterns and inspiration to understand their natures so that they will grab a line of action and go with it. This was a very conscious effort on our part. From the time they were small, we were determined that they would make the most of their talents and abilities.
            Leora was most helpful. She did a tremendous job with those little kids. As they got older my influence began to have a larger bearing on it, but in those early stages she was magnificent.

Leora: However, in those early stages, let me tell you, he'd come home from work in the evenings and after dinner he'd gather those little ones around him and sit on the sofa and tell them stories. They weren't the stories from the story books. They were stories he made up in his own mind, often as he went along, and they always had a point. They would sit there enthralled, listening to his stories.

Jack: Well, I had read a tremendous amount and knew so many stories that it was not difficult to improvise. I would remember the main plot or theme and would be able to tell it to them in an interesting way. There was always a helpful or learning point to the stories—not a heavy moral, not preachy.

We took a deep interest. We gave them full backing in Scouting and in other activities and they loved it. Along with it was always this view of developing their talents. There were many things that we encouraged them to do without ever forcing them. One boy saved his money for a long while until he could buy his own bicycle. He's now a capable businessman doing very well—partly, we think, because he went through that period of saving to buy a bicycle when money was hard to get. At an early age, they chose their own life insurance policies and kept them up.

Jack's father died in 1940, his mother in 1954. During the years in between their deaths, Jack contributed heavily to the support of his mother. His two sisters, who lived in Logan, took care of her comfort and physical needs.

Reaching the Top

Jack's belief had always been that he should use imagination and careful thought before he acted. This included for him a continuous attempt to do his own job well and to understand the demands and perspective of his boss' job. This was not always easy, since many managers in the company were not inclined to discuss their jobs with their subordinates. Jack, however, encouraged his own employees to consider and reflect on the problems that faced the treasurer's office.

During the mid-1950s, Jack, as treasurer, was traveling with the president of PSPL making presentations to stock analysts and fighting off merger attempts. The Eisenhower administration defused the furor over the PUD takeovers so that the company no longer had to worry so much about that threat. Repeated questions about the nature of Harold's personal life and disposition during this period were always answered with descriptions of what was happening at the company. It was as if his personal life had merged into his corporate life.

While on one of the eastern trips, the president of PSPL was advised by one of the financial institutions that unless he soon made provisions for his succession, the firm would withdraw its very substantial investment. It was not apparent to the analysts who would provide the leadership of the company in the future. This was a "bolt" to both the president and to Jack. Jack had never thought of being president of the company before, and he realized for the first time that he was one of the few people in the company who was capable and familiar enough with the job to handle it.

The result of the investment firm's statement was a period of active review by the president. As the word that a successor was being selected got around, there was a lot of politicking among the senior officers of PSPL. In Jack's terms, this was characterized by a great deal of secrecy and game playing, but Jack's approach was to avoid that and to continue to attend to the financial affairs of the business.

Puget often used consultants on matters of major importance, and the succession to the presidency was no exception. At least two firms were retained to evaluate top management and their skills. The president of Puget agreed with their conclusions, and made Jack senior vice president in 1959. This promotion was an interim one designed to prepare Jack and ease the shock to the two or three people who considered themselves in line between Jack and the presidency. Jack was made president of the company in 1960. A year later, he was elected chairman of the board and chief executive officer.

Chief Executive Officer

During his incumbency as CEO, Jack felt that his most important contribution was to change the nature of executive management in the company from one of relative secrecy and authoritarianism to one of mutual participation. He felt that the other top executives, as a result of his efforts, enjoyed their work better, were happier, and performed better.

The atmosphere and work became one of mutual cooperation rather than one of hard discipline and dictatorship. That was the first big job that I saw I had to do. I was not there long enough to carry out fully the long-range planning required by the physical operations of the utility business, but we set the stage for that to go on.

When faced with difficult problems, Jack would frequently lie awake at four or five in the morning and mentally probe various alternative means of solving them. This was a very important time for him in which he could explore these action plan scenarios without the interruptions of the office routines. The pressures of his job were demanding but not debilitating to Jack.

Yes, there is a lot of stress, but there's another aspect of it. The executive who works hard and carries lots of responsibility and concerns ... it isn't necessarily *that* which causes him to have ill health and break down as many do. It's more a matter of their personal nature or state of mind. It is true that "hard work never hurt anybody." Stress itself won't hurt you unless you let it. I don't think that the stress hurt me. I liked challenges and when I had problems that were really serious, I labored over them very hard. There were many problems where decisions had to be made. There were a lot of decisions that whichever way you went, you were partly wrong. It was as they say, "Like being caught between a rock and a hard place."

There are a lot of people who evaluate what distinguishes a successful executive by his decisions. With all of the tough ones he has to make, if the majority of them are right, he's a good executive. No executive makes them all right. He is going to make some wrong, and then he is going to have to work to straighten them out. If you've made the wrong decision, and you know you've made the wrong decision, you have to know how to reverse your field and still not lose face in your organization. The best way to do it is to be frank about it and not start covering up, or somebody will find out. Then you lose faith, which is worse than being wrong and correcting your mistake.

Jack's concern with his mental agility and education focused on another aspect of working as a CEO:

As a chief executive officer, you are waited upon. You can lose touch with the normal activities of life. May I tell you what happened to me? When I was chief executive, I had secretaries and assistants to do practically everything. Before that I used to take care of all my own financial affairs, write my own letters, and checks, and everything. When I was CEO they did everything for me. I didn't do any arithmetic. Didn't need a computer, didn't even know to use one. At one time, having been an accountant, I could add up a string of figures like nothing at all. By the time I retired, would you believe it, I could hardly remember a telephone number long enough to dial it! I hadn't kept accustomed to the relationship of numbers. I could feel it, and it was just enough of a warning to me. From that point on, I began to practice with figures and writing. I *felt* that slippage. It GOES. You get away from your skills a few years, and they leave you.

In 1965, Jack reached retirement age and stepped down from the top job. He retained a seat on the board of directors for several years and took an active role in the planning and implementation of management changes over the next five years.

Retirement

Jack had few reservations about retiring:

Look at it this way. I went through some really tough years when I was working with the president of the company. I practically had no vacations. Something was always coming up. He'd call me from New York on a Saturday evening about ten o'clock and want me to get on a plane at eleven and be back there Sunday at noon. In those days it took fourteen hours by plane to get back to New York.

That was all right. I didn't mind; it was the nature of my job, but it *was* strenuous work. There was a lot of travel. One year, I was in New York staying in a hotel for eleven out of the twelve months. It was not easy. There were lots of early and long hours.

So, having been successful in my financial strategy, I looked forward to retirement so that I could engage in other activities that were more enjoyable.

I've had no problems keeping busy. The first year we took a little vacation and rest in Europe. We spent the summer over there. Then I had lunch with the president of one of the local television/radio stations here. We became good friends, and he invited me to be on the board of directors and on the management committee of the television station.

One day the telephone rang while I was out in the garden, and I was asked if I would like to go to Iran. And I said, "Fine." The caller said, "I am speaking for the U.S. State Department, and we have a team of experts going to Iran to study its national electric system to determine what sources of energy should be used to produce electricity. They've got oil, gas, and water power. They also need to know what kind of transmission and distribution lines to put in. The team will study what the growth of the country's going to be, how big a system should be built, and related matters."

I was invited to head up the team. They needed a name and a position to deal with the cabinet-level officials in Iran. When I got over there it was more than that. I was paid well, but it was darn hard work. It was interesting, and I got a lot out of it, but it was very hard on me and Leora. It was so hot in that 119-degree weather at an altitude of 4,000 or 5,000 feet.

The following year we made a trip of about a month to South America for the Chamber of Commerce. About that time, we also made a swing with another official group for a couple of months to Japan, Hong Kong, Manila, and then down to Australia. I came back all bugged out from that. I mean, we went so *much.* We had a whale of a good time and enjoyed it.

During these years, the drugstore business was expanding rapidly, and it went public. The owner, my friend, had tried to keep it a family business. Since he and I were very close, he asked me to be on the board of directors so he would not have to take an outsider. So, I was on the board of directors there.

Then a local hospital asked me to be on the advisory board. I was involved in Boy Scouts, too. I was active in my church work, business, and community activities. After awhile I had to begin gradually unloading some of these responsibilities so I could have a little time for my family and myself. I began playing golf once a week. So I have been as busy as I ever was at the office.

Leora: If he had retired as treasurer of the company, he still would have enjoyed retirement and doing the things he likes to do. He loves the garden. He loves his golf. He loves being active.

Jack: He loves spending time with his wife a little bit, too! (*Laughter.*)

Leora: No matter what happened, that man would be busy. He'd be doing something. And he'd be enjoying it.

His sons call him for advice when they have a problem, a business deal, a decision or something. They ask him, "Hey, Dad, what about this?" And they spend an hour talking on the telephone. That's awfully nice. It's good for the relationship between father and son, and it keeps him thinking about things. And it's good for the boys because they have respect for his years of experience.

In 1979, Jack returned to his alma mater, Utah State University, to accept an honorary doctor's degree in business management. This was a rewarding and satisfying experience for him.

As the Clawsons continued to reflect on their fifty years of marriage and career, Jack was asked how he would describe himself:

One thing I have, I reckon, is a pretty fair mental capacity and ability. I do not learn very rapidly. There are a lot of people who can learn faster than I, but I'm persistent and orderly in it so that in the long run I will probably come out even or on top. I may not be the first, but I am thinking about difficult problems and I can stick with it for a long time until I get an answer. A lot of others may get lost in the complexity of the problems.

Leora: He says he doesn't learn rapidly, and yet I've seen him take a thick book, receive it at 5:00 P.M. and go and give a report on it at a meeting the next morning. He doesn't learn rapidly??!

Jack: Most executives have to be able to do that. I learned that in making presentation to a superior, you have to get to the vital point at once and supply the additional data if you are asked for it. When I was chief executive, each day I'd get a stack of reports, business magazines, and papers to go through on my desk every morning. But I'd have people coming in for long conferences, discussing very serious problems all day long. Come five o'clock, the stack of papers was still there. Then I would have to bring that stack home at night to go through them. If you want understanding, you have just got to look at the reports yourself.

As a student journalist, I learned that in writing a newspaper article one has to say in the first paragraph what the whole story is about because a lot of people just read the first line or two. The first sentence of every paragraph normally is the essential point. The rest is secondary information regarding that particular idea and if you don't need it, you go to the next one and on down. That is a kind of speed reading that I've done a lot of and still do because I want to cover a lot of information.

Beyond this matter of my mental capacity, the next thing is I think I have imagination. Looking ahead and visualizing events and problems in the future, and solving them in advance or planning steps to be taken. I have solved a great many problems the first hour of the day when I wake up at 4 or 5 o'clock. It's surprising how looking at all the angles of a particular problem at that hour would bring out things I'd never thought about.

When I was a kid, I read many of Horatio Alger's talks. I began thinking about accomplishing things in life—right from the start. Even when I was 8 or 10 years old, I began imagining myself doing what the Horatio Alger boys did. As I continued on in life I could always visualize myself doing things. I think I have done this all of my life—this projecting of myself. In doing so, I have visualized the problems in advance, before they happened or had to be settled. This has been a great help. Having done that early in my life—first it was to be a teacher, then it was to be a lawyer, then it was to be a businessman—at each stage I was using my imagination and saying: "What do I do so I'll be the best or at least good at it?" And then I would begin to do those things.

I had serious setbacks and times when it looked as though I were a failure and not making the grade, very off-base with serious shortcomings. I think this is a common experience, psychological ups and downs. Little things will set us back, but somehow the sun will shine, next month anyway, and better things will come up to get us going. Sacrifice comes before miracles—sometimes you have to go through the hardships in order to achieve your goals. We often learn more from our mistakes and our bad times than we do from all our successes. I have had confidence that there's always another side beyond the dark times.

I've made a lot of mistakes, but I don't dwell on them. I don't think it's wholesome, I don't think that helps any except to recognize that most of them have been very good for us. I can't conceive of anybody getting on without setbacks of various kinds. You learn from them.

I have a good sense of responsibility. My first motivation was unhappiness with a life in which I was born and raised, rural people with low incomes and virtually no prospects of employment in the area. This disturbed me, and I had a feeling that I wanted something better. This became a source of great motivation to me. I was determined to achieve something better. From reading and observing, I knew it was available. There had to be a way, and I was going to find it.

I was very awkward and self-conscious in dealing with people, especially groups. I didn't have that natural inclination.

I've been described as, "He is not able to accept compliments graciously. He's embarrassed by it." When I was growing up, I had a feeling of inadequacy. An inability to deal with people. I didn't feel at ease. Not in school or classes where I had a feeling of ability with effort to match anybody, even at the Harvard Business School. However, I always felt I lacked personality. I just didn't seem to have the personality to feel at ease with other people.

When I was made president of the company, I attended a meeting of top executives in a big hotel. I found it difficult to go up to some of them and find anything intelligent to talk about. For one thing, I hadn't been brought into it gradually. I also felt, "Here's the head of Boeing over here, a billion-dollar business, and here are all these top bankers. They're top men in their businesses. I'm top man in mine, but heck I'm just an old country boy." That took time to get over. I worked hard to develop the ability to be gracious and to get along with everyone. I did, and that made a big difference. I found that they were just men, talking little talk like you and me.

Leora: This seems like a contradiction to me. I've never seen him with a person or a group that he hasn't been able to carry on a fine conversation. He's said that for years but I never see it—it's never evident.

Jack: Here's another thing. I have an innermost urge to take over and run things in directions in which I am interested or feel I have an ability. In Boy Scouts, I wanted to be the troop leader, and became a troop leader. In school, when there was

a question, I didn't mind holding up my hand. I have to hold myself down in groups because when I think I know more about it than anybody else, I want to tell them. I want to give them another point of view. I try to stimulate their thinking.

I am also curious. I can't sit down where there's any kind of a book without having a pick it up and see what it is about—whether it's a women's magazine, a magazine in a dentist's office, whatever it is. I want to pick it up and read it and see what it's about. I have a lot of mental curiousity.

Leora: That all got in the way a little bit. Especially when he was so loaded with responsibilities—both company and church. I felt very neglected. I felt that I had to do something about it. It couldn't continue the way it was. There was always somebody calling him for time and attention, so I had to work it out.

There's one thing that I might change in him, though I might be sorry if I did.

Jack: Besides, now it's fifty years too late!

Leora: I'd try to have him be more aware of other people's feelings, moods, needs. He's very aware of his own, and the need to work and to do and to deliver (pause), but I wonder sometimes if he even sees my needs.

Jack: Some people have thin "insulation," and they are very sensitive to everything that people do and say and think. Other people have a thick insulation mentally, spiritually, and physically. They're built that way, and no matter what they do they'll never be as thoughtful as those who are naturally sensitive. In my personal drive, I become insensitive and hurt her. She thinks it's because I don't care. She feels it through her whole system. To me, I feel I'm going quite a ways with my level of sensitivity. Often, I'm thinking more in terms of what I'm doing than of the feelings that are involved. I'm thinking of the programs, aspirations, and that sort of thing—the management of affairs, not of the feelings. In thinking about what needs to be done all the time, I am not so careful about managing the feelings.

It's very difficult for a person who is thin-skinned to be running the management of a business without getting into trouble, because one cannot be that sensitive. On the other hand, one has to be considerate, but if you get too sensitive, you're in trouble.

Leora: Well, that's very true. I've never been in business, but I've been in management positions (in the church) where you don't get paid for the job but where you have to manage well. I've been an executive in that sense for twenty-five years. It's been my sensitiveness, not touchiness (and there's a difference) that has kept people coordinating with good feelings. I think some say, "This is the way I am, so just take it or leave it. This is me." I know I'm extremely aware and sensitive, and many times I tell myself, "That's just none of my business, just stay quiet and don't let your feelings take over."

We recognize these characteristics in ourselves and in recognizing them, we have to know also that there are advantages and disadvantages. We can't play it always just the way we want it. We have to discipline ourselves to try to know, and in all integrity, to do what we feel is the right thing to do. If you don't have feelings, if you don't see these things, and you just tell yourself that's not one of your characteristics, you build and build and build this indifference rather than saying, "Now, for one hour today I'm just going to watch and do whatever I can and to help...." I mean you can justify yourself in being inconsiderate.

But, too, there isn't a day that goes by that he doesn't come up and put his arms around me and tell me how sweet I am and how much he loves me, and what could he have done without me. Sometimes, I say to him in humor, "You have a hell of a way of showing it!" Words alone are not enough.

Jack: For me, even if I do it, I don't feel so deeply as she does. When I'm working with people, I try to be mindful of the things they're interested in, so I can inspire them to move ahead. I may not be quite as sensitive in some of the things I say to them and perhaps even offend some of them because I am not so sensitive. Lorie does it spontaneously. I cannot change completely, but I can change my ways of doing things but it's like teaching my muscles to do something that doesn't come naturally.

I don't mean to offend. But quite often I'm so set on accomplishing something that I think is more important than maybe hurting their feelings a little bit. Actually on rare occasions, I have deliberately shocked or startled someone a little bit in order to impress them—which is a different thing than Lorie might do by loving them into doing it—perhaps both ways get results.

Having finished his self-description, Harold volunteered his view of his wife:

Among Leora's qualities, and constant endeavors, let me list a few—not necessarily in any order of importance:

Deep concern for other people, including especially her own family.

Constantly seeking improvement.

Outgoing friendliness and *helpfulness* to everyone. Everyone who knows her, loves her.

Generous to a fault, really!

Indefatigable, sets highest standards of performance for herself—encourages others in same direction.

Considerate and highly sensitive to the needs and feelings of others.

Constantly striving to improve in cultural things and refinement, and encouraging others in that direction.

Inveterate "student" (reader) to improve and increase in knowledge, particularly in all phases of life—health, activities, as well as cultural things.

A competent teacher, speaker and leader—confident and winning.

Tremendous supporter of family *and* friends.

Constantly holding to highest standards in goals, performance, conduct *ideals.*

Well-liked and admired wherever she goes, with a multitude of friends.

During the latter part of his administration, Jack had begun having even more serious abdominal pains. He had lived with them for 55 years, excusing himself at times to go lie down and massage his stomach. Leora had made it her crusade to ease that burden and had researched diet and exercise programs constantly over the years. Jack described Leora's help in one sentence: "I could *not* have achieved what I did without the help, advice, counsel and support Leora gave me in every way, nor would I even be alive today, I am sure, without her tremendous interest and concern in everything having to do with health, and personal concern in all matters." About five years after he had retired, though, the pain was too much, so the doctors advised exploratory surgery. They found, to their surprise, that Jack's intestines had fused almost shut in several places—the result of bovine tuberculosis contracted in Jack's tenth year. After corrective surgery, Jack regained his strength and felt better than he had for his entire working career.

After the interview, Jack arose, and motioning to the casewriter, ambled down to the lake by his home, climbed in his 17-foot runabout, and said: "Let's go waterskiing!" And they did.

ASPECT CARDS

FINANCIAL (Money)	INTELLECTUAL
FAMILIAL (Parents, siblings)	EMOTIONAL
RECREATIONAL	PHYSICAL
SOCIAL (Friends, parties, meeting people)	POLITICAL (Campaigns, public office)
MARITAL (Spouses, live-in partners)	SPIRITUAL (Meaning of life, God, cosmos)

ASPECT CARDS

PROFESSIONAL (Occupation, career)	**MATERIAL** (Possessions)
SOCIETAL (Community service)	**ECCLESIASTICAL** (Church work) .
PARENTAL (Children)	**IDENTITY** (Clarity of self-image)

VALUES CARDS

BEING INDEPENDENT	BEING CLOSE TO OTHERS
BEING PRAISED BY COLLEAGUES AT WORK	GAINING PUBLIC RECOGNITION
ACHIEVING A GOAL	FINISHING A TASK
BEING PRAISED BY SPOUSE	GETTING REWARDED FAIRLY FOR MY EFFORTS
BEING PRAISED BY PARENTS	HAVING AS MUCH (MANY) AS POSSIBLE

VALUES CARDS

ENJOYING THE ACTIVITY	USING MY ENERGY AND RESOURCES WISELY
CONCENTRATING ON ONE THING	DOING BETTER THAN THE NEXT PERSON
FOLLOWING DIRECTIONS	DIRECTING THE NEXT PERSON
DECIDING WHAT TO DO NEXT	CHANGING ACTIVITIES DAILY
MOVING QUICKLY	CHANGING ACTIVITIES WEEKLY

VALUES CARDS

MOVING SLOWLY	CHANGING ACTIVITIES MONTHLY
ORGANIZING THINGS	LOOKING AHEAD
BEING ENCOURAGED	PLANNING AHEAD
CREATING NEW THINGS	LOOKING BACK
FEELING EXPERT (especially at __)	THE TRANQUILITY

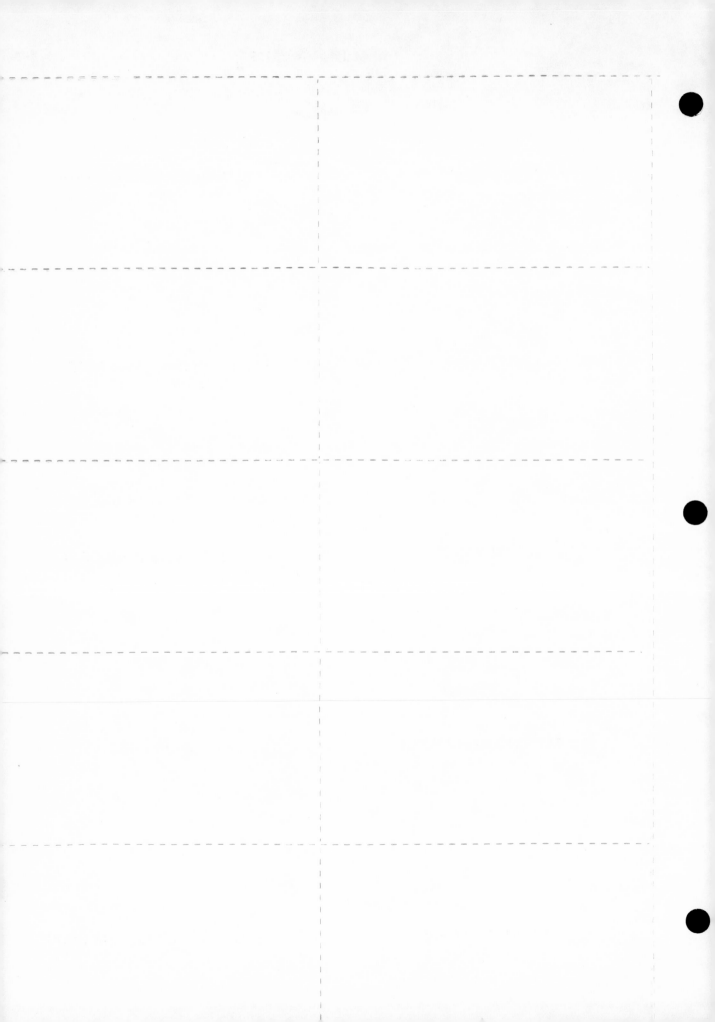

VALUES CARDS

WORKING ON DETAILS	TACKLING A CHALLENGE
WORKING ON THE BROAD ISSUES	BEING SEEN AS AN EXPERT (especially at __)
GETTING AHEAD	ADMIRING THE BEAUTY OF IT ALL
LEARNING NEW THINGS (especially __)	BEING FREE
MEETING PEOPLE	FEELING A PART OF THE GROUP

VALUES CARDS

HELPING PEOPLE	TAKING RISKS
TEACHING PEOPLE	BUILDING THINGS
EXPANDING INFLUENCE	WATCHING PEOPLE GROW
HAVING A SET SCHEDULE OR ROUTINE	RELAXING
BEING ABLE TO _____	HAVING _____

VALUES CARDS

FEELING ____

BEING ____

Self- SECOND EDITION
Assessment
and Career
Development

James G. Clawson • John P. Kotter
Victor A. Faux • Charles C. McArthur

In this new edition, the authors focus on self-assessment and career development skills to help you to match job/career goals. They stress development of key managerial skills of inductive logic, planning, and implementation. These skills are essential to conducting more effective job-searches, including interviewing and correspondence, and in guiding the careers of others.

Special new and retained features:

* self-contained instruments for easy use
* more material on women in management and on dual-career couples
* now includes cases from a variety of sources
* additional material on mentoring/developmental relationships anticipates key management development issues
* material on managing the transition from school to the working world
* real-life cases reveal actual events and dilemmas in career development

The book is based on a Harvard Business School program that won the first EXXON Award for educational innovation in graduate education for business administration and management. The program combines student self-assessment of interests and potential with practical instruction in job identification and career management.

PRENTICE-HALL, INC., Englewood Cliffs, N.J. 07632

ISBN 0-13-80310